595

Christians Only

Christians Only

A History of the Restoration Movement

James DeForest Murch

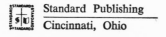
Standard Publishing
Cincinnati, Ohio

© MCMLXII
The Standard Publishing Company
Cincinnati, Ohio

Library of Congress Catalog Card Number: 61-18657

Printed in the United States of America

Preface

FOR fifty years there has been need for a comprehensive, but not too ponderous, history of the American movement to restore the New Testament church in doctrine, ordinances, and life. Many other competent histories have been written, but the more recent ones appear to be severely limited in scope and motivated by modern scientific and theological theories foreign to the genius of the Restoration movement.

I have long had a secret desire to write such a volume in the frame of reference afforded by Thomas Campbell's *Declaration and Address,* a document as vital to this movement as the Declaration of Independence is to the United States of America. I rejoice and thank God that He has permitted me to realize my purpose in this book.

As Kenneth Scott LaTourette confesses in the Introduction to his monumental work, *A History of the Expansion of Christianity,* "No historian can write without bias, and he who professes to do so is either deceiving or self-deceived. The very selection of facts out of the endless and infinitely multiple stream of daily happenings in itself involves judgment as to what is significant."

In this present work I have sought to portray the Restoration movement in the traditional historical view, which sees in history the hand of God and evaluates and interprets facts in the light of His Word. I have little regard for the modern school of history which looks askance at the supernatural and which sees in the flow of events simply mechanical and human factors—geographical, climatic, economic, political, social, cultural, and intellectual. I see the Restoration movement as a part of the plan of God to preserve and perpetuate "the faith which was once delivered unto the saints" in its purity and power, and visibly to restore the one body in Christ. I believe that unless the movement remains true to the principles and purposes which brought it into being, it has no reason to exist.

This book frankly presents an irenic personal view of the historical facts implicit in the events of 150 years in the life of a great people, now approximately five million strong. It seeks to interpret the processes

v

whereby they have achieved their distinctive position and character as one of the leading religious communions in the Christian world, to point out their failures and shortcomings, and to highlight the unique opportunities which lie before them in the new ecumenical era in the larger history of the church universal.

I am deeply in debt to many sources for the information which the book contains. The bibliography at the end of each chapter acknowledges some of these sources. Among the individuals with whom I have consulted and who have assisted in many ways are Dean E. Walker, Joseph H. Dampier, Jesse M. Bader, Claude H. Spencer, Burris Butler, Edwin V. Hayden, Ronald A. Merritt, Athens Clay Pullias, M. Norvel Young, George S. Benson, Don H. Morris, B. C. Goodpasture, Frank S. Smith, Orvel Crowder, Fred P. Thompson, Verda Bloomhuff, James W. Nichols, LeRoy Garrett, E. L. Jorgenson, and John W. Wade.

Christians Only is sent forth with a prayer that it may in some small way be used by the Lord to advance His cause and kingdom and to achieve the unity of all God's people for which He prayed.

—JAMES DeFOREST MURCH

WASHINGTON, D. C.

Contents

Introduction

The Preservation of the Faith

WHEN Christ announced His intention to establish His church (Matthew 16:18), He certainly intimated His intention to preserve and perpetuate it in all its pristine purity and power. This He has done, as history abundantly attests.

The church of Christ is the mystical body of Christ. He is the head, the king, the lawgiver, and those who are members of His body are under His direction and government. In the words of Alexander Campbell, "The true Christian church, or house of God, is composed of all those in every place that do publicly acknowledge Jesus of Nazareth as the true Messiah, and the only Saviour of men, and building themselves *upon the foundation of the apostles and prophets, associate under the constitution which He himself granted and authorized in the New Testament,* and are walking in His ordinances and commandments—and of none else."

It was not long after the church was established that departure from the original pattern caused division and it became necessary to rebuke heresy and restore the declaration and practice of the true faith.

True to His promise, our Lord has, in every time of declension, raised up men to restore apostolic preaching and practice by an appeal to the revealed Word of God. The story of that apostolic succession is one of the most thrilling in the annals of man.

Holy Scripture is the first to record the cycle of purity, power, apostasy, and restoration in the church of Christ. The earliest forms of apostasy were advocated by the Judaizers, the Greek philosophers, and the devotees of worldly lust. The Jewish hierarchy vigorously and effectively opposed the new church from without, but Jews who became Christians sought to bring their brethren under the Mosaic law. From the book of Acts and the epistle to the Galatians, one can see that this serious development threatened not only to nullify the basic doctrine of justification by faith, but also to confine the church within the limits of a Jewish sect and to destroy its power and liberty to bring the gospel to the world. Greek philosophy, widely accepted by the intelligentsia throughout the Roman Empire in New

Testament times, had a tremendous influence upon religion. Gnostic systems seeking a satisfactory theory of God, explanation of nature, and codes of conduct, formed the basis of many religious heresies. These invaded the Christian churches and turned people from the revealed gospel to speculations, debates, and divisions. Sincere efforts of faithful brethren to combat these heresies sometimes took the form of unwise assertion of ecclesiastical power and control that later developed into episcopal systems and seriously modified the character of the churches. Ever present were the temptations of the flesh, aggravated and encouraged by the popular vile practices of a pagan society.

Pietistic Christianity demanded that the life square with the profession. When church leaders succumbed to worldly practices, whole churches were affected and lost their testimony to the superiority of the Christian way of life. In the midst of these departures from the faith, the apostle Paul stands out as God's man of the hour, branding the heresies and the heretics, calling the churches back to the divine pattern, and inspiring them to pursue the evangelization of the world with consecration and sacrifice.

Following the martyr deaths of the apostles and the murderous and devastating persecutions under the Roman emperors, the church faced new threats to its purity and power. Bishops assumed authority over groups of churches, weakening the Scriptural eldership and congregational independence. The baptism of infants began to take the place of the baptism of believers, and the doctrine of baptismal regeneration arose. Catholicism, the doctrine of one authoritative, humanly devised church institution to which all the churches must submit, was widely accepted by the bishops. The union of church and state found its beginnings in the benevolent protectorate of Constantine, the first Christian emperor of the Roman Empire.

These departures from primitive practice were by no means universal, nor were they condoned by many noble Christian leaders in the churches. Clement of Rome reminded the faithful that salvation is not by wisdom or works, but by faith. Tertullian warned against the infiltration of Greek heresy, opposed the practice of infant baptism and baptismal regeneration, and denounced transubstantiation and the substitution of a human ecclesiasticism for the power and working of the Holy Spirit and the guidance of the Holy Scriptures. Montanus sought to raise up congregations that would restore the primitive piety, wait for the Lord's return, and give the Holy Spirit His rightful place in the churches. In his closing years, Tertullian became a member of one of these churches seeking to restore apostolic practice.

E. H. Broadbent in *The Pilgrim Church* says,

> Departure from the original pattern given in the New Testament for the churches met very early with strenuous resistance, leading in some cases to the formation within the decadent churches of circles which kept themselves free from the evil and hoped to be a means of restoration to the whole. Some of them were cast out and met as separate congregations. Some, finding conformity to the prevailing conditions impossible, left and formed fresh

companies. These would often reinforce those others which, from the beginning, had maintained primitive practice. There is frequent reference in later centuries to those churches that had adhered to Apostolic doctrine, and which claimed unbroken succession of testimony from the time of the Apostles. They often received, both before and after the time of Constantine, the name of Cathars, or Puritans, though it does not appear that they took this name themselves.

Departures from the faith were largely responsible for the convening of the Council of Nicea and five other general church councils, the last of which was held in 680. They were occupied mostly with questions as to the divine nature, the relations of the Father, Son, and Holy Spirit. In the course of the discussion, new extrabiblical creeds were devised which became tests of fellowship. Thus the Bible was no longer considered sufficient for the guidance of the churches without the addition of tradition and church dogma.

Prior to the councils, the New Testament canon consisted of those books which had been generally accepted by the churches under the guidance of the Holy Spirit. This acceptance was confirmed by the councils and by every later competent critical comparison of the canonical with the apocryphal and noncanonical books, the difference in value and power being evident. Although copies of the books were available only in limited numbers, and both the Roman and the Greek Catholic church authorities did not permit individual interpretation of the Scriptures, sufficient copies were available to enable intelligent men to know the truth and detect error.

In the fourth century, Priscillian appeared as God's man to urge a return to apostolic practice. The Roman church destroyed most of his writings, but those that remain show extensive quotations of Scripture. He and his friends habitually gathered for Bible reading and the observance of the Lord's Supper in independent assemblies. The circles of those who shared their faith increased rapidly, but soon they were subject to persecution and were practically exterminated.

As in the case of the Priscillians, thousands of Christians or brethren who sought to restore and maintain the church of the New Testament were destroyed to the full extent of the ecclesiastical and political power of their persecutors. It is difficult to trace their history with accuracy because their writings were ruthlessly destroyed. The extant references to them in Catholic church literature depict them as heretics and guilty of all sorts of evil teachings and practices. Undoubtedly some of these descriptions are true, because every independent movement includes a wide variety of thought and expression and makes it possible for its enemies to brand it with extremist characteristics. In spite of severe limitations, a large body of trustworthy evidence enables us to trace through history the fact that the true church, often a remnant flock, has existed continuously since Pentecost.

From the middle of the seventh to the middle of the ninth century "the true Christians," as they called themselves (otherwise known as the Paulicians) labored to maintain the apostolic faith. A record of their beliefs and practices is to be found in an ancient Armenian work entitled *The Key of Truth.* They practiced baptism of believers in open streams, requiring antecedent repentance and faith; met for Bible study and the observance of the Lord's Supper under the guidance of duly-ordained elders; and laid great emphasis on the empowerment of the Holy Spirit and living a godly life. Scattered by persecutions under the Empress Theodora, they established assemblies wherever they went.

In the Slavic lands the Bogomils, meaning "friends of God," sustained the true church. Under Emperor Alexius Comnenus they were cruelly persecuted and imprisoned. They were accused by their enemies of all sorts of vile practices, yet some writers of this time, notably Gregory of Narek, attributed high motives to them. Said Gregory, "From a negative position as regards the Church this sect has taken up a positive line of thinking and has begun to search out the foundation itself, the Holy Scriptures, seeking there pure teaching and sound guidance for the moral life."

Indications are that these primitive churches and the older churches in Armenia and Asia Minor maintained lines of communication with the Albigenses in France, the Waldenses in Italy, and the Hussites in Bohemia until the fifteenth century. They recognized a common ground of faith and practice that bound them together.

In the early part of the twelfth century, God raised up Pierre de Bruys, an able and diligent preacher of the Word, who traveled through Dauphine, Provence, Languedoc, and Gascony and established churches after the New Testament pattern. Joining forces with Henri of Cluny, whose oratory moved the people against the established church, De Bruys caught the imagination of the common people and initiated a mass movement for the true faith. The name *Albigenses,* taken from the district of Albi in which they were especially numerous, came to designate this movement. Toward the close of the century, terrible persecutions directed by the Roman church liquidated them by the tens of thousands.

Churches that never departed from the faith and were not influenced by the evils prevailing in the Catholic system existed in the Alpine valleys of the Piedmont from the earliest days of the Christian era. Probably from these faithful disciples, the wealthy Peter Waldo, of Lyons, became interested in the study of the Scriptures and led in a movement known as "the poor men of Lyons," which taught the Scriptures to the masses. This God-called man put new life into the churches and led an expansion of the true faith into surrounding areas, reaching even to Bohemia, where Waldo died in 1217. The Waldenses, though ravaged by persecutions and often reported to be extinct, have persisted in their testimony to the New Testament faith even until today.

The doctrines and practices of these brethren were grounded in the Scriptures. Apart from the Bible, they had no confession of faith, no rules nor any authority of men. To follow Christ was their chief desire. In matters of church order they practiced simplicity, electing elders who became the overseers of the flock, observing the Lord's Supper for all believers, and practicing baptism of believers, reiterating the Scripture, "He that believeth and is baptized shall be saved." Their apostles were consecrated businessmen who traveled by twos and did the work of evangelists. Regular individual reading of the Bible and daily family worship characterized their home life.

John Wycliffe was raised up in England to point the way out of a corrupt church back to the Word of God. In his treatise, *The Kingdom of God,* and in other writings, he showed that "the gospel of Jesus Christ is the only source of true religion" and that "the Scripture alone is truth." He is believed to be the author of the classic guide to the proper interpretation of Scripture:

It shall greatly helpe ye to understande Scripture,
If thou mark
Not only what is spoken or wrytten,
But of whom,
And to whom,
With what words,
At what tyme,
Where,
To what intent,
With what circumstances,
Considering what goeth before
And what followeth.

With indefatigable zeal he preached Bible doctrine and translated the Bible into the language of the common people. His English Bible wrought a revolution in English thought and proved most effective in restoring New Testament practice. As he grew increasingly familiar with the Scriptures, Wycliffe came to acknowledge their infallibility and exclusive authority, and set forth this teaching in his book, *Of the Truth of Scripture.* He held that only by the observance of the pure law of Christ as revealed in the Scriptures, without mixture of human tradition, could the church grow and prosper. Summoned to appear before the pope because of his heresy, Wycliffe declined. He died quietly in 1384. Although his followers became involved in political disputes and considerably nullified the immediate effect of his courageous ministry, his work was used by God in later years.

In Hungary, by the way of Wycliffe's lectures at Oxford University, God raised up John Huss, theological doctor, preacher of Prague, and confessor to the queen of Bohemia. His expositions from the Holy Scriptures and his appeals for the restoration of apostolic practices so moved the people who heard him that he was summoned to the Council of Constance to answer for his heresies. There he was seized, cast into a dungeon, and condemned to die by burning. He died with the prayer on his lips, "God give me a fearless heart, a right faith, a firm hope, a perfect love that for Thy sake I may lay down my life with patience and joy." Among those who followed in his train was Jan Zizka, of the little town of Tabor, where tens of thousands of people met regularly to celebrate the Lord's Supper, taking both the bread and the wine. This practice became so well known that the cup became the symbol of the "Taborites." At the foot of Tabor hill is the pool, still called Jordan, where great numbers were immersed upon profession of their faith in the Lord Jesus Christ.

The concept of restoring the foundations of the New Testament church is well set forth in a book by Peter Cheltschizki, *The Net of Faith*. Cheltschizki says,

> Nothing else is sought in this book but that we, who come last, desire to see the first things and to return to them in so far as God enables us. We are like people who have come to a house that has been burned down and try to find the original foundations. This is the more difficult in that the ruins are grown over with all sorts of growths, and many think that these growths are the foundation . . . There is no other foundation than that which is laid which is Jesus Christ from whom the many have turned away and turned to other gods and made foundations of them . . . In the Apostles times when the Apostles preached, the believers were separated from the unbelievers and they were assemblies of believers, of one faith . . . and they had fellowship with each other in spiritual things and in the Word of God.

In the midst of the dark ages of the church, God raised up another spiritual Moses to deliver His people from bondage—Martin Luther. His major work was the translation and publication of the Scriptures for wide distribution among the common people. Trained in a monastery and attaining to the doctorate, he devoted himself to the study of the Bible, in which he found freedom from the scholastic theology, the dogmatic authority of the church with its hierarchy and traditions, the power of prejudice, and from every human ordinance. He desired to impart this freedom to all men. Since he had learned it from the Scriptures, he knew that the best way to disseminate it was to make the Bible available for the widest possible reading and study. "Scripture without comment is the sun whence all teachers receive light," said the great reformer. After years of laborious effort, thousands of copies were circulated and the most important epoch in the Reformation was attained.

In the earlier years of Luther's attempt to establish the Reformation church, he adhered rather faithfully to the principle of *sola scriptura*. This led him to defy the pope, abolish the mass, teach the principle of justification by faith, abrogate the celibacy of the clergy, restore the preaching office, and discard compulsory fasts and many other Romish practices. At one time he favored the practice of immersion, and sought in other ways to recreate without compromise the original New Testament church. But national, political, and economic pressures eventually conspired to swerve him from this course of action.

Luther's spirit and Luther's translation of the Bible, however, brought a new day with repercussions far beyond anything he envisioned. In many ways the Anabaptist movement was the culmination of the principles Luther espoused. He would have been the last to admit this, for he zealously opposed and even persecuted all Anabaptists until his dying day.

The aberrations of many Anabaptists must, of course, be condemned;

but the movement as a whole contributed much to the ultimate restoration of the New Testament church. Its passion was to discover in the pages of Holy Writ, the pattern of the church of the first century, and to renew original Christianity in doctrine, ordinances, and life. Anabaptist leaders took Luther's Bible and made it their constant companion and guide. Haled into court by their persecutors, the Anabaptists' knowledge of the Scriptures was more than a match for both Catholic and Protestant theologians. As Thomas von Imbroich stood in the court in Cologne about 1556, he declared, "The Scripture cannot be broken, nor shall anything be added to or subtracted from the Word of God which remains in eternity." Menno Simons' colleague, Dirk Phillips, wrote in his *Vindication*: "From these words it is evident that whatever God has not commanded and has not instituted by express command of Scripture, He does not want observed nor does He want to be served therewith, nor will He have His Word set aside nor made to suit the pleasure of men." The Anabaptists had a keen discernment of the relative importance of the New Testament over the Old, and insisted that all doctrine and practice in the church have New Testament support. Pilgrim Marpeck compiled a book of more than eight hundred pages on the theme of Old and New Testament contrasts. Dirk Phillips pointed out that "the false prophets cover and disguise their deceptive doctrines by appealing to the letter of the Old Testament consisting of shadows and types. For whatever they cannot defend from the New Testament Scriptures they try to establish by the Old Testament . . . and this has given rise to many sects and to many false religious forms." Anabaptists commonly practiced baptism of believers, and their preference for immersion resulted in their nickname. They preferred to be known simply as brethren in Christ. Their services were simple with great emphasis on the Lord's Supper and the fellowship exhibiting love, peace, and good will to all men. They insisted upon personal holiness and evidence of the new birth in daily living, rejecting completely the institutional concept of salvation common to the major churches of the Reformation.

In France and Switzerland, God raised up a great company of Bible believers from 1500-1800 so that there was much searching of the Scriptures, and many churches after the New Testament pattern were established. The great names of Farel, Le Fevre, Roussel, Calvin, Zwingli, and others were written on the pages of church history for ages to come. Unfortunately, political and social problems persuaded Reformation leaders to build a church-state system organized largely on an Old Testament pattern. In Geneva, Calvin ruled with an iron hand, the city council having absolute power over religion as well as civil matters. Churches of the New Testament pattern almost disappeared in the general organization. Nevertheless, the translation of the Scriptures into the vernacular and the free discussion of the tenets of the Christian religion were great influences which spread throughout Europe.

Though the work of Wycliffe had been quite effectively smothered in England, independent groups of Bible Christians still persisted. The state church had transferred its allegiance from the pope to the king, who was acknowledged as its supreme head. Some evangelical influences resulted in the adoption of Reformation principles, however. The Puritans working from within sought to purify completely the doctrine and order of the state church, but with little success. Finally, Robert Browne issued a notable book, *A Treatise of Reformation Without Tarrying for Anie,* in which he advised all those who desired a church of the New Testament pattern to leave the established church. Thus arose English Congregationalism from which came the Puritans who settled in New England in 1620 and thereafter. Many of their churches wore the name *Church of Christ* and took the Bible only as their rule of faith and practice.

Alongside the "Brownites," Baptist congregations developed, some of which traced their history as far back as 1580. These churches practiced immersion of believers and accepted the sole authority of the Scriptures in doctrine and life. They stressed the principles of soul freedom, the separation of church and state, and the universal priesthood of believers. The local church was sovereign. The name of John Smyth stands out as the great Baptist leader in the English movement. John Clark, Mark Lucar, and Roger Williams brought this remarkable Bible faith to North American shores in the early 1600's, where it has been the means of stimulating great interest in Bible doctrine and practice.

Of special interest is the remarkable Bible ministry of the Haldane brothers, whom God raised up in Scotland in the 1700's, when the spiritual climate of the land was exceedingly low. Dr. Robert Richardson, the biographer of Alexander Campbell, devotes two chapters of the *Memoirs* to the Haldane movement which he credits with giving Mr. Campbell "his first impulse as a religious reformer, and which may be justly regarded as the *first phase* of that religious reformation which he carried out so successfully to its legitimate issues."

Robert and James A. Haldane were of distinguished Scottish ancestry and sons of a very pious mother. Robert, the older brother, entered the navy and served with unusual distinction, retiring at length to his fine estate. Here his early religious impressions revived as under the Spirit of God and he began a daily study of the Holy Scriptures. Though devoted to the kirk, he attributed to a lowly stonemason his first clear concepts of "the important truth that faith must cast away all reliance on frames and feelings and rest only on Christ." His full surrender to the Lord led him to dedicate all his time and his immense wealth to Christian pursuits. One might write a whole volume on his benevolence, much of which was devoted to carrying the gospel to the heathen.

James Haldane was not stirred as was his brother until, while attending the General Assembly of the Church of Scotland, he heard the discussions which eventuated in an adverse vote on a resolution, "That it is the duty of Christians to send the gospel to the heathen world." He was so stirred at this exhibition of smug self-righteousness and lack of concern for the unsaved that he joined his brother Robert in studying the Bible "in a childlike spirit, without seeking any interpretation that should agree with his own ideas." Both brothers were strongly attached to each other and

16

agreed in the religious changes which their Bible study led them to make.

Having heard of the coldness and immorality among the ministers and churches in northern Scotland, they set out in 1797 to distribute Bibles and tracts and hold open-air meetings in which they taught the Word of God. They based their right to preach "upon the indispensable duty of every Christian to warn sinners to flee from the wrath to come, and to point out Jesus as the way, the truth and the life." The Presbyterian clergy viciously opposed them, but the populace followed them with large audiences. Their activities came to the attention of Rowland Hill, celebrated independent evangelist, whom they at length commissioned to open services in the great Circus in Edinburgh. This move caused tremendous religious excitement: as many as fifteen to twenty thousand persons attended the meetings. Thrilled by the responses of the people to the simple gospel, Robert Haldane proceeded to erect tabernacles in the chief cities and towns of Scotland and to provide preachers. Not desiring to start a new denomination, it was agreed among the Haldanes and their co-laborers to associate themselves with the Congregationalists of England. James A. Haldane became the minister of the church in Edinburgh; Greville Ewing in Glasgow. Robert preferred to travel, covering Scotland many times, encouraging brethren of like faith in Bible study and good works. The most interesting of his journeys took him to Switzerland where he conducted Bible classes, chiefly in Geneva. Among the young men he inspired to lives of Christian service were Merle D'Aubigne, the historian of the Reformation; M. Malan, the hymn writer; F. Monod; Henri Pytt; and Felix Neff.

Taking the Bible and the Bible alone as their rule of faith and practice, the Haldanes and their associates eventually came to grave decisions involving not only a break with the Church of Scotland but also with the Congregationalists. Naturally these decisions had far-reaching consequences and led to divisions in the Haldane movement. However, the brothers had never sought to establish a denomination and viewed many of these changes in local church fellowship as normal results in a search for Scriptural truth. The often dramatic disagreements among their followers served to awaken wide interest in the study of the Scriptures and resulted in tremendous changes in the thinking and practice of leaders in the established churches.

Among the radical decisions made by the Haldanes was the rejection of extracongregational church government. They came to teach that Christ was the sole head of the church and that local church government should be vested in a plurality of elders. Abandoning the doctrine of infant baptism, they eventually decided that only immersion of believers was sustained by the Scriptures. They early introduced the practice of every-Sunday observance of the Lord's Supper and of weekly meetings for social worship in which all members were allowed to participate with prayers and testimonies. They were strongly insistent upon the necessity of a pious Christian life by all professors of religion, and frequently resorted to strict disciplinary measures in their congregations.

Several years earlier, a somewhat similar movement gained headway in Scotland under the leadership of Glas, Sandeman, and Walker. While these men held to noble views of a free gospel and simplicity of faith, they were coldly intellectual in their concepts of salvation and legalistic in their application of divine truth. The Haldanes believed that faith is more than intellectual assent to Bible truth. They regarded faith as resting upon the evidence furnished by the Holy Spirit in the Scriptures, but as embracing not only the understanding but the heart. Both brothers often said that "faith is trust or confidence in Christ," implying a willingness to submit to His authority and consisting in a heartfelt, personal trust in Him as the Son of God and Saviour of mankind. Much of the Haldane preaching in later years was devoted to combating the "evils of Sandemanianism."

While the Haldane movement disappeared with the lengthening of the years, except for its somewhat nebulous relationship to the Plymouth Brethren, its influence not only in the British Isles but around the world still remains to a large degree.

Richardson's view that the Haldane movement was "the first phase" of the American movement, which is the subject of this volume, attests the historical fact that restoration is a continuing mark of the divine order. Whenever error or apostasy threaten the purity and effectiveness of the church of Christ, God raises up a restoration movement to accomplish His purpose. Should "the current reformation" fail in its mission, God will assuredly raise up another. The "gates of hell shall not prevail" against His church.

BIBLIOGRAPHY: Introduction

Babut, E. C., *Priscillian et le Priscillianisme*.
Beausobre, *Histoire Critique de Manichee et du Manicheeisme*.
Broadbent, E. H., *The Pilgrim Church* (see Preface for additional historical source material).
Burkitt, F. C., *The Religion of the Manichees*.
Cheltschizki, Peter, *The Net of Faith*.
Combo, E., *Histoire des Vaudois*.
Conybeare, Fred C., *The Key of Faith* (translated from the Armenian).
D'Aubigne, J. H. Merle, *History of the Reformation*.
Faber, G. S., *The Ancient Vallenses and Albigenses*.
Haldane, Alexander, *Memoirs of R. and J. A. Haldane*.
Harnack, Ad. V., *Marcion das Evangelium vom Fromden Gott*.
Hershberger, Guy F., *The Recovery of the Anabaptist Vision* (see Introduction for additional historical source material).
Keller, Ludwig, *Die Reformation und die alteren Reformparteien*.
LaTourette, Kenneth Scott, *A History of the Expansion of Christianity* (Vols. I and II).
Moshiem, Johann Lorenz von, *Institute of Ecclesiastical History*.
Ramsey, W. M., *The Church in the Roman Empire Before A.D. 170*.
Richardson, Robert, *Memoirs of Alexander Campbell*. (Chapters 10 and 11).
Rowe, John F., *History of Reformatory Movements*.
Schepss, Georg, *Priscillian ein Neuaufgefundener*.

Chapter 1

A Great Awakening

in America

As the eighteenth century drew to a close in America, signs of a tremendous moving of the Spirit of God appeared in what Dorchester had called "the darkest period spiritually and morally in the history of American Christianity."

This tragic declension had many causes, among which were the collapse of stable and responsible government, a fluctuating economy, and the infiltration of French infidelity.

The French and Indian War and the American Revolution had so disturbed the ideals and customs of the people that their regular observance of the Lord's Day and the ministry of the churches had been widely disregarded. The British and French soldiers had exhibited an extremely low order of morality and introduced a tide of godless skepticism. The part played by France in the liberation of the new nation from the tyranny of Britain had induced a special affection for the country of Lafayette. The writings of Voltaire were welcomed by the intelligentsia as the means of emancipating mankind from religious tyranny and the introduction of a new age of reason.

According to Cunningham, these early Americans, bewitched by Voltaire, denounced religion as a "system of fraud and trick" imposed upon the ignorant multitude by priestcraft. They found no authority, no evidence whatever for a divine revelation. To them moral obligation seemed "a cobweb, which might indeed tangle flies, but by which creatures of a stronger wing nobly disdained to be confined." The world, they decided, had probably been eternal; and matter was the only existence. Man must have sprung, like a mushroom, out of the earth by some chance chemical process; and his powers of thinking, choice, and motivity were merely the result of "elective affinities." If there had been a God, and if man were a created being, he had been created only to be happy. Animal pleasure being the only happiness, it was, in infidel eyes, the only end of man's creation.

Infidel clubs were popular. They were made up of men and women who studied the works of Voltaire, Volney, and Paine, and indulged in all sorts of base and lascivious practices. In one such club it was said that "the conduct of the females was such as to illustrate the practical effects of their beliefs. Not one of them could or would pretend to know who was the father of their offspring. Perhaps hell could not produce more disgusting objects . . ." Joel Parker wrote:

> We are fast becoming a nation of drunkards. We could ascertain that there are 300,000 drunkards in our land and that from ten to twenty thousand were annually assigned to drunkards' graves . . . Piety seems to be flying out of our land; religion declined, morality extinguished, vice grew bold, profaneness, revelling, dishonesty and sinful amusements greatly increased, universalism, infidelity, atheism, scoffing at all serious godliness, contempt for the holy Sabbath, deflections from public worship, omission of family religion and disregard of divine ordinances, have spread in a degree, which calls for tears of grief, threatening in progress to waste all the valuable interests of society.

Dr. Timothy Dwight, president of Yale, wrote in his *Travels*:

> Youths, particularly those who have been liberally educated, and who, with strong passions and feeble principles, were votaries of sensuality and ambition, delighted in the prospect of unrestrained gratification, and, panting to be enrolled with men of passion and splendor, became enamored of the new [infidel] doctrines. The tenor of opinion, and even of conversation, was to a considerable extent changed at once. Striplings scarcely fledged suddenly found that the world had been enveloped in general darkness through the long succession of preceding ages, and that the light of wisdom had just begun to dawn on the human race. All the science, all the information that had been acquired before the last thirty or forty years stood in their view for nothing. Experience they proclaimed a plotting instructress who taught in manners, morals and government nothing but abecedarian lessons fitted for children only.

The religious decline was not by any means confined to the eastern states. In Kentucky, many towns were named for infidels, such as Altamont, Bourbon, and Rousseau. Peter Cartwright, the noted Methodist circuit rider, wrote:

> Logan County, Kentucky, when my father moved there, was called Rogue's Harbor. Here many refugees from all parts of the Union fled to escape punishment or justice, for, although there was law, it could not be executed, and it was a desperate state of society. Murderers, horse thieves, highway robbers, and counterfeiters fled there until they combined and actually formed a majority. Those who favored a better state of morals were called regulators, but they encountered fierce opposition from the rogues. A battle was fought with guns, pistols, dirks, knives, and clubs in which the regulators were defeated.

West of the Alleghenies there were groups of twenty to fifty thousand people without a church or minister. Yet these communities were filled with infidel works such as the *System de La Nature*, the *Philosophical Dictionary*, *Political Justice*, and the *Age of Reason*. The churches of the eastern states did little or nothing to establish congregations in the West, while it is said that the infidels of France raised among themselves three million francs for the purpose of printing and distributing books to corrupt the minds of the American people.

The effect of this situation upon the state of this nation became a growing concern of thinking people. An intimate friend wrote to George Washington in 1796, "Our affairs seem to lead to some crisis, some revolution; something that I cannot forsee or conjecture. I am more uneasy than during the war." Washington replied, "Your sentiment that we are drawing to a crisis accords with mine. What the event will be is beyond my foresight."

Washington was one of the woeful minority who still held to the ancient moral and spiritual landmarks. In his Farewell Address, he said:

> Of all the dispositions and habits which lead to political prosperity, religion and morality are indispensible supports. In vain would that man claim the tribute of patriotism, who would labor to subvert these great pillars of the duties of men and of citizens. The mere politician equally with the pious man ought to respect and cherish them (Strickland, p. 30).

Patrick Henry, who abhorred infidelity, wrote an unpublished work against the *Age of Reason*. Benjamin Franklin, who is often classified as an opponent of religion, wrote Tom Paine, refusing to publish one of his tracts:

> I would advise you not to attempt unchaining the tiger, but to burn this piece before it is seen by any other person . . . You yourself may find it easy to live a virtuous life without the assistance afforded by religion, . . . but think how great a proportion of mankind consists of weak and ignorant men and women and of inexperienced, inconsiderate youth of both sexes who have need of the motives of religion to restrain them from vice, to support their virtue and retain them in the practice of it until it become habitual, which is the great point of security (Strickland, p. 31).

Others of this high-minded and courageous mold were little more effective in their instruction than King Canute with the tide.

The churches were impotent. Lengthy and theologically abstruse creeds were made rigid tests of fellowship. The clergy usurped the interpretation of Scripture and assumed priestly functions. The Bible was virtually a closed book to the masses, and it was not regarded to be a systematic and progressive revelation of God's plan of redemption. The doctrine of total depravity was carried to disgusting extremes. Bitter debate accentuated sectarian division that turned the forces of righteousness upon one another in the face of a moral and spiritual situation which called for united action on the part of all the friends of God. Methodism was checked in its effective growth. In three years—1793-1795—the denomination suffered an average loss of about four thousand members annually. There was a general decline in all church membership. So discouraging was the situation in the Episcopal church that the bishop of New York resigned, believing the church would not continue much longer. Bishop Madison, of Virginia, shared the despairing conviction of Chief Justice Marshall that the church had gone too far to be revived.

Church colleges were no longer worthy of the name. Yale's charter clearly stated that it must uphold the Christian religion and one of its laws stated that "if any scholar shall deny the Holy Scriptures, or any part thereof, to be of divine authority; or shall assist and endeavor to propagate among the students any error or heresy subverting the foundations of the Christian religion, and shall persist therein, after admonition, he shall be dismissed." Yet when the Freshman class entered Yale in the fall of 1796, only one was a professing Christian; the Sophomore class contained none; the Junior one; and the Senior only eight or ten. The college church had dwindled to two members. On a Communion Sunday, scoffers in the dining hall cut the bread in pieces, and with unctuous mockery forced the element upon a solitary student who had just come in from divine worship. Infidelity dominated the College of William and Mary in Virginia. Harvard went so far in its liberalism that it eventually elected Henry Ware, an avowed Unitarian, to the divinity professorship. Princeton in 1792 had only one student who was a professed Christian. Professors who were rank infidels infected with their godless philosophies every church educational institution of any consequence in the young nation.

In the midst of these dark and discouraging days came the Great Revival (1800-1860). This major phenomenon in American church history prepared the way for the movement which is the theme of this work. Previous volumes have taken too slight note of the Great Revival and have failed to differentiate between the fruits of that Revival and the distinctive features of the Restoration movement.

Spiritual revivals occur periodically in the life of the church and often result not only in a quickening of the people of God but also in the amelioration of the ills of society in general. There is no more vivid example of this than the Wesleyan Revival in Great Britain.

Burns, in *Revivals, Their Laws and Leaders* (pp. 13, 14), describes prerevival conditions in general which might well picture America before the Holy Spirit moved at the close of the eighteenth and the beginning of the nineteenth century. Says Burns:

A period of gloom sets in, a weariness and exhaustion invade the heart, the pleasures of the world no longer satisfy, they set up a deep distaste and satiety. Sick in soul man turns with a sigh to God; dimly they awake to the consciousness that, in bartering heaven for earthly joys, they have encountered irremediable loss; that in the decay of spiritual vision the world has lost its soul of loveliness. Slowly this aching grows, the heart of man begins to cry out for God, for spiritual certainties, for fresh visions. From a faint desire this widens until it becomes a great human need; until in its urgency, it seems to beat with violence at the very gates of heaven.

Within the church itself, also, throughout all its day of defection, there have been many who have not bowed the knee to Baal, who have mourned its loss of spiritual power, and who have never ceased to pray earnestly for a revival of its spiritual life. Gradually, however, their numbers are found to increase; prayer becomes more urgent and more confident . . . Men begin to gather in companies to pray. They cease not to importune God, day and night, often with tears beseeching him to visit them with his divine power. In many different places, quite unconnected with each other, the spirit of intercession awakes and with it an expectancy that will not be denied, a premonition that there is at hand the dawn of a new day.

The Great Revival in America was preceded by concerted prayer. A group of twenty-three New England ministers, including Stephen Gano, of Providence, and Isaac Backus, of Middleboro, issued a "Circular Letter" calling the ministers and churches to pray for revival. The Circular Letter contains the following interesting paragraphs:

> To the ministers and churches of every Christian denomination in the United States, [a call] to unite in their endeavors to carry into execution the humble attempt to promote explicit agreement and visible union of God's people in extraordinary prayer for the revival of religion and the advancement of Christ's Kingdom on earth.
> In execution of this plan, it is proposed that the ministers and churches of every Christian denomination should be invited to maintain public prayer and praise, accompanied with such instruction from God's Word, as might be judged proper, on every first Tuesday, of the four quarters of the year, beginning with the first Tuesday of January, 1795, at two o'clock in the afternoon, if the plan of concert should then be ripe for a beginning, and so continuing from quarter to quarter, and from year to year, until the good providence of God prospering our endeavors, we shall obtain the blessings for which we pray (Strickland, p. 45).

The historic awakening began in New England, not on the western frontiers. Dr. Edward O. Griffin, president of Williams College, fixed the beginning date as 1792, and described an unbroken series of revivals lasting well into the new century. The fire fell in New England and spread like a conflagration throughout the nation.

Strangely enough, the colleges became the centers of the spiritual phenomenon. Head and shoulders above the distinguished educators who furnished leadership was President Timothy Dwight, of Yale. So important was the contribution of Dwight to a changed climate in American thought and life that no attempt to delineate the America of 1792-1810 can in any sense be adequate without extensive recognition of that contribution. He scarcely had begun his administration until he started to preach evangelistic sermons in the college church. At first the students resisted the gospel messages, but finally confessions of faith in Christ began to mark the services.

It was customary for the president or the professor of divinity "to deliver a discourse to the candidates for the baccalaureate on the Sabbath preceding the public commencement." In 1796, Dwight preached on "The Nature and Danger of Infidel Philosophy." His text was Colossians 2:8: "Beware lest any man spoil you through philosophy and vain deceit, after the tradition of men, after the rudiments of the world, and not after Christ." In the opening of this famous baccalaureate sermon, Dwight said:

> The philosophy which has opposed Christianity in every succeeding age has uniformly worn the same character, with that described in the text. It has rested on the same foundations, proceeded from the same disposition, aimed at the same ends and produced the same means. Satisfied with the justice of

23

these assertions, I feel it, young gentlemen, to be my duty on this occasion to exhort you to beware lest you become a prey to the philosophy which opposes the Gospel; to prove to you that this philosophy is vain and deceitful; to show you that you are in danger of becoming a prey to it; and to dissuade you by several arguments from thus yielding yourself a prey.

He showed them that the infidel philosophy of their day was merely a revival of what other philosophers taught. In this sermon he put these philosophers, as it were, in a procession. He made them march, one by one, before his listeners as he unfolded their teaching and the character it produced.

Mr. Hume declares that man is a mere machine, that is, an object operated on by external causes; that suicide or self-murder is lawful and commendable and of course virtuous; that adultery must be practiced, if we would obtain all the advantages of life; that female infidelity (or adultery) when known is a small thing, when unknown, nothing; that skepticism is the true and only wisdom of man; that it is unreasonable to believe God to be wise and good.

Such is the skepticism of Hume; the mortality and materiality of the soul; the doctrine that man is a mere animal, that animal gratification is the chief end of our being, that right and wrong depend solely on the decision of the magistrate; that ridicule is the test of truth; that we may lawfully get all things, if we get them safely; that modesty is inspired only by prejudice and has its foundation in the mere desire of appearing to be superior to animals. Adultery is lawful according to the religion of nature. . . . When we view the pernicious tendency of these doctrines, we may safely say that thoroughly practiced, they would overwhelm the world with that misery which the Scriptures exhibit as experienced only in hell.

Lord Bolingbroke declared that man is only a superior animal; that man's chief end is to gratify the appetites and inclinations of the flesh. Adultery is no violation of the Law, or religion of nature; that there is no wrong in lewdness except in the highest incest; that the law or religion of nature forbids no incest except between the nearest relations and plainly supposes that all men and women are unchaste and that there is no such thing as conjugal fidelity.

These doctrines served as specimens of the philosophy which then existed.

Dwight brought the old pagan philosophies before the graduates. He said:

Both Zeno and Cleanthes taught that children may lawfully roast and eat their own parents as any other food; Diogenes and the cynics generally taught that parents may lawfully sacrifice and eat their children. Plato taught that lewdness was justifiable, and Cicero, that it was a crime of small magnitude. Aristippus taught that both theft and adultery were lawful.

Dwight went on to show that the man who seriously believes in the rectitude of lying, cruelty, fraud, lewdness, and impurity cannot be virtuous. He showed this to be the case in the lives of Tindal, Blount, and others. The ancient philosophers were adulterous and lewd. He cited the cases of Seneca, Aristippus, Zeno, and Zenophen to show that many of the ancient philosophers were noted for sodomy. "These are among the most

24

respectful of those men," said he, "whose theological and moral systems modern philosophers prefer to that of Christ and his apostles."

He warned the graduates to beware of the infidel arguments against the Scriptures, and the confidence with which they asserted their philosophies, and the boast that their opinions were embraced by the great body of mankind, especially of the ingenious and the learned.

Christians believe, and infidels do not, that the Scriptures are a divine revelation. Neither they nor we know, both classes merely believe. The only question to be decided between the contending parties is which believes on the best evidence . . . The faith therefore which is best supported is most rational and ought to confer the superiority of character . . .

I cheerfully admit, young gentlemen, that many infidels have been ingenious men; that some of them have been learned men, and that a few of them have been great men. Hume, Tindal and a few others have been distinguished for superior strength of mind, Bolingbroke for eloquence of the pen, Voltaire for brilliancy of imagination, and various others for respectable talents of different kinds. But I am wholly unable to form a list of infidels, which can, without extreme disadvantage, be compared with the two Bacons, Erasmus, Cumberland, Stiblingfleet, Grotius, Locke, Butler, Newton, Boyle, Berkley, Milton, Johnson . . . In no walk of genius, in no path of knowledge, can infidels support a claim to superiority or equality with Christians. . . .

But what, let me ask, would have been our situation had these and many other able men of past ages never lived? How much of all we know is contained in their works and derived solely from their talents and labors. Can it be just, can it be decent to forget the hand that feeds us, and treat with contempt those without whose assistance we should have been savages and blockheads? . . .

Because the vast majority believe false philosophy is no argument. So in days when all believed Aristotle's philosophy, was it true? or disbelieved the Copernican system and Galileo, was it false? . . .

Heathenism formerly overspread the world and numbered in its votaries nearly all the learned and unlearned of the human race. . . . When Christianity first began to progress, it could boast of only twelve poor, uneducated men as its champions with perhaps less than a thousand followers. By the labors of this little band, in less than three centuries, it overturned most of the superstition, power, learning and philosophy of the known world.

Dwight warned them against another source of danger: namely, the contempt and ridicule with which Christianity is opposed. Lord Shaftesbury was a master in ridicule. Voltaire said, "Render those pedants as enormously ridiculous as you can. Ridicule will do everything." To this Dwight replied, "The cause which needs these weapons cannot be just; the doctrine which cannot be supported without them must be false."

He warned them against the bias of the world toward infidelity. This is seen in history since the Reformation revival, especially in Europe. He warned them of the certain bias in their own hearts against Christianity. Said he:

The restraints of Christianity you, like others, at times feel with impatience and pain. Unbelief and infidelity seem to give freedom.

Circumstances had filled every Christian, every friend of the human race with alarm, not for the permanence of Christianity, but for the continuance of peace, the safety of every right and the existence of every valuable interest. This infidel philosophy presents no efficacious means of restraining vice or promoting virtue; on the contrary, it encourages vice, and discourages virtue. . . . Philosophy will not and Christianity will increase your comfort and lessen your distress here, and save you from misery and confer on you happiness hereafter.

The summary of this sermon is remarkable:

As mere infidelity [philosophy] teaches nothing but to contest all principles and to add none. As skepticism it is an ocean of doubt and agitation, in which there are no soundings, and to which there is no shore. As animalism and atheism it completes the ravage and ruin of man, which in its preceding forms, it had so successfully begun. It now holds out the rank Circerean draught, and sends the deluded wretches, who are allured, to taste, to bustle and wallow with the swine, to play tricks with the monkey, to rage and rend with the tiger and to purify into nothing with the herd of kindred brutes.

Christianity, with an influence infinitely more benevolent, enhances the value of your present life beyond the search of calculation. It informs you that you are intelligent and moral creatures of the all-perfect Jehovah, who made, who preserved, who rules the universe, who is present in all places, who beholds all things, who is eternal and immutable, infinitely benevolent, infinitely beneficent, the faithful friend of the virtuous, the unchanging enemy of sin, the rewarder and the reward of all returning sinners, who diligently seek him. In this character, it presents to you a direct, clear and perfect system of rules for all your moral conduct; rules of thinking, speaking and acting; rules reaching every possible case and removing every rational doubt. Here is no uncertainty, no wavering, no rolling on the billows of anxiety, no plunging into the gulf of despair. Your path is a straight and beaten way and were you wayfaring, and fools, you need not err therein.

As you pass through the various stages of your journey, you are furnished with aids and motives infinite to check your delay, to recall your wanderings, to cheer fatigue, to refresh your languidy, to lessen your difficulties, to renew your strength, and to prolong your perseverance to the end. Should you at any time through ignorance, inattention or allurement, dangerously diverge from your course, a sweet and charming Voice behind you cries, "This is the way, walk ye therein." Should you hereafter have families, your communication of the principles and your practice of the duties of Christianity will beyond all things else insure to you domestic peace and prosperity. . . . The friends who visit you will esteem and love you, for they will find in your character something to be esteemed and loved. . . . To the neighborhood around you, you will be esteemed benefactions and blessings. The poor, the sick, the outcast, the friendless and disconsolate, will especially acknowledge you as their patrons. Enemies you will find . . . Compare your friends with your enemies and you will find nothing to be regretted.

Nor will you be less useful to your country. Rational freedom cannot be preserved without the aid of Christianity . . . In this country, the freest and the happiest, which the world has hitherto seen, the whole system of policy originated, has continued, and stands on the single basis of Christianity. Good subjects have been formed here by forming good men; and none but good subjects can long be governed by persuasion. The learning, peace, mild intercourse and universally happy state of society, enjoyed here, all have the same origin. Would you preserve these blessings during your own life, would you hand them down to posterity, increasing multitudes of those who are not Christian, and all those who with one voice tell you, EMBRACE CHRISTIANITY (Strickland, pp. 66-70).

Revival in the highest definition of that term came to the Yale campus in 1802, and under the preaching of Dwight hundreds of students gave themselves to Christ as Lord and Saviour. At Williams College, so strong was the wave of commitment to Christ that the famous "Haystack Meeting" eventuated, often considered the beginning of American foreign missions. In Andover College, the lives of Judson, Rice, and Hull were touched and led to the formation of the American Board of Foreign Missions and the American Baptist Foreign Mission Society.

In the West, where the Restoration movement had its rise, the Great Revival started among the Presbyterians in Kentucky. While Barton W. Stone, one of the noted early leaders in the Restoration movement, figured in this spiritual awakening, he was by no means the leader in it. That distinction belongs to James McGready. He was ably assisted by William McGee, William Hodge, Robert Marshall, John Rankin, and Stone.

James McGready was born in Pennsylvania about 1760. His parents moved to Guilford County, North Carolina, where he spent his boyhood days. As a lad he was exemplary in conduct. He was so sedate that his uncle put him under the training of John McMillan, a Presbyterian minister in western Pennsylvania. J. M. Howard writes in Hay's *Presbyterians*:

About 1786, he, by accident, overheard a conversation between two friends, of which he was the subject. They freely expressed their views about his religious character, declaring that although a minister in the Presbyterian Church, he was a mere formalist and a stranger to regenerating grace. This led him to earnest self-examination and prayer, and at a sacramental meeting, near the Monongahela River, he found the new spiritual life which his friends had declared he lacked. This new experience transformed his whole life. Thenceforth he made it his mission to arouse false professors, to awaken a dead church and warn sinners and lead them to seek the new spiritual life which he himself had found. In North Carolina, where he went as pastor, extensive revivals were kindled. His ministry also aroused fierce opposition. He was licensed by the Redstone Presbytery. Wherever he preached revivals broke out. He was accused of "running people distracted." His life was threatened, in a letter written in blood. His pulpit was burned down. Because of this opposition he went west in 1796, and accepted a call from some of his former hearers who had settled in Kentucky. He became pastor of three churches in Logan County: Gasper River, Muddy River and Red River. Here his sermons stirred the ungodly and aroused opposition. The people had been told by his enemies not to give any trouble to experimental religion.

Barton W. Stone described McGready:

His person was not prepossessing, nor his appearance interesting, except his remarkable gravity and small piercing eyes. His coarse tremulous voice excited in me the idea of something unearthly. His gestures were *sui generis*, the perfect reverse of elegance. Everything appeared by him forgotten but the salvation of souls. Such earnestness, such zeal, such powerful persuasion, I had never before witnessed.

Logan county was the scene of the initiatory meeting which set the pattern for the regional revivals fanning out through Kentucky into Tennessee, the Ohio country, western Virginia, and the Carolinas. As in New

England, there was first a call to prayer. McGready drew up the following covenant which bound all its signers to offer special prayer at definite times:

> When we consider the word and promise of a compassionate God, to the poor lost family of Adam, we find the strongest encouragement for Christians to pray in faith—to ask in the name of Jesus for the conversion of their fellow-men. None ever went to Christ, when on earth, with the case of their friends that were denied, and although the days of his humiliation are ended, yet for encouragement of his people, he had left it on record, that where two or three agree upon earth to ask in prayer believing, it shall be done. Again "whatsoever ye shall ask the Father in my name that will I do, that the Father may be glorified in the Son." With these promises before us we feel encouraged to unite ·our supplications to a prayer-hearing God, for the outpouring of his Spirit, that his people may be quickened and comforted, and that our children and sinners generally may be converted. Therefore we bind ourselves to observe the third Saturday of each month, for one year, as a day of fasting and prayer, for the conversion of sinners in Logan County and throughout the world. We also engage to spend one-half hour every Saturday evening, beginning at the setting of the sun, and one-half hour every Sabbath morning, at the rising of the sun, in pleading with God to revive his work.

The first big break came in Presbyterian pre-Communion services at Red River, Gasper River, and Muddy River. As McGready called on people to examine themselves, confess their shortcomings, and give testimony to their Christian faith as requisite to participation in the Lord's Supper, "many persons were so struck with deep, heart-piercing convictions that their bodily strength was quite overcome so that they fell to the ground and could not refrain from bitter groans and outcries for mercy." Then the movement of the Spirit seemed to take the ensuing events out of human hands. Daily and through the nights for weeks on end, thousands gathered in the churches and in the open fields to confess their sins and to call on the name of the Lord for salvation.

Barton W. Stone, Presbyterian minister at Concord and Cane Ridge in Bourbon County, journeyed across the state to witness a revival in McGready's field. He wrote to friends at home:

> There on the edge of a prairie in Logan County, Kentucky, the multitudes came together and continued a number of days and nights encamped on the ground, during which time worship was carried on in some part of the encampment. The scene was new to me and passing strange. It baffled description. Many, very many, fell down as men slain in battle and continued for hours together in an apparently breathless and motionless state, sometimes for a few minutes reviving and exhibiting symptoms of life by a deep groan or a piercing shriek, or by a prayer for mercy, fervently uttered. After lying there for hours, they obtained deliverance. The gloomy cloud that had covered their faces seemed gradually and visibly to disappear, and hope in smiles brightened into joy. They would rise shouting deliverance, and then would address the surrounding multitudes in language truly eloquent and impressive. With astonishment did I hear men, women and children declaring the wonderful works of God and the glorious mysteries of the Gospel (Quoted by Candler, *Great Revivals and the Great Republic*, pp. 178, 179).

Shortly afterward, in August, 1801, Stone witnessed similar scenes in his own churchyard and in the great canebrake surrounding it—probably the greatest demonstration of revival power ever seen in America. Stone disclaimed any credit for what happened, but he was an active participant in it, preaching day and night alongside Methodist, Baptist, and independent preachers from western states. The roads for miles were clogged with wagons, carriages, horsemen, and people who had walked miles to attend. Military men on the ground estimated that between twenty and thirty thousand people were present on the peak days. The multitudes remained in their primitive surroundings until all food supplies were exhausted and they were faced with starvation.

Stone in his autobiography (*A Short History of the Life of Barton W. Stone Written by Himself*) describes the phenomenon of the Cane Ridge revival:

The bodily agitation or exercises, attending the excitement in the beginning of this century, were various, and called by various names;—as, the falling exercise—the jerks—the dancing exercise—the barking exercise—the laughing and singing exercise, etc. The falling exercise was very common among all classes, the saints and sinners of every age and of every grade, from the philosopher to the clown. The subject of this exercise would, generally, with a piercing scream, fall like a log on the floor, earth, or mud, and appear as dead. Of thousands of similar cases, I will mention one. At a meeting, two gay young ladies, sisters, were standing together attending to the exercises and preaching at the time. Instantly they both fell, with a shriek of distress, and lay for more than an hour apparently in a lifeless state. Their mother, a pious Baptist, was in great distress, fearing they would not revive. At length they began to exhibit symptoms of life, by crying fervently for mercy, and then relapsed into the same death-like state, with an awful gloom on their countenances. After awhile, the gloom on the face of one was succeeded by a heavenly smile, and she cried out, precious Jesus, and rose up and spoke of the love of God—the preciousness of Jesus, and of the glory of the gospel, to the surrounding crowd, in language almost superhuman, and pathetically exhorted all to repentance. In a little while after, the other sister was similarly exercised. From that time they became remarkably pious members of the church.

I have seen very many pious persons fall in the same way, from a sense of the danger of their unconverted children, brothers, or sisters—from a sense of the danger of their neighbors, and of the sinful world. I have heard them agonizing in tears and strong crying for mercy to be shown to sinners, and speaking like angels to all around.

The jerks cannot be so easily described. Sometimes the subject of the jerks would be affected in some one member of the body, and sometimes in the whole system. When the head alone was affected, it would be jerked backward and forward, or from side to side, so quickly that the features of the face could not be distinguished. When the whole system was affected, I have seen the person stand in one place, and   jerk backward and forward in quick succession, their head nearly touching the floor behind and before. All classes, saints and sinners, the strong as well as the weak, were thus affected. I have inquired of those thus affected. They could not account for it; but some have told me that those were among the happiest seasons of their lives. I have seen some wicked persons thus affected, and all the time cursing the jerks, while they were thrown to the earth with violence. Though so awful to behold, I do not remember that any one of the thousands I have seen ever sustained an injury in body. This was as strange as the exercise itself.

The dancing exercise. This generally began with the jerks, and was peculiar to professors of religion. The subject, after jerking awhile, began to dance, and then the jerks would cease. Such dancing was indeed heavenly to the spectators; there was nothing in it like levity, nor calculated to excite levity in the beholders. The smile of heaven shone on the countenance of the subject, and assimilated to angels appeared the whole person. Sometimes the motion was quick and sometimes slow. Thus they continued to move forward and backward in the same track or alley till nature seemed exhausted, and they would fall prostrate on the floor or earth, unless caught by those standing by. While thus exercised, I have heard their solemn praises and prayers ascending to God.

The barking exercise (as opposers contemptuously called it) was nothing but the jerks. A person affected with the jerks, especially in his head, would often make a grunt, or bark, if you please, from the suddenness of the jerk. This name of barking seems to have had its origin from an old Presbyterian preacher of East Tennessee. He had gone into the woods for private devotion, and was seized with the jerks. Standing near a sapling, he caught hold of it, to prevent his falling, and as his head jerked back, he uttered a grunt or kind of noise similar to a bark, his face being turned upwards. Some wag discovered him in this position, and reported that he found him barking up a tree.

The laughing exercise was frequent, confined solely with the religious. It was a loud, hearty laughter, but one *sui generis;* it excited laughter in none else. The subject appeared rapturously solemn, and his laughter excited solemnity in saints and sinners. It is truly indescribable.

The running exercise was nothing more than, that persons feeling something of these bodily agitations, through fear, attempted to run away, and thus escape from them; but it commonly happened that they ran not far, before they fell, or became so greatly agitated that they could proceed no farther. I knew a young physician of a celebrated family, who came some distance to a big meeting to see the strange things he had heard of. He and a young lady had sportively agreed to watch over, and take care of each other, if either should fall. At length the physician felt something very uncommon, and started from the congregation to run into the woods; he was discovered running as for life, but did not proceed far till he fell down, and there lay till he submitted to the Lord, and afterwards became a zealous member of the church. Such cases were common.

I shall close this chapter with the singing exercise. This is more unaccountable than anything else I ever saw. The subject in a very happy state of mind would sing most melodiously, not from the mouth or nose, but entirely in the breast, the sounds issuing thence. Such music silenced everything, and attracted the attention of all. It was most heavenly. None could ever be tired of hearing it. Doctor J. P. Campbell and myself were together at a meeting, and were attending to a pious lady thus exercised, and concluded it to be something surpassing any thing we had known in nature.

Thus have I given a brief account of the wonderful things that appeared in the great excitement in the beginning of this century. That there were many eccentricities, and much fanaticism in this excitement, was acknowledged by its warmest advocates; indeed it would have been a wonder, if such things had not appeared, in the circumstances of that time. Yet the good effects were seen and acknowledged in every neighborhood, and among the different sects it silenced contention, and promoted unity for awhile; and these blessed effects would have continued, had not men put forth their unhallowed hands to hold up their tottering ark, mistaking it for the ark of God.

The Great American Revival, sometimes called the "Second Awakening," did not mark the beginning of the Restoration movement in America, as some have indicated in their anxiety to predate its advent and credit Stone with its major initiatory thrust. This revival was not characteristic of the Restoration movement, yet is significant in that it was responsible for certain thought reactions of Restoration leaders. Unquestionably, the revival created an atmosphere favorable or unfavorable to the Christian religion which immensely facilitated the progress of the Restoration.

The over-all results of this great awakening are well described by Leonard Bacon in his *History of American Christianity*:

> The widespread revivals of the first decades of the nineteenth century saved the church in America from its low estate and girded it for stupendous tasks that were about to be devolved on it. In the glow of this renewed fervor, the churches of New England successfully made the difficult transition from establishment to self-support and to the costly enterprises of aggressive evangelization into which, in company with other churches to the South and West, they were about to enter. The Christianity of the country was prepared and equipped to attend with equal pace the prodigious rush of population across the breadth of the Great Valley, and to give welcome to the invading host of immigrants, which, before the end of a half century, was to effect its entrance into our territory at the rate of a thousand a day. It was to accommodate itself to changing social conditions as the once agricultural population began to concentrate itself in factory villages and commercial towns. It was to carry on systematic campaigns against instituted social wrong, such as the drinking usages of society, the savage code of dueling and the public sanction of slavery. And it was to enter the "effectual door" which from the beginning of the century opened wider and wider to admit the Gospel and the church to every nation under heaven.

The churches began to make phenomenal growth. Dorchester wrote: "Nothing like such an increase had ever been known, though it has since been paralleled and even.exceeded for the new revival era has continued to our time."

By 1850, the Presbyterians grew to 487,691 members; the Congregationalists to 197,197; the Baptists to 815,212; and the Methodists to 1,323,631. In 1800, there was one church to 1,751; one minister to 2,001; and one communicant to 14.50 inhabitants. In 1850, there was one church to 538; one minister to 900; and one communicant to 6.57 inhabitants.

Presbyterian growth in the West was severely restricted by the rise of the Cumberland Presbyterian church, which was a protest against hyper-Calvinism. The Christian Connection likewise flourished because of defections from strait-laced Presbyterianism. Throughout the nation the old-line denominations became subject to severe scrutiny and critical evaluation, and numerous new fellowships of Christians arose outside the aegis of the traditional churches.

In 1800, pietists of the German Reformed heritage established the United Brethren in Christ. The Evangelical Association—destined many years later to merge with the United Brethren in the present Evangelical United Brethren church—was formed under the leadership of Jacob Albright, who had been a Lutheran. Kentucky Baptists, deploring the hairsplitting theology of the times, began to stress the necessity for a return to the simple gospel of the New Testament. The South Kentucky Association of Separate Baptists in 1787 numbered eleven churches which were "constituted on the Bible" alone. The oldest Baptist church in Indiana, established in 1789, took as its name "The Church of Christ on Owen's Creek" (Knox County). The Free Will Baptists in the eastern states (1727-1801) protested the hyper-Calvinism which negated the freedom of the individual to accept or reject salvation and to read and interpret the New Testament for himself. The Methodist church in Maryland, Virginia, and North Carolina faced a revolt against the episcopacy of Francis Asbury, led by James O'Kelly. When the first Methodist General Conference, in 1792, turned down his resolutions demanding the right of appeal to the conference by preachers who felt themselves unjustly treated by the bishops, he organized the Republican Methodist church. Later, in 1794, these dissidents adopted the name *Christian church,* declared that the Bible should be their only creed, and adopted a measure of congregational polity. This significant secession did not mean that there was any departure from Methodist theology or evangelistic methodology. A "Christian" movement in New England began in 1801. It revolved about the ministries of two men—Elias Smith and Abner Jones.

Smith was born in 1769 at Lyme, Connecticut, but was a resident of Vermont when he professed conversion when he accidentally fell from a horse. He joined the Baptist church and two years later, despite a woeful lack of education, was ordained to the ministry. Disgusted by the hyper-Calvinism of many of his brother ministers, he soon came to the conviction that all man-devised creeds should be abandoned as tests of fellowship and that overhead ecclesiastical organizations were inadequate guarantees of unity. He soon began to advocate a return to the Holy Scriptures and the preaching of the simple gospel of Christ and the apostles.

Jones was born at Royalton, Massachusetts, in 1772, but also became a resident of Vermont where he, too, professed conversion and joined the Baptist church, preaching as opportunity offered. As a young man he took a short course in the Thompsonian theory of medicine, practiced for a time, and finally became an agent for its inventor, Samuel Thompson. As a student of the Bible, he conceived the idea of a fundamental simplicity in Christian doctrine which would eliminate the necessity of elaborate creeds. Hearing Smith expound his views, Jones decided to put them into action by organizing the first "Christian church" in New England, at Lyndon, Vermont, in September, 1801. Smith reported a Christian church was organized in Portsmouth, New Hampshire, in March, 1803. By 1807 there were fourteen such churches and twelve ordained ministers of this persuasion. For some forty years the two kindred spirits worked together.

In 1827 a writer in the *Advocate and Messenger* declared that "nearly one hundred companies of free brethren met together to worship God in the name of Christ without the addition of any other name." He added that

32

"we mean to be New Testament Christians, without any sectarian name connected with it, without sectarian creeds, articles or confessions, or discipline to illuminate the Scriptures. . . . It is our design to remain free from all human laws, confederations, and unscriptural combinations; and to stand fast in the liberty wherewith Christ has made us free." These New England churches, having originated in dissent from the hyper-Calvinism of the Baptists, retained for a time the Baptist practice of the immersion of penitent believers. Later they came to make only "Christian character" a test of fellowship.

In September, 1808, Elias Smith had the distinction of founding the *Herald of Gospel Liberty,* the first American religious newspaper. After a checkered career, the journal became the official organ of the so-called Christian Connection, which finally merged with the Congregationalists to form the Congregational-Christian denomination. The *Herald* was merged with the *Congregationalist* in 1931. Under Smith's editorship, the *Herald* reflected his wavering views on religion. His weakness for Unitarianism's idea of religious liberty led him in and out of that fold with the result that the New England Christians became known as "Evangelical Unitarians." In a pamphlet entitled "An Account of the Christian Denomination in the United States," Simon Clough, corresponding secretary of the United States General Christian Conference and pastor of one of these churches in New York City, wrote:

> It will be seen from this short statement of our faith that we are strictly Unitarian in our sentiments. We, however, choose to be known by the name Christian. . . . Our mode of preaching and applying these doctrines is very different from that of the body of Christians usually denominated as Unitarians. We are evangelical Unitarians in preaching and applying the Unitarian doctrine; and we are frequently denominated Evangelical Unitarians to distinguish us from the Unitarians in this country and in England.

So definitely did the New England Christians find an affinity in their views that in 1844 they joined with the Unitarians in the establishment of the Meadville Theological School, at Meadville, Pennsylvania.

The Christian churches of New England, and their progeny in Canada, New York, New Jersey, Pennsylvania, and northern Ohio, later joined with the Christian churches of the O'Kelly persuasion on the Middle Atlantic seaboard and the Christian churches of Kentucky, Ohio, and Indiana, to form the Christian Connection with headquarters in Dayton, Ohio. Reference will be made later to the Kentucky "Christians" and to a partial union with the Restoration movement, but the main stream of these people of rather mixed beliefs persisted to the time of their union with the Congregationalists, 122 years after the days of Elias Smith and Abner Jones.

The Great Revival not only created many new churches but also many new seminaries for the training of ministers: Andover, in 1808; Bangor, in 1816; Auburn, in 1821; Yale, in 1822; Union, in 1836; Newton, in 1825; and others too numerous to mention.

33

Great co-operative Christian enterprises were born. Samuel Mills helped to bring the American Bible Society into existence in 1816 by a union of twenty-eight Bible societies that had been formed in Philadelphia, Massachusetts, Connecticut, New York, and elsewhere in the young nation. The American Tract Society united similar organizations in an effective unit in 1825. The Sunday-school movement had its rise in this same period in Virginia, South Carolina, Pennsylvania, and other states. The first Sunday-school union was formed in Philadelphia in 1791, the forerunner of the American Sunday-School Union organized in 1824.

The revival's moral impact on society was tremendous. George A. Baxter wrote to Archibald Alexander, of Princeton, that "the character of Kentucky was entirely changed," the people now being as "remarkable for sobriety as they had formerly been for dissoluteness and immorality." Elaphalet Nott, John Mason Peck, and Lyman Beecher initiated legislation outlawing dueling. The entire abstinence from the use of beverage alcohol became a growing practice. The Total Abstinence Society was organized in 1820 and the American Society for the Promotion of Temperance in 1826. Slavery came under severe criticism. Barton W. Stone, of Kentucky, emancipated his slaves during the revival. In 1818, the General Assembly of the Presbyterian church issued its historic indictment of human bondage. Social and economic progress came as a fruitage of saved men.

The blessings of God were apparent in material gain. The power of steam was soon to transform means of travel and communication. The discoveries of gold, silver, iron, copper, and coal in America's bountiful storehouse made for the greater wealth, comfort, and convenience of humanity. The period following the Great Revival was one of unprecedented national prosperity, and no serious student of history can separate social and economic betterment from their essential spiritual roots.

Thus did God prepare the seed bed for the birth and development of the greatest single Christian movement of distinctly American origin in the religious world.

BIBLIOGRAPHY: Chapter 1

Bacon, Leonard, *History of American Christianity*.
Beardsley, Frank G., *A History of American Revivals*.
Cleveland, Catherine C., *The Great Revival in the West, 1797-1805*.
Cunningham, Charles E., *Timothy Dwight*.
Dwight, Timothy, *Embrace Christianity*.
Finney, Charles G., *Lectures on Revivals of Religion*.
Garrison, W. E., *Religion Follows the Frontier*.
March, Angier, *Increase of Piety, or the Revival of Religion in the United States of America*.
MacClenny, Wilbur E., *The Life of Reverend James O'Kelly*.
Rogers, James R., *The Cane Ridge Meeting House*.
Stone, Barton W., *A Short History of the Life of Barton W. Stone*.
Strickland, Arthur B., *The Great American Revival*.
Sweet, William Warren, *The Story of Religion in America*.
Thompson, Rhodes, *Voices of Cane Ridge*.
Tracy, Joseph, *The Great Awakening*.

Chapter 2

Thomas Campbell and

the *Declaration and Address*

IN 1807 there came from Ireland to America a man of great humility and deep Christian convictions, who was destined to initiate the greatest religious movement of peculiarly American origin in the history of the Christian church.

Other men had the same urges and the same aims, but it remained for him to state in the earliest and a most important document in the background of the modern Ecumenical movement, the basic Biblical principles by which the union of all Christians might be accomplished.

This man was Thomas Campbell.

His ancestors were originally from western Scotland. Emigrating to Ireland, they settled in County Down where Thomas was born February 1, 1763. His father, Archibald, was originally a Roman Catholic and served in the British army. After his return from the wars, he repudiated Romanism and became a strict member of the Church of England. Besides Thomas, there were three younger sons—James, Archibald and Enos—all of whom received an excellent elementary English education in a nearby military regimental school. There were also four daughters, all of whom died in infancy.

In his youth, Thomas became the subject of deep religious impressions and acquired a deep devotion for the Holy Scriptures. The cold formality of the Episcopal ritual never appealed to him, and he was deeply concerned about the want of vital piety in the state church. Attracted to the society of the more rigid and devotional Covenanter and Seceder Presbyterians, he began to attend their religious services. Soon he experienced deep concern for his salvation and began to wrestle with doubts and misgivings and a sense of sin. Then one day as he was walking alone in the fields, in the midst of his prayerful anxieties and longings, "he felt a divine peace suddenly diffuse itself throughout his soul, and the love of God seemed to be shed abroad in his heart . . . He was enabled to see and to trust in the merits of a crucified Christ and to enjoy a divine sense of reconciliation, that filled him with rapture and seemed to determine his destiny forever." At this time, Thomas Campbell believed he was divinely "called" to serve the Lord, and soon afterward decided to devote himself to the ministry in the Secession church. His father at first opposed his decision, but eventually acquiesced.

Entering Glasgow University, Thomas began his required studies in the liberal arts. Upon their completion, he enrolled in the theological school of that branch of the Secession known as the Anti-Burghers. In order to gain admission into Divinity Hall, it was required by the Synod that he should be examined by his Presbytery as to his proficiency in Latin and Greek. He was also examined on the various branches of philosophy he had studied in the University and on his personal religious experience. Then ensued five years of further study, during which time he was permitted to teach or preach. Upon the completion of his theological training, Campbell submitted to examinations and trials for license before the Presbytery in Ireland and was made a probationer. He immediately began a roving ministry in mission churches under the supervision of the Synod, often occupying himself in teaching school.

It was during this period of his ministry that he met Jane Corneigle, the daughter of a devout Huguenot family whose ancestors had settled on the borders of Lough Neagh in County Antrim. In June, 1787, Thomas married Jane. Their first child, Alexander, was born September 12, 1788. Shortly afterward, the family moved to Sheepbridge where Thomas taught school and preached for Seceder churches in the vicinity until 1789, when he accepted a call to the church at Ahorey.

While Thomas was devoting himself to the care of his congregation and to the education of his children, his family continued to increase. Two daughters, Dorothea and Nancy, had been born before the move to Ahorey. To these were added a third daughter, Jane, and then a son, Thomas, another son, Archibald, and finally Alicia. The family resided at Rich Hill until their great adventure to America.

The home life of the Campbells was deeply religious and they raised their children "in the nurture and admonition of the Lord." The Seceder Synod required that a minister "should worship God in his family by singing, reading, and prayer, morning and evening; that he should catechise and instruct them at least once a week in religion; endeavoring to cause every member of the family to pray in secret morning and evening; and that he should remember the Lord's day to keep it holy, and should himself maintain a conversation becoming the gospel." In all these requirements the young minister was faithful, and found in his wife an able assistant. Every day, each member of the family memorized some portion of the Scriptures to recite at evening worship. On the Lord's Day, all attended worship and upon their return home were expected to give an account of the text and of the sermon in all its leading points. That evening at family worship, all the Bible texts memorized during the week were repeated. These exercises were not carried out in a merely perfunctory manner, but in a spirit of love and affectionate interest in the welfare of each person. In later years the children testified of their indebtedness to their parents for their knowledge of the Scriptures and their high concepts of morality and religion.

As preacher, Thomas Campbell was popular not only in the churches and communities he served but was highly honored throughout the Seceder denomination. In addition to his ministerial duties at Ahorey, he became principal of the school at Rich Hill. His son, Alexander, later joined him as a teacher.

Being a man of a kindly and generous spirit, he became deeply concerned over the narrowness and intolerance of the religious leaders who perpetuated old traditions and ecclesiastical quarrels to the harm of the broader mission of the gospel. His own denomination was a case in point. To understand the situation which troubled Campbell's soul it is necessary to recount the history of Presbyterianism in Scotland and the disgraceful rise of narrow party spirit in the church.

Following the martyrdom of Patrick Hamilton at St. Andrew's, February 29, 1528, the Reformed faith gradually gained ascendancy over the Roman church. In the year 1560, the intrepid John Knox established the Presbyterian church, and, after a series of political and ecclesiastical wars, it became firmly established as the state church of Scotland. The famous National Covenant pledged church and state to maintain the Calvinistic religion free from all innovations, but when in 1643 it became politically expedient to modify the terms of the Covenant, the dissenters set up independent societies and churches under the name *Covenanters* or *Reformed Presbyterians*. Later, when the state assumed the right to appoint ministers without the consent of the churches, Alexander Erskine and several other eminent ministers seceded from the established church in 1733 and formed the Seceder Presbyterian church. This denomination then divided in 1747 over the question whether certain oaths required of the burgesses of towns, binding them to support "the religion presently professed within the realms," sanctioned the abuses in the state church which the Seceders protested. Those who considered the oath unlawful became the "Anti-Burghers" and those who approved it the "Burghers." Each party insisted it was "the true church." But their differences did not end there. In 1795 the power of the civil magistrates in religion, as asserted in the twenty-third chapter of the Westminster Confession and also in the original National Covenant, was questioned with the result that the Burghers divided into the "Old Light Burghers" and the "New Light Burghers," and the Anti-Burghers split into the "Old Light Anti-Burghers" and the "New Light Anti-Burghers," each contending that it was the only true church. To complicate matters and to point up the utter foolishness of such ecclesiastical hairsplitting, the Old-Light Anti-Burgher Seceder Presbyterian church in Ireland, in which Thomas Campbell ministered and to which he belonged, insisted on perpetuating the division despite the fact that the Burgher oath was purely a Scottish issue and never required in Ireland.

The sage of Ahorey, in October, 1804 was host to a "Committee on

Consultation" at Rich Hill, composed of ministers who had become restive under this ridiculous situation. They agreed on the wisdom of uniting the Burgher and Anti-Burgher groups in Ireland and prepared an overture to the Synod of Ireland, which was received with great favor. When the General Associate Synod in Scotland met in 1806, however, Thomas Campbell's earnest and forceful plea in behalf of Irish reunion was ignored. Campbell's effort failed, but his experience with hidebound sectarianism, "fraught with the awful consequences of distracting, disturbing and dividing the flock of the Lord's heritage and of sowing discord among the brethren," as he said in his address to the Anti-Burgher Synod of Ireland, served to prepare him for the great decisions he was soon to make in America.

Another influence that made a deep impression on the soul of Thomas Campbell was the work of James Gibson and the Rich Hill congregation of "Independents," or Puritans. The pulpit of this church was always open to Bible-believing ministers. Among those who preached there were Rowland Hill, celebrated English evangelist, James Alexander Haldane, Alexander Carson, and John Walker. These men were generally Calvinistic in basic doctrine but held to the right of private judgment, the independence of the local congregation, and an evangelical type of preaching with a view to creating a greater public interest in the subject of religion. The Rich Hill Independents observed the Lord's Supper every Lord's Day, received weekly contributions, opposed going to theatres or places of public amusement, and encouraged Bible study apart from catechetical instruction. Much was said of the recently organized Evangelical Society, which numbered in its membership people of all the churches, and had for its purpose the promotion of union meetings held in halls and in the open air in which the gospel was preached and men invited to accept Christ. Thomas Campbell joined the society despite the criticism of his brethren, and prayed for the blessing of God on the ministries of the evangelists.

Heavily burdened because of the division and strife in the Presbyterian church and the responsibilities to the church and school in County Antrim, Campbell grew extremely pale, dyspeptic, and weak. Finally his physician prescribed an extended sea voyage and rest. At length, Alexander offered to take over the Rich Hill school and prevailed upon him to go to America. It was agreed that if the new land was found to be favorable for settlement, the whole family would later join him there. On April 8, 1807, he sailed from Malin-Head, the most northern point of Ireland, and after thirty-five days, landed in the city of Philadelphia.

The Anti-Burgher Synod of North America was assembled on that very day in the "City of Brotherly Love." Presenting his credentials from the Presbytery of Market Hill and the church at Ahorey, Campbell was duly received and assigned by the Synod of Philadelphia to the Presbytery of Chartiers in the western part of the state. Here he found several of his old neighbors from Ireland and began a new ministry under auspicious circumstances. Advising his family of virtues of "the promised land," he

38

awaited their arrival, thrusting himself immediately into his new parish duties.

It was not long, however, before Thomas Campbell discovered that something of the same problems he faced in his denomination in northern Ireland existed also in America. His friendliness with the Independents and members of other denominations was looked upon with growing doubt as to his doctrinal soundness. In 1796, the Associate Synod had passed an act prohibiting "occasional Communion" or Communion with other bodies of Christians (Presbyterians). Presbyterians of whatever persuasion were widely scattered in this newly settled country, and with one accord they began to seek the ministrations of Mr. Campbell. When asked to visit a few isolated Anti-Burghers at Cannamaugh, on the Allegheny River about Pittsburgh, he officiated at a Communion service. Many who belonged to other branches of the Presbyterian church attended, sincerely desiring to partake of the emblems which they had not received in many years. In his sermon of preparation, often called "the fencing of the Communion table," Campbell felt it his duty to express regret at the existing divisions in the church and to suggest to all present, who felt so disposed and were duly prepared, to partake of the elements regardless of presbyterial connection. A Seceder minister, William Wilson, who accompanied him on the trip, reported this heresy. At the regular session of the presbytery, October 27-29, 1807, charges of deviation from orthodoxy` were preferred against him; and the Cannamaugh incident soon loomed as an ecclesiastical scandal of the first order. The lengthy and involved proceedings in presbytery and synod are thoroughly documented in William Herbert Hanna's *Thomas Campbell, Seceder and Christian Union Advocate* and constitute a sad commentary on the state of the church at that time. On September 14, 1808, Mr. Campbell, through the medium of a letter addressed to the synod, declined "all ministerial connection with, or subjection to, the Associate Synod of North America," and after some subsequent legal maneuvering, their relationship was finally dissolved May 23, 1809, almost two years from the day when he was received.

Now in his forty-sixth year and after eleven years or more as an ordained minister of the Seceder church, Campbell found himself in a strange country, his family still in Ireland, forsaken by his Anti-Burgher brethren and without any official ministerial connection. But he still had God and the respect of a host of Christian people in the community who gloried in his bold stand for the unalloyed "faith which was once delivered unto the saints."

Large groups of friends and acquaintances invited him to address them in homes and halls throughout Washington and Allegheny Counties. With his new-found freedom in Christ, he began to plead for the union of the divided church on the basis of the Bible and the Bible alone. He deplored the sectarianism of the time and pleaded with the people to co-operate with one another in the great objects of the kingdom. Summer meetings were held in arbors under the trees after the fashion of the missions of the Evangelical Society in the British Isles. Campbell's following soon began to emerge as a clear-cut Christian fellowship with an increasing need for a permanent organization.

Finally plans were announced for a meeting of all interested persons in the house of Abraham Altars, located between Mount Pleasant and Washington. Altars was not a member of any church but, in common with many like him, was definitely interested in Campbell's proposition. The exact date of this gathering is unknown, but it probably occurred in the early summer of 1809. Dr. Robert Richardson, in his *Memoirs of Alexander Campbell,* thus describes the historic moment which marked "the formal and actual commencement of the Reformation . . . which has produced such important changes in religious society over a large portion of the world":

> All seemed to feel the importance of the occasion and to realize the responsibilities of their position. A deep feeling of solemnity pervaded the assembly when Thomas Campbell, having opened the meeting in the usual manner, and, in earnest prayer, specially invoked the Divine guidance, proceeded to rehearse the matter from the beginning, and to dwell with unusual force upon the manifold evils resulting from the divisions in religious society— divisions which, he urged, were as unnecessary as they were injurious, since God had provided, in his sacred Word, an infallible standard, which was all-sufficient and alone-sufficient, as a basis of union and Christian co-operation. He showed, however, that men had not been satisfied with its teachings, but had gone outside of the Bible, to frame for themselves religious theories, opinions and speculations, which were the real occasions of the unhappy controversies and strifes which had so long desolated the religious world. He, therefore, insisted with great earnestness upon a return to the simple teachings of the Scriptures, and upon the entire abandonment of everything in religion for which there could not be produced a Divine warrant. Finally, after having again and again reviewed the ground they occupied in the reformation which they felt it their duty to urge upon religious society, he went on to announce, in the most simple and emphatic terms, the great principle or rule upon which he understood they were then acting, and, upon which, he trusted, they would continue to act, consistently and perseveringly to the end. "That rule, my highly respected hearers," said he in conclusion, "is this, that *WHERE THE SCRIPTURES SPEAK, WE SPEAK; AND WHERE THE SCRIPTURES ARE SILENT, WE ARE SILENT.*"
>
> Upon this annunciation a solemn silence pervaded the assembly. Never before had religious duty been presented to them in so simple a form. Never before had the great principle on which this religious enterprise rested been so clearly presented to their minds. It was to many of them as a new revelation, and those simple words, which embodied a rule so decisive of all religious strifes and of all distressing doubts, were forever engraven upon their hearts. Henceforth, the plain and simple teaching of the Word of God itself was to be their guide. God himself should speak to them, and they should receive and repeat His words alone. No remote inferences, no fanciful interpretations, no religious theories of any kind, were to be allowed to alter or pervert its obvious meaning. Having God's Word in their possession, they must speak it faithfully. There should be no contention, henceforth, in regard to the opinions of men, however wise and learned. Whatever private opinion might be entertained upon matters not clearly revealed must be retained in silence, and no effort must be made to impose them upon others. Thus the *silence* of the Bible was to be respected equally with its revelations, which were by Divine authority declared to be able to "make the man of God perfect and thoroughly furnished unto every good work." Anything more, then, must

be an incumbrance. Anything less than "the whole counsel of God" would be a dangerous deficiency. Simply, reverentially, confidingly, they would speak of Bible things in Bible words, adding nothing thereto and omitting nothing given by inspiration. They had thus a clear and well-defined basis of action, and the hearts of all who were truly interested re-echoed the resolve: "Where the Scriptures speak, we speak; where the Scriptures are silent we are silent. . . ."

It was some time after Mr. Campbell sat down to afford opportunity to those present to give, as he had requested, a free and candid expression of their views, before anyone presumed to break the silence. At length, a shrewd Scotch Seceder, Andrew Munro, who was a bookseller and postmaster at Canonsburg, arose and said: "Mr. Campbell, if we adopt *that* as a basis, then there is an end to infant baptism." That remark, and the conviction it seemed to carry with it, produced a profound sensation. "Of course," said Mr. Campbell in reply, "if infant baptism be not found in the Scripture, we can have nothing to do with it." Upon this, Thomas Acheson, of Washington, who was a man of warm impulses, rose, and advancing a short distance, greatly excited, exclaimed, laying his hand upon his heart: "I hope I may never see the day when my heart will renounce the blessed saying of the Scripture, 'Suffer little children to come unto me, and forbid them not, for of such is the kingdom of heaven.'" Upon saying this he was so much affected that he burst into tears, and while a deep sympathetic feeling pervaded the entire assembly, he was about to retire to an adjoined room, when James Foster, not willing that this misapplication of Scripture should pass unchallenged, cried out, "Mr. Acheson, I would remark that in the portion of Scripture you have quoted there is no reference, whatever, to infant baptism." Without offering a reply, Mr. Acheson passed out to weep alone; but this incident, while it foreshadowed some of the trials which the future had in store, failed to abate, in the least, the confidence which the majority of those present placed in the principles to which they were committed. The rule which Mr. Campbell had announced seemed to cover the whole ground, and to be so obviously just and proper, that after further discussion and conference, it was adopted with apparent unanimity, no valid objection being urged against it (pp. 235-238).

This meeting was followed by wide repercussions. Some refused to attend Campbell's services. Campbell himself began to realize that he had enunciated a principle which would likely result in sweeping changes in his own concepts of Christian faith and practice. James Foster, an old-time friend in Ireland, confronted him one day with this startling question, "Father Campbell, how could you, in the absence of any authority in the Word of God, baptize a child in the name of the Father, and of the Son and of the Holy Spirit?" Mr. Campbell was quite confounded. His face colored, he became for a moment irritated and replied in an offended tone of voice, "Sir, you are the most intractable person I ever met." Despite this and other incidents, a considerable group felt themselves cordially united in a great crusade for Christian union and peace in the religious world. In order to carry out this purpose more effectively, a meeting was called at the headwaters of Buffalo creek, August 17, 1809, to form a fellowship to be known as "The Christian Association of Washington." Twenty-one of their number were appointed to work out with Mr. Campbell a statement of purpose, principles, and program for the new organization. A log building was constructed to be used for future meetings of the Association and for school purposes. Near this meeting house, in the home of a Dr. Welch, Mr. Campbell was assigned an upper room in which he began to compose a *Declaration and Address,* according to the directive of the meeting. When it was finished, he called a meeting of the chief members and read it to them for their approval and adoption. By unanimous action it was agreed upon and ordered to be printed, September 7, 1809. There was little drama attached to the incident. It was an isolated event occurring in the mountainous backwoods of the American frontier, among a small group of earnest but ordinary people led by a recently unfrocked minister. But God was to use it marvelously to His glory within the next one hundred fifty years.

In the midst of his labors over the *Declaration and Address* Thomas Campbell received word that his family had arrived safely from Scotland. After a voyage of fifty-four days and much stormy weather they landed in New York City on September 29, 1809, and set out by wagon for the West. Eager preparations were made to house them and, in company with his good friend, John McElroy, Campbell set out to intercept the travelers. On October 19, on the road to Philadelphia, the happy meeting took place. With ardent love Thomas embraced Jane and the children. Alexander was twenty-one, tall and athletic with an air of frankness and self-reliance. Dorothea was sixteen and resembled Alexander. Nancy, thirteen, was more like her father. Jane was nine, Thomas six, and the two youngest, Archibald six, and Alicia four. Two lead horses equipped with side saddles were provided, an agreeable change from confinement in the wagon and the fatigue of walking. There was much interchange of information about happenings in Ireland and Scotland and the startling developments in America. The critical two years in the life of Alexander will be recounted in the chapters dealing with his life and labors. Suffice to say, the Lord had so moved in the development of father and son that they were prepared to join hearts and hands in the accomplishment of His purposes. When the proof sheets of the *Declaration and Address* were placed in Alexander's hands, he was greatly impressed with the fact that his father had here fully expressed the ideas and principles which he had come to believe.

The *Declaration and Address* is so basic to the development of the American movement to restore New Testament Christianity that it needs to be presented and considered in its entirety. In its first published form, it was a pamphlet of fifty-six pages consisting of four parts: (1) *The Declaration* stating briefly the reasons for the organization of the Christian Association of Washington and proposing a tentative constitution; (2) the *Address,* setting forth in logical form the principles of Christian unity and the means by which it might be attained; (3) the *Appendix* in which certain points in the *Address* are amplified and possible criticisms are answered; and (4) a *Postscript* suggesting steps that should be taken for the promotion of the crusade.

Certain important principles are set forth in the *Declaration* which are basic to the whole document. They give Mr. Campbell's ground of reasoning and intimate his ultimate conclusions about matters of faith.

1. *The authority of the Holy Scriptures.* In the opening sentence Campbell stated that "it is high time for us . . . to take all our measures directly and immediately from the Divine Standard. To this alone we feel ourselves divinely bound to be conformed, as by this alone we must be judged."

2. *The individual Christian's responsibility before God and the right of private judgment.* Mr. Campbell was "persuaded that as no man can be judged for his brother: so no man can judge for his brother; but that every man must be allowed to judge for himself, as every man must bear his own judgment, must give an account of himself to God." Lest the writer be misunderstood as to the implications of this broad assertion he immediately says, "The divine Word is equally binding upon all, so all lie under an equal obligation to be bound by it, and it alone; and not by any human interpretation of it: and that, therefore, no man has a right to judge his brother, except in so far as he manifestly violates the express letter of the law."

3. *The evil of sectarianism.* The "heinous nature, and pernicious tendency of religious controversy among Christians" were soundly condemned. But Mr. Campbell despaired of peace and unity at any time in the foreseeable future within the ranks of the established churches because of "the diversity and rancour of party contentions, the veering uncertainty and clashings of human opinions"; nor, said he, "can we reasonably expect to find it anywhere, but in Christ and His simple word, which is the same yesterday, and today and forever." He therefore declared that "for ourselves and our brethren" we must reject "human opinions and the inventions of men as of any authority, or as having any place in the Church of God."

4. *The way to peace and unity in the body of Christ is through conformity to the teachings of the Holy Scriptures.* Continuing, Mr. Campbell says we must "forever cease from [further] contentions . . . returning to, and holding fast by, the original standard; taking the divine word alone for our rule; the Holy Spirit for our teacher and guide, to lead us into all truth; and Christ alone, as exhibited in the word, for our salvation . . ."

After this statement of fundamental principles, nine resolutions are set forth which were intended to serve as a constitution of the Christian Association and to provide a program for the propagation and promotion of simple "evangelical Christianity."

The *Address* bears this salutation: "To all that love our Lord Jesus Christ in sincerity, throughout all the Churches . . . Dearly Beloved Brethren." In these few words, the writer's spirit of love and concern for all Christians is abundantly set forth. He held no rancour in his heart toward anyone who claimed Christ as Saviour and Lord. The document was to go first of all to his Presbyterian friends who had so shamefully treated him and then to all evangelical Christians of whatever denominational persuasion. He reminds them that "it is the grand design and native tendency of our holy religion, to reconcile and unite man to God, and to each other, in truth and love to the glory of God, and their own present and eternal good . . . In so far, then, as this holy unity and unanimity in faith and love is attained; just in the same degree, is the glory of God, and the happiness of man promoted and secured."

In contrast with this desire for the unity of all God's people, Mr. Campbell then portrays "the awful and distressing effects" of the "adversions, reproaches, backbitings, evil surmisings, angry contentions, enmities, excommunications and persecutions" being carried on in and between the existing churches, while whole areas of the land were without gospel preaching and worship. He comments on the favorable situation for the spreading of the gospel in America, where democracy and freedom of religion prevail.

"Dearly beloved brethren," he says, "why should we deem it a thing incredible that the church of Christ, in this highly favored country, should resume that original unity, peace and purity, which belongs to its constitution, and constitutes its glory? Or, is there anything that can be justly deemed necessary for this desirable purpose, but to conform to the model, and adopt the practice of the primitive church, expressly exhibited in the New Testament?"

In his exuberant vision of a church united on the Bible and the Bible alone, he sees within the existing churches essential doctrinal agreement:

> It is, to us, a pleasing consideration that all the churches of Christ, which mutually acknowledge each other as such, are not only agreed in the great doctrines of faith and holiness; but are also materially agreed, as to the positive ordinances of Gospel institution; so that our differences, at most, are about the things in which the kingdom of God does not consist, that is, about matters of private opinion, or human invention. What a pity, that the kingdom of God should be divided about such things! . . . Our dear brethren, of all denominations, will please to consider, that we have our educational prejudices, and particular customs to struggle with as well as they. But this we do sincerely declare, that there is nothing we have hitherto received as matter of faith or practice, which is not expressly taught and enjoined in the word of God, either in express terms, or approved precedent, that we would not heartily relinquish, that so we might return to the original constitutional unity of the Christian church.

It is clear from this and other passages in the *Address,* that Mr. Campbell had no desire to set up a new denomination. He regarded his friends in the churches as Christians. Indeed if he had not so regarded them he would not have been interested in seeing them united. Minimizing the prevalence and power of bigotry among the rank and file of the people and their sentimental loyalty to their denominational traditions, Mr. Campbell assumed the existence of an inherent desire for a united church. In a passionate appeal he writes.

> You are all, dear brethren, equally included as the object of our love and esteem. With you all we desire to unite in the bonds of an entire Christian unity, Christ alone being the head, the centre; his word the

rule . . . We humbly presume then, dear brethren, you can have no relevant objection to meet us upon this ground. . . .

Are we not all praying for that happy event, when there shall be but one fold, as there is but one Chief Shepherd. What! shall we pray for a thing, and not strive to obtain it! not use the necessary means to have it accomplished! What said the Lord to Moses upon a piece of conduct somewhat similar? "Why criest thou unto me? Speak unto the children of Israel that they go forward" (pp. 11, 12).

Mr. Campbell based the authority for his appeal in "Jesus Christ and God the Father, who raised him from the dead. By this authority are you called to raise up the tabernacle of David, that is fallen down among us, and to set it up upon its own base." The method of approach to the problem, he says, involves unselfish, friendly, and independent association for consultation and advice, free from subjection to any authority but Christ in order to discover "a permanent scriptural unity amongst the friends and lovers of truth and peace throughout the churches."

With some hesitancy, Mr. Campbell set up thirteen propositions for consideration, all of which point toward the restoration of the New Testament church so that true Christians might "stand with evidence upon the same ground on which the church stood at the beginning." These propositions are so important that they are produced verbatim in their entirety:

1. That the church of Christ upon earth is essentially, intentionally, and constitutionally one; consisting of all those in every place that profess their faith in Christ and obedience to him in all things according to the scriptures, and that manifest the same by their tempers and conduct, and of none else, as none else can be truly and properly called Christians.

2. That although the church of Christ upon earth must necessarily exist in particular and distinct societies, locally separate one from another; yet there ought to be no schisms, no uncharitable divisions among them. They ought to receive each other as Christ Jesus hath also received them to the glory of God. And for this purpose, they ought all to walk by the same rule, to mind and speak the same thing; and to be perfectly joined together in the same mind, and the same judgment.

3. That in order to this, nothing ought to be inculcated upon christians as articles of faith; nor required of them as terms of communion; but what is expressly taught and enjoined upon them, in the word of God. Nor ought any thing be admitted, as of divine obligation, in their church constitution and managements, but what is expressly enjoined by the authority of our Lord Jesus Christ and his Apostles upon the New Testament church; either in express terms, or by approved precedent.

4. That although the scriptures of the Old and New Testament are inseparably connected, making together but one perfect and entire revelation of the Divine will, for the edification and salvation of the church; and therefore in that respect cannot be separated; yet as to what directly and properly belongs to their immediate object, the New Testament is as perfect a constitution for the worship, discipline and government of the New Testament church, and as perfect a rule for the particular duties of its members; as the Old Testament was for the worship, discipline and government of the Old Testament church, and the particular duties of its members.

5. That with respect to the commands and ordinances of our Lord Jesus Christ, where the Scriptures are silent, as to the express time or manner of

performance, if any such there be; no human authority has power to interfere, in order to supply the supposed deficiency, by making laws for the church; nor can any thing more be required of christians in such cases, but only that they *so* observe these commands and ordinances, as will evidently answer the declared and obvious end of their institution. Much less has any human authority power to impose new commands or ordinances upon the church, which our Lord Jesus Christ has not enjoined. Nothing ought to be received into the faith or worship of the church; or be made a term of communion among christians, that is not as old as the New Testament.

6. That although inferences and deductions from scripture premises, when fairly inferred, may be truly called the doctrine of God's holy word: yet are they not formally binding upon the consciences of christians farther than they perceive the connection, and evidently see that they are so; for their faith must not stand in the wisdom of men; but in the power and veracity of God—therefore no such deduction can be made terms of communion, but do properly belong to the after and progressive edification of the church. Hence it is evident that no such deductions or inferential truths ought to have any place in the church's confession.

7. That although doctrinal exhibitions of the great system of divine truths, and defensive testimonies in opposition to prevailing errors, be highly expedient; and the more full and explicit they be, for those purposes, the better; yet as these must be in a great measure the effect of human reasoning, and of course must contain many inferential truths, they ought not to be made terms of christian communion: unless we suppose, what is contrary to fact, that none have a right to the communion of the church, but such as possess a very clear and decisive judgment; or are come to a very high degree of doctrinal information; whereas the church from the beginning did, and ever will, consist of little children and young men, as well as fathers.

8. That as it is not necessary that persons should have a particular knowledge or distinct apprehension of all divinely revealed truths in order to entitle them to a place in the church; neither should they, for this purpose, be required to make a profession more extensive than their knowledge: but that, on the contrary, their having a due measure of scriptural self-knowledge respecting their lost and perishing condition by nature and practice; and of the way of salvation through Jesus Christ, accompanied with a profession of their faith in, and obedience to him, in all things according to his word, is all that is absolutely necessary to qualify them for admission into his church.

9. That all that are enabled, through grace, to make such a profession, and to manifest the reality of it in their tempers and conduct, should consider each other as the precious saints of God, should love each other as brethren, children of the same family and father, temples of the same spirit, members of the same body, subjects of the same grace, objects of the same divine love, bought with the same price, and joint heirs of the same inheritance. Whom God hath thus joined together no man should dare to put asunder.

10. That division among christians is a horrid evil, fraught with many evils. It is antichristian, as it destroys the visible unity of the body of Christ; as if he were divided against himself, excluding and excommunicating a part of himself. It is antiscriptural, as being strictly prohibited by his sovereign authority; a direct violation of his express command. It is antinatural, as it excites christians to contemn, to hate and oppose one another, who are bound by the highest and most endearing obligations to love each other as brethren, even as Christ has loved them. In a word, it is productive of confusion, and of every evil work.

11. That, in some instances, a partial neglect of the expressly revealed will of God; and, in others, an assumed authority for making the approbation of human opinions, and human inventions, a term of communion, by introducing

them into the constitution, faith, or worship, of the church; are, and have been, the immediate, obvious, and universally acknowledged causes, of all the corruptions and divisions that ever have taken place in the church of God.

12. That all that is necessary to the highest state of perfection and purity of the church upon earth is, first, that none be received as members, but such as having that due measure of scriptural self-knowledge described above, do profess their faith in Christ and obedience to him in all things according to the scriptures; nor, secondly, that any be retained in her communion longer than they continue to manifest the reality of their profession by their tempers and conduct. Thirdly, that her ministers, duly and scripturally qualified, inculcate none other things than those very articles of faith and holiness expressly revealed and enjoined in the word of God. Lastly, that in all their administrations they keep close by the observance of all divine ordinances, after the example of the primitive church, exhibited in the New Testament; without any additions whatsoever of human opinions or inventions of men.

13. Lastly. That if any circumstantials indispensably necessary to the observance of divine ordinances be not found upon the page of express revelation, such, and such only, as are absolutely necessary for this purpose, should be adopted, under the title of human expedients, without any pretence to a more sacred origin;—so that any subsequent alteration or difference in the observance of these things might produce no contention nor division in the church (pp. 16-18).

These propositions have been summarized by Frederick D. Kershner as follows:

1. That the church of Christ is "essentially, intentionally and constitutionally one."

2. That although this unity presupposes and permits the existence of separate congregations or societies, there should be perfect harmony and unity of spirit among all of them.

3. That the Bible is the only rule of faith and practice for Christians.

4. That the Old and New Testaments alone contain the authoritative constitution of the church of Christ.

5. That no human authority has power to amend or change the original constitution and laws of the church.

6. That inferences and deductions from the Scriptures, however valuable, can not be made binding upon the consciences of Christians.

7. That differences of opinion with regard to such inferences shall not be made tests of fellowship or communion.

8. That faith in Jesus Christ as the Son of God is a sufficient profession to entitle a man or woman to become a member of the church of Christ.

9. That all who have made such a profession, and who manifest their sincerity by their conduct, should love each other as brethren and as members of the same body and joint-heirs of the same inheritance.

10. That division among Christians is anti-christian, anti-scriptural, unnatural and to be abhorred.

11. That neglect of the revealed will of God and the introduction of human innovations are and have been the cause of all the corruptions and divisions that have ever taken place in the church of God.

12. That all that is necessary to secure the highest state of purity and perfection in the church is to restore the original ordinances and constitution as exhibited in the New Testament.

13. That any additions to the New Testament program which circumstances may seem to require, shall be regarded as human expedients and shall not be given a place of higher authority in the church than is permitted by the fallible character of their origin.

In the concluding paragraphs of the *Address,* Mr. Campbell, still laboring under the belief that all lovers of the Lord were equally desirous of unity, again made a soul-stirring appeal:

> Ye lovers of Jesus, and beloved of him, however scattered in this cloudy and dark day, ye love the truth as it is in Jesus, if our hearts deceive us not; so do we. Ye desire union in Christ, with all them that love him; so do we. Ye lament and bewail our sad divisions; so do we. Ye reject the doctrines and commandments of men that ye may keep the law of Christ; so do we. Ye believe the alone sufficiency of his word; so do we. Ye believe that the word itself ought to be our rule and not any human explication of it; so do we. Ye believe that no man has a right to judge, to exclude, or reject, his professing christian brother; except in so far as he stands condemned, or rejected, by the express letter of the law:—so do we. Ye believe that the great fundamental law of unity and love ought not to be violated to make way for exalting human opinions to an equality with express revelation, by making them articles of faith and terms of communion—so do we. Ye sincere and impartial followers of Jesus, friends of truth and peace, we dare not, we cannot, think otherwise of you;—it would be doing violence to your character; it would be inconsistent with your prayers and profession, so to do. We shall therefore have *your* hearty concurrence. But if any of our dear brethren, from whom we should expect better things, should, through weakness or prejudice, be in any thing otherwise minded, than we have ventured to suppose, we charitably hope, that, in due time, God will reveal even this unto them:—Only let such neither refuse to come to the light; nor yet through prejudice, reject it, when it shines upon them. Let them rather seriously consider what we have thus most seriously and respectfully submitted to their consideration, weigh every sentiment in the balance of the sanctuary, as in the sight of God, with earnest prayer for, and humble reliance upon his spirit; and not in the spirit of self-sufficiency and party zeal,—and, in so doing, we rest assured, the consequences will be happy, both for their own, and the church's peace (p. 21).

The great document ends on an apologetic note. Under the heading *Appendix,* Mr. Campbell explained, interpreted, and reiterated his views. He seemed to anticipate the reception his propositions would receive in certain quarters.

One of the first questions he presaged was, "What is your attitude toward the Westminster Confession of Faith and similar creeds of Christendom?" He replied,

> As to creeds and confessions, although we may appear to our brethren to oppose them, yet this is to be understood only in *so far* as they oppose the unity of the church, by containing sentiments not expressly revealed in the word of God; or, by the way of using them, become the instruments of a human or implicit faith: or, oppress the weak of God's heritage: where they are liable to none of those objections, we have nothing against them. It is the *abuse* and not the *lawful use* of such compilations that we oppose (pp. 24, 25).

He said further,

> We are by no means to be understood as at all wishing to deprive our fellow-christians of any necessary and possible assistance to understand the scriptures: or to come to a distinct and particular knowledge of every truth they contain; for which purpose the Westminster Confession and Catechisms, may, with many other excellent performances, prove eminently useful (p. 42).

Mr. Campbell then emphasized that all human creeds must be constantly scrutinized to determine whether the doctrines they teach are true to the Bible. He advised that we "take the Scripture in its connection on these subjects, so as to understand one part of it by the assistance of another . . . manifesting our self-knowledge, our knowledge of the way of salvation, and of the mystery of the christian life, in the express light of divine revelation; by a direct and immediate reference to, and correct repetition of, what it declares upon these subjects."

Another criticism that Mr. Campbell foresaw was that he had succumbed to latitudinarianism or liberalism. He made it clear that the divine law as enunciated in the Holy Scriptures is the basis of judgment in dealing with both doctrine and discipline. He would be as broad as the Scriptures and as narrow as the Scriptures. The criticism was expected to come largely from the creedalists, so he turned the tables against them by intimating that they were the real liberals. He charged they took greater latitude than the divine law allowed when they expressed their own human opinions and made them of equal importance with Holy Writ and tests of church fellowship.

Mr. Campbell insisted that his position presupposed "the existence of a fixed and certain standard of divine original; in which everything that that wisdom of God saw meet to reveal and determine, for *these,* and all other purposes, is expressly defined and determined; betwixt the Christian and which, no medium of human determination ought to be interposed. . . . We have no intention whatsoever of substituting a vague indefinite approbation of the Scriptures, as an alternative for creeds, confessions and testimonies; for the purpose of restoring the church to her original constitutional unity and purity." Having made it clear that fundamental orthodox Christian doctrine is essential to the fellowship of Christians, he then proceeded to deal with the matter of moral discipline:

> We have supposed in the first place, the true discrimination of christian character to consist in an intelligent profession of our faith in Christ and obedience to him in all things according to the Scriptures; the reality of which profession is manifested in the holy consistency of the tempers and conduct of the professors, with the express dictates, and approved examples of the Divine word. Hence we have humility, faith, piety, temperance, justice, charity, etc., professed and manifested in the first instance, by the persons' professing with self-application the convincing, humbling, encouraging, pious, temperate, just and charitable doctrines and precepts of the inspired volume, as exhibited and enforced in its holy and approved examples . . . [and] in case of any visible failure, by an apparently sincere repentance, and evident reformation. Such professors, and such only, have we supposed to be, by common consent, truly worthy of the Christian name (p. 47).

In the *Appendix,* Mr. Campbell repeatedly appealed to the Word of God as full and final authority and an adequate foundation for Christian unity. Divisions may be healed, he said,

> . . . by simply returning to the original standard of christianity—the profession and practice of the primitive church, as expressly exhibited upon

the sacred page of New Testament scripture . . . we humbly think that a uniform agreement in *that* for the preservation of charity would be infinitely preferable to our contention and divisions: nay, that such a uniformity is the very thing that the Lord requires, if the New Testament be a perfect model—a sufficient formula for the worship, discipline and government of the christian church. Let *us* do, as we are there expressly told *they* did, say as *they* said: that is, profess and practice as therein expressly enjoined by precept and precedent, in every possible instance, after *their* approved example; and in so doing we shall realize, and exhibit, all that unity and uniformity, that the primitive church possessed, or that the law of Christ requires. But if after all, our brethren can point out a better way to regain and preserve that christian unity and charity expressly enjoined upon the church of God, we shall thank them for the discovery, and cheerfully embrace it (p. 35).

Finally, in the concluding portion of the *Appendix,* Mr. Campbell says,

The New Testament is the proper and immediate rule, directory, and formula, for the New Testament church, and for the particular duties of christians; as the Old Testament was for the Old Testament church, and for the particular duties of the subject under that dispensation; at the same time by no means excluding the old as fundamental to, illustrative of, and inseparably connected with, the new; and as being every way of equal authority, as well as of an entire sameness with it, in every point of moral natural duty; though not immediately our rule, without the intervention and coincidence of the new; in which our Lord has taught his people, by the ministry of his holy Apostles, all things whatsoever they should observe and do, till the end of the world. Thus we come to the one rule, taking the Old Testament as explained and perfected by the new, and the new as illustrated and enforced by the old; assuming the latter as the proper and immediate directory for the christian church, as also for the positive and particular duties of christians, as to all things whatsoever they should observe and do. Farther, that in the observance of this Divine rule—this authentic and infallible directory, all such may come to the desirable coincidence of holy unity and uniformity of profession and practice; we have overtured that they all speak, profess, and practice, the very same things, that are exhibited upon the sacred page of New Testament Scripture, as spoken and done by the Divine appointment and approbation; and that this be extended to every possible instance of uniformity, without addition or diminution; without introducing any thing of private opinion, or doubtful disputation, into the public profession or practice of the church (pp. 49, 50).

Upon the publication of the *Declaration and Address,* there was much favorable comment within the little circle of brethren composing the Christian Association of Washington, but cold silence on the part of ministers and leaders in the denominational churches. Though earnestly and repeatedly invited to consider the propositions submitted, and to make any corrections or amendments to them that might be supported by the Scriptures, they did not respond. The religious climate remained unchanged and religious leaders remained unaware that the ecumenical principle here enunciated would have amazing consequence in the years to come.

Indeed, Mr. Campbell and those associated with him were unconscious of the changes that must be made in their own beliefs and practices if they were to carry the principles they had espoused to their logical application and conclusion.

The Christian Association, adopting the document as its charter, sought in 1810 to become affiliated with the regular Presbyterian church. At the Synod of Pittsburgh, meeting at Washington, October 2, 1810, Mr. Campbell presented his *Declaration and Address* and made application as the representative of the Association to be received "into Christian and ministerial communion." This is a further evidence of his purpose to avoid separate denominational status. He told his Presbyterian friends that the purpose of the Association was to promote Biblical Christian union and was not a church. The pastor of the Presbyterian church at Upper Buffalo, a close friend of Campbell's, expressed confidence that the Synod would act favorably on his petition, but after brief consideration the august body frigidly decided that "it is not consistent with the regulations of the Presbyterian Church that Synod should form a connection with any ministers, churches, and associations."

By the spring of 1811, Mr. Campbell, with some reluctance, came to feel that the Christian Association must become an independent church if it were to serve its members properly. Accordingly, on May 4, 1811, in the meeting house near Mount Pleasant, Pennsylvania, the group constituted itself into a local church, congregational in form of government. Thomas Campbell was chosen elder and his son Alexander was licensed to preach the gospel. On the next day, Sunday, May 5, the Lord's Supper was observed for the first time, and it was observed weekly thereafter, since this was believed to have been the practice of the apostolic church. Thus the Association became a distinct church, seeking to restore the New Testament pattern, being guided in all things solely by the Scriptures.

William Gilcrist offered a site for the construction of a meeting house. The Association had been meeting in a community building near Mount Pleasant and it was thought best to have its own property. The new frame structure was located about two miles southeast of West Middleton, Pennsylvania. The location gave the congregation the name of the Brush Run church. The first service in the new building was held June 19, 1811.

Adventuring in the quest of apostolic faith and practice, the new church was to meet grave problems.

It appears from the records of the young Brush Run church, and from extant copies of some of the sermons delivered by Thomas and Alexander Campbell, that in doctrine and practice the Christian Association was quite similar to the independent churches established by the Haldanes in Scotland.

It regarded the religious bodies around them as possessing the substance of Christianity, but as having failed to preserve "the form of sound words" in which it was originally presented.

The abandonment of every human system and a return to the Bible and the Bible alone as the rule of faith and practice were its chief objectives.

It regarded each local church as an independent organization, having its own local government by bishops and deacons, yet not so absolutely independent of other churches as not to be bound to them by fraternal relations.

In function it ministered to the sick and needy, was evangelistic, gave itself to teaching and preaching, provided "the breaking of bread and the prayers," and promoted Christian fellowship.

Considering "lay preaching" as authorized, it denied the distinction between clergy and laity to be Scriptural.

Although it looked upon infant baptism as without direct Bible authority, it countenanced it for conscience' sake, as Paul and James permitted circumcision for a time in deference to Jewish prejudice. Immersion was practiced as Scriptural baptism for all those accepting Christ upon profession of faith.

It observed the Lord's Supper every Lord's Day.

Receiving no doctrine but that which was expressly revealed, it gradually realized that many things considered precious and important in the traditional churches must inevitably be abandoned.

Paying no respect whatever to the doctrinal and theological controversies which had raged in the churches since the times of the apostles, it proposed a restudy of the Scriptures to discover the foundations of the New Testament church and rebuild the entire structure of primitive Christianity.

At this point in the development of the new movement, Alexander Campbell began to assume aspects of leadership through which he greatly distinguished himself and gained wide acceptance. The close and harmonious relationship between father and son continued undiminished, but Alexander came to be regarded as the Moses of the hour. The story of this man and the circumstances under which this change took place can best be told in the next two chapters.

BIBLIOGRAPHY: Chapter 2

Campbell, Alexander, *Memoirs of Elder Thomas Campbell.*
Campbell, Thomas, *Declaration and Address* (Centennial edition).
Hanna, W. H., *Thomas Campbell, Seceder and Christian Union Advocate.*
Kershner, Frederick D., *Christian Union Overture.*
Kershner, Frederick D., *Restoration Handbook.*
McAllister, Lester G., *Thomas Campbell: A Man of the Book.*
McLean, Archibald, *Thomas and Alexander Campbell.*
Richardson, Robert, *Memoirs of Alexander Campbell.*

Chapter 3

Alexander Campbell and
His Sermon on the Law

$\mathbf{T}$HOMAS CAMPBELL'S greatest ally in his crusade for Christian unity through a return to the New Testament pattern was his son, Alexander. Indeed, the son was destined to be its chief advocate in the formative years.

Something of his home life as a child has already been indicated. His naturally active and lively temperament led him to participate freely in the recreations of youth. Fishing, hunting, and swimming were his delight and he possessed remarkable physical health and vigor. His father, a teacher of no mean ability, superintended his literary education and also his religious training. The Campbell home followed strict Seceder Presbyterian custom and worshiped God at the family altar in the singing of hymns, Bible reading, and prayer, morning and evening. The children were catechised and instructed once each week in the fundamentals of the Christian faith and were expected to pray in secret and "maintain a conversation becoming the gospel." Alexander's mother, who was of Huguenot ancestry, co-operated in the spiritual improvement and welfare of the family. It was their rule that every member of the family should memorize, during each day, some portion of the Holy Scriptures. Alexander testified that in his early life he memorized almost all the Proverbs, Ecclesiastes, and the Psalms, to say nothing of all the appropriate Scriptures related to the catechism. In this connection he paid a rich tribute to his mother:

> Having a peculiarly ready and retentive memory, she treasured up the Scriptures in early life, and could quote and apply them with great fluency and pertinency from childhood to old age. She, indeed, possessed a mental independence which I have rarely seen equaled, and certainly never surpassed, by any woman of my acquaintance. Greatly devoted to her children, and especially to their proper training for public usefulness, and for their own individual and social enjoyment, she was indefatigable in her labors of love, and in her attention to their physical, intellectual, moral and religious training and development (*Memoirs*, Vol. I, pp. 36, 37).

Alexander's first formal schooling was received in an elementary school in Market Hill, Ireland. Later he attended an academy in Newry, under the instruction of his uncles, Archibald and Enos. When Thomas Campbell accepted the church at Ahorey, the family moved to Rich Hill, two miles away. Here he opened a school under the patronage of the Honorable William Richardson, M. P., and lord of the manor. Soon Alexander, at the age of seventeen, was assisting as an instructor, although pursuing his own special course of study under his father's guidance.

It was while in Rich Hill that Alexander received Christ as his Saviour. He had by this time an unusually excellent knowledge of the Scriptures and had a clear concept of the chief points in the divine plan of salvation. Many matters puzzled him, however, and he began to take lonely walks in the fields and to pray in secluded spots, to seek divine guidance and approval. It was universally held by the Seceders that "an assured persuasion of the truth of God's promise in the gospel, with respect to one's self in particular, is implied in the very nature of saving faith." Alexander's own account of the outcome of this experience states that from the time he could read the Scriptures he became convinced that Jesus was the Son of God. He continues,

> I was also fully persuaded that I was a sinner, and must obtain pardon through the merits of Christ or be lost for ever. This caused me great distress of soul, and I had much exercise of mind under the awakenings of a guilty conscience. Finally, after many strugglings, I was enabled to put my trust in the Saviour, and to feel my reliance on him as the only Saviour of sinners. From the moment I was able to feel this reliance on the Lord Jesus Christ, I obtained and enjoyed peace of mind. It never entered my head to investigate the subject of baptism or the doctrines of the creed (*Memoirs*, Vol. I, p. 49).

Shortly after this he was received as a regular communicant of the church at Ahorey and almost immediately began to give much attention to theological studies, particularly ecclesiastical history, with a view to becoming a Presbyterian minister.

Without departing from strict Presbyterian faith and practice, Thomas and Alexander Campbell manifested a fine spirit of toleration toward other religious communions. Alexander was particularly enamored with the principle of "independency" which was advocated by the church in Rich Hill. It was connected with the Puritan movement in England, and its pulpit was frequently filled by Alexander Carson, John Walker, James Alexander Haldane, and on one occasion, by the celebrated Rowland Hill. The Rich Hill Independents observed the Lord's Supper in the "evangelical style," reflecting an earnestness and zeal for the saving of souls. Contrasting their freedom of thought and action, within the limits of Scriptural authority, with the spiritual despotism and denominational prejudice of the extreme Presbyterianism of his day, Campbell was moved to consider seriously the claims of independency.

Books were the young man's constant delight, and he had a passion for the improvement of his mind. He yearned for a university education, but owing to his father's large family there seemed but little prospect. Glasgow was favored because of its relationship to the Seceder church. Its only theological seminary was located there. An additional barrier to advanced learning now came in the serious illness of his father.

Thomas Campbell's physician ordered him to take a protracted sea voyage, as indispensable to his recovery. At first he resisted the idea, but finally on Alexander's persuasion and his promise to take over the Rich Hill school, the senior Campbell sailed for America April 8, 1807.

About a year later, the American climate, freedom and opportunity having completely won the heart of Thomas Campbell, he urged his family to join him in the new world. Almost immediately Alexander set out for Londonderry to arrange passage. On the first day of October, 1808, the family sailed on the *Hibernia*. Several days later a storm was encountered near the rocky coast of Scotland and the ship put into Lochin-Daal Bay on the Island of Islay. On the evening of October 7, Alexander was reading to his sister. The weather was calm. At length he fell asleep. Waking suddenly with evident marks of alarm on his face, he told his mother and sisters that he had had a dream in which he thought the ship had struck a rock and sunk into the sea. He had by the most strenuous effort been able to save the family. So deep an impression had been made upon him that he did not undress for bed and determined to be ready if an emergency might arise. In the midst of the night, when all on board were asleep, a terrific storm hit the ship, tearing it from its anchors and dashing it upon a sunken rock; timbers crashed and water began to rush into the main hold. Utter confusion reigned as terrified passengers crowded to the deck and were exposed to the fury of the storm. As the hours passed, prospects for rescue dimmed. Sailors and strong men became drunken in their despair.

Campbell, in the near prospect of death, felt as never before, the vanity of the aims and ambitions of human life, and envisioned the true purposes of man's creation. He thought of his father's noble life, devoted to God and to the salvation of men, and was gripped with an overwhelming desire to give himself in full surrender to Christ to be used in any way His Spirit might direct. If he had any doubts about entering the ministry they were all dissolved in this hour. Calmly submitting himself to the dispensations of heaven, he proceeded to make definite plans for the rescue of his mother and sisters. When a rescue was finally effected, they found themselves on the Isle of Islay in the midst of the Campbell clan who graciously entertained them and aided them in salvaging their goods from the wreckage of the ship. Laird Campbell, of Shawfield, the chief owner of Islay, was particularly gracious to them. Observing that Alexander had many books in his baggage he invited him to the manor, treating him more like a relative than a stranger.

This providential experience—Campbell always believed it was exactly that—enabled him to enter Glasgow University for his long-cherished encounter with higher education. The family was transported to Scotland's chief city by the ship's owners, who had returned their passage money. Almost immediately Alexander contacted Greville Ewing, minister of the

Independent church, whose acquaintance he had formed on a visit to Rich Hill. Through Ewing's courtesy, the young seeker after knowledge was introduced to the different professors of the University and entered classes on November 8. Among the fifteen hundred students enrolled, Alexander formed many warm and lasting friendships.

Classes in Greek, logic, *belles lettres,* experimental philosophy, French, Latin, and elocution occupied his chief interest. Among his professors were Young, Jardine, and Ure. In a diary written chiefly in Latin, young Campbell recorded in great detail the happenings of his 4:00 A.M. to 10:00 P.M. days and added whole reams of observations on a wide range of subjects from art to theology. The document reveals the intellectual and spiritual breadth and depth of his mind which was soon to be completely devoted to a great religious movement in America.

Little has been said of Campbell's deep spiritual commitment, which his diary reveals. In a meditation on the inquiry of the psalmist, "Who can understand his errors?" and his prayer to God, "Cleanse thou me from secret faults," he plumbs the depths of human motives and feelings and rises by faith to the heights of complete commitment to Christ. He realized his own weakness and inability and despaired of the perfection which God requires. He sought in prayer the divine aid to "work in him both to will and to do his own good pleasure" and for that strength which is made perfect in human weakness. He put his hope not in self-righteousness, but in the merits of Christ, and looked to him whom God has made wisdom and righteousness, sanctification and redemption.

Mr. Ewing, of the great Independent church in Glasgow, formed a strong attachment to the young university student and invited him to his home for discussions on religion and for social gatherings.

As the time approached for the family to make its second attempt to sail to America, Alexander began to have qualms of conscience about his affiliation with the Seceders. It was while he was in this unsettled state of mind that the semiannual Communion season approached. He wished to comply with all his religious obligations but felt himself crippled by allegiance to all the petty decisions of domineering synods and general assemblies. At the time of preparation, he finally concluded to go the elders of the Glasgow Seceder church and get a metallic token, which all communicants were required to obtain. The elders asked for his credentials and when informed that his membership was with the church in Ireland forced him to appear before the session for examination. He passed the test and was given his token. When the Supper was served, however, he was still wrestling with his conscience. As the plate was passed he tossed in his token, but when the elements were passed he refused to partake. This crucial act was, however, still a matter of his inner life. At the close of the university session in May, having fully complied with the rules of the church, he asked for and received his certificate of good standing, which he carried with him to America.

The Campbells left Greenock, Scotland, on August 4, 1809, and arrived in the harbor of New York, September 29. After attending worship services and viewing the city, the family set out on October 5 to join Thomas Campbell in Washington, Pennsylvania. They traveled by foot and horseback, wagon and stage, through a sparsely settled country over mountains and valleys surrounded by a forest rich in autumn colors. On the tenth day of their journey they were surprised to see Thomas riding toward them, and a most affectionate meeting took place. At Williamsport they entered Washington County, and were entertained overnight by the Reverend Samuel Ralston, president of the trustees of Jefferson College. Next day they reached the town of Washington, which was to be their home.

Through long days and nights father and son poured out their hearts concerning their religious experiences. Thomas Campbell had met Alexander with some trepidation of spirit, wondering how Alexander would receive the story of Thomas' unjust treatment by the American Presbytery and Synod and his decision to preach independently to audiences made up of people from all denominations. Strangely enough, Alexander, thousands of miles away, had been led by the Holy Spirit to an almost identical position. Finding themselves of one mind, they next began to discuss the *Declaration and Address*. Alexander gave his hearty approval to all the propositions. Captivated by its clear and decisive position, and thrilled by the opportunity to cast his lot with such a noble Christian enterprise, he shortly after informed his father that he had determined to consecrate his life to the dissemination and support of the principles and views set forth in the masterly document.

Soon after, he entered upon a rigid course of Biblical and theological study under his father's guidance to prepare himself for the gospel ministry. From 8:00 to 9:00 each morning he read Greek, from 11:00 to 12:00 Latin, and from 12:00 to 1:00 Hebrew. Ten verses of Scripture were committed to memory each day, read in the original languages, and interpreted by the help of Henry and Scott's notes and practical observations. The remainder of his educational schedule was employed in the study of church history and other required subjects in a standard seminary curriculum. In the course of his labors, he wrote reams of essays and compositions.

In the spring of 1810, the young man made his first public talk to a gathering in a private home. So favorably were his remarks received that an appointment was arranged on July 15 to address a public assembly in a grove on the farm of Major Templeton, eight miles from Washington. Taking Matthew 7:24-27 as his text, the twenty-two-year-old preacher was able to rivet the attention of his audience and hold it with marked effectiveness. There were immediate demands for more appointments, and with the encouragement of his father he embarked upon a preaching schedule under the auspices of the, newly formed Christian Association that kept him busy for many days to come.

Thomas Campbell still entertained hopes that the rift between him and the Presbyterian Synod might be healed. In October, 1810, he appeared before the Synod of Pittsburgh, meeting in Washington, and applied to "be taken into Christian and ministerial communion." Bypassing the real issue at stake, the Synod passed a resolution to the effect that "it is not consistent with the regulations of the Presbyterian church that Synod should make a connection with any ministers, churches, or associations." Thus, on the ground that Mr. Campbell was affiliated with the Christian Association, his application was rejected. His treatment was curt, harsh, and it resulted in a final open separation.

Alexander was so stirred by this ecclesiastical insult to his father that he announced his intention to reply to the Synod in the next semiannual meeting of the Christian Association, in Washington on November 1. At the appointed time he addressed a large assembly, taking as his text Isaiah 57:14 and 62:10. In his introduction he praised the timeliness of the proposals set forth in the *Declaration* and condemned those who opposed the overtures.

> The reception this attempt has experienced has evinced its origin. It has met with the approbation of no party as such. Had it fared otherwise, it would have evinced itself not catholic, original and pure, for no party can, with any show of decency, pretend to these properties and yet refuse to be measured by the pure, original and catholic standard of the Holy Scriptures. They will only submit to be tried by their own standards; that is, in other words, by their own opinions, as if the word has no certain, fixed or express meaning of its own, but just what they are pleased to give it (*Memoirs*, Vol. I, p. 338).

The young preacher proceeded to make a proper division of the text and to elucidate it under different heads. Then he dealt item by item with the objections which had been leveled at the Christian Association. The principles he enunciated were substantially those his father had set forth in the *Declaration and Address* and may be summarized as follows:

1. The existing denominations possess the substance of Christianity, but in many respects have failed to preserve the Scriptural form in which it was originally expressed. The chief object of the new reformation is to persuade Christians to abandon human statements and adopt "the form of sound words" as the true basis of union.

2. Each congregation should have its own internal government by elders and deacons and, while regarded as an independent body, should have fellowship with other churches of like faith.

3. The distinction between clergy and laity is unauthorized by Scripture and should be abandoned.

4. Infant baptism is without direct Scriptural authority, but the practice should be a matter of forbearance, permissible, as circumcision was approved by Paul and James for a time in deference to Jewish prejudices.

5. Should religious parties refuse to accept the overtures of the Christian Association, it might be necessary to resolve it into a distinct church or congregation in order for its members to carry out for themselves the duties and obligations laid upon them by the Holy Scriptures.

6. The principle of receiving or practicing nothing but what was expressly taught in the Scriptures was likely to result in the abandonment of many things deemed precious and important by the existing churches.

Thomas Campbell could not have made this address because of the personal aspects of the situation and his natural humility of spirit. It was not in his nature to debate issues nor to challenge the opposition aggressively. Yet it was essential, if the *Declaration and Address* were to be more than a mere essay, that its principles should be boldly championed and effectively implemented. Those who heard Alexander on this occasion were impressed that he possessed the qualities of leadership that were essential for the task. From that day forward, Thomas Campbell joyfully realized that Alexander must increase and he must decrease in the achievement of their common aims.

Now Alexander was overwhelmed with invitations to discuss this challenge to the established churches. He visited in many homes and with individual persons and groups of interested persons. Among the homes was the capacious and impressive dwelling of a wealthy Mr. John Brown, a somewhat liberal-minded Presbyterian who had a reputation for great kindness of disposition, piety, and integrity, and a remarkable love for simplicity and plainness in dress and mode of living. In repeated visits all phases of the Christian system were discussed with great mutual pleasure and profit. Alexander soon formed a friendly acquaintance with Mr. Brown's daughter, Margaret, that ripened into love. On March 12, 1811, they were married and decided to make their home with her father.

About this time it was agreed by the members of the Christian Association that they should assume the character of an independent local church. Accordingly, on May 4, 1811, Thomas Campbell was appointed elder, and Alexander was licensed to preach. Four deacons were chosen: John Dawson, George Sharp, William Gilcrist, and James Foster. The congregation then joined in singing Psalm 118:13-29, in the old metrical version, Seceder style, and in offering prayer. On the following Lord's Day, the church held its first Communion service, and Alexander preached from John 6:48, 58. Afterward his father delivered a discourse on Romans 8:32. A new meeting house constructed on Brush Run was occupied on June 16, Alexander preaching the sermon on Galatians 1:4. Shortly afterward, three persons presented themselves for baptism—Margaret Fullerton, Abraham Altars, and Joseph Bryant.

Immediately the problem arose about the form of baptism. The principles of the *Declaration and Address* required that the question should be settled not by appeal to Protestant tradition but to the Holy Scriptures. Thomas Campbell, Thomas Sharp, and Joseph Bryant conferred earnestly on the subject. Bryant had been convinced through careful study that immersion was the only baptism taught in the New Testament. Campbell admitted that in the primitive age candidates went down into the water and were buried in it. "Water," said he, "is water; and earth is earth. We certainly could not call a person buried in earth if only a little dust were sprinkled on him." He consented, therefore, to perform the ceremony by immersion, even though he himself had never been immersed. The baptism took place July 4 in a deep pool of Buffalo Creek, about two miles above the mouth of Brush Run. It was a moving, if somewhat incongruous, event. Thomas Campbell had never immersed anyone and he did not know exactly how to proceed. He was, however, determined to conform to what his newly discovered principles seemed to require. He asked the candidates to stand in the pool at shoulder depth. Then, standing on the root of a tree which projected over the pool, he bent down their heads until they were buried in the liquid grave, repeating at the same time in each case, the baptismal formula.

The baptismal issue now assumed large proportions in the Brush Run church. Thomas Campbell was criticized for being inconsistent and unqualified to administer the ordinance because he had never been immersed. Alexander at first believed the matter was inconsequential, since baptism was not required as a term of Communion at Brush Run. Indeed, he delivered three sermons to defend his position. But the question would not down. The birth of his first child brought Alexander face to face with the matter: should the child be "baptized" or not?

Finally, after much prayer and study of the original Greek texts, he was convinced that infant baptism was unauthorized by Scripture and that immersion of believers could be substantiated. Once convinced, he resolved at once to obey the divine command. Having formed an aquaintance with Matthias Luce, a Baptist minister who lived near Washington, Campbell asked him to perform the rite, June 12, 1812. Thomas was still noncommittal, being loath for sentimental reasons to depart from the old Presbyterian tradition. But when the hour arrived and a large audience was assembled, it appeared that Thomas Campbell, his wife, and daughter Dorothea had come prepared to be immersed. He requested the privilege of making a statement and proceeded to make a lengthy address on his reasons for his step. He frankly told of his severe mental struggles, arising not only from his early education and the fact that he had been a pedobaptist minister for about twenty-five years, but from the natural desire to avoid any controversy that would be likely to frustrate his dream of a united church. He said he had no idea that to take the Bible and the Bible alone as a rule of faith and practice would lead to such a crucial choice, but since his first allegiance was to his Lord and to His revealed will in the Holy Scriptures, he had no alternative but to obey the clear teaching of the Word. He reviewed at length all the Scriptures pertaining to the divine ordinance and confessed himself fully prepared to obey his Lord.

This address was followed by another of similar length by Alexander Campbell which made a profound impression on the large assemblage. He said he had stipulated with Elder Luce that the ceremony should be performed precisely according to the pattern in the New Testament, and that, as there was no account of any of the first converts being called upon to give what is called a "religious experience," this modern custom should be omitted and that the candidates should be admitted on the simple confession that "Jesus is the Son of God." Thereupon, the service proceeded in which Thomas Campbell, his wife, and daughter, Dorothea, Alexander Campbell, and his wife, and Mr. and Mrs. James Hanen were baptized according to the New Testament practice. The meeting lasted seven hours. The community was so stirred by this amazing development that the ministers were invited to the homes to discuss further the subject of baptism until a very late hour that night. On the following Lord's Day at Brush Run, thirteen others presented themselves for Scriptural baptism, among them James Foster. Thomas Campbell administered the ordinance, each candidate making a simple confession of Christ as Son of God.

This sensational development at Brush Run instigated a broad restudy of the Scriptures with regard to all the basic tenets of the Christian faith apart from the traditional creeds of Christendom.

The subject of *faith* was a case in point. Many persons in the religious world believed that faith was miraculously imparted by the Holy Spirit and that a satisfactory experience was necessary to prove that saving faith had been obtained. The Brush Run brethren discovered that the primitive Christian faith was a simple trust in Christ as Lord and Saviour; that "faith cometh by hearing, and hearing by the Word of God"; that this was all that was required for discipleship, and that its validity was attested by a willingness to obey the divine commands and by the regenerate life.

The subject of the *Sabbath* came under review. The religious community looked upon the first day of the week as a sort of Jewish Sabbath moved up one day on the calendar, and they applied many of the old Sabbath laws in its observance. They could show no Scripture authorizing the change. The Brush Run brethren discovered that the early church met on the first day of the week for fellowship, the breaking of bread and prayers, and observed it as the Lord's Day commemorating His death, burial, and resurrection. They discovered no rabbinical prohibitions as applicable to it, and chose to busy themselves with all such concerns as might advance the kingdom of God.

In these and many other matters the new church daily examined their traditional beliefs and practices in the light of the Scriptures to determine whether "these things were so."

There was, however, a certain loneliness in congregational independence and the brethren yearned for fellowship with others of like mind and heart. There had been and was now no intention to set up a new and separate communion or denomination. Alexander Campbell was pleased with the Baptists more than any other community of Christians. They were a Bible people, strongly evangelistic, and committed to Bible doctrine. They often invited him to preach in their churches, where they accepted him enthusiastically. In late 1812, he visited their Association meeting at Uniontown, Pennsylvania, as an observer. He was invited to preach but declined. He was unhappy about some of the sermons, but he found that other people were also disappointed. Many urged him to join the Redstone Association which held views more in accord with his. He laid the matter before the Brush Run church in the fall of 1813, and after much discussion they finally concluded to make an overture, at the same time setting forth a full statement of their sentiments. The paper, some eight or ten pages in length, was drawn making plain Brush Run's opposition to human creeds as bonds of communion and expressing a willingness to co-operate or unite with the Redstone Association provided they be allowed to preach whatever they learned from the Holy Scriptures, regardless of any creed or formula of Christendom. After much discussion, Brush Run was received by a considerable majority, and the new fellowship was established.

In this limited history it is impossible to discuss all the interesting experiences of the Campbells with their Baptist brethren. They were frequently under fire, especially by those Baptist creedalists committed to the Philadelphia Confession of Faith and extreme Calvinistic theology. The Campbells were basically Calvinistic in their theology, but they refused the brand and the limitations on liberty in Christ.

Sectarian bigotry and petty personal jealousies were often manifest in the meetings of the Redstone Association, but Alexander Campbell was well respected. On August 30, 1816, the Association held its regular meeting at Cross Creek, with Campbell as one of the preachers on the Lord's Day. This proved to be a memorable occasion. A large concourse of people gathered outdoors, because the church house was inadequate. There, under the shade of beautiful, leafy elms and towering plane trees at the edge of Cross Creek, Campbell arose and delivered a discourse founded on Romans 8:3: "What the law could not do, in that it was weak through the flesh, God sending his own Son in the likeness of sinful flesh, and for sin, condemned sin in the flesh." He then launched into the famous "Sermon on the Law" which created widespread repercussions in the Baptist community and set a basic pattern for the interpretation of Scripture in the Restoration movement.

The general purpose of the sermon was to show that Christians are under the law to Christ and not to Moses. Campbell first ascertained the true meaning of the phrase *the law* in the text and in similar portions of Scriptures. Then he pointed out those things which the law could not accomplish; demonstrated the reason the law failed to accomplish these objectives; illustrated how God had remedied these relative defects of the law; and deduced such conclusions from the premises as should be obvious to every unbiased and intelligent person.

This was no impromptu message. Campbell had evidently thought it out carefully. Immediately after its delivery he wrote it *in extenso,* printed it in pamphlet form, and reprinted it thirty years later in the *Millennial Harbinger* (1846, p. 493 ff.). Indeed, it was a sort of declaration of independence for the whole Christian church.

In the outset Campbell showed that *the law* signifies the whole Mosaic dispensation. He said that there were great and immutable principles upon which the Mosaic law was based, but he maintained that the Mosaic code did not originate them; it simply embodied some of the applications of these principles and was a distinct and peculiar institution designed for special ends and for a limited time.

The great principles above mentioned were set forth by Christ: "Thou shalt love the Lord thy God with all thy heart, . . . soul, . . . mind, . . . and . . . strength; . . . and thy neighbour as thyself." And the Lord

62

added, "On these two commandments hang all the law and the prophets." These laws are not mentioned in the Decalogue and are of universal and immutable obligation. Said Campbell,

> Angels and men, good and bad, are forever under them. God, as our Creator, cannot require less; nor can we, as creatures and fellow-creatures, propose or exact less, as the standard of duty and perfection. These are coeval with angels and men. They are engraven with more or less clearness on every human heart. These are the groundwork or basis of the law, . . . which constitute their conscience or knowledge of right or wrong. By these their thoughts mutually accuse or else excuse one another (Romans 2:14, 15). By these they shall be judged, or, at least, all who have never heard or seen a written law or gospel. Let it then be remembered that in the Scriptures these precepts are considered the basis of all law and prophecy; consequently, when we speak of the law of Moses, we do not include these commandments.

Campbell condemned the generally accepted theological distinctions of moral, judicial, and ceremonial law as so involved as to perplex the average mind and proceeded in Scriptural terms to eliminate the whole Mosaic code as binding upon Christians.

Under the second head of his discourse he pointed out the things which the law could not accomplish. He said it could not give righteousness and life. Citing Paul's argument in the Galatian letter, he insisted that if the law could do this, Christ had died in vain. He also said the law could not exhibit the malignity or demerit of sin. Laws against sinful actions such as theft, murder, and adultery did not and could not deal with the vast problem of sin which underlies man's sinful actions. He believed that the Mosaic law was designed for the Jewish nation and in its specifically detailed rules was wholly inadequate for universal application. He said its inadequacies were remedied in the sending of God's only begotten Son in the likeness of sinful flesh to make "reconciliation for iniquity," so that the spiritual seed of Abraham might find "righteousness and eternal life, not by legal works or observances, in whole or in part, but through the abundance of grace and the gift of righteousness which is by him." Thus Christ became "the end of the law for righteousness to everyone that believeth. Nor is He, on this account, the minister of sin, for thus the righteousness, the perfect righteousness, of the law is fulfilled in us who walk not after the flesh but after the Spirit. Do we then make void the law or destroy the righteousness of it by faith? God forbid; we establish the law."

At this point Mr. Campbell elaborated on the events of the life of Christ involving the atonement and showed how it was a full exhibition of the malignant nature of sin and its destructive consequences as well as the overwhelming and everlasting mercy, love, and grace of God. In this tremendous section of the discourse, Mr. Campbell further showed that the failure of the law as a rule of life was remedied in the perfect life and teachings of Christ. In the transfiguration, Moses, the giver of the law, and Elijah, the restorer of the law, are witnesses to the voice of the Father, saying, "This is my beloved Son, in whom I am well pleased, *hear ye him.*"

63

Christ was thus ordained to displace the Mosaic law through a new rule of grace and truth. Mr. Campbell then proceeded to show the essential difference between the law and the gospel and that Christians were not under law but under grace.

He then, in the third place, presented another conclusion: there is no necessity to preach the law in order to prepare men to receive the gospel. "This conclusion," said Campbell, "corresponds perfectly with the commission given by our Lord to the apostles, and with their practices under the commission." "Go," He said, "into all the world, and preach the gospel to every creature . . . [Teaching the disciples] to observe all things whatsoever *I* have commanded you." Thus they were constituted ministers of Christ and not of Moses, of the new covenant, not of the old. Sacred history in the Acts of the Apostles demonstrates this fact. The apostles went forth preaching the gospel to *all nations* and they preached not one word which called for acceptance of the law. This conclusion further corresponds with the nature of the church:

> The Christian dispensation is called the ministration of the Spirit, and, accordingly, everything in the salvation of the Church is accomplished by the immediate energy of the Spirit. Jesus Christ taught his disciples that the testimony concerning himself was that only which the Spirit would use, in converting such of the human family as should be saved. He would not speak of himself, but what he knew of Christ. Now he was to convince the world of sin, of righteousness, and of judgment; not by applying the law of Moses, but the facts concerning Christ, to the consciences of the people. The Spirit accompanying the words which the apostles preached would convince the world of sin; not by the ten precepts but because they believed not in him— of righteousness because he went to the Father—and of judgment because the prince of the world was judged by him. So that Christ, and not law, was the Alpha and Omega of their sermons; and this the Spirit made effectual to the salvation of thousands. Three thousand were convinced of sin, of righteousness, and of judgment, in this precise way of hearing of Christ, on the day of Pentecost; and we read of many afterward. Indeed, we repeat it again, in the whole history of primitive preaching we have not one example of preaching the law as preparatory to the preaching or reception of the gospel.

Then Campbell trained his verbal guns on the weakness of traditional Protestantism, which had built much of its creedal doctrine on arguments and motives drawn from the Old Testament, and condemned infant baptism, observance of holy days and fasts as preparatory to observing the Lord's Supper, sanctifying the Sabbath, the union of church and state, establishing religion by civil law, and the imitation of Jewish customs such as circumcision in infant baptism. He specifically condemned all religious practices which were not enjoined or countenanced by the authority of Jesus Christ.

In his final climactic moments, he lifted up Christ, calling upon his hearers "to venerate in the highest degree the Lord Jesus Christ; . . . to receive Him as the great prophet and the 'Lord of all righteousness,' " concluding that "if we continue in His word, then we are His disciples indeed, and we shall know the truth, and the truth shall make us free:

and if the Son shall make us free, we shall be free indeed." After a few practical reflections, the sermon closed with the petition, "May he that hath the key of David, who opened and no man shutteth, and shutteth that none can open, open your hearts to receive the truth in the love of it, and incline you to walk in the light of it, and then you shall know that the ways thereof are pleasantness, and all the paths thereof are peace. Amen."

Had this sermon been preached before many Baptist associations in our day there would have been little objection. Most Christians recognize a clear division between the Old Testament, with its Jewish institutions and ordinances, and the New Testament or Covenant, with its Christian church, a new institution, with distinctly Christian ordinances having meanings which could not possibly have existed before Christ. They believe that the New Testament is the norm by which the Old Testament must be interpreted. The Old Testament shows that God has exercised providential care over men and has provided ways of salvation for them, but does not determine what the way of salvation is or what the commands of God are under the Christian dispensation. The specific beliefs and practices of the Christian church or the duties of individual Christians cannot be validated by drawing analogies between them and the requirements of Hebrew law. Furthermore, the interpretation of Scripture requires the recognition of at least three dispensational lines—the Patriarchal, the Jewish, and the Christian—for any intelligent understanding of what portions are applicable to Christian life.

But the Baptist ministers at Cross Creek were very unhappy and proposed to bring the sermon to trial at the next meeting of the Redstone Association at Peter's Creek in 1817. While the question was dismissed, cries of "heresy" and "heterodoxy" were hurled against Campbell. As a result pulpits were closed against him.

Interestingly, Thomas Campbell presented at the same Cross Creek meeting a paper on the Trinity, which was read and accepted without amendment. Even the keenest minds of the opposition could find no fault with its orthodoxy. This profound subject, however, was dealt with almost exclusively in terms of the Scripture with the result that the term *Trinity* or the usual theological vocabulary was missing. Campbell sought to frame his thesis not in "words that man's wisdom teacheth" but in those which the Holy Spirit employed in Holy Writ. His views on this important doctrine are in marked contrast to the weak and vacillating ideas held by Barton W. Stone, whose important role in the Restoration movement is yet to be discussed.

The "Sermon on the Law" marked the beginning of a brief but tremendously effective period of Alexander Campbell's ministry. Entrenched denominationalism resented him and his revolutionary biblicism. The clergy treated him with contempt or willfully ignored him. In this situation he realized the need of some drastic strategy if the reformatory movement he represented were not speedily to disappear from view. He began coldly to contemplate and diagnose the illness of contemporary sectarianism and the ecclesiastical institutions which coddled and protected it. He determined that regardless of the feelings of his friends he would discover and destroy the virus of theological infallibility and religious bigotry.

In this resolution Campbell displayed all the boldness of Farel and the uncompromising spirit of Knox in their battle with Rome in the Protestant Reformation. In his new role he was to employ the weapons of sarcasm and irony, incisive and desolating logic, and the idol-smashing tactics of the true iconoclast. While he realized that he would incur the everlasting hatred of entrenched ecclesiastics, he believed he had to destroy false religious concepts and clear the ground of their debris before he could build constructively on the one foundation, the church after the divine pattern. At heart he still maintained his affectionate sympathy for all men and yearned for their salvation, but he believed the time had come to declare all-out war on sectarianism and to challenge its leaders to battle.

BIBLIOGRAPHY: Chapter 3

Athearn, Clarence R., *The Religious Education of Alexander Campbell.*
Campbell, Alexander, *The Sermon on the Law.*
Campbell, Selina Huntington, *Home Life and Reminiscences of Alexander Campbell.*
McLean, Archibald, *Thomas and Alexander Campbell.*
McLean, Archibald, *Alexander Campbell as a Preacher.*
Richardson, Robert, *Memoirs of Alexander Campbell.*

Chapter 4

Alexander Campbell and
the *Christian Baptist*

T HE "Sermon on the Law" was delivered at Cross Creek, far from the sophisticated centers of religious thought and action on the Eastern seaboard. Not a single "religious leader" in America at that time was aware of it, nor destined to be concerned about it. But "God moves in a mysterious way his wonders to perform." He went into the wilderness town of Tekoa for a great reformer in the person of Amos, to confront the kings of Judah with their social sins. He chose a rough, uncouth hair-shirted man of the wilderness, John the Baptist, to introduce the Son of God to the world. The "Sermon on the Law" and Alexander Campbell, the man who delivered it, were destined to be known far beyond Cross Creek. Indeed, this preacher was now beginning to throw off all the limitations of Brush Run, Buffalo Creek, the Redstone Association, and the provincialisms that had hitherto bound him.

Thomas Campbell had moved into Guernsey County, Ohio, to start a new church and school. Later he was to go to Pittsburgh to serve a church after the New Testament pattern. Alexander became the moving spirit in establishing a congregation at nearby Wellsburg, Virginia.

When the narrow creedalists in the Redstone Association moved to unfrock Campbell because of Cross Creek and other transgressions of the law, the Wellsburg congregation proved a refuge and a help. On one of Alexander's excursions into Ohio, he preached in the Baptist church at Warren, where Adamson Bentley was minister. He was so well received that when the Baptists of the Ohio country organized the Mahoning Association, they invited him and the Wellsburg church to affiliate.

Redstone met in September, 1823. A large crowd attended to witness Campbell's downfall. The Brush Run messengers were announced; Alexander Campbell's name was not among the number. He was present, but only as an observer. Campbell was requested after a lengthy debate to state why he was not, as usual, a messenger from Brush Run. He arose and expressed his regret that the Association should have spent so much of its precious time considering him and his status and begged to relieve

67

the Association from all further trouble since the Wellsburg church of which he was now a member was not connected with the Redstone Association. The heresy hunters were completely foiled, and their elaborate strategy by which they expected to oust Campbell in disgrace was rendered futile. A solemn stillness ensued and, for a time, it seemed as though the Association had nothing to do.

Campbell's relationship with the Mahoning Association was most rewarding. The majority of its members were friendly to his views and he was recognized as a leader and counselor in all its deliberations. He frequently addressed its sessions and some of his greatest sermons were preached to his Mahoning brethren. At Canfield (1826) he spoke on a theme which was regarded as a sequel to the "Sermon on the Law." Among the ministers attending were Thomas Campbell, Walter Scott, Sidney Rigdon, Thomas Miller, William West, Corbley Martin, and Jacob Osborne. The meeting was held in the Congregational meeting house in the center of the town. The following extract from the *History of the Disciples in the Western Reserve* gives this vivid description of what took place:

> At a very early hour [the building] was filled, and many around it endeavored to hear. Mr. Campbell . . . founded his discourse on Malachi 4:2: "Unto you that fear my name, shall the Sun of righteousness arise with healing in his wings." He announced his theme, "The Progress of Revealed Light." His discourse abounded in thoughts so fresh, and he made his theme so luminous and instructive that the most rapt attention followed him throughout the delivery.
>
> Seizing on the evident analogy between light and knowledge, and using the former, as the Scripture everywhere does, as a metaphor for the latter, the eloquent preacher exhibited the gradual and progressive unfolding of divine revelation under four successive periods of development, which he characterized as First, The Starlight Age; Second, The Moonlight Age; Third, The Twilight Age; and Fourth, The Sunlight Age; and employed these respectively to explain, First, The Patriarchal; Second, The Jewish Dispensation; Third, The Ministry of John the Baptist, with the personal ministry of the Lord on the earth; and Fourth, The full glory of the perfect system of salvation under the apostles when the Holy Spirit was poured out on them, after the ascension and coronation of Jesus as Lord of all. Under his remarks, and applications of the theme, the whole Bible became luminous with a light it never before seemed to possess. The scope of the whole book appeared clear and intelligible; its parts were so shown to be in harmony with each other, and with the whole, that the exhibition of the subject seemed little else to many than a new revelation, like a "second sun risen on midnoon," shedding a flood of light on a book hitherto looked upon as dark and mysterious. The style of the preacher was plain, common sense, manly. His argumentation was sweeping, powerful and convincing; and above all, and better, his manner of preaching formed so pleasing and instructive a contrast with the customary style of taking a text merely . . . that the assembly listened to the last of a long address scarcely conscious of the lapse of time. At the conclusion [he dwelt] with earnest and thrilling eloquence on the glory of the gospel dispensation, the consummation of all the revelations of God, the Son of Righteousness "now risen with healing in his wings," putting an end to the moonlight and starlight ages . . . The discourse was never forgotten . . .

Indeed, it was not forgotten but went far beyond the Western Reserve of Ohio to "the uttermost parts of the earth," even as his "Sermon on the Law."

The news of this Savonarola of the Alleghenies spread abroad to such an extent that the clergy of the traditional churches challenged him to debate. At first the new Christian community felt that controversy was not favorable to the promotion of Christian union. In the spring of 1820, Campbell was urged to meet John Walker, a Presbyterian minister, in a discussion of baptism. He at first refused, but finally yielded to the strong persuasion of John Birch and the Baptist church at Mount Pleasant, Ohio. Accordingly, Mr. Walker chose Samuel Findley as moderator and Mr. Campbell chose Jacob Martin as joint moderator. According to Richardson in his *Memoirs,* the following rules for discussion were adopted by mutual consent:

> 1. Each speaker shall have the privilege of speaking forty minutes without interruption, if he thinks proper to use them all. 2. Mr. Walker shall open the debate and Mr. Campbell shall close it. 3. The moderators are merely to keep order, not to pronounce judgment on the merits of the debate. 4. The proper subject of the ordinance of baptism is first to be discussed, then the mode of baptism. 5. This debate must be conducted with decorum, and all improper allusions or passionate language guarded against. 6. The debate shall be continued from day to day, until the people are satisfied, or until the moderators think that enough has been said on each topic of debate.

Since this was the first of many important debates in which Campbell engaged; it may be well to give it more consideration than its actual importance might indicate. The rules adopted became a pattern for future technique.

On Monday morning, June 19, Mr. Campbell, accompanied by his father and a few friends, arrived in Mount Pleasant and was greeted by a large audience. Walker's first speech was very short and simply stated his argument:

> I maintain that baptism came in the room of circumcision; that the covenant on which the Jewish church was built, and to which circumcision is the seal, is the same with the covenant on which the Christian church is built, and to which baptism is the seal; that the Jews and the Christians are the same body politic, under the same lawgiver and husband; hence the Jews were called the congregation of the Lord; and the Bridegroom of the Church says, "My love, my undefiled one"—consequently the infants of believers have a right to baptism.

The protagonists immediately joined in discussing the basic issue of the Jewish and Christian covenants, Mr. Campbell employing the arguments in his "Sermon on the Law." Walker was driven from pillar to post to defend his wholesale assertions, as Campbell poured Scripture after Scripture into the discussion. Finally, Walker was forced to abandon his ground and with it any Scriptural authority for infant baptism. He then moved to the discussion of the action of baptism. The rout was now so complete that it was proposed by Findley that each debater be given only one address each on the subject. Campbell insisted on at least two. Walker then went on with the usual arguments to prove that sprinkling and pouring are Scriptural modes of baptism. Campbell answered not only with Scripture but with quotations from the noted Presbyterian scholar, Dr. George Campbell, as to the root meaning of the word in the original. After a feeble rejoinder by Walker, Campbell took over completely. It was evident to everyone that Walker had failed miserably to prove infant baptism a divine ordinance and Campbell concluded his final address by issuing this general challenge: "I this day publish to all present that I feel disposed to meet any paedobaptist minister of any denomination, of good standing in his party, and I engage to prove in a debate with him, either *viva voce* or with the pen, that infant sprinkling is a human tradition and injurious to the well-being of society, religious and political."

Prior to the debate a large number of pedobaptists around Mount Pleasant had been immersed following a Baptist revival. Indeed, this is what had precipitated the debate. Now another large company requested immersion. So depleted were the pedobaptist churches that after they had recovered some aplomb they began a search for one of their most noted preachers who might meet Mr. Campbell and retrieve their fortunes.

The Campbell-Walker debate was published, amid wild charges and countercharges, and had a large circulation, further enhancing the reputation of Campbell and extending the cause he represented. The printed page was now to be the medium by which the whole Western country was to be challenged by the new reformation.

In the spring of 1823, after conferring with his father and with Walter Scott and other friends, Alexander Campbell issued a prospectus for a proposed journal to be called *The Christian Baptist,* a title adopted not without some debate, since the term *Baptist* was a party designation. They finally decided, however, that to allay possible religious prejudice among their Baptist brethren, the designation should be added. In the prospectus, the nature and aims of the publication were set forth as follows:

> *The Christian Baptist* shall espouse the cause of no religious sect, excepting that ancient sect "called Christians first at Antioch." Its sole object shall be the eviction of truth, and the exposure of error in doctrine and practice. The editor acknowledging no standard of religious faith or works, other than the Old and New Testaments, and the latter as the only standard of the religion of Jesus Christ, will, intentionally at least, oppose nothing which it contains and recommend nothing which it does not enjoin. Having no worldly interest at stake from the adoption or reprobation of any article of faith or religious practice—having no gift nor religious emolument to blind his eyes or to pervert his judgment, he hopes to manifest that he is an impartial advocate of truth.

The number of subscribers answering the prospectus was small, but Campbell determined to go ahead with the project. In order that he might not be under obligation even to a printer who might influence his work or under certain circumstances halt publication, he purchased a complete printing establishment and set it up at Bethany, Virginia, where he was then residing. Reflecting his prodigious capabilities (for he was now a successful farmer, businessman, and minister of the gospel), he soon became an expert proofreader, printer, editor, and publisher. Indeed, he conducted his printing business with such economy and successful activity that in the first seven years he had issued forty-six thousand volumes of his own work.

The first issue of *The Christian Baptist* appeared on July 4, 1823, when clerical opposition was at an all-time high. This situation may have been somewhat responsible for the editor's emphasis on the exposition of existing corruptions of the religious community. In his Preface he wrote:

> We expect to prove whether a paper perfectly independent, free from any controlling jurisdiction except the Bible, will be read; or whether it will be blasted by the poisonous breath of sectarian zeal and of an aspiring priesthood (p. vi).

At the masthead he carried these quotations:

> Style no man on earth your father, for He alone is your Father who is in heaven; and all ye are brethren. Assume not the title of Rabbi; for ye have only One Teacher: neither assume the title of Leader; for ye have only One Leader—the Messiah. *Matth. xxiii, 8-10.*
> Prove all things: hold fast that which is good. *Paul the Apostle.*

The leading article was a brief review of the Christian religion as first established, showing the prophetic background of the Messiah, His lowly advent and His glorious victory in the atonement as the suffering Saviour. He dwelt on the perfection of His teaching; the life and conduct of His disciples and of the apostles; and contrasted them with modern religious teachers. He then described the New Testament churches as to their unity, their faith and love of Christ, their independence as local congregations, and their devotion to good works. By contrast, he presented a scathing picture of modern Christianity with its corruptions and divisions. This article became a pattern for the content of future issues.

His series on "The Restoration of the Ancient Order of Things" set forth in great detail the nature and work of the church of the New Testament. He then urged the abandonment of everything not in use among early Christians, such as creeds, unscriptural words and phrases, theological theories; and the adoption of everything sanctioned by primitive practice, as the weekly breaking of the loaf, the fellowship, the simple order of public worship, and the independence of each church under a plurality of bishops (elders) and deacons. In overthrowing clerical and ecclesiastical power, however, Campbell sought to make it clear that "all things be done to edification" and "in decency and in order." The position of ministers was to be on the order of that of the elders, with their proper position and authority, and worthy of pecuniary support. In one of this series of articles he wrote:

The bishop of a christian congregation will find much to do that never enters the mind of a modern preacher or "minister." The duties he is to discharge to Christ's flock in the capacity of teacher and president, will engross much of his time and attention. Therefore the idea of remuneration for his services was attached to the office from the first institution. This is indisputably plain, not only from the positive commands delivered to the congregations, but from the hints uttered with reference to the office itself (Vol. III, p. 360).

Nevertheless Campbell utterly denied the "propriety of the distinction between clergy and laity." He believed that the modern clergy had been responsible for the development of extra-Scriptural ecclesiastical machinery, liturgy, and theological lore in order to make themselves indispensable to a denominational system. They had made the system so complicated that only a special class of experts could handle it. These "hireling priests" had come between the people and the Bible and claimed that they alone could properly interpret its teachings to the masses. He later wrote a series of scathing articles under the general theme of "A Looking Glass for the Clergy," which aroused the unbridled hatred of the profession. However, he exempted the Baptists: "Amongst the Baptists it is to be hoped that there are few clergy, and would to God there were none! The grand and distinguishing views of the Baptists must be grossly perverted before they could tolerate one such creature."

The series on the "Ancient Order" dealt extensively with unscriptural organizations in which category Campbell included Bible societies, missionary societies, Sunday schools, synods, presbyteries, conferences, and general assemblies that claimed administrative or legislative control of local congregations. He even included Baptist associations which assumed such prerogatives. He allowed that no functions which the Scriptures ascribe to the local church should be usurped by organizations not mentioned or described in Holy Writ. At this time most Baptist associations on the frontier were voluntary associations of churches for mutual aid, edification, and fellowship. The actions of the messengers sent to associations were understood to be advisory only and not in any way to determine or direct the policies of the local church. In some cases, associations were beginning to assume legislative and judicial functions and this trend came under the *Christian Baptist's* strong condemnation.

The condemnation of human creeds called for a restoration of universal Bible study, contended Campbell. To this end he proposed a "proper method of studying the Word of God." He assumed that God had "revealed himself, his will and our salvation in human language" to be "used by his Spirit in the common received sense among mankind generally; else it could not have been a revelation." The reader was advised to begin with Matthew's gospel, read the whole of it at one reading or two, marking the passages that are not easily understood. Then read it again with special attention to the marked passages until their meaning is clear. Follow by reading the other gospels. "Then read the Acts of the Apostles, which is the key to all the Epistles; then the

Epistles in a similar manner . . . Always before reading an Epistle, read everything about the people addressed in the Epistle which you find in the Acts of the Apostles." This restudy was to be undertaken without "any commentator or system before your eyes or mind" and without any preconceived notions. The Old Testament was to be read as background. Campbell advised that it would be advantageous to find a group of earnest seekers after the truth to join in such an exploratory study. Then he added the injunction to ask "the Father of Lights"

> for that instruction which he has graciously promised to all that ask him, praying that "the God of our Lord Jesus Christ, the Father of glory, may give unto you the spirit of wisdom and revelation in the knowledge of Him; the eyes of your understanding being enlightened, that ye may know what is the hope of his calling, and what the riches of glory of his inheritance in the saints, and what the exceeding greatness of his power to usward who believe, according to the working of his mighty power, which he wrought in Christ when he raised him from the dead and set him at his own right hand in the heavenly places . . . that Christ may dwell in your hearts by faith, that ye, being rooted and grounded in love, may be able to comprehend with all saints what is the breadth, and length, and depth and height, and to know the love of Christ which passeth knowledge, that ye may be filled with all the fulness of God."

The editor was beset with a tidal wave of criticism because of the radical views expressed in the "Ancient Order" series. This came from both Baptist and pedobaptist sources. Among the queries that were directed against him was the frequent one, "How can you remain in fellowship with Baptist churches and hold such beliefs?" To which, says Richardson, he was wont to reply:

> I do intend to continue my connection with this people so long as they permit me to say what I believe; to teach what I am assured of, and to censure what is amiss in their views and practices. I have no idea of adding to the catalog of new sects . . . I labor to see sectarianism abolished and all Christians of every name united upon the one foundation upon which the apostolic church was founded. To bring Baptists and paedo-Baptists to this is my supreme end . . .
> When I unite in prayer with a society of disciples, I have full communion with them in certain petitions, confessions and thanksgivings, but requests may be presented, confessions made and thanksgivings offered in which I have not full communion. The same may be said of any other social act of worship. All I intend by the phrase is that I will unite with any Baptist society in the United States in any act of social worship, such as prayer, praise or breaking bread in commemoration of the Lord's death, if they confess the one Lord, the one faith, the one hope and the one baptism; provided always that as far as I can judge, they piously and morally conform to their profession . . . I frankly and boldly declare to them, as Paul did to the Corinthians, the things in which I praise them, and the things in which I praise them not. And I know of no way, of no course that any Christian can pursue consistently with the New Testament, consistently with his serving God and his own generation, but this one. Therefore, I advocate it and practice it.

Campbell was accused also of being a Socinian and denying the Scriptural teaching of the work and office of the Holy Spirit. This, as

73

well as other unfounded criticism, was dealt with in the *Christian Baptist* on several occasions. He presented alone the simple teaching of the Scriptures, refraining from human speculations. He traced the work of the Spirit in revealing all that is known of God, and in attesting and confirming, by prophecy, by miracle, and by supernatural gifts, the mission of Christ and the apostles, thus providing the infallible testimony by which alone faith can be produced. He believed that these manifestations of divine wisdom and power were confined to the apostolic age and to a portion of the saints then living and that "the influences of the Spirit as the Spirit of all goodness were felt and experienced by all the primitive saints, and are now felt by all true believers." He was always cautious and reticent as to his views of the manner in which the Holy Spirit accomplished His work. He rejoiced in the promise that God would "give his Holy Spirit to them that ask him"; he believed in the reality of this gift as the true seal of the covenant and the source of the fruits that adorn the Christian life, but he refused to offer any opinion or to propound any theory as to the manner in which the Holy Spirit exerted His power. He readily recognized the evidences of special or added influences exerted by the Spirit in believers:

> I am not to be understood as asserting that there is no divine influence exercised over the minds and bodies of men. This would be to assert in contradiction to a thousand facts and declarations in the volume of revelation; this would be to destroy the idea of any divine government exercised over the human race; this would be to make prayer a useless and irrational exercise; this would be to deprive Christians of all the consolation derived from a sense of the superintending care, guidance and protection of the Most High. But to resolve everything into a "divine influence" is the other extreme. This divests man of every attribute that renders him accountable to his Maker, and assimilates all his actions to the bending of trees or the tumults of the ocean occasioned by the temptest (*Christian Baptist,* April, 1825).

The crucial issue in the discussions on the Holy Spirit was the so-called "irresistible operation" of the Spirit in conversion. This doctrine had, in Campbell's opinion, been responsible for all the untoward emotional demonstrations in current revivalism and the refusal of intelligent men to accept Christ as their Saviour. In his famous discussion with Andrew Broaddus in the *Christian Baptist,* there was a remarkable meeting of minds on the subject. Said Broaddus in one of his letters:

> That the Word of God is the instrument of our regeneration and sanctification, I have no doubt; nor would I think of saying it is his usual method (whatever in some cases he may choose to do) to operate on the soul independent of the word. But that there is a living, divine agent, giving life and energy to the word, and actually operating on the soul, is, in my view, a truth which forms one of the glorious peculiarities of the religion of Jesus: and this I would say, in the language of the apostle, we are "born again not of corruptible seed, but of incorruptible, by the word of God, which lives and abides forever" (*Memoirs,* Vol. II, p. 152 ff.).

To which Campbell replied,

I am not conscious that there is one point of controversy between us in all the items of the practical truth embraced in your letter. Whatever diversity of opinion might possibly exist between us in carrying out some principles to their legitimate issue, I am conscious of none in the premises . . . Were it not for the pernicious influence of the theories afloat on this subject, I would assert my concurrence in opinion with you. This may appear to be a strange saying; but it is in accordance with the genius of this work. I have taken a stand which I am determined, by the grace of God, not to abandon. I will lay down no new theories in religion, contend for no old theories, nor aid any theory now in existence . . . Because no *theory* is the gospel of Jesus the Messiah.

Campbell further stated:

If any man accustomed to speculate on religion as a mere science should infer from anything that I have said on these theories, that I contend for a religion in which the Holy Spirit has nothing to do; in which there is no need of prayer for the Holy Spirit; in which there is no communion of the Holy Spirit; in which there is no peace and joy in the Holy Spirit—he does me the greatest injustice . . . All whom I baptize, I baptize in the name of the Father, and of the Son, and of the Holy Spirit. I pray for the love of the Father, the grace of the Son, and the communion of the Holy Spirit to remain with all the saints. A religion of which the Holy Spirit is not the author, the subject matter, and the perfecter is sheer Deism. To a man that teaches otherwise, I would say, "Art thou a teacher in Israel and knowest not these things?" . . . The incontrovertible fact is, that men must be born from above; and for this purpose the glad tidings are announced. Let us simply promulgate them in all their simplicity and force, unmixed with theory, uncorrupted with philosophy, uncomplicated with speculation, and unfettered by system, and mark the issues.

There was basic agreement but Campbell's refusal to enter the field of theological speculation in any way left Broaddus and many others in grave doubt concerning his orthodoxy.

In his "Six Letters to a Skeptic," Campbell presented a remarkable argument for the basic evidence of Christianity and a Christian view of the world. He held that the Bible must be a revelation of God because man cannot even form an idea of God by his own powers; not one of the terms peculiarly expressive of the idea of God such as *spirit, eternity,* or *immortality,* is to be found in any people prior to their being possessed of an oral or written revelation; no nation without such a revelation can be found with a single idea of any item of the deist's creed; not one of the idolatrous nations pretends to have derived its religion from reason. From historical and prophetic evidence and from a study of the genius and tendency of Christianity, he argued that the only hope of the world lies in its acceptance of Jesus Christ as Saviour and Lord. From this ground he moved to the position that men must be changed, regenerated, and reformed by the love of God if society is to reach the apex of morality and prosperity. These ideas produced a profound respect for the writer and were widely circulated among educators and statesmen.

A whole volume could be filled with Campbell's new approach to the problems of the religious and political community. His father and many of his followers from that day to this regretted his often iconoclastic tirades against the *status quo*. His classic "Third Epistle of Peter," "The Parable of the Iron Bedstead," and "A Looking Glass for the Clergy" were examples of a keen ironic wit that was devastating. But taken as a whole, this journalistic venture made him a national figure who was never again ignored and gave the reformation which he espoused a public forum that challenged the whole religious community.

The Campbell-Walker debate was such a signal defeat for the pedobaptist forces on the frontier that another debate on infant baptism was bound to be forthcoming. After much searching, the Presbyterians finally found a man of greater scholarship and ability than Walker, W. L. McCalla, minister of their church in Augusta, Kentucky. After rules of the discussion were adopted, Campbell chose Jeremiah Vardeman, one of the most popular Baptist preachers in Kentucky, as his moderator; McCalla chose James K. Birch; and they in turn chose Major William Roper. The debate was held in Washington, Mason County, Kentucky, beginning October 14, 1823. Campbell rode more than three hundred miles on horseback to be present. Sidney Rigdon accompanied him. The sage of Bethany opened the discussion on a high spiritual level and challenged his opponent to point out any advantages of infant sprinkling.

McCalla then promised to produce (1) a divine command for infant baptism, (2) *probable* evidence of apostolic practice, and (3) *positive* evidence of apostolic practice of the rite. Then Campbell in a strategic approach assured his pedobaptist friends that he was not there to widen the breach by inflaming their passions but that he intended to proceed from the base laid down in the Westminster Confession of Faith:

> All things in Scripture are not alike plain in themselves, nor alike clear unto all; yet those things which are necessary to be known, believed, and observed for salvation, are so clearly propounded and opened in some place of Scripture or other, that not only the learned but the unlearned, in a due use of ordinary means, may attain unto a sufficient understanding of them.

He then proceeded to quote from the same chapter, section nine:

> The infallible rule of interpretation of Scripture is the Scripture itself; and, therefore, when there is a question about the true and full sense of any Scripture which is not manifold, but one, it may be searched and known by other places that speak more clearly.

Campbell challenged McCalla to be loyal to this principle laid down in his own confession of faith. Campbell then proceeded to take as a text the declaration of the Westminster Confession: "Baptism is a sacrament of the New Testament, ordained by Jesus Christ." Defining *sacrament* as a "holy ordinance," he said appeal must be made "to the New Testament and not to the Old to ascertain the nature, design and subjects of the ordinance. Furthermore, this appeal must be to the words of Jesus Christ for the institution of baptism, because the text says it is an ordinance of Jesus Christ; we shall have nothing to do with Moses in this matter, however useful he may be in others. No doubt our opponent will feel honored and will acquiesce in our method as correct."

76

The battle throughout the debate was fought on this ground, and, try as he might, McCalla could not extricate himself from the web of his own Westminster Confession in which Campbell had enmeshed him. Being completely outmaneuvered and unable to present a New Testament case for infant baptism, McCalla at length refused to reply to Campbell's arguments and confined himself to the reading of extensive manuscripts which he had prepared prior to the debate. Finding his efforts to elicit debate quite futile, Campbell began to devote his addresses to the design of baptism. This was a new adventure in the study of the Word and was to contribute to an extensive treatise on baptism at a later time. The platform meetings continued for seven days and closed with Mr. Campbell issuing the same challenge to the pedobaptist community that he had issued at Mount Pleasant.

The rout was complete. The Baptist preachers were so much pleased with the results that they besieged Campbell with requests to remain in Kentucky and preach in all the most prominent pulpits. The pedobaptists in the area never recovered from the blow with the result that adult-immersionist bodies dominate the state to this day. Campbell was so pleased by the results of the encounter that he wrote, "This is, we are convinced, one of the best means of propagating the truth and exposing error in doctrine or practice." Lexington, "The Athens of the West," received Campbell in a veritable ovation. He was recognized by Dr. Horace Holley, president of Transylvania University, Henry Clay, and other distinguished citizens as being the mightiest intellect who had ever visited the city.

Campbell's contacts with the Baptists of Kentucky were especially cordial, because his views coincided with those that they had held for many years. The Separate Baptists were descendants of Shubail Starnes, who was born in Boston and migrated to North Carolina in 1754. The church he established in the Southland refused to adopt or formulate articles of faith, taking the Bible alone as its rule of faith and practice. One author of Baptist history states that Starnes and those who followed his leadership had a "doctrine and practice . . . substantially the same as that now held by the Campbellites." Three of the first Baptist preachers to enter Kentucky in 1780 were of the Starnes persuasion—William Marshall, Benjamin Lyn, and James Skaggs. In 1785 the churches they established were described as mostly Arminian in doctrinal belief, practiced believer immersion, called themselves "churches of Christ," opposed all human creeds, practiced open Communion, took the Bible alone as their rule of faith and practice, and were so wedded to the idea of congregational polity that their associations were restricted to fellowship and mutual encouragement.

The Concord Association stated in its code of government printed in 1825 that "this body shall have no power to lord it over God's heritage, neither shall it have any classical power or infringe upon any of the internal rights of the churches." The document went on to say:

We understand this sentence as saying that the Association has no power to determine what any church shall receive as her creed; or whether she shall have any creed or confession at all other than the Bible; and, consequently, that she has no power to lord it over God's heritage as to condemn any church for holding or teaching any scriptural truths, though they be at variance with the opinions of this body concerning such truths.

All the Concord Baptists were enthusiastic followers of Campbell and read his *Christian Baptist* avidly. J. A. Spencer, author of a *History of Kentucky Baptists,* claimed that by 1827 "Campbellism was a raging fanaticism in Northern Kentucky." He further observed that in 1829 and 1830 "there were severed from the Baptists eight or ten thousand people" who joined the Restoration movement. In trying to account for the virtual disappearance of the Separate Baptists in Kentucky, Spencer puts it in one brief but trite sentence, "They were sluft off to the Campbellites." Some of these churches had been absorbed by the "Stonites" (of which more will be said in the next chapter), but it was Campbell who appealed to their sensibilities and convictions so that it was almost a case of "love at first sight" on the part of both parties.

Upon Campbell's return to Bethany, the debate with McCalla was put into book form and had a wide circulation with salutary results.

In 1827, Mrs. Campbell, whose health had steadily declined, died. Her five surviving children, all daughters, and her husband heard her tranquilly and cheerfully confess her faith in Christ and add, "I die without an anxiety about anything upon the earth, having committed all that interests me into the hands of my faithful and gracious heavenly Father, and the confident expectation of a glorious resurrection when the Lord Jesus appears unto the salvation of all who trust in Him." It was her request, if he were so inclined, that Campbell should take her dearest friend and frequent visitor at Bethany, Miss Selina Bakewell, to be the mother of her children. Some two years later, not only in deference to his wife's earnest wish but also in accordance with his own deliberate judgment and tender regard, Campbell married Miss Bakewell. The wisdom of his choice was to be amply confirmed in the years to come.

Meanwhile, Thomas Campbell and the churches at Brush Run, Washington, Pigeon Creek, and others that held to the views of the Restoration movement, became victims of the creedalists of the Redstone Baptist Association and were denounced as Arian, Socinian, Arminian, Antinomian, and with every evil word their enemies could devise. Accordingly, they formed the Washington Association on September 7, 1827. Soon after, the Brush Run church disbanded because of emigration, the remnant members affiliating with the Washington church and a new congregation near Buffalo (Bethany), Alexander Campbell's home.

Campbell had now become, in the eyes of many, the foremost champion of true Christianity in America. Infidelity was still rampant and it had recently gained an outstanding advocate in the person of Robert Owen. Owen was the son-in-law of Robert Dale, proprietor of the New Lanark Mills in Scotland. Dale had done much for the advancement and happiness of the working classes, and Owen had generously financed co-operative societies and communities in many places. Coming to America, he established such communities as Kendal, Ohio, and New Harmony, Indiana. At the same time he denounced Christianity as an opiate of the masses and preached the doctrines of atheism with brilliant reasoning and eloquent oratory. He issued frequent challenges to the clergy to meet him in debate on the evidences of Christianity, but no one was brave enough to accept him. Campbell accepted Owen's challenge on April 25, 1828, and the two agreed to meet in Cincinnati on April 13 of the following year.

Great national interest was manifested in the engagement. Owen chose as moderators the Reverend Timothy Flint, Francis Carr, and Henry Starr. Campbell selected Judge David S. Burnet, Colonel Samuel W. Davis, and Major Daniel Gano. These six chose the Reverend Oliver M. Spencer. Then Judge Burnet was appointed chairman. The debate continued for eight days and was attended by great crowds, many coming from New York, Pennsylvania, Virginia, Tennessee, Mississippi, and other states. The metropolitan press gave extensive accounts of the arguments; and Mrs. Anthony Trollope, celebrated English author of the time, described the debate at some length in her *Domestic Manners of the Americans.*

Owen undertook to prove that all religions are founded on ignorance and fear; that they are in conflict with science and natural law; that they are a source of strife, vice, and misery; that they hinder the development of a society embodying virtue, intelligence, and goodwill; and that they are perpetuated only by the tyranny of the unscrupulous few over the ignorant masses. He built his arguments on twelve natural laws which he had worked out with great exactness.

Campbell had prepared only his opening address in order that he might be free to deal effectively with Owen's arguments. In his opening he apologized for bringing the evidences of the Christian religion into debate, as though they were matters to be contested. He stated that he had no hope of convincing Owen of the error of his ways, but he had accepted the challenge for the sake of the doubting, wavering public who were in danger of being swept off their feet by infidel theories. In classic and thoughtful language he dealt with basic questions such as "What is man? Whence came he? Whither does he go?" He dwelt eloquently on the history of Christianity and the blessings it had imparted to the nations in comparison with the materialistic schemes and degrading principles which had plunged society into disbelief, sensual indulgence, and everlasting death. His powerful grasp of the subject made a marked impression on the audience and from that hour until the debate closed Campbell was in full command of the situation.

Owen expected him to defend traditional Christianity as represented in the established churches and was nonplused to find the ground shifted to the New Testament revelation in its simplicity and purity. Somewhat as McCalla, he found himself driven to the use of manuscripts which he had prepared beforehand, the content of which became less and less relevant to the discussion as time went on. Nothing could divert him from his "twelve laws of human nature." His rout was so complete that on Friday, April 17, he conceded to Campbell the remainder of the time. In a speech which lasted *twelve hours,* Campbell reviewed the nature and evidences of Christianity, the grandeur, the power, and the adaptability of the gospel to mankind in all relationships and conditions of human society. He showed that Christianity was a reasonable religion—not seeking to make men happy or reformed by legal enactments or vain theories, but by implanting in the human heart, through the discovery of the divine philanthropy, that principle of love which fulfills every moral precept. Presenting the gospel as a series of connected historical facts, resting on the infallible testimony of witnesses and prophecy, he dwelt upon its simplicity (as opposed to human authoritative creeds and systems) and the distinctive views of the gospel which the Restoration movement espoused. He then proceeded to show that all that was good in Owen's social schemes had been plagiarized from the teachings of Christ and all the evil in them was the fruit of the devil.

At the conclusion of the debate, Campbell called upon all in the audience "who believe in the Christian religion, or who feel so much interest in it as to wish to see it pervade the world" to stand. Almost everyone rose to his feet. He then asked all those who were "doubtful of the truth of the Christian religion or who do not believe it, and who are not friendly to its spread and prevalence over the world" to arise. Only three persons stood.

It was almost unanimously agreed by those who heard him that the cogency of Campbell's arguments had never been surpassed, if ever equaled. He was the sensation of the moment. On the Lord's Day he was invited to preach in the Methodist church (the largest in the city) and the house could not contain the people who came to hear him.

For a time at least, denominational feelings were abated and all parties agreed that they owed an everlasting debt to Campbell. A number of prominent people in the community made confession of faith and were immersed. Young college men who had been converted in the meetings went on foot and horseback through the countryside preaching in homes and schoolhouses, their work resulting in the establishment of many churches after the New Testament pattern. The debate was published and had an immense circulation throughout the English-speaking world.

Upon his return home, Campbell's friends and neighbors prevailed upon him to be a candidate for election to the Virginia Constitutional Convention of 1829. He had become a large landowner and had distinguished himself in public affairs to such an extent that he was easily elected. His main interest in going to Richmond for the long, grueling sessions was to introduce legislation for the emancipation of the slaves. Later he was to free his own slaves and provide generously for their future needs. Arriving in the capital city, he found all political power in the hands of the slave-owning aristocracy. Representation was heavily weighted in favor of the eastern counties. Leading an effort to democratize the government and thus make possible the abolition of slavery he found himself opposed by such men as James Madison, James Monroe, John Marshall, and John Randolph—all landed aristocrats and on the side of the oligarchy controlling the convention.

Campbell, however, acquitted himself with such eloquence and intelligent argument on the floor of the assembly, and revealed such a fine understanding of the principles of a democratic society, that he earned the respect of all. He was frequently invited to speak in the churches of the city, and many of his fellow delegates went to hear him. President Monroe is quoted as saying that he heard him often and regarded him as "the ablest and most original expounder of the Scriptures" he had ever heard. The friendships he made among the political leaders of the nation were later to result in an invitation to preach before a joint session of the House of Representatives and the Senate of the United States, the only minister of the gospel to be extended such a courtesy in the history of the republic.

BIBLIOGRAPHY: Chapter 4

Campbell, Alexander, *The Christian Baptist* (1823-1829) (seven volumes in one; revised by D. S. Burnet with Alexander Campbell's last corrections).

Campbell, Alexander, and Robert Owen, *Debate on the Evidences of Christianity*.

Campbell, Alexander, and John Walker, *A Debate on Christian Baptism*.

Campbell, Alexander, and W. L. McCalla, *A Debate on Christian Baptism*.

Garrison, W. E., *Alexander Campbell's Theology, Its Sources and Historical Setting*.

Grafton, T. W., *Life of Alexander Campbell*.

Hayden, W. L., *Alexander Campbell, Matchless Defender of the Protestant Faith*.

Haley, J. J., *Debates That Made History*.

Kellems, Jesse R., *Alexander Campbell and the Disciples*.

Lowber, J. W., *Alexander Campbell and the Disciples*.

Rice, N. L., *Campbellism: Its Rise, Progress, Character and Influence*.

Richardson, Robert, *Memoirs of Alexander Campbell*.

Smith, Benjamin L., *Alexander Campbell*.

Spencer, J. H., *A History of Kentucky Baptists* (Vols. I and II).

Walker, Granville, *Preaching in the Thought of Alexander Campbell*.

Warren, Louis A., *The Influence of the Separatists on Disciples' Heritage* (an address).

Chapter 5

Barton W. Stone and
the Christian Connection

AS God in His providence was moving in America to infuse the church with new life, He touched among others the life of Barton Warren Stone. He was to have a large part in shaping the destiny of the movement to restore New Testament Christianity and point the way to Christian unity. His major contribution lay in his irenic spirit, his bent to practical unity, and his deep concern for the saving of lost souls.

Stone was born December 24, 1772, near Port Tobacco, Charles County, in southern Maryland, the son of John and Mary Warren Stone. He was a fifth generation American. The Stones were members of the Church of England and were active in Christ Church in Port Tobacco. Here Barton submitted to "infant sprinkling" at the hands of the Reverend Thomas Thornton. In his autobiography, Stone gives only three short sentences to the first years of his life in Maryland. He considered himself a Virginian. Following the death of his father in 1775, his mother abandoned the manoral life of southern Maryland and settled with her seven sons and one daughter in Pittsylvania County, near the Dan River, about eighty miles south of the Blue Ridge Mountains.

At the impressionable age of nine, Bart, as he was called, was surrounded by the events and experiences of the Revolutionary War. In the war zone he saw the tented fields with the attending thievery, promiscuity, swearing, drunkenness, and gambling which demoralized his Pittsylvania "Garden of Eden." From that day on he was a confirmed pacifist, hating the causes and effects of war in all its forms.

His early education was that usual to the frontier. When the Stone estate was divided, Barton took his share and invested it in higher learning, enrolling in the famous David Caldwell Academy, near Greensboro, North Carolina. Here the majority of Carolina Presbyterian preachers, trained in the classics, had been students. Five of Caldwell's graduates became governors of states. Konkle called Caldwell "one of the greatest natural teachers that America has ever produced" and said that his school was "a veritable seminary to the whole South." A dominant factor of life at Caldwell was religion in the Calvinistic pattern. So keen a student was Stone that he was able to complete the classical course in three years.

To the religious atmosphere of Caldwell came many evangelists. James McGready was the most popular. He was a strict Calvinist and preached the doctrines of total depravity, the judgment of God, and the necessity of a new birth that only God could give. On one of McGready's visits, Stone came under deep conviction but could not find salvation in the horrific hell-fire and brimstone preaching to which he listened. It remained for William Hodge, preaching in the Alamance church nearby, to touch his heart and lead him into full surrender to Christ. That night the text was "God is love." Stone reported that "with much animation and with many tears he spoke of the love of God for sinners, and of what that love had done for sinners. My heart warmed with love for that lovely character he described, and momentary hope and joy would rise in my troubled breast." When the service was over Stone retired to the woods alone with his Bible. With the theme of Hodges' discourse, "God is love," ringing in his ears, he yielded, and, as Stone tells the story in his autobiography:

> I . . . sunk at his feet a willing subject. I loved him—I adored him—I praised him aloud in the silent night, in the echoing grove around. I confessed to the Lord my sin in disbelieving his word so long and in following so long the devices of men. I now saw that a poor sinner was as much authorized to believe in Jesus at first, as at last—that *now* was the accepted time, and the day of salvation.

His was not an orthodox conversion according to the preaching of his time but it was real. From this commitment he never departed.

Young Stone desired to enter the ministry, but he had no miraculous call. Caldwell told him that his overwhelming desire was sufficient and assigned him the complex subject of the Trinity for a dissertation, to be presented at the next meeting of the Orange Presbytery. The more he read *The Divine Economy* by the Dutch theologian Herman Witsius, the more confused he became. Finally he found an assuring treatise on the subject by Isaac Watts, prepared his discourse, and awaited the examination. Fortunately, the Reverend Henry Patillo, who accepted Watts' view, presided at the next meeting of the Presbytery. He tactfully worded his queries so that Stone answered satisfactorily, and passed the examination.

In the months before the presbytery could confirm his license, Stone decided to visit his older brother in Georgia. There he was unexpectedly invited to teach in Succoth Academy, at Washington, where he remained for a year. The principal of the academy was Hope Hull, a Methodist who had supported James O'Kelly's campaign against Asbury which resulted in the Republican Methodists in 1792. Stone accompanied Hull to a district conference in South Carolina in 1795, and they became friends. Another man who influenced Stone in this formative period was John Springer, a New Light Presbyterian, to whom sectarian lines meant little.

Returning from Georgia, Stone received his license from Henry Patillo and immediately began a preaching tour into North Carolina and Virginia. Returning west through Tennessee and into Kentucky, he came to Cane Ridge and Concord, near Lexington, where he became supply minister. In these frontier Presbyterian churches he met with more success than in Virginia and Carolina. Within a few months, fifty new members were received at Concord, and thirty at Cane Ridge. The next year (1798) he was called to the stated ministry of the two churches he had been serving. This involved an examination by the Presbytery of Transylvania, the prospect of which disturbed him. Stone still held views on basic doctrines which were not acceptable in some quarters.

On the day of his ordination, he resolved to face examination frankly and honestly and leave the results with the Lord. Dr. James Blythe and Robert Marshall, whom he had first met in Virginia, were his examiners. They asked him how far he was willing to go in receiving the Westminster Confession. He told them, "As far as I see it consistent with the Word of God." This seemed to satisfy the examiners. When the question was proposed in Presbytery, "Do you receive and adopt the Confession of Faith, as containing the systematic doctrine taught in the Bible?" Stone answered aloud so the entire congregation might hear, "I do, as far as I see it consistent with the Word of God." No objection was made and he was ordained. The exact answer was not made a matter of record in the minutes and that caused difficulty later.

At this time the Presbyterians were the strongest religious body on the frontier. Next numerically were the Baptists and Methodists. But the masses were either deistic, atheistic, or in a state of religious apathy. In Kentucky in 1800, statistics showed that only ten thousand out of a population of 221,000 were church members. This situation was the seed bed for the great revivals which were soon to come. Strangely enough, it was James McGready who was to be the "John the Baptist" of this great awakening in the West—the man whose fire and brimstone preaching back in Virginia had repelled Stone rather than won him to Christ. Stone, however, went to hear him preach and became convinced that such preaching was essential in a society committed to crass materialism. McGready attacked "the flesh-pleasing idols" of the frontiersmen, their Sabbath-breaking, cursing, balls, parties, horse-racing, gambling, drunkenness, and the like. He could consign them to the lower regions with such tremendous effectiveness that they came on their knees pleading for forgiveness and salvation. Soon he was followed everywhere he went with hundreds, then thousands of suppliants, and the great revival was on. Stone was baffled by the piercing shrieks, the jerks and the epilepsy-like strokes that left men and women like dead bodies. He did not approve the method, but he could not deny its effectiveness in changing lives.

After a visit to Logan County, where McGready was in the midst of his greatest revival, Stone returned to his parish to find the strange manifestations already at work among his people. At Concord, where he preached, two little girls were "struck down," and at Cane Ridge an old friend, Nathaniel Rogers, "praised God aloud for his conversion." In

June, a "protracted meeting" began in the open air at Concord, with some four thousand persons from all denominations in attendance. Stone was not active in this demonstration. He was concerned, but his Presbyterian nature was slow to respond.

In the midst of this tornadolike religious excitement, Stone, now in his twenty-ninth year, journeyed two hundred miles from Cane Ridge to Greenville, Kentucky, to marry Eliza Campbell, who was "pious and much engaged in religion." He had one hundred acres of land five miles east of the Cane Ridge meeting house, and there constructed a log cabin. To this primitive place he brought his bride, scarcely in time for the historic Cane Ridge Revival. Stone did not plan it. Stone was not responsible for its success. While he participated in it and encouraged it, he was never too convinced that this was God's permanent and perpetual way of winning men to Christ, and of building and extending the borders of the church of God.

The "fire fell" on this wise. The meeting was called on Thursday or Friday, "before the first Lord's Day in August, 1801." The call went out from a group of Presbyterian preachers, but Methodist and Baptist ministers also responded. From all parts of Kentucky, Tennessee, and Ohio the people came—twenty-five thousand of them, it is said. The roads were jammed. The woods were filled with people, horses, wagons, carts, and arbors. Preachers were preaching all around, night and day. The singing, shouting, and demonstrations were never ending, until food supplies ran out, and the starving, happy people were forced to go back home. The Cane Ridge Revival will remain one of the great events in the history of religion in America. But this was not and is not in any way characteristic of the movement of which this volume is a record. It had its proper setting in the Great Western Revival (see pp. 22-27), without which it is altogether likely the Restoration movement in America might not have come into being at this time.

The sympathetic and extensive report of the Cane Ridge meetings in Stone's autobiography (see Chapter I) was misinterpreted by many and proved embarrassing to his followers in later years. Because of it, his Presbyterian brethren accused him as "the ringleader in these disorders." Elder John Rogers, who published Stone's autobiography with "additions and reflections," asserted that none of Stone's associates saw him actively participate in the Cane Ridge exercises. His type of evangelism, and he was intensely evangelistic, was something different, and will be considered later in this chapter.

After the Great Revival began to subside, the Presbyterian church was beset by schisms. The authority of presbyteries and synods had been flouted by pastors and laymen who participated in the revival. Strong ties of fellowship were formed with revival friends of other theological views. The Cumberland Presbyterians came into being in 1810, and the "New Lights" formed new presbyteries or were lukewarm in their fellowship with the old ones.

Stone had come to know the importance and the joy of a firsthand

Christian experience. He believed it was possible for the Holy Spirit to enlighten and guide men in the study of the Word of God apart from the traditional creeds of Christendom. He saw the sinfulness of division in the body of Christ. He shared the democratic liberty of the frontier and was growingly restive under ecclesiastical authority. He had seen a demonstration of Christian unity among men of common faith in a common objective.

After six years as a Presbyterian pastor at Concord and Cane Ridge, Stone dramatically called his congregations together and informed them that he "could no longer conscientiously preach to support the Presbyterian Church" and that his

> labors should henceforth be directed to advance the Redeemer's Kingdom, irrespective of party; that I absolved them from all obligations in a pecuniary point of view, and then in their presence tore up their salary obligation to me, in order to free their minds from all fear of being called upon hereafter for aid.

Concurrently, the associates of Stone in the so-called "Revival movement" faced similar decisions. Among them were Robert Marshall, John Dunlavy, Richard McNemar, and John Thompson. McNemar's views were early made an issue in the Washington Presbytery. He was accused of holding "dangerous and pernicious ideas" that deviated from the doctrines "contained in the Confession of Faith of the Presbyterian Church." A committee of elders was appointed to prefer charges and to offer him an opportunity to affirm his allegiance. After long and circuitous proceedings, the issue finally came to a focus in the sessions of the Synod of Kentucky at Lexington, September 7, 1803. The Synod reproved the Washington Presbytery for its leniency toward McNemar. In the vote, the antirevivalists prevailed over the revivalists, and the latter announced their withdrawal from the jurisdiction of the Synod. The statement signed by Marshall, Stone, McNemar, Thompson, and Dunlavy expressed a deeply rooted commitment to the Bible as full, final, and complete authority and a desire for freedom in interpreting the Confession. After feeble efforts at reconciliation, the Synod voted September 13, 1803, to suspend the signatories on the ground that the dissenters (1) had separated themselves from the jurisdiction of the synod; (2) had seceded from the Confession of Faith; (3) had refused to return to the doctrines and standards of the church; and (4) had constituted themselves into a separate presbytery.

The formation of the Springfield Presbytery actually took place sometime after September. In January, 1804, it published *An Apology for Renouncing the Jurisdiction of the Synod of Kentucky*. Robert Marshall was the author of the first part which attempted to justify the separation. The second part, written by Stone, was a critique of certain doctrines in the Confession of Faith, and the third part, by Thompson, was a defense of the Bible against the authority of human creeds. The independent Springfield Presbytery survived only nine months. While essentially

Presbyterian in its polity and operation, it was not recognized by established Presbyterianism. Its member churches were all Presbyterian in background and consisted of fifteen congregations. In Ohio were Turtle Creek, Eagle Creek, Springfield (the modern Springdale, Cincinnati), Orangedale, Salem, Beaver Creek, and Clear Creek; in Kentucky: Cane Ridge, Concord, Cabin Creek, Flemingsburg, Indian Creek, Bethel, Paint Lick, and Shawnee Run. While there were other churches of like views and many groups unorganized and unidentified where the revival preachers were welcome, there seemed to be little disposition among them to submit to any kind of ecclesiastical authority. The men who organized the presbytery were soon in the throes of a doctrinal discussion of the atonement and other issues, and it was becoming increasingly apparent that there was little real unity or stability among them. Stone was almost the only stable and dependable man in the group, as time was to reveal.

Nevertheless the somewhat shadowy and nominal Springfield Presbytery lived long enough to issue a document of dissolution which will long live in church history, *The Last Will and Testament of the Springfield Presbytery*. Both Stone and McNemar have been credited with its authorship, with the weight of probability on the side of Stone. It was read on June 28, 1804, at Cane Ridge in the final meeting of the organization. The text follows:

The Presbytery of Springfield, sitting at Cane Ridge, in the county of Bourbon, being, through a gracious Providence, in more than ordinary bodily health, growing in strength and size daily; and in perfect soundness and composure of mind; and knowing that it is appointed for all delegated bodies once to die; and considering that the life of every such body is very uncertain, do make and ordain this our last Will and Testament, in manner and form following, viz.:

Imprimis. We *will,* that this body die, be dissolved, and sink into union with the Body of Christ at large; for there is but one body, and one Spirit, even as we are called in one hope of our calling.

Item. We *will,* that our name of distinction, with its Reverend title, be forgotten, that there be but one Lord over God's heritage and his name one.

Item. We *will,* that our power of making laws for the government of the church, and executing them by delegated authority, forever cease; that the people may have free course to the Bible, and adopt *the law of the Spirit of life in Christ Jesus.*

Item. We *will,* that candidates for the Gospel ministry henceforth study the Holy Scriptures with fervent prayer, and obtain license from God to preach the simple Gospel, with the Holy Ghost sent down from heaven, without any mixture of philosophy, vain deceit, traditions of men or the rudiments of the world. And let none henceforth take this honor to himself, but he that is called of God, as was Aaron.

Item. We *will,* that the church of Christ resume her native right of internal government—try her candidates for the ministry, as to the soundness of their faith, acquaintance with experimental religion, gravity and aptness to teach; and admit no other proof of their authority but Christ speaking in them. We will, that the church of Christ look to the Lord of the harvest to send forth laborers into his harvest; and that she resume her primitive right of trying these who say they are apostles, and are not.

Item. We *will,* that each particular church, as a body, actuated by the same spirit, choose her own preacher, and support him by a freewill offering, without a written *call* or *subscription*—admit members—remove offenses; and never henceforth delegate her right of government to any man or set of men whatever.

Item. We *will,* that the people henceforth take the Bible as the only sure guide to heaven; and as many as are offended with other books, which stand in competition with it, may cast them into the fire if they choose; for it is better to enter into life having one book, than having many to be cast into hell.

Item. We *will,* that preachers and people, cultivate a spirit of mutual forbearance; pray more and dispute less; and while they behold the signs of the times, look up, and confidently expect that redemption draweth nigh.

Item. We *will,* that our weak brethren, who may have been wishing to make the Presbytery of Springfield their king, and wot not what is now become of it, betake themselves to the Rock of Ages, and follow Jesus for the future.

Item. We *will,* that the Synod of Kentucky examine every member, who may be suspected of having departed from the Confession of Faith, and suspend every such suspected heretic immediately, in order that the oppressed may go free, and taste the sweets of Gospel liberty.

Item. We *will,* that Ja . . . . . . , the author of two letters lately published in Lexington, be encouraged in his zeal to destroy partyism. We will, moreover, that our past conduct be examined into by all who may have correct information; but let foreigners beware of speaking evil of things which they know not.

Item. Finally we *will,* that all our *sister bodies* read their Bibles carefully, that they may see their fate there determined, and prepare for death before it is too late.

Springfield Presbytery: L.S.
June 28, 1804:

Robert Marshall
John Dunlavy
Richard M'Nemar
B. W. Stone
John Thompson
David Purviance

The Last Will and Testament in its published form included an "Address" which reiterated the opposition of the witnesses to "church sessions, presbyteries, synods, general assemblies, etc." as without precedent or example in the New Testament and closed with an appeal for the unity of all believers: "We heartily unite with our Christian brethren of every name, in thanksgiving to God for the display of his goodness in the glorious work he is carrying on in our Western country."

At the same meeting in Cane Ridge, it was agreed that the name *Christian* be adopted to the exclusion of all sectarian names for the church. It is interesting to note that one Rice Haggard proposed this resolution. Haggard was a leader in a similar movement in the East and had persuaded it to accept the name *Christian* instead of *Republican Methodist.* After some years as one of their ministers in Virginia and North Carolina, he had come to Kentucky and cast his lot with Stone and his company. Through his instrumentality and that of others, a lasting fellowship was established between the two movements.

James O'Kelly was the leader of the Eastern movement. He was of Irish extraction, and lived from 1739 to 1826. In 1792 he led a secession from the Methodist church of which he was a member because the Baltimore conference would not accept his views on democracy in church government and the appointment of preachers. Although he was an affusionist, many of his followers favored immersion as the only Scriptural baptism. In 1809 the southern "Christians" established relations with a northern group of "Christians" founded by Abner Jones and Elias Smith. Jones (1772-1841), founded the "first free Christian Church" in New England in Lyndon, Vermont, in the autumn of 1801. Smith (1769-1846) joined with him in 1802 to organize a Christian church at Portsmouth, New Hampshire. The latter was a publisher and established *The Herald of Gospel Liberty* on September 1, 1808. This was said to be "the first religious newspaper published in the world." Its first issue carried a reprint of the *Last Will and Testament of the Springfield Presbytery* together with a commendation of the work of Stone and his friends in the West. This journal eventually became the official organ of the Christian Connection.

There seemed to be a tragic instability and inconstancy in Stone's associates. McNemar and Dunlavy were looking for a millennial church and were speedily entranced by the strange gospel of Shakerism. The mother church of the disciples of Ann Lee, at New Lebanon, New York, hearing of the Kentucky revival, sent three missionaries—Benjamin Seth Youngs, Issachar Bates, and John Meacham—to contact the revivalist leaders. The religion of the Shakers was a combination of asceticism, communism, spiritualism, and paternalism. They forbade marriage and the perpetuation of the race. Dancing in worship was considered a "sacred exercise." They pleaded for the unity of all God's people under their "United Society of Believers in Christ's Second Appearing" headed by two elders and two elderesses. The pledge of union began, "We do by these presents covenant and agree to renounce and disannual every bond, tie and relation of the flesh, and to hold ourselves free and separate from all that pertains to the corrupt generation of fallen man." They claimed that their faith and practice was summarized in seven principles: innocence and purity, love, peace, justice, holiness, goodness, and truth. Ann Lee was hailed as representing in her person the second coming of Christ; that as God had appeared in a man as Jesus, a sex cycle has eventuated in the second presence of God in a woman. When the missionaries of this strange sect contacted Stone and "a number more" at Cane Ridge in 1805, they reported progress in winning the Christians to Shakerism. At Turtle Creek they converted Malcom Worley, who gave them the 4,500-acre estate that was to become the main site of the Shaker establishment west of the Alleghenies. Also at Turtle Creek, Richard McNemar and his family united with them. At Eagle Creek, John Dunlavy was converted. Then Matthew Houston succumbed. When Stone resisted, Dunlavy taunted him in a letter concerning his first favorable impressions of Issachar Bates and his doctrines. A year later Stone wrote: "[The Shakers] are a set of worldly minded, cunning deceivers, whose religion is earthly, sensual and devilish."

The remaining "witnesses" to the *Last Will and Testament* then became embroiled in theological controversies. Stone's views on the atonement and the trinity were constantly under fire by the Presbyterians, and he was driven to the defensive if not defeat on these issues by John Poague Campbell's strong critique. Robert Marshall converted Stone to the Baptist position on baptism, then returned to his own pedobaptist views. The worst blow to the Christian movement in the West was the decision of Marshall and Thompson to rejoin the Presbyterian church. Except for Purviance, Stone was the only one left of the original signatories.

David Purviance (1766-1847) was born in North Carolina, but early moved with his family to Bourbon County, Kentucky, where they became part of the Cumberland Presbyterian church. He was well-educated and entered politics, being elected several times to the Kentucky Legislature. He withdrew from politics, temporarily, to preach. He was active in the Cane Ridge church, and was ordained by it to preach. It is said that he was the first preacher publicly to repudiate infant baptism and to insist that immersion of adult believers was the only baptism taught in the New Testament. He moved to Ohio in 1807, and was elected to the state Legislature. He and Stone met for the last time in 1843 at the church in New Paris, Ohio.

Stone was not to be discouraged. He believed he was called by God to his prophetic ministry. He had seen many evidences of His blessing. His commitment was complete, and like the apostle Paul "neither height nor depth nor things present nor things to come" could separate him from his fellowship with Christ in the salvation of precious souls. Stone was at his best as an evangelist. In 1811, he went with Reuben Dooly on an evangelistic tour in Ohio. At Eaton, the county seat of Preble County, they converted "almost the whole town." In Adams County, he converted Matthew Gardner who became a giant in evangelism. In this area many churches sprang up which Stone visited every year for twenty years. In Meigs County, he went to baptize William Caldwell, with whom he had a long correspondence, and stayed to bring almost every Baptist church in the county into the "Christian Connection." In southern Indiana, traveling with Clement Nance and James Robeson, he established scores of churches following revival meetings in which hundreds were converted and baptized.

Stone's chief evangelizing ministry, however, remained in Kentucky. While his ministerial associates of the early days deserted him, the people did not. Everywhere he went, great audiences greeted him. Yet he did not seek the multitudes. He was just as much at home preaching in a kitchen to a family, or in a barn to which a farmer had invited his neighbors. So fully committed were his converts that they themselves became evangelists. Soon his correspondence was greater than he could handle. People would write him telling of new churches that had been organized, or asking his advice in problems that arose. This was one of the factors that led him to publish a journal, the name of which was *The Christian Messenger*. The first issue of his twenty-four-page monthly appeared in November, 1826. It continued for the remainder of Stone's life and for a short period beyond. There were some intermissions in 1838-1840, 1842, and 1843, due to illness and financial difficulties. The little journal was a reflection of the heart of its editor. It breathed the spirit of Christian unity and evangelism. Practically every idea that Stone entertained appeared in print. He was opposed to slavery and Masonry, and believed in plain dress. His beliefs and his doubts about the great doctrines of the church were aired, and these articles were the source of much confusion and debate. His positions were often fuzzy and characteristic of a man who has not made up his mind. Stone had an untrained frontier mind when it came to subtle theological distinctions. Unlike Alexander Campbell, he lacked the background of a university education and also a logical mental equipment to deal with premises, equations, implications, and conclusions.

As to the nature and work of Christ, Stone believed that Christ was not God, but the Son of God. He was not an Arian, but he used many arguments and phrases associated with Arian views. He rejected the creedal terms *eternal Son* and *eternally begotten,* because he could not find them in the Bible. He believed in the pre-existence of Christ as the Son, but he also believed that Christ had a beginning. The Father alone was eternal; the Son had the stature of a creature. The Son was not a mere man; since His creation was the work of the Father alone, He was not a creature like other creatures; in fact, He was supreme above all other creatures. He is not deity in the full sense, because the Godhead in Him is derived from God, and he is not fully man because the Godhead is united with a human body having no human mind or spirit. The position of Isaac Watts on this subject seemed most acceptable to Stone, but he was not prepared slavishly to follow the opinions of any man.

Stone believed concerning the atonement that the word *atonement* in the Scriptures meant reconciliation. In Old Testament history, man sinned and was separated from God. The sacrifice was made to cleanse the transgressor. The consequence of the death of Christ on the cross was that a reconciliation took place between God and the "purified offender." He believed that no man can be saved without the benefit of the atonement, but he denied the substitutionary theory as contrary to the true nature of Christianity. He taught that atonement had a moral influence exerted on man, but not on God; that the death of Christ had a moral tendency to lead men to repentance, obedience, and love. While Stone himself indulged in much speculation on the subject, he made clear to his followers that it was unnecessary for the common man to have an intellectual understanding of the death of Christ before he could become a member of the church. If the sinning soul discovered the love of God in the face of Jesus, he could trust the Father to forgive him his sins.

Concerning conversion, Stone believed that man is depraved, but he rejected the total depravity theory on the ground that it devitalized moral activity and turned men away from the love of God. "All mankind," wrote Stone, "are polluted and unclean—all bearing iniquity—all guilty. God's holy nature stands in opposition to our unholy nature, and our sins have separated us and our God." Man, he taught, is not born with a corrupt nature. He is neither good nor bad in infancy, but he has a predisposition to sin because "a law of sin" dwells in every man. He also has "a willingness to do good, to hate and shun evil—to be pleased with the law of God" and to accept salvation through Christ. Stone held that man must be born again, or "renewed in knowledge, righteousness and true holiness after the image of God." He accepted Paul's language about casting off the old man and putting on the new. He insisted that human wisdom and power can never affect regeneration, but that men become new creatures through the will of God after the similitude of a birth. He rejected the doctrine that man can do nothing to be saved until God works faith and repentance in him by his creative power, because he could not understand how a God of love could grant this power to some and withhold it from others. He insisted on man's response as absolutely essential in conversion. This response involved: (1) the hearing of the gospel as revealed in the Holy Scriptures; (2) the acceptance of the gospel; and (3) the obedience to the terms of the gospel. Only then can the sinner be "quickened, renewed and sanctified."

Stone was often misunderstood in his insistence on the role of the Scriptures in conversion. He preached with great persuasiveness concerning the activity of the Spirit in conversion and often said that to make the Scriptures *everything* in regeneration was just as extreme as to make them nothing." He was a strong believer in the work of the Spirit in the life of the Christian and in the life of the church. He stressed preaching "in the spirit on the Lord's Day" in contrast to the more sedate theological discourses of the learned Presbyterian ministers. Indeed, he often accused them of having the Word of God "not so much in their hearts as in their heads."

At first Stone gave little attention to the subject of baptism. He even considered it an optional practice. When controversy arose among his followers, he finally began a study of the Scriptures which led him to the conclusion that immersion of believers was the divinely ordained baptism, and he himself was immersed. Thereafter he began to preach that baptism "is ordained by the King" and that the Bible clearly taught the ordinance was "for the remission of sins." Most of the Christian churches in Kentucky became strictly immersionist. He opposed the practice of excluding the unimmersed from Communion and fellowship, however, and urged "patience and forbearance toward such pious persons as cannot be convinced" they should be immersed.

Eliza Campbell Stone died May 30, 1810, after an illness of a year. She bore five children in eight years, an ordinary accomplishment for a pioneer woman, but this was perhaps partially responsible for her death. In October the following year, Stone married her cousin, Celia Wilson Bowen, of Mansker Creek, Tennessee. Her father was a man of some means; and his family, with its various connections, was prominent in the life of the Volunteer State.

Stone had nineteen children. Eleven died childless, but Stone had a total of forty-nine grandchildren in the families of the remaining eight. Celia, it was said, "was a woman of great strength of character and many excellencies whose life was given to good works." Stone was not at home much. Traveling in his wide evangelistic ministry, he had little time for domestic affairs. Both Eliza and Celia deserve great credit for making his ministry possible by bearing the burdens of home-making and rearing his children in "the nurture and admonition of the Lord."

When Alexander Campbell visited Kentucky in 1824, he met Stone at Georgetown. The two men at once formed a warm personal attachment to each other, which was to continue through life. They recognized the fact that they were engaged in identical ministries with the same general objectives.

It is estimated that the Christian Connection had grown to a constituency of approximately fifteen thousand by 1830. No authentic figures are available, but various estimates appeared in the *Christian Register,* the *Morning Star and City Watchman,* and the *Herald of Gospel Liberty.* The population west of the Alleghenies was constantly on the move. Families that stopped in Kentucky long enough to affiliate with the Christian Connection eventually settled in other states and carried their distinctive faith and practice with them. Churches were thus established in Tennessee, Alabama, Ohio, Indiana, Illinois, and Missouri, and the "Stonites" became increasingly well known as a part of the Western community. Kentucky and Indiana had the largest membership, probably four thousand or more in each of these states. When one realizes that the total population of Kentucky was only 688,000 at this time, and that the traditional denominations were well entrenched in the area, the extent of Stone's influence is amazing.

Three miles from Georgetown, in the Great Crossings community, lived John T. Johnson, a Baptist preacher who was greatly enamored of Campbell's views on the Scriptures. Johnson and Stone became friends and began to talk about the possibilities of union between the "Christians" and the "Reformers." In 1831, Johnson invited "Raccoon" John Smith, another Christian-Baptist evangelist, to hold a meeting for him at Great Crossings. As the Spirit of the Lord moved, Johnson, Stone, Smith, and John Rogers, a Christian Connection evangelist, got together for prayer and discussion about union. They agreed to call their people and see if they wanted union. If so, Smith and Rogers would travel and preach for it. Stone wrote of the incident in the *Christian Messenger,*

We who have taken the word of God alone for our rule of faith and practice, are the only people that dare to speak out fearlessly. We have no name to lose—already it is cast out as evil. We have no salaries at stake—this might be a temptation to be silent. We have no fear of offending our brethren, and fellow-sufferers for the Kingdom of Christ, while we walk in truth and keep within the Bible.

94

Johnson soon became co-editor of the *Messenger* and its pages were filled with propaganda for union.

Alexander Campbell, hearing of these portentous developments, wrote:

In Kentucky and the Southwest generally . . . many congregations called "Christians" are just as sound in the faith of Jesus as the only-begotten Son of God, in the plain import of these terms, as any congregation with which I am acquainted. With all such, I as an individual, am united, and would rejoice in seeing all immersed disciples of the Son of God called "Christians" and walking in all the commandments of the Lord and Saviour. We plead for the union, communion and co-operation of all such; and wherever there are in any vicinity a remnant of those who keep the commandments of Jesus whatever may have been their former designation, they ought to rally under Jesus and the apostles and bury all dissensions about such unprofitable subjects as those long-vexed questions about trinity, atonement, depravity, election, effectual calling, etc. . . . With all such I am united in heart and in hand, and with all such I will, with the help of God, co-operate in any measure which can conduce to the furtherance of the gospel of Christ . . .

These sentiments brought forth a hearty response from Stone and the Kentucky Christians. Stone wrote:

Oh my brethren, let us repent and do the first works, let us seek for more holiness, rather than trouble ourselves and others with schemes and plans of union. The love of God, shed abroad in our hearts by the Holy Ghost given unto us, will more effectually unite than all the wisdom of the world combined.

These great truths began to be uppermost in the prayers and the thinking and the conversation of the two communions in Kentucky. Union sentiments grew by leaps and bounds. They both opposed sectarian bigotry in others and recognized the fact that they might be guilty of it themselves if they refused to consider unity with any Christians of like mind and heart. They both desired to build on the Bible and the Bible alone; were opposed to creeds as terms of Communion; desired to win souls to Christ and to disseminate the apostolic gospel; were persecuted and maligned by the established churches; and had no overhead organization that could prevent them from full fellowship and co-operation if they desired it.

This people of God had a growing conviction that they were on the verge of a great demonstration of the validity of their contention that Christian union could come by a return to the Bible alone as a rule of faith and practice—a Restoration of the New Testament church in doctrine, ordinances, and life.

BIBLIOGRAPHY: Chapter 5

Badger, Joseph, editor, and others, *Christian Palladium* (1832-1861).

Campbell, Alexander, editor, *Millennial Harbinger* (1830-1844).

Campbell, John Poage, *Strictures on Two Letters*, published by Barton W. Stone.

Dunlavy, John, *The Manifesto, or a Declaration of the Doctrine and Practice of the Church of Christ.*

Hall, Colby D., *The New Light Christians.*
MacClenny, Wilbur E., *The Life of Reverend James O'Kelly.*
MacLean, John P., *A Sketch of the Life and Labors of Richard McNemar.*
McGready, James, *The Posthumous Works of the Reverend and Pious James McGready* (Vols. I and II).
Morrill, M. T., *A History of the Christian Denomination in America.*
McNemar, Richard, *The Kentucky Revival.*
Purviance, David, *The Biography of David Purviance.*
Richardson, Robert, *Memoirs of Alexander Campbell.*
Rogers, John, *The Biography of Elder Barton W. Stone.*
Smith, Elias, *The Life, Conversion, Preaching, Travels and Sufferings of Elias Smith.*
Stone, Barton Warren, *An Address to the Christian Churches of Kentucky, Tennessee and Ohio.*
Stone, Barton Warren, editor, and others, *Christian Messenger* (1826-1844).
Stone, Barton Warren, *Works of Elder B. W. Stone.*
Summerbell, Nicholas, *History of the Christian Church to 1870.*
Ware, Charles C., *Barton Warren Stone.*
West, William G., *Barton Warren Stone.*

Chapter 6

Walter Scott and
the *Gospel Restored*

W ALTER SCOTT was the youngest of the four men who are generally credited with laying the foundations of the Restoration movement in America. He came out of backgrounds similar to those of Alexander Campbell, and the two became warm friends and close associates in a common task. They complemented one another in that Campbell furnished the intellectual and theological guidance; and Scott, the practical evangelistic promotion necessary to any great religious movement. It is often said that without the ministry of Walter Scott the work of the Campbells might soon have been forgotten.

Scott was born in Dumfriesshire, Scotland, October 31, 1796, of the same family as the world-renowned author Sir Walter Scott. His parents were John and Mary Innes Scott, and Walter was one of ten children. John Scott was a music teacher, and the whole family were devout members of the Presbyterian church. At an early age, Walter gave such promise of superior talents that his parents determined to send him to the University of Edinburgh. Accordingly, he went to live with his aunt who resided in Edinburgh, and pursued his studies there with great zeal and success. Inheriting considerable musical talent from his father, he learned to play the flute as an avocation and became known as the finest flutist in the city.

Soon after Scott completed his education, his mother's brother, George Innes, a successful businessman in the United States, offered to further his interests if he would come to this country. His family agreed to the arrangement, and on July 7, 1818, he arrived in New York City. His first undertaking was as Latin tutor in a Long Island classical academy. However, he did not remain there long. Friends he had made upon his arrival urged him to go to the Allegheny country where opportunity for future advancement was far greater than in the East. He and a companion set out on foot for the long journey. They reached Pittsburgh on May 7, 1819. Scott found employment almost immediately, as an assistant to George Forrester, a fellow Scotsman who operated an academy. Forrester was also the leader of a small church which took the Bible alone as its rule of faith and practice. Somewhat akin to the churches of the Haldane movement, it sought to restore the doctrine and practice of the apostolic church. The Pittsburgh congregation practiced immersion and also such debatable customs as feet washing and the holy kiss. They were locally nicknamed "the kissing Baptists."

Scott was greatly impressed with Forrester's piety and sincere devotion to the study of the Word of God—so much so that he began a restudy of the Scriptures apart from the Westminster Confession or any other theological guide. He soon came to the conclusion that infant baptism was without a divine warrant and that "wherever baptism was enjoined, it was a personal, and not a relative duty; that it was a matter that no more admitted of a proxy than faith, repentance, or any other act of obedience"; and that since as a Presbyterian infant he had rendered no service, nor obeyed no command, he had not been Scripturally baptized. He then sought through his Greek New Testament to ascertain how he might be baptized. He found no justification for sprinkling or pouring in the original text, but abundant evidence for immersion. Accordingly, he requested Forrester to immerse him. Shortly afterward, he joined the little New Testament church and proved a valuable member. His superior education, his gifts, talents, zeal, and piety soon won him the respect and love of his brethren. So thankful was he for the satisfaction of soul he had attained that he began to share his convictions with others, with the result that scores of new members were received.

A change in Forrester's plans made it necessary for him to give up his academy, and, as Scott had proven himself eminently well qualified, the entire management of the school fell into his hands. Despite this encouraging change in his fortunes, he was increasingly obsessed with his Bible studies and the conviction that the salvation of the world was more important than any other work to which he could give his talents. Having come upon a pamphlet on baptism written by Henry Errett, father of Isaac Errett, and published by a New York congregation of Scotch Baptists, Scott was intrigued by the view that baptism is definitely related to remission of sins and salvation. As new vistas of Bible truth thus opened to him, Scott decided to sell his Pittsburgh academy and go to New York to gain further instruction from the church there. After three months in Gotham, he became disappointed with the narrowness and pettiness of the church, and, moving on to Paterson, New Jersey, he found another band of Bible believers to whom he ministered. From there he drifted to Baltimore and Washington for brief evangelistic meetings, but everywhere he was impressed with the confusion in religious thought.

One day he climbed to the top of the Capitol building in Washington to commune with God. He was filled with sorrow "at the miserable desolation of the Church of God" and in a spirit of dejection determined to go back to Pittsburgh. He had been entreated by Nathaniel Richardson, a substantial businessman, to become the tutor of his son Robert and a

98

few other boys. (Robert was later to become a professor in Bethany College and Alexander Campbell's biographer.) In this new situation Scott became so well and favorably known that he soon had a new academy with an enrollment of 140 boys from the best families in the city. He also resumed the care of the little church he had left for the New York adventure and continued to grow "in the knowledge of the truth."

It was in 1821 that he became fully convinced that the great central idea of the Christian religion was to be found in the Messiahship of Jesus; and that an all-sufficient creed might be stated in the words of Peter's confession, "Thou art the Christ, the Son of the living God." Was not this the rock upon which Christ had said He would build His church? It was a proposition, Scott held, around which all other truths in the Bible grouped themselves, revolving as planets about the sun. To prove this, he referred to the fourfold purpose of the evangelists in the four Gospels, climaxed by the words of the apostle John, "These [things] are written that ye might believe that Jesus is the Christ, the Son of God; and that believing ye might have life through his name" (20:31).

During the winter of 1821-22, Scott first met Alexander Campbell. Scott was twenty-five and Campbell was thirty-three. Campbell had come to Pittsburgh to meet business and religious acquaintances. Writing in later years, he often referred to their meeting as most fortuitous. Campbell said, "Our age and our feelings alike rendered us susceptible of a mutual attachment, and that was formed, I trust, on the best of principles. If the regard which we cherished for each other was exalted by anything purely incidental, that thing was an ardent desire in the bosom of both to reform the Christian profession, which to each of us appeared in a state of the most miserable destitution." After hours of prayer and discussion they were indissolubly united in mind and heart for the great mission to which they had been divinely called.

Robert Richardson, who was probably more intimately acquainted with both men than any other person, wrote in his *Memoirs of Alexander Campbell*:

> The different hues in the characters of these two eminent men were such as to be, so to speak, complementary to each other, and to form, by their harmonious blending, a completeness and a brilliancy which rendered their society peculiarly delightful to each other. Thus, while Mr. Campbell was fearless, self-reliant and firm, Mr. Scott was naturally timid, diffident and yielding; and, while the former was calm, steady and prudent, the latter was excitable, variable and precipitate. The one like the north star was ever in position, unaffected by terrestrial influences; the other, like the magnetic needle, was often disturbed and trembling on its center, yet ever returning or seeking to return to its true direction. Both were nobly endowed with the powers of higher reason—a delicate self-consciousness, a decided will and a clear perception of truth. . . . If the tendency of the one was to generalize, to take wide and extended views and to group a multitude of particulars under a single head of principle, that of the other was to analyze, to divide subjects into their particulars and consider their details. If the one was disposed to trace analogies and evolve the remotest correspondences of

relations, the other delighted in comparisons and sought for resemblances of things. If the one possessed the inductive power of the philosopher, the other had, in a more delicate musical faculty and more active ideality, a larger share of the attributes of the poet. In a word, in almost all these qualities of mind and character, which might be regarded differential or distinctive, they were singularly fitted to supply each other's wants and to form a rare and delightful companionship (Vol. I, pp. 510, 511).

On January 3, 1823, Scott married Sarah Whitsett, a Covenanter Presbyterian, who later joined her husband's congregation and became an ardent participant in his ministry. Their home was blessed by five children—four sons and a daughter. Each morning the household was instructed in the Scriptures and the passages of Holy Writ memorized the previous day were recited. Every member participated in prayer. Visitors to the Scott home were always deeply impressed with its fine spiritual atmosphere and its high regard for the Holy Scriptures.

Also in 1823, when Scott's new-found friend Alexander Campbell projected his first journal, he consulted Scott as to the name and the format. He had planned to call it *The Christian,* but Scott felt that it would have a wider acceptance among the Baptists if it were named *The Christian Baptist.* The suggestion met Campbell's approval and the first issue appeared in August of that year. Included was an article by Scott entitled, "A Divinely Authorized Plan of Teaching the Christian Religion." He continued his contributions, producing three other articles on the same subject, and frequently writing on a wide range of themes during the seven years of the paper's existence.

Three years later, Scott and his family moved from Pittsburgh to Steubenville, Ohio, where he opened an academy. Here he found three churches holding views comparable to his own. One was known as the church of Christ and was of the Haldane persuasion. The second was the Christian church similar to the congregations in Kentucky under the leadership of Stone. The third was of the Campbell movement, related to the Mahoning Baptist Association. All professed to be seeking the restoration of original Christianity.

In the summer of 1826, the Mahoning Baptist Association held its annual meeting nearby and Scott attended. Although not a member, he was by courtesy invited to participate as "a teaching brother." On Sunday he delivered the morning sermon based on Matthew 11 and made a deep impression on his hearers. Alexander Campbell was present and was much impressed by Scott's eloquence and the finished nature of his address. When the Association met the following year in Lisbon, Campbell traveled through Steubenville and urged Scott to accompany him. Scott was at first inclined to remain away because he was not a member, but his decision to go was to prove one of the most important steps of his life. During the proceedings it was determined that the Association should employ an evangelist "to labor among the churches." A committee was appointed to find the man, and unanimously recommended Walter Scott. The invitation appealed to him and he accepted.

From the beginning of Scott's ministry he made history. His first appointment was at Lisbon, Columbiana County, Ohio. Upon his arrival, every seat in the Baptist chapel was filled. He took as the theme for his sermon the confession of Peter as recorded in Matthew 16:16, "Thou art the Christ, the son of the living God." This was familiar ground to him in view of his decision in Pittsburgh years before to take this as the all-sufficient creed of the church. In his sermon, he first discussed the text as a fact which the four gospels were written to establish; to which type and prophecy in the Old Testament had pointed; which the eternal Father had announced from heaven at Christ's baptism and transfiguration. Scott then showed that the foundation truth of Christianity was the deity of Jesus Christ and that belief in Him was essential to salvation. He insisted that this belief would produce such love in the heart of the believer that he would be led to true obedience in all things necessary to the acceptance of Christ as Saviour and Redeemer. The speaker then showed that this same Peter was the first to declare the terms of pardon under the new dispensation of God's grace. It is said that as Scott spoke he was gripped with the idea that if what he was saying was true, the Spirit-guided answer of Peter to the cry of the people, "What must we do?" was the only answer that any minister of Christ had a right to give to the same question now. With great boldness of spirit, Scott thereupon concluded his discourse with these words, "Repent and be baptized, every one of you in the name of Jesus Christ, for the remission of sins, and ye shall receive the gift of the Holy Ghost."

In New Lisbon was a pious and God-fearing man, William Amend, a member of the Presbyterian church. In his study of the Scriptures, he had come to conclusions similar to those thus stated by Scott, although he had never seen or heard of the man. Having been invited to attend the services on this particular evening, he heard most of the discourse with great approval. When the preacher stated the terms of pardon in the words of Scripture, without the usual Baptist exhortations, Amend was thrilled in his heart and immediately pressed his way through the crowded aisle and made a public declaration of his belief in the Lord Jesus Christ and his purpose to obey Him in the same way the three thousand had obeyed on the Day of Pentecost. On the same day, in the beautiful stream at the edge of Lisbon, Amend was buried with his Lord in Christian baptism and rose to walk in newness of life. The city was stirred to its depths. The meetings became the talk of the market place and the point of daily discussion in every home. Thereafter, Scott used the divine formula with great effectiveness in his evangelistic ministry. He often referred to the date, November 18, 1827, as the time when the ordinance of Christian baptism was for the first time in modern history received in perfect accordance with apostolic teaching and practice.

After some months of evangelizing in the Steubenville area, Scott moved to Canfield to be nearer the center of strength of the Mahoning Baptists. The strongest church was at Warren under the ministry of Adamson Bentley, a close friend of the Campbells. Bentley was at first

101

wary of the strange evangelism of Scott and closed his church against him. Finally convinced that only the New Testament pattern was being followed, Bentley permitted Scott to hold a series of meetings at Warren, which stirred the whole community and resulted in a large ingathering.

Among the converts was John Tait, a man of great stature and a strong Presbyterian. Tait's wife had attended the services and was convinced that she should be immersed. Her husband vowed that if Scott attempted to baptize her, he would tear the preacher limb from limb. He strode into a room where Scott and some other preaching brethren were talking and threatened violence. Scott made it clear that if Tait's wife presented herself for baptism nothing could stop him from performing the ordinance. He then began to reason with Tait, and as the explanation of the Scriptures proceeded, he asked for prayer. When the group rose from their knees, Tait asked for baptism and was immersed with his wife. One by one the Baptist churches in the area accepted the New Testament view of conversion, and it was said that the Mahoning River became a veritable Jordan as Scott immersed hundreds of believers.

There were, however, those who insisted that Scott was guilty of preaching and practicing a new heresy. These rumors reached his friend, Alexander Campbell, who feared that the enthusiastic nature of Scott might have carried him beyond the bounds of prudence. Accordingly he asked Thomas Campbell to visit the scene of Scott's labors and observe the new phenomenon first hand. In the spring of 1828 Thomas reported to his son (*Memoirs,* Vol. II, p. 219, 220):

> I perceive that theory and practice in religion, as well as in all other things, are matters of distinct consideration. It is one thing to know concerning the art of fishing—for instance the rod, the line, the hook, and the bait, too; and quite another thing to handle them dexterously when thrown into the water, so as to make it take. We have spoken and published many things correctly concerning the ancient gospel, its simplicity and perfect adaptation to the present state of mankind, for the benign and gracious purposes of its immediate relief and complete salvation; but I must confess that, in respect to the direct exhibition and application of it for that blessed purpose, I am at present, for the first time, upon the ground where the thing has appeared to be practically exhibited to the proper purpose. . . .
>
> Mr. Scott has made a bold push to accomplish this object, by simply and boldly stating the ancient gospel and insisting upon it; and then by putting the question generally and particularly to males and females, old and young— Will you come to Christ and be baptized for the remission of your sins and the gift of the Holy Spirit? Don't you believe this blessed gospel? Then come away . . . This elicits a personal conversation; some confess faith in the testimony—beg time to think; others consent—give their hands to be baptized as soon as convenient; others debate the matter friendly; some go straight to the water, be it day or night and, upon the whole none appear offended.

Following Campbell's visit, so many invitations for meetings came that Scott could not answer half of them. Individual Christians opened their homes and barns for meetings and new churches began to form in each community. It is said that one of Scott's favorite methods of announcing his meetings was to go to the schoolhouse and after dismissal meet the children. He would introduce himself and ask them if they would like to learn a new five-finger exercise. Thereupon he would say, "Lift your left hand. Now beginning with your thumb repeat after me: Faith, repentance, baptism, remission of sins, gift of the Holy Spirit; that takes up all your fingers. Now again: Faith, repentance, baptism, remission of sins, gift of the Holy Spirit. Now again, faster, altogether." After the drill he would advise the children to go home, repeat this to their parents and tell them that the man who taught them would be preaching that night and all were invited. Immediately the whole neighborhood would be alerted and the meeting place filled to overflowing on the first night. His sermons were always pitched at the level of the common man and avoided deep theological analysis, yet this graduate of the University of Edinburgh spoke with clear and erudite precision the teaching of Christ and the apostles. The frontier had never heard anything like it before, and religion began to take on a new interest and meaning wherever he went.

When the Mahoning Association met in August, 1828, Scott reported membership of churches more than doubled, to say nothing of hundreds who had been immersed, but were unable to affiliate with any church. In his written statement he said:

> The results of your appointment have been important and peculiar. God has greatly blessed your good work. Many of the saints of the Mahoning churches have been strengthening during the last year. Much error has been corrected; backsliders have been reclaimed, and many hundreds of all ranks have actually been converted and baptized into the name of Jesus Christ, our Lord.
>
> While these blessed results are connected with immense personal labors, by day and by night in every minister concerned, yet we cannot and would not avoid attributing them ultimately to the grace of God our Father, in turning our attention to the gospel in its original terms.
>
> The publication of the gospel in the express form given it by the Apostles on Pentecost, and the public ministration of its spirit on their inspired plan, viz., in immersion, are facts which in the development of reforming principles, are perhaps more intimately connected with the unity of the body of Christ, and the abolition of sects; the destruction of systematic divinity and the conversion of the world, than any other piece of solid knowledge which has been recovered by the church during the progress of three hundred years of reformation.
>
> To persuade men to act upon the divine testimony, rather than to wait upon uncertain and remote influences; to accept disciples upon a simple confession of repentance toward God and faith in the Lord Jesus Christ, and to baptize them for an immediate personal acquittal from their sins through the blood of Christ, and for the Holy Spirit, are matters which have caused great public excitement. This excitement, however, has only turned out to the furtherance of the gospel; and we bless God, who has taught us by his Apostles, that, as the divine testimony may be received when understood, and understood when honestly listened to; so it may be acted upon the very moment it is received. Therefore, the enjoyment of remission and of the Holy Spirit, is not a thing of tomorrow, but of today—"today," says God, "if you will hear my voice" . . . "and there were added unto them that very day three thousand souls . . ."

The attendance at Warren was the largest in the history of the

Association and there was great rejoicing and praise to God. It was unanimously voted to add William Hayden to the evangelistic team. Later, Adamson Bentley and Marcus Bosworth took to the field. The Western Reserve of Ohio was on fire with the restoration of New Testament Christianity.

The Austintown meeting of the Association in August, 1830, will long be remembered. The organization was now under bitter attack by the whole Baptist community. The Mahoning churches were shaking off their allegiance to the Philadelphia Confession of Faith and were determined to give up every man-made tradition and practice that could not be supported by a "thus saith the Lord." The idea of an association, they had come to believe, was unscriptural. Perhaps at Scott's instigation, certainly with his support, John Henry introduced a resolution "that the Mahoning Association, as an advisory council, or an ecclesiastical tribunal, should cease to exist." Alexander Campbell opposed the motion but was dissuaded by Scott. The Association adopted the resolution and adjourned *sine die.* Thus was broken the last official tie of the Reformers or Disciples, as they were called, with the Baptists. The action at Austintown did not change the general situation existing across the nation. The views of the reformation continued to be preached in many Baptist churches, but the die had been cast and complete separation was seen as an early eventuality.

New evangelism swept the churches. "Raccoon" John Smith's three churches in Kentucky had 392 baptisms during the year 1827-1828. In additional meetings, he reported nearly one thousand. In the same year, in the *Christian Baptist,* Jeremiah Vardeman reported 550 persons immersed from November 1 to May 1, and other evangelists recorded scores and hundreds added to the churches. The North District Association, flooded with Reformers, followed Mahoning's example and adjourned *sine die.* Tate's Creek Association withdrew fellowship with all "Campbellite churches." The Beaver Association voted an anathema on "Campbellites' errors." Sulphur Fork, in 1829, recorded its approval of Beaver's action. The Goshen Association passed a resolution "that the doctrines of A. Campbell are anti-christian" and requested Baptist churches to bar their doors to all who held such heresy. In 1830, the Long Run Association passed firm but courteous resolutions condemning Campbell's position. And so the walls of separation were built higher and higher.

In 1831, Scott, much depressed in spirit because of a constantly recurring dyspepsia, went to Cincinnati where he had close fellowship with James Challen, minister of the church there. Eventually he located in nearby Carthage where he remained for many years, organizing a church, and acting as its pastor, evangelizing as his health would permit. His education and culture enabled him to make contacts with many of the leading citizens, a number of whom he converted to the faith.

Eager to disseminate his views to the widest possible audience, Scott, in 1832, began the publication of his renowned monthly journal, *The Evangelist.* In its columns he discussed many of the religious questions of the day. His essays were widely reprinted both in America and abroad.

Important pamphlets and books resulted from his studies in the Word of God.

One of the most important of these was his *Discourse on the Holy Spirit*. The incentive to this undertaking was the tendency of many Reformers to resolve religion entirely into a system of abstract beliefs; to disbelieve the actual indwelling of the Holy Spirit in believers; and to deny special providence and guidings and the efficacy of prayer. This was perhaps due to an extreme reaction against the wild demonstrations of converts in popular revivalism which were attributed to the workings of the Holy Spirit. Richardson spoke of such Reformers or Disciples as taking the philosophy of John Locke in his *Essay on the Human Understanding* as their Bible; denying to the Creator any access to the human soul except by "words and arguments," while conceding to the devil a direct approach; preaching more about "the laws of human nature" than about the gospel of Christ.

Scott, in this work, endeavored to show that "Christianity, as developed in the sacred oracles, is sustained by three divine missions—the mission of the Lord Jesus, the mission of the apostles, and the mission of the Holy Spirit." He said that although the mission of Christ was to the Jews, that of the apostles was to the world, and that of the Holy Spirit was to the church. He showed that the Spirit descended on the Day of Pentecost, remaining in the church, dwelling in all its members, and acting through them in comforting the saints and convincing the world of sin, righteousness, and judgment. He exposed the incorrectness of the common notion that the Spirit was sent to the world, as being opposed to Christ's clear declaration that the world could not receive him. He insisted upon the absolute need of the indwelling of the Holy Spirit in every believer in order to realize a permanent union with Christ. The mission of the Spirit, he held, is permanent in nature and He will abide in the church forever. "There is no member of the body of Christ," said he, "in whom the Holy Spirit dwelleth not; for it will hold as good at the end of the world as it does now, and it holds as good now as it did on the Day of Pentecost and afterward—that 'if any man have not the Spirit of Christ he is none of his.' "

When Alexander Campbell read the *Discourse* he wrote:

> Brother Walter Scott who in the fall of 1827, arranged the several items of faith, repentance, baptism, remission of sins, the Holy Spirit and eternal life, restored them in this order to the Church under the title of the Ancient Gospel, and successfully preached it for the conversion of the world— has written on the fifth point (viz., the Holy Spirit), which presents the subject in such an attitude as cannot fail to make all who read it understand the views entertained by us, and, as we think, taught by the apostles in their writings. We can recommend to all the disciples this discourse as most worthy of a place in their families, because it perspicuously, forcibly and with brevity favorable to an early apprehension of its meaning, presents the subject to the mind of the reader. Our opponents, too, who are continually misrepresenting, and many of them no doubt misconceiving, our views on this subject, if they would be advised by us, we would request to furnish themselves a copy, that they may be better informed on this topic, and, if they should still be

conscientiously opposed, that they may oppose that which we teach, and not a phantom of their own creation.

Another of Scott's works, *The Gospel Restored,* was written to give a systematic view of the Christian religion as taught in the Scriptures. The plan of the work is: (1) an analysis of sin, (2) the gospel, the means of recovery of man from its power and punishment. Scott summarizes the treatise in a paragraph:

> In regard to the sinners and sin, six things are to be considered: the love of it, the practice of it, the state of it, the guilt of it, the power of it, and the punishment of it. The first three relate to the sinner; the last three to sin. Now, faith, repentance, and baptism, refer to the first three—the love, the practice, and the state of sin; while remission, the Holy Spirit, and the resurrection, relate to the last three—the guilt, the power, and the punishment of sin; in other words, to make us see the beauty and perfection of the gospel theory, as devised by God: faith is to destroy the love of sin, repentance to destroy the practice of it; baptism, the state of sin; remission, the guilt of it; the Spirit, the power of it; and the resurrection to destroy the punishment of sin; so that the last enemy, death, will be destroyed.

Scott considered his book *The Messiahship* the crowning achievement of his literary career. It presented with logical force and deep spiritual power the centrality of Christ in the whole economy of God. Campbell said it was the best treatise on the divinity of Christ that he had read in forty years. Scott followed it by a short tract on *The Death of Christ* which made clear his devout belief in the atonement and closed with a tender and deeply spiritual paean of praise to God for His provision for our salvation through the precious blood of Christ.

His talents in the field of education were widely recognized. The College of Teachers and Western Literary Institute of Cincinnati requested him to address its meetings. Among the distinguished members were Dr. Daniel Drake, Joseph Ray, Professor William McGuffey, Archbishop Purcell, Dr. Calvin E. Stowe (husband of Harriett Beecher Stowe) and Dr. A. Kinmont. The governor of Ohio appointed him to the Board of Trustees of Miami University. He served as first president of Bacon College in Georgetown, Kentucky. Active as a Christian citizen, he led in many social reforms. The church at Carthage under his leadership voted to have no Christian communion with those who used liquor or those who sold wine or strong drink. He opposed slavery and favored the deportation of Negroes to a colony in their native Africa, financed and sponsored by American means.

As the Restoration movement approached full-fledged stature among the Christian communions of America, it was led by four of the most intelligent and educationally well-equipped ministers of the nation. The Campbells were trained in the University of Glasgow and the theological school of the Seceder Presbyterian church. Stone was a graduate of the Caldwell Academy and had been professor of languages in Succoth Academy. Scott was a graduate of the University of Edinburgh and

106

recognized as an educational leader. Associated with "the four horsemen" were outstanding religious leaders and business and professional men in every major community on the frontier. Although they were all under fire from the established churches and cordially hated by their clergy, they felt called by God to give a testimony and a challenge for "the faith which was once delivered unto the saints" and to plead for the union of all God's people on the basis of "the Bible and the Bible alone as an all-sufficient rule of faith and practice."

BIBLIOGRAPHY: Chapter 6

Baxter, William, *Life of Elder Walter Scott.*
Campbell, Alexander, editor, *Millennial Harbinger* (1830-1861).
Kershner, Frederick D., *The Prophet of New Testament Evangelism.*
Richardson, Robert, *Memoirs of Alexander Campbell.*
Scott, Walter, *A Discourse on the Holy Spirit.*
Scott, Walter, editor, *The Evangelist* (1832-1838).
Scott, Walter, *The Gospel Restored.*
Scott, Walter, *The Messiahship.*
Stevenson, Dwight E., *Voice of the Golden Oracle.*

Chapter 7

Christian Unity in Practice

IN a marvelous way, God had raised up a people to His name in many places throughout America prior to 1830. Without consultation with or prior knowledge of each other, men had been led by the Holy Spirit to abandon human dogmas and traditions and turn to the Bible as their only rule of faith and practice. A remarkable similarity in the views of these people was evident, and usually when they confronted one another, they came to common ground and gladly worked together to further the kingdom of God.

Among the groups that now began to coalesce into one body were Free Will Baptists, Scotch Baptists, Regular Baptists, German Baptists (Dunkards), Separate Baptists, Republican Methodists, Christians, and Reformers or Disciples. Their ministers often exchanged pulpits and the churches were open to fellowship with one another in evangelistic meetings and gatherings for the study of the Bible.

As an example, at Deerfield, Portage County, Ohio, was a little society formed for the purpose of examining the Scriptures. It was composed of Cornelius Finch, a Methodist preacher, and his wife; Ephraim P. Hubbard, an active Methodist, and his wife, who was a Baptist; Samuel McGowan, a Baptist, and his wife who was a Presbyterian; Peter Hartzell, a Presbyterian, and his wife, a Baptist; Jonas Hartzell, a Presbyterian, and his wife, a Methodist; Gideon Hoadley, an active member of the Methodist church, and a few others. Each professed a love for the Word of God and had come to the conclusion that only their party names and creeds separated them. Their studies brought many changes in their thinking and a complete harmony in their association.

One of the members, Ephraim Hubbard, had joined the Methodist church with the stipulation that he would not be bound by the *Book of Discipline* except as it agreed with the Scriptures. He requested immersion of several Methodist preachers, but all refused on the ground that such an act would be a denial of the efficacy of sprinkling to which he had been subjected in infancy. Finally, he and his brother, who was a Methodist pastor, were immersed by a Baptist minister. In other matters he was deeply dissatisfied with his church relationship. His example was typical of the experiences of all those in the little flock at Deerfield.

Hearing that there was a church after the New Testament pattern at Braceville, Hubbard and Finch paid it a visit. As a result, Adamson Bentley, of the church at Warren, and Marcus Bosworth, of Braceville, visited them, "taught them the way of the Lord more perfectly," and set the church in order. Almost all the male members of the Deerfield congregation became ministers and, in co-operation with Walter Scott, then evangelist in the Mahoning area, led many persons to Christ.

There was constant fraternization between the ministers of the Christian church and the Reformers. In 1828, J. E. Church, a Christian preacher, wrote of his meeting with Walter Scott at Fairfield, Ohio. Church heard Scott preach and was at first disposed to consider him heretical. He told Barton W. Stone that Scott "seems to suppose the apostolical Gospel to consist of the five following particulars, viz.: faith, repentance, baptism for the remission of sins, the gift of the Holy Ghost, and eternal life. Thus, you see, he baptizes the subject previous to the remission of his sins, or the receiving of the Holy Spirit." Stone replied, "We have for sometime practiced in this way throughout our country. Many of the most successful Baptists pursue the same course. I have no doubt that it will become the universal practice, though vehemently opposed." Thus began a close fellowship with Church and Scott in the Ohio country.

Scott tells of his meeting with Joseph Gaston, another Christian evangelist,

> I had appointed a certain day in which to break bread with the Baptist Church at Salem. Brother Gaston was a resident of Columbiana County, and was at that time in the vicinity of Salem. The Baptist brethren regarded him as a good man and a true disciple; but he was a Christian or New Light, and contended for open communion—things which they greatly disliked. Before meeting, the principal brethren requested me to converse with him on the subject, saying they were sure I could convert him.

An all-day discussion resulted in which the two men examined the Scriptures together. They both agreed that it was silly to dispute about open or close Communion when they were in such close agreement on all the essentials of the gospel. To climax their fellowship, they went together to the home of an inquiring couple and led them to accept Christ as their Saviour.

At this time, the two major groups of New Testament Christians were the Reformers or Disciples, under the leadership of the Campbells and Scott, and the Christians, under Stone. It is variously estimated that each group numbered from eight to ten thousand members. Their center of numerical strength was in Kentucky. Providentially the Great Crossings church, shepherded by John T. Johnson, a Reformer, and the Georgetown church, served by Barton W. Stone, were within a "stone's throw" of one another, and the two men had a common passion for Christian unity.

Their abilities and leadership were widely recognized among the two bodies of Christians. In solemn prayer and pledge they agreed to promote national union.

When "Raccoon" John Smith, another Reformer preacher of great power, was invited by Johnson to hold a meeting at Great Crossings in November, 1831, a conference developed between the three preachers and one of Stone's warmest co-laborers, John Rogers. They agreed to announce their plan of union to their respective congregations and see if they approved it. Finding almost unanimous approval, the four men determined to write and preach for Christian union. Stone wrote in the *Christian Messenger,*

> We who have taken the word of God alone for our rule of faith and practice are the only people that dare to speak out fearlessly. We have no name to lose—already it is cast out as evil. We have no salaries at stake—that might be a temptation to be silent. We have no fear of offending our brethren, and fellow-sufferers for the Kingdom of Christ, while we walk in the truth, and keep within the Bible.

Stone, Johnson, Rogers, and Smith arranged dates and places for joint meetings of Christians and Reformers. Usually three or four days were spent in each community. Christmas, 1831, coming on the Lord's Day, they decided they would celebrate Christ's birthday and the birth of the New Year by a festival of unity. For Georgetown, the meeting would be December 23-26 and for Lexington, December 30-January 2. No minutes of these meetings were kept, or if so, they were burned. It was the custom after reading minutes, to burn them, since records might be construed as a return to the formalism, legalism, and ecclesiasticism from which they had so recently been emancipated. From the scattered references in the *Messenger* and the *Christian Baptist,* in correspondence, and from tradition, a fairly good picture can be constructed of what took place in Lexington, the historic culminating meeting.

The Christian church there had dedicated a new building on Hill Street, October 16, 1831, which they gladly opened for the occasion. The Reformers in Lexington were few in number, meeting in a renovated chair factory. Brethren came from far and near and overflowed the new church. John Augustus Williams, in his *Life of John Smith,* called it "a mass meeting of the brethren." There was no formal agenda. There were no commissions to report. Fellowship and speech making were spontaneous. A representative speaker from each communion was to speak. Smith spoke for the Reformers; Stone, for the Christians. In conference, Smith agreed to speak first. He stressed the fact that Christian union must be in the one faith and built upon the Holy Scriptures. He opposed human speculation, unprofitable discussions, and the tyranny of ecclesiastical courts.

Williams reports that Smith insisted that the Scriptures made it plain that all true Christians must be one:

> God has but one people on earth. He has given them but one Book, and therein exhorts and commends them to be one family. A union such as we

plead for—a union of God's people on that one Book—must, then be practicable.

Every Christian desires to stand complete in the whole will of God. The prayer of the Saviour, and the whole tenor of his teaching, clearly show that it is God's will that his children should be united.

Then Smith dwelt on the many occasions of fellowship with men of like mind and heart in both camps. In conclusion he said, "Let us, then, my brethren, be no longer Campbellites, or Stonites, New Lights or Old Lights, or any other kind of lights, but let us come to the Bible, and to the Bible alone, as the only book in the world that can give us all the light that we need."

Stone was emotionally stirred and, according to tradition, "spoke with irresistable tenderness." He agreed that the basis of unity could never be on speculative or controversial subjects. He confessed his own weakness in becoming involved in theological speculation,

> after we [the Christians] had given up all creeds and taken the Bible and the Bible alone as our rule of faith and practice, we met with so much opposition, that by force of circumstances, I was led to deliver some speculative discourses upon certain subjects. But I never preached a sermon of that kind that once feasted my heart; I always felt a barrenness of soul afterwards. I perfectly accord with Brother Smith that those speculations should never be taken into the pulpit; but that when compelled to speak of them at all, we should do so in the words of inspiration.

His moving address was climaxed when Stone declared, "I have not one objection to the ground laid down by Brother Smith as the true Scriptural basis of union among God's people; and I am willing to give him, now and here, my hand." The seal of the great Commonwealth of Kentucky flashed into his mind with the figures of two men clasping hands under the motto: "United we stand, divided we fall." With a sense of the dramatic, Stone turned to Smith and the two men shook hands as the great audience stood and joined in unuttered prayer and sang as they had never sung before one of the great hymns of Zion. On Sunday, the two bodies joined in a Communion service as a token of unity formed by a great spiritual imperative. There were no formal motions made, no documents or agreements signed. The Spirit of God seemed to move at Lexington and to keep moving in great waves of power into the surrounding churches.

Stone wrote in the *Christian Messenger*:

> They were united by no written compact, no association, no conventional constitution. . . . They were free to think for themselves without the dictation of ghostly bishops . . . were drawn together by the spirit of truth as taught by our common Lord and experienced by us, the subjects of his kingdom.
>
> Johnson testified, "What could we do but unite? We both compared notes. We found ourselves congregated on the same divine creed, the Bible. We had the same King—the same faith—the same law. We, reciprocally, had discarded all human speculations and opinions, as foreign to the gospel, and unworthy of the serious attention of Christians. The name under which we rallied was the same. We could not do otherwise than unite in Christian love, fellowship and effort in the glorious work of reform.

112

Johnson joined forces with Stone in the editorship of the *Christian Messenger*. Their first joint editorial said:

> Will the Christians and Reformers thus unite in other states and sections of our country? We answer—if they are sincere in their profession and destitute of party spirit they will undoubtedly unite. . . . But should all in other states and sections act inconsistently with their profession, we are determined to do what we are convinced is right in the sight of God. Nothing can move us from this purpose, unless we should make shipwreck of faith and good conscience. From which may our merciful God preserve us.

Many obstacles had to be overcome. Lexington was a case in point. On the Sunday the union was consummated in the observance of the Lord's Supper, there was no difficulty because the elders officiated as usual. But when it was proposed to unite the two local congregations the matter of administering the service became a point at issue. On February 12, 1832, it seemed that agreement had been reached and a time two weeks later was set for the enrollment of names in the united church. Meeting on February 19, the Reformers had no preacher present. Thomas Smith, the regular preacher for the Christians, was also absent. Reformers expected the observance of the Supper, but since there was no ordained minister present, the Christians forestalled it. It was the belief of the latter group that local elders or deacons could not officiate. Because of dissension on this matter, plans for the union of the two congregations were dropped for the time being. It was not until Thomas Miller Allen was called to be the minister of the Lexington Christians that actual union came. At his advice "they waived all prejudice and differences of opinion on the subject of order and clerical privilege—if, indeed, any such differences still remained—and not only consented to union but nobly proposed it." Accordingly, the two congregations formally united in July, 1835. Similar disagreements were reported in many places, but union sentiment prevailed.

During this period Stone and Alexander Campbell had extensive correspondence on the subject of union. Campbell was now wary. He had heard too much about Stone's theological speculations and about some practices of the Christians "which had gone past Jerusalem after departing from Babylon." He said he would be honored by a merger with the "larger" and "respectable" Christian denomination, but he would refuse if it meant in any way the submerging of "the ancient gospel and the ancient order of things." Campbell was not ready to admit that Stone and his followers had antedated the Reformers in their discovery of the pure and unadulterated gospel and the restoration of the pure church of the New Testament in doctrine, ordinances, and polity.

When the news of the happenings at Lexington and beyond came to his ears, Campbell was stunned. While he earnestly desired Christian union, he was not ready for such precipitate action. He published the news in his new *Millennial Harbinger* but he spoke words of caution:

> These brethren need not to be told that to convert persons is not merely to baptize them, to loose them and let them go; nor to give them the name

Christian, and induce them to protest against human leaders, against human creeds, and to extol the sufficiency of the inspired writings; but "to turn them from darkness to light, and from the power of Satan to God, that they may receive forgiveness of sins and an inheritance amongst them that are sanctified"—*to teach them to observe and do all* that the Lord has commanded.

Campbell said nothing in favor of or in open opposition to the union, but he strongly urged the necessity of bringing all concerned into the full truth and practice of the New Testament.

Indeed, differences in opinion on central doctrines needed to be resolved. They did not affect so much the membership of the local churches as the leadership of the two movements. Campbell and Stone were the central figures in controversy and others tended to follow in their train. Among these central issues were the Trinity, the atonement, the name of the church, church government, revivalism and the work of the Holy Spirit in conversion, and Christian baptism.

The Trinity. The views of Stone on this subject have already been mentioned (Chapter 5, p. 84 ff). They were not Unitarian but of such a fuzzy nature as to seem to minimize the status of Christ and the Holy Spirit.

Thomas Campbell had written a discourse on the Trinity for the Redstone Baptist Association, which had been received as thoroughly orthodox, although he avoided theological terms and adhered to strictly Scriptural forms of expression. Alexander's views coincided with those of his father so much so that Stone saw no difference between them and those held by the Calvinists.

Campbell laid down three basic principles which must be considered in discussing the Trinity (a word which he avoided because it was not in the Scriptures):

1. The pretensions of the Bible to divine authority are to be decided by reason alone.
2. When reason decides this question, the truths of the Bible are to be received as first principles not to be tested by reason, but from which man is to reason.
3. Terms in the Bible are to be understood as reason suggests their meaning, but the things taught are to be received not because they have been proved by reason, but because God has revealed them.

He countered Stone's contention that it is unreasonable to believe that three persons can be one God and yet each of the persons be supreme God. Campbell said it is not more unreasonable than to believe that there can be a God at all, or an Eternal First Cause,

because in all the dominions of reason there is nothing that could suggest the idea; and because it is contrary to all the facts before us in the whole world that a cause can be the cause of itself, or not the effect of some other cause. Not many from analogy, can reason further that every cause is the effect of another, ad infinitum. Here reason shuts the door. Here analogy puts down her rule, and shuts her case of instruments.

Stone was no match for the logic and intellectual depth of Campbell and was at last content to abandon all speculation for the simple statements of the Bible on the subject.

The eastern Christians, however, were definitely unitarian in their views of the subject. Campbell was always careful to state that his fellowship with the Christians did not include the eastern brethren. His aversion to the use of the name *Christian* instead of *Disciple* was largely grounded in his fear that the general religious community would assume that their views on the Trinity were unorthodox.

The atonement. Stone's views on the Trinity affected his thinking on the nature and work of Christ. In 1839-40 he carried on a lengthy correspondence with Thomas Campbell in which he held, in effect, that the death of Christ exerted a chiefly moral influence producing repentance and love in the sinner. Campbell maintained that the death of Christ was a unique event in history and that in the economy of God it was necessary for Christ to die as a substitutionary sacrifice, that in his blood, remission of sins might be made available to sinful men.

Alexander Campbell took up his father's view, but agreed with Stone that such terms as *expiation, pacified,* and *propitiate* were of human theological origin and should be discarded in any strictly Biblical discussion of the issue. The main difference between the two men finally centered in the question of whether or not the death of Christ reconciled God to men. They both agreed that it reconciled man to God. Campbell insisted that Stone was in grave error in omitting the greatest design of the death of Christ, namely, "to expiate sin." When Stone announced at Lexington that he was willing to abandon speculation and accept all the teaching of Scripture in the words of Scripture, Campbell was satisfied, and the matter never became a serious issue.

The name. In 1804, Stone and his group had settled on the name *Christian* as being the proper designation for the followers of Christ and the name of the church. He and other leaders believed that the name was of divine origin and often quoted Dr. Philip Doddridge's translation of Acts 11:26, "The disciples were by divine appointment first named Christians at Antioch."

Alexander Campbell preferred the name *Disciples of Christ,* and as late as 1839 he stated four reasons in the *Millennial Harbinger*:

> 1. It is more ancient. The disciples were called disciples in Judea, Galilee, Samaria, and among the Gentiles before they were called Christians at Antioch.
> 2. It is more descriptive. A person may be named after a country or a political leader and feel it "an insult to be called the pupils or disciples of the person whose name they wear." A stranger might imagine that Christian, like American or Roman, had some reference to a country, rather than a scholarship. Disciples of Christ is a more accurate designation than Christian.
> 3. It is more scriptural. In the Acts, the term "Disciple" is used thirty times and "Christian" but twice.
> 4. It is more unappropriated. Unitarians and Arians use "Christian" but no other people use "Disciples of Christ."

The Stone view, however, was favored by Thomas Campbell and by

Walter Scott, and the name *Christian* prevailed over much of the nation. Disciples or Reformers came to use the name *Christian* to designate the church and the name *Disciple* to designate the individual Christian. Those who saw the controversy as useless held that "any name that is a Scriptural name is a proper name for the church."

Church government. The status of ordination and the superior place of the clergy was another point of difference. The Christians maintained that the Lord's Supper and baptism could not be properly administered except by an ordained minister. The Reformers, arguing from the principle of "the priesthood of all believers," held that this was the prerogative of any member of the church.

Stone was a regularly ordained minister in the Presbyterian church, and he insisted that all congregations of Christians should admit no minister to leadership who was not properly ordained. Campbell was not a formally ordained minister and this may have colored his thinking. He had inveighed against the traditional clergy in the *Christian Baptist*, and he had a mortal fear that the hierarchical system would gain a foothold in the new movement. Countering Stone's view, he pictured a situation in which the church is dependent upon an ordained orator,

> who superadds to his eloquence the charms of being called and sent by divine authority "to preach to Christians" and "to administer ordinances," so that his authority is irresistible and his presence indispensable to Christian worship. When he is absent, the church can do nothing. Like a widow forlorn and desolate, she is solitary and silent. But the presence of this oratorial Pastor is like the meeting of the bridegroom and the bride.

Both Christians and Reformers rejected human creeds and church disciplines and agreed that the Bible alone contained the true standard of church government.

Revivalism. The Stone movement was born in revival and continued to thrive on these periods of religious excitement. In fact, the Christians in some places had a tendency toward the camp-meeting revivalism of the Methodists.

Campbell has a distaste for emotionalism and "mystical impulses." He felt that the tumult and the shouting of revival orators, the tears, and the pleadings of the mourner's bench were an insult to the intelligence of men and the dignity of the Holy Spirit. He branded popular revivalism as "the greatest delusion of our age, and one of the most prolific causes of the infidelity, immorality, and irreligion of our contemporaries." It was this fear of the introduction of undue emotionalism into the Restoration movement that led him to send his father to the Western Reserve of Ohio to investigate the strange new evangelism of Walter Scott. Wherever Scott and his "school of evangelists" went, however, the idea of revivals or "protracted meetings," as the Reformers preferred to call them, appealed to the churches.

The action and interaction of the two groups tended to favor the Scott type of revival and even Campbell himself came to admit the value

116

of these special seasons of refreshing and soulsaving. Writing in the *Harbinger* in 1840 he said,

> To fix the mind for a long time on the subject of religion, to abandon the business, and care, and perplexity, and pleasures of this life for some days in succession, and to turn all our thoughts to religious truth, to things unseen and eternal, is, in my judgment, sound wisdom and discretion. But on such occasions the people must be fed with the bread and water of life.

The infusion of the spirit of evangelism from both Stone and Scott insured the rapid and amazing growth of a movement which might have degenerated into an abstract adventure in Biblical polemics.

The Holy Spirit. Somewhat related to the revival issue was the question of the work and office of the Holy Spirit in conversion. Stone and his followers were committed to the belief that the Spirit had been sent into the world "to operate as a reprover of the wicked, and a comforter of the good, which holy influence will continue until the coming of the Son of God to judge the world." They acknowledged the Spirit as operating in harmony with the teaching of the Word, but as a personality apart from the Word.

Campbell's views, which have already been mentioned, were branded as those of a "Bible worshiper." Badger's *Christian Palladium* asserted that the sage of Bethany denied all activity of the Spirit since the time of the apostles except through the written Word. Said the editor, "If God communicated to Christians only by the Bible, all spiritual experience would cease and Christianity would become a 'spiritless system.'" Some of Campbell's followers undoubtedly held such views, saying that the Bible was the only Holy Spirit they knew about. The fact is, that at this time Campbell was concerned with the popular doctrine of regeneration without the Word, and experiential salvation which considered "impressions" and "operations" as superior to the clear instruction of the Scriptures.

Probably the clearest proof of Campbell's belief in the operation of the Spirit of God in conversion is to be found in a letter to Mr. Meredith, editor of the *Baptist Interpreter,* when he said:

> The human heart must be changed and renovated by some cause; for unless the heart be reconciled to God, purified, cleansed, no man can be admitted into the society of heaven. Those views I have always presented to the public. But the question is, How is the moral change to be effected? By the Spirit alone? By the gospel facts alone? By the Word alone? I do not affirm any one of these propositions. I never did affirm any one of them.
>
> How the Spirit operates in the Word, through the Word, by the Word, or with the Word, I do not affirm. I only oppose the idea that anyone is changed in heart or renewed in the spirit of his mind by the Spirit without the Word.

Christian baptism. Both Stone and Campbell believed that immersion was the Scriptural mode of baptism and that baptism was for the remission of sins. The point at issue with them was whether or not there could be fellowship with the unimmersed in churches of the New Testament pattern.

Campbell felt that the fate of the unimmersed was in the hands of God; that it is not ours to judge whether or not they will be saved; but that if the testimony of the Restoration was to be pure and undefiled, the unimmersed must not be admitted to local congregations "after the New Testament pattern."

His famous "Lunenburg Letter," written in 1837, is often quoted to show his liberal view on the subject. A devout lady of Lunenburg, Virginia, inquired whether he thought the unimmersed were Christians and he replied, in part:

> Who is a Christian? I answer, Everyone that believes in his heart that Jesus of Nazareth is the Messiah, the Son of God; repents of his sins, and obeys him in all things according to his measure of knowledge of his will. A *perfect man in Christ*, or a perfect Christian, is one thing; and "a babe in Christ," a stripling in the faith, or an imperfect Christian, is another. The New Testament recognizes both the perfect man and the imperfect man in Christ . . .
>
> I cannot . . . make any one duty the standard of Christian state or character, not even immersion into the name of the Father, of the Son, and of the Holy Spirit, and in my heart regard all that have been sprinkled in infancy without their own knowledge and consent, as aliens from Christ and the well-grounded hope of heaven . . .
>
> Should I find a paedo-baptist more intelligent in the Christian Scriptures, more spiritually-minded and more devoted to the Lord than a Baptist, or one immersed on a profession of the ancient faith, I could not hesitate a moment in giving the preference of my heart to him that loveth most. Did I act otherwise, I would be a pure sectarian, a Pharisee among Christians. Still I will be asked, How do I know that anyone loves my Master but by his obedience to his commandments? I answer, In no other way. But mark, I do not substitute obedience to one commandment, for universal or even general obedience. And should I see a sectarian Baptist or a paedo-baptist more spiritually minded, more generally conformed to the requisitions of the Messiah, than the one who precisely acquiesces with me in the theory or practice of immersion as I teach, doubtless the former rather than the latter, would have my cordial approbation and love as a Christian. So I judge, and so I feel. It is the image of Christ the Christian looks for and loves; and this does not consist in being exact in a few items, but in general devotion to the whole truth as far as known. . . .

Many narrow-minded followers of Campbell immediately protested this generous attitude, but he reiterated it in the columns of the *Harbinger* and quoted extensively from the *Christian Baptist* and his other published works to show that this had always been his position. What many people failed to see in the statement was that he was expressing his personal judgment and feeling in the matter. This irenic spirit always characterized his life and work. But he drew a line between his personal feelings and the clear teaching of the Word of God. His love and respect for Christians did not go beyond their willingness to investigate and learn the whole truth about baptism, and to comply with the truth as they discovered it. Neither was he willing to call a church a New Testament church that compromised the express teaching of the Scriptures by admitting the unimmersed to membership.

118

It was precisely at this point that Campbell and Stone disagreed. Stone favored fellowship in the Christian churches on an equal basis between the immersed and the unimmersed, making Christian character the sole test of fellowship. The Christian churches had many unimmersed in fellowship and, in fact, some who held to the Quaker view that only "spiritual baptism" met all Scriptural requirements.

Despite all these and minor differences, the union of Disciples and Christians moved toward consummation. There were several reasons for this.

The foremost of these was the spirit and will of Christian unity which pervaded the ministry and the churches. Stone put it in a homely way when he said there are four kinds of union: (1) Book Union—that is under a creed, authoritative and in adaptation uncertain; (2) Head Union, founded on opinion, variable, tyrannous, and no better than the first; (3) Water Union, based on immersion, an unstable compact; and (4) Fire Union, "a union founded on the spirit of truth"—a worthy and permanent union. "This is the very union for which Jesus prayed, and by which the world will believe that he is the Christ of God." He further explained—"in retrospect," writing in his *Christian Messenger* (1833):

> How vain are all human attempts to unite a bundle of twigs together, so as to make them grow together, and bear fruit. They must first be united with the living stock, and receive its sap, and spirit, before they can ever be united with one another. The members of the body cannot live unless by union with the head—nor can the members of the church live united, unless first united with Christ, the living head. His spirit is the bond of union. Men have devised many plans to unite Christians—all are vain. There is but one effectual plan, which is, that all be united with Christ and walk in him.

Another reason for unity was the lack of any denominational or overhead authority or organization to prevent it. It is true that there were two rather well-defined groups and sets of leaders involved; but there was no debate about terms of institutional mergers or whether the Christians were joining the Disciples, or the Disciples the Christians.

There was a unanimous acceptance of the Holy Scriptures as ultimate authority and a guide in apostolic practice. There was a common desire to restore the New Testament church in doctrine and life. Human creeds had been rejected and the opinions of men were properly discounted. Even the views of Campbell and Stone were treated as of secondary importance and were not allowed to interfere with an independent study of the New Testament and the adoption of its directives.

Finally, there was a mutually generous and patient attitude accorded all those who held divergent views. They had all "come out of Babylon" and "under great tribulation," and they were conscious of the fact that they had yet a long way to go before they were to discover and to practice the whole will and way of God.

Nevertheless, there were those who were so obsessed by party spirit that they refused to join the union movement. Stone was unable to win all of the so-called Christian Connection. The Unitarian wing in New

England, led by Joseph Badger, editor of the *Christian Palladium,* bitterly opposed Stone. Badger branded Campbell as a Calvinist and a Trinitarian, and his views on baptism as Roman Catholic. In southern Ohio, David Purviance and Matthew Gardner led many churches in refusing to abandon the "open membership" position. In North Carolina, where old Republican Methodist doctrine was still firmly entrenched among the Christians, there was strong opposition to union. While the great mass of the Christian Connection joined the movement in the West, the majority of Eastern churches kept their identity. Finally, dissidents effected a denominational union with headquarters in Dayton, Ohio, with an official organ, *The Herald of Gospel Liberty.* In organization, they followed the Republican Methodist pattern with conference supervision and local church autonomy. Two colleges, Defiance in Ohio and Elon in North Carolina, trained their ministry. Growth was limited, and eventually, under stress of financial obligations and a steadily diminishing membership, the General Convention of Christian Churches united with the Congregationalists in 1931 to form the Congregational Christian denomination (now part of the United Church of Christ).

At the time of the Christian-Disciples union in Lexington, two rather significant incidents occurred in the ranks of the latter: the defection of Sidney Rigdon to Mormonism, and of Dr. John Thomas to form the Christadelphians. Rigdon had been active in the early days of the Disciples in Pennsylvania and Ohio, and Dr. Thomas, in Virginia. Both had been guilty of many erratic actions.

Rigdon had often expressed the view that the Old and New Testaments might not be the complete and final revelation of God to man and that a new revelation might reasonably be expected as world conditions warrant. Campbell had reproved him publicly, but this concept seemed to remain fixed in his thought. In 1830, Mormonism was introduced into northern Ohio and found an eager convert in Rigdon. He was especially interested in the news that Joseph Smith, the movement's Methodist founder, had discovered golden plates near Palmyra, New York, inscribed in "reformed Egyptian characters," containing important divine communications, an account of the "twelve lost tribes of Israel" and revelations designed to usher in "the latter days" of the Christian era. It is said that Rigdon collaborated with Smith to produce the *Book of Commandments* and the essential Christian theological doctrine of the Church of Jesus Christ of Latter Day Saints.

It must be admitted that many of the Christian teachings in Mormonism contain a strange resemblance to Restoration principles. Restorationism in Mormonism is concerned chiefly with the restoration of the Aaronic and the Melchisedekan priesthoods. Rigdon immersed a number of the Mormon leaders, and led them in formulating their baptismal doctrine. Rigdon's church at Kirtland, Ohio, eventually became Mormon headquarters, and a great temple was erected there which stands to this day, the property of the Reorganized Church of Latter Day Saints. Upon the death of Smith, Rigdon was for a time considered as the new head of the

Mormon church, but when Brigham Young was chosen, Rigdon was banished and died a lonely and disappointed man in Allegheny City, New York.

Dr. John Thomas was a physician who had been immersed by Walter Scott in Cincinnati. After preaching in Philadelphia and other eastern cities, he located in Virginia, where he began the publication of the *Apostolic Advocate*. His narrow views on baptism led him to advocate reimmersion for forgiveness of sins. Soon he began to make tests of fellowship out of his strange opinions on the Trinity, the nature of the human soul, the state of the dead, the final destiny of the wicked, and eternal life. After his discussion in Painesville, Ohio, with a Presbyterian minister, the brethren there passed a resolution indicating that Thomas' views did not represent the congregation and were "likely to produce a division among us." They recommended that Thomas "discontinue the discussion of them." This protest and later advice from Alexander Campbell failed to deter him. Soon he was reported as spreading his peculiar views in England, and later in Illinois, by means of a new journal called the *Investigator*. Finally, Campbell felt impelled to denounce him publicly as having departed from the Reformation and seeking to form a new party. Thomas' ideas culminated in the development of the strange cult known as the Christadelphians (Christ's Brethren).

The years that followed the historic union of the forces of Campbell and Stone in Lexington were marked by a uniform pattern of evangelism and church planting that exceeded anything that hitherto had been experienced. The travels of the evangelists, the circulation of periodicals, the establishment of colleges, and the mouth-to-mouth propaganda of converts created a spirit of unity and fellowship in a common cause that was electrifying. The story of that spectacular expansion is told in the following chapter.

BIBLIOGRAPHY: Chapter 7

Badger, Joseph, editor, and others, *Christian Palladium* (1832-1861).
Campbell, Alexander, editor, *Millennial Harbinger* (1832-1835).
Haggard, Rice, *An Address . . . on the Sacred Import of the Christian Name*.
Hayden, A. S., *Early History of the Disciples on the Western Reserve, Ohio*.
Richardson, Robert, *Memoirs of Alexander Campbell*.
Shaw, Henry K., *Buckeye Disciples*.
Stone, Barton W., editor, *Christian Messenger* (1831-1835).
Ware, Charles C., *Barton Warren Stone*.
West, William G., *Barton Warren Stone*.
Williams, John Augustus, *Life of John Smith*.

Chapter 8

A Movement
of National Significance

THE American unity movement seeking to restore the New Testament church by an appeal to the Bible alone as a rule of faith and practice began to achieve national importance. Hitherto it had been characterized by a series of regional or community efforts with remarkably similar aims, grouped around a few outstanding leaders. Once contacts were established and co-operative endeavors undertaken, a new confidence was born. The vision of a united church seemed well within the realm of possibility. The common man responded to this leadership in a remarkable way. Everywhere people were restudying the Scriptures, getting a clear grasp of the nature of the New Testament church, questioning all human innovations in the traditional churches, and joining in the crusade for Christian unity.

The frontier, where the movements were really active, was in a state of flux. People were, for the most part, not permanently settled, and were on the outlook for new locations where they might better themselves. Adherents to the new crusade carried their convictions with them wherever they went and propagandized their new-found faith. Churches of the New Testament pattern were set up in homes; and the Lord's Supper was observed every Lord's Day, Bible studies pursued, and "social meetings" held. These churches often grew to full stature in the religious life of the communities and became centers of evangelism.

Only a brief review can be given of the development of the movement in the various states during the years prior to 1860. The states of Ohio and Kentucky at first were the chief centers of activity. Bordering states of Pennsylvania, Virginia, Indiana, Illinois, and Tennessee next began to feel the impact of the crusade.

Kentucky. After the union of Christians and Reformers at Lexington in 1832, Kentucky led all the states in number of churches and members. Men like John T. Johnson, John Smith, and Barton W. Stone garnered in a continued harvest of souls that ran into the thousands every year. In 1847, a state report showed 403 known churches with some thirty-five thousand members and many remote areas unreported. Three years previous to that date, the *Christian Journal* stated that the Christian church had the largest membership of any communion in the state. Co-operative meetings were held in various areas and the churches made contributions for the support of general evangelists. In 1840 a state-wide meeting, held in Harrodsburg, continued for ten days and resulted in forty-eight conversions. Every year thereafter, such a meeting was held, finally resulting in a regularly established Kentucky Annual State Meeting, organized in May, 1850. A decade later, the annual meeting reports showed more than forty-five thousand members in the state.

Ohio. The northern section of the state was the chief center of strength for the Reformers or Disciples. The south had a number of such churches, but the Christians were predominant. Yearly meetings, which took the place of the old Mahoning Baptist Association, drew an attendance of two thousand to five thousand, and a fine spirit of co-operation existed. In 1848, this area of the state reported seventy-one churches with a total of 4,508 members. In 1852, the first attempt at a state-wide meeting was made in Wooster. Alexander Campbell was present to deliver the chief address. Reports indicated twenty-five thousand members in three hundred churches. "A School of Preachers," which was set up at New Lisbon in 1835, met annually for several years. This appears to have been the first attempt at a training program for Christian ministers. Several schools under Reformer auspices were established in the state, including the Hygeia Female Atheneum; the Mount Vernon Male Academy, and the Vernon Female Institute; the Bedford Christian Institute; and the McNeeley Normal School. In November, 1850, the Western Reserve Eclectic Institute was opened, which eventuated in the establishment of Hiram College. A number of magazines were published in Ohio for the purpose of promoting the Restoration cause, chief of which was Walter Scott's *Evangelist,* published at Cincinnati. This city, because of its strategic location as "The Queen City of the West" and "The Gateway to the South," soon became a center for meetings of national significance for the whole movement.

Indiana. Absalom Littell, a Presbyterian who became a reader of the *Christian Baptist,* migrated from Pittsburgh to a point on the Ohio River opposite the city of Louisville, and in 1829 led a Regular Baptist church at Silver Creek, Clark County, Indiana, to the New Testament position. Several other churches claim as early a beginning. Free Will Baptists, German Baptists (Dunkards), and independent churches joined the movement by scores. The Christian church emigres from Kentucky were responsible for establishing many new churches. Union and co-operation were first effected by John Wright in a conference in New Albany in 1823. The first Indiana state convention, held at Indianapolis in 1839 with fifty "public speakers," reported 115 churches, with 7,110 members in fellowship. The Indiana Christian Missionary Society was organized in 1849. When Alexander Campbell visited the state the following year, he reported the Disciples "second only to the Methodists in number, wealth and influence." Scores of public discussions were held, chiefly with Methodists and Universalists. Henry B. Pritchard, O. A. Burgess, Benjamin Franklin, J. M. Mathes, Thomas P. Connelly, and Elijah Goodwin were among the chief polemicists of their time. Mathes and Franklin were also editors of some influence. Mathes edited the *Christian Record,* and Franklin, several magazines which eventuated in the *American Christian Review* in 1856. Hall's *Christian Register* reported 19,914 members of the Christian church in the state in 1848. In 1860, between twenty-five and thirty thousand were enrolled.

Illinois. The Christians organized their first church in this state at Barney's Prairie in 1819. Then came Coffee Creek (Keensburg), the "Christian Settlement" in Lawrence County, near Vincennes, Indiana, and Antioch (Cantrall) in Sangamon County. Growth came rapidly, and the Disciples were soon one of the major religious communions in the state. When Edward Baker, one of their ministers, defeated Abraham Lincoln as a candidate for Congress in a Sangamon County election, Lincoln's biographer wrote, "Baker and wife belonged to that numerous and powerful sect which has several times played so important a part in Western politics—the Disciples."

Eureka College was established in 1855, having its origin in the Walnut Grove Academy conducted by John T. Jones. It was the first coeducational institution of higher learning in the state. In the twenty years preceding 1860, twenty major debates were held in which the New Testament position was defended by such able men as Clark Braden. The first state meeting was held in Pittsfield in 1839. The Illinois State Missionary Society was organized at Shelbyville in 1850. Arny's report in the *Millennial Harbinger* in 1848 claimed 11,636 members in the state. In 1843, a follower of Dr. Thomas founded a church in the mushrooming town of Chicago. When Thomas' strange views caused division, Campbell's followers organized a separate church in 1849. This latter congregation grew to a position of strength in Chicago under the leadership of Lathrop Cooley, of Cleveland, Ohio. The Honore family, pillars of the church, had two daughters who married prominent men: Potter Palmer, of Chicago, and Frederick Grant, of Washington, son of President Ulysses S. Grant. Palmer, founder of the Palmer House, was a deacon in the Chicago church. By 1860, the Disciples numbered about fifteen thousand in Illinois.

Tennessee. The Christian church at Post Oak Springs, organized in 1812 and still alive today, claims to have been the first congregation after the New Testament pattern in the state. A large number of Christians from Kentucky poured into Tennessee and took their convictions with them. Baptist churches by the scores warmly advocated the views expressed in the *Christian Baptist.* Alexander Campbell's six visits to Nashville won him countless friends and resulted in many strong Baptist churches joining his movement. P. S. Fall, Tolbert Fanning, and David Lipscomb were outstanding leaders, the latter two strongly opposing any form of interchurch association. Mr. and Mrs. Fanning established a

Female Academy at Franklin in 1837. Franklin College was opened at Elm Crag in 1845. Minerva College for Women was established four years later on the same grounds. Burritt College near Spencer was opened in 1849. In 1860, Tennessee was credited with a membership of 12,285.

Michigan. John Martindale, Reuben Wilson, and David D. Miller began preaching the Restoration message in 1840. The first church was "set in order" on Plum Street, in Detroit, in 1841. Isaac Errett, who was to have such wide national influence in years to come, organized the church at Ionia in 1859, and preached for groups at Muir, Woodward Lake, and North Plains. In 1858, Elias Sias read the widely disseminated tract, *Sincerity Seeking the Way to Heaven*, sought baptism from Errett, and became the state's most successful evangelist, winning thousands to Christ. In 1856, Benjamin Franklin evangelized in southern Michigan. Only about one thousand members were reported in 1860.

Wisconsin. The shifting nature of the population in these early days kept well-organized churches from being formed. There was, however, much evangelistic activity and many persons won to Christ. Henry Howe, David Evans, and J. P. Lancaster were among the early preachers. The oldest surviving congregation in the state is Viroqua, begun by Daniel Parkinson in 1852. Only five hundred members were reported in 1860.

In the eastern section of the nation there were many strong local and regional centers of the faith, but they were widely scattered.

New England. The Christian churches in this area were strongly tinctured with Unitarian and Universalist views, and refused almost in their entirety to come into the Lexington union. When Alexander Campbell visited New England in 1836, he preached in the famous Baptist Tremont Temple in Boston, and the first Reformer church was established there in 1843. A few Christian churches in Massachusetts, notably Haverhill, Lynn, and Worcester, joined the Restoration movement. An independent church at Danbury, Connecticut, visited by Campbell, decided to join the movement and became the strongest church of the Disciples in New England. In Vermont, Campbell's visit eventuated in the churches in Pawlet and West Rupert, but the cause did not grow. Dr. Charles J. White was largely responsible for maintaining and perpetuating these congregations. Two small churches in the region of Lubec, Maine, were the sole representatives of the movement in that state. Even today with the strong Roman Catholic, Unitarian, and liberal Congregational influences in New England, Bible doctrine does not seem to thrive.

New York. The oldest existing congregation had its beginnings in Scotch Baptist antecedents in New York City long before the *Declaration and Address*. It early (1810) became a "reforming" body and contributed a number of leaders to the national movement. Throopsville (1830), North Lancaster (1833), and Pompey (1834) were the next to join. In 1850, fourteen churches were reported with about two thousand members, and a state missionary society is known to have been operating in 1855.

Pennsylvania. The first church organized by the Campbells was at Brush Run in 1811. The churches at Somerset (1817) and at Johnstown

(1830) were early bulwarks of the cause. A number of men of distinction who came into the fold included Congressman Charles Ogle, Judge Francis M. Kimmell, United States Attorney General Jeremiah Sullivan Black, and William Ballentine, noted Hebraist. The church at Philadelphia was organized in 1832. N. J. Mitchell in the same year formed a congregation at Howard, which became a center for church-organizing activity. At this time, other known churches were operating at Canton, Smithfield, Columbia, Troy, Ridgeburg, and Luzerne County. In 1834, several churches dismissed from the Central Christian Conference of New York assembled in Lewisburg in eastern Pennsylvania and organized a state conference from which dates the Pennsylvania Christian Missionary Society. Western Pennsylvania churches organized a missionary society in 1850. The two co-operative bodies finally merged after 1860. Dependable figures are unavailable, but it is estimated that in 1860 there were forty-five hundred members.

Virginia. West Virginia did not become a state until 1863. Reformation activity was in the western section of Virginia and is historically credited to West Virginia. In 1815, a group from the Brush Run church moved to Charlestown, Virginia (Wellsburg), and organized a church of which Alexander Campbell became the minister. Bethany, the home of Campbell, was only seven miles away, and became the center of the whole reform movement for many years. The O'Kelly and Christian church movements simultaneously furnished leaders for many churches in eastern Virginia which came together after the Lexington union. Among these were Dr. Chester Bullard and Robert Ferguson. After the famous "Dover Decrees," which anathematized Campbell among the Baptists, there was a constant stream of Baptist churches entering the movement. The Sycamore (Seventh Street) church in Richmond was founded in 1832 as a result of a split in the leading Baptist church of the city. The first Peter Ainslee was sent out as an evangelist of the Tidewater churches in that same year. In April, 1833, eastern Virginia churches held their first "co-operation meeting" at Acquitain, with sixteen preachers and seven hundred persons present. Another meeting in Richmond in October of the same year reported sixteen congregations represented and twelve hundred persons in attendance. Alexander Campbell was elected president of one of these "co-operation meetings" held in western Virginia in April, 1835. He attended a similar meeting in Charlottesville in 1840, when fifty-six churches reported with three thousand members. It was at this meeting that the "Bullardites" were received into fellowship and Campbell first met Bullard, with whom he formed a very close friendship. Bullard was responsible for the establishment of many churches in Virginia. The *Christian Baptist,* and later the *Millennial Harbinger* and the *Christian Intelligencer* (Richmond), were published in the state. It is estimated that there were eight thousand members in the Virginia of 1860.

Maryland. Growing out of a small Haldane congregation founded by a young preacher by the name of Farquharson, the First Christian Church of Baltimore was organized in 1831. When Campbell visited the city in 1833, he held a meeting which won them to the Disciples. Among those

127

he baptized was Theodotus Garlick, eminent sculptor and plastic surgeon, who made the first daguerreotype photograph in America. Robert R. Ferguson, the first settled minister, also served congregations at Gunpowder, Hyattstown, and Rockville. A number of New Light Christians joined forces with the Disciples after the Lexington union. The conversion of a Lutheran minister, Samuel K. Hoshour, resulted in churches of the New Testament pattern at Hagerstown and Beaver Creek. In Washington, D. C., the first congregation was organized in 1843 in the home of Dr. James T. Barclay. There were about one thousand members in this area by 1860.

North Carolina. Dr. B. F. Hall, dentist and evangelist, read the Campbell-McCalla debate and began preaching the restoration program among the Baptists. Opposed by his brethren, Hall invited Thomas Campbell to North Carolina for aid and comfort. The church at Edenton, where Hall served, thus became the first to take an independent stand. Campbell then went to Greenville for a visit with General William Clark, the first subscriber to the *Millennial Harbinger* in the state. The general and Jeremiah Leggett led the revolt against the Philadelphia Confession in the Kehukee Regular Baptist Association and the Neuse Baptist Association with the result that many churches withdrew, forming a Union Meeting of Disciples in 1833. The oldest continuous Christian church organization in the state is Wheat Swamp, which was founded as a Baptist church in 1752. Besides Hall and Clark, Dexter A. Snow and Thurston Crane were leaders in the North Carolina advance. There were approximately twenty-five hundred members in the state by 1860.

South Carolina. To Evergreen, Pendleton County, goes the distinction of being the earliest congregation of Disciples. It was established in 1831. Captain Samuel G. Earle, called "the first of all the Disciples in the state," lived in this area and his several sons graduated with honors from Bethany College. Two distinguished Baptist laymen, Dr. William R. Erwin and his brother, General James D. Erwin, were excluded from the Kirkland Baptist Church because they held *Christian Baptist* views. They built a new church edifice at nearby Antioch and thus the second congregation in the state was established in 1833. Alexander Campbell visited the state in 1838 and gave impetus to the cause. In 1860 there were about three hundred members.

Georgia. A group of Republican Methodists, or Christians, was established at Scull Shoals, near Athens, in 1807. This congregation later (1842) became a church "according to the New Testament pattern" and the first church of the Restoration movement in Georgia. In 1838, Alexander Campbell visited Savannah, where Shelton C. Dunning and Christian H. Dasher had formed a New Testament church in 1819. This church and the one in Augusta lay rival claim to being the second. The eminent physician and mayor of the city, Dr. Daniel Hook, aided by the wealthy Mrs. Emily Harvey Tubman, led in organizing the church in 1835. Upon Campbell's visit to Augusta in 1845, the governors of two states were in his audience despite the boycott on the meetings by Methodist, Baptist, and Presbyterian churches. The winning of Cyrus White, eminent Free Will Baptist, resulted in many of those churches joining the movement. James S. Lamar, of

Georgia, founded the state's first journal, *Christian Union*, and became the biographer of Isaac Errett. His son, Joseph, became a justice of the United States Supreme Court. In 1860 there were only eleven hundred members in Georgia, but they were wielding an influence in the religious and public affairs of the state far beyond their numbers.

Farther west in the Southland the influence of the movement grew.

Alabama. The Christian church movement laid the foundation for advance in this state. James E. Matthews, William McGauhy, and E. D. Moore were the first preachers in the northern tier of counties. Matthews converted Tolbert Fanning there. In 1827 an "Annual Meeting of the Christian Conference" was held at Antioch, Jackson County, with twenty-one ministers and three hundred members present. In 1841, Prior Reeves brought nine of sixteen Baptist churches in one east Alabama association into the movement. Alexander Campbell visited the state in 1839, 1857, and 1859. In 1860 there were forty-one churches and 2,458 members.

Mississippi. William Matthews, a Baptist preacher and medical doctor, whom Alexander Campbell referred to as "that distinguished Christian philosopher," entered the state from Alabama in 1828, and within a year, three congregations were having fellowship in the Restoration movement. The church at Jackson celebrated its one-hundredth anniversary in 1925 and laid claim to being the oldest church in the state. Jefferson Johnson established the Utica Church in 1836; and Tolbert Fanning, the Columbus church in 1838. In February, 1839, Alexander Campbell visited the state and spoke of visiting churches at Woodville, Consolation, and Natchez. There were state evangelists at work from 1841 to the days of the Civil War. The United States census of 1860 recorded twenty-four churches in Mississippi with 2,450 members.

Louisiana. Jacob Creath preached the first sermon for the Disciples near Bayou Sara in October, 1826. The first congregation was established at Jackson, fifty miles north of Baton Rouge, in 1836. James Shannon, president of the State Teachers College there, was its first minister. He later was president of Bacon College and of the University of Missouri. Alexander Campbell delivered eight lectures at Jackson in 1839. Wappenoekee (1840), Cheneyville (1843), and Claiborne (1843) were next in line. Campbell spoke in the Baton Rouge church (1848) on his visit to the capital in 1857, and was entertained in the home of Governor Wickliffe. The known strength of the congregations in the state in 1860 was six hundred.

Missouri. A wave of immigrants from Kentucky settled in Missouri following its admittance to the Union as a state in 1821. Among them were many Christians of the Stone movement. Everywhere they went they set up Christian churches until it became the second strongest state for the Disciples. Among the preachers of the early days were Thomas McBride, Samuel Rogers, Joel Haden, T. M. Allen, Allen Wright, George Waters, M. P. Wills, F. R. Palmer, Absalom Rice, James Love, and Jacob Creath, Jr., all men of great ability. The first church was probably established in Howard County in 1813. "After the flood," they began to be reported by the scores. Annual meetings for co-operation began in 1837 at Bear Creek church, Boone County. Succeeding meetings were held at Paris in 1838 and Fulton in 1839. The first state meeting was held at Fayette in 1841. An old report of the gathering shows seventy-one churches with 4,753 members and 1,587 additions during the year. J. P. Lancaster and Allen Wright were appointed state evangelists. St. Louis was entered in 1837 and Westport Landing (Kansas City) in 1858. Alexander Campbell spoke at the 1845 state meeting and received an offering of four hundred dollars for Bethany College. Alexander Proctor, a Missouri boy graduated from Bethany in 1848, became the first college graduate among Missouri Christian ministers. His later leadership in the state and nation proved the wisdom of an educated ministry. G. A. Hoffman, in John T. Brown's *Churches of Christ*, gives a table indicating that Missouri had sixteen thousand members in 1850; twenty-five thousand in 1860.

Arkansas. Little Rock was the site of the first church. Its story reads like many others on the new frontier. A Baptist church was established by Silas Toncray in the home of Major Isaac Watkins in 1824. Benjamin F. Hall came to the city in 1832 from Kentucky and led the church in its decision to "renounce their creed, rules of decorum, name and every other appendage of human invention, taking only Jesus as their King and Lawgiver." William Wilson Stevenson, who became the first pastor at Little Rock, was independently wealthy and served without remuneration. At the same time, he became mayor of the city and president of the Arkansas Antiquarian and Historical Association. Elder John T. Johnson (brother of Richard M. Johnson, then vice-president of the United States), of Kentucky, held a meeting in Little Rock in 1845, which resulted in more than one hundred additions. Robert Graham, whom Alexander Campbell called "the greatest discovery I ever made," founded the church at Fayetteville and also Arkansas College. State-wide co-operative meetings began in 1852, when E. M. Northrum was chosen state evangelist. In 1860, according to the United States census, there were thirty-three Christian churches in the state with 2,257 members.

Even in "the far west" the influence of the Restoration movement was felt.

Iowa. Three years after the Black Hawk War ended, the Disciples organized their first church in Dubuque, October 1, 1835. The cause grew "notwithstanding the slander and opposition of its enemies," says an early report. At Fort Madison, the second congregation was established in 1836. Twenty-one churches were known to exist before Iowa achieved statehood in 1846. Despite the "California gold fever," which decimated whole congregations, the cause advanced. Co-operative meetings were reported as early as 1842. The "first great state meeting" was held at Marion in 1850. In 1856 it was agreed to open a college in Oskaloosa; but because of the panic of 1857, it did not matriculate students until 1861. Oskaloosa College was the forerunner of Drake University at Des Moines. In 1860 there were more than one hundred fifty congregations with a membership of ten thousand persons related to the movement.

Texas. Collin McKinney, a Stoneite minister from Kentucky, migrated to Texas at the head of a large company, settling on Hickman's Prairie in Bowie County in 1831. Here in the winter of 1841-42 at McKinney's Landing, a Disciple, G. Gates of Jeffersonville, Indiana, organized Texas' first church. Collin McKinney was a great Texas leader, leaving his name in Collin County and in McKinney, its county seat. He was elected to Congress and occupied many high offices. The first congregation to be perpetuated until the present, however, was transported bodily from Tennessee via Alabama and Mississippi with the famous "Davy" Crockett as a guide. It was led by Dr. Mansil W. Matthews and Lynn D'Spain. The church traveled every day except Sunday, when it stopped for worship and the observance of the Lord's Supper. The church was duly constituted at Clarksville, January 17, 1846. Out of this church came Addison and Randolph Clark, who founded Add-Ran College, now Texas Christian University. In 1857, Elder James Sandford Muse formed the old Muse Academy at McKinney, which produced many of the early Christian church ministers in Texas. Though the forces were scattered over wide-open spaces, it is estimated that there were twenty-five hundred Disciples in Texas in 1860.

Nebraska. Reformer ministers were first to preach the gospel to the white settlers of the Nebraska country long before it became a state. There is a record of the forty-wagon train of Joel Palmer, pausing near the present town of Martin, in 1845, to hear a sermon by a Disciple preacher by the name of Foster. The first town (Brownville) in Nebraska was established by a Disciple, Richard Brown, in 1854. With the aid of Joel M. Wood and John Mullis, a church was organized in January, 1855. Brown and Wood were members of the first territorial legislature. When D. R. Dungan entered the state to evangelize, with Rock Bluff as his center of operations, he was appointed chaplain of the last territorial legislature in Omaha, and Governor Saunders aided greatly in establishing the church in Omaha in 1861. Only a few churches were recorded as existing in Nebraska at this time, but foundations were well laid for future expansion.

Kansas. Pardee Butler is the name usually associated with the beginnings of the Restoration movement in "bloody Kansas." He did not, however, begin his work there until 1855. Prior to that, John Graces settled in Atchison County in 1854; Duke Young organized the first church in what is now Potter; W. S. Yohe a few months later founded the Leavenworth church; and John Fremont established the congregation in Iola. Butler laid out the town of Pardee and organized the church there in 1857. He called the first co-operative meeting at Leavenworth in the same year, and the next year a state missionary society was organized at Old Union. There were nine members present from three churches, and they chose Butler as state evangelist. He organized seven new churches in his first year, but his strong antislavery position hindered his work. At Atchison he was barely saved from an angry mob bent on hanging him. They finally compromised by tarring and feathering him and setting him adrift on the Missouri River. In later years, he was widely honored through the state and the nation for his antislavery leadership. In 1860 there were twenty churches in Kansas with about one thousand members.

California. Sutter's discovery of gold in 1847 opened California to a great influx of immigrants and fortune hunters. Thomas Thompson, of Missouri, long a reader of the *Christian Baptist*, arrived at Gold Run, Placer County, that year and immediately began a lifelong career of independent evangelization. In the winter of 1850-51, he organized the church at Stockton. James Anderson, who came to California the same year, married Thompson's only daughter and joined him in his work. The first governor of California, Peter H. Burnett, was a Disciple and his brother, Glenn, became a preacher for the Reformation on the Pacific coast. Among the ministers who came to California in these halcyon days were J. P. McCorkle, Joshua Lawson, William Brown, W. W. Stevenson, J. P. Rose, J. N. Pendergast, Byrum Lewis, J. K. Rule, George Kinkaid, John O. White, and Edward Dickinson Baker. Churches were established at Sebastapol (Yountville) in 1853; Cacheville (Woodland), Santa Rosa, Vaca Valley, and Gilroy in 1854. The first state meeting was held at Stockton in 1855. The second such meeting was held in 1856 on the ranch of A. C. Hawkins, who acted as host for the Vacaville church, with a free table and entertainment for all. This was the beginning of a series of state encampments. At the encampment at Mark West, near Santa Rosa, in 1860, twenty-seven churches were reported with 1,223 members. During the week, one hundred persons responded to the gospel invitation and were baptized, including Linsey Carson, brother of the famed "Kit" Carson. In 1858, W. W. Stevenson began to issue the *Western Evangelist*. In 1860, Hesperian College (now Chapman College) was organized at Woodland.

Oregon. Following closely upon the heels of Jason Lee and Marcus Whitman in the settlement of the Oregon country, a wagon train with one thousand persons arrived from Missouri to make their homes there. Many of them were Disciples. In 1846, Amos Harvey organized the first church "on the banks of the Yamhill River," later located at Whiteson, now at Amity. A number of other churches were established, but the settlements were unstable and few of them remain. The oldest continuing church in the state is the Blackhawk congregation, now McMinnville. So rapidly did the Restoration plea spread that a common by-word was, "The Campbellites and the fern are taking the Willamette Valley." Today the largest religious communion in the state is the Christian church. In 1852, Glenn Burnett called the first state meeting at McCoy, and shortly afterward, John Rigdon was appointed state evangelist. Edward Dickinson Baker, Disciple minister who had defeated Lincoln in the Whig primary election in Sangamon County, Illinois, in 1842 (p. 125), came to Oregon in 1860 and campaigned for Lincoln for the Presidency. He was a famous orator and is credited with turning Oregon into the Lincoln camp. He became

United States senator from Oregon and it was he who introduced Lincoln at his first inaugural. The known number of churches in the state at this time was thirty-eight with an estimated thirteen hundred members.

The total number of members in the United States in 1860 was likely more than two hundred thousand. Robert Richardson estimated approximately that number in 1844. An optimistic reporter in the *Millennial Harbinger* in 1854 insisted there were three hundred thousand.

During this period of expansion, Alexander Campbell became a veritable apostle Paul in his indefatigable labors as businessman, farmer, editor, author, educator, preacher, and evangelist. It is almost inconceivable that one man, with all the handicaps of early transportation and communication, could do what he did for the dissemination of the Restoration plea. This chapter would not be complete without some record of his "journeyings oft" for the "care of the churches."

During the spring of 1830, Campbell paid a short visit to Cincinnati and nearby points in Kentucky. That fall he took a more extensive journey through Ohio and Kentucky to Nashville, Tennessee. He preached in Zanesville and Wilmington, Ohio. At the latter, the whole Baptist church, excepting one member, had joined the reformation. Samuel Rogers, highly esteemed by Campbell, was the moving spirit of the expansion that was taking place in this area. On November 5, Campbell visited James Challen's church of some three hundred members in Cincinnati and spoke at nearby Mill Creek and Covington, Kentucky. There were baptisms at all these services. Cynthiana, Leesburg, Versailles, Great Crossings, and Lexington, Kentucky, were visited. At Lexington, he dined with Dr. Woods, president of Transylvania University, before moving on to Athens, Nicholasville, Harrodsburg, Danville, Columbia, Glasgow, and Bowling Green, to deliver discourses to the multitudes who came to hear him. On Friday, December 10, in Nashville, Tennessee, he delivered a discourse on the characteristics of apostasy and the mystery of iniquity to an audience including most of the clergy of the city. A discussion followed in which Dr. Obadiah Jenkins of the Presbyterian church attacked his views, and several days of debate ensued. During Campbell's stay in Nashville, more than thirty persons became obedient to the faith. The large Baptist church, led by P. S. Fall, came into fellowship with the Restoration movement.

An eastern journey in 1831 took Campbell to Richmond, Fredericksburg, Bowling Green, Norfolk, and other points in Virginia. In Baltimore, Maryland, he held several meetings. Finding the New York church divided over extreme views of church order, he labored to bring unity among the brethren. During his stay in the city he addressed large audiences of skeptics in Tammany Hall and Concert Hall and made a deep impression, although Baptist churches in the city were closed against him. In Philadelphia he found a similar situation, and had to speak in the Universalist church. During his stay there, some sixteen persons were added to the Bank Street church. This eastern journey took some three months, covered seventeen hundred miles, and included eighty discourses. D. S. Burnet

133

who visited the Baltimore church shortly afterward, received fifty new members and attributed much of his success to the work Campbell had previously done there.

In February, 1835, in company with Lavinia, his daughter, Campbell made another tour to Nashville. Everywhere he went audiences were so great that no auditorium could contain them. Among the interesting features of this trip were meetings with Walter Scott in Carthage; addresses to the Choctaw Indian Academy and Transylvania University; contacts with John O'Kane, who later became state evangelist in Indiana; conferences with Bishop James Otey, of the Episcopal church in Tennessee; and scores of baptisms in the churches where he preached.

In the spring of 1836 he set out on a journey into the northeast. At Ravenna, Ohio, his addresses were largely concerned with popular skepticism. Dr. Samuel Underhill engaged him in several discussions which resulted in the strengthening of New Testament Christianity throughout the Western Reserve of Ohio. Speaking at Cleveland and Buffalo, he moved on to Rochester, New York, where he opened a series of lectures in the courthouse on June 24. Later he visited Syracuse, Saratoga Springs, and moved on into Vermont and New Hampshire where he contacted many readers of his magazine. In Boston, Lynn, and Salem, Massachusetts, he addressed groups of the Christian churches. After meetings in Philadelphia and Baltimore, he reached home in September, having been absent ninety-four days, traveling two thousand miles, and delivering ninety-three discourses, "averaging one hour and twenty minutes each."

Having received an urgent call to visit the Southern states, he left Bethany, October 8, 1838, passing through Virginia and North and South Carolina, and visiting churches and brethren in Georgia, Alabama, Mississippi, and Louisiana. Toward the end of January, 1839, he left New Orleans and headed northward, stopping in Kentucky before landing in Bethany, March 28. Six months were engaged in this journey in which he averaged speaking once a day, baptizing many persons.

In June, 1840, Campbell's notes indicate he went to Charlottesville, Virginia, where he spoke at a general meeting of the churches. Fifty-six congregations were represented. The meetings lasted seven days, with most of the leading ministers of the state participating in the preaching services. It was here that Campbell formed his lasting friendship for Chester Bullard, bulwark of the cause in the state. This incident is typical of many short journeys for the strengthening of the churches. At other times he made short trips to raise funds for Bethany College, but they usually resolved themselves into evangelistic and teaching missions. On one of such journeys into Kentucky in 1842, he found the Lexington church erecting the largest meetinghouse in the state and the president and many of the leading professors in Transylvania University co-operating in the enterprise. In Madison, Lincoln, and Garrard counties, people were obeying the gospel by the hundreds. It was estimated that some forty thousand people were then enrolled in the churches of the state. Campbell's services were marked by many persons accepting Christ as Saviour.

134

After a trip through Virginia, Georgia, and North and South Carolina, in 1845, he embarked on a journey to the "far west." He visited St. Louis, where Jacob Creath was then ministering. The two then set out by stage-coach to Columbia for a state gathering of the churches. About 150 churches reported. After speaking there, Campbell filled engagements at Lexington, Booneville, Liberty, Fayette, and many other places. While in Hannibal, he visited the apartment where Barton W. Stone had died in November, 1844. He paid high tribute to the work of Stone as "the honored instrument of bringing many out of the ranks of human traditions, and putting into their hands the Book of books as their only confession of faith and rule of life." He purchased an oil painting of Stone and took it to Bethany, where it remained for many years in the parlor of his home. In Illinois, Campbell visited Winchester, Jacksonville, Springfield, Bloomington, and other cities, returning to St. Louis where he took passage on a boat for his home. On this journey he covered seven thousand miles, speaking in churches from Georgia to western Missouri.

Campbell had long desired to visit his native land, and in the spring of 1847, he acceded to the wishes of the churches in Great Britain and Ireland and addressed a series of meetings there. At Baltimore he was met by James Henshall, who accompanied him on the trip. They sailed from New York on May 4 on a voyage which took twenty-five days. Campbell spoke many times on the "good ship Siddons." Landing at Liverpool he was met by J. Davis, of Mollington, who represented the church. For several days he was entertained in Davis' home on the River Dee. When meetings began at Chester, large audiences greeted him in the building where Matthew Henry, the Bible commentator, had preached. At Wrexman in Wales he spoke to a group from which the churches in Wales developed. In Shrewsbury he formed the acquaintance of some Plymouth Brethren "of whom he formed a high opinion as a spiritually-minded and intelligent people." In Liverpool, Eaton Hall, Leicester, London, and other cities, he was greeted with splendid audiences that manifested great interest in the Restoration plea. After a brief sojourn in France, he came to Edinburgh, where he had anticipated meeting James Haldane, but Haldane was absent from the city. He engaged rooms for a series of lectures, but his plans had been anticipated by a group of rabid "Independents" and Congregationalists who had heard of his work in America. They formed an alliance with the "Scotch Antislavery Society" and filled the city with posters warning the populace against Campbell as one who had been a former slave holder and "is still a defender of manstealers." Great crowds attended his meetings where he attempted to explain his views on the slavery issue despite the confusion aroused by the Reverend Mr. James Robertson and his cohorts. Then followed most encouraging meetings in Aberdeen, Montrose, Dundee, Cupar, Auchtermuchty, Dumferline, Glasgow, Paisley, Kilmarnock, Ayr, and Irvine. As he was about to begin a series of lectures in Glasgow, the same group that had attempted to boycott his meetings in Edinburgh appeared with the police and served him a warrant to prevent him from leaving

Scotland, and notified him that the Reverend Mr. Robertson had entered a suit for slander against him for five thousand pounds. A series of legal actions ensued, resulting in Campbell's being thrown in jail. The brethren at Glasgow offered to protect him from this humiliation, but he insisted that he was not guilty of any of the charges made against him and that he would pursue due course of law until he was justified. Finally judgment was given against Robertson by Lord Murray, confirmed by all the lords in the "court of sessions," and the gentleman was condemned to pay court costs for both sides in the dispute. Although winning his point, Campbell was mentally and physically distressed. His voice was weakened and it was with difficulty that he addressed meetings in Ireland at Belfast, Dungannon, Cockestown, and Morse. At Rich Hill, where the Campbell family had spent so many delightful years, he addressed a congregation in the old Presbyterian meetinghouse where he had heard his father give his farewell sermon in April, 1807. Returning to Mollington in England, he rested before a co-operation meeting of Disciples at Chester, where the brethren presented him with elegant copies of the Polyglot Bible and a generous purse more than sufficient to pay his expenses. This largess he donated to Bethany College. At the close of the meeting he immersed two Wesleyan ministers from Wales, and Samuel Davies of Mollington. During this trip, Campbell and Henshall had the privilege to present $1,326.72 from the churches in America for the suffering poor of Ireland and Scotland. After a rough return sea voyage, they arrived in Boston, October 19, to learn of the death of Campbell's son, Wickliffe. While the journey had its trials and sorrows as well as its joys, it was eminently worthwhile, as it set alight lamps of restoration in the British Isles which have never gone out.

BIBLIOGRAPHY: Chapter 8

Cauble, C. W., *Disciples of Christ in Indiana*.
Cole, Clifford A., *The Christian Churches of Southern California*.
Davis, M. M., *How the Disciples Began and Grew*.
Fortune, Alonzo W., *The Disciples in Kentucky*.
Garrison, W. E., and Alfred T. DeGroot, *The Disciples of Christ: A History*.
Gates, Errett, *The Early Relation and Separation of Baptists and Disciples*.
Haley, T. P., *The Dawn of the Reformation in Missouri*.
Hall, Alex W., *The Christian Register*.
Harmon, M. F., *A History of Christian Churches in Mississippi*.
Hayden, A. S., *Early History of the Disciples in the Western Reserve, Ohio*.
Haynes, N. S., *History of the Disciples of Christ in Illinois*.
Hodge, Frederick A., *The Plea and the Pioneers in Virginia*.
Hudson, Charles R., *The Disciples in Southern California*.
Longan, G. W., *Origin of the Disciples of Christ*.
McPherson, Chalmers, *Disciples of Christ in Texas*.
Moseley, Joseph Edward, *Disciples of Christ in Georgia*.
Pekra, George L., *The Disciples of Christ in Missouri*.
Shaw, Henry K., *Buckeye Disciples*.
Swander, Clarence F., *Making Disciples in Oregon*.
Ware, Charles C., *North Carolina Disciples of Christ*.
Wilcox, Alanson, *A History of the Disciples of Christ in Ohio*.
Zimmerman, John D., *Sunflower Disciples, the Story of a Century*.

Chapter 9

Definitive Developments

IN the period from 1830 to 1860 the Restoration movement not only attained national proportions, but its message and its practices became more clearly defined.

Alexander Campbell, acknowledged as the most outstanding leader of the movement, was under constant fire. As the advocate of the "ancient order of things" and as the higher critic of the established denominations, he was forced to defend himself against their widely publicized charges that he was a heretic. The movement as a whole was nicknamed *Campbellite*, branded as denying "the proper divinity of our Lord and the scriptural doctrine of the atonement," and as rejecting "all the fundamental doctrines of the gospel."

In 1836 Campbell published *The Christian System,* in which he endeavored to set forth comprehensively, systematically, and constructively the doctrines he believed were taught in the New Testament. He thought that this would achieve two main purposes: (1) effectively answer his critics and (2) provide the Disciples with an intelligent grasp of the fundamentals of the Christian faith. In the Preface he said:

> Having paid a very candid and considerate regard to all that has been offered against these principles, as well as having been admonished from the extremes into which some of our friends and brethren have carried some points, I undertake this work with a deep sense of its necessity, and with much anticipation of its utility, in exhibiting a concentrated view of the whole ground we occupy, of rectifying some extremes, of furnishing new means of defence to those engaged in contending with this generation for primitive Christianity (pp. xiv, xv).

The work was divided into three major parts: (1) "the principles by which the Christian institution may be certainly and satisfactorily ascertained," (2) "the principles upon which all Christians may form one communion," and (3) "the elements or principles which constitute original Christianity."

Campbell disclaimed any *ex cathedra* omniscience and warned that the Bible alone revealed the Christian institution in its infallible perfection:

> The Christian institution has its facts, its precepts, its promises, its ordinances, and their meaning or doctrine. These are not matters of policy, of arrangement, or expediency, but of divine and immutable ordination and continuance. Hence the faith, the worship and the righteousness, or the doctrine, the piety, and the morality of the gospel institution, are not legitimate subjects of human legislation, alteration or arrangement. No man nor community can touch these and be innocent. These rest upon the wisdom and authority of Jehovah (p. 57).

Yet Campbell believed that the human intelligence demanded proper interpretation, discussion, and application of God's revelation. In this frame of reference, he and his father recognized the value of human creeds and frequently expressed their agreement with some of their statements of Christian doctrine. They also recognized the errors of man-made doctrines and utterly rejected them as infallible guides or tests of fellowship. *The Christian System* sought to state Christian doctrine in Biblical terms without human authority, private opinion, or theological speculation, and to contribute something of value to the dialogue of those who were committed to "the faith which was once delivered unto the saints."

The book began with a consideration of the universe, and Bible interpretation, and moved on to the nature of God and man, sin, the atonement, faith, repentance, baptism, conversion, the gift of the Holy Spirit, the Christian hope, the church, the ministry, and Christian discipline. In the section on Christian union, the Bible alone is shown to be the norm by which all doctrine, ordinances, polity, and piety are to be judged. Three lengthy treatises on the kingdom of heaven, remission of sins, and regeneration are included, because these seemed to be the areas in which discussion was most crucial.

Campbell's enemies immediately hailed *The Christian System* as "the Campbellite creed," but his friends, and the Restoration movement as a whole, received it for what he intended it to be—a statement of his own views. It was never a very popular book. The churches seldom mentioned it and certainly required no one to accept it, or even read it. The preachers welcomed it as a help, but often disagreed in public with some of its statements. Today it is practically unknown. In 1830-1860 it quite well represented the body of opinion held by the movement, and is still helpful as a book of reference.

The Christian System did not, however, allay the criticism that Campbell was a heretic. Although he usually ignored criticism, he was always willing to make a forthright statement when sincere people asked him what he believed about the fundamentals of the Christian faith. In 1846 he set forth the following articles in answer to an inquiry:

> 1. I believe all Scripture is given by inspiration of God, is profitable for teaching, conviction, instruction in righteousness, that the man of God may be perfect and thoroughly accomplished for every good work.

2. I believe in one God as manifested in the Father, the Son and the Holy Spirit, who are therefore one in power, nature and volition.

3. I believe that every human being participates in all the consequences of the fall of Adam, and is born into the world frail and depraved in all his moral powers and capacities. So that without faith in Christ it is impossible for him, while in that state, to please God.

4. I believe the Word which from the beginning was with God, and which was God, became flesh and dwelt among us as Emmanuel, or "God manifest in the flesh," and did make an expiation of sins by the sacrifice of himself, which no being could have done that was not possessed of superhuman, superangelic and divine nature.

5. I believe in the justification of sinners by faith without the deeds of the law; and of a Christian, not by faith alone, but by the obedience of faith.

6. I believe in the operation of the Holy Spirit through the Word, but not without it in the conversion and sanctification of the sinner . . .

7. I believe in the right and duty of exercising our own judgment in the interpretation of the Holy Scriptures.

8. I believe in the divine institution of the evangelical ministry, the authority and perpetuity of baptism and the Lord's Supper.

Campbell believed in a vertebrate Christianity that stood for a body of New Testament doctrine. He opposed statements of faith only as they opposed the unity of the church by "containing human opinions not expressly revealed in the Word of God" and as they were imposed as tests of fellowship in the churches.

In this connection, his approval of the World Evangelical Alliance may be understood. Several articles in favor of it appeared in the *Millennial Harbinger* in 1846. The Alliance was an interdenominational body formed in Britain at a time when Roman Catholicism was enjoying a new ascendancy (evident in the Oxford Movement and the defection of Newman and Manning from the Church of England), and when religious intolerance in Estonia, Latvia, Lithuania, Turkey, Persia, Spain, and Portugal had resulted in imprisonment and death to many Protestants. There was a universal demand for some sort of united action to oppose these threats and offer a channel for the future co-operation of all Protestants in matters of common concern. In the United States, Protestants were becoming increasingly aware of an extreme fragmentation that had militated against the evangelization of the masses and rendered them almost impotent in the face of Romanism's rising power. Theologically there were the basic differences of Calvinism, Arminianism, and Lutheranism. Organizationally, there were such varied polities as congregationalism, presbyterianism, and the episcopacy. Differences in languages, race, nationality, provincialism, confessions, and traditions were being emphasized to the detriment of the church universal. Politics, pride, selfishness, personal ambition, fanaticism, bigotry, and intolerance were all playing their part in what tended to become a public scandal in the name of Christ. Men of Christian spirit on both sides of the Atlantic who had upon their hearts the best interests of the cause of Christ and the accomplishment of the ultimate purposes of the kingdom of God saw the Alliance as a method of unitedly meeting the issues of the times.

Protestants from all parts of the world gathered in London in August, 1846, and unanimously adopted the following resolution:

That the members of this Conference are deeply convinced of the desirableness of forming a confederation, on the basis of the great evangelical principles held in common by them, which may afford an opportunity to the members of the church of Christ of cultivating brotherly love, enjoying Christian intercourse, and promoting such objects as they may hereafter agree to prosecute together; and they hereby form such a confederation, under the name of The Evangelical Alliance (*Millennial Harbinger*, 1846, p. 627).

A constitution was adopted with a rather lengthy set of doctrinal principles which were believed essential to co-operation. The first two of these principles were: (1) the divine inspiration, authority, and sufficiency of the Holy Scriptures; and (2) the right and the duty of private judgment in the interpretation of the Scriptures. In other matters there was expressed a synthesis of prevailing orthodox creeds with the Apostles' Creed as a standard.

Campbell did not endorse everything in the constitution. He noted that the Alliance was not a church and had a right to state doctrinal terms or fellowship for its peculiar purposes. His chief reason for approving it is stated in the following significant paragraph:

I thank God and take courage from every effort, however imperfect it may be, to open the eyes of the community to the impotency and wickedness of schism, and to impress upon the conscientious and benevolent portion of the Christian profession the excellency, the beauty, and the importance of union and co-operation in the cause of Christ, as prerequisite to the diffusion of Christianity throughout the nations of the earth (*Millennial Harbinger*, 1847, p. 253).

In another statement, Campbell thanked God for the Alliance and declared that he would "co-operate with [it] just as far and as long as they please to permit me" (p. 255). His irenic spirit was further expressed in another article referring to the Alliance when he said:

The signs of the times are, in some respects, more auspicious now than in any former period in the memory of the living generation. When, before, since the great apostasy, did the world, European and American, hold a convention for the furtherance of union among Christians, and for the purpose of forming an alliance in favour of catholic truth against sectarian heresies and error? When did the heathen world before ever stretch out its hands to Christendom, imploring them to come over and help them to extricate themselves from the snares and toils of Paganism? The world without the Christian profession, and the world within it, are alike discontent with themselves and their condition and are alike calling for help. Ought we not, then, to be more earnest, more sanguine and more laborious than ever before in the furtherance of the Gospel, and in the maintenance of our truly enviable position?

Campbell's optimism about the World Evangelical Alliance and his championship of basic Protestant principles did not, however, cause him

140

to weaken his strictly Biblical position nor deflect him from his purpose to restore the New Testament church in his day and time.

During 1836, Campbell rendered a great service to Protestantism in taking strong exceptions to Roman Catholicism. Bishop (later Archbishop) John B. Purcell, of Cincinnati, had openly objected to an address before the College of Teachers in that city in which Campbell had connected the rapid march of modern progress with the spirit of inquiry produced by the Protestant Reformation. Many Protestants in Cincinnati petitioned Campbell to challenge the bishop to a debate on the Roman Catholic religion. Finally a discussion was arranged, one of the very few in history between a responsible member of the Roman hierarchy and a Protestant minister.

Seven propositions were arranged:

> (1) The Roman Catholic institution is not now or never was catholic, apostolic or holy, but is a sect; (2) her notion of apostolic succession is without any foundation in the Bible; (3) she is not uniform in her faith, or united in her members; but mutable and fallible, as any other sect; (4) she is the Babylon of John's Revelation; (5) her notions of purgatory, indulgences, auricular confession, remission of sins, transubstantiation, supererogation, etc., . . . are immoral in tendency and injurious to . . . society; (6) despite her pretensions of having given us the Bible, we are independent of her in knowledge and evidences of that book; (7) Romanism . . . is essentially anti-American, being opposed to the genius of all free institutions, and positively subversive of them . . .

Despite all the political and social pressures brought against Campbell during the discussions, he acquitted himself with honor. The whole city and the three adjoining states were aroused with a high degree of excitement. Charges and countercharges filled the air. At the close of the discussion a great mass meeting of citizens, led by the celebrated Lyman Beecher, adopted resolutions of appreciation of Campbell's work and requested that the debate be published. The book had a tremendous sale and had a powerful effect in exposing to the nation the false pretenses and dangerous tendencies of the Roman system. For many years it remained the standard non-Catholic work on Romanism.

The debate with Bishop Purcell served to awaken a considerable degree of sympathy and good will toward Campbell, since Protestants in general were made to realize that the man they had mistaken for a foe was in reality a defender of the great truths and doctrines they cherished in common. In many areas, both the clergy and the laity began to recognize the Christians, or Disciples of Christ, as strange but essentially orthodox members of the Christian community.

The Presbyterians in Kentucky, having suffered stinging defeats in Campbell's debates with Walker and McCalla and having lost large numbers of members to the Christian churches, were determined that another discussion was imperative if their status was to be maintained as a major denomination in the area. Accordingly, they approached Campbell with a set of propositions for discussion and designated the Reverend

Mr. N. L. Rice, of Paris, as their representative. A statement of the issues was finally agreed upon as follows:

(1) The immersion in water of a proper subject into the name of the Father, the Son and the Holy Spirit is the one and only apostolic or Christian baptism. Campbell affirms. (2) The infant of a believing parent is a scriptural subject of baptism. Rice affirms. (3) Christian baptism is for the remission of past sins. Campbell affirms. (4) Baptism is to be administered only by a bishop or an ordained presbyter. Rice affirms. (5) In conversion and sanctification, the Spirit of God operates on persons only through the Word of truth. Campbell affirms. (6) Human creeds, as bonds of union and communion, are necessarily heretical and schismatical. Campbell affirms.

The affair immediately assumed the proportions of a grand church council. Judge Robertson was chosen by Rice as his moderator. Colonel Speed Smith was Campbell's choice. The two selected the Honorable Henry Clay as president. The largest auditorium in Lexington, Kentucky, was chosen as the location.

Campbell, dealing with the first proposition in fine Christian spirit, showed exceptional skill in stating comprehensive views and broad fundamental truths, coupled with scholarly research and the establishment of general laws of translation and interpretation. Rice, on the other hand, manifested a prejudiced and hostile spirit and dealt with the subject by raising small, critical exceptions and technicalities. In this he displayed a cleverness which often won his audience and caused some to believe that he had the advantage of his opponent.

Two-thirds of the printed debate is concerned with the subject of baptism and makes a tremendously convincing case for the immersion of the penitent believer. Four of the six propositions were in this field. The place of the ordinances in the church and their proper Scriptural observance were shown to be essential to Christian unity.

In Proposition 5, Campbell inveighed against popular "camp-meeting Christianity" and regeneration by the Holy Spirit without the clear teaching of the Word of God. His contention that "the Holy Spirit in conversion and sanctification operates only through the Word" was so well reasoned that it is said Henry Clay, carried away with the argument, leaned forward in his chair and began to nod assent, waving his hand toward Campbell in the graceful and approving manner which was peculiar to him. Finally he recovered himself, drawing back and looking to see whether any one had noticed that he was off his guard. A high dignitary in the Episcopal church, writing soon after in the *Protestant Churchman,* said that this portion of Campbell's address "is one of the most splendid specimens of logical and eloquent reasoning" he had ever read. This Episcopalian went on to say that "Rice is wholly incapable of this sort of thing. His imagination is as barren as the surface of granite."

In Proposition 6, Campbell stated the case for Christian union in such a manner that the debate was given a permanent and lasting significance for the Christian church. In dealing with the elaborate creeds of the Protestant churches, he inveighed against "intellectual opinions and dogmas," called for a return to the Bible, and emphasized the centrality of Christ in the Christian system. Said Campbell: "It is not the object of our efforts to make men think alike on a thousand themes. Let them think as they like on any matters of human opinion and upon 'doctrines of religion,' provided only they hold the Head, Christ, and keep his commandments."

Campbell made it clear that this obedience to Christ involved obedience to the revelation of His will in the Holy Scriptures:

We regard the Lord Jesus Christ as King, Lord, Lawgiver and Prophet of the church, and well qualified by the power of the Holy Spirit, to give us all a perfect volume—one in substance and form exactly adapted as he would have it for just such a family as the great family of man; we believe the Lord Jesus was wiser and more benevolent than all his followers in their united wisdom and benevolence, and that he could and would give them such a book as they needed. It is both the light of salvation and the bond of union among the saved. We abjure creeds simply as substitutes—directly or indirectly, substitutes—for the book of inspiration. In other respects we have no objection to any people publishing their tenets and views or practices to the world. I have no more objection to writing my opinions than to speaking them. But mark it well, it is the making of such compends of views, in the ecclesiastic sense, *Creeds* (that is, terms of communion and bonds of union) that we abjure. . . .

Christianity is a liberal institution . . . Surely, then, that ought to be a large house, on a broad foundation, that has in it a table for saved men from every nation under heaven . . . We receive men of all denominations under heaven, of all sects and parties, who will make the good confession on which Jesus Christ builded his church . . . On a sincere confession of this faith we immerse all persons, and then present them with God's own book as their book of faith, piety and morality.

This was Campbell's last major debate. From this time forward, he gave himself to what he believed were more constructive concerns. The Campbell-Rice discussion became a major work of reference—a clear delineation of the great, basic, broad principles of the reform movement. At first the Presbyterians claimed they had won the battle, overlooking the fact that when Campbell spoke he baptized great numbers, including a Lutheran minister of the city. J. H. Brown, a Presbyterian, in his enthusiasm purchased the copyright of the printed debate for $2,000 and circulated it assiduously. Soon it became apparent, however, that readers were leaving the Presbyterian church or at least requesting their pastors for immersion. Mr. Brown soon sold his rights to C. D. Roberts, of the Christian church at Jacksonville, Illinois, who printed and circulated the debate in large quantities for many years.

Campbell and Stone early saw the necessity of education in the life of the movement. In the preface of the *Harbinger* of 1840 Campbell wrote:

The cause of education becomes a more and more interesting object in the pursuance of this plan. We must begin at the nursery. We must have family, school, college, and church education, adapted to the entire physical, intellectual, moral and religious constitution of man. Of these the first in time, place, and importance, is the domestic and family training. We have been dreaming for ages, and are only just now awakening to the importance of education—not merely to its importance, but to the *rationale*—the philosophy of the thing called Education.

To this subject, as essentially connected with the speed and progress of the current reformation, a more full and marked attention should be paid. An uneducated person is not competent to the full display of Christian excellence—to the full manifestation of Christian character. No person is well educated—is properly taught or trained, that is not a Christian (p. 4).

Campbell had come from a home which gave much attention to Christian culture; and, realizing the importance of family training, he wrote a series of articles, under the title "Conversations at the Carlton House," to promote family education. His interest in education did not end here. He was already dreaming about founding a college at Bethany.

In the autumn of 1836, Bacon College, the first institution for higher education under Christian church auspices, was established at Georgetown, Kentucky. The principal promoter of the project was John T. Johnson, then editor of the *Christian*. He was ably seconded in his plans by B. W. Stone, editor of the *Christian Messenger*. They chose Walter Scott to be president pro tem and opened sessions in meager quarters with a limited faculty. The college was patterned after traditional liberal-arts institutions. In 1840, the brethren at Harrodsburg promised more generous support if Bacon were moved there. Coincidental with the move, James Shannon was elected president; Samuel Hatch, professor of natural science; Samuel H. Mullins, professor of ancient languages; Henry H. White, professor of mathematics and civil engineering; and George Matthews, principal of the elementary school. About one hundred students were enrolled.

President Shannon, who later became president of the University of Missouri, was a highly educated man of strong character. A graduate of the Royal Institution of Belfast, Ireland, he had received highest honors in Latin, Greek, and all the liberal arts. In 1821, he became principal of Sunbury Academy in Georgia, and after serving with distinction, was made a full professor in the Theological Baptist Institution at Newton, Massachusetts. In 1830 he was appointed professor of ancient languages in the University of Georgia, and in 1836, became president of Louisiana State College, at Jackson. It was while he was in Jackson that he met Alexander Campbell and became a warm supporter of the reformation.

Bacon College had a checkered career. It closed its doors in 1850, but one of its graduates would not let it die. John B. Bowman reopened it in Harrodsburg in 1857 under the name Kentucky University and secured a permanent endowment of $200,000 for the institution. Transylvania University at nearby Lexington, the oldest institution of higher learning west of the Alleghenies, was on the verge of closing. In 1865 Bowman engineered a merger of the two universities. Transylvania had been successively under the control of the Presbyterians, the Episcopalians, the Baptists, and the Methodists. It now became a Christian church institution of great distinction with a large endowment and an impressive campus. Robert Milligan was chosen as president. Its influence on the life of Kentucky and the nation is a matter of history.

144

It remained, however, for Alexander Campbell to develop a distinctively Christian type of higher education, which was later to characterize the colleges of the reformation. Dr. Richardson, in his *Memoirs,* gives an impressive digest of Campbell's concept of the rationale of Christian higher education:

> In the College, he proposed a liberal course of studies, giving somewhat more prominence than usual to the physical sciences, and contemplating the most liberal provisions for thorough instruction, so as to prepare young men to enter upon the study of the learned professions. In this department, however, . . . moral and religious training was to form a principal feature and the Bible was to be made one of the regular text-books, so that no one could receive the honors of the institution without being thoroughly acquainted with the Sacred Oracles, which were to be taught regularly every day—not with the design of evolving from them any system of doctrines, but for the purpose of familiarizing the mind with Bible facts and institutions (vol. 2, p. 464).

Campbell conceived of the Bible as the basis of all moral culture. He felt "the relations of the great principles taught in the Bible to human rights and political and social freedom" were being ignored by the educators of his time. "No one had assigned to it its proper position in respect to moral science, which had, as yet, found no better foundation than philosophy, and the study of [that] had been postponed to the latest period" in the curriculum. The Bible, in Campbell's thinking, was the center around which any true Christian college must be constructed, with its sacred truths accepted as the normative and modifying standard for the entire educational operation.

In his early fifties, he accordingly announced his plans to establish a college at Bethany, and promised to devote a major portion of his time to the project. Indeed, he determined to invest thousands of dollars of his own money in the school, provided the brethren would support it generously with their prayers, their money, and their children. During the winter of 1840, a charter was granted in the name of Bethany College. Mr. Campbell was elected president and was requested by the board of trustees to prepare the curriculum. Buildings were constructed on land donated by Campbell, and the collegiate department opened for the reception of students on October 21, 1841. The faculty consisted of A. F. Ross, professor of ancient languages and ancient history; Charles Stewart, professor of algebra and general mathematics; Robert Richardson, professor of chemistry, geology, and the kindred sciences; W. K. Pendleton, professor of natural philosophy; the chair of English literature remained to be filled. Alexander Campbell himself became professor of mental philosophy, evidences of Christianity, moral and political economy.

It was a small beginning, but with the leadership of Campbell, Bethany almost immediately became a great power for good in the whole brotherhood. His morning lectures on the Bible soon became famous. He began the sessions each year with Genesis and closed with lectures on the New Testament. These lectures were not particularly critical or exegetical, but rather discursive, highlighting the great moral and religious principles which he considered essential to the building of Christian character. They broke through the conventionalities of most college curricula, going to the very center of life and making a tremendous impact on the lives of the students. There were twenty classes a day, the first beginning at 6:30 in the morning and the last continuing to 4:30 in the afternoon. About one hundred fifty students were enrolled. At the first college commencement, July 4, 1843, more than fifteen hundred persons were present.

Soon a steady stream of well-equipped ministers of the gospel was flowing out to give leadership to the churches from coast to coast. These men reflected a methodology in preaching that was peculiar to Bethany. They carried their Bibles with them and their great familiarity with the passages pertaining to salvation and the pattern of the New Testament church amazed their listeners. The gospel which they preached was characterized by simplicity. All abstruse and metaphysical theology was put aside, and "Christ and him crucified" was exalted in every sermon. To believe in Christ as the Son of the living God and to obey His commands were all that were necessary, on the human side, to make Christians and to keep them in the pathway of everlasting life. Every statement made was bolstered by passages of Scripture. If a "thus saith the Lord" could not be produced for the preacher's teaching, it was forthwith rejected by the elders and the people who came to the services with their Bibles and "thumbed the references" to "see if these things were so." People from the community marveled, and said, "We never heard so much Scripture in sermons anywhere." Along with the message was an inevitable appeal for the unity of all Christians on the Bible alone.

It was an entirely new idea to build a college with the Bible as its chief textbook and to emphasize its teaching as more important than the teaching of all the other books in the world. Thus at Bethany was born the idea that created a whole family of Bible schools, colleges, and "Bible chairs" distinctively characteristic of the early work of higher education among the Christian churches.

Other colleges were established in several places by men of varying talents. The frontier was lacking in proper means of higher education, and ministers often took the leadership in local community efforts to establish academies and colleges. Some of these institutions died, but others lived to become the precursors of schools of some standing. Franklin College was opened by Tolbert Fanning near Nashville, Tennessee, in 1837, but was one of the casualties of the Civil War. Kentucky Female Orphan School was organized at Midway in 1849, and has survived as Midway Junior College for girls. Western Reserve Eclectic Institute founded in 1850 later became Hiram College at Hiram, Ohio. Fairview Academy (1843) became the nucleus of Butler University, Indianapolis, Indiana. Walnut Grove Academy (1848) and Abingdon College (1854) were antecedent to Eureka College, Eureka, Illinois. Arkansas College, founded in 1852, was a casualty of the Civil War, but is credited as being responsible for the establishment of the state university at Fayetteville. Camden Point Female Academy (1848) later became Missouri Christian College and survived for eighty-one years. Christian College, a school for girls, was established at Columbia, Missouri, in 1852. Christian University (now Culver-Stockton College) was chartered in 1853 and opened in 1855 at Canton, Missouri. Chapman College, at Los Angeles, California, was first chartered as Hesperian College in 1860. Oskaloosa College, predecessor of Drake University, was opened at Oskaloosa, Iowa, in 1861. Scores of others of varying longevity might be mentioned. Despite the fact that they soon passed into oblivion, they left a heritage of substantial accomplishment in individual lives and in their communities.

W. T. Moore, in his *Comprehensive History of the Disciples of Christ,* whimsically said that "the Disciples do not have bishops: they have editors." From their beginning their thinking and works were pretty largely determined by what they read in the columns of their periodicals. Alexander Campbell in *The Christian Baptist* and the *Millennial Harbinger;* Barton W. Stone in the *Christian Messenger;* and Walter Scott and John T. Johnson in *The Christian* were the oracles to which the brethren listened with respect, but these were by no means the only influences in the field of Restoration journalism. The *Herald of Gospel Liberty,* the world's first religious newspaper, was founded in 1808. Edited by Elias Smith, this paper was the organ of the New England Christians whom Alexander Campbell branded as Unitarians and who finally failed to join with their western friends in the union initiated at Lexington. Alexander Hall began to publish the *Gospel Proclamation* in 1847. It later joined with Benjamin Franklin's *Western Reformer,* to become the *Proclamation and Reformer* in 1850. Other papers that were born and soon died were: *The Northern Reformer, Heretic Detector and Evangelical Review* edited by Arthur Crihfield (1837-1842); *Apostolic Advocate,* John Thomas (1834-39); *Christian Panoplist,* B. F. Hall and John T. Johnson (1837); *Christian Preacher,* D. S. Burnet (1836-40); *Christian Publisher,* J. Henshall (1839); *The Disciple,* Alexander Graham, J. A. Butler, and J. H. Curtis (1836); *Christian Reformer,* J. R. Howard (1836); *Christian Review,* Tolbert Fanning (1844-48); *Morning Watch,* J. M. Barnes and C. F. R. Shelburne (1837-40); *Christian Age,* T. J. Mellish and others (1845-53).

The *Christian Age* became an object of some controversy. There was mild agitation for "one [publication] society of the brotherhood at large." Benjamin Franklin led the movement. The Cincinnati Christian Tract Society, created in 1846, was the first step toward the goal. In 1851 it became the American Christian Publication Society, and in 1853 purchased the *Christian Age* with the intention of making it the one great voice of the movement. The financing of the proposition through a $40,000 stock company came upon evil days, and Alexander Campbell's *Millennial Harbinger,* the unquestioned leader in the publications field, turned its guns on the *Age.* The dangers of the A.C.P.S. to the freedom of the churches was masterfully presented by W. K. Pendleton, associate editor of the *Harbinger,* and the proposal died, not to be revived until the twentieth century was well advanced.

The idea of organized co-operation on state and national levels was now much in the minds of leaders in the new reformation. In 1845, D. S. Burnet, of Cincinnati, led in the organization of the American Christian Bible Society "to aid in the distribution of the Sacred Scriptures, without note or comment, among all nations." It was opposed by certain reactionary elements on the ground that it was a society and not a church. Campbell was lukewarm about the idea because he felt that similar work was being carried on effectively by other religious groups, but he did not oppose the Society. All its officers and members were his friends and he hoped that their labors would be crowned with success. The A.C.B.S. never amounted to much, but it spearheaded a movement for organized co-operation on a larger scale.

Charles Louis Loos, commenting on this new development, said:

> It was urged on all sides, and by our wisest men, that it was of great importance that a closer acquaintance and fellowship of mind, heart and hand should now be established among us, because of the increasing number and the widespread extent of our people. But furthermore also because we are beginning to awaken to the duty of executing the command of our King to carry the gospel to all parts of the world.

Alexander Hall urged that a general convention be held in the autumn of 1849. He suggested that Cincinnati be the place and that Alexander Campbell be the convener and set the date. Finally the A.C.B.S. acted and called all the brethren to come to Cincinnati on October 23 of that year to discuss the proposal.

Immediately a hue and cry went up demanding specific New Testament authority for the move. Campbell gave answer:

> To ask for a positive precept for everything in the details of duties growing out of the various exigencies of the Christian church and the world, would be quite as irrational and unscriptural as to ask for an immutable wardrobe or a uniform standard of apparel for all persons and ages in the Christian Church. . . . In all things pertaining to public interest, not of Christian faith, piety or morality, the church of Jesus Christ in its aggregate character is left free and unshackled by any apostolic authority. This is the great point which I assert as of capital importance in any great convention movement or cooperation in advancing the public interests of a common salvation.

Despite a plague of cholera, more than one hundred brethren from one hundred churches and eleven states gathered in Cincinnati, October 23-28. The meeting was held in the Christian church at the corner of Fourth and Walnut Streets. Alexander Campbell, although absent, was elected president; Walter Scott, D. S. Burnet, John O'Kane, John T. Johnson, W. K. Pendleton, Tolbert Fanning, and fourteen other brethren were elected vice presidents. James Challen was made corresponding secretary and Archibald Trowbridge treasurer. The name *General Convention of the Christian Churches of the United States of America* was chosen on the first day, but before the meeting had adjourned it became clear that this was too pretentious a title to suit the brethren. They were determined that the convention was not to be *the official organization* of the churches or an ecclesiastical tribunal with any power whatsoever over the churches. They turned down the idea that it should be composed of delegates officially representing the churches. Every person who had come was voted a delegate. It was made clear that this was a voluntary mass meeting of interested brethren and that their actions and resolutions were only advisory in character. When someone proposed "that this convention recommend to our churches not to countenance as a preacher any man who is not sustained or acknowledged by two or more churches," Walter Scott immediately arose and said, "I never feel so much like being angry, as when I am compelled to sit in the pulpit with a man of doubtful character. I feel degraded by the contact." Others expressed similar opinions, but the resolution was killed. In fact, all efforts to have the convention hand down directives, or strong expressions of general opinion, were lost on the assumption that disputatious issues were only causes for division.

As the sessions progressed, it became evident that the real reason the delegates had come together was to discover ways and means of developing a foreign missionary enterprise. One reporter of the proceedings said, "It might without serious inaccuracy be said that the missionary society was organized to send Dr. Barclay to Jerusalem."

Dr. J. T. Barclay was a graduate in medicine from the University of Pennsylvania and received his classical education in the University of Virginia. He desired to become a missionary, and following the Acts account of missions "beginning at Jerusalem," he believed that a Bible people should undertake their first mission work in the Holy City. The assembly was so stirred by this thought that, in a dramatic moment, $2,550 was made available to send Dr. Barclay as the first foreign missionary of the Christian churches. This incident, coupled with the trends of the discussions concerning the character of the organization, determined the name finally chosen—*The American Christian Missionary Society. American* indicated the supporting field and *Missionary,* the purpose of the organization. Dr. Barclay was formally appointed June 11, 1850, "to engage in teaching, preaching and the practice of medicine among the Jews at Jerusalem." He sailed from New York on September 11, and arrived in Jerusalem, February 7, 1851. The mission was quite barren of results and closed, but the brethren had made an important move toward the fulfillment of the great commission to go into all the world and make disciples.

The resolutions adopted at Cincinnati covered a wide range of subjects, but were of such a mild and apologetic tone as to be of meager effect. They included suggestions for the inauguration of state and regional missionary societies, care in the ordination of ministers, the organization of Sunday schools, proper observance of the Lord's Day, and the necessity of personal piety and devotion.

An annual meeting for the A.C.M.S. was set for the Wednesday after the third Lord's Day in October at Cincinnati, "or at such time and place as shall have been designated by a previous annual meeting."

Campbell greatly rejoiced at the results of the Cincinnati meeting and wrote a lengthy commendatory editorial in the December, 1849, *Harbinger.* Among other things he said:

> Our expectations from the Convention have more than been realized. We are much pleased with the result, and regard it as a very happy pledge of good times to come. The unanimity, cordiality, and generous concurrence of the brethren in all the important subjects before them, was worthy of themselves and the great cause in which they are all enlisted (p. 694).

He rejoiced in the approval of the American Christian Bible Society and without exception expressed agreement with every item in the report of the resolutions committee.

There was, however, far from unanimous approval of the convention in the brotherhood at large. Jacob Creath, Jr., and others objected on principle to the formation of any society of churches or individuals designed to do work that local churches should do. It was strongly asserted that the Scriptures contained no precept or example that would authorize the organization of a missionary society. Creath proposed that a "general meeting" be held in May or June, 1850, to consider whether "conventions and missionary or Bible societies" were Scriptural or in any Christian sense legitimate. The elders of the church at Connellsville, Pennsylvania, protested that "the church is the only missionary society and can admit no rivals." Using the dictum of Thomas Campbell, "Where the Scriptures speak we speak, and where the Scriptures are silent we are silent," the critics of the Society gave it literal and rigid application and called for the dissolution of the organization in the interests of a pure church.

The A.C.B.S. and the A.C.M.S. withstood the attacks and enjoyed a season of unusual prosperity, but the "cloud on the horizon" that was no larger than a man's hand grew with the ensuing years and was destined not only to hinder the cause of missions but to foster disunity and open division in the Restoration movement at home and abroad.

By 1860, the movement had a clearly defined testimony, which it was declaring effectively, to the religious world. It was riding the wave of westward expansion and seemed destined to grow phenomenally for years.

BIBLIOGRAPHY: Chapter 9

Campbell, Alexander, *The Christian System.*
Campbell, Alexander, and John B. Purcell, *Debate on the Roman Catholic Religion.*
Campbell, Alexander, and N. L. Rice, *A Debate on the Action, Subject, Design and Administrator of Christian Baptism.*
Campbell, Alexander, editor, *Millennial Harbinger* (1840-1846).
Ewing, J. W., *Goodly Fellowship, the Centenary Record and History of the Alliance.*
Garrison, W. E., *An American Religious Movement.*
Hayden, W. L., *Church Polity.*
Keith, Noel, *The Story of D. S. Burnet.*
Lewis, Grant K., *The American Christian Missionary Society.*
Lowber, J. W., *The Who and the What of the Disciples of Christ.*
Moore, W. T., *Comprehensive History of Disciples of Christ.*
Peter, Robert, *Transylvania University: Its Origin, Rise, Decline and Fall.*
Richardson, Robert, *Memoirs of Alexander Campbell.*

Chapter 10

The Civil War and
Growing Tensions

BY 1860, Negro slavery had become a national issue of major importance. The United States were divided into "slave states" and "free states." The slave states were largely in the South, the free states in the North. There was a growing sentiment in the South for the right of the states to deal with their own domestic affairs and to secede from the Union, if necessary, to preserve an institution they considered vital to their prosperity. Newly elected President Abraham Lincoln, of Illinois, came from a Christian church home. Opposed to slavery he was elected on a platform for "the preservation of the Union."

Shortly after the election, South Carolina seceded from the Union. By February, 1861, Mississippi, Florida, Georgia, Louisiana, and Texas withdrew. On February 4, a new federal government, for the Confederate States of America, was set up at Montgomery, Alabama, with Jefferson Davis, a graduate of Transylvania University, as president. In April, Confederate guns fired on the Union's Fort Sumpter off the Carolina coast. A few days later Lincoln called out the northern militia and one of the bloodiest civil wars in history was on.

Such a violent social and political conflict was certain to affect the churches. Methodist and Baptist denominations had divided over the slavery issue sixteen years before the war. In 1857 the "New School" Presbyterians divided, followed closely by the "Old School" in 1861. The Protestant Episcopal church of the South seceded from the northern church in 1861, although the division was never recognized by the General Conference. The Free Will Baptists, the Christian Connection, and practically every other Protestant denomination in America were sundered in bitterness and hate.

The Christian churches were the only major Protestant body having sizeable numbers of constituency in both the North and the South that did not divide. The tensions were strong, but there were a number of factors which kept the brotherhood together. They were, first of all, a unity movement which recognized that Christians were one in Christ and not in

151

a denomination. In a hostile denominational world they had been closely knit together in the one faith. Long ago they had decided that matters of opinion beyond the clear teaching of the Bible should not divide Christians. Slavery was considered a matter of opinion, of ethics, but not of faith. Their slogan, "In faith, unity; in opinions, liberty; in all things, charity," took on greater significance in the crisis. Many of the early leaders were pacifists. Events surrounding the unpopular Mexican War had been largely responsible for this widely held view. There was no authoritative body above the local congregation that could legislate on the slavery issue. Occasionally the issue threatened to divide local churches, and did in some remote instances, but the brotherhood at large was preserved. Another factor was the location of Christian church strength in the nation. They were not strong in the so-called "deep South." They were almost without representation in abolitionist New England. It has been estimated that of the 2,068 churches, 827 were in the slave states and 1,241 were in free states.

Alexander Campbell, as might be expected, wielded a tremendous influence in shaping the thinking of the brethren. He was a large land-holder in Virginia. At one time he owned slaves, but had freed them. Selina Campbell, in *Home Life and Reminiscences of Alexander Campbell,* says that shortly before their marriage, Campbell "had purchased . . . two brothers, men without family, James and Charley Pool, from a Methodist preacher in the neighborhood. They were about eighteen and twenty years of age, respectively, and he promised them their freedom when they should arrive at the age of twenty-eight. This he gave them." Two other Negroes, Mary and Ben, whom he inherited from the Brown estate, had been freed and aided in securing modest homes of their own.

In the *Millennial Harbinger,* 1845, he wrote:

> We are the only religious community in the civilized world whose principles . . . can preserve us from [division]. It may be . . . lawful and expedient to form an Abolition, or a Liberty, or a Pro-Slavery party . . . But . . . Christian union and communion are not in the least to be affected by such parties, any more than by other political denominations. . . .
>
> To preserve unity of spirit among Christians of the South and of the North is my grand object, and for that purpose I am endeavoring to show that the New Testament does not authorize any interference or legislation upon the relation of master and slave, nor does it either in letter or spirit authorize Christians to make it a term of communion (pp. 51, 194, 195).

Benjamin Franklin, of the *American Christian Review,* an influential journal of the times, championed the same view. Of all the papers circulating in the movement, only one—John Boggs' *Northwestern Christian Magazine*—was openly abolitionist. The New Testament book of Philemon was frequently referred to by church leaders as setting forth the principles which should motivate Christian thinking on the slavery issue.

Individual Disciples of Christ reacted to the controversy and the war as everybody else in the nation. The eldest son of Alexander Campbell wore the gray of the Confederate cavalry. Dr. W. H. Hopson, whose church at Lexington, Kentucky, almost divided over slavery, became a chaplain with General Morgan's troops. T. W. Caskey, of Texas, carried a double-cylinder, sixteen-shooter revolver and a Colt rifle and was known as the "fighting parson." Dr. B. F. Hall was a chaplain with the company commanded by Barton W. Stone, Jr. In the North, Isaac Errett, strongly antislavery, urged support of the war and himself obtained a chaplain's commission in the Union army. J. W. Errett, his brother, became a major. James A. Garfield, at first a pacifist, offered his service to the Union and came out of the war a general. The Forty-second Ohio Regiment, which Garfield commanded, was said to have been composed almost entirely of Disciples. He made recruiting speeches on the steps of many Christian churches in the Western Reserve, where abolition sentiment was high. J. Harrison Jones, a noted Christian minister, was chaplain of the regiment. Some two hundred fifty Hiram College students served in Union armies. It is said that W. T. Moore, later author of *A Comprehensive History of the Disciples of Christ,* persuaded four out of five undecided state representatives who were members of his church in Frankfort, to vote for Kentucky's loyalty to the Union, thus breaking a deadlock in the Legislature. Lincoln's Christian preacher friend, Edward Dickinson Baker, senator from Oregon and a colonel in the Union army, lost his life in the battle of Ball's Bluff, Virginia.

J. W. McGarvey exemplified the strong pacifist sentiment in the brotherhood. He vigorously opposed the participation of Christians in armed conflict and refused to take sides in the war. It is interesting to note that he began his famed *Commentary on Acts* in 1860, while he was still in Missouri, and completed it in Kentucky in 1863. While almost everyone around him was worked up to white heat about the war, he calmly devoted his talents to the problems of exegesis. Twice he was interrupted by military operations: once when a Confederate force under General Sterling Price attacked a Union force stationed in Missouri; and later when Confederate General Kirby Smith attacked Richmond, Kentucky, on August 30, 1862. McGarvey had moved to Kentucky on the urgent request of Dr. W. H. Hopson to forestall a split over the slavery issue in the Lexington church. Both factions joined in supporting McGarvey as their minister.

Among the noted Restoration leaders committed to Christian pacifism were Benjamin Franklin, T. P. Haley, J. J. Everest, T. M. Allen, and Moses E. Lard. Alexander Campbell, David S. Burnet, John T. Walsh, Robert Milligan, and Barton W. Stone might be added to the list, although they might better be characterized as "peace advocates." There was a widespread determination among Disciples in both the North and the South to avoid fighting or killing their brethren with whom they had labored for twenty years in building the kingdom of God. There were many touching incidents reported in which army rules were broken to spare the lives of Christian brethren.

It was at the point of the organized life of the brotherhood that the war tensions were most apparent. The American Christian Missionary

Society met in Cincinnati in the fall of 1861. During one of the sessions, Dr. J. P. Robinson presented a resolution:

Resolved, That we deeply sympathize with the loyal and patriotic in our country in the present efforts to sustain the government of the United States, and we feel it our duty as Christians to ask our brethren to do all in their power to sustain the proper and constitutional authorities of the Union.

It was seconded by L. L. Pinkerton, of Kentucky. D. S. Burnet questioned whether it was consistent with the second article of the Constitution which read, "The object of this Society shall be to promote the Gospel in destitute places of our own and foreign lands." Isaac Errett, who was presiding, ruled the resolution in order. John Smith, of Kentucky, then moved to appeal the decision to the house and it was voted "not germane" to the purposes of the convention whereupon a ten-minute recess was declared during which a "mass meeting" was called to consider the resolution. It then passed with only one dissenting vote. Since the convention was held in Ohio and the representation from the state was particularly large, the brotherhood referred to the incident as representing "the Ohio point of view."

In 1863, the A.C.M.S. again met in Cincinnati and again received a resolution phrased in stronger terms calling for loyalty to magistrates and deploring "the attempts of armed traitors to overthrow our government." After a heated debate, it passed with several negative votes. Such actions could have caused an open split among the churches were it not for the fact that the convention was universally considered a purely voluntary association of brethren without any authority over the churches and likely to reflect the views of the local area in which its meetings were held. State societies experienced similar problems during the war but came through the conflict organizationally unimpaired.

Two interesting developments are worth noting in this connection. An "antislavery convention" was held in Cleveland in January, 1854, which made a headline in the *Christian Age,* "Trouble Among the Disciples." But a correspondent in the *Harbinger* reported that not more than thirty-three persons attended. In 1859, an antislavery missionary society was formed in Indianapolis, upon call of a petition bearing six hundred names, to support Pardee Butler as an evangelist in Kansas. Butler was a rabid abolitionist although responsible for establishing many churches under the auspices of the A.C.M.S. Finally the society admonished him to keep his political and social views to himself. Ovid Butler, who had founded what later became Butler University, disagreed with this policy and consented to become the president of the antislavery society. Its receipts were small and when war partisanship cooled, it died.

As the war drew to a close, it remained for Abraham Lincoln to free the slaves by his historic "Emancipation Proclamation." Lincoln's father and stepmother were members of the Christian church. While living in Kentucky, the Lincolns were surrounded by Scotch Baptist churches, which later became Christian churches. In Indiana, they found their

154

religious fellowship among such Baptists. When they finally settled in Illinois, they joined the Christian church. Lincoln, in his youthful years, was an agnostic, but as he grew older he developed a love for a Biblical faith. He had little use for the denominations and never formally affiliated with a church. There is a tradition among Illinois Disciples that John O'Kane, when state evangelist, discussed the state of Lincoln's soul with him on several occasions; finally he was convicted and wished to be immersed. He reportedly knew that his wife, who had strong Episcopal and Presbyterian social obligations in Springfield, would be greatly embarrassed if it were known that a "Campbellite" evangelist had baptized him. But one night, Lincoln slipped away from the house with proper garments for baptism, met O'Kane and was immersed in the waters of the Sangamon River. Whether this story is true or not, there are many evidences of Lincoln's strong Christian Biblical convictions. (Another version tells of his baptism in Virginia while he was President.) The Bible and prayer were his strength while he led the nation in its most crucial years. He believed that he was called of God to preserve the Union and to free the slaves. Today the whole free world recognizes him as one of the greatest statesmen who ever lived.

When the conflict was over, the Northern churches raised thousands of dollars to alleviate the suffering and poverty of their brethren in the South. The spirit of true Christian unity was demonstrated both north and south of the "Mason and Dixon Line," and the churches continued in close fellowship in Christ and in those things which make for peace and progress in the kingdom of God.

In these formative years, death came to several early leaders of the movement. Barton W. Stone died November 9, 1844. Thomas Campbell died January 4, 1854. Walter Scott was the next to fall. He had been in failing health for a number of years and finally died April 23, 1861. On March 4, 1866, Alexander Campbell was taken.

In Campbell, the Disciples of Christ lost their most cherished and capable leader. Until he was seventy years of age, he continued to visit the churches and the conventions and to write voluminously. In his later years he retired to his home in Bethany. Here he continued to meet his friends and the stream of visitors who came from all over the nation to confer with him. In December, 1865, he preached his final sermon. On February 11, 1866, he made his last public appearance. His last illness and death were characterized by the same calm confidence in God and humble reliance on his divine Redeemer that he had demonstrated throughout his life.

With an unbounded influence over a Christian community of hundreds of thousands, he never sought ecclesiastical control. The telegram from Wheeling, West Virginia, to the press of the nation, spoke of him as "Bishop Campbell," but had the readers only known, that designation referred to the fact that he was one of the bishops or elders of the local church at Bethany. Campbell was by nature a leader and would have occupied such a position in any area of life he might have chosen. He often corrected the press when it alluded to him as "the founder of the Christian church." He insisted that he had founded nothing in the field of religion, but had sought to restore the church that Jesus built. In this task he often showed that the things he taught were in the Bible and that they had been repeatedly recognized by leaders in the church in many periods in its history. The error that roused his ire more than anything else was to use the term *Campbellite* to designate the movement to restore the church of the New Testament. It must nevertheless be admitted that he had been the prime factor in creating the momentum for the greatest single religious movement in America of strictly American origins. As the years pass he is increasingly recognized as the greatest religious leader of his time.

With the passing of Alexander Campbell it became clear that there was no comparable leader upon which his mantle could immediately fall. This vacuum drew several good men into prominence, largely because they were editors of journals of considerable circulation. Each operated independently and there was little agreement among them on matters of opinion. Their readers and followers in the churches were soon plunged into controversies. With no voice from Bethany to arbitrate or ameliorate the differences, a grave situation confronted the brotherhood.

At the death of Campbell, Professor W. K. Pendleton had become editor-in-chief of the *Millennial Harbinger,* as well as president of Bethany College. He had been closely associated with Isaac Errett and Robert Richardson in the editorship for some years. They were of one mind on controversial matters, and they continued to work together, shaping brotherhood opinion along Biblical inclusivist lines.

William Kimbrough Pendleton was born in Louisa County, Virginia, September 8, 1817, and died September 1, 1899. He was of English descent, the son of Colonel Edmond Pendleton. He had a fine education in the best preparatory schools and the University of Virginia. He studied law for two years and was licensed to practice. Alexander Campbell was a warm friend of the family. In June, 1840, he immersed Pendleton, and in the fall of that year gave him the hand of his daughter, Lavinia, in marriage. The first Mrs. Pendleton died in 1846, and Pendleton then married Clarinda, another daughter of Campbell, in 1848. Campbell's celebrated letters from Europe were addressed to this daughter. Pendleton distinguished himself as a professor in Bethany College, and was later promoted to the vice-presidency. He was a cultured gentleman of the old school and always made a favorable impression wherever he went. He was a deep student of the Scriptures, inclined to state their truths in philosophical terms. He was a linguist and possessed literary qualities of the highest caliber. He was fond of classical music, and was an excellent judge of paintings, sculpture, and beauty in nature. He was not in any sense aggressive and was a constant demonstration of the Scriptural saying, "In quietness and confidence shall be your strength." He was an effective preacher, but was overshadowed by his distinguished father-in-law. While he made a valuable contribution to the life of the brotherhood and inherited the position and much of the property of Campbell, the mantle of the sage of Bethany did not fall to him, nor was he recognized for his true worth. It was inevitable that the *Harbinger* under his editorship was to become just another journal in a plethora of Disciple literature.

Three other journals beside the *Harbinger* had wide influence. Moses E. Lard published a *Quarterly* which expressed extreme conservative views. In his personality and his contentions he presented a complete contradiction. He was cordial and gracious and on occasion voiced such left-wing concepts as pacifism and universalism. But when it came to maintaining the ground that Campbell held in his *Christian Baptist* days, he was adamant. In his writings he was extremely pessimistic, especially about minor concerns.

Benjamin Franklin, who published the *American Christian Review,* was a splendid type of man for the work he undertook to do. His character was above reproach; he was indefatigable in his labors and willing to make great sacrifice for the cause he loved. For a time he expressed a generous spirit toward those with whom he disagreed, but later violently opposed all those who disagreed with his ultraconservative views. He was the author of two volumes of sermons which became the homiletical pattern for conservative preaching not only for his time but for generations to come.

Tolbert Fanning's *Gospel Advocate* supported Franklin's views and their united influence made the advocacy of their journals a very deciding factor in the future history of the Restoration movement. Fanning was the acknowledged leader of thought in the South and founded Franklin College, near Nashville, Tennessee, the forerunner of David Lipscomb College.

The frontier was now changing rapidly. Higher cultural and social progress was evident everywhere. Railroads had superseded the stagecoach. All the luxuries of modern living were to be found in every center of population, even the small villages. Many rural mansions had been built by prosperous farmers and stockmen. Organs, chandeliers, imported furniture, rugs, and wall paper graced many Christian church homes. A college education was considered essential to community and national leadership. Church buildings were now assuming pretentious proportions, displacing the little clapboard tabernacles common to pioneer days. Progressives within the brotherhood recognized these changes and realized that while matters of faith and moral convictions could not be compromised, the churches must keep abreast of the times.

The introduction of organs as aids to church worship produced one of the most serious controversies that plagued the brotherhood. Other matters of tension involved close Communion, open membership, attitudes toward denominational bodies, the paid ministry, and extracongregational organizations. Other restoration movements in history had faced the problem of adaptation to the ever-changing conditions of new eras with varying results. What would happen to the American analogue?

Many historians, writing from a superficial and prejudicial viewpoint, have attributed all the troubles of the brotherhood to ignorance, prejudice, personal ambition, reactionism, and sociological conditions. Undoubtedly these factors were present in some degree, but if we approach the situation objectively in a spirit of Christian love and good will, we must admit that the causes of disagreement lay much deeper in the realm of sincere and earnest conviction and in a desire to do God's will and to further His kingdom. The trouble came largely in the absence of deeply spiritual commitment to Christ and in an inability to discern between matters of opinion and matters of faith.

Robert Richardson, in his *Principles and Objects of the Religious Reformation,* set forth that distinction clearly:

> Without a proper recognition of the difference between *faith* and *opinion* it is impossible to make any progress in a just knowledge of divine things, or to obtain any clue by which the mind can be extricated from the complexed labyrinth of sectarianism. . . . The fallible deductions of human reason are continually mistaken for the unerring dictates of inspiration and human authority is blended with that which is Divine. . . . A theory consisting of any number of favourite opinions, smoothly intertwined, forms the thread upon which various Scripture doctrines and texts are strung and curiously interwoven, so as to assume a form and meaning wholly artificial and unauthorized. When men thus fail to make any distinction between the express *revelation* of God and the *opinions* which men have superadded, and when they have already committed the great error of adopting indiscriminately, in the religious system of a party, an incongruous mixture of opinions with the things of faith, the mistiness and obscurity which surround the former overspread by degrees the latter also. . . .
>
> In opposition to views and practices so erroneous we urge:
>
> 1. That the Scriptures mean precisely what they say, when construed in conformity with the established laws of languages.
>
> 2. That the Bible contains the only Divine revelations to which man has access; and that these revelations are perfectly suited by their Divine author to the circumstances and capacity of man to whom they are addressed.
>
> 3. That true religious faith can be founded upon this Divine testimony alone.
>
> 4. That opinions are mere inferences of human reason from insufficient and uncertain premises, or conjectures in regard to matters not revealed, and that they are not entitled to the slightest authority in religion by whomsoever they may be propounded. . . .
>
> The measure of faith is, then, precisely the amount of Scripture testimony, neither more nor less. What this distinctly reveals is to be implicitly believed. Where this is obscure or silent, reason must not attempt to elaborate theories or supply conclusions and impose them on the conscience as of Divine authority. . . .
>
> It is preposterous to expect that men will ever agree in their religious opinions. It is neither necessary nor desirable that they should do so. It is nowhere commanded in the Scriptures that men should be of one opinion. On the contrary, differences of opinion are distinctively recognized, and Christians are expressly commanded to receive one another without regard to them (Rom. xiv:1). As well might we expect to conform the features of the human face to a single standard, as to secure a perfect agreement of men's minds. Hence, there can be no peace, unless there be *liberty of opinion.* Each individual must have a perfect right to entertain what opinions he pleases, but he must not attempt to enforce them upon others, or make them a term of communion or religious fellowship. They can do no harm so long as they are

private property and are regarded in their true light, as human reasons possessed on no Divine authority or infallibility. . . .

Every proposition or doctrine, then, for which there is not clear Scriptural evidence, is to be regarded as a matter of opinion; and everything for which such evidence can be adduced, is a matter of faith—a fact or a truth to be believed.

This basic doctrine was generally accepted and had become a Disciple shibboleth: "Where the Scriptures speak, we speak; where the Scriptures are silent, we are silent." It became apparent, however, that there was a difference of opinion as to the meaning of this rule. One school of thought believed that it opened the way for free church action in all matters not expressly mentioned in the Scriptures. The other school held that where the Scriptures failed to speak on any matter, the churches had no right to act. There were all sorts of views as to whether particular matters, such as the worship, were fully revealed in a fixed Divine pattern.

Moses E. Lard was of the school that viewed any change of "apostolic practice" as a dangerous and disloyal "innovation." In his *Quarterly* he said:

The spirit of innovation is a peculiar spirit. While coming in it is the meekest and gentlest of spirits; only it is marvellously firm and persistent. But when going out, no term but fiendish can describe it. It comes in humming the sweetest notes of Zion; it goes out amid the ruin it works, howling like an exorcised demon. At first it is supple as a willow twig; you can bend it, mould it, shape it, to anything; only it will have its way. But when once it has fully got its way, then mark how it keeps its footing. It now calls for reason, for argument, for Scripture; but no more has it an ear for reason, argument or Scripture than has the image of Baal. Argue with the spirit of innovation indeed! I would as soon be caught cracking syllogisms over the head of the man of sin. Never. Rebuke it in the name of the Lord; if it go not out *expel it*. This only will cure it. . . .

He is a poor observer of men and things who does not see slowly growing up among us a class of men who can no longer be satisfied with the ancient gospel and the ancient order of things. These men must have changes; and silently they are preparing the mind of the brotherhood to receive changes. Be not deceived, brethren, the Devil is not sleeping. If you refuse to see the danger till ruin is upon you, then it will be too late. The wise seaman catches the first whiff of the distant storm, and adjusts his ship at once. Let us profit by this example.

Let us agree to commune with the sprinkled sects around us, and soon we shall come to recognize them as Christians. Let us agree to recognize them as Christians, and immersion, with its deep significance, is buried in the grave of our folly. Then in not one whit will we be better than others. Let us countenance political charlatans as preachers, and we at once become corrupt as the loathsome nest on which Beecher sets to hatch the things he calls Christians. . . . Let us agree to admit organs, and soon churches will become gay worldly things, literal Noah's arks, full of clean and unclean beasts. To all this let us yet add, by way of dessert, and as a sort of spice to the dish, a few volumes as inner light speculations, and a cargo or two of reverend dandies dubbed pastors, and we may congratulate ourselves on having completed the trip in a wonderfully short time. We can now take rooms in Rome, and chuckle over the fact that we are as orthodox as the rankest heretic in the land.

Lard and his like nicknamed the opposition *digressives;* and the *progressives* (the opposition "digressives") not to be outdone, flung back the byword *anti.* The battle was on. A consideration of the major issues must be recorded in any true history of this era.

The organ controversy was not peculiar to the Disciples. All the denominations of Protestantism had been torn by it. In the early days of the Reformation in Europe, Calvin and Zwingli were opposed to the use of the organ in worship. The Methodists lost a small group known as Free Methodists; the Presbyterians, antiorgan bodies such as the Reformed and United Presbyterian, which also insisted on singing only the metric version of the psalms; the Baptists, the Primitive Baptists; and many others. The Christians in New England passed a conference resolution: "We recommend to the churches and preachers that they use their influence to prevent the introduction of instrumental music into our meetings and worship, and to suppress them where they have already been introduced." In some groups there was opposition to the use of written music in hymnbooks. In the churches of Christ, those who opposed the organ did so on the ground that there was a distinct revelation of a divine pattern of worship which did not include instrumental music. Some of these churches are still wrangling over the supposed consecutive order in which prayer, praise, offering, Communion, et cetera, should occur on the Lord's Day. Those who favored the organ called attention to the use of instruments in worship in the Old Testament order, and the lack of any injunction in the New Testament against it; indeed, they insisted, instrumental music is repeatedly mentioned in John's description in his Revelation of worship in the church triumphant. Some scholars called attention to the instrumental connotations of the words *psallo* and *zimmer,* often translated "sing." There was no open division over this issue at the time, except in separate local congregations that continued to recognize each other as "erring brethren" in a common fellowship before the Lord.

Also involved in the worship was the question of close Communion. Benjamin Franklin and G. W. Elley were its protagonists. In the *Review* Franklin contended:

> There are individuals among the sects who are not sectarians or who are more than sectarians—they are Christians or persons who have believed the Gospel, submitted to it, and in spite of the leaders been constituted Christians according to the Scriptures. That these individuals have a right to commune there can be no doubt. But this is not communion with the sects.
>
> What is the use of parleying over the question of communion with unimmersed persons? Did the first Christians commune with unimmersed persons? It is admitted that they did not. Shall we then deliberately do what we admit they did not do?
>
> When an unimmersed person communes without any inviting or excluding that is his own act, not ours, and we are not responsible for it. We do not see that any harm is done to him or us, and we need make no exclusive remarks to keep him away, and we certainly have no authority for inviting him to come.
>
> If it is to be maintained that "except a man be born of the water and of the Spirit he cannot enter the kingdom of God"; that "as many of us as

have been baptized into Christ have put on Christ," as we have it in the Scriptures, and that none were in the Church or recognized as Christians in apostolic times who were not immersed, it is useless for us to be talking about *unimmersed Christians,* and thus weakening the hands of those who are labouring to induce all to enter the kingdom of God according to the Scriptures.

We have nothing to do with any *open* communion or *close* communion. The communion is for the Lord's people, and nobody else. But if some imagine themselves to have become Christians according to the Scriptures, when they have not, and commune, as we have said before, that is their act and not ours. We commune with the Lord and his people, and certainly not in spirit with any ones who are not his people, whether immersed or unimmersed. We take no responsibility in the matter, for we neither invite nor exclude.

Isaac Errett went on record unqualifiedly for open Communion. He recognized that there had always been a people of God in Babylon. In the *Millennial Harbinger* he took advanced ground:

At one and another trumpet call of Reformation, multitudes came forth from Babylon. They did not reach Jerusalem. But they wrought great deeds for God and for his Word. They talked much and they suffered much for the name of Christ. We inherited the blessed fruit of their labors. We follow them through the scenes of their superhuman toil, to the dungeon where they suffered, and to the stakes where they won the glories of martyrdom, and whence they ascended in chariots of fire to the heavens; and as we embrace the chains they wore, and take up the ashes from the altar-fires of spiritual freedom, we ask not whether these lofty heroes of the church militant, to whom we owe *our* heritage of spiritual freedom, may commune with us—but rather, if we are at all worthy to commune with them! We feel honored to call them brethren. Our reformation movement is the legitimate offspring of theirs. . . . We felt the need of further reformation. We have seen the mischievous and wicked tendencies of the sect spirit and life. We have eschewed it. We invite all who love the Saviour to a Scriptural basis of union. We do not, meanwhile, deny nor refuse their prayers, their songs, their exhortations, nor their sympathy with truth and goodness. Whilst we cannot endorse their position nor their practice, as lacking immersion, and as practicing infant baptism, but lift up a loud and constant voice against it—we must still deal with them as *Christians in error,* and seek to right them. To ignore their faith and obedience and to deal with them as heathen men and publicans, will be indeed to "weaken the hands" of the pleaders for Reformation and expose ourselves, by a judgment of extreme narrowness and harshness, to the pity, if not the scorn, of good men everywhere.

The whole problem of open or close Communion impinged upon church membership. The Franklin school finally came to insist upon rebaptism even though the candidate for church membership had been immersed in a denominational church. These brethren saw that, in order to be consistent on the Communion question, they could not accept immersion which had been performed according to usages and doctrines and by the hands of administrators alien to reformation practice. They eventually refused to have any religious fellowship whatsoever with anyone outside their own churches. The Errett school recognized the original willingness of the immersed believer to obey the ordinance of Christ as valid in His sight, and acceptable as a qualification of church membership. They

161

refused, however, to accept the unimmersed as members of the local church on the ground that they had not been Scripturally baptized and that to receive such would tend to destroy the testimony of the churches as congregations after the New Testament pattern. These brethren conceived of their churches as demonstrations to the Christian world of apostolic unity and practice. The Communion question did not divide the Disciples, but the question of open membership was destined to destroy the fellowship of brethren in years to come.

Among the "innovations" opposed by Lard and others was that of the paid or located ministry. Alexander Campbell, a wealthy man, refused to accept a stipend for his services and looked with disfavor upon pastors of local congregations. It will be remembered that his attacks upon the clergy in the *Christian Baptist* assumed that such men were chiefly to blame for perpetuity of the ecclesiastical structures which had divided the churches. Like the Baptists, the Disciples held the Scriptural position that all Christians are "kings and priests" in the kingdom of God. There was no clergy nor laity in the Restoration movement. The "preaching brethren" were chosen by congregations to have "oversight of one voluntary society, who, when he leaves that society, has no office in any other in consequence of his being an officer in that." The common title or term of address for preachers was *elder* and for nonpreaching elders, *brother.* Soon a distinction arose, but the preaching elder was always considered answerable to the plurality of elders in the local church. They "hired him and fired him." There was certainly no "lording it over God's heritage" on the part of the minister. The title *reverend* was universally eschewed. The multiplication and growth of the churches, however, and their need for full-time shepherding, coupled with the problem of securing men who were morally and doctrinally sound, led to the practice of ordained, full-time, resident ministers, functionally distinct from the membership or the local eldership. Tolbert Fanning, of the *Gospel Advocate,* was one of the chief opponents of this innovation. He wrote, "The brethren who advocate the salary system lose sight of the fact that we professed in years past to adopt the Scripture as our only rule of faith and practice. There is not a word in the Scriptures favoring such views; the brethren have adopted their views and practices from the sectarian views of those around them." Other right-wing leaders joined him in branding the churches that condoned such "heresy" as being "priest-ridden" and succumbing to "clerical domination." The salaries were pitiably small. The churches kept their ministers poor and humble. But still these men assumed the role of an ecclesiastical aristocracy in the eyes of the opposition. Despite the furor in the press and in the conventions on this issue, it did not divide the brotherhood. Local churches settled the problem to suit themselves.

The Restoration movement was passing through a dark period, but so was the nation just emerging from one of the bitterest and bloodiest civil wars in the history of the world. It was only natural that parties should arise among a democratic people. Their controversies contributed

162

to a deeper understanding of the nature of the movement, revealed the consequences implicit in certain types of reasoning, and for a time, at least, were helpful in promoting its vigor and growth.

Opposing forces do not necessarily bring disaster. The American way of life is an outstanding example of this fact. The two-party system has been the strength of the nation when both parties are dedicated to uphold the Declaration of Independence and the Constitution and work for the higher good of the people. In commercial life, we do not hesitate to say that competition is the life of trade. In nature, we see that the best developed men and women, both intellectually and physically, are to be found in the "temperate zone" around the world, where the seasons are in eternal conflict. Protestantism in its purest form is constantly testing its doctrines in the crucible of communication and discussion, while growing more numerous and more effective in its impact upon the world. It is true that there are dangers implicit in opposing forces, but only death is a refuge from all danger.

BIBLIOGRAPHY: Chapter 10

Boggs, John, editor, *Northwestern Christian Magazine* (1854-1858).
Borden, E. M., and G. H. P. Showalter, *Church History Showing the Origin of the Church of Christ.*
Campbell, Selina Huntington, *Home Life and Reminiscences of Alexander Campbell.*
Franklin, Benjamin, editor, *American Christian Review* (1856-1865).
Campbell, Alexander, W. K. Pendleton, and others, *Millennial Harbinger* (1845-1870).
Fanning, Tolbert, William Lipscomb, and others, *Gospel Advocate* (1855-1868).
Garrison, W. F., and Alfred T. DeGroot, *The Disciples of Christ: A History.*
Lamar, J. S., *Memoirs of Isaac Errett.*
Lard, Moses E., editor, *Lard's Quarterly* (1863-1868).
Longan, George W., *Origin of the Disciples of Christ.*
Moore, W. T., *Comprehensive History of the Disciples of Christ.*
Morro, W. C., *Brother McGarvey.*
Richardson, Robert, *Principles and Objects of the Religious Reformation.*
Rowe, John F., *History of Reformatory Movements.*
Shaw, Henry K., *Buckeye Disciples.*
Shepherd, J. W., *The Church, the Falling Away and the Reformation.*
West, Earl Irvin, *Search for the Ancient Order.*

Chapter 11

Isaac Errett and
Our Position

A FIGURE now arose who was in many respects as significant to the Restoration movement as Alexander Campbell in his day. In the midst of controversy and confusion, a leader of understanding, insight, and broad vision was essential to preserve and perpetuate the original purposes of the movement. Isaac Errett possessed all these qualities and more. Because of his wisdom and guidance, a measure of unity was to be preserved until the one hundredth anniversary of the *Declaration and Address.*

Isaac Errett was born in New York City, January 2, 1820. He was the son of the Ireland-born Henry and Sophia Kemmish Errett, leaders in the strait-laced church of Christ in the great metropolis, which was so well known to the Campbells and Walter Scott. It was Henry Errett who, in 1818, initiated an "Epistolary Correspondence between Christian Churches in Europe and America" by addressing a letter, signed by the officers of the congregation, "to the Churches of Christ throughout the earth." He was "of the strictest sect of the Pharisees" but had great clarity of intellect and lived a pure and exemplary life. Upon Henry Errett's death in 1825, his widow married a Scotsman named Sauter. The family then moved to a farm in Somerset County, New Jersey, and later to Pittsburgh, Pennsylvania, where Sauter built a sawmill. There was a church "after the New Testament pattern" in Pittsburgh, and the family regularly attended worship and Bible studies.

Isaac was apprenticed to the owner of a bookstore and later to a printer, A. A. Anderson, who edited a paper called *The Intelligencer.* Errett's formal education was limited, but he had a fine mind, read all the good literature he could obtain, and was soon writing articles for *The Intelligencer* that revealed superior talent, elegance of style, and power of diction which were truly amazing.

In the spring of 1833, Isaac and his brother Russell, hearing the gospel through the preaching of Elder Robert McLaren, were baptized by him in the Allegheny River and received into the Pittsburgh church.

It was the practice of the church to have "social meetings" in which the young people, as well as adults, were allowed to speak. Errett's talks soon indicated a great store of Bible knowledge and a depth of understanding and spiritual power, with the result that the elders "set apart" the young man in a solemn ceremony, and he became a "minister of the Word" on June 18, 1840. It was the good fortune of the Pittsburgh church to have as frequent guest preachers such men as Thomas Campbell, Alexander Campbell, and Walter Scott. Errett became acquainted with these men, studied their pulpit manners and their homiletical methods. Soon he was being complimented as measuring up to the preaching abilities of these great leaders of the Restoration movement. When a new congregation was established on Smithfield Street, Errett became its full-time evangelist; and his ministerial career was launched. Here he baptized his first convert, Mrs. Sarah Ann King. Here, too, he married Harriett Reeder, October 18, 1841.

The young preacher's friendship with the leaders of the movement soon (1844) resulted in his call to the New Lisbon (Ohio) church where the eloquent Walter Scott had first declared "the divine plan of salvation." After a prosperous ministry, he went to North Bloomfield and on to Warren, the great church which had been led into the Restoration by Adamson Bentley. During this latter ministry, Errett was in great demand as an evangelist, even being called to Bethany to conduct a series of meetings and preach in the College. While still at Warren, he debated the noted Joel Tiffany, a Universalist, on the destiny of man.

In 1851, during the agitation over the Fugitive Slave Law, he preached a controversial sermon on "The Design of Civil Government and the Extent of Its Authority," which displeased Alexander Campbell and made Errett an outspoken leader of the antislavery movement. It was during this period that he became a warm friend of James A. Garfield. When the Civil War came, he threw his influence solidly behind the North and incurred the displeasure of many of the brethren in the South.

When the Ohio Christian Missionary Society was founded at Wooster in 1852, the minister from Warren helped frame the constitution. Later, he was elected its third president. In 1857 he became the corresponding secretary of the American Christian Missionary Society. In 1855 he was selected to make the annual address to the American Bible Union in New York City. Here he met many distinguished American religious leaders, including Henry Ward Beecher. Errett's address made so great an impression upon his hearers that it was ordered published and was widely copied by the religious periodicals of the day. These facts are indicative of the great respect Errett commanded, not only among his brethren but the whole American Christian community.

In 1856 a group of Christian businessmen, whom Errett trusted, persuaded him to embark upon a great real estate and lumber development expedition to Michigan. When the large Springfield (Illinois) church heard there was some possibility of his leaving Warren, Judge Logan, a man of great wealth and influence, was dispatched with a tempting offer to secure him as its minister. But Errett would not listen to the pleadings of his brethren to "remain in civilization" and proceeded to bury his talents in rural Michigan for nearly ten years.

His withdrawal from active leadership in brotherhood life was unfortunate. Reactionary elements in the churches were bringing controversial issues to the fore. Among these people debates were considered to be more important than the preaching of the gospel and the salvation of souls. They regarded those who disagreed with their opinions, not as erring brethren, but as their enemies and the enemies of the truth. Incompetent leaders founded a whole flock of new reactionary journals by which they disseminated their views. Hobbies were brought to the front, subordinate and insignificant points were magnified, and the rights of churches and individuals to hold new and progressive ideas in the realm of expediency were vigorously denied. Lines of communication were kept open with Michigan, but the widely recognized and trusted leader who might have maintained a measure of unity and peace was to all intents and purposes withdrawn from the field of battle. The venerable Campbell was too old to speak the needed words. Seemingly interminable controversy and confusion reigned.

In 1862, a group of cultured and well-to-do Disciples in Detroit persuaded Errett to go to this burgeoning city and establish a new church. A property was purchased from the Congregationalists and refurbished into one of the most attractive church edifices in the city. Large audiences soon came to hear the outstanding preacher.

In order to acquaint the Christian community with the simple New Testament position of the church at Jefferson Avenue and Beaubien Street, Errett issued what he called "A Synopsis of the Faith and Practice of the Church of Christ." The little brochure consisted of ten articles which stated in concise form exactly what the Restoration stood for. In addition there was a series of bylaws which the congregation had adopted that its affairs might be conducted "in decency and in order." Reactionary elements in the brotherhood immediately hailed the document as "a creed" and proceeded to brand Errett as a heretic who had "departed from the faith."

Moses E. Lard published the "Synopsis" in his *Quarterly* (September, 1863) and attacked it bitterly:

> There is not a sound man in our ranks who has seen the Synopsis that has not felt scandalized about it. I wish we possessed even one decent apology for its appearance. It is a deep offense against the brotherhood—an offense tossed into the teeth of the people who, for forty years, have been working against the divisive and evil tendency of creeds. . . . We are told that this Declaration is not to be taken as a creed. But will this caveat prevent its being so taken? Never. When Aaron's calf came out, and he called it a bird, still all Israel, seeing it stand on four legs, with horns and parted hoofs, would have shouted, A calf, a calf, a calf. . . . The brethren . . . may call their work in classic phrase a Synopsis, or gently a Declaration, but still we cry, A creed, a creed, a creed. It is not the mere title of the work that

constitutes it a creed, but its matter and form, together with the manner in which it was issued, and the sanctions by which it is accompanied. . . . It has a painful significance—painful because symptomatic of the following items:

(1) That some of our brethren have lost their well grounded opposition to creeds, and are ready to traffic in these unholy things. This indicates a diseased state of the body. How far this disease extends will be seen by the extent to which the Synopsis is endorsed.

(2) That these brethren are no longer willing to be styled heretics for the truth's sake, but now wish to avoid that odium by adopting the customs and views of the sects of the day, and thus to become themselves a sect.

(3) That what the world needs in order to learn the faith of these brethren is not the Bible alone, but the Bible and a "Synopsis of their faith and practice." With them, then, the Bible is an insufficient enlightener of the human family.

For all these symptoms of degeneracy our brotherhood will feel something more than mere regret. They will feel profoundly ashamed.

Benjamin Franklin in his *American Christian Review* also voiced his opposition to the "Synopsis."

The little brochure had, of course, stated very clearly that it was not a creed. Errett himself utterly rejected all human creeds. He had written:

This declaration of our faith and aims is not to be taken as a creed. We assume no right to bind the conscience with any stereotyped formula. Vital religion is a thing of growth in the heart of the individual Christian. We design a mere statement, for general information, of the purposes which induced us to band together, and the principles we propose to develop. We have no sectarian shackles with which to bind Christ's freemen—no spiritual prison house for the confinement of the soul. We present no authoritative standard of interpretation of the Bible. The Spirit that indicted the Word can best bring home to the heart the significance of its truths. The practice of the divine precepts furnishes the best interpretation. We repudiate all human authority in spiritual concerns (Matt. xxiii. 8-12; John vii. 16, 17).

Mr. Errett was not alarmed by the "tempest in a teapot" over the document. He perfectly understood his ground and knew that he was completely in line with the historic position of the movement. He had expected to· be misunderstood by his enemies but had faith that the intelligent majority of his brethren would approve his intentions. The "Synopsis" served its purpose in such an admirable fashion in Detroit that the church soon came to occupy a place of respect in the community and grew in numbers and spiritual power. The reception of the document, which was accorded in the brotherhood at large, led Errett later to produce on a broader scale a statement of "our position," which will be presented later in some detail.

After a comparatively brief ministry in Detroit, the great preacher again retired to his Michigan wilderness. He was not idle, in any sense of the word. Besides his business obligations, he preached at Ionia, Muir, and other communities. These labors resulted in a pocket of well-indoctrinated churches in that section of the state which have continued to the present day.

Finally, in 1865, he was persuaded to come to the Western Reserve Eclectic Institute (later Hiram College) to occupy the position of principal and professor of evangelical and pastoral training, preparation and delivery of sermons, and church government. The men who brought him out of hibernation were James A. Garfield, J. P. Robinson, Harmon Austin, and the wealthy Phillips brothers of Western Pennsylvania—Thomas W., Charles M., I. N., and John T. The brotherhood owes these men an everlasting debt of appreciation. When it was bruited about that Errett had entree to the confidence of such wealthy and distinguished men, he was offered the presidencies of Northwestern Christian University (later Butler University) and Kentucky University (Transylvania), both of which he declined.

Scarcely had Errett entered upon his new duties at Hiram when some associates proposed to launch a new magazine which would take the place of the declining *Millennial Harbinger* and counter the baneful influences of some reactionary and legalistic determinism. The Phillips mansion in New Castle was the scene of the first conference to consider seriously this project on December 22, 1865. A joint stock company was formed and a committee was named to obtain a charter and necessary papers for organization under the title of the Christian Publishing Association. Isaac Errett was chosen editor-in-chief and the journal was named the *Christian Standard* because, in his words,

> We propose to lift up the Christian Standard, as a rallying point for the scattered hosts of spiritual Israel; to know only "Jesus Christ and Him crucified": His cross, His word, His church, His ordinances, His laws and the interests of His kingdom.

The board of directors consisted of James A. Garfield, W. S. Streator, J. P. Robinson, T. W. Phillips, C. M. Phillips, G. W. N. Yost, and W. J. Ford. Streator was elected president; W. J. Ford, secretary; and J. P. Robinson, treasurer.

The first issue of the *Standard* came from the press on April 7, 1866, with the motto on its masthead, "Set Up a Standard; Publish and Conceal Not." It contained, besides the usual doctrinal, devotional, and news articles of the current journals in the brotherhood, discussions of the moral and religious aspects of public issues in the fields of literature, art, education, science, commerce, and government. It recognized its relationship to the whole Christian community and carried information concerning the views and proceedings of all denominations and interchurch organizations. It was immediately hailed as a distinct addition to the religious journalism of the nation.

The *Standard* enjoyed a wide and favorable acceptance, until the days following the War brought general economic ruin to the nation, and financial difficulties beset the new venture. The checkered career of the Christian Publishing Association cannot be detailed here. Suffice to say that, at a meeting of the executive committee in 1868, the ownership of the paper was transferred to Errett. To fend off bankruptcy he accepted the presidency of Alliance College; but when similar financial problems beset that institution, the editor decided to give up publication. It was at this juncture that God providentially provided a Good Samaritan in the person of R. W. Carroll, a Quaker, in Cincinnati, Ohio. He had been impressed by the high quality of journalism evident in the new publication. His experience in printing many books by Christian church ministers and educators had been rewarding, and he felt led to underwrite the *Standard* and issue it on the presses of R. W. Carroll and Company. Errett gladly accepted this offer, and the first issue from Cincinnati appeared on July 31, 1869. J. S. Lamar, of the distinguished Georgia family of that name, became associate editor.

The *Standard* restored the Restoration movement to its pristine dignity and rescued its living principles from perversion. The petty controversies about matters of opinion and expediency had given a false direction to the whole movement. The broad, majestic concepts of a united church built on the Bible as its rule of faith and practice were now restated and elaborated with intelligent and constructive articles and editorials.

Errett did not shun the issues of instrumental music in the worship, extracongregational organizations, the located ministry, open Communion, and the like; but the tone of each issue was pitched at a level that inspired and lifted the reader to a higher concept of Christian discipleship. The great tasks of the church in the fields of evangelism, education, benevolence, Christian fellowship, Bible study, and piety got top billing in the headlines.

When the editor dealt with the controversialists he did so in a Christian spirit. Sometimes the editors of the *Review* and the *Gospel Advocate* vexed him, but he gave them as good as they sent.

In 1869 the *Apostolic Times* appeared to counteract the growing popularity of the *Standard*. It was edited by Moses E. Lard, Robert Graham, Winthrop Hopson, Lanceford B. Wilkes, and John W. McGarvey. This was truly a formidable array of talent. There was not a stain upon the reputation of one of them. Circumstances had brought them together in the Lexington area, and they each held places of distinction in the churches and the university. They announced that the *Times* was dedicated "to the primitive faith, and the primitive practice, without enlargement or diminution, without innovation or modification." Their alliance in common agreement about the controversial issues, took almost the nature of a *Quinqueviri* with the force and authority of divine law. So certain were they of their ability to slay the Cincinnati dragon that they so announced on many occasions. They said that no such array of talent had ever been brought together in one periodical and that their influence alone would assure the largest subscription list in the brotherhood. Circulation reached a total of about one thousand before its early demise. During the years of its existence, it was conducted with much ability, considering the fact that its editorials and articles were limited in scope and were almost all controversial.

The *Times* made it clear that the brotherhood was "upon the eve of a falling away, which no phrase but partial apostasy will describe," the said

170

apostasy involving "expediency, progress, organs, recognition, palatial edifices, and societies." Errett denied that there was any apostasy:

Are there any among us who are subverting the faith of the Disciples in the divinity of the Lord Jesus—in his sacrifice for sin; his resurrection, or his rightful authority? We are happy to say that we know of none such in our ranks.

It is held that every applicant for membership, upon the confession of his faith in Christ, and repentance toward God, should be immersed into the name of the Father, and of the Son, and of the Holy Ghost; and that this baptism is for the remission of sins.

Do any among us deny this? Are we seeking to persuade men to the contrary? . . . Any attempt to introduce and enforce anything as a matter of faith or duty, which the Apostles did not enforce in the name of our Lord, would be a step in apostasy. And any attempt to compel uniformity in thinking or in practice, where the Apostles have left us free, is virtual apostasy . . .

Continuing his argument the editor of the *Standard* said:

The germs of apostasy from Christ are found in the presumptuous spirit that seeks to dictate where Christ has not dictated. Division and its bitter fruits may come as readily through the attempt to forbid that which Christ has not forbidden, as through an attempt to impose that which Christ has not imposed. . . . Two things, it strikes us, must carefully be kept in mind, if we would legitimately work out the spiritual emancipation contemplated in the reformation which we plead.

1. The necessity for free and unembarrassed research with a view to grow in grace and knowledge. It is fatal to assume that we have certainly learned all that the Bible teaches. This has been the silly and baneful conceit of all that have gone before us. Shall we repeat the folly, and superinduce a necessity for another people to be raised up to sound a new battle-cry of reformation? Must every man be branded with heresy or apostasy whose ripe investigations lead him out of our ruts? Must free investigation be smothered by a timid conservatism or a presumptuous bigotry, that takes alarm at every step for progress? Grant that errors may sometimes be thrust upon us. Free and kind discussion will soon correct them. . . . Murderous stifling of free thought and free speech . . . not only renders union worthless by the sacrifice of liberty, but will defeat its own purpose and compel, in time, new revolutionary movements.

2. The absence of all right to control our brethren where Christ has left them free. Such freedom may sometimes alarm us. Creedbound communities may lift their hands in holy horror at the "latitudinarianism" that we allow. But it is not worthwhile to accept principles unless we are willing to follow them to their legitimate results; and we insist that Romans xiv. allows a very large liberty which we have no right to trench on except with the plea of the demands of Christian love.

On this statement of editorial principles, Errett took on the editors of the *Times* and all his other opponents and effectively dealt with the controversies. He favored all expediencies that would advance the cause of Christ. He favored all progress within a strictly Biblical frame of reference. He asked for Christian consideration in dealing with the question of instrumental music, which he neither endorsed nor opposed. He pleaded for the organized work in the field of missions and evangelism. He believed in a paid, full-time local ministry. He co-operated in union meetings and urged an irenic spirit in relations with denominational churches. Yet there was not a more powerful exponent of the Biblical faith and the plea for Christian unity by the restoration of New Testament Christianity. Gradually the majority of brotherhood leadership stood firmly with him.

His broad view of the Restoration plea is best summarized in the small tract entitled *Our Position,* which has been distributed by the millions of copies. We devote several pages to quotations from this classic document because it, more than any other factor in the life of the churches from 1870-1909, gave balance and direction to the movement and preserved its unity and peace. Even today it remains the most competent and adequate brief summary of "the plea" of the Disciples of Christ.

It deals with "our position" under three heads: (1) that in which we agree with the parties known as evangelical, (2) that in which we disagree with them all, and (3) that in which we differ from some, but not all of them. Then follows a consideration of the question of Christian union.

The first section bravely stated the fundamentals of the Christian faith as revealed in the Scriptures:

1. The divine inspiration of the Holy Scriptures of the Old and New Testaments.
2. The revelation of God, especially in the New Testament, in the tri-personality of Father, Son, and Holy Spirit.
3. The alone-sufficiency and all-sufficiency of the Bible, as a revelation of the divine character and will, and of the gospel of grace by which we are saved; and as a rule of faith and practice.
4. The divine excellency and worthiness of Jesus as the Son of God; his perfect humanity as the Son of man; and his official authority and glory as the Christ—the Anointed Prophet, Priest and King, who is to instruct us in the way of life, redeem us from sin and death, and reign in and over us as the rightful Sovereign of our being and Disposer of our destiny. We accept, therefore, in good faith, the supernatural religion presented to us in the New Testament, embracing in its revelations,—
    (1) The incarnation of the Logos—the eternal Word of God—in the person of Jesus of Nazareth.
    (2) The life and teachings of this divinely anointed Lord and Saviour, as the highest and completest unfolding of the divine character and purposes, as they relate to our sinful and perishing race, and as an end of controversy touching all questions of salvation, duty and destiny.
    (3) The death of Jesus as a sin-offering, bringing us redemption through his blood, even the forgiveness of sins.
    (4) His resurrection from the dead, abolishing death and bringing life and immorality clearly to light.
    (5) His ascension to heaven, and glorification in the heavens, where He ever liveth, the Mediator between God and men; our great High Priest to intercede for His people; and our King, to rule until His foes are all subdued and all the sublime purposes of His mediatorial reign are accomplished.
    (6) His supreme authority as Lord of all.
5. The personal and perpetual mission of the Holy Spirit, to convict the world of sin, righteousness and judgment, and to dwell in believers as their Comforter, Strengthener and Sanctifier.
6. The alienation of the race from God, and their entire dependence on the truth, mercy and grace of God, as manifested in Jesus, the Christ, and

revealed and confirmed to us by the Holy Spirit in the gospel, for regeneration, sanctification, adoption, and life eternal.

7. The necessity of faith and repentance in order to the enjoyment of salvation here, and of a life of obedience in order to the attainment of everlasting life.

8. The perpetuity of Baptism and the Lord's Supper, as divine ordinances, through all ages, to the end of time.

9. The obligation to observe the first day of the week as the Lord's day, in commemoration of the death and resurrection of Jesus Christ, by acts of worship such as the New Testament teaches, and by spiritual culture such as befits this memorial day.

10. The Church of Christ, a divine institution, composed of such as, by faith and baptism, have openly confessed the name of Christ; with its appointed rulers, ministers and services, for the edification of Christians and the conversion of the world.

11. The necessity of righteousness, benevolence and holiness on the part of professed Christians, alike in view of their own final salvation and of their mission to turn the world to God.

12. The fullness and freeness of the salvation offered in the gospel to all who accept it on the terms proposed.

13. The final punishment of the ungodly by an everlasting destruction from the presence of the Lord and from the glory of His power.

Errett asserted that

. . . from the first day that this plea for a return to primitive Christianity began, until this day, there has been no doubt and no controversy among its leading advocates, and none among the mass of its intelligent adherents, on the thirteen points we have named. Not only have they accepted these teachings, but they have been ready at all times to advocate and defend them against all unbelievers and errorists (pp. 3-7).

The second section frankly stated certain differences existing between the Disciples and the Protestant world:

1. While agreeing as to the divine *inspiration* of the Old and New Testaments, we differ on the question of their equal binding of *authority* on Christians. In our view, the Old Testament was of authority with *Jews,* the New Testament *is now* of authority with *Christians.* We accept the Old Testament as true, and as essential to a proper understanding of the New, and as containing many invaluable lessons in righteousness and holiness which are of equal preciousness under all dispensations; but as a *book of authority* to teach *us* what *we* are to do, the New Testament alone, as embodying the teachings of Christ and his apostles, is our standard.

2. While accepting fully and unequivocally the Scripture statements concerning what is usually called the trinity of persons in the Godhead, we repudiate alike the philosophical and theological speculations of Trinitarians and Unitarians, and all unauthorized forms of speech on a question which transcends human reason, and on which it becomes us to speak "in words which the Holy Spirit teacheth." . . .

3. While agreeing that the Bible furnishes an all-sufficient revelation of the Divine will, and a perfect rule of faith and practice, we disagree practically in this: *We act consistently with this principle,* and repudiate all human *authoritative* creeds. We object not to publishing, for information, what we believe and practice, in whole or in part, as circumstances may demand, with the reasons therefor. But we stoutly refuse to accept of any

173

such statement as authoritative, or as a test of fellowship, since Jesus Christ alone is Lord of the conscience, and His word alone can rightfully bind us. What He has revealed and enjoined, either personally or by His apostles, we acknowledge as binding; where He has not bound us, we are free; and we insist on standing fast in the liberty wherewith Christ hath made us free, carefully guarding against all perversions of said liberty into means or occasions of strife.

4. With us, the Divinity and Christhood of Jesus is more than a mere item of doctrine—it is the central truth of the Christian system, and, in an important sense, the Creed of Christianity. It is the one fundamental truth which we are jealously careful to guard against all compromise. To persuade men to trust, and love, and obey a Divine Saviour, is the one great end for which we labor in preaching the gospel; assured that if men are right about Christ, Christ will bring them right about everything else. We therefore preach Jesus Christ and Him crucified. We demand no other faith, in order to baptism and church membership, than the faith of the heart in Jesus as the Christ, the Son of the living God; nor have we any term or bond of fellowship but faith in this Divine Redeemer, and obedience to Him. All who trust in the Son of God, and obey Him are our brethren, however wrong they may be about any thing else; and those who do not trust in this divine Saviour for salvation; and obey His commandments, are not our brethren, however intelligent and excellent they may be in all beside. Faith in the unequivocal testimonies concerning Jesus—His incarnation, life, teachings, sufferings, death for sin, resurrection, exaltation, and Divine sovereignty and priesthood; and obedience to the plain commands He has given us, are with us, therefore, the basis and bond of Christian fellowship. In judgments merely inferential, we reach conclusions as nearly unanimous as we can; and where we fail, exercise forbearance, in confidence that God will lead us into final agreement. In matters of expediency, where we are left free to follow our own best judgment, we allow the majority to rule. In matters of opinion—that is, matters touching which the Bible is either silent or so obscure in its revelations as not to admit of definite conclusions—we allow the largest liberty, so long as none judges his brother, or insists on forcing his own opinion on others, or making them an occasion of strife.

5. While heartily recognizing the perpetual agency of the Holy Spirit in the work of conversion—or, to use a broader term, regeneration—we repudiate all theories of spiritual operations and all theories of the Divine and human natures which logically rule out the word of God as the instrument of regeneration and conversion; or which make the sinner passive and helpless, regarding regeneration as a miracle, and leading men to seek the evidence of acceptance with God in supernatural tokens or special revelations, rather than in the definite and unchangeable testimonies and promises of the gospel. We require assent to no *theory* of regeneration, or of spiritual influence; but insist that men shall hear, believe, repent, and obey the gospel— assured that if we are faithful to God's requirements on the *human* side of things, He will ever be true to Himself and to us in accomplishing what is needful on the *Divine* side. . . .

6. While agreeing with all the evangelical in the necessity of faith and repentance, we differ in this: We submit *no other tests* but faith and repentance, in admitting persons to baptism and church membership. We represent to them no Articles of Faith other than the one article concerning the Divinity and Christhood of Jesus; we demand no narration of a religious experience other than is expressed in a voluntary confession of faith in Jesus; we demand no probation to determine their fitness to come into the church; but instantly, on their voluntary confession of the Christ, and avowed desire to leave their sins and serve the Lord Christ, unless there are good reasons to doubt their sincerity, they are accepted and baptized, in the name of the

Lord Jesus, and *into* the name of the Father, the Son, and the Holy Spirit. They are thus wedded to *Christ,* and not to a set of doctrines or to a party.

7. We not only acknowledge the perpetuity of Baptism, but insist on its meaning, according to the Divine testimonies: "He that believeth and is baptized, *shall be saved.*" "Repent and be baptized, every one of you, in the name of Jesus Christ, *for the remission of sins,* and you shall receive the gift of the Holy Spirit." We therefore teach the believing penitent to seek, through baptism, the divine assurance of the forgiveness of sins, and that gift of the Holy Spirit which the Lord has promised to them that obey Him. . . .

The Lord's Supper, too, holds a different place with us from that which is usually allowed to it. We invest it not with the awfulness of a sacrament, but regard it as a sweet and precious feast of holy memories, designed to quicken our love of Christ and cement the ties of our common brotherhood. We therefore observe it as a part of our regular worship, every Lord's day, and hold it a solemn, but joyful and refreshing feast of love, in which all the disciples of our Lord should feel it to be a great privilege to unite. . . .

8. The *Lord's* day—not the Jewish Sabbath—is a New Testament observance, which is not governed by statute, but by apostolic example and the devotion of loyal and loving hearts.

9. *The Church of Christ*—not sects—is a Divine institution. We do not recognize sects, with sectarian names and symbols and terms of fellowship, as *branches* of the Church of Christ but as unscriptural and antiscriptural and therefore to be abandoned for the One Church of God which the New Testament reveals. That God has a people among these sects, we believe; call on them to come out from all party organizations, to renounce all party names and party tests, and seek only for *Christian* union and fellowship according to apostolic teaching. . . .

It will thus be seen that our differential character is found not in the advocacy of new doctrines or practices, but in rejecting that which has been added to the original simple faith and practices of the Church of God. Could all return to this, it would not only end many unhappy strifes and unite forces now scattered and wasted, but would revive the spirituality and enthusiasm of the early Church; as we should no longer need, as in the weakness of sectism, to cater to the world's fashions and follies to maintain a precarious existence. Zion could again put on her beautiful garments and shine in the light of God, and go out in resistless strength to the conquest of the world . . . (pp. 8-15).

In the fourth section Errett stated the doctrine of Christian union, which is the testimony of the Disciples to Christendom:

Let us now state the doctrine of Christian union as taught and practiced by us.

1. It frankly avows not only the folly, but the *sin* of sectarianism, and teaches that, just as any other sin, it must be abandoned. It proposes no compromise whatever with denominationalism, but insists that party names, party creeds, and party organizations, being in direct contravention of the teachings of Christ, must be forsaken. It distinguishes between sects going away from the Church of God into Babylon, and sects coming back from Babylon, seeking to find the Church of God. With these latter it has much sympathy, and offers for their imperfect yet important and salutary movements in reformation, many apologies. Still it insists that the return from Babylon to Jerusalem is incomplete so long as rival and jarring sects are found in place of the one catholic apostolical Church of primitive times.

2. It insists that unity and union are practicable; that in the first age of

the Church our Lord and his apostles did establish one grand spiritual brotherhood, and did embrace in it men of all classes and nationalities, however diverse or antagonistical their sentiments, tastes and habits may previously have been; and that the Christless condition of society at that time presented much greater obstacles in the way of such a union than any that are found now among the professed followers of Christ. The difficulties should therefore be manfully met in the face and overcome.

3. It proposes simply a return, "in letter and in spirit, in principle and practice," to the original basis of doctrine and of fellowship. Seeking after this it finds—

(1) That all who put their trust in Jesus as the Christ, the Son of God, and for His sake left their sins and renounced all other lordships, were at once accepted as worthy to enter this fellowship. *Faith in the Divine Lord and Saviour was the one essential condition of entrance.* None could enter without faith—infant membership was therefore impossible. None who had faith could be refused admission—no other test was allowed but that of faith in and submission to Jesus, the Christ. We therefore proclaim, in opposition to all big and little creeds in Christendom, *that the original creed has but one article of faith in it, namely*: That Jesus is the Christ, the Son of God. All doctrinal tests but this must be abandoned.

(2) That all such believers were admitted into this fellowship by baptism, upon the authority of Jesus Christ, into the name of the Father, and of the Son, and of the Holy Spirit. . . .

(3) That among these baptized believers there was no ecclesiastical caste—no distinction of clergy and laity; but all were brethren, and none was to be called Master or Father. The order of the church must harmonize with this. . . .

(4) In all matters where there is no express precept or precedent, the law of love should lead us to that which will promote edification and peace.

a. In matters merely inferential, unanimity is to be sought, but not forced.

b. In matters merely prudential, the majority should rule, care being had, however, not to transcend the limits of expediency by contravening any Divine precept; and regard always being had to the prejudices and the welfare of all.

c. Where Christ has left us free, no man has a right to judge his brother. The largest liberty is here allowed, limited only by the spirit of the apostolic teaching: "If meat cause my brother to stumble, I will eat no meat while the world stands" (pp. 24-27).

The third section considered points of partial agreement or disagreement with other communions; the fifth section dealt with common objections to the position of the Disciples current in that day.

The broad, irenic spirit of Isaac Errett, firmly contained within a Biblical frame of reference, pervaded the whole brotherhood, except for a small minority of dissidents. The *Christian Standard* saved the movement from becoming an isolationist sect with a few peculiar customs as their chief claim to superior piety and doctrinal purity. The distinctive message of the Disciples was widely recognized as intellectually respectable. It was widely admitted that the Disciples had a valid right conscientiously to contend for that message within the framework of evangelical Christianity.

The *Millennial Harbinger* ceased publication in 1870, and the *Standard* assumed its mantle of leadership. W. K. Pendleton, the *Harbinger's* last editor, joined the *Standard* in 1874, adding his ripe scholarship and graceful writing abilities to the editorial staff. Russell Errett, Isaac's son, also became associated with the journal as a writer and in a managerial capacity. On July 29, 1873, the Standard Publishing Company was incorporated as a separate entity, with Isaac Errett as president, although R. W. Carroll remained a stockholder and treasurer. In 1874, the Carroll interest was sold to the Erretts. Their Quaker benefactor was always held in highest esteem.

Errett was now often in the public eye. As a warm friend of the Honore and Palmer families in Chicago, he was called upon to officiate at the wedding of Ida Marie Honore to Frederick Dent Grant, son of the President. Later he was to give the funeral oration for President James A. Garfield. When religious issues were before the nation, Errett's views were sought by the *New York Tribune* and leading magazines. Such prestige was not lost on his brethren who increasingly looked to him for wise counsel and leadership. His contributions toward co-operative efforts will figure largely in the history of the brotherhood to be recounted in the following chapter, but some of them should be at least mentioned in this digest of his life work.

Errett was president of the Ohio Christian Missionary Society, secretary of the American Society and the General Convention. When Mrs. S. E. Pearre proposed a woman's missionary board, Errett championed their cause in his famous editorial, "Help Those Women," proposing that "the sisters" hold a convention and organize. Without his support it is doubtful that "the brethren" would have consented to any such move. For years, Errett had ardently hoped for the organization of a society completely devoted to the evangelization of the world. He prepared the way through a series of editorials to educate the minds and consciences of the general brotherhood. Dissident elements contended that the churches had enough to do at home without scattering their talents to "the uttermost parts of the earth." In 1875, the Foreign Christian Missionary Society came into being, and Isaac Errett became its first president, a position he held for many years.

Errett's books were of a broad evangelical nature and not exclusively identified with the Restoration movement. They were designed to serve not only the constructive interests of the brotherhood, but to reach a larger audience. Among them were *Talks to Bereans, Letters to a Young Christian,* and *Evenings With the Bible.* They reveal a man of deep spiritual insights who saw beyond the machinery of brotherhood and the hard logic of Scripture propositions into the very heart of God, tempering justice with mercy and love. He was able to think Godly thoughts and to express them with sincerity and beauty in the broad terms of universal faith.

When Isaac Errett died, December 19, 1888, he, like Alexander Campbell, had no successor. He had been "called to the kingdom for such a time as this," had set up a standard for his and for future generations, and received his "crown of life" which "fadeth not away."

W. T. Moore, in his great address, "Isaac Errett: The Man and His Work," characterized him as "a real man" of unwavering faith, moral courage, an open mind, genuine culture, childlike spirit, insight, and vision. Moore's eulogy reached its climax with this statement:

We can scarcely claim to be men unless we can stand the test with respect to at least three things: We must see the invisible, know the unknowable, and do the impossible. Almost any one can accomplish the ordinary; but only a magnificent character can accomplish the extraordinary. It is precisely at this point that true greatness is separated from mediocrity.

Isaac Errett . . . was almost a prophet in his ability to interpret the facts of the day in which he lived. He saw at a glance the needs of the religious movement with which he had become identified, and he at once set for himself the task of providing those needs.

Moore proceeded to specify the contribution Errett made to the Restoration movement: (1) he did much to deliver it from the atavism and despotism of reactionary forces; (2) he gave the brotherhood a high view of Christian union; and (3) he projected a nobler conception of the task of the church and the responsibilities it imposed.

BIBLIOGRAPHY: Chapter 11

Errett, Isaac, editor, *Christian Standard* (1866-1888).
Errett, Isaac, *Our Position.*
Errett, Isaac, *A Synopsis.*
Hayden, A. S., *Early History of the Disciples of Christ in the Western Reserve, Ohio.*
Lamar, J. S., *Memoirs of Isaac Errett* (Vols. I and II).
Lard, Moses E., editor, *Lard's Quarterly* (1863-1868).
Moore, W. T., *Comprehensive History of the Disciples of Christ.*
Shaw, Henry K., *Buckeye Disciples.*
Wilcox, Alanson, *A History of the Disciples of Christ in Ohio.*

Chapter 12

The Rise of
Conventions and Agencies

AS the Restoration movement spread into new states and territories, the small groups of weak churches felt the need of co-operative agencies for mutual fellowship and united evangelistic advance. Conventions were the first expression of this need. In chapter 9 appears a record of these early gatherings and organizations. State meetings, particularly in Indiana, had reached a mature stage, and the churches were jointly supporting state evangelists. There was a growing feeling that there should be some sort of general society where the brethren could confer and deal realistically with the problem of evangelizing America and the world.

Around 1840, Alexander Campbell not only sensed this feeling but became an ardent advocate of the brotherhood-wide co-operation. In the *Millennial Harbinger* in November, 1842, he advocated "a more rational and scriptural organization":

1. We can do comparatively nothing in distributing the Bible abroad without co-operation.
2. We can do comparatively but little in the great missionary field of the world either at home or abroad without co-operation.
3. We can do little or nothing to improve and elevate the Christian ministry without co-operation.
4. We can do little to check, restrain, and remove the flood of imposture and fraud committed upon the benevolence of the brethren by irresponsible, plausible, and deceptious persons without co-operation.
5. We cannot concentrate the action of the tens of thousands of Israel in any great Christian effort, but by co-operation.
6. We can have no thorough co-operation without a more ample, extensive, and thorough church organization (p. 523).

In 1844, a conference on the subject was called at Steubenville, Ohio, at the request of a number of churches in Virginia and Ohio. The discussions prepared the way for future co-operation.

Regardless of previous emphasis on the place of the Bible in the reformation, the Disciples felt themselves to be peculiarly obligated to

179

publish and disseminate the Word of God. Inspired by the Steubenville meeting, D. S. Burnet, James Challen, and J. J. Moses, of Cincinnati, published an "Address" in 1845 calling for the organization of a new American Christian Bible Society. On January 27, in Cincinnati, a constitution was adopted and Burnet was chosen president. Strangely enough, Alexander Campbell at first opposed the organization. He was primarily interested in promoting Bethany College and a general brotherhood organization on broader lines. He finally withdrew his opposition, however, and became a generous supporter of its objectives. The Society distributed thousands of copies of the Scriptures, raising its funds largely in individual contributions in the form of "Life Memberships." It co-operated with the Baptist Bible Union and the American and Foreign Bible Society, and finally disbanded to work through the latter organization.

Almost simultaneously with the advent of the Bible society, a group of Cincinnati Disciples announced the organization of a Sunday School and Tract Society, the objects of which were "to diffuse the knowledge of the Christian religion, by the publication and circulation of religious tracts, and a Sunday School library, with special reference to the wants of our brotherhood, and the interests of our children." At its second annual meeting in 1849, the Society's president, B. S. Lawson, announced that the Society owned nine tracts with the following titles: "The Hundred Witnesses"; "Manifestations of the Son of God"; "On Faith"; "On Baptism"; "Conversion of the Eunuch"; "Positive Divine Institutions"; "On Repentance"; "Duty of Repentance"; and "On Dancing." D. S. Burnet was the chief promoter of the Tract Society, as well as the Bible Society.

About the year 1849 there seemed to be a general feeling that some kind of organization should be formed which would enable all the Christian communities to work together. Mr. Campbell sensed this feeling and began to formulate plans which he hoped would make possible co-operation on a large scale. In a series of articles, published in the *Millennial Harbinger* during 1849, entitled "Church Organization," Mr. Campbell proceeded to discuss the organization of the local church and pointed out the advantages of co-operation on a larger basis.

He began this series with a discussion of the word *ecclesia* showing the various implications which lie within its meaning. He pointed out how it was used to refer to the whole Christian community in Matthew 16:18, and at other times, referred to one local group such as the seven churches in Asia.

After having laid the foundation from the Scriptures, Mr. Campbell proceeded to make the following comments in the May issue:

A church of Jesus Christ is an organized body, or company of disciples of Christ, meeting statedly in some one place to worship God through Jesus Christ, and to edify and comfort one another; and . . . the church of Christ, in the aggregate, is the same as the kingdom of Jesus Christ—or the whole Christian community on earth composed of all them in every place that are baptized into Christ.

The officers or servants of the church are therefore of two classes;—Those

180

who belong to a particular community; and those that belong to the whole kingdom of Jesus Christ. Each community has its own bishops and deacons, its own presbytery and diaconate . . .

But besides these, there were also officers that belonged to the whole Christian community.—Such were the Apostles, Prophets, Evangelists, and public messengers of the Apostolic age, and such still are the missionaries and messengers belonging to the communities of any one state, nation or province (p. 269).

Campbell proposed that a standing committee call a meeting "in Cincinnati, Lexington, Louisville or Pittsburgh" to set up a new organization. The meeting was finally held in Cincinnati, October 23, 1849, with L. L. Pinkerton in the chair and John M. Bramwell acting as secretary. Campbell could not be present because of illness, but he was immediately elected honorary president of the meeting. The four vice-presidents were David S. Burnet, John O'Kane, John T. Johnson, and Walter Scott. James Challen was made corresponding secretary. A committee was appointed to determine the agenda. On October 24, Burnet, one of the most ardent advocates of a national organization, took the chair in the absence of Campbell. Discussions as to the nature, aims, and program of such an organization revealed all sorts of ideas. Finally a committee on constitution was appointed. Their report, which came before the body on October 25, resulted in the birth of the American Christian Missionary Society. The constitution consisted of thirteen articles and was "fearfully and wonderfully made." Campbell was elected permanent president, with twenty vice-presidents and twenty-five managers. James Challen was named secretary; George S. Jenkins, recording secretary; and Archibald Trowbridge, treasurer. On the closing day, October 26, some ecclesiastically-minded brethren were restrained from taking action which might have restricted the congregational rights of local churches—such as, the recommendation of ministers to pulpits and the ordination of evangelists. Altogether, some fifty-eight resolutions were presented. The 156 brethren present from one hundred churches were almost unanimous in their approval of the decisions made, and returned to their homes with new hopes for the final outcome of the movement.

Campbell himself seemed much pleased with the outcome and wrote in the December *Harbinger*: "Our expectations from the Convention have been more than realized. We are much pleased with the result, and regard it as a very happy pledge of good things to come. . . . I am peculiarly gratified with the great issues of deliberation" (p. 694).

There was, however, mild opposition to any sort of extracongregational organization. Many individuals such as J. B. Ferguson, Archibald McLean, and Jacob Creath, Jr., published protests insisting that delegates from churches, paid memberships, ecclesiastical tribunals, and extracongregational missionary societies were without support in Scripture. The church at Connellsville, Pennsylvania, passed resolutions, which Campbell printed in the *Harbinger*, expressing its opposition under ten heads. The most significant items were:

4. That, conscientiously, we can neither aid nor sanction any society, for this or other purposes, apart from the church, much less one which would exclude from its membership many of our brethren and all of the apostles, if now on earth, because silver and gold had they not.

5. That we consider the introduction of all such societies a dangerous precedent—a departure from the principles for which we have always contended as sanctioning the charter of expediency—the evil and pernicious effects of which the past history of the church fully proves.

6. That we also consider them necessarily heretical and schismatical, as much so as human creeds and confessions of faith, when made bonds of union and communion.

The Connellsville document also commented: "The church of Jesus Christ is, in constitution and design, essentially missionary . . . not *a* missionary society, but emphatically and pre-eminently *the* missionary society—the only one authorized by Jesus Christ or sanctioned by the apostles." This view was later to be adopted by a growing segment of the movement and eventually to result in open division; but at the time the counsels of Campbell, Burnet, Johnson, O'Kane, Goodwin, Errett, and others overwhelmingly prevailed and a new era of progress was initiated. The A.C.M.S. was not the ultimate solution of the problem of co-operation, but it was a beginning.

In this period, the first venture looking to an "official brotherhood publishing house" was made. The *Christian Age* was originally published by T. J. Mellish from 1845-48. Walter Scott bought it in 1848. D. S. Burnet of the Bible and Tract Societies, in partnership with Benjamin Franklin, acquired it in 1850, but sold it in 1852 to Jethro Jackson. The General Convention in 1852, largely on Burnet's advice and with little understanding of the action, established the American Christian Publishing Society. The Society immediately took over from Jethro Jackson the *Age,* the new *Sunday School Journal,* all his books, tracts, stereotype plates, and the right to publish. Offices, set up in Cincinnati, were well stocked with religious books and the works of the American Tract Society. The publication of a history of Dr. Barclay's Jerusalem mission was announced and an elaborate publishing program was undertaken. The *Millennial Harbinger* announced the new venture in its June, 1853, issue, but accompanied it with a stinging editorial critique on "The Publication House of the Brethren," signed "A. W. C.," who probably was Archibald W. Campbell, one of the co-editors. The editor called attention to the frequent changes in the ownership and policies of the *Age,* and branded the whole project as an ill-timed experiment. In June, 1854, the *Harbinger* accused the A.C.P.S. of misappropriating the funds of the Missionary Society in some way, virtual bankruptcy, and perverting their sacred trust. While the Convention appointed a committee to investigate the charges and gave the A.C.P.S. a clean bill, the Publication Society never recovered from the attacks emanating from Bethany.

The 1856 Convention received a resolution from W. K. Pendleton which read, *"Resolved,* That it is inexpedient to continue the existence of the American Christian Bible Society, and that it should be dissolved."

Before the annual meeting was adjourned both the Bible Society and the Publication Society were dead.

Many persons are quick to charge that the whole incident was the result of rival ambitions of editors and publishing interests. A valid principle was involved, however. In a religious movement which acknowledges no official overhead controls, the power of the press is as dangerous to freedom as the power of bishops. As long as the journals which serve it are privately owned, their influences are discounted accordingly. Once a single publishing house is acknowledged as having some quasi-official status in the life of the movement, the concept of ministerial and congregational freedom is endangered.

Lack of financial support was one of the first snags struck by the American Christian Missionary Society. The paid memberships were insufficient and offerings from the churches were meager. The Society sent Dr. J. T. Barclay as its first missionary to evangelize Jerusalem, on the ground that the apostolic church in its evangelizing program began "first at Jerusalem." Barclay was a graduate in medicine from the University of Pennsylvania and was previously a classical student at the University of Virginia. The mission was a pitiable failure and an indication that more than sentimental legalism was essential to the salvation of the world. Campbell and others, reviewing the situation, felt that the Society should have a broader purpose and be more representative of the churches. Dissatisfaction with A.C.M.S. accomplishment was so great by 1868 that definite steps were taken to provide a better means of national cooperation. A committee of twenty was chosen to study the problem. The group was composed of able men such as Pendleton, Proctor, Errett, Moore, Belding, Longan, Loos, Caskey, Lamar, Reynolds, Graham, and Franklin. They made their report at the Louisville convention of the A.C.M.S. in 1869.

The "Louisville Plan" called for a general convention composed of messengers from state conventions, who were to be the chosen representatives of the churches and district conventions, the latter being composed of messengers from the churches. There were to be general, state, and district boards corresponding to the several conventions, and each constituent body was to have a corresponding secretary and an executive officer. Each state was entitled to two delegates, plus one additional for each five thousand members in the state. Churches were to pledge definite sums annually for missions and pay it to the district treasurer who was to divide it into two equal sums for the district and the general board.

Article II of the "Louisville Plan" read:

Its object shall be the spread of the Gospel in this and in other lands, according to the following plan of church co-operation:

Section 1. (a) There shall be a General Board and Corresponding Secretary. (b) A Board and Corresponding Secretary for each State to co-operate with the General Board. (c) District boards in each State, and a Secretary in each district whose duty it shall be to visit all the churches in his district, in order to induce them to accept the missionary work as a part of their Christian duty.

Section 2. There shall be an annual convention in each district, the business of which shall be transacted by messengers appointed by the churches; an annual convention in each State, the business of which shall be conducted by messengers sent from the churches of the State, it being understood, however, that two or more churches, or all the churches of a district, may be represented by messengers mutually agreed upon; and an annual general convention, the business of which shall be conducted by messengers from the State conventions.

Section 3. The General Convention shall annually appoint nine brethren, who, together with the Corresponding Secretaries of the States and the Presidents of the State Boards, shall constitute a General Board, who shall meet annually to transact the general missionary business, and appoint a committee of five to superintend the work in the intervals between their annual meetings.

This elaborate machinery would have stirred the hearts of some modern-day Disciples who prefer and plan ecclesiastical organization. How men of supposedly good judgment, committed to the principle of congregational freedom, could have been persuaded that this was the solution to the problems of the brotherhood continues to be a marvel. Nevertheless, it was unanimously adopted (except for two negative votes). Even Benjamin Franklin, who had been one of the most vocal in his opposition to the A.C.M.S., gave open assent to the Louisville Plan.

When the news of the "Plan" was read by the churches they were literally stunned. Confusion inevitably followed. The people could not understand why they should have an elaborate ecclesiastical system of this sort foisted upon them so soon after their liberation from denominationalism. Funds were not forthcoming. The machinery could not operate.

At this point it is well to consider at some length the general opposition to extracongregational associations. This adverse reaction was never completely overcome and finally became one of the factors in a major open break in the fellowship of the churches.

The chief opposition came from Jacob Creath, Jr. He began his perennial onslaughts in a series of mild articles in the *Millennial Harbinger* in which he quoted at length from the noted Dr. W. E. Channing, of Boston, who had brilliantly espoused the principle of congregational freedom. But when Editor Campbell replied in his series on "Dr. William E. Channing's Opinions of Conventions," Creath unsheathed his sword and declared war. Answering the assumption that conventions were acceptable to the majority of Disciples, Creath answered, "I suppose the golden calf was acceptable to all the Jews, *except Moses*. I believe the calves set up at Dan and Bethel were popular with Jereboam and the ten tribes. The report of the spies was acceptable to all the Jews, *except Caleb and Joshua*. The Pope is very acceptable to the Catholics; so are creeds and clerical conventions to all the Protestant parties. But does all this prove that they are accountable to God?" (August, 1850, pp. 470, 471). Challenging Campbell, he said:

You place conventions on the level of the church of God and civil governments. From the Acts of the Apostles, we have authority for the organization of all the early Christian churches. Paul says the governments that exist are ordained of God—Rom., ch. 13. Now, if you will produce as good authority for conventions as I have for the congregations of God and civil governments, *I will yield the controversy to you.* . . .

You say that our Saviour and the apostles did not denounce conventions, as such. Did they denounce Popery and corrupt Protestantism, as such? Did they denounce infant baptism, or creed making, or auricular confession, as such? It is for you to show that they authorized conventions (September, 1850, pp. 496, 497).

John T. Johnson, who early favored conventions and societies, wrote in the *American Christian Review,* shortly before his death:

The congregation plan is the divine arrangement. It works best. It accomplishes most good, by calling forth all the energies and resources of each congregation, and the least injury is the result . . .

I am yet to learn that an ecclesiastical establishment, by its messengers, has the divine right to select and ordain evangelists, to sit in judgment on evangelists, on congregations and their difficulties; to try heresies, to declare fellowship, non-fellowship, etc. . . .

Tolbert Fanning joined with William Lipscomb in July, 1855, to establish the *Gospel Advocate,* announcing that he intended to give the "subject of co-operation a thorough examination." In February, 1857, he announced:

We regard the church of Christ as the only divinely authorized Bible, Missionary and Temperance Society on earth; and furthermore, we believe that it is in and by means of the church the world is to be converted, and Christians are to labor for the Lord. . . . In all the efforts to do the service of the Lord through human institutions, it has seemed to us that the church is degraded, and rendered indeed useless.

Three months later he reiterated:

We believe and teach that the Church of Christ is fully competent to most profitably employ all of our powers, physical, intellectual and spiritual; that she is the only divinely authorized Missionary, Bible, Sunday School, Temperance and Cooperation Society on earth. It is, has been, and we suppose, always will be our honest conviction, that the true and genuine service of God can be properly performed only in and through the church. Hence we have questioned the propriety of the brethren's efforts to work most successfully by means of State, district and county organizations, "Missionary," "Publication" and "Bible Societies" or "Bible Unions," "Temperance Societies," "Free-Mason and Odd-Fellowship Societies" to "visit" the fatherless and widow in their affliction, or any other human organization for the accomplishing of the legitimate labor of the church.

Benjamin Franklin, wavering in his views on co-operative endeavors, was first in, then out of the society complex. His basic views were, however, expressed early in his editorship of the *American Christian Review* (December, 1849):

We are perfectly aware that if we wish to put the Christian communities in the power of men, to control them, wield them, and make them engines to honor man, we need some kind of an organization of the New Testament; but the simple independent church, for keeping the ordinances, religious instruction and saving the world, is all-sufficient for the good of the saints and the glory of God. Indeed, one of the principle reasons why this question of organization has perplexed the minds of so many is, that they are looking for, and trying to make out something unknown to the whole of the New Testament. They overlook the simple, easy and common-sense arrangement of the New Testament, and complain that we have no arrangement . . .

The opposition to extracongregational agencies fell into three classifications: (1) the conviction that human ecclesiastical organizations were unauthorized by the Scriptures, and were therefore unscriptural; (2) the potential danger of the societies infringing upon the independence of the local congregation; and (3) the making of a particular kind of co-operative endeavor a test of Christian fellowship. There were often lower motives involved, examples of which could be cited *ad infinitum*, but primarily the controversy hinged on great issues of principle common to all other restoration movements in the history of the Christian church.

Alexander Campbell was thoroughly committed to the creation of all essential means of united action in the Lord's work, provided the independence of the local churches was maintained and the Biblical faith was preserved and declared. Prophetically he saw the Restoration movement rising to a position of great influence for Christian unity in the religious world:

We have seen the tremendous community arise. . . . They have renounced the tyranny of opinionism—they have repudiated the schismatic tenets of a morbid Protestantism—they have abjured allegiance to papistical traditions—they have rallied around a few cardinal salutary and sublime truths, and have vowed to build their faith, their hope, their love upon the firm foundation of the Apostles and Prophets; and without regard to differences in mere opinions, they have resolved to receive, cherish and sustain one another as brethren in the family of God.

But among these thousands and myriads of men, formerly of all creeds and parties, there are all sorts of spirits, all conceivable varieties of intellect and disposition—some that require a bridle, and some that demand a spur. We have the diffidence and tardiness of age, and the waywardness and impetuosity of youth. Some must preach, and some must hear; some must write, and some must read; and who can say to A, Do this, and he does it; or to D, Withold thy hand, and he obeys. In such a conflicting state of affairs, the harmlessness of the dove and the wisdom of the serpent are of the greatest importance. Indeed, all the graces of the spirit of Christ are indispensable to setting in order of the things that are wanting and to the maintenance of "a unity of spirit in the bonds of peace."

Campbell knew that progress could be purchased only at a great price in human opposition and controversy, but he prayed for an understanding and generosity of spirit among all who loved the Lord, that peace and brotherhood might prevail despite differences of opinion. If that concept could have been realized in the life of the brotherhood, society and

186

nonsociety brethren might have lived together and prayed together in a united testimony for "the faith which was once delivered."

The "Louisville Plan" failed miserably, but it temporarily convinced the Disciples that complicated ecclesiastical machinery is not according to their genius as a religious movement; that individual freedom and congregational independence cannot be discounted; that missionary contributions must be voluntary and elicited by the merit of the work; that co-operation of the churches must be a purely voluntary matter and that any plan of federating them into an official organization would be unacceptable to many of them; that the support of extracongregational societies or conventions cannot be made a test of fellowship if any semblance of unity and brotherhood are to be maintained; and that sometimes things have to get worse before they can be better. It did not prove that the brethren were opposed to co-operation or to missionary work, but only that new patterns must be devised which would accomplish these laudable ends without threatening the genius of the movement.

Various changes were made from time to time in the framework of the General Christian Missionary Convention until finally it retained but little of the objectionable features of the "Louisville Plan." Its missionary work eventually resumed the old name of the American Christian Missionary Society and continued until its absorption in the United Christian Missionary Society in 1920. Thomas Munnell was corresponding secretary of the General Christian Missionary Convention from 1868 to 1877, when he was succeeded by F. M. Green.

In 1874 two encouraging developments in co-operation began. Both the organization of the Christian Woman's Board of Missions and the meeting that eventuated in the organization of the Foreign Christian Missionary Society took place in the Richmond Street church in Cincinnati (which was succeeded by the Western Hills Church of Christ).

In July, 1874, Caroline Neville (Mrs. S. E.) Pearre, well known in Kentucky and Missouri but then residing in Iowa City, Iowa, proposed the idea of enlisting the ladies of the Christian churches in the support of their own program of missionary endeavor. When Isaac Errett visited the Iowa City church, he learned of Mrs. Pearre's plan and decided to support the calling of a mass meeting of women in Cincinnati for the formation of a new society. His editorial, "Help Those Women," in the *Christian Standard* of July 11, 1874, prepared the brotherhood for generous acceptance of the idea. Mesdames Pearre, Milligan, Sloan, Goodwin, Dickinson, King, Brown, Norris, and others attended the meeting which convened October 22, 1874. The Christian Woman's Board of Missions was organized upon a pattern similar in constitution and bylaws to the Woman's Missionary Society of the Congregational churches. Headquarters were established in Indianapolis, and plans were made to establish missions in the West, in India, in Jamaica, and among the American Negroes. The first officers were Maria Jameson, president; Sarah Wallace, recording secretary; Mrs. S. E. Pearre, corresponding secretary; and Mrs. O. A. Burgess, treasurer. An offering of $430 was received.

The C.W.B.M.'s first full year's receipts, for 1875, were $770.35. The figures for 1880 were $5,050; for 1890, $42,116; for 1900, $106,722. W. J. Williams and family became the first missionaries, going to Jamaica in 1876 and reorganizing the scattered remnants of the work begun earlier by the A.C.M.S. In 1880, the women joined with the A.C.M.S. in a mission to France. Then followed undertakings in India, China, and Mexico, and missionary and education projects in America. Societies were organized in local churches for women, young people, and children, and the funds poured in. *Missionary Tidings,* an official journal, was started in 1883. *Junior Builders* magazine, begun in 1890, served the children's societies. A leaflet and book literature were created to give an educational impact to missions.

Also in 1874, during the Cincinnati General Convention, Joseph King gave a stirring address on "The Importance of Foreign Missions." Many brethren privately urged the formation of a foreign society. When the "powers that be" failed to do anything about a new society, W. T. Moore left the auditorium and went to a basement room in the Richmond Street church, where he spent some time in prayer over the matter. He then contacted several like-minded brethren; and, in an independent meeting, a committee was set up with Moore as chairman to draft a plan of organization. Among those present were B. B. Tyler, Thomas Munnell, F. M. Green, J. B. Bowman, W. F. Black, J. C. Reynolds, Robert Moffett, J. S. Lamar, R. M. Bishop, W. S. Dickinson, John Shackleford, and David Walk. Isaac Errett was president of the General Society and was presiding over its sessions at the time. Later he associated himself with the move, heartily promoted it in the columns of the *Standard,* and served on the committee that drafted the first constitution.

The formal organization of the Foreign Christian Missionary Society took place at the convention in Louisville, in 1875. Isaac Errett was elected president; W. T. Moore, J. S. Lamar, and Jacob Burnett, vice presidents; Robert Moffett, secretary; B. B. Tyler, recording secretary; and W. S. Dickinson, treasurer. Among the first missionaries sent out by the society was Dr. A. Holck who went to Denmark; Henry Earle, to England; and Jules DeLaunay and wife, to France. M. D. Todd and W. T. Moore then joined Henry Earle in England. In 1882, the India mission was established (in connection with the C.W.B.M.) with G. L. Wharton and wife, Albert Norton and wife, and Misses Mary Greybiel, Ada Boyd, Laura Kinzie, and Mary Kingsbury. E. T. C. Bennett and C. A. Moore, assisted by J. W. McGarvey and O. A. Carr, were sent as evangelists to Australia. In 1883, W. H. Williams was sent to Panama; and George T. Smith and wife, and Charles E. Garst and wife went out to Japan. In eight years, eleven missions were established. In that time some thirteen hundred persons were baptized. Property worth $79,000 was acquired.

The brotherhood was amazed and heartened at the signal success attending its representatives around the globe. Then came China, Africa, Cuba, Hawaii, and the Philippine Islands in rapid succession, with such heroic missionaries as W. E. Macklin, F. E. Meigs, Emma Lyon, E. I.

Osgood, James Butchart, E. E. Faris, D. N. Biddle, L. C. McPherson, Melvin Menges, A. E. Cory, W. H. Hanna, H. P. Williams, and scores of others, thrilling young Disciples and inspiring them to volunteer for Christian service abroad. By 1900 the F.C.M.S. receipts were $180,016.16.

Behind the scenes in this rapid development was Archibald McLean, who devoted himself unselfishly and sacrificially to missionary promotion. McLean was elected secretary of the Foreign Society in 1882. He was a blunt Scotsman from Prince Edward Island, endowed with great abilities as an executive and a promoter. Foreign missions was an obsession with him. He felt that Christ's directive to "go . . . make disciples of all the nations" was the supreme business of the church. Immersing himself in a study of world needs and acquiring a knowledge of the history and techniques of Christian missions, he became one of the most capable missions executives in Christendom. The ministers and the churches of the Disciples in that day had little interest in the evangelization of the world. His task of creating a climate in which successfully to solicit and obtain support for the Society's program was prodigious. And gradually the brotherhood became missions conscious and the money came. McLean introduced scientific and standardized methods in missionary service and the F.C.M.S. eventually became one of the major Christian missionary societies of the world.

Numerous state missionary societies came into being in the evangelistic tradition of Walter Scott and the Mahoning Baptist Association. Scott was charged to preach the gospel "in destitute places," in such churches as desired "protracted. meetings"; to "travel and labor" among the brethren for the advancement of the cause, and "to receive voluntary and liberal contributions" for his support. These contributions were generally received in quarterly meetings and his report to the churches was made in the yearly meetings.

Ohio having been the mother of the idea, it was natural that she led the way in establishing the pattern of state societies. The Ohio Christian Missionary Society was organized at Wooster, May, 1852. Prior to that there had been sporadic state meetings in which such leaders as D. S. Burnet, T. J. Mellish, Benjamin Franklin, William Hayden, R. R. Sloan, J. P. Robinson, J. H. Jones, J. J. Moss, and Jacob Hoffman had been prominent. Alexander Campbell occasionally attended these meetings, encouraging the churches in such co-operative efforts. Names such as "The Convention of Churches of Christ in the State of Ohio" and "The Christian Missionary Society of Ohio" were chosen for organizations that came and went. In this trial-and-error period, the churches came to the conclusion that they did not want any superorganization or exercise of quasi-official authority by its evangelists. They rejected the delegate idea and favored mass meetings of interested brethren. Churches or ministers that doubted the wisdom of such co-operation, disapproved policies, or simply neglected the fellowship, were still considered brethren.

Only fifty-five churches, from twenty-three of Ohio's eighty-eight counties were represented at Wooster when the Ohio Christian Missionary

Society was formed. The adopted constitution avowed as its purpose: "The only object of this Convention shall be to devise ways and means for the furtherance of the original gospel within the bounds of the State of Ohio by assisting weak churches and disseminating the truth in destitute regions." "Delegates," similar to Baptist Association "messengers," were to compose its meetings. Officers and a board of managers were to direct the affairs of the Society. A committee was appointed to divide the state into nine districts to assure "grassroots" co-operation and to keep the state society from becoming too dominant in church affairs. Two state evangelists or missionaries were appointed to "ascertain the statistics of every church." D. S. Burnet was elected the first president; John Campbell, vice-president; T. J. Mellish, secretary; and W. B. Hillman, treasurer.

In succeeding years, the names of J. P. Robinson, R. M. Bishop, Isaac Errett, Robert Moffatt, and Alanson Wilcox stood out as the great leaders of Ohio Disciples. Ohio moved from a total membership of approximately twenty-five thousand in 1860 to eighty thousand in 250 churches in 1890.

The Illinois Christian Missionary Society was organized in 1856; New York, in 1861; Michigan and Nebraska, in 1868; Iowa, in 1869; West Virginia, in 1870; Virginia, in 1876; California, in 1876; Maryland, in 1877; Georgia and Oregon, in 1879; Wisconsin, in 1880; Pennsylvania, in 1882; and Arkansas, North Carolina, Texas, Colorado, and Kansas, in 1883. Eventually all the states were organized in a more or less effective manner for the propagation of the gospel.

There was no thought of building ecclesiasticisms. In fact, the opposition to all forms of co-operation on the part of some kept the state society leaders busy explaining in definitive terms the moderate nature of their undertaking. It is probable that this opposition was providentially permitted to act as a sort of breakwater against the flood of schemes constantly proposed in these conventions that might have resulted in the development of an ecclesiastical hierarchy and the destruction of congregational freedom. It is a significant fact of later history that when this opposition was withdrawn, dangerous trends toward ecclesiasticism developed to the weakening of the society system.

In 1888, the Board of Church Extension was organized to meet the church construction needs of 1,628 homeless mission churches. The A.C.M.S. launched the work, locating the offices of the Board in Kansas City, Missouri, because it was considered the center of the territory in which most of the loans would be needed. Later, the Board became a separate and independent organization. At first it was recommended that five hundred dollars should be the amount of the largest loan. Then one thousand dollars was fixed as the maximum on a property costing five thousand dollars. Soon loans of five thousand dollars were being permitted for city properties. When the Board lent fifteen thousand dollars to secure a sixty thousand dollar property in New York City, they were roundly criticized for prodigal waste. But as a result of the wise management of this "building and loan society," splendid church buildings began to spring up in strategic centers. A hitherto largely rural people began to challenge the populations of such cities as Los Angeles, Seattle, Tacoma, Spokane, Minneapolis, Chicago, Cleveland, Pittsburgh, Boston, Baltimore, Washington, Richmond, Houston, Dallas, Oklahoma City, St. Louis, Omaha, and Denver. Beginning in 1888 with $10,662.80, the Fund soon grew to a half million dollars. Within twenty years the Board had lent $1,516,500 to 1,228 churches, which had expended more than three million dollars for their edifices and grounds. Here was a type of co-operation which no one could oppose. It involved no doctrinal position and operated on a purely business basis. It soon became one of the most important organizations of the brotherhood and accomplished a work that told mightily in the extension of the movement.

Little had been done even in local churches in the field of Christian benevolence and philanthropy until the year 1886, when the National Benevolent Association of the Christian Churches was organized. Here, again, was a type of agency which elicited little opposition. The primitive church was distinguished for its ministries to the widows and orphans and took frequent collections to provide food and clothing for the needy. Such a project as the N.B.A. was both Scriptural and apostolic. The Association was chartered under the laws of the state of Missouri and opened its first home in St. Louis in January, 1889. This home was "for children only, until such time as knowledge of the association and its purposes, on the part of the brotherhood-at-large, should justify the enlargement of its work." Two improvements were soon made by the addition of a babies' home and a hospital. The development of the N.B.A. into a multimillion-dollar operation was yet to come.

The conscience of the brotherhood next began to be exercised about the plight of its retired ministers, many of whom were ill and poverty stricken. The Colorado brethren, under the leadership of R. H. Sawyer, projected an "Old Preachers Home." While the idea did not come to fruition, it initiated an action in the state convention which eventuated in national action. The General Missionary Convention in Richmond, Virginia, in 1894, appointed a committee on ministerial relief consisting of W. S. Priest, A. M. Atkinson, W. F. Cowden, W. F. Richardson, and N. S. Haynes. In May, 1895, ex-Governor Ira J. Chase, of Indiana, one of the state's greatly admired preachers, died suddenly in Lubec, Maine, while in the midst of an evangelistic meeting. Atkinson was charged with the task of providing support for Chase's destitute family and his dramatic appeal to the brotherhood crystalized sentiment for a new agency. The general convention in Dallas, Texas, in October, 1895, established the Board of Ministerial Relief with offices in Indianapolis, Indiana. Thus began a ministry which later developed into the Pension Fund of the Disciples of Christ.

With the rise of conventions and agencies came an unprecedented wave of brotherhood progress, prosperity, and expansion.

BIBLIOGRAPHY: Chapter 12

Campbell, Alexander, W. K. Pendleton, and others, *Millennial Harbinger* (1831-1870).
Davis, M. M., *Restoration Movement of the Nineteenth Century.*
Errett, Isaac, editor, *Christian Standard* (1866-1888).
Garrison, J. H., *The Story of a Century.*
Garrison, W. E., and Alfred T. DeGroot, *The Disciples of Christ: A History.*
Green, Francis Marion, *Christian Missions and Historical Sketches.*
Harrison, Ida Withers, *The Christian Women's Board of Missions.*
Haynes, N. S., *History of the Disciples of Christ in Illinois.*
Keith, Noel, *The Story of D. S. Burnet.*
Lewis, Grant K., *The American Christian Missionary Society.*
Loos, C. L., *Our First General Convention.*
McLean, Archibald, *The History of the Foreign Christian Missionary Society.*
Moore, A. B., *Alexander Campbell and the General Convention.*
Moore, W. T., *Comprehensive History of the Disciples of Christ.*
Richardson, Robert, *Memoirs of Alexander Campbell.*
Shaw, Henry K., *Buckeye Disciples.*
Tyler, B. B., *A History of the Disciples of Christ.*

Chapter 13

Like a Mighty Army

IN the days immediately following the Civil War, the Restoration movement numbered about two hundred thousand members. In 1875, it was credited with four hundred thousand communicants. By 1900 it had a membership of 1,120,000. The restoration moved "like a mighty army"—a religious force that America could not discount or ignore.

The Disciples credited their success to the unadulterated gospel, "the power of God unto salvation." They had disposed of the excess baggage of Roman Catholic and Protestant ecclesiastical dogma and tradition, and in their newly found freedom in Christ were evangelizing and baptizing hundreds every day. They had also unwittingly capitalized on "the American dream" of a bourgeoning "Utopia." Theirs was a "free church" in a "free land."

By 1870, the American frontier was beginning to disappear. St. Louis claimed to be "third largest city." The 1876 Centennial Exposition in Philadelphia drew three million visitors, and Colorado became the Centennial State. Kansas, Oklahoma, and Texas had real-estate booms that drew thousands to new homesteads in the West. The major denominations with headquarters in the Eastern cities contributed little to this settlement program, but Disciples joined the trekking companies by the thousands. Primarily a rural people, they talked the language of the settlers. Everywhere they went they set up churches, preached Christian unity, and became an important factor in the life of the new states.

The thrilling story of the Disciple invasion of Oklahoma has become an epic. The first opening was in 1889, with the Cheyenne and Arapahoe territories added in 1892 and the "Strip" in 1893. J. M. Monroe was the hero of the story. He organized the first Christian church at Guthrie, then the capital, in 1889, less than two weeks after the official opening. The following Sunday he established the church in Oklahoma City. Before official statehood was reached, the Disciples boasted a congregation in every county and in every town of more than one thousand population. On September 16, 1893, the famous "Run" into the Cherokee Strip occurred. It is said that one hundred fifty thousand people awaited the sound of the gun that would start them across the border to stake claims for new homes. Monroe held a revival among the waiting throngs and baptized about four hundred converts. With the co-operation of the Board of Church Extension, E. F. Boggess, minister at Guthrie, was given a Kentucky thoroughbred racing horse to make the run. Within thirty-nine minutes after the gun sounded Boggess had staked a claim for a church lot in Perry, the capital of the Strip. Other properties were immediately acquired in all strategic locations. For many years the Disciples were the leading religious force in Oklahoma.

In Colorado, the first Christian church was organized in 1868 at Golden City. J. H. and Bertie Stoner brought the Restoration plea to the mountain mining camps and pioneer settlements under thrillingly romantic situations. In 1882, there were congregations established at Golden, Boulder, Denver, Loveland, and Colorado Springs. Dr. William Bayard Craig, later chancellor of Drake University, characterized as "a steam engine in boots," arrived in Colorado in 1882. A town and a mountain bear his name today. Under his leadership, the Central Christian Church in Denver erected a fine edifice, which was dedicated by Isaac Errett in 1883. The state society was organized the next day (March 26) with Craig as president. In the next four and one-half years, the state evangelist organized churches in Lake City, Grand Junction, Aspen, Glenwood Springs, Buena Vista, Salida, Monta Vista, and Lamar. In 1897 there were thirty-eight churches with 4,495 members.

In Montana, Thomas F. Campbell (not related to the Bethany Campbells except through marriage to a niece of Thomas) was responsible for introducing the plea in 1865 at Helena. Here he established a school for boys and was later chosen as president of Monmouth College in Oregon. Intensive church planting in Montana can be attributed to G. A. Hoffman and J. Z. Tyler. In 1900, there were seventeen churches with 1,019 members in this vast, sparsely-settled territory of one hundred fifty thousand square miles.

John C. Hay established the first congregation in New Mexico at Roswell, in August, 1893. Congregations followed at Albuquerque, Carlsbad, Artesia, Clovis, Deming, Hagerman, Las Vegas, Lordsburg, Raton, Roy, and Tucumcari, until in 1909 there were nineteen churches with fifteen hundred members.

Disciples entered even Utah, the stronghold of Mormonism, in 1890. The first church was located in Salt Lake City, Utah, after Judge J. M. Breeze had stimulated an interest, and William F. Cowden, evangelist of the General Missionary Society, had been sent to hold an organizing meeting. At Ogden, Leonard G. Thompson, with aid from the Christian Women's Board of Missions, set a church in order in October, 1890.

When there were less than one hundred thousand inhabitants of Wyoming, the Disciples had already been in Laramie for two years. In 1890, L. I. Mercer established churches in Buffalo and Beckton. K. H. Sickafoose entered the Big Horn Valley in 1901. Soon there were ten churches "holding forth the word of life" to the territory's residents. In 1886, the American Christian Missionary Society sent Thomas H. Mullin to Arizona where he organized Central church in Phoenix. R. A. Hopper began the work in Tempe in 1898. Then followed Douglas, Bisbee, Tuscon, and the development of the Arizona Christian Missionary Society.

Thus the last frontiers were entered. Churches in almost every state became bases for further operation.

The debaters were the shock troops of "the army of the Lord." In this art of religious discussion, the Disciples had taken Alexander Campbell as their guide and were ready to challenge everyone who disagreed with them. Their debates covered the whole range of Christian doctrine and the beliefs of the cultists and infidels. T. W. Caskey (1816-96) held fifty-six public discussions; Henry Pritchard (1819-1900) engaged in forty debates and is credited with destroying Universalism in Indiana; Benjamin Franklin (1812-78) held thirty regular discussions and engaged in many more written debates; Clark Braden (1831-1917) met E. L. Kelley, a Mormon elder, in Ohio in 1884 and virtually exterminated Mormonism in that state: W. D. Moore met Universalism's brilliant Dr. S. P. Carleton in Indiana and Ohio with the result that many Universalist churches closed their doors; John S. Sweeney (1832-1908) specialized in Methodists; O. A. Burgess (1829-82) was mighty against old-world Calvinism as represented in the Presbyterian and Baptist churches. D. R. Dungan, J. W. McGarvey, J. M. Mathes, L. B. Wilkes, and many others too numerous to mention were experienced debaters. So "mighty in the Scriptures" were these advocates of the apostolic faith that by 1900 it was almost impossible to find opponents to keep up this form of "military operation," and religious debate became largely a matter of history.

A change in modes of preaching came in this period. In the early days of the movement, preaching was almost exclusively polemical and evangelistic. Preachers were under attack by the denominations and were driven to defend their simple New Testament position. They constantly inveighed against the evils of denominationalism and called upon members of other churches to "come out from Babylon." The proof-text method was popular. Sermons portrayed the glories of a united church and the religious millennium that would come on earth when all God's people were one. In the so-called protracted meetings, they preached expository sermons largely drawn from the book of Acts and concluded with a "gospel invitation." This invitation to accept Christ at the close of every sermon has remained until this day a distinctive feature of Disciples' preaching and worship services.

As the movement grew in general acceptance, preaching began to emphasize such themes as the lordship of Christ, Christian living, and the distinctive messages of the various books of the Bible. Christian doctrine was presented in a broader Biblical context, but there was still major emphasis on such themes as sin, redemption, faith, forgiveness, conversion, baptism, the New Testament pattern of the church, and

Christian unity. Sermons soon began to reflect the traditional laws of homiletics. Classic sermonic quality is noted in W. T. Moore's collection of sermons in the *Living Pulpit* (Volumes I and II).

This homiletical development was probably encouraged by the appearance of such books as Robert Milligan's *Scheme of Redemption* (1868), H. W. Everest's *Divine Demonstration* (1884), J. W. McGarvey's *Evidences of Christianity* (1886), and J. H. Garrison's *The Old Faith Restated* (1891). These volumes were doctrinally sound and "true to the plea," but evidenced a systematic knowledge and understanding of Christianity in its larger and more irenic aspects. The preaching and writing of Isaac Errett and J. H. Garrison guided preachers into deeper spiritual thought and provided wider concepts of the mission of the church in the world.

Beginning with Walter Scott, the Disciples always had a number of itinerant evangelists in the field. At this period the more successful were Knowles Shaw, who wrote "Bringing in the Sheaves," T. D. Garvin, and J. V. Updike. In 1879, Updike left the Church of God (Winebrennerian) and became a flaming evangelist of the Restoration movement. James E. Hawes joined him as singing evangelist. The Updike-Hawes team greatly advanced the cause wherever they went. They specialized in visiting communities where there was no "church after the New Testament pattern" or a very weak congregation. Invariably they would receive around one hundred new members and leave a strong church of Christ. These invasions of denominational strongholds often resulted in violence. Their tents were sometimes wrecked or burned and they were threatened with bodily harm. They were especially successful in Ohio and the Midwest. Hawes kept a record of baptisms and at the conclusion of their ministry had more than ten thousand names in his book.

Toward the end of the period, a new type of evangelistic preaching was introduced which had a tremendous appeal to the masses. Dwight L. Moody, the union evangelist, was drawing great crowds in all the metropolitan centers from coast to coast. He preached a "faith only" gospel, with emphasis on "the new birth," and moved thousands of people to his "inquiry rooms" for further instruction on "the way of salvation." Not many Disciples participated in these union meetings because the "terms of salvation," particularly baptism, were omitted from Moody's preaching. Lesser evangelists adopted Moody's methods and were enjoying wide acceptance. Charles Reign Scoville conceived the idea that the good in Moody's mass methods could be appropriated by the Disciples and utilized in connection with their usual presentation of the "gospel plan of salvation." His experiments in the new evangelism were amazingly successful. His first meeting, held in the little rural church at South Scott, Steuben County, Indiana, in the fall of 1892, resulted in forty-two additions. As Scoville's experience grew, local church campaigns seldom saw less than one hundred persons added. Then at Anderson, Indiana, there was a "veritable Pentecost" with 1,269 additions to the local church. At Oklahoma City, First church received more than fifteen hundred new

196

members; and so the fabulous wave of evangelism began to spread. Each campaign was preceded by intensive organization, promotion, and advertising. Cottage prayer meetings were held. Prospect lists were prepared. Visitation teams were trained to get results in personal evangelism. Mass choirs sang evangelistic songs. The sermons were popular and sentimental in tone and psychologically aimed at immediate decisions for Christ. The "steps into the kingdom" were clearly though briefly stated and "baptism the same hour of the night" was advised. This new school of evangelists included such men as S. M. Martin, W. T. Brooks, James Small, H. E. Wilhite, Herbert Yuell, Roger Fife and sons, W. E. Harlow, and William J. Lockhart.

The role of the Disciples in the life of the nation now assumed marked significance.

Chief among its noted leaders was James A. Garfield. He was born in Orange, Cuyahoga County, Ohio, in 1831. Although of excellent New England stock, his parents were poor. When he was two years old, his father died, leaving the widow with four small children. Garfield grew to young manhood as the chief supporter of the family. The Restoration plea challenged him under the preaching of W. A. Lilly. He was immersed shortly before he entered Western Reserve Eclectic Institute (later Hiram College) in 1851. He further pursued his education in Williams College, graduating with high honors in 1856. He began to preach while a student in Hiram, and soon became one of the outstanding ministers of the brotherhood. From 1857 to 1861 Garfield was principal of the Western Reserve Institute. He distinguished himself both as a teacher and an administrator. The principles of the new Republican Party appealed to him, particularly its stand on the slavery question, and he was in demand as a speaker in its behalf. In 1859, he was elected to the senate of Ohio, but at the outbreak of the Civil War in 1861, entered the army as colonel of the Forty-second Regiment Ohio Volunteers. Here his abilities took him rapidly to the top echelons of service, and when he resigned in 1863, Garfield was a general, chief of staff to General Rosencrans, of the Army of the Cumberland. He was nine times chosen representative of the Nineteenth Ohio Congressional District and became known by the high moral tone of his addresses on current issues. His name will ever be associated with legislation creating the civil service in opposition to the political doctrine "to the victor belongs the spoils of office." Legislation dealing with the army, reconstruction, the currency, the tariff, and resumption of specie payments bore the mark of Garfield's wise counsel. In 1880 he was elected to the United States Senate from Ohio; and in the same year was nominated and elected to the Presidency of the United States, being the only minister of the gospel ever to occupy this high office. The great expectations of the people for his administration were, however, shockingly dashed by Garfield's assassination by a disappointed office seeker. Thus he became a martyr to his ideals of clean government and the civil service. During his meteoric rise in the public esteem, he was loyal to his commitment to the Restoration movement. In Washing-

197

ton, against the wishes of his political advisers, he regularly attended divine worship in the humble clapboard chapel of the Christian church on a side street. Because of the many inquiries about the religious views of the Disciples he wrote that classic statement, "What We Stand For."

1. We call ourselves Christians, or Disciples of Christ.
2. We believe in God the Father.
3. We believe that Jesus is the Christ, the Son of the living God, and our Saviour. We regard the divinity of Christ as the fundamental truth of the Christian system.
4. We believe in the Holy Spirit, both as to his agency in conversion and as indwelling in the heart of the Christian.
5. We accept both the Old and the New Testament Scriptures as the inspired Word of God.
6. We believe in the future punishment of the wicked and the future reward of the righteous.
7. We believe that the Deity is a prayer hearing and a prayer answering God.
8. We observe the institution of the Lord's Supper on the Lord's Day. To this table we neither invite nor debar; we say it is the Lord's Supper for all of the Lord's children.
9. We plead for the union of God's people on the Bible and the Bible alone.
10. The Christ is our only creed.
11. We maintain that all the ordinances should be observed as they were in the days of the Apostles.

When the Archbishop of Canterbury preached at the memorial service for Garfield in the church of St. Martin's-in-the-Lane in London, it is said he made references to this simple statement of faith in most laudatory terms. Following this service, some five thousand Englishmen gathered in silence in the church yard of the Cathedral while the great bell sounded the Requiem, the only time it had ever been tolled except for deaths in the royal family.

Among the other national leaders of the period was Judge Jeremiah Sullivan Black (1810-1883), of Somerset, Pennsylvania. Early in his career he became a distinguished advocate and served as presiding judge of the Sixteenth Judicial District and as judge of the Supreme Court of Pennsylvania. In 1857, because of his great ability and incorruptible integrity, he was appointed by President James Buchanan as Attorney General of the United States. In his later years he conducted a written debate with the renowned infidel, Robert G. Ingersoll, in the columns of the *American Christian Review,* on the evidences of the Christian faith.

Numbers of Disciples were elected governors of states, among them such distinguished statesmen as Richard M. Bishop, of Ohio; General Francis M. Drake, of Iowa; Benton McMillan, of Tennessee; Alvin Saunders, of Nebraska; and Ira J. Chase, of Indiana. Bishop at one time served as president of the American Christian Missionary Society. Drake, through his generous giving, made possible the great university in Des Moines which bears his name.

Many senators such as George M. Oliver, of Pennsylvania, brought honor to the brotherhood. Representatives in the Congress were elected by the score, among them James Allen and H. D. Morely of Mississippi; W. H. Graham, Thomas W. Phillips, Sr., and Russell Errett, of Pennsylvania; A. M. Lay, Benjamin Franklin, Joshua Alexander, Champ Clark, and Thomas Hackney, of Missouri; James D. Richardson, William C. Houston, and C. E. Snodgrass, of Tennessee; R. M. A. Hawk, of Illinois; Albert T. Willis and John D. White, of Kentucky; R. F. Armfield, J. D. New, Charles Cooper, and E. D. Crumpacker, of Indiana; J. A. Hughes, of West Virginia; and "Cyclone" Davis, of Texas. Champ Clark was for many years Speaker of the House of Representatives and lost the nomination for President on the Democratic ticket by only a narrow margin to Woodrow Wilson. Tom L. Johnson, noted reform mayor of Cleveland, Ohio, was a member of the Crawford Road church there for many years. In diplomacy were such men as General Z. T. Sweeney, ambassador to Turkey and brilliant preacher of the gospel.

Disciples in the business field included R. A. Long, of the monolithic Long-Bell Lumber Company; Ovid Butler, for whom Butler University was named; Timothy Coop, of England; W. S. Dickinson, A. M. Atkinson, John B. Bowman, Joseph I. Irwin, Albert Allen, C. H. Gould, B. F. Coulter, G. W. N. Yost, Charles C. Chapman ("The Orange King of the World"), R. H. Stockton, J. H. Allen, and Claude L. Garth. The roll is far too long even to begin to list the names, not of mere church members who distinguished themselves in the market place, but men who took an active and intelligent part in promoting the plea for a united church by a return to the Bible alone as the rule of faith and practice.

One name deserves to be written high on the list—Thomas W. Phillips, Sr. Probably no minister among the Disciples had a clearer grasp of the genius of the movement or the essential elements of the Christian faith than this multimillionaire oil and gas man from Pennsylvania. He could have had any office he desired in the gift of the state of Pennsylvania, and briefly served his state in the halls of Congress, but he preferred to give most of his time apart from his business duties to his church. He made possible the launching of the *Christian Standard* under the editorship of Isaac Errett. He gave liberally of his wealth to Bethany and Hiram Colleges, and backed E. V. Zollars in founding Oklahoma Christian University (later to bear the Phillips name). His largess was freely invested in all the rising agencies of the brotherhood. But probably his greatest contribution to the movement was his book *The Church of Christ,* which clearly, simply, and in depth describes the church that Christ and the apostles built. It was first issued anonymously ("By A Layman") by Funk and Wagnalls, then one of America's leading book publishers. It was soon acclaimed by religious leaders of all denominations and had a circulation approaching a million copies. Thousands of volumes are still in circulation, telling the simple story of what might be today if the Christian world would return to the simplicity of the New Testament church.

The amazing story of the educational contribution of the Disciples to the frontier country, commonly called the Middle West, could well be recorded in these pages. In the period immediately following the Civil War, Christian church ministers and educators founded more than two hundred private or church-owned colleges, seminaries, academies, and institutes. In 1946, Dr. Claude E. Spencer, curator of the Disciples of Christ Historical Society, compiled a list of 256 such schools organized to that date.

The situation which made this possible was the absence of any comprehensive and adequate public policy in the establishment and maintenance of secondary and collegiate education in much of the area west of the Allegheny Mountains. Indeed, there were only eight hundred high schools in the entire nation in 1880.

Ohio is an excellent example of what happened in many states. The chief educational institution which received the support of the churches was Western Reserve Eclectic Institute, which became Hiram College in 1867. It began in 1850 with A. S. Hayden as principal and drew its students largely from families who were members of Christian churches. Its self-perpetuating board was composed of Christian church men, but the school had no official relationship to any church or group of churches. In this respect it was like all educational institutions serving the churches throughout the nation. Later, they may have been endorsed by conventions or agencies, but control always remained with individuals. Even before the Civil War, Hiram had a student enrollment of more than five hundred and grew to substantial proportions, becoming under J. M. Atwater, B. A. Hinsdale, and E. V. Zollars one of the outstanding educational institutions of the brotherhood.

But Ohio needed other educational institutions, and Disciples felt called to provide them. In the fall of 1865, T. D., Hugh, and James Garvin started Franklin College at Wilmington. In a whirlwind promotional campaign, the funds were promised for the purchase of a thirty-three-acre site and the construction of a college building. In the hard times which followed the Civil War, the property was sold to the Society of Friends, who still operate the institution as Wilmington College.

In 1868, a group of Disciples in Alliance urged Isaac Errett to move his recently-launched *Christian Standard* to their city and accept the presidency of a new college they had projected. Alliance College opened that summer. In August, 1869, a splendid four-story main building was dedicated and prospects seemed excellent. However, shortly after Errett's decision to move to Cincinnati, the institution closed its doors, and in 1887 the buildings and campus were sold to the Alliance Board of Education. Alliance College was indirectly the precursor of Mount Union College, which has had a prosperous history in that location.

J. S. Lower, J. Fraise Richards, Warren Darst, and H. S. Lehr, seeing the need of "normal colleges" for the training of teachers, started schools at Hopedale, Geneva, Republic, Fostoria, Mansfield, and Ada. The school at Ada, under the capable direction of Lehr, became the Northwestern Ohio Normal School, with an enrollment in 1880 of fourteen hundred.

While the graduates were mostly teachers, under the personal guidance of Lehr and Professor Parks many became ministers in the Christian churches. In 1900, the institution was purchased by the Methodists and became Ohio Northern University. In that year it enrolled three thousand students.

Other educational plants founded in this "golden age" of the Disciples in Ohio included Bedford Christian Institute, Central Ohio Classical and Business College, Fayette Normal, Music, and Business College, Hygiea Female Atheneum, McNeeley Normal School, Mount Vernon Male Academy, Vernon Female Institute, and, later, Phillips Bible Institute.

In far-west Texas a similar development was taking place. Add-Ran College had been founded by Addison and Randolph Clark in 1873, and was the breeding-ground of Christian leadership for the Texas churches. Out of this background came Texas Christian University at Waco, and later in Fort Worth. But there were a score of other educational institutions under various Disciples' auspices—Muse Academy, Mount Enterprise Academy, Patroon College, Burnetta College, Carlton College, Carr-Burdette College, Jarvis Institute, Randolph College, Hereford-Panhandle Christian College, Add-Ran Jarvis College, Midland College, Lockney College, Gunter College, Southwestern Christian College, Lingleville College, Childress Classical Institute, and Sabinal College.

Indiana, Illinois, Kentucky, Missouri, and other states had similar educational experiences with scores of failures but some major successes. W. T. Moore, in his *Comprehensive History of the Disciples of Christ,* pays tribute to this generation of educators:

> Their ambition was very great at the beginning, so much so, indeed, that it sometimes becomes ridiculous, such as calling what was little more than a grammar school a university. But even that absurd way of styling things must be regarded as evidence of the hope which the founders of these institutions had with respect to the future. These men ought to be honored for the very absurdities which they committed in the name of a great faith which they had in their brethren to build up and sustain their educational institutions.

Gradually the Disciples began to realize the relationship between sacrificial stewardship and higher education. Standards of scholarship were raised and adequate buildings and equipment began to be provided. Co-operation took the place of competition, and colleges began to insist upon well-trained leadership. Toward the end of 1900, some thirty-five major institutions of higher education enrolled around eight thousand students and owned property worth more than six million dollars. Among these were Bethany College, Hiram College, Bible College of Missouri, Drake University, Johnson Bible College, Transylvania University, College of the Bible (Lexington), Butler College, Virginia Christian College, Eureka College, Oklahoma Christian University, Milligan College, Atlantic Christian College, Christian University, Eugene Bible University, Kentucky Female Orphan School, William Woods College, Hamilton College, Missouri Christian College, Campbell-Hagerman College, West Kentucky

College, Nebraska Christian University, Christian College, and the Disciples Divinity House at the University of Chicago.

A unique type of educational institution had its rise in the latter years of this period—the Bible chair. Tax-supported universities were beginning to draw thousands of students. In 1882, Leonard Bacon proposed the establishment of a limited college program in connection with the University of Michigan. In 1898, a committee was appointed by the Missouri state convention to look into the planting of a Bible chair or a Bible college in connection with the state university at Columbia. In 1893, the Michigan dream became a reality with "Father" T. M. Iden supported in a Bible chair through joint co-operation of the Michigan Christian Missionary Association and the Christian Woman's Board of Missions.

In 1896, the plan was inaugurated (formally established in 1906) at the University of Virginia. In 1900, Bible chairs were established at the University of Kansas and the University of Texas. Projects for the University of Pennsylvania and the University of Georgia were not adequately supported and were abandoned. Thus was inaugurated an idea which, with some modifications, was later adopted by all the major denominations of the nation. Most state universities are ringed now with splendid buildings housing special educational and social programs under Methodist, Presbyterian, Lutheran, and other auspices.

The influence of religious journalism continued to be a major factor in guiding the destinies of the Restoration movement. There were scores of periodicals in the field but the *Christian Standard* and the *Christian-Evangelist* led in quality of product, services rendered the churches, and rightness and logic of their policies. Isaac Errett, of the *Standard,* and J. H. Garrison, of the *Evangelist,* were warm personal friends and were in substantial agreement on most of the doctrinal and practical issues involving the life of the brotherhood. The *Christian-Evangelist* came into being with the merger of B. W. Johnson's *Evangelist* and Garrison's *Christian* in 1882, with both men as co-editors until Johnson's death in 1894. After the death of Isaac Errett in 1888, the *Standard* and the *Evangelist* began to manifest somewhat different points of view representing the two growingly distinct schools of thought in the mainstream of the movement.

Under the wise business management of Russell Errett, son of Isaac Errett, the Standard Publishing Company rapidly forged ahead in the journalistic field to become one of the leading houses in America. It was first in the field with special literature services to the Sunday schools and Christian Endeavor Societies. It provided a wide range of study quarterlies, weekly periodicals for distribution in all the graded classes, and methods books of all kinds. To cope with the demand for this literature, the buildings at Cincinnati were expanded and the latest and best printing equipment installed. A great library of religious paintings and prints was acquired as the basis for full-color reproductions of Christian art. Standard was the first religious publishing house in the nation to introduce offset color printing and eventually came to be the supplier of Bible art in color

202

to some thirty denominational houses. The *Young People's Standard,* later named *The Lookout,* rivaled and finally exceeded the *Christian Standard* in circulation to become the most widely read periodical in the brotherhood. Among Standard's services to the churches were elders' and deacons' conferences, Bible-school conventions, doctrinal congresses, and evangelistic conferences, in which experts trained church leaders for more efficient work.

The *Christian Standard* under the successive editorship of Hugh McDiarmid (1888-1896) and J. A. Lord (1896-1910), became known as "the guardian of the faith." It was free and independent of the conventions and agencies, though at this time in substantial agreement with their policies. J. W. McGarvey's department of Biblical criticism was one of the strong features of the journal and had a tremendous influence in keeping the movement true to its original principles.

On the right fringe of the movement there were two widely read periodicals—*The Christian Leader and The Way,* edited by John F. Rowe, and the *Gospel Advocate,* edited by David Lipscomb. Others in this conservative category were the *Octographic Review, the Firm Foundation,* the *Christian Messenger,* the *Christian Preacher,* the *Primitive Christian,* and the *Gospel Echo.*

On the left fringe a new magazine made its appearance in 1884 bearing the name *Christian Oracle,* which was destined later, under the nomen *Christian Century* and an extremely liberal policy, to play an influential role in the affairs of the brotherhood and the whole Protestant world.

The period from 1879-1900 was marked by a building boom. The colleges erected great halls of learning. The churches tore down their small and inadequate frame buildings and replaced them with structures of gothic and classic beauty. One of the first of these was the edifice constructed by Central Christian Church, Cincinnati, Ohio. It was a copy, at least in part, of a small French cathedral, with a celebrated rose window, and an audience room seating more than fifteen hundred persons. It was long considered the finest church edifice in the brotherhood. A great hue and cry went up from rural and village Disciples, roundly condemning the Cincinnati "aristocrats" for seeking the "habiliments of Rome" and spending an extravagant $150,000 which might well have been given either to the poor or to the evangelization of the world. Other beautiful buildings were erected in St. Louis, Kansas City, Louisville, Lexington, and other large cities in which the Disciples were numerically strong. In many centers of population there had been rapid accumulation of wealth and leading members gave generously to help provide church facilities which would compare favorably with those of their religious neighbors. Pipe organs, Sunday-school buildings, lecture rooms, and institutional features were added to the old-time single room "auditoriums."

"Like a mighty army" the Disciples sang. They not only sang the great traditional hymns of the church with zest, but they loved their own "Bringing in the Sheaves," "There Is a Habitation," "The Beautiful

Garden of Prayer," "The Way of the Cross Leads Home," "Tell Mother I'll Be There," and "His Eye Is on the Sparrow." As the new evangelism began to sweep the brotherhood, professional song evangelists began to multiply. In this period the more familiar names were J. H. Fillmore, J. H. Rosecrans, A. J. Showalter, Charles M. Fillmore, W. E. M. Hackleman, and C. C. Cline. A plethora of hymnals and songbooks became available, including the *Christian Hymn and Tune Book, Christian Psaltery, The Christian Hymnal, The Praise Hymnal, Silver and Gold,* and *Songs of Evangelism.* The state and national conventions were veritable songfests symbolic of happy throngs on the victory highway.

Sunday schools, or Bible schools as many preferred to call them, began to be a significant arm of the churches. For some time, despite the approval of Alexander Campbell and Isaac Errett, church leaders doubted these organizations had the authority or sanction of Scripture. In the first stage of their popularity they were seen as agencies for teaching evangelism. Full-time workers were called "Bible-school evangelists." In Indiana, the Disciples formed their own Indiana State Sunday-School Association in 1861. In 1870, at Wabash, the I.S.S.S.A. reported more than four hundred delegates in its convention. In 1865, the Ohio state society employed a Sunday-school evangelist, and the Ohio Christian Sunday-School Association was organized in 1867. Then followed the Illinois Association in 1874; Kentucky in 1873, with J. W. McGarvey as its first president; Missouri in 1876; Kansas in 1880; Texas in 1887; and Oregon in 1892. In 1882, an independent General Christian Sunday-School Association was organized which sponsored national gatherings. At Detroit in 1903, a more comprehensive organization, called the National Bible-School Association was established, and thus was launched one of the most inspiring developments in the life of the churches resulting in the reaching of millions for Christ through the Sunday school.

As the first one hundred years of history came to a close, there was a measure of real unity among the more than one million Disciples in America. They still held inviolate their glorious ideal—the union of all Christians. They were sincerely seeking to demonstrate in churches after the New Testament pattern that they had the plan for a united, aggressive, invincible, and glorious church. They were building not on a catechism, or creed of man's formulation, but on the Holy Scriptures, the gospel of salvation. These "called out" people were seeking the evangelization of the world and the realization of the great commission program in their day and generation. "Like a mighty army" moved the church of God!

BIBLIOGRAPHY: Chapter 13

Abbott, B. A., *The Disciples: An Interpretation*.
American Home Missionary Year Books (1903-1909).
Brown, John T., *Churches of Christ*.
Edwards, J. H., editor, *Orthodoxy in the Civil Courts*.
Errett, Isaac, Hugh McDiarmid, and James A. Lord, editors, *Christian Standard* (1870-1901).
Garrison, J. H., editor, *Christian-Evangelist* (1890-1901).
Garrison, W. E., and Alfred T. DeGroot, *The Disciples of Christ: A History*.
Green, F. M., *The Life of James A. Garfield*.
Hall, Colby D., *Texas Disciples*.
Lamar, J. S., *Memoirs of Isaac Errett*.
Moore, W. T., *Comprehensive History of the Disciples of Christ*.
Peters, H. H., *Charles Reign Scoville*.
Ridpath, J. C., *The Life and Work of James A. Garfield*.
Shaw, Henry K., *Buckeye Disciples*.
Smith, Theodore Clarke, *The Life and Letters of James Abram Garfield*.
Updike, J. V., *Sermons*.
Wilcox, Alanson, *A History of the Disciples of Christ in Ohio*.

Chapter 14

One Hundred Years—
Crest and Crisis

IN 1909 approximately thirty thousand Disciples of Christ gathered in Pittsburgh, Pennsylvania, for the centennial celebration of Thomas Campbell's *Declaration and Address*.

The choice of Pittsburgh for this mammoth demonstration was peculiarly fitting. The main stream of the movement began in western Pennsylvania. The *Declaration and Address* was written in a house that was then still standing in Washington, Pennsylvania. Pittsburgh was not far from Brush Run and Bethany. Walter Scott began his public ministry in Pittsburgh, and Robert Richardson practiced medicine there before becoming the trusted associate of Alexander Campbell at Bethany. Many strong Christian churches were located in the area.

The centennial celebration formed a historic promontory, marking the accomplishments of the past, the status of the movement at the beginning of the twentieth century, and the prospects for its future. It proved to be the last time that brethren of the three rapidly developing schools of thought in the movement were to be represented in a major national gathering. An event of such significance demands the historian's extended attention.

The history of the Disciples to this point is a phenomenal record. They had grown from some twenty persons associated with Thomas Campbell, to nearly one and one-half million. God had seemingly called these people to a distinctive testimony and mission, which He had providentially protected and advanced. There had been dark days as well as bright, and almost insurmountable problems were yet to be solved, but all this was to be expected in any undertaking. God has not assured immunity from evil influences, but He has given grace and guidance in meeting these influences. There are centrifugal and centripetal forces in every movement. Conflict is the law of progress. When men surrender their spirits and wills to God, He can weld them together in the bond of faith, hope, and love, and make them a real brotherhood in

Him. Prior to Pittsburgh, this had been accomplished in a truly marvelous way.

In 1901 at the Minneapolis convention of the American Christian Missionary Society and its associated agencies, the Centennial Convention idea was first proposed. J. H. Garrison moved that a committee be appointed to explore the possibilities. Garrison was named chairman and Helen E. Moses, Benjamin L. Smith, A. McLean, and Judge C. P. Kane were appointed to work with him. In 1905 it was decided to go to Pittsburgh, and a local committee consisting of R. S. Latimer, Wallace Tharp, George T. Oliver, T. E. Cramblet, William H. Graham, and W. R. Warren was established. Later, Thomas W. Phillips, Sr., O. H. Phillips, and M. M. Cochran were added. Finally the national and local committees were amalgamated by the choice of an executive committee with Thomas W. Phillips as chairman.

The Centennial Convention was then made the culminating feature of a Centennial Campaign with individual, congregational, and institutional goals to be accomplished by the entire brotherhood. The individual goals included: daily worship in every home; each person to win another to Christ; two Christian papers, state and national, in every home; not less than a tithe to God; an offering from every disciple to some Christian college; every home to be an antisaloon territory. Goals for congregations were: all the church membership and as many more in the Bible school; all the church in the prayer meeting; every church its mission; every preacher preaching; every church well housed and every church debt paid; every church in the state missionary co-operation; a men's organization in every church. Finally the institutional goals required: two million dollars for missions, benevolence, and education, with specific goals for the major agencies. There were also general goals which included: a thousand recruits to the ministry; ten thousand organized adult Bible classes; two hundred thousand trained workers; first place in the Christian Endeavor movement; fifty thousand at Pittsburgh; the promotion of Christian union by its practice.

The headquarters in Pittsburgh mailed some 208,000 letters. Posters were distributed. In the last year of promotion, the *Christian Standard* issued nine great centennial specials which were sent by the thousands to people in all denominations. The *Christian-Evangelist* gave much space to the project. Two editions of the *Declaration and Address* were reproduced in facsimile from the original and had a circulation of more than twenty thousand copies. A million copies of twenty-three leaflets and tracts appropriate to the observance were distributed free. The secular press joined in publicity for the event.

Long before the opening session on October 11, 1909, great crowds of people began to arrive in Pittsburgh. Every hotel and rooming facility in the city and its suburbs was employed to take care of the unofficial delegates to this giant mass meeting. The Kansas City delegation chartered a train for the trip and leased the entire Schenley Hotel as their headquarters. Hundreds of special trains and chartered cars from California,

208

Missouri, Indiana, Iowa, Kentucky, Oklahoma, Texas, and Kansas jammed the railyards. Ohio, West Virginia, and Pennsylvania furnished a steady stream of arrivals. Registration and entertainment clerks were swamped, and worked in relays night and day to serve the people. The spacious auditorium of Carnegie Hall was too small to accommodate the crowds at the main sessions. Simultaneous programs were provided in nearby churches and with outdoor meetings in Duquesne Garden, Luna Park, and Forbes Field. Thousands could not get into the meetings and stood in great throngs in the streets and parks enjoying the fellowship of brethren. Two hundred fifty Pittsburgh churches of all denominations opened their pulpits to leading preaching brethren on the Lord's Day. The closing Communion service in Forbes Field drew twenty thousand persons in the three-tiered grandstand. Thousands more filled the bleachers and stood on the ball field to remember the death and suffering of their Saviour. Pittsburgh, even America, had never seen such a mass demonstration to the glory of God. The religious world stood amazed and asked what manner of people these were who so zealously contended "for the faith which was once delivered unto the saints." The aim of the centennial committee to "tell the story of the Restoration movement, giving the principles of the plea, and voicing a message of Christian unity to the people of this generation" was fully accomplished.

Fifty noted speakers in five simultaneous sessions gave challenging messages. With only a few exceptions there was a remarkable unanimity in declaring the principles of the movement.

Archibald McLean, the veteran secretary of the Foreign Christian Missionary Society, said,

> In this Centennial year we honor [our fathers] by contending earnestly for the very thing for which they contended—*the union of all believers*. This is a glorious ideal in perfect harmony with the spirit of the age and the spirit of our Lord . . . *On a basis of Holy Scripture*. We build not on a catechism, or creed, or confession of man's formulation but on the word of truth, the gospel of our salvation. We read that God has magnified his word above all his name. It is for us to do likewise. *To the end that the world may be evangelized*. This is the end for which the Word became flesh and tabernacled among us; the end for which he died in agony on the cross and rose and ascended to the Father; the end for which the church was instituted and commissioned . . . (*Souvenir Program*, Centennial Convention, p. 46).

Robert M. Campbell, the grandson of Alexander Campbell, paid this tribute:

> Our fathers took their stand upon God's word, and God's word alone, and they felt that they stood upon the mountain-top, and by faith they could put their hands to their ears and could hear the tramp of millions coming to take their stand upon the Bible, and the Bible alone, as our rule of faith. . . .
> They, like the apostles of old, were characterized by the purity of their doctrine, by the piety of their lives, and by their patience under suffering. . . .
> And let us stand upon the Bible, on the mountain-top, and let us say to the multitudes, We fear not the whole universe, because we can stand here and feel secure, and as our fathers have said, feel the strength of mountains as they stood with the everlasting hills (*Centennial Convention Report*, p. 90).

R. A. Long, the distinguished Christian businessman who had given so liberally to the cause, gave no uncertain testimony:

The principles laid down by the leaders in this movement have done more in the last hundred years to bring the minds of Christian thinkers generally to a sense of the necessity of the union of God's people than any other single influence . . .
While it should be . . . our disposition to compromise matters that are not vital, God forbid that for any cause we may exercise such liberality as is not justified by the teachings of God's holy book.
We have been hearing a great deal lately about a new religion proposed by Dr. Eliot, the ex-president of Harvard. . . . what we want is not a new religion, but a closer adherence to the old religion that has been tested and found meeting the wants of mankind. . . . the principles of the gospel, of individual and social redemption, must remain the same as when Jesus declared, "No man cometh to the Father but by me" (*Centennial Convention Report*, p. 77, 78).

Charles S. Medbury thrilled the audience that heard him with a clarion call:

I plead with all the strength of my life for this continued heralding of the simple gospel of our Christ because it seems to me that the glorious record of the days agone places the stamp of divine approval upon this ministry. I know not where to turn for another universal message. . . .
I wish it were within my power to sound . . . the call of a new crusade. I wish we might become so lost in one sublime purpose that the world looking to us as a people might be moved to depths as yet unsounded. If only loyalty to the word of our God and the Christ of the Scriptures, and a spirit like the Master's own, and a passion for souls such as characterized him, could dominate us, happy would we be and blessed the world because of us (*Centennial Convention Report*, p. 178).

George Hamilton Combs said the program of the movement was clear cut:

We ask all Christians to unite by wearing a name at once catholic, Scriptural, the name that is the glory and inspiration of all our churches—the name of Christ. We ask all Christians to unite upon a creed bearing also the marks of Scripturalness and catholicity, a creed living, vital, unchanging—the person of Christ. We ask all Christians to unite upon the observances of the ordinances of the church as they are revealed in Scripture and in the catholic recognitions of the churches.
In a word, we hold that if the churches were to strip themselves of all that is specially distinctive and sectarian, that, so divested, they would have all the marks of the catholic, which is the apostolic, which is the united church. Scripturalness, catholicity, these are the twin fixed stars in whose light we journey as we seek the restoration of the united church (*Centennial Convention Report*, p. 27).

J. J. Haley, long recognized as a pulpiteer of note, summarized the plea for unity as "simple, Scriptural and catholic":

(1) The catholic creed of Christendom, the central and cardinal

proposition of Christianity [is this]—"I believe that Jesus is the Christ, the Son of the living God, the Saviour and Lord of men."

(2) The catholic rule of faith and practice, the word of God contained in the Old and New Testament Scriptures.

(3) The catholic ordinances, baptism and the Lord's Supper.

(4) The catholic name, "Christian."

(5) The catholic life, the ethics of the kingdom of God, "Whatsoever things are true, whatsoever things are honest, whatsoever things are just, whatsoever things are pure, whatsoever things are lovely, whatsoever things are of good report, if there be any virtue, if there be any praise, think on these things." . . .

If the churches ever get together, it will be on the basis of this universal New Testament Christianity (*Centennial Convention Report*, p. 336).

J. W. McGarvey, in his eightieth year, a living link with the early leaders of the movement, vigorously declared:

[Our] supreme, controlling rule of thought and action . . . was the rule so tersely and admirably expressed by Thomas Campbell: "Where the Scriptures speak, we speak, and where the Scriptures are silent, we are silent." It was this that led Walter Scott, when he was informed of Thomas Campbell's teaching, to devote himself night and day to the study, not of volumes in which his spiritual forefathers had expounded and defended the ancestral creed, but to the Scriptures alone, determined to follow them whithersoever they might lead. It was this that led Alexander Campbell, after accepting it from his father, to insist on the abandonment of infant baptism, and then to go on abandoning traditions, one by one, until he was freed from them all. It was this that led Barton W. Stone, before he heard of either of the Campbells, and before he fully realized what he said, to proclaim to sinners moaning and weeping in the dark, the Scriptural way of peace and pardon. It was this supreme devotion to the word of God that developed a movement having at first only the union of believers in view, into one having in view the complete restoration of primitive Christianity in its faith, its ordinances and its life, with union as a necessary result. For it was soon seen that the union for which Christ prayed, and upon which the apostles insisted, could be brought about only in this way. This, then, became, and has continued to be, the leading thought and purpose of the brotherhood, being the only practicable way of bringing about the union of God's people. It has made what we call our Reformation the mightiest instrument for the furtherance of Christian unity thus far known to history (*Centennial Convention Report*, p. 383).

Thomas W. Phillips, Sr., rejoiced at the growing interest in the Bible throughout the nation and called for a united testimony in the spirit of the *Declaration*:

It was here [in Pennsylvania] that a declaration of freedom from ecclesiasticism was made, one hundred years ago. In making this [our fathers] put emphasis on the Bible, and stated that "Where the Bible speaks, we speak; where the Bible is silent, we are silent." Now, this great rule has become more and more appreciated as the years have advanced. We find now the Y.M.C.A. teaching nothing but the Bible. . . . We find Bible classes in all the great congregations, and it is so taught and so understood that creeds and confessions of faith are practically ignored. . . . Now, in regard to the other great propositions, that all shall be united in one, that the prayer of Christ may be fulfilled; that all may be united in one, that the

211

world may believe. This great plea went out over the country and over the world, proclaiming unity upon the word of God . . . The world will never believe until God's people are united. A divided church has never saved a country, a city or a State, and never can. . . . In advocating this great plea, we do not claim to be the only Christians, but we do claim to be Christians only. We have no authority but the Bible; . . . and we have no creed but Christ (*Centennial Convention Report,* p. 22).

Brethren from England and Australia and New Zealand included Leslie W. Morgan, Thomas Hagger, W. J. Hastie, and many others, all bearing fraternal greetings. Scores of missionaries brought stories of the triumphs of the gospel.

The whole Christian community in the United States joined in the celebration. Denominations that had once so vigorously opposed their right to preach "the plea" now hailed the Disciples as having made a great contribution to the religious life of America.

The Baptist churches of New England and members of the Baptist Ministerial Conference of Boston headed by Cortland Myers, of Boston's Tremont Temple, sent greetings to the convention. Their communication was highlighted by the expression of the hope that "the two bodies of Christians, known as Disciples of Christ and Baptists, should be united in one body as speedily as possible to bring it about consistently with the principles of both" and rejoiced "in the advance that has already been made to that end, as seen in the actual union of churches in various localities as well as in fraternal commingling in congresses and conventions and evangelistic efforts." L. A. Crandall was the official fraternal delegate of the Northern Baptist Convention. In his felicitous address he remarked,

[We are met here] upon a fundamental contention of both Disciples and Baptists. We have steadily refused to be bound by formulated statements of doctrine, insisting that the Bible is "our only rule of faith and practice." Every human soul has the right to stand face to face with God and interpret him for himself. Creeds may have been created by those of our fellowship, but they are simply the expressions of opinion without other authority than that which is inherent in the truth that they may embody. We give respectful attention to the opinions of Augustine and Calvin and Luther, but deny their right to decide for us in any matter which concerns the religion of Jesus. . . . but for us there is only one Teacher whose instruction abides unchallenged through all changes in human thought (*Centennial Convention Report,* p. 484).

James M. Barkley brought greetings for the Presbyterians, J. T. McCrory for the United Presbyterians, Bishop Charles W. Smith for the Methodists, and J. H. Lucas for the Congregationalists.

One of the greatest causes of rejoicing at Pittsburgh was the reports of the missionary societies and the other agencies claiming the support of the brotherhood.

The Christian Woman's Board of Missions was first on the program. It was growing rapidly with 545 new societies being organized in the churches during Centennial year for a total membership of 73,608. Receipts for all purposes during the centennial period were $1,165,675.

212

The C.W.B.M. was maintaining fifty-nine schools of all kinds, including mountain schools and schools for Negroes, Bible chairs at the gates of state universities in the United States, and elementary schools and junior colleges on the foreign fields. Orphanages, hospitals, and zenana homes (for women) ministered to thousands. Thousands of members were reported in new churches with many baptisms each year. The missionary staff of the Board included 244 workers in the homeland and 256 in Jamaica, India, Puerto Rico, South America, Mexico, New Zealand, Canada, and Africa. Mission properties were estimated to be worth $500,000.

In the sessions of the Foreign Christian Missionary Society there was great rejoicing over thrilling reports from Japan, Africa, the Philippines, Tibet, and other lands. The work was going forward on four continents and in 13 countries with a missions staff of 167 missionaries and 594 native helpers in 48 stations and 128 outstations. There were 117 organized churches with 10,435 members, and reporting 1,314 converts for the year. The F.C.M.S. was maintaining 130 Bible schools and 62 elementary schools and colleges. Seventeen hospitals and dispensaries had treated 127,882 patients. There were 149 nationals studying for the Christian ministry. Financial receipts for the work of the Society in 1908-1909 were $350,685, an increase over the previous year of $76,360. A dramatic feature of the foreign missions report was the dedication of the new mission steamer, *Oregon,* for use on the Congo and Bosira rivers in Africa. Six thousand delegates assembled at the shipyards of James Rees and Sons in Pittsburgh for the unique services. "No such service was ever held on the continent, if, indeed, in the world," stated the official report.

The American Christian Missionary Society, the direct descendant of the old General Christian Missionary Convention, had finally been reorganized into an agency for the evangelization of America in co-operation with the state missionary societies. At Pittsburgh, it reported 108 evangelists directly employed, and 584 employed in contractual arrangements with the states. The first group reported 5,556 additions for the year, and the latter, 29,707. It was estimated that a total of 3,600 churches "after the New Testament pattern" had been organized during the lifetime of the Society. The report pointed out that about two-thirds of the population of America was unchurched and that a great work was yet to be done to win souls to Christ.

The Board of Church Extension, during the twenty-one years of its operation, had aided 1,261 congregations scattered over 43 states, Canada, and Hawaii, in constructing new buildings and saving others from mortgage foreclosure. The total amount in the fund stood at $757,621 and nearly a million dollars had been returned on loans. The receipts from the brotherhood for the year were almost $100,000.

The National Benevolent Association rejoiced in twelve institutions of mercy: two hospitals—St. Louis, Missouri, and Valparaiso, Indiana; three homes for the aged—East Aurora, New York, Jacksonville, Illinois, and Eugene, Oregon; seven homes for orphans—Cleveland, Ohio, Grand

Prairie, Texas, Denver, Colorado, Baldwin, Georgia, Walla Walla, Washington, and the Christian Orphan's Home and the Mother's and Babies' Home in St. Louis. It had aided 21,684 persons in distress and owned real estate and securities valued at $325,606.

Thirty-six colleges and universities reported 7,658 students and property valued at $6,004,053. Great banquets were held where alumni, students, and friends of these institutions gathered. Probably the largest of these was held by Bethany College and attended by some eight hundred diners. United States Senator George S. Oliver, a Bethany alumnus, presided and announced that $6,000 had been raised for an endowment fund of $125,000 to be presented to the College as a centennial gift.

Other agencies reported substantial progress. Interesting sessions were devoted to Christian Endeavor, temperance, and ministerial relief.

The great centennial celebration was a demonstration of the fact that the Restoration movement had impressed its message upon America and the world and had become one of the most aggressive and rapidly growing religious communions in Christendom. The spirit of the meetings was a constant recognition of the fact that all achievements had been the blessings of divine providence, and that the future could only hold promise of greater accomplishment if the Disciples were loyal to Christ and to the faith. As the thousands of brethren trekked back to their homes and their local churches, they went with an unsurpassed faith and enthusiasm.

Unfortunately, Pittsburgh was the crest of a wave which was to break in fifty years of controversy and division.

Those who were gifted with prophetic insight and had properly evaluated the trends in the brotherhood at large were aware that there were "rifts within the lute." All was not harmony at Pittsburgh. The missionary societies were criticized because of evidences of *centralization of authority*. Many persons felt that the centennial idea had been commercialized by money-raising schemes to fill the coffers of the agencies. The critics also sensed something on the verge of corporate or denominational pride and hierarchical pretensions in many of the pronouncements of agency leaders.

Delegates noted the *rise of liberalism in Christian doctrine* in several of the addresses, notably those of Samuel Hardin Church, Perry J. Rice, and Herbert L. Willett. These men represented a developing school of religious thought based on certain premises of the currently popular scientific naturalism. The casual listener at Pittsburgh who was unaware of current trends in theology and philosophy might not have detected anything heretical in these addresses. However, when Colonel Church (who was curator of the great Carnegie Museum and a grandson of Walter Scott) proposed that the churches adopt the practice of receiving the unimmersed as members, a wave of hisses and boos greeted the idea. The Standard Publishing Company, publisher of the *Centennial Convention Report*, refused to print the Church address and disclaimed all responsibility for the Rice and Willett messages. These happenings were symptomatic of a disease which was infesting all Protestantism and which will be treated

214

at length in the following chapter, considering "The Great Apostasy."

The third rift was even more realistic. There were only a few brethren present at Pittsburgh who opposed the use of instrumental music in the worship, missionary organizations, and other such "innovations." J. W. McGarvey and Fred L. Rowe of the *Christian Leader* were the only men of national reputation representing this viewpoint. In 1906, J. W. Shepherd and others had made representations to the Census Bureau of the United States government that churches of this persuasion should no longer be listed with the Disciples of Christ but be designated as *Church of Christ*. The dissidents had received the tacit approval of the three major exponents of this school of thought, *The Gospel Advocate, The Firm Foundation,* and the *Octographic Review.* The move was disapproved by many right-wing brethren, but they had no effective means of expressing what little influence they had. The *Christian Standard* and the *Christian-Evangelist* were, of course, against the open break but foolishly "wrote it off" as an insignificant event. While the main stream of the movement was smugly celebrating its victories at Pittsburgh, a very determined minority was planning a forward movement under another banner. So important is this third "rift" that much of the remainder of this chapter is devoted to a brief history of it and some of the reasons for it the unfortunate development.

The beginnings of this separate people can be traced in the thought and action of their forebears as recorded in Chapter 10. Moses E. Lard, Benjamin Franklin, Tolbert E. Fanning, and others had opposed the introduction of organs, open Communion, a paid and located ministry, missionary societies, and every doctrine and practice that was not specifically approved in the words of Scripture. Robert Richardson, Isaac Errett, and others had pointed out that in matters of faith, Scriptural approval was essential, but in matters of opinion and method, there should be freedom, and that such matters should never be made tests of fellowship. These brethren felt the legalistic view of the Scriptures requiring strict obedience and conformity to a written code of law had missed the inner spirit or purpose of God's revealed will. Indeed, they felt that irrevocable law had been made out of the silences of the Scriptures without regard to the demands of common sense and human progress. They sensed the development of a Pharisaical trust in obedience to law rather than grace as the ultimate hope of redemption.

Both groups of brethren were actuated by the highest motives, and believed that their course of action was necessary if they were to be loyal to Christ and teachings of the Holy Scriptures. Strangely enough they found themselves quarreling, not over the Scriptures themselves but over interpretations of a methodology of unity set up by Thomas Campbell: "Where the Scriptures speak, we speak; where the Scriptures are silent, we are silent." The argument appeared to be interminable, and as tempers flared and personalities clashed, division seemed inevitable. Breaks first came in congregations—two churches in a community having little or no fellowship but still considering themselves part of the same family.

Then on Sunday, August 18, 1889, the controversy took a more serious turn. The brethren in Shelby County, Illinois, had been gathering at Sand Creek for a yearly meeting since 1873. On this occasion it is said that six thousand persons were present. Daniel Sommer, editor of the *Octographic Review,* had been invited to address the assembly; and he harangued them for an hour and forty minutes on the state of the brotherhood charging the "innovators" with being responsible for all the existing division, bitterness and strife. In the midst of the address P. D. Warren, one of the elders of the Sand Creek congregation arose and read a document which claimed to represent the views of Sand Creek, Liberty, Ash Grove, Union, and Mode churches. In brief it stated:

[Once] we were of one heart and soul; we lived at peace and prospered in the things pertaining to the kingdom of God and the name of our Lord Jesus Christ. Then, what was written as doctrine and for practice was taught and observed by the disciples of our Lord Jesus Christ . . . We as a people discarded all man-made laws, rules, and disciplines and confessions of faith as means of governing the church. We have always acknowledged and do now acknowledge the all-sufficiency of the Holy Scriptures to govern us as individuals and congregations.

[Now] there are among us those who do teach and practice things not taught or found in the New Testament, which have been received by many well-meaning disciples, but rejected by those more thoughtful, and in most instances, better informed in the Scriptures, and who have repeatedly protested against this false teaching and those corrupt practices among the disciples. Some of these things of which we hereby complain, and against which we protest, are the unlawful methods resorted to in order to raise or get money for religious purposes . . . the use of instrumental music in the worship and the select choir, to the virtual, if not the real abandonment of congregational singing. Likewise, the man-made society for missionary work and the one-man imported preacher pastor to feed and watch over the flock. These with many other objectionable and unauthorized things, are now taught and practiced in many of the congregations, and that to the great grief and mortification of some of the members of said congregations. . . .

And now, in closing this address and declaration, we state that we are impelled from a sense of duty to say that all such as are guilty of teaching or allowing and practicing the many innovations and corruptions to which we have referred, after having had sufficient time for meditation and reflection, if they will not turn away from such abominations, that we cannot and will not regard them as brethren.

This was followed by an open break between the churches in Shelby County. Daniel Sommer, in reporting the event in his journal, made it clear that this mass-meeting was not a convention, nor in any sense a representative body of the churches of Christ. He said the Sand Creek Declaration was an expression only of the will of the churches that were responsible for it, and that it was presented only after the brethren who signed it felt that there was no other solution but separation.

Alfred Ellmore, writing in the *Christian Leader,* felt that the time had come to cut out "the cancer" of innovation or "the body would be ruined." He listed possible courses open to the churches:

216

1. Ask the "progressive" men to return to our original plea in all things, viz., speak where the Bible speaks, and be silent when the Bible is silent.
2. The brethren who are yet loyal to this plea, leave it, and go with the party who declare us only a religious movement.
3. Remain together as we are and go on in endless confusion and strife; or
4. Separate and have peace.

The *Christian Standard* strongly denounced the Sand Creek Declaration. It called it a "new confession of faith" and suggested that all adherents to its doctrines must separate themselves from other brethren where the organ is used or the missionary societies supported. Of Sommer the editor said, "Daniel Sommer has abandoned apostolic ground and is no more identified with the Disciples of Christ than Sidney Rigdon." The *Standard* of June 25, 1892, advised "without reservation" that Sommer should not be admitted to the churches as a preacher or evangelist because of his tirades "against the progressive Christianity we teach."

The *Gospel Advocate* was lukewarm to the proceedings. David Lipscomb was opposed to all kinds of meetings above the level of the local church and to pronouncements in which the churches associated themselves. J. C. McQuiddy wrote:

> The Sand Creek manifesto was manifest folly and the *Advocate* emphatically denies any sympathy with Sommerism—whatever that is—Sand Creekism, sandlotism, Standardism, or any other partyism in religion. The *Advocate* is for Christ and his church (chosen ones) and is in ardent sympathy with all those who are drawing their life from Him who is the true vine . . .

It was evident that the *Advocate,* while approving local church division to maintain the faith, was not ready for any open break of a wholesale nature. Through T. R. Burnett, one of its contributing editors, it said:

> Ephraim is joined to his idols, and he would rather have his society and music idols than any kind of Christian union known to the Bible. Brethren, proceed to re-establish the ancient order of things, just as if there was never a Church of Christ in your town. Gather all the brethren together who love the Bible order better than modern fads and foolishness and start the work and worship of the church in the old apostolic way. Do not go to law over church property. It is better to suffer wrong than to do wrong . . . It is better to have one dozen true disciples in a cheap house than a thousand apostate pretenders in a palace who love modern innovations better than Bible truth. The battles of the reformation have yet to be fought.

As time went on, the numbers of those who advocated middle ground steadily decreased. Among the giants who once held this position were J. W. McGarvey, Moses E. Lard, W. H. Hopson, L. B. Wilkes, and Robert Graham. All were opposed to innovations but held varying views as to what constituted innovations. They believed that all the brethren could stay together in advocacy of a common faith and not make matters of opinion a test of fellowship. The *Apostolic Times* best expressed this view and seldom indulged in controversy. When it died, F. G. Allen carried on with a similar policy in the *Old Path Guide,* persuading McGarvey and M. C. Kurfees to join him. In 1889, McGarvey joined the

Standard's staff of contributing editors, still retaining his views on instrumental music in worship and holding his membership in a noninstrument congregation until his death in 1911. Fred L. Rowe, of the *Christian Leader,* held his membership in a church using the instrument in worship, although he for many years personally opposed the practice. In this "no man's land," brethren were under constant crossfire from opposing camps until finally their kind completely disappeared.

There was, however, a wide range of disagreement among those who refused to co-operate with the "progressives." Practices which were innovations to some persons were not considered innovations by others. Some objected to the Sunday school, others did not. Some favored quarterlies and helps for the study of the Scriptures, others insisted on using the Bible alone. Some favored the use of one cup in the Communion service, others could see no harm in using individual cups. Some opposed Christian colleges, others advocated them; the advocates could not agree among themselves as to how to support them. Some opposed all missionary work, others favored missionary work provided it could be done by the local church. Still others sent missionaries to foreign lands. There was as little agreement as before separation about the proper interpretation of, "Where the Scriptures are silent, we are silent." By 1906, when J. W. Shepherd and his advisers took their drastic step for national separation, there seemed to be a fair degree of unanimity on making the test of fellowship the organ and the missionary society. Wide ranges of disagreement on other matters were not suffered to keep churches and church membership from appearing in the annual reports to the government. By 1909, the centennial year, some three hundred thousand members were listed under "Churches of Christ," in comparison with 1,300,000 listed as "Disciples of Christ."

Despite these unfortunate developments there was still much to be thankful for. The Restoration movement was young as compared with other developments in the history of the world church, and its accomplishments to date had been little short of marvelous.

Generous critics in American Protestantism had credited the Disciples with having given the denominations a *vision of Christian unity* and having changed the thought and practice of many. Sects and denominations remained, but the divisive spirit which hitherto maintained them was manifestly weakening. A host of leaders in all religious bodies were beginning to talk seriously about Christian union on a New Testament basis. Party walls were crumbling. The great historic creeds, while still of vast influence, were beginning to lose their sacrosanct significance and were being measured more thoughtfully by the teachings of Scripture. The person of Christ was being exalted above human doctrine. In community union meetings, when the Christian church minister had his turn to speak, he usually waxed eloquent on the subject of unity and was almost always hailed as a prophet of the new day in church relationships. The Disciples themselves had changed their attitude toward the denominations. They were still fully convinced of the evils of sectarianism, but they were

218

beginning to find kindred spirits in the ranks of other churches who were as eager as they to advance the kingdom of God and to do only the will of Christ as revealed in the New Testament. They found that there were scores of things, which did not involve doctrine, that all the churches could do better together than separately. In community life and in the larger affairs of society at large, they joined in many projects with a mutually rewarding camaradarie in Christ.

The Restoration movement had made the Bible live again in the churches. There was less tendency among denominational preachers to preach on obscure theological themes and to refer to the historic creeds to support their views. Their people had been exposed to many years of the simple Bible preaching of Restoration ministers or evangelists in their local communities, and they relished it. Community Bible classes became popular, first under Christian church auspices, and then (sometimes in self-defense) under sponsorship of the Y.M.C.A. or ministerial associations. W. C. Pearce and Herbert Moninger popularized the teacher-training movement in the Sunday schools of the nation through Bible studies. Many of the community classes used their textbooks that were Bible centered and taught people more about the Holy Scriptures than they had ever known before. It was common talk in many communities that "if you want to hear a real Bible sermon you should hear the Christian church preacher." The constant challenge to take "the Bible and the Bible alone as the authoritative rule of faith and practice" was having its effect. The Disciples were willing to put the Bible on the conference table and meet all comers on exactly what it said. Those who were honestly seeking the truth, the whole truth, and nothing but the truth, found it. In the best tradition of the movement, Disciples did not ask others to come to them, did not proselytize, but asked seekers to join *Christ* and *His* church and to do *His* will as revealed in the New Testament. They maintained that when all Christians are in Christ and in the church of the New Testament, they are automatically one with each other. Sometimes the Disciples did not practice their principle too well, but the principle gained acceptance far beyond their borders among people they had never met.

Disciples had originally organized their own churches to preach an unalloyed gospel and to practice simple New Testament Christianity. Now that they were a separate people, they had a tendency to develop some of the marks of a denomination themselves. But where they sincerely practiced undenominational Christianity and had fellowship with all others of like mind, they were most effective in their ministry of calling the religious world back to pure Bible doctrine and practice. The Bible, and the Christ of the Bible, were the source of their popular appeal.

The Restoration movement had also contributed much to the religious world in teaching how "rightly to divide" the Scriptures. Alexander Campbell's "starlight age, moonlight age, and sunlight age" made clear the three great dispensations of God's grace. The difference between the law and the gospel was an early feature of all Restoration Bible study and preaching. It was for the emphasis on these distinctions that the Redstone

Baptist Association sought to discipline Campbell. His "Sermon on the Law" was, one hundred years later, conceded by all intelligent and unprejudiced religious thinkers to be the only proper principle of Biblical interpretation: that is, that the modern man is not under Moses, but under Christ; not under the law, but under the gospel; not under the Jewish dispensation, but under the Christian dispensation. The whole Bible was accepted without question as the revealed Word of God, but required these clear distinctions to make its message understood logically.

Distinguished writers in the nineteenth century had expressed views similar to those of Campbell but they were not widely accepted and promulgated. It can be affirmed without successful contradiction that the Disciples emphasized these distinctions much more vigorously and showed their bearing upon a proper understanding of the Christian religion with more clarity, than any other religious people, before or since the hundred years of their existence. To the Disciples belonged the credit for a new day in an intelligent understanding of the Bible by the common man.

The Disciples in one hundred years of history had focused Christian thought on the proper distinction between faith and opinion. From the beginning they held that, for the most part, the great creeds of Christendom were expressions of human opinion. They contained much philosophical and theological speculation about Bible facts, despite the expression of wide consensus. Consensus among Calvinists was different from consensus among Arminians, and consensus among either of these theological camps was not consensus among Lutherans. All professed to base their doctrines on the Holy Scriptures, but they were not couched exclusively in Bible terminology. The Disciples had contended that philosophy and theology are not necessarily opposed to true religion, nor did they hesitate to offer explanations of the facts of religion, even when these facts were far removed from the sphere of conclusive investigation. They strongly urged that human philosophies and theologies must not be made tests of fellowship. The rule of Thomas Campbell was effectively applied as the Disciples began to meet the practical issues of a growing communion. "Where the Scriptures speak, we speak" kept them on the main track of progress. Its corollary, "Where the Scriptures are silent, we are silent," was unfortunately carried to extremes; but even this rule, when rightly interpreted, saved the movement from making untaught questions matters of vital importance. The Disciples contended that whatever is necessary to salvation is clearly revealed in the words of Scripture, and if anything more were necessary it would have been revealed. Thus, any addition to the Word of God would not only be nonessential to salvation but could be regarded as impertinent. One might have his own opinions, but these must be treated with indifference and be admitted only for the exercise of religious liberty. Here, again, the principle had not been too well practiced by the Disciples, but its validity had been tested and proved many times and gave promise of being the means of eventually bringing true Christian unity to pass. Their experience had added new meaning to Comenius' dictum, "In faith, unity; in opinions, liberty; and in all things, charity."

220

The Disciples had made another important contribution to Christian thought and practice by their insistence that the faith of the gospel is not primarily doctrinal but personal. They found that Christ is the center of the Bible revelation, that He, in His death, burial, and resurrection, is the gospel, and that the church is His body. Faith in the Lord Jesus Christ necessarily implies all that belongs to His personality and His will for mankind. The Disciples held, therefore, that "Christ is our creed," and required no other confession on the part of the penitent sinner than Peter's confession, "Thou art the Christ, the Son of the living God." In this faith the Disciples stood almost alone throughout the nineteenth century, but the beauty and simplicity of it caused the religious world to see the folly of involved philosophical and theological statements as essential to church membership and to broader ecumenical fellowship. The premise for Disciples' faith was divine revelation in Holy Scripture and therefore fully comprehensive and meaningful. It was not a nebulous human concept of a Christ that satisfied emotional or intellectual fads or fancies, but the historic Christ of the New Testament, living and reigning today and forever.

While the principles of the freedom of the local church and soul liberty were not distinctive to the Disciples, they as fiercely contended for these principles as the Baptists, Congregationalists, and others. Indeed, it was doubtful whether there could be found anywhere a body of Christian people who had better demonstrated their commitment to those tenets. They made clear that this freedom is in Christ and limited by His will and that in obedience to Him is to be found the largest liberty. Because of this commitment, the Disciples recognized no extracongregational authority. Denominational peoples marveled at this freedom and found it difficult to understand. Indeed, it was one of the appeals that led multiplied thousands into their fellowship—a place where men were free to serve Christ and His church without the limitations of ecclesiastical overlordship and predetermined courses of action.

Thus at the end of one hundred years a called-out people had contributed largely to the coming glory of a united Christian church serving God and humanity.

BIBLIOGRAPHY: Chapter 14
Abbott, B. A., *The Disciples: An Interpretation.*
Centennial Convention Report.
Disciples of Christ: One Hundredth Anniversary.
Ellmore, Alfred, *Christian Leader, Octographic Review, Christian Advocate.*
Fortune, Alonzo W., *Origin and Development of the Disciples.*
Garrison, J. H., editor, *Christian-Evangelist* (1908-1909).
Garrison, J. H., *The Story of a Century.*
Hill, John L., *As Others See Us and As We Are.*
Lord, J. A., editor, *Christian Standard* (1908-1909).
Moore, W. T., *Comprehensive History of the Disciples of Christ.*
Tyler, B. B., *A History of the Disciples of Christ.*
Warren, W. R., *The Life and Labors of A. McLean.*
West, Earl Irvin, *Search for the Ancient Order.*
Willett, Herbert L., *Our Plea for Union and the Present Crisis.*

Chapter 15

The Great Apostasy

As the origins of the Restoration movement in America cannot be fully understood without the background of the Great Awakening, so the events of the fifty years from 1909-1959 cannot be adequately comprehended and evaluated without the background of the Great Apostasy in world Protestantism.

The climate of the Christian community had undergone an amazing change between 1809 and 1909. Because of their comparative isolation from the mainstream of this community, the Disciples were scarcely aware of what had taken place. At the beginning of the nineteenth century almost all Protestants believed that the Holy Scriptures were the infallible revelation of the true religion. If the Campbells, Stone, and Scott had been told that there would come a day when the Bible would cease to be the bulwark of Christian doctrine and practice in the churches and its very authenticity doubted by the vaunted leaders of Christendom, they would scarcely have believed it. But by 1909 such was the situation.

Textual criticism of the Scriptures had long been recognized as a legitimate field of theological study, but the early critics were men who revered the Word of God and sought only to provide a valid text. Darwin's evolutionary hypothesis had upset the whole scientific world. Scientists began to accept the principle of the uniformity of nature and forced the idea with growing insistence upon all thought. Protestant theologians, particularly in Germany, had been strongly influenced by Kant and Hegel and were ready to desert Biblical theology. The new interpreters of religion were Schleiermacher (1768-1834) and Ritschl (1822-1889) and, somewhat later, Troeltsch (1865-1923). Under the spell of the evolutionary principle and a philosophy of immanence, the influential Christian theologians came to view Christianity as the highest expression of an essence common to all religions and to regard Christian experience as fully explainable from the study of naturalistic and behavioristic psychology. In the spirit of immanental idealism they merged special with general revelation and blended humanity with God. The Bible was all but abandoned, and they turned to the universal movements of thought for the most significant disclosures of God and moral and spiritual absolutes.

Ferdinand Christian Bauer, of Tubingen, could not quite bring himself to an entire acceptance of the rationalistic view of the Scriptures, but, accepting a destructive textual criticism as his frame of reference, he proceeded to tear the Bible to shreds. From the remains, he deduced that early Christianity—the religion of Christ and the apostles—was wholly Judaistic in tone and practice. He rejected Paul as possessing true Christianity and credited "Paulinism" with having changed the original movement into a separate sect. The Gospels and Acts were held to be distorted versions of original Christian history, although Matthew was credited with retaining many features unaltered from the Judaistic original. The Tubingen school founded by Bauer dominated the theological criticism of the New Testament during the greater part of the nineteenth century.

The process of destroying faith in the authenticity and credibility of the Scriptures involved all sorts of speculation. Leading higher critics developed the theory that a lost document, "the logia" or "Q" was the source of much of the Gospels. The Johannine writings were attributed to "some Christian teacher who seems to have lived and written in Asia Minor." The eschatological passages and writings were ignored or explained away by ingenious theories in an attempt to reconstruct "the historical Jesus." Legends and sayings from Essene, Mithraic, and other sources were adduced to prove that there was nothing unique about the religion set forth in the Gospels. The "tales of Jesus" were said to have been devised to meet the needs of Christian missionary endeavor of the early Hellenistic church. The genealogies of Christ and the chronology of events in the Gospels were distorted with all the ingenuity of radical skeptics and infidels. The Old and New Testament canons were held up to ridicule. Elohim and Yahweh were assumed to be tribal deities and not the true God. The trustworthiness of the Chronicles was impugned. Deuteronomy was consigned to the seventh century B.C., and the idea of the Mosaic origin of all the institutions described in the Pentateuch was considered inadmissible. Old Testament prophecies of Christ were eliminated on the ground that there was no definite proof of specific relationship.

In the great universities of Germany, scientific objections to the basic doctrines of the Christian faith gained such credence in intellectual circles that theologians were forced to re-examine their traditional views. The historic creeds, which rested their claims to authority on the Holy Scriptures, were scrapped or reinterpreted in terms of evolutionary naturalism or divine immanence. Abandoned to the new culture were the inspiration of the Scriptures, the unique deity of Christ, the miracles, the atonement for sin, the bodily resurrection, the individual resurrection of the saints, the second coming of Christ unto final judgment, heaven, hell, and every vestige of the supernatural elements of the Christian faith. The mind of man was made the court of final appeal.

The schools of theological thought which grew out of this religious revolution were many and varied but they might all be grouped under the banner of *liberalism* or *modernism*. No two liberals thought exactly alike, but the general principles were the same. The Bible was to them merely a historical record of the developing religious consciousness of the Jewish people. Liberals did not accept Jesus as one to be worshiped but as an example, a prophet, a teacher, and a moral pioneer. They were willing to accept the religion of Jesus as a means by which men can come to God, as Jesus came to God, but not to accept the Biblical revelation about Jesus as the Son of God and himself very God, the only Saviour of mankind. They refused to recognize that this same "moral" teacher claimed to be sinless and that He also had a Messianic conscience.

Liberals made the cross merely a thought form of the apostolic era in which the truth of the love of God was demonstrated. The New Testament interpretation of the cross of Christ must pass even as the doctrine of the atonement had changed through the time of the scholastics and the Protestant reformers. Miracles, to the liberals, were merely the legendary clothing of a great man. They were the ages' high estimate of one who left a great impact on his contemporaries. In order to express the greatness of his personality they clothed him in the supernatural habiliments of events that really did not occur or that probably could be explained by natural law if all the facts were known.

The gospel, for liberals, was utterly changed from the means of reconciliation with God, or the redemption of the soul from sin, or the liberation of man from the bondage of evil, to a sense of filial piety, or brotherhood, or of mutual understanding and human betterment. If the cross was considered involved in the gospel it was mentioned only as a way of sacrificial living. The church became, for liberals, merely a fraternal society with certain social benefits. It was no longer the assembly of called-out people who were saved by grace through faith in Christ. Liberals no longer considered the church to be the body of Christ, the organism of which He is the head and which enjoys mystical union with Him. Liberals saw the church as a movement which in every age becomes the vanguard for the social and spiritual development of mankind. Biblical Christianity was utterly repudiated by the liberals and new doctrines were substituted for the old.

Among the notable names who have been involved in the critiques and theologies were Bauer, Driver, Tholuck, Feuerbach, Strauss, Dorner, Muller, Roth, Biederman, Mansel, Royce, James, Harnack, Herrmann, Pfleiderer, Otto, Kierkegaard, Bultmann, Eichorn, Geddes, DeWette, Niebuhr, Fosdick, Ames, Hayden, Case, Wieman, Matthews, Smith, Van Deusen, Bennett, Vatke, Graf, Wellhausen, Duhm, Streeter, Loisy. This list, including some contemporaries, could be expanded at great length. It includes men of various types of liberalism.

Defending the faith from varied viewpoints were such scholars as Orr, Wace, Knox, Fox, Koeberle, Theilcke, Schlink, Merz, Elert, Sauer, Taylor, Forsyth, Tennant, Mackay, Maclean, Hoskyns, Manley, Hammond, Lamont, Machen, Vos, Mullins, McGarvey, Keyser, Patton,

Wilson, Delitsch, and Torrey, who set forth the Biblical fundamentals. Not only the authority of the Scriptures was flouted but also the authority of Christ as revealed in the Scriptures. Dr. Augustus Strong saw the conflict as centered in the person and nature of our Lord:

> We need a supernatural Christ; not simply the man of Nazareth, but the Lord of Glory; not the Christ of the Synoptics alone, but also the Christ of John's Gospel; not merely a human example and leader, but one who "was declared to be the Son of God with power by the resurrection of the dead"; not simply Jesus according to the flesh, but "the Word who was with God and was God" in eternity past; not simply God manifest in human life nineteen centuries ago, but the God who is "the same yesterday today and forever"; not simply the humbled, but also the glorified Saviour, who sits now on the throne of the universe, all power in heaven and earth being given into His hand. When we believe in an ascended Lord at God's right hand, the God of Creation, of Providence, and of Redemption, we have a faith that can conquer the world.

The liberals somehow failed to see that the very theme of the Bible is the incarnate Word in whom alone man can find truth, freedom, and salvation, and to whom the written Word conforms in divine and human structure. They missed the fact that the Holy Bible is of God and from God and is its own self-witness by which all views of inspiration must be tested, corrected, strengthened, and empowered. The prophetic and apostolic Word is the word of divine wisdom by which the rationalism of man is summoned to repentance and renewal. The historical record in the Scripture is the account of God's dealings with man, which alone gives meaning and direction to all history. In the last analysis the credibility and inspiration of the Scriptures is the work of the Holy Spirit, whose operation cannot finally be subjected to human analysis, repudiation, or control, but who remains the internal master of that which He himself has given, guaranteeing its authenticity and declaring its message with quickening and compelling power. Indeed, there is no other concept of the Word of God which can explain its preservation and perpetuation through the ages and its effect on the lives of men and human institutions.

Nevertheless, the liberal movement swept Christendom as wildfire, carried along by the growingly popular evolutionary philosophy and the upsurge of modern science and invention. Higher education abandoned the Christian philosophy upon which it had grown to mammoth proportions. God-centered education was exchanged for a man-centered process. God's will was no longer the basic norm. Man's mind became the measure of all things. The moral and spiritual ultimates, even truth itself, were scrapped for relative values. Human social welfare became a matter of primary concern. The goal of education was no longer to fit men to live in harmony with the will of God. Education, in the new view, became an instrument by which the developing and changing person might continue in the quest for certainty. Genuine values and tenable ends and ideals could be found, said the liberals, only within the movement of experience and not from authority, human or supernatural.

In the atmosphere of the colleges and universities and their associated theological seminaries, the new intellectual movement found its most effective breeding ground. The new Baptist-related University of Chicago, backed by the Rockefeller millions, and headed by Dr. William Rainey Harper, educated in the German universities, became the center of liberal influence in the United States. Theological liberals first attacked strategic chairs of religion and the well-endowed seminaries of the leading Protestant denominations. Bible-believing professors were discredited by a well-directed propaganda which made them appear as naive, obscurantist, unscholarly, and reactionary. In many instances liberals falsely represented themselves to be evangelical, accepting under oath evangelical confessions of faith "with mental reservations," using orthodox words to convey liberal thought, and moving with caution until circumstances afforded safe opportunity to take an open stand for the new doctrines. Often they used so-called "inclusivist" strategy—persuading orthodox institutions to admit liberals to their faculties on the ground that the principle of academic freedom required presentation of all viewpoints. When liberals attained majority status they set up new standards and by various devices eliminated all Bible-believing professors. Once firmly intrenched in the institutions that trained the leadership of the churches, they next directed their strategies to obtain control of important boards and commissions, and finally the administrative machinery of whole denominations.

A classic example of the liberal method of capturing colleges and seminaries was the looting of historic Andover. Andover Theological Seminary was founded especially to combat the Unitarian doctrines which had made such inroads on the orthodox Congregationalism of New England. In the charter of the Associate Foundation were written such passages as:

> Every professor . . . shall be . . . an ordained minister of the Congregational or Presbyterian denomination . . . an orthodox Calvinist. . . . He shall on the day of his inauguration publicly make and subscribe a solemn declaration of his faith in divine revelation and in the fundamental and distinguishing doctrines of the Gospel as expressed in the following creed.

Then followed eight clauses, which would seem, even in our day, to guarantee the orthodoxy of the institution forever. Evangelicals had faith in Andover and gave it many rich bequests through the nineteenth century until it became a plum ripe for picking. The story of jockeying which finally delivered Andover to the liberals is too long to tell here. Many high-minded liberal professors, such as J. Henry Thayer, when confronted with the necessity of conforming to the "Andover creed," withdrew for conscience sake. But there came a time when E. C. Smith and four other faculty members conspired to take the oath "with mental reservations," set up a liberal cell within the school and collaborated with unfaithful members of the board to achieve their purposes. Evangelicals were deceived into believing that the school was still orthodox until the famous case of the "Visitors of the Theological Institution at Andover vs. Trustees of

Andover Theological Seminary" was tried in the courts of Massachusetts. The liberals won by specious devices which will ever be a blot on the escutcheon of Christendom.

An interesting footnote to the story was written by an Institute of Unitarian Ministers which after "the rape of Andover" met in the halls long sacred to the orthodox Christian faith. In the assignment of rooms in the dormitories cards were used with jocose names such as Tophet, Canaan, Babylon, and the Dead Sea. A mock trial was staged in which "Albertus Carolus Diffenbachus" was finally acquitted of the charge of "fundamentalism." The loss of Andover shocked Bible-believing people of all churches from one end of the nation to the other. It proved but the beginning of scores of similar episodes in which almost all the leading seminaries, colleges, and universities of American Protestantism were taken over by liberalism, in most instances without resort to the courts and with the consent of denominational and interdenominational authorities. Only a few conservative denominations were able to keep their educational institutions free from this fatal virus.

The strange new liberal gospel gradually found its way into the field of Christian missions. Mission boards in most denominations were, along with boards of education and publication, very wealthy and very influential. Liberals were not interested in carrying out the imperative of the great commission, but they were vitally concerned with control of machinery that would give them world influence and an opportunity to remake the international social order. Prior to the Great Apostasy, the missionary leadership of the world was united in the belief that Jesus Christ, God and Saviour, is the only hope of a world lost in sin and shame. They believed that Christianity was the divinely revealed ultimate religion and is not merely one of the evolving religions of the world engaged in a common search of mankind for God. They believed that Christianity is God's offer of himself to men in Christ, who was not a "fellow seeker with us after God," but "the fulness of the Godhead bodily" without whom no man can be saved. Liberalism came into the missionary picture as a parasite, living on the boards, institutions, and missions built up by evangelicals, and undermining the Scriptural beliefs and practices that have made Christian missions a vital force in the world. Liberals denied that men are lost without Christ, in the full New Testament sense. They looked upon the authentic historical facts of the New Testament as "symbolic and imaginative expressions" of Christianity. They considered non-Christians as brothers in a common quest for ultimate truth. They linked the name of Jesus with Buddha and Mohammed, as one of the great founders and teachers of religion. Rejecting the deity of Christ, the doctrine of redemption through His blood, the justification of the sinner by faith, and other facts of the gospel, liberals had no distinctly Christian motivation for missionary crusade.

The strategy by which liberals proceeded to take over the mission boards was also backed by Rockefeller money. It was called the Laymen's Foreign Missions Inquiry. W. E. Hocking, noted humanist philosopher of Harvard, headed the project. Its theological findings and its proposed revolutionary program of action originated in the minds of highly placed liberal clergymen in mission boards who, daring not to make known their unorthodox views to their own denominations, took advantage of lay anonymity to spread their poison. But the Protestant world was not yet ready to yield to their pressures. Such great missionary leaders as Robert E. Speer, of the Presbyterian (U.S.A.) Board of Foreign Missions, took the field against the Laymen's Inquiry report, *Rethinking Missions*. Dr. Speer covered the nation and wrote voluminously for the preservation of evangelical Christian missions, appearing in practically every city where Dr. Hocking went with his liberal propaganda. The liberals lost the battle, but they won the war, as eventual changes in denominational missions policy fully attest.

In 1893 the majority of all Protestant missionary boards and societies (102) had organized the Foreign Missions Conference of North America. They were one in their basic missionary theology and philosophy and found in such an organization opportunity for fellowship in a common task, the discussion of effective methods of administration and united action in dealing with governments and crucial issues of many kinds. As liberal influences began to be felt in this co-operative body, frictions arose that eventually split the Conference, causing Southern Baptists and some Lutheran bodies to withdraw. The Conference reports began to show a decline in the number of new missionaries sent out. The number of ordained ministers and evangelistic personnel on the missionary rolls fell by hundreds, while those registered in the fields of teaching and technical supervision increased by more than 50 per cent. Eventually two new co-operative missionary agencies in the interchurch field—the Evangelical Foreign Missions Association and the Interdenominational Foreign Missions Association—came into being to carry on the original purposes of the Foreign Missions Conference.

The Methodist Episcopal church (now the Methodist church) is a perfect example in liberal achievement with respect to control of the denominational apparatus. A small group of liberals met in Boston early in the 1900's and agreed to work together in liberalizing the church. A four-point program was adopted: (1) place a rationalist in every chair of English Bible in the various church colleges, (2) liberalize the Book Concern, (3) liberalize the church rituals and the Discipline, (4) liberalize the approved course of study for the training of the ministry. Strongly evangelical Bishop Thomas B. Neeley said of this program,

> There is an anti-Methodist school of thought working through a few aggressive individuals to compel the Church to accept its views and, at the present time, to accomplish this without constitutionally changing the Articles of Religion or other standards of doctrine. The method is not that of frontal or open attack but of the sapper and the miner.

The strategy was overwhelmingly successful. In a generation the denomination was firmly in the control of the liberals. Every Methodist college and university was in their hands. The Sunday-school board had eliminated all its old evangelical leadership and was sending its emissaries to every conference in the land spreading the new educational philosophy. Exerting its influence in the production of Sunday-school literature in the Book Concern, liberalism was able to reach and misteach the more than four million children and youth in Methodist Sunday schools. Anti-Wesleyan doctrine soon began to appear in the books bearing the imprint of related publishers. The Foreign Missions Board was taken over, and the evangelical missionary testimony of this great communion became a thing of the past. Finally, through political manipulations, the bishopric came under liberal domination, and the whole episcopal framework of the church, down through the district superintendents, began to operate to the embarrassment of every evangelical pastor. This was made possible through handpicked conference delegates chosen from graduates of liberal Methodist colleges and seminaries. A large evangelical constituency remained in the denomination, especially among the rank-and-file of the local church membership; but they were the unvoiced millions, helpless and hopeless when it came to determining the policies of the ecclesiastical machine. The tragic situation confronting Bible-believing Wesleyans led to wholesale desertions to newer and smaller bodies such as the Church of the Nazarene, the Free Methodist church, the Wesleyan Methodist church, and to other holiness groups.

The Presbyterian Church in the U.S.A. was one of the citadels of the evangelical faith in the early days of the century. With such stalwart theologians as Robert Dick Wilson and B. B. Warfield; missionary leaders like Robert E. Speer; lay leaders like William Jennings Bryan and John Wanamaker; and clergymen of the stature of Maitland Alexander and Clarence E. Macartney, it seemed that these descendants of John Calvin and John Knox might be impervious to the onslaughts of liberalism. The General Assembly frequently warned the church to be on guard to preserve the faith as set forth in the Westminster Confession and the Holy Scriptures. Then the Union Theological Seminary, of New York, became the spawning ground for the new faith. Despite the fact that the institution came under scathing attack from denominational leaders, its influence, by strange and devious means, infiltrated other Presbyterian institutions. Before denominational leaders were aware of it, liberalism had sufficient strength in Presbyterianism to declare itself in the notorious "Auburn Affirmation" (1923). This document, signed by 1,292 ministers, said, in effect, (1) we do not believe in the inerrancy of the Holy Scriptures or accept them as final authority in faith and practice; (2) we accept the incarnation of Christ as a fact but deny the Biblical doctrine of His virgin birth; (3) we deny that on the cross Christ "satisfied divine justice and reconciled man to God"; (4) we doubt that Christ rose from the dead "in the same body in which He suffered"; (5) we deny the supernatural element in Christ's miracles and (by inference) the supernatural element in His redemptive work. The text of the Affirmation, like many liberal pronouncements of that period, taken alone seemed comparatively harm-

230

less. It must, however, be understood in its true meaning when it is compared with the doctrinal statements in the Westminster Confession of Faith and "The Five Points of Christian Doctrine," adopted by the General Assembly in 1923.

Within the Presbyterian church were still many individual congregations that were veritable garrisons of orthodoxy, and a whole host of ministers and laymembers, but by processes similar to those used in the Methodist Episcopal church, the Presbyterian ecclesiastical structure came under eventual control by liberals. The staunch *Presbyterian,* the *Presbyterian Banner,* and other orthodox journals of the denomination were squeezed out of business. The church-related colleges and seminaries, with a few exceptions, became liberal. The loss of Princeton University and Princeton Theological Seminary precipitated a quarrel that had wide repercussions and resulted in the establishment of the Westminster Theological Seminary in Philadelphia under the leadership of the distinguished evangelical scholar, J. Gresham Machen. Two new Presbyterian denominations, the Orthodox Presbyterian church and the Bible Presbyterian church were organized by dissidents who left the fold of the Northern church.

The story of apostasy in the American (Northern) Baptist churches, the denomination with which early Restoration leaders so vigorously contended, began with John D. Rockefeller's munificent gift of the University of Chicago. This center of the whole liberal movement in America immediately became a bone of contention. The Divinity School of the University numbered such notable liberals as Shailer Matthews and Gerald Birney Smith in its faculty, and frequently heard lecturers from the English and German theological seminaries which were the birthplaces of naturalistic and rationalistic theology and the destructive Biblical criticism. In 1913 the Northern Baptist Theological Seminary of Chicago was formed as a visible evidence of the disapproval of Bible-believing Baptists and a determination to train a ministry true to the traditional Baptist faith. When Rochester, Colgate, and the other Eastern seminaries capitulated to liberalism, the Eastern Baptist Seminary was founded in Philadelphia.

Soon the mission boards of the Northern church were under fire because of their compromises with liberalism. When the evangelical Baptist churches refused to support liberal missionaries, John D. Rockefeller, Jr., an ardent liberal, came forward with millions of dollars to make up the mission board deficits.

In 1919 the Missouri Convention withdrew its six hundred churches and joined the Southern Baptists. The following year, the evangelicals, or "fundamentalists" of the Northern Convention, called a preconvention conference in Buffalo to restate the "fundamentals of the Baptist faith." Among them were such noble names as J. C. Massee, Curtis Lee Laws, John Roach Stratton, A. C. Dixon, W. B. Hinson, W. B. Riley, and Cortland Myers. This proved to be the turning-point in the history of the denomination. From this time forward there were wholesale desertions to the Southern Convention. Minnesota, Oregon, and Arizona conventions withdrew to become independent. The General Association of Regular

Baptist Churches, and at a later date the Conservative Baptist Association of America, were organized by still other dissidents (each new denomination numbering more than one thousand churches and supporting its own colleges, seminaries, and missionary societies). Hundreds of Northern churches and pastors set up "independent" Baptist churches, having no affiliation with any denominational body, determined to preserve and perpetuate "the church of the New Testament" in doctrine, ordinances, and life. Individual Bible-believing Baptists withdrew by the thousands, feeling that if their testimony were to count for "the faith which was once delivered unto the saints" they must find fellowship with other Christians outside the aegis of the Northern Baptist Convention. Many good people remained in nominal relationship in the hope that the day might come when the Convention and its agencies would return to their original orthodox position.

Scarcely a single evangelical Protestant denomination anywhere in the world escaped the devastating apostasy. An entire volume could be devoted to the tragic story of controversy, lawsuits, and divisions that made Christians the laughingstock of the enemies of the faith.

Liberalism now projected itself into the ranks of interchurch co-operation. The World Evangelical Alliance, which Alexander Campbell looked upon with favor, stood like a Rock of Gibraltar for the orthodox faith, and liberals began to desert it. John A. Hutchison, in his history of interchurch co-operation in America, said that the credo of the Alliance was a "theological straight jacket" and on that account no longer appealed to American churchmen. He continued:

> One of the clues to the failure of the Evangelical Alliance was the theological rigidity which prevented it from adjusting itself to one of the major transitions in the history of the American church. . . . Educated people began to demand that religion put off the crudities of an earlier day and put on the garments of refinement and culture.

Again Dr. Hutchison commented that

> the nineteenth century liberal revolt in New England brought into American Christianity currents of humane and ethical thought which before the end of the century had influenced even the most orthodox denominations. Nineteenth century scientific thought, with its concepts of evolution and progress, likewise made its mark on the churches . . .

Accordingly, an invitation was sent out early in 1905 by a committee of the National Federation of Churches and Christian Workers calling for a conference of official representatives of all denominations. They proposed that a new organization be set up "to express the visible unity of the Christian churches, to record their agreement on issues where they do agree and to co-operate in common tasks." Official delegates representing thirty denominations gathered in Carnegie Hall, New York City, during the week of November 15-21, and organized the Federal Council of Churches of Christ in America. The nearest semblance of a statement of

232

faith upon which the conferees could agree was contained in the Preamble of the Plan in which Jesus Christ was acknowledged as "divine Lord and Saviour." Even the word *divine* was not in the original draft, but Samuel J. Nichols (Presbyterian) demanded its insertion to assure the "evangelical character" of the organization. After considerable discussion it was unanimously voted. Evangelicals were scarcely aware, in that early day, that in the "weasel word" vocabulary of liberals the word had a double meaning. Historically it carried the connotation of deity, but the rationalists used it as indicating that Christ was divine as men may be divine, that His divinity may differ from man's only in degree. The liberals would permit no mention of the Bible in the Preamble.

In the early days of the Council the cleavage between evangelicals and liberals was quite evident. William H. Roberts, a self-styled "old-fashioned Presbyterian" constantly championed "fundamental Christian doctrine," while William Hayes Ward spearheaded for liberalism. John Wanamaker stood for Bible-centered education against the pleadings of George Richards for "a more intelligent and progressive type of education with less reference to emotional evangelism." Dean George Hodges, of Yale Divinity School, pled for "an honest reception of new truth in both science and religion as a mode of God's progressive revelation of himself to man," while David H. Bauslin declared that the present age needed salvation from "rationalism, Voltaire, and Tom Paine."

Herbert L. Willett, accepting the findings of the "higher critics" of the Bible and covering his attacks on its infallibility with beautiful weasel words of tribute, was confronted by his fellow Disciple, Frederick D. Power, who believed the Bible "from cover to cover." Frank Mason North made eloquent appeals for church action in industrial situations based on a claim of Christ's sovereignty over social as well as individual life, while Henry Van Dyke held that "removal of ignorance," "better character," and "the improvement of human nature," and not "legal enactment," would produce a better society. Whenever the Council met in these early days there was debate. Yet there was a fierce determination not to permit differences to wreck this new attempt at Christian co-operation. Naive evangelicals hoped that liberalism was only a passing fad soon to be absorbed in the approach of some new millennium, while liberals, biding their time, traded concessions in theology for concessions in social ethics and action, and negotiated a stranglehold on the Council's commissions and administrative machinery. While the organization maintained an "inclusive policy" with regard to membership, it tended to practice an "exclusive policy" with regard to leadership. Harry Emerson Fosdick, widely acknowledged liberal leader, said in his *Adventurous Religion* (1926) that "the liberals are gaining, and if not stopped now, will soon be in control." In the latter days of the Federal Council, before it was merged into the comprehensive National Council of Churches of Christ in the U.S.A., liberals were in complete control of leadership, policy, and program.

The blight of liberalism was evident in almost every phase of the

233

Council's activities, and evangelicals were finally forced to admit that it could no longer qualify as the representative of American Protestantism or of historic Protestant principles and essential Christian doctrine. In the Council's Cleveland convention in 1942, Metropolitan Antony Bashir, of the Syrian Antiochian Archdiocese of New York and North America, a constituent church, led a worship service in which he invoked the intercessions of "our all-immaculate Theotokos and ever Virgin Mary" and the great ecumenical teachers, hierarchs, and saints of the Eastern Orthodox church. In a resolution passed at the same convention, the Roman Catholic church was referred to as a "sister communion."

While its leaders still professed on occasion that the Council was evangelical in doctrine, the liberal views of its key leaders were a matter of abundant record. Onetime president Francis J. McConnell said concerning the deity of Christ:

> Critics point out to us that in the early days of the church it was quite common even for popular thought to deify a man. On that memorable occasion in Paul's missionary journey through south Galatia when multitudes called Barnabas Zeus and Paul Mercury they were acting true to the idea of the time which conceived of gods as capable of appearing in human form and found it easy to believe that man could become god. Is not this tendency to deify Jesus more heathen than Christian? Are we not most truly Christian when we cut loose from a heathen propensity and take Jesus simply for the character he was and for the ideal he is?

Henry Sloane Coffin's writings were filled with denials of the historic Christian faith. He rejected the Bible as the infallible Word of God. In his volume, *What to Preach,* he called the virgin birth an "unscriptural exaggeration." G. Bromley Oxnam, another Federal Council president, shocked evangelicals by this paragraph from his book, *Preaching in a Revolutionary Age*:

> Hugh Walpole, in *Wintersmoon*, tells of a father and son at church. The aged rector read from the Old Testament, and the boy learned of the terrible God who sent plagues upon people and created fiery serpents to assault them. That night the father passed the boy's bedroom, the boy called him, put his arms around his father's neck, and drawing him close, said, "Father, you hate Jehovah. So do I. I loathe him, the dirty bully!" We have long since rejected a conception of reconciliation associated historically with an ideal of Deity that is loathsome. God, for us, cannot be thought of as an angry, awful, avenging Being who because of Adam's sin must have his Shylockian pound of flesh. No wonder the honest boy in justifiable repugnance could say, "Dirty bully."

While these pronouncements were not officially representative of the Council itself, the Council shared responsibility for them in the sense that it habitually and almost exclusively chose such liberal thinkers for its positions of trust.

Instead of contributing to the unity of the churches, the Council promoted division. Bible-believing, Christ-honoring Protestants in all denominations began to consider ways and means to set up a new interchurch

234

body for co-operation and action, which would have a clear and unequivocal testimony for the historic Christian faith. In a few short years the National Association of Evangelicals (1942) was created to fill this need.

The Restoration movement which had put so much emphasis on the Scriptural authority and norm in doctrine, ordinances, and life and was pleading for Christian unity on the Bible alone was suddenly confronted with a new climate in which to carry on its program. Increasingly large areas of Protestantism were convinced of the infallibility of Wellhausen and his ilk and felt that the Bible might be untrustworthy not only in cosmology and history but also in faith and practice. With the Biblical foundations crumbling, Christian theologians and educators began to talk of a Christian theology apart from the Biblical theology. They sneered at those who refused to admit the validity of destructive criticism and who clung to the Scriptures, calling them "bibliolaters" and repudiators of "true revelation." The popular concept of the Bible was that it is in some of its parts a "sign" or a "witness" to revelation but not in its Old and New Testament canon "the true Word of God." Some Disciples accepted the new theories. The mainstream of the movement did not. Thus ensued the bitter controversies which threatened to undermine and destroy the distinctive Restoration message and program and to dissipate all the gains of one hundred years.

BIBLIOGRAPHY: Chapter 15

Bettex, F., *The Bible the Word of God.*
Bettex, F., *Science and Christianity.*
Bryan, William Jennings, *Orthodox Christianity vs. Modernism.*
Eucken, Rudolph, *Main Currents in Modern Thought.*
Gordon, Ernest, *Leaven of the Sadducees.*
Henry, Carl F. H., *Fifty Years of Protestant Theology.*
Keyser, Leander S., *Contending for the Faith.*
Knudson, Albert C., *Present Tendencies in Religious Thought.*
Laws, Curtis Lee, editor, *The Watchman-Examiner.*
Machen, J. Gresham, *Christianity and Liberalism.*
McGarvey, J. W., "Biblical Criticism," *Christian Standard* (1893-1911).
McIntosh, Douglas Clyde, *The Problem of Religious Knowledge.*
Morgan, J. Vyrnwy, editor, *Theology at the Dawn of the Twentieth Century.*
Mullins, E. Y., *Christianity at the Crossroads.*
Patton, F. L., *Fundamental Christianity.*
Rian, Edwin H., *The Presbyterian Conflict.*
Smith, Gerald Birney, *Religious Thought in the Last Quarter Century.*
Strong, Augustus H., *Fifty Years in Theology.*
Torrey, R. A., editor, *The Fundamentals: A Testimony to the Truth. A Symposium* (four volumes).

Chapter 16

The Great Controversy

FOR one hundred years the Disciples of Christ had been a Bible people. They knew the Scriptures, prided themselves on knowing how to "rightly divide the Word," and delighted in receiving and doing "the whole counsel of God." They had no question about basic doctrines as revealed in the words of Scripture. They sought to "adorn the doctrine" with the labor of souls and bodies which bore the marks of God's grace. They believed that the unity of all God's people could be achieved by a return to the Bible alone as the authoritative rule of faith and practice.

Now, suddenly, in their hour of greatest achievement, they began to recognize the infiltration of "another gospel" which denied the credibility, inspiration, and authority of the Bible in the name of science and modern culture. The Disciples had not accepted any clear-cut theological system or intellectual statement of faith. They knew nothing but the Bible and had yet to plumb its depths. The rank-and-file members were for the most part oblivious to the scientific and theological influences which were undermining the faith of millions in the Holy Scriptures. When they heard about these modern views they lumped them together with the man-made creeds of Christendom and discounted them as unworthy of their concern. What they could understand were the evidences of departure from the faith. If the Bible said one thing and one of the brethren said something else, that was heresy. With their failure to see beyond surface digressions and to understand the nature of the new apostasy, the defenders of the faith were greatly handicapped in the controversy that was about to ensue.

The right wing of the movement, the Churches of Christ, had so isolated itself from the mainstream of the Christian world and from the cultural and scientific movements of society in general that it was almost wholly unaffected by the controversy. It was to reach the Churches of Christ later in the twentieth century when they were able to take advantage of the experiences, the strategies, and the victories of the evangelical scholars. Liberalism was introduced to the mainstream of the Restoration movement by the Disciples Divinity House, the *Christian Century,* the Campbell Institute, and the Congresses promoted by a small coterie of "forward looking" brethren.

The Disciples Divinity House had its beginnings in the mind of Herbert L. Willett, who had wholeheartedly expoused the liberal cause. In 1893 he suggested the establishment of a seminary in connection with the University of Chicago, the great Rockefeller-endowed citadel of liberalism. Through Willett's influence, President Harper of the University was asked to address the National Convention of the Disciples in Chicago in October of that year. Harper explained the advantages the University could offer any theological school established in affiliation with it. In accordance with his terms, the Divinity House was founded in 1894, with Willett as dean. Since the Disciples had no graduate school in theology, a large group of graduates from their colleges began to flock to Chicago where they eagerly imbibed liberal ideas and doctrines. Others went to Yale, which was also controlled by liberals.

The liberals needed an organ through which they could propagandize the brotherhood. The *Christian Standard* was opposed to their views. The *Christian-Evangelist* was lukewarm. A small journal known as the *Christian Oracle,* founded in Iowa in 1884, had moved to Chicago. It was having financial problems, so the liberals took it over and renamed it the *Christian Century.* From 1901-1908 its editors included George A. Campbell, Charles A. Young, Herbert L. Willett, and J. J. Haley. Among the names of its writers were Arthur Hall, Errett Gates, Hiram Van Kirk, C. C. Rowlinson, Edward Scribner Ames, Charles Clayton Morrison, and others. At first the owners were afraid to state frankly their heretical views for fear of alienating their subscribers. It was proposed to get out an "extra," which might circulate among the liberals of the denominational churches who were more "enlightened" than the Disciples, but this proved impractical.

Finally, in 1908, Morrison bought the *Century* and a new policy of frank and open commitment to liberalism was inaugurated. His guns were trained on the *Christian Standard,* which he rightly figured was the one great barrier to the liberal program. He accused its publisher and its editors of "vicious propaganda," "falsehood," and "bigotry," and of causing the "dissension" which "racked the brotherhood." When the controversy arose over Willett's appearance on the program of the Centennial Convention, Morrison wrote his first editorial on public affairs, "Shall Professor Willett Resign?" and forced the opponents of Willett into a compromise. Morrison thus achieved a position of importance, which his great talents as a writer and thinker fully warranted.

In 1911 Morrison ran a series of articles advocating the reception of the unimmersed into the churches, thus creating the major issue of the Great Controversy—"open membership." This and other liberal views he espoused were arrived at in his own thinking because of the liberal premises he had accepted. At this time the doctrines of the Morrison-Willett school of thought were so repulsive to the Disciples that the *Century* lost many subscribers and came to the verge of bankruptcy.

238

Liberals in other communions, meanwhile, began to subscribe for the paper and showered Morrison with praise for his courageous and scholarly presentation of the liberal position. In 1918 the paper assumed the subtitle of "An Undenominational Journal of Religion" and launched into the open field of interdenominational journalism where it was to become the outstanding advocate of liberal thought and ecumenical unity in American Protestantism. Morrison did not, however, relax his interest in the crusade to infiltrate and capture the Disciples of Christ for liberalism.

The medium for the development of a liberal strategy for the capture of the schools and agencies of the Disciples was the Campbell Institute. This fellowship of college and university trained ministers and workers was organized in 1892 as the Campbell Club by five graduate students in Yale Divinity School. Its original purpose was to promote "a scholarly spirit, . . . quiet self-culture and the development of a higher spirituality," and to make "contributions of permanent value to the literature and thought of the Disciples." Since all its members had been duly exposed to the liberal philosophy and theology, it was a natural breeding ground for liberal ecclesiastical action. Gradually the few evangelicals who were in the original organization withdrew, though their names continued to be used for years as a camouflage of orthodoxy.

In 1896 some Yale and Chicago men organized the Campbell Institute, which grew to a membership of several hundred representing most of the colleges of the Disciples. They met as occasion demanded, especially at state and national conventions. Significantly, W. E. Garrison and A. T. DeGroot, two good members, in their *Disciples of Christ: A History,* say that "through this fellowship there flowed much of the vital substance nourishing the growing edge of the Disciples. Many of the most successful pastors serving notable congregations were in its company. A neglected theme is the achievement in practical affairs of the churches, in evangelism and other promotional work, by men of this fellowship." In 1939 the *Christian Standard* pointed out that "six of the last eight presidents of the International Convention" were members of the Institute. A list of prominent men in the work of all the colleges and agencies covering a period of fifty years from 1909 reveals the extent to which Institute men and their friends came to control the organizational life of the brotherhood.

One other item in the liberal apparatus should be mentioned—the Congresses. Liberals got their idea from the Parliament of Religions held in connection with the World Fair in Chicago in 1893. Here Christian ministers and scholars mingled with Jews, Buddhists, Mohammedans, Shintoists, Confucianists, and persons of other heathen faiths. Liberal Disciples who participated developed "feelings of almost racy heterodoxy." Individual denominational meetings or "congresses" were held as adjuncts of the larger Parliament. Following one of the interdenominational meetings at Macatawa Park, on Lake Michigan, a group of liberal Disciples laid plans for a series of Congresses where religious, theological, scientific, and social problems could be discussed at length. The first one was held in St. Louis in 1899. J. H. Garrison, editor of the *Christian-Evangelist,* presided. Edward Scribner Ames gave the first address on "The Value of Theology," which set the tone for the meeting. Conservative leaders were invited, and a few came, notably J. B. Briney. There was full freedom of discussion.

In 1912 at Kansas City, a constitution was adopted which widened the orbit of the Congresses to include "the Baptist and other denominations." Liberal domination of these meetings and their purpose to use them for liberal propaganda was blatantly demonstrated in the program for 1914. Liberal Baptist George B. Foster spoke that year on "The Need for a New Apologetic," which, a reporter stated, "covered ground which would have been good for at least six months of acrimonious newspaper controversy." This was too much for even the irenic conservatives, with the result that this was the last year any appreciable number of them attended. Even Herbert L. Willett admitted in *Progress* in 1917 that in Congress programs, "a large proportion [of the papers] have been contributed by members of the Campbell Institute." From this time on the propaganda value of the Congresses decreased until in 1926, under the presidency of Alva W. Taylor, they folded. An important aftermath of these meetings were the dinners set up by "converts" in their regional areas. A key liberal would speak, taking advanced theological and social ground, followed by an open forum in which the reasonableness and propriety of the "new gospel" were driven home.

Conservatives were slow to see what was happening in their Zion. Some were naive enough to be taken in by the liberal propaganda. Most of them trusted in a false security. It is related that a young man from Ohio came to register in the College of the Bible in Lexington in the days of J. W. McGarvey's presidency. The eager candidate for the ministry said, "Brother McGarvey, I have come here to learn how to defend the Bible." To which the aging scholar replied, "Then, young man, you better pack your collar box and go back home. The Bible needs no defense. It will take care of itself." McGarvey, was, however, soon stabbed wide awake by moves to take over Transylvania and the College of the Bible, and he became a foremost effective protagonist for the "faith which was once delivered."

In 1893 McGarvey began a department in *Christian Standard* under the title, "Biblical Criticism." He had previously sought the co-operation of a number of scholars of various denominations in founding a magazine devoted to this subject. There was, however, no Rockefeller money or any other financial support for such an enterprise. The *Standard* offered the space and McGarvey's monumental work began. The very nature of the *Standard's* constituency made it impossible for him to deal with the issues except in a very popular way. His writings made thousands of active church members at least conscious of liberalism's threat to the cause they loved and gave them tools to deal with it when it reared its head in their local congregations. The weakness of the undertaking was, as McGarvey well knew, its failure to fight scholarship with scholarship and deal with the basic intellectual issues. Occasionally in his department he would take "pot shots" at President Harper, Lyman Abbott, Washington Gladden, and other leading liberals; but his answer to the scholars was to be heard in the classrooms at Lexington and in his books, *Evidences of Christianity, The Authorship of Deuteronomy, Jesus and Jonah, The Text and Canon of the New Testament,* and *Credibility and Inspiration.* In their time these books were very effective although they were discredited by liberal scholars.

It is said that when George Foote Moore, of Yale, read McGarvey's book on Deuteronomy he remarked that it would be useless for him to reply until he and McGarvey could "go far back of his arguments and discuss and agree upon certain fundamental assumptions." The metaphysical approach to the issues of Biblical criticism is, after all, the root of the whole controversy. McGarvey believed his Bible because of his approach in faith; Moore did not, because of his primary assumptions. McGarvey never hesitated to meet liberals and confront them with their errors. He frequently spoke in the Congresses and participated in the discussions. He debated with Washington Gladden in the daily press on the book of Esther. He challenged the Chicago coterie of liberals frequently and seldom came off second best. The *Christian Century* and the *Christian-Evangelist* were so unfair to him and the things he stood for that finally McGarvey accused them of "a lack of honesty, reverence, and intelligence." It was at great personal sacrifice that he carried on his "battle for truth and right." He paid both in weakening physical health and in personal and scholarly disapprobation. But it was McGarvey, above all others in the brotherhood, who sensed the real issues at stake in both the Great Apostasy and the Great Controversy and dealt effectively with them. Without him the conservatives would have been dispersed and overcome.

Another stalwart was Alfred Fairhurst, professor in Kentucky University at Lexington. While McGarvey was challenging the textual critics, Fairhurst was defying the scientific naturalists in his classroom and in his books, *Organic Evolution Considered* and *Theistic Evolution.* Both had a wide sale throughout the English-speaking religious world. He, too, did not hesitate to meet the evolutionists in the Congresses and show up the weaknesses of their hypotheses.

It is small wonder that at the death of McGarvey (1911) and others of "the old school" at Lexington, the liberals moved in for "the kill." At all odds the faculties had to be cleared of this threat to "progress." Hall L. Calhoun, a Ph.D. from Harvard, had been tagged by McGarvey to succeed him as president of the College of the Bible. Other conservatives were being prepared in schools of comparable and unquestioned scholarship, to carry on the tradition of sound Biblical training. Dr. A. W. Fortune and certain liberals on the board had other ideas. Almost immediately R. H. Crossfield, a liberal, was chosen president not only of the College of the Bible but of Transylvania College as well. Calhoun was made dean of the seminary in 1912 and proceeded to do the best he could to maintain orthodox Biblical standards. But the inexorable liberal purge was on. S. M. Jefferson, Charles Louis Loos, and I. B. Grubbs were succeeded by such liberals as A. W. Fortune, William Clayton

Bower, G. W. Hemry, and Elmer E. Snoddy. All of these men accepted many of the conclusions of destructive criticism and also the theory of evolution as applied to religion.

The liberal strategy at Lexington was exactly the same as that used by educators in all Protestant denominations. They insisted that the educational standing of the College needed to be improved. There were too many students who had received improper preparatory training. Some men were beyond the "teaching age." Teaching methods in use were obsolete. Professors were needed who could lecture and conduct "cooperative" inquiry between student and teacher, with much reading and broad research on "all sides of a question." There ought to be much freedom of discussion (as if there had never been any) and stimulation of students to come to "their own conclusions." Motive and viewpoint in studying the Bible had changed, and the "new approach" was essential if the school was not to be "typed" and ostracized by the accrediting agencies. Furthermore, if changes were not made, the graduate ministry would become "negative, obscurantist, and defeatist," and make a "negligible contribution to the ecumenicity, religious scholarship, art, and culture of our time."

At first in the name of academic freedom, the liberals appealed only for a place or two on the faculty in fairness to a new theological viewpoint that had attained wide acceptance. Later they maintained that there was no other viewpoint than theirs which had any scholarly standing. The liberal position was buttressed by action of the educational accrediting agencies, now in almost complete control of the liberals. These actions did not involve doctrine, but they created standards which eliminated much Biblical and doctrinal instruction from the curriculum and disqualified the older scholars and professors from holding a place on the faculty. In fact, the real basic issues of the educational controversy were not allowed to appear, and when evangelicals raised them they were branded as "troublemakers" bent on "destroying the peace" of the brotherhood.

What the liberal strategy "soft pedaled" was the fact that a new system of thought—an apostasy from the clearly revealed essence of the Christian faith—had come upon the horizon. It was not difference on a few points, but the old and the new diverged radically all along the line. Indeed, Charles Clayton Morrison put it incisively in his editorial, "Fundamentalism and Modernism: Two Religions," in the *Christian Century* in January, 1924:

> There is a clash here as grim as between Christianity and Confucianism. . . . The God of the fundamentalist is one God; the God of the modernist is another. The Bible of the fundamentalist is one Bible; the Bible of the modernist is another. The church, the kingdom, the salvation, the consummation of all things—these are one thing to the fundamentalists and another thing to the modernists . . . Which is the true religion? . . . The future will tell.

Liberal educational strategists used many clever feints to keep the

242

facts from the people who supported the schools, most of whom were evangelicals in dense ignorance of the battle going on behind the scenes. Some of the less honorable liberals (and there were many honorable and honest men among them) deliberately misled inquiring brethren as to their stand on the issues. The favorite tactic, however, was to assume an aggrieved demeanor because inquiry was made and faith questioned, thus relieving the one questioned of the necessity of making a frank and honest answer. All of these tried and usually successful strategies were applied in Transylvania and the College of the Bible controversy with eminent success.

Dean Calhoun was now surrounded by a faculty that was completely opposed to his emphasis on the Bible as a textbook and to his evangelical theology. His statements in the classroom were held up to ridicule by his comrades who were supposed to believe in the principle of "academic freedom." Calhoun's friends in the student body then began to take notes on statements of the liberal professors. These "devout and scholarly men" were reported as follows:

A. W. Fortune: The virgin birth and the bodily resurrection have nothing to do with my acceptance of Jesus Christ . . . If we are to have Christian unity the time must come when we accept all forms of baptism, sprinkling, pouring and immersion.

George V. Moore: The divinity of Christ is not one of kind but of degree. He was simply divine to a greater degree than any other man.

E. E. Snoddy: If Jesus is a kind of meteor come down from heaven, then he has nothing in common with me and cannot help me solve my problems.

These and scores of other statements indicating the kind of instruction being offered at Lexington were sent to the *Christian Standard* with an appeal for help. On March 31, 1917, Editor George P. Rutledge published pages of letters of protest against the liberal invasion of this noble institution and called for an investigation of the charges. Under the chairmanship of Mark Collis, the College of the Bible board undertook an investigation and announced that it had cleared the professors of blame. Shortly afterward, Collis dissociated himself with the report and resigned from the board. Calhoun also resigned, leaving the institution completely in the hands of the liberals. An attempt was made to set up a Bible department in Bethany College with Calhoun, S. S. Lappin, W. R. Walker, and other conservatives composing the faculty, but that move was a failure. Calhoun, disillusioned by the perfidy of men he counted as brethren, finally joined the Church of Christ wing of the Restoration movement, where he served on the faculties of Freed-Hardeman and David Lipscomb Colleges until his death in 1935.

The liberal attack on Transylvania and the College of the Bible struck at the very heart of the higher educational program of the Disciples. It affected two of the oldest and most popular training schools for the Christian ministry. The outcome turned the tide toward liberalism. What the liberals stood for at Lexington became mainly the convictions and working principles of the faculties of all the schools holding membership in the Board of Higher Education of Disciples of Christ. An entire volume could be written and documented showing the method of infiltration, the strategy of purging evangelical professors, and the change of educational policy. Always this was accomplished under the guise of intellectual and religious liberty and of advancing the best interests of the brotherhood. There were always protests of innocence to charges of disloyalty to the Word of God and to the historic principles of the Restoration movement.

It became evident to Bible-believing, Christ-honoring evangelicals that the time had come for a "crash program" of new schools for the training of a sound ministry. Pursuing the Lexington story, in this connection, a group of men trained in the College of the Bible under McGarvey, Loos, Grubbs, and others of like mind, decided to establish a new school at Louisville. Accordingly McGarvey Bible College opened classes in the fall of 1923. Henry J. Lutz was chosen president. Serving with him on the faculty were Ralph L. Records, R. C. Foster, and other visiting lecturers. They had little or no financial undergirding, inadequate buildings and equipment, but they had scholarship and great faith in the promises of God. They reminded themselves of Garfield's definition of a college: "Mark Hopkins on one end of a log, and a student on the other." Some eighty students were enrolled in a curriculum reminiscent of that used by McGarvey at the College of the Bible.

At exactly the same time, each without knowledge of the plans of the other, the Cincinnati Bible Institute opened its doors. This school was the outgrowth of the program of the Clarke Fund, an evangelistic agency, headed by James DeForest Murch. Many new churches were being established and educational prospects indicated that these pulpits would eventually be filled by liberal preachers. The only solution seemed to be to set up a school, after the order of the old Phillips Bible Institute, of Canton, Ohio, and train a new generation of ministers. John W. Tyndall was called as president and was assisted by Murch and L. G. Tomlinson. On the faculty were a group of part-time teachers recruited largely from the editorial staff of the Standard Publishing Company: E. W. Thornton, Traverce Harrison, J. E. Sturgis, Robert E. Elmore, C. J. Sharp, Edwin R. Errett, and Orval W. Baylor. More than one hundred students enrolled. This school likewise had its financial problems but was determined to become a permanent institution.

It was not long until the leaders of both McGarvey and Cincinnati began to think in terms of merger by which their resources and student bodies might be combined. Negotiations began toward the close of the school year with the result that in 1924 the Cincinnati Bible Seminary was formed—a school destined to grow into the largest ministerial training school among the Disciples of Christ. Murch, by reason of his position as president of the newly formed Christian Restoration Association, was chosen acting president; and Ralph Records was dean As soon re-organization plans were completed the school was set up as an independent corporation and Records was elected president, in 1926.

244

The Cincinnati Bible Seminary became a pattern for many other new schools. In 1927 Manhattan Bible College was established at Manhattan, Kansas; in 1928 Atlanta Christian College at Atlanta, Georgia; in the same year Pacific Bible Seminary at Long Beach, California; Alberta Bible College at Calgary, Alberta, Canada, in 1932; San Jose Bible College, San Jose, California, in 1939; Ozark Bible College, Joplin, Missouri, in 1942; Dakota Bible College, Arlington, South Dakota in the same year; Lincoln Bible Institute, Lincoln, Illinois, and Nebraska Christian College, Norfolk, Nebraska in 1944. Wherever there was apostasy in education a new evangelical school sprang up to produce a ministry "true to the Bible" and to the mission of the Restoration movement.

Simultaneously the foreign missionary work, as well as education, of the Disciples was infiltrated by liberals. Here again, the strategy was to keep the real issues from the masses. Unfortunately, those who opposed this penetration did not hold the ensuing controversies to the basic issues but allowed secondary considerations to obscure the real ones. The only histories of the tragic encounter have thus emphasized the fringe debate and left the impression that only selfish ambition, false pride, ignorance, publishing-house rivalries, and reactionary influences were the cause of the trouble.

There had been controversy in the Foreign Christian Missionary Society for some time. In 1907 the *Christian Standard* discovered that John D. Rockefeller had made several gifts to the Society and immediately raised objection. The real issue, generally obscured, was that Rockefeller, benefactor of the liberal University of Chicago, the very center of aggressive modernism, was making such gifts to the foreign boards of all the leading denominations. This was a part of the liberal strategy to obtain control of these boards. Later the Rockefellers were to back the Laymen's Missionary Inquiry, which sought to change the whole motivating missionary theology and philosophy of American Protestantism. Evangelicals among the Disciples were determined that this golden pipeline to liberalism should be plugged.

At about this same time Ida M. Tarbell had written in *McClure's Magazine* a series of exposures of the machinations of Rockefeller's Standard Oil Company by which it had attained a monopoly on the American oil business. Unfortunately the public issues overshadowed the religious issues. Thomas W. Phillips, Sr., of the T. W. Phillips Gas and Oil Company, had been marked for slaughter by Rockefeller. Only because of his profound business sagacity had he been able to survive cut-throat competition. Phillips was persuaded to enter the foreign missions controversy. Soon A. McLean, the noble veteran of foreign missionary endeavor among the Disciples, was forced to defend the Society. Russell Errett, head of the Standard Publishing Company, long a warm friend of McLean, replied. The debate seemed to resolve itself into charges of "tainted money" and personal Errett-McLean diatribe. Finally, the only way to stop the interminable charges and counter charges was for the *Standard* to close its columns to any further discussion. When Phillips carried the issue to the 1907 National Convention in Norfolk he received a cold reception and the F.C.M.S. kept the Rockefeller money.

In 1908 a young man named Guy W. Sarvis was appointed as a missionary to China with special assignment as a teacher in the University of Nanking. He was a graduate of the University of Chicago and had been an assistant to Edward Scribner Ames in the liberal, open-membership Hyde Park (now University) church. Editorials began to appear in the *Standard* in 1911 attacking the F.C.M.S. for sending this liberal to the China mission. Sarvis was a proved liberal, but by devious strategies he remained in the employ of the Society on a promise to conform to its policies and not propagate his personal opinions. At the Louisville National Convention in 1912, Ames posed as conciliator and magnanimously withdrew the "living-link" support of Sarvis by the Hyde Park congregation. The *Christian-Evangelist,* then under the managing editorship of A. C. Smither with J. H. Garrison as editor-emeritus, exulted over "this happy solution" and recorded the fact "the convention rose and sang, 'Praise God, from whom all blessings flow.' " Later conventions were to sing the "Doxology" and rejoice over such phyrric victories that had nothing to do with basic issues. An interesting footnote to the Sarvis incident was his eventual retirement in Florida, where he and his wife became active members in the Orlando Unitarian Church, which, of course, stands for the central Unitarian doctrines of "the fatherhood of God, the brotherhood of man, the leadership of Jesus, salvation by character, and the progress of man onward and upward forever" and denies the deity and atonement of Christ.

In 1919 plans were announced for merger of all the "brotherhood agencies," including the Foreign Society, into one huge ecclesiastical body. This was done in the name of greater efficiency, the elimination of overlapping organization, and "constant and conflicting appeals to the churches for money." Again *Christian Standard* sensed the liberal strategy as a move to control not only the Foreign Society, but all the organized life of the brotherhood, as an apparatus to accomplish the liberals' ultimate purposes. Realizing that protests in a well-controlled Convention would not be given a fair and unlimited hearing, the *Standard* publicized a call of evangelical brethren for a preconvention rally. The call was significant. Among other things it pointed out

that there is an impending crisis in the affairs of the Restoration movement, coincident with the spread of modern rationalism . . .

1. Under this influence the Scriptural unity of doctrine is disturbed, among other evils, by the attempted introduction of "open membership," threatening the peace of all our congregations, and the very integrity of the Restoration plea.

2. As a result, our evangelistic work has been well-nigh brought to a standstill.

3. Our wonderful Bible-school progress has been halted.

4. In most of our colleges classes for the ministry have dwindled alarmingly.

5. In several instances, public journals, professedly loyal, champion the

cause as a separate denomination, or sect rather than as the divine cure for sectarianism.

6. Instead of forming a training force sufficient for a great Bible ministry, our colleges are too largely spending their energies in feeble rivalry of State institutions, under secular and not under Scriptural, standards of efficiency.

7. With a foreign element of 40,000,000 souls within our borders, we are doing next to nothing to win them to Christ, and through them, to open the way for the promulgation of the gospel in their home lands.

A great outpouring of brethren came to Cincinnati that year. The Odd Fellows' Temple was so crowded that the "rump convention," as the liberals called it, had to move to a larger auditorium. All the basic issues were discussed at length and strong opposition was registered against the merger of the agencies. Nevertheless, the United Christian Missionary Society was organized and began its operations in the following year.

In this chapter we are now primarily concerned with Foreign Missions and will confine our allusions to the U.C.M.S. in this frame of reference. The F.C.M.S. was now a mere "department" and answerable to a "higher power." Liberal infiltration now proceeded at a much more rapid rate.

The China Mission, to which Sarvis had been sent, proved to be a hotbed of liberal missionary philosophy and practice. Robert E. Elmore, who had succeeded A. W. Fortune as minister of the Walnut Hills church, Cincinnati, when this avowed liberal went to Lexington, was also recording secretary of the Foreign Society. He had vigorously opposed all liberal trends in the Society. In 1920, after futile efforts to forestall approval, Elmore revealed that Frank Garrett, secretary of the China Mission, had proposed the union of the Mission with the new liberal Church of Christ in China. He also revealed the practice of open membership in the China Mission. The *Christian Century*, in a boasting mood, confirmed the Elmore charges (August 26, 1920):

> The mission churches have already exercised their congregational prerogatives and taken action.
> Most, if not all, of the mission churches of Disciples in China have been for some time receiving unimmersed Christians into their membership. . . .
> The membership reports sent to missionary headquarters in America have made no distinction between the immersed and unimmersed members.

Morrison's revelation was based on good solid facts furnished him by George Baird, head of the mission at Luchowfu, and other liberals who were constantly in touch with him by correspondence.

The U.C.M.S. denied that there was any open membership in China and another battle was on. As usual, a secondary consideration was allowed to act as a smoke screen to the real issue of liberalism versus Biblical Christianity. From 1920, almost all the controversy over foreign missions centered on open membership. Was it practiced in China or was it not practiced in China? The contention of the Society was that unimmersed persons had the same status in the work and worship of native congregations as they had in the American churches; that a few stations had "associate membership" lists, but not many.

The 1920 International Convention at St. Louis heard a resolution presented from the floor by Mark Collis, calling for the resignation of Garrett. In an effort to stifle controversy, Charles Medbury, minister of the great University church, Des Moines, and universally loved, presented what later became known as "The Medbury Resolution." It quoted a former action of the Society and proposed an additional safeguard:

> That the Executive Committee is committed to the program of the organization and maintenance of work on the mission field in consonance with the teaching and practice of the disciples of Christ in the United States.
>
> These resolutions can have but one meaning, and that is that the Executive Committee does not approve of any control of the local churches by a district association (United Church of Christ) or of the advocacy or practice of open membership among the missionaries or mission stations supported by the Foreign Society.
>
> *Resolved,* That this statement of the Foreign Christian Missionary Society voicing, as we believe it does, the heart of our brotherhood as to the points at issue, be submitted by the United Society to men and women engaged in service under their direction, whose teaching or practice have been called in question, to the end that their open avowal of loyal support of such an expression of the thought and life of the brotherhood, may restore in the hearts of all, complete confidence in them, or, if in liberty of conscience such avowal is impossible, may indicate the wisdom of a prompt cessation of service as representatives of the disciples of Christ.

The resolution passed by a resounding majority. It was sent to the missionaries on all foreign fields and the Society announced that there was no dissent from it, i.e., "the missionaries were all willing to follow explicitly the accepted position of the Society."

It was at St. Louis that S. S. Lappin, former editor of the *Christian Standard,* had declared on the convention floor that open membership was being practiced in China. His charge was met by vigorous, almost insulting, denial by U.C.M.S. officials. In the interest of fairness, the *Century's* Morrison asked for the floor and read a personal letter from Baird unequivocally stating that open membership was being practiced in the mission. It was also at St. Louis that an exhibit of an "independent agency," the Christian Woman's Benevolent Association, was ordered thrown into an alley and those in charge ejected by police. The conservatives went home in a mood to "take with a grain of salt" any further protestations of innocence from the Executive Committee of the U.C.M.S. Disbelief and unrest caused trusted evangelical John T. Brown, a member of the U.C.M.S. Board of Managers to propose an on-the-field investigation of the India, China, and Philippine missions.

Upon his return from the Orient, Brown reported that India was all right; that E. K. Higdon and the Taft Avenue church were involved in open membership; and that the practice was widespread in China. At the same time he stated his belief that "most of the missionaries on the foreign field will agree, or have agreed, to work in harmony with the policy of the society." This belief was later renounced. His full report to the Society was then released to the *Standard,* with its damning evidence, and was

248

circulated far and wide in the brotherhood, contributing to the rift. Z. T. Sweeney, one of the wisest and most intelligent leaders of the evangelical opposition and member of the U.C.M.S. Board of Managers, sought to allay the rising storm of indignation in the brotherhood by proposing a "Peace Resolution" at the Oklahoma City International Convention in October, 1925:

> 1. That no person be employed by the United Christian Missionary Society as its representative who has committed himself or herself to belief in, or practice of, the reception of unimmersed persons into the membership of churches of Christ.
> 2. That if any person is now in the employment of the United Christian Missionary Society as a representative who has committed himself or herself to belief in, or practice of, the reception of unimmersed persons into the membership of churches of Christ, the relationship of that person to the United Christian Missionary Society be severed as employee. And this be done as soon as possible, with full consideration given to the interests of the person involved without jeopardy to the work of the Society (*Year Book*, 1925, p. 8).

This was like a bombshell to the liberals, many of whom held high offices in the Society and practiced open membership. Everything was done to keep the resolution from the floor of the convention. They called it a "new creed," insisted that it had to do with "personal convictions" and would require "intellectual and ecclesiastical policing." They sought to change the clause "committed . . . to belief in," but to no avail. Among those who opposed it in the debate were F. W. Burnham, C. M. Chilton, Mrs. W. H. Hart, Edgar DeWitt Jones, Edwin Marx (one of the liberal China missionaries), H. O. Pritchard, and A. D. Rogers. Speaking in favor of it were J. B. Briney, Claude E. Hill, R. A. Long, Charles S. Medbury, George A. Miller, Sam I. Smith, Z. T. Sweeney, and P. H. Welshimer. Never had the Convention witnessed such open demonstration of liberal and evangelical commitment. The resolution almost penetrated the smoke screen which had kept the brethren from realizing what the Great Controversy was about. After every parliamentary road block had been exhausted, R. A. Long moved for a vote and the Peace Resolution passed by an overwhelming majority. If it had been faithfully carried out, one of the greatest obstacles to unity and brotherhood would have been hurdled. But it was not implemented. If it had been, the entire official family would have been disrupted. Several, including Stephen J. Corey, had already prepared their resignations. Burnham devised the ignominious "Interpretation" of the Peace Resolution in which it was stated that the open-membership question had been settled in 1922 at the Winona Lake convention and that "there was no such practice under the United Society anywhere." The action of the Oklahoma City convention was held to have been purely advisory. The Burnham document interpreted "committed to belief in" as "not intended to invade the right of private judgment, but only to apply to such open agitation as would prove divisive." Evangelicals greeted this move as revealing the utter perfidy of the liberal cabal now in control of the foreign missionary program of the Society. It was all the

249

peacemakers could do to keep evangelicals from deserting the Convention and its associated agencies en toto and setting up their own co-operative program. They went in some strength to one more such gathering in Memphis in 1926. The story of that debacle needs some background for a complete understanding of the events which took place.

With the "official" missionary agencies under fire, thousands of Disciples had lost faith in their programs and withdrawn support. The people were not antimissionary, but they were completely at a loss to know where they could invest their money in doctrinally sound work. The principle of "independent missions" had long been established but seldom practiced. Isaac Errett, ardent supporter and promoter of the early societies, had said in an editorial, March 2, 1867:

> We have no idolatrous attachment for the General Missionary Society. If it can do the work proposed, we will encourage it. If it fails to command sufficient confidence and sympathy to enable it to do its work wisely and well, we shall go in for whatever form of associated effort the general wisdom of the brotherhood may approve (*Christian Standard*, p. 68).

There were several independent missions which had received considerable support such as the Cunningham (Yotsuya) Mission and the Azbill Mission in Japan. The Clarke Estate, established by Sidney S. Clarke, of Cincinnati, had been operating as a home missionary agency since 1871. James D. Murch, chairman of the Estate trustees, conceived the idea of enlarging its work to establish churches and to "cover America with the Plea." Attorneys advised against enlarging the original trust but approved the idea of setting up a similar Clarke Fund for this purpose. Contributions were received as a number of evangelists took the field, organizing in some years as many as one new church a month. It was under the aegis of the Fund that the Cincinnati Bible Institute was founded.

As the missionary situation in the official agencies continued to get worse, it was proposed that the Clarke Fund should be reorganized to serve as a clearinghouse for a whole new agency complex. In 1919, after the comity agreement in Mexico, Enrique T. Westrup had organized the Mexican Christian Missionary Society and salvaged the work in Monterrey and other cities. In the same year, M. B. Madden, who had disagreements with the F.C.M.S. Japan mission, set up the Osaka Christian Mission in Japan's second largest city. The Christian Woman's Benevolent Association, of St. Louis, was operating an independent Mothers' and Babies' Home, Christian Hospital, and Christian Old People's Home. The Christian Normal Institute, of Grayson, Kentucky, and other independent schools of a distinctly evangelical character were also in this growing orbit of so-called independent agencies.

Upon the advice of leading brethren, the Clarke Fund trustees issued a call for a general meeting in the historic Richmond Street church in Cincinnati, the site of the organization of the Christian Woman's Board of Missions, and the prayer meeting which eventuated in the founding of the Foreign Christian Missionary Society. On September 1, 1925, the Christian Restoration Association was organized. Murch was elected president. Other trustees were L. L. Faris, Horace W. Vaile, E. W. Thornton, Ralph L. Records, Cameron Meacham, O. A. Trinkle, Ransom Perry, and Ira M. Boswell. An advisory board of representative brethren was headed by P. H. Welshimer, minister of the largest congregation in the brotherhood, First church, Canton, Ohio. Four departments were set up: home missions, foreign missions, education, and a clearing house for as many "associated free agencies" as might wish to avail themselves of its services. The *Restoration Herald,* a new missionary magazine, was launched with Murch as editor. Its first issue featured the work of the Cunningham Mission. "Restoration Rallies" were held in all parts of the nation, in which the work of the associated agencies was explained and promoted. More than one hundred such rallies were held with representatives of the agencies and friendly ministers supplying the programs. A semiannual national missionary assembly was set up, holding its first meeting in Central Christian Church, Cincinnati.

In September, 1925, the Standard Publishing Company began the publication of a new monthly periodical devoted entirely to the Great Controversy. The first issue was called *The Spotlight,* but because another journal had pre-empted that name, the October issue bore the nomen, *The Touchstone.* Robert E. Elmore was the editor. It proposed to "turn the full light of publicity upon departures from the faith and polity of the New Testament Church." The John Brown Report seemed to furnish the groundwork for a "no-holds-barred" attack on the United Christian Missionary Society.

Unfortunately the missions controversy was permitted to deteriorate from a discussion of fundamental principles to base political jockeying and personal insult and diatribe. The spirit of Christ was seldom displayed and there was little prayer seeking the guidance of the Holy Spirit. The *Touchstone,* while rendering a real service in telling the brotherhood facts about liberal aggression that might otherwise not have been disclosed, included bitter tirade and unwholesome attitude. The *United Society News,* launched in December, 1925, and edited by W. M. Williams, was equally guilty of vicious propaganda. It was mainly concerned with attacks on the Christian Restoration Association and its president (whom Williams called "Smurch"), the *Touchstone,* and the *Christian Standard.* The *News* lumped the whole opposition under the heading of "Theological Tomcats":

> If the garrulous bunch of tomcats in the back yard were at home catching mice, where they ought to be, there would be much more peace in the neighborhood. And if those theological tomcats who are raising a rumpus in our Zion were preaching and practicing the Christian religion instead of posing as the only defenders of the faith and sole custodians of the oracles of God, we would have less disturbance and division and make far better progress in the Kingdom of God.

Fortunately the venom of each of these journalistic misadventures eventually killed the other and they soon disappeared from the scene. The masses of the people resented such an approach to problems that had to do with the most sacred things in their Christian faith and of the kingdom. The crisis in the Philippine mission now came to the fore. The liberal policy of the Society was forcing the abandonment of the evangelistic work in Aparri in northern Luzon, the surrender of the distinctly Biblical ministerial training school, Manila Bible Institute, and participation in an interdenominational missionary program for the future. The Higdon-Taft Avenue church open-membership situation had not cleared. Leslie Wolfe, the secretary of the Mission, had at first consented, in the interests of peace and harmony, to some of these moves and in his official capacity as secretary had signed several official documents. Meanwhile the struggle to satisfy his conscience as a convinced conservative went on. Finally, he decided to resign and return to America. The trustees of the Christian Restoration Association, learning of the situation authorized President Murch to cable Wolfe five-hundred dollars as a first month's payment on support of a new independent Philippine Mission, provided he would decide to remain in the Islands. Wolfe accepted and the new work was set up with the overwhelming majority of the natives supporting Wolfe.

When the Gastambide church, largest in the Islands, led by Felina S. Orlina, went independent, the U.C.M.S. mission put a padlock on the property and engaged policemen to keep the church from meeting in the edifice which had largely been paid for out of their own meagre income. Aparri was reopened. The Ilocano churches entered the new fellowship almost en masse. The Manila Bible Institute was reorganized with Juan S. Baronia as president. The incident was a tremendous demonstration of the desire of the native people to follow the teachings of the Bible rather than the opinions of men. Imagine the sensation caused in America by these events in the Philippines. Punitive measures were immediately taken by the Society to neutralize the effect of the debacle. The Memphis Convention was approaching, and the leaders had much explaining to do about the "Burnham Interpretation" of the Peace Resolution, to say nothing of this new crisis. The liberals who were in complete control of the Convention tightened their cordon and determined to save their gains regardless of. the cost.

Leading conservatives proposed that Wolfe, Peneyra, and Baronia come to America and state their case at Memphis. Another preconvention rally was set up by a Committee on Future Action and widely publicized in the *Christian Standard* and *Touchstone*. The First Methodist Church was rented for the meeting, but Disciple liberals were able to get the Methodists to annul their agreement. Accordingly the Pantages Theatre was procured. On November 10 and 11, 1926, the ambassadors from the Philippines told their story and leading ministers and educators restated the case of the opposition to liberalism and open membership and the perfidy of the U.C.M.S. The liberal smear campaign against Wolfe, Peneyra, and Baronia was set in motion in an attempt to defame the characters of these men and prove that they were dissemblers and fakes. Burnham asked Edwin R. Errett, S. S. Lappin, and a picked group of conservatives to meet him in advance of the Convention attack and in a

252

great show of piety and Christian concern presented the documents which proved the liberal case. The evangelicals examined the evidence and deplored the fact that it was to be misinterpreted in a campaign of slander. As "lambs for the slaughter," the Philippine delegation was easily disposed of in the main convention, November 11, 1926. The U.C.M.S.'s own white-wash of the open-membership charges was featured in a report of a "Commission to the Orient," headed by Cleveland J. Kleihauer, minister of the open-membership University church, Seattle. Mark Collis, W. D. Cunningham, and other evangelicals who dared take the platform to state their grievances were insulted and made to appear as fools. The official Memphis Convention was a complete "vindication" and victory for the liberal cause, and many conservatives went home determined that they would never again set foot in such a national gathering.

The "independent missionary" idea now spread like wildfire. In 1926 Thomas Kalane, a native trained in America, was sent as a missionary to South Africa. Later O. E. Payne and C. B. Titus were sent to reinforce and enlarge the work. In the same year, Jesse Kellems and Charles Richards, a popular evangelistic team, were sent to South Africa to set up New Testament churches in Johannesburg, Durban, and other leading cities. In the same year, the S. G. Rothermels set up a mission in the United Provinces of India. In 1928 the Harry Schaeffers opened the Central Provinces India Mission. In 1929 the J. Russell Morses began a work among the Lisus on the Tibetan border, continuing the mission of the late Dr. A. L. Shelton. The story of the closing of Shelton's Batang Mission by the U.C.M.S. was one of the most tragic in the history of Christian church missions. Shelton had induced Morse to give his life to missionary endeavor on "the roof of the world." The record of his sacrificial service has been an inspiration to hundreds of young people who have followed in his train. The record of this new development in missionary work will be treated at greater length in a later chapter.

The high hopes of the founders of the Christian Restoration Association, however, were not to be realized. Despite the splendid accomplishments of the Association and the impetus it had given to independent missions at home and abroad, to education and to benevolences, conservative elements in the brotherhood were so disillusioned by the failure of the older agencies that they doubted any co-operative agency program was free from the dangers of heresy, ecclesiasticism and compromise. Murch received an invitation to return to the Standard Publishing Company in 1933 and resigned the presidency. He was succeeded by Leon L. Meyers, and a reactionary program was adopted which severely limited C. R. A. influence and prestige. Robert E. Elmore became editor of the *Herald* and soon it adopted a sniping policy criticizing all those both in and out of the evangelical fold who failed to agree with the editor. The completely independent idea in Christian missions, somewhat comparable to the method used by the Churches of Christ, soon gained ascendancy among the conservatives.

The United Society now became a test of fellowship which sundered old ties at local as well as national and state levels. Many liberal ministers and churches had fellowship only with those who supported the Society. Many evangelical ministers and churches had fellowship only with those who boycotted the Society. The traditional view that freedom in missionary giving was the inalienable right of free churches and free brethren was flouted by both parties.

Now the International Convention itself became a target of controversy.

Convention organization had continued to be a matter of controversy and division from the days of the so-called Louisville Plan. This grand design for an all-inclusive, centralized national and state organization was almost immediately rejected as inimical to the freedom and autonomy of the churches. In weakened form, however, it continued until 1895, when the name of the General Christian Missionary Convention was changed, and the organization again became the American Christian Missionary Society. The National Convention became a huge mass meeting, largely under the aegis of the A.C.M.S. but open to all agencies. The chief concern of the National Convention was the preaching of the gospel and Christian fellowship.

The missionary and benevolent agencies of the brotherhood, growing in prestige and wealth, were, however, increasingly influential in Convention affairs. There was much competition among them for financial support. So incessant were their demands upon the congregations and on the state and national conventions that, finally, an unwholesome reaction set in. In 1893 representatives of the agencies met to resolve internal misunderstandings and work out a plan to resolve general criticism. This meeting drafted a constitution for a "united society," but the action was rejected by all parties concerned. In 1899 a further attempt was made which likewise failed. The agencies now eyed the National Convention as a medium through which their purposes might eventually be achieved.

In 1907 at Norfolk, Virginia, the constitution and bylaws of the American Christian Missionary Society were revised to set up a "delegate convention." Instead of the mass meeting, the National Convention was to become a representative body composed of delegates from contributing churches, state missionary societies, Sunday schools, and other organizations; and it was specified that "all members must furnish credentials in order to exercise the right to vote." At New Orleans in 1908, the constitution was amended providing for a delegate convention in which every church, whether contributing or not, should have the right of representation. This amendment was never implemented, largely because of the opposition of the *Christian Standard*. The *Standard*, sensing the popular reaction in the brotherhood at large, opposed the delegate idea on the ground that "a convention made up of delegates representing the churches is an ecclesiasticism." The whole matter was dropped in the interest of a display of unity in the great centennial celebration in Pittsburgh in 1909.

The believers in centralization resumed their activities the next year at Topeka. Peter Ainslee was president of the A.C.M.S. and the Convention. He announced that the sessions would be conducted in harmony with the specifications of the constitution, which provided for a definite membership, including accredited delegates. A. B. Philputt, chairman of the committee on unification, announced that his group would recommend a general convention to which all agencies would report, a delegate membership, and the unification of all the agencies into three units—home, foreign, and women's. The *Evangelist* approved. The *Standard* vigorously objected, now seeing not only an ecclesiastical threat, but also an organization which could deliver the brotherhood into compromising situations in increasingly popular interchurch bodies. The Topeka convention was not a delegate gathering and the unification committee's report was rejected.

Still the advocates of centralization persisted. At Toronto in 1913 it was stated that "no persons but accredited representatives of the Churches will have part in these assemblies." The dictum was not fully enforced but fully enough to get approval of a new constitution with the delegate idea firmly planted in the text. The centralizers were still unhappy, however, because the document contained a disclaimer of authority not only over the churches but over the agencies as well. The Convention thus became only an advisory body. In 1916, the agitation for a Convention with greater authority and for a united missionary society including all the agencies became so strong that Russell Errett let loose a broadside charging that the Convention had now become a "sect":

(1) It has been perverted from its avowed purpose—i.e., to unify our voluntary association of individuals—into the formation of an ecclesiasticism, with our free congregations as units in an organization which intends to control officially the missionary and other interests of the brotherhood.

(2) It was "adopted" (not by the congregations themselves but by a few hundred votes in a mass-meeting of four thousand) as a *delegate* Convention. . . .

(3) While it is wholly irresponsible, and, in the eyes of the law, is a pure nonentity, it has planned to take charge of our largest corporate interests and announces its intention to assume control of all affairs of the brotherhood, or "church," as it prefers to call it . . .

(4) Its pretense of regard for the authority of the churches is only a pretense . . .

At the Des Moines Convention that year, Z. T. Sweeney offered a resolution asking for a committee of five to meet with the officers of the Convention, representatives of the societies, editors and owners of the newspapers, to provide changes in the constitution for the peace of the brotherhood. The resolution was passed and the committee drafted an entirely new constitution for an International Convention of Disciples of Christ. The Preamble read:

WHEREAS, There is a widespread feeling among Disciples of Christ that a closer co-operation among their various missionary, educational, benevolent, and other agencies, and a more general fellowship in their common efforts for the extension of the kingdom of God in the world, would result in greater efficiency:

Therefore, We, members of the churches of Christ in convention assembled, reaffirming our steadfast adherence to the independence and autonomy of the local churches and disavowing any control over our congregations or missionary, educational and benevolent agencies other than that which is advisory, and inviting the fellowship of all our brethren in the accomplishment of these ends, do hereby adopt the following constitution.

The Convention became merely a voluntary association of individuals, the delegate idea was abandoned, all members of the churches attending the Convention were given the privilege of voting on all matters. At Kansas City, Missouri, in 1917, the new constitution was adopted amid great rejoicing throughout the brotherhood, including the *Standard*. In an editorial November 10, 1917, it said,

> It is our conviction that the Kansas City Convention mapped out a program on which we can depend for unity and substantial results for several years to come, and likewise a program that will expand and bear fruit a generation hence (p. 10).

But the centralizers were not finished. Amendments to the Constitution were immediately proposed which strengthened the Convention and created relationships to the agencies similar to those obtaining in purely denominational patterns of government. Among these was a set of specifications for the affiliation of agencies. The original Article VI of the constitution stated that "any general brotherhood missionary, educational, or philanthropic organization may become a co-operating organization . . . provided it will . . . submit its reports to the Convention and . . . hold its books, accounts, and all its records open to . . . inspection." Actually under these terms the old agencies could not maintain their exclusive status, and independent agencies might be recognized as worthy of support. The convention centralizers and the agency exclusivists now combined to prevent such a possibility, though they did so in sufficiently mild proposals to divert suspicion as to their real intents. Plans were also initiated which eventuated in the organization of the United Christian Missionary Society (designed to include all national agencies under one head). Considering these moves as acts of bad faith, the *Standard* refused to be represented at the 1922 Winona Lake Convention, and after the Memphis Convention in 1926, refused to recognize it as a legitimate brotherhood agency.

After many years of earnest effort to correct the departures from the faith evident in the Convention and in its reporting agencies, the evangelical elements of the brotherhood present at Memphis called a postconvention meeting, November 12, 1926, to set up a Committee on Future Action. Named to the committee were P. H. Welshimer, chairman, W. R. Walker, O. A. Trinkle, W. E. Sweeney, F. S. Dowdy, Robert S. Tuck, and Mark Collis. The committee later decided to issue a call for a "North American Christian Convention" to be held in Indianapolis, October 12-16, 1927. The gathering proposed was to be a mass meeting of "believers" which would "cause the enemies of truth and righteousness to take notice." It was to be a convention, not in the usual sense, but of all those who belong to the one church whose members are born from above, who walk according to the Spirit, and whose names are written in the Lamb's book of life.

It was not to be a denominational assembly. No form of rationalism, unitarianism, or unbelief was to be expressed from the platform. Principles, rather than causes or agencies, would be represented. Ample arrangements were to be made for conferences for elders and deacons, church finances, Bible study, women's work, and other matters which pertain to the health and growth of local congregations. Great themes were to be discussed on the program such as the deity of Christ, the integrity of the Scriptures, the church, Christian evangelism, the Restoration movement, and Christian unity. The Convention was to close with a great Communion service in which those assembled should pledge themselves in greater love and loyalty to Christ their Lord and Saviour. There were to be no resolutions, no business sessions, no official or agency convention machinery, no bitterness, wrangling, or protesting. Some thirty-five hundred brethren gathered. So happy were the people with their experiment that they authorized a continuation committee to arrange for a similar meeting the following year at Kansas City. The committee was composed of Edwin R. Errett, J. H. Stambaugh, W. S. Martin, C. C. Taylor, Ira M. Boswell, and J. H. O. Smith. This group reiterated the aims of the Convention:

> To honor the Scriptures as the only ground for the unity of followers of Christ.
> Disclaiming all affiliations with parties, factions, and special interests, to put forward the truths and objects common to the whole brotherhood of believers.
> To provide opportunity for loyal followers of the cross to show their colors under the banner, "Where the Scriptures speak, we speak; where the Scriptures are silent, we are silent."
> To exalt Christ as the creed that needs no revision.
> To exhibit a fellowship that springs from absolute freedom in Christ and freedom from ecclesiastical assumptions and machinations.

True to these aims the North American has met annually (with a few exceptions) for many years. It has frequently had men on its programs who have supported the International Convention or some of its related agencies and has not sought to create friction or division among those who are basically sound in the faith but disagree on secondary matters. The *Standard* has usually approved its policies. The *Christian-Evangelist,* while opposed to the idea of a separate convention, has frequently lauded the aims and the spirit of the North American. Editor Raphael H. Miller, after Indianapolis, May 8-12, 1927, wrote:

> The unprejudiced observer could not but be impressed by the attendance at all the sessions of the convention, estimated at from three to four thousand; the predominance of younger preachers; the full-voiced singing; the cordial fellowship in and the earnestness with which both speakers and listeners were seeking God's Word and way . . .
> It gives us matter for serious consideration that our divisions and contentions, our misrepresentation of one another's motives, our voiced suspicions which carelessly are set flying, our failure to recognize the honesty and sincerity of differing points of view, our divergencies in methods for carrying out the Great Commission, our failure to provide forums for presentation

and discussion of conscientiously-held convictions, and our competitions in educational ideals have created a felt need for group-conscious conventions and assemblies to give emphasis to what seems to be neglected in other conventions and assemblies of Disciples. . . .

Other conventions similar to the North American, but regional or community in character, have grown up in many sections of the nation—such as the Southwest Christian Convention, the Southern Christian Convention, and the Midwest Christian Convention. The Cincinnati Bible Seminary has promoted for many years a Conference on Evangelism which is national in scope and quite largely attended. Such developments indicate a strong desire among evangelicals for fellowship and co-operation. They might be termed *Biblical inclusivists* seeking unofficial united action with all those who are uncompromisingly committed to the teachings and practices of the New Testament.

The organization controversy extended to the state missionary societies. Because of their close relationship to the American Christian Missionary Society, they gradually tended to become branches of the national Society. Their programs were filled with promotional addresses for the national agencies and the speaking personnel was either provided by or approved by the agencies involved. The original purpose of the state societies was to hold evangelistic meetings for the purpose of organizing new churches or encouraging weak churches. State or district evangelists, rather than executive secretaries, were their chief employees. As the years passed evangelism became a minor concern of these societies. They began to exercise authority over the churches, though they denied any such design. Their services to the churches included telling them how to conduct their affairs. The advice of the state officials was sought in calling ministers, arranging budgets, setting up departmental activities, and solving internal problems. From this rather harmless and often very helpful relationship slowly evolved a shepherding or overlording species of control. The state organizations began to tell the churches whom they should or should not call as their ministers; what agencies they should and should not support. The practice of ordaining ministers, which had for more than a hundred years been the prerogative of local congregations, was now taken over by the state conventions, or services were held in the churches with the state secretary or official representative of the Society officiating. The state society concept of local church autonomy was narrowed down to freedom in internal domestic affairs exclusively, an abridgement of the historic rights of the congregations.

For more than a century there had been no limitations to this freedom; it pertained to brotherhood-wide, world-wide matters; it involved association with other local churches, groups of churches, conventions, and interchurch agencies. The free churches did not look upon district conventions or state conventions as subdivisions of a superchurch controlled by one constitution. They set up co-operative groups among themselves as occasion seemed to warrant without being warned that they were transgressing the rights of the state societies. They had banded themselves

258

together at will in evangelizing projects; now they were warned that the control of such affairs was vested in superchurch bodies and that the direction of these concerns was no longer considered part of the "sphere of autonomy" of the local church. It became increasingly difficult for the churches to distinguish between ecclesiastical control by the state societies and what the societies called "recommended procedures, purely descriptive and not arbitrary and regulatory." When there was a division of opinion about the support of the state societies or the International Convention agencies, the state secretaries would come to the defense of the state society parties and, if necessary, advise or supervise lawsuits to oust the "independents." Two classic examples of such court action are to be found in Eldora, Iowa, and Brookville, Indiana. Fortunately all such suits have eventually been decided in favor of the majority party and not on the ground of supercongregational control or authority.

As a result of these frictions, and to preserve their autonomy, hundreds of churches withdrew support from the state societies and reverted to co-operative gatherings of their own, patterned on the plan of the old-time fifth Sunday or yearly meetings; or they set up independent Bible conferences and Christian service camps. Occasionally, as in the case of Arizona, the old state societies were taken over by the evangelicals, causing the International Convention or the United Christian Missionary Society to encourage and officially recognize new state organizations.

In still another area of the co-operative life of the churches, the Great Controversy raged—the area of interchurch relations.

Alexander Campbell had approved the work of the World Evangelical Alliance. Isaac Errett and J. H. Garrison were enthusiastic about co-operation in such interdenominational agencies as the International Sunday School Association, the United Society of Christian Endeavor, and the Young Men's Christian Association.

When the National Federation of Churches and Christian Workers was established in 1901, the *Christian-Evangelist* proposed that Disciples should join it. E. B. Sanford, secretary of the new organization, addressed the 1902 National Convention in Omaha, stating the principles of the Federation. J. H. Garrison presented a resolution expressing "our cordial approval of the effort to bring the Churches of this country into closer co-operation and to give truer expression to the degree of unity which already exists." J. A. Lord, editor of the *Standard*, spoke against it, inquiring if such action would not be "recognizing the denominations." After some confusion and opposition the resolution was adopted. *Federation* was a bad word in many quarters due to the fact that the A.C.M.S. had given up plans to establish new churches in some important centers, because Methodists or Presbyterians had pre-empted them.

There was also the "federated church" idea, which involved the establishment of only one church in each community, to be composed of people of all denominations without regard to the clear teachings of the Scriptures. The *Standard* contended that the "Federation is not a union in Christ, but union in denominationalism, union in an order of things

259

which Christ and his apostles condemn as carnal and as an enemy to Christian union or union in Christ." New Testament churches had no stomach for this sort of compromise and they rightly assumed that this was the idealism of the N.F.C.C.W. Only liberals supported the Federation.

In 1905 the Federal Council of Churches of Christ in America was organized to take the place of the N.F.C.C.W. Thirty or more Disciples of Christ took part in the New York founding proceedings. These brethren were mostly liberal in their theological views, but there were also staunch evangelicals who felt that Campbell was right when he said "approaches are better than reproaches." A special mass meeting was called at the time of the Norfolk Convention in 1907 to determine where the Disciples would join. Frederick D. Power, a true evangelical, reported for a committee recommending favorable action and approving the appointment of delegates to the Federal Council. There was only one dissenting vote, that of J. B. Briney. It should be noted that there was nothing official about these actions. The men who went to New York were not "officially appointed." The action at Norfolk was outside the regular sessions of the National Convention. In those days all concerned recognized the fact that, in view of the voluntary character of all the co-operative agencies and conventions, there was no authority which could designate official representatives of the whole body of Disciples. Nevertheless the Disciples were "in" to all intents and purposes.

The conviction of advocates of this course of action was well expressed by W. T. Moore in his *Comprehensive History of the Disciples of Christ.*

> There has been a growing feeling that Christian union cannot be realized by simply contending for a platform that requires immediate conformity to all the conditions of Scriptural union; consequently the advocates of federation hold to the notion that this Scriptural platform must be approached by successive steps rather than by one step which will embrace everything that ought to be considered. These advocates claim that federation will bring the denominational leaders together, and that this is an important step in the right direction. . . . They think it is well to emphasize the points of agreement rather than the points of disagreement. They think that the points of disagreement will not be long in disappearing entirely if the points of agreement are sufficiently brought in view . . .
>
> Now whether this view of the matter is correct or not, it is certain that this is all that the friends of Federation mean by entering into cooperation with the denominations. There are a great many things that can be done in common, and it is believed that while these things are being done, the various religious bodies will become acquainted with one another, and will learn to love one another; and as love is greater than either faith or hope, this can ultimately conquer sectarianism and bring about the union of all God's people . . .
>
> [These men who favor Federation] are still thoroughly committed to Restoration principles; nor will they surrender these for any compromise which, in the slightest degree, discounts the great truths for which they have contended. But they have come to believe that Christian union can be effected more readily by working from the heart life than from a purely intellectual point of view. . . .

The *Christian Standard* and its very considerable constituency were opposed to entering upon this new adventure primarily because they believed there was no guarantee whatsoever that the Council would adhere to even a minimum of essential belief as a basis for fellowship or the discussion of true Christian unity. The Bible had been rejected as a basis, thus repudiating the principle laid down in the old Evangelical Alliance.

These evangelicals in the Restoration movement were determined that nothing should compromise their historic and Scriptural plan for the union of all believers. Said the *Standard*:

> The plan for unity was to return to the pattern of New Testament Christianity revealed in the Acts and the Epistles. As [the fathers] studied the New Testament they found that this pattern is twofold. They spoke of "the ancient gospel" and "the ancient order." The ancient gospel centered in the proposition that Jesus is the Christ, the Son of the living God. This is the creed of the New Testament church, the only proper test of faith and fellowship. This proposition was proved, not by theological speculations and opinions, but by the facts of the gospel divinely interposed in the stream of human history; namely, the death of Christ for our sins, His burial and His resurrection from the grave as the ground of our hope. These gospel facts were appropriated by faith in Christ, repentance toward Christ, confession of Christ and baptism into Christ. This is the divinely appointed, unchanging means and method of coming into fellowship with Christ and His church. . . . As these men honestly studied their New Testament they found the New Testament church differing in design from all the "churches" of their day. They conceived that the pathway to Christian unity lay along the line of restoring the polity of the church according to the pattern. . . . Denominationalists generally hold that it is not. They maintain generally two different theories of the church. One is the authoritarian concept of the Catholic groups, based on the authority of the clergy, vested in them by right of apostolic succession. The other is the evolutionary . . . concept, that the church is divinely molded to fit the needs of the time and place where it found itself and that its polity and forms are adaptable to the *mores* of succeeding generations.

Conservatives saw the Federal Council as committed to one or the other of these concepts which were completely foreign to the Biblical concept of the Restoration plea. They felt that to commit the Disciples to this heretical complex was to surrender to denominationalism.

Furthermore, the conservatives saw the names of a host of liberals in positions of prominence in the new organization. They knew these men were committed to a theology and philosophy which were anti-Christian in the Biblical sense. There was talk that the Eastern Orthodox Catholic churches were soon to be received into full membership, with their heterodox doctrines completely foreign to the basic principles of Protestantism. Evangelicals also saw the threat of superchurch influence through an interchurch organization of this nature bringing pressures and exerting authority over member churches to the extent that liberty in preaching the gospel and carrying on church programs might be threatened.

At this same time there were related developments in foreign lands. A conference of foreign missionaries in China was planning for cooperative work in China, Japan, the Philippines, India, and other countries.

261

This involved the surrender of the distinctive schools of the Disciples in these areas and some mission stations in the name of "comity." In July, 1910, British and American Disciples had sponsored an Anglo-American Conference on Christian Union, in London. Liberal representatives of Baptists, Congregationalists, Friends, Wesleyans, and Anglicans were on the program. The note of compromise was struck by Leslie W. Morgan, Errett Gates, Charles Clayton Morrison, and J. H. Garrison, along with a complete abandonment of the principles of the Restoration movement. All these movements, taken with the plans for the Federal Council, created fears in the hearts of thousands that the Disciples were being "sold out" and were slated to become "a disappearing brotherhood."

As a result only a few Disciples actively supported the Federal Council. Nevertheless, the International Convention cloaked its representatives with sufficient prestige and authority to give them status with the denominational world. Disciples who did not co-operate with the Council were branded as "mavericks" and "off-brand" and discredited because of "narrow" and "sectarian" views. The Restoration plea of the Disciples for Christian unity on the Bible alone was not presented before the Council with wholehearted commitment.

With all these unfortunate controversies in the years of liberal ascendancy, the work of the churches was slowed to a halt. There was little gain in membership. In 1900 there were 1,120,000 members reported in government statistics. In 1920 there were 1,178,079. There was a slight gain by 1930—1,554,678 but the old-time drive was gone. So shocking were these figures that leaders in all camps felt some effort should be made to bury their differences and unite for advance. Many believed that not even radical differences in opinion should necessitate division among Disciples of Christ so long as they are not made tests of fellowship. So began a new era of attempts at reconciliation.

BIBLIOGRAPHY: Chapter 16

Ames, Edward Scribner, *Beyond Theology.*
Campbell, George A., *Friends Are My Story.*
Corey, Stephen J., *Fifty Years of Attack and Controversy.*
DeGroot, Alfred T., *The Grounds of Divisions Among the Disciples of Christ.*
Elmore, Robert E., *The Corey Manuscript.*
Elmore, Robert E., editor, *The Touchstone* (1925-1926).
Garrison, J. H., W. R. Warren, A. C. Smither, Frederick D. Kershner, B. A. Abbott, editors, *Christian-Evangelist* (1908-1926).
Hayden, Edwin V., *Fifty Years of Digression and Disturbance.*
Lord, J. A., S. S. Lappin, George P. Rutledge, and Willard Mohorter, editors, *Christian Standard* (1908-1926).
Morrison, Charles Clayton, editor, *Christian Century* (1908-1926).
Murch, James DeForest, editor, *The Restoration Herald* (1925-1926).
Williams, W. M., editor, *United Society News* (1925-1926).
Thornton, E. W., editor, *Watchword of the Restoration Vindicated: A Symposium.*

Chapter 17

Attempts at Reconciliation

SENSING the grass-roots demand that something be done to bring about better understanding and unity among the brethren, the 1934 International Convention at Des Moines authorized the appointment of the Commission on Restudy of the Disciples of Christ. The resolution said,

> In view of the passion for unity which gave birth to the brotherhood of Disciples of Christ; in view of the irenic spirit which characterized our early movement; in view of the many union movements arising in Protestant Christianity; in view of the need of an aroused passion for unity among ourselves and in further view of the new frontiers and of the new challenge which the world is giving to the church for a deeper spiritual interpretation of God and the Gospel faced not only by the Disciples of Christ but by all other communions;
>
> It is hereby recommended that after a century and a quarter of history the convention, by its regularly constituted methods, appoint a commission to restudy the origin, history, slogans, methods, successes and failures of the movement of the Disciples of Christ, and with the purpose of a more effective and a more united program and a closer Christian fellowship among us.
>
> The Commission, which will be appointed, shall be composed of twenty members, proportionately representing the varied phases and schools of thought in the institutional life among us.
>
> It is recommended that this committee proceed at once to restudy our whole Disciple movement and, if possible, to recommend a future program.

The following persons served on the Commission during a part or all of its existence: Edward Scribner Ames, L. D. Anderson, H. C. Armstrong, Eugene C. Beach, R. M. Bell, George Walker Buckner, Jr., F. W. Burnham, George A. Campbell, Homer W. Carpenter, C. M. Chilton, Abram E. Cory, J. H. Dampier, Virgil L. Elliott, Stephen J. England, Edwin R. Errett, A. W. Fortune, Graham Frank, Winfred Ernest Garrison, Henry G. Harmon, Claude E. Hill, Edgar DeWitt Jones, Frederick D. Kershner, Hugh B. Kilgour, Clarence E. Lemmon, Raphael Harwood

Miller, Orval M. Morgan, Charles Clayton Morrison, James DeForest Murch, William F. Rothenburger, M. E. Sadler, O. L. Shelton, Willard E. Shelton, G. Gerald Sias, T. K. Smith, George H. Stewart, W. E. Sweeney, Robert S. Tuck, Dean E. Walker, L. N. D. Wells, P. H. Welshimer, and J. J. Whitehouse.

The first formal report was presented to the Convention in 1946. It sought to give an objective and impartial statement of the viewpoints held by the varying schools of thought in the brotherhood. So significant is the statement to any valid interpretation of the history of this period of the Restoration movement that its most important sections are reproduced *in toto*:

I. Denomination or Movement?

It is agreed that in our inception we were a movement rather than a denomination; that historically we have endeavored to avoid denominational status; and that to be content with occupying a status as one among many denominations is to abandon our attempt to realize unsectarian Christianity.

Some of us hold that we must therefore refuse to accept any denominational status, and rather seek to occupy non-partisan and ultimate ground in all points of faith and order.

Others hold that we are compelled by the existing order of Protestant denominationalism to be a denomination, while at the same time testifying against denominationalism and exploring all possibilities of finding common ground on which all Christians may stand.

Still others, in the judgment of this commission few in number, hold that we have in the processes of history become a denomination, possessing peculiarities and identity in a manner similar to the denominations round about us.

II. Local Church Autonomy

We are agreed that from the beginning we have emphasized the autonomy of the local church.

Some among us hold that there is a tendency on the part of the agencies and conventions to assume and to exercise authority over the local churches.

Others interpret the utterances and policies of the agencies and conventions as, in the main, the exercise of the responsibility of leadership which the churches desire them to undertake and to which the churches respond voluntarily with no sense of constraint by official authority.

III. The New Testament Church

We are agreed that the New Testament affords the sufficient basis and norm of evangelism and church life. But there are differences of understanding at certain points as to what the New Testament requires. The differences arise largely from two considerations. The first has to do with the bearing of the New Testament upon the structure of the local church.

Some among us find in the New Testament the divinely authoritative pattern for the form and organization of the local church, and affirm that, historically, we set out to restore this New Testament pattern and that our local churches essentially represent its restoration.

Others among us recognize in the New Testament certain *principles* which inherently belong to any local church that calls itself Christian, but they do not find any evidence that the particular *forms* of organization or procedure prevailing in the primitive church, were authoritatively prescribed as a pattern which the Christian church is obligated to reproduce in detail, everywhere and throughout all time.

The second consideration has to do with the relations among local churches. We are agreed that the New Testament distinctly discloses a clear conception of the *Church* as distinguished from the local churches and a profound sense of interdependence among all the churches. But the New Testament gives no clear evidence of an organization of local churches in a general or connexional relationship. From these facts two alternative conclusions are drawn.

Some believe that our churches would therefore deviate from the New Testament norm should they (1) recognize such a relationship, or (2) consent to create a recognized agency as their exclusive instrument for the united administration of their missionary or benevolent enterprises, or (3) create a single representative convention or council for the formation and expression of their united convictions on (a) matters which concern the churches and their agencies, or (b) our witness to Christian unity, or (c) our witness to the gospel in relation to the moral and human problems of our time. But they would leave to the brethren freedom to create any number of agencies for the expression of any or all of these above ends, as may seem to them expedient.

Others believe that the absence of an authoritative pattern leaves the churches free, and their relation to each other in the *Church* renders it their duty, (a) to create such agencies or organs as may be needed in order unitedly to carry on their missionary and benevolent enterprises and their plea for Christian unity in the most adequate and responsible manner; and (b) to constitute a genuinely representative convention or council through which the united voice of the brotherhood may be expressed—provided, always, that such agencies or organs and such convention or council shall not be clothed with nor allowed to assume any independent authority over the churches, but shall operate only under the consent of the churches whose rightful duty it is to participate in the democratic process by which their consent is enlisted and expressed.

IV. Conventions

We are agreed that our conventions have a highly important place in the life of our churches. As occasions for fellowship and witness-bearing, they have served to enlarge the vision of the local churches by exchange of views and experiences and by keeping the churches conscious of belonging to one another. We are also agreed that our people have not yet found a type of convention which fully satisfies their tradition, their convictions and their sense of obligation to give united expression to the interests of Christ's kingdom. The dissatisfaction which we all share has, however, in recent years, found expression in the holding of other conventions sponsored by those who desire to protest against certain features of the existing International Convention, as well as to exemplify, by contrast, a convention of a different type.

This development is an expression of the dissatisfaction and is also a cause of tension and of possible peril to the unity of our brotherhood. We believe that the sponsors of the North American [Christian] Convention deplore what seemed to them, in good conscience, the necessity of holding another type of assemblage. In view of the dissatisfaction, not only on the part of dissenters, but of supporters also, it seems evident that the brotherhood has a clear call to provide itself with a convention that will unite our people wholeheartedly, instead of tending to divide them.

V. Unity and Restoration

We are agreed that from our beginning we have cherished no purpose more steadfastly than to exercise a potent influence on behalf of Christian unity. Our movement began under this impulsion, and the passion for the unity of the whole church has never been lost. We are agreed, however, that we stand in need of Christ's forgiveness that our witness on behalf of this great consummation has not been more consistently proclaimed and, especially, more appealingly exemplified. We are embarrassed in our testimony and humbled in our hearts by the divisions that have already occurred in our own fellowship, and by the present tensions which gave rise to the creation of our commission.

Our study of the history and ideals of our people has led us to the conclusion that a basic cause of our divsions and our more serious dissensions, both past and present, lies in a difference of understanding with respect to the fundamental purpose of our movement.

Our commission agrees that the two concepts of unity and restoration have been, from the beginning, held together in a parity of mutual dependence. The fathers believed that they had discovered in the New Testament the pattern of the true church, that this pattern was authoritative for the Church of Christ in all time, and that Christian unity could be attained only by its restoration. Throughout our history this conception of our plea has persisted. During the past half century, however, in the thinking of a considerable section of our people, the ideals of union and restoration have tended to fall apart as two concepts that are not coordinate or mutually dependent. This, the commission believes, is a principal cause of the major dissensions which disturb us.

Some among us maintain that these two conceptions of union and restoration must be held together, essentially unchanged, in the form in which we traditionally conceived them. It is affirmed that Christian unity is possible only on the basis of the restoration of the primitive church in this form.

Others among us are content to abandon the concept of the restoration of the primitive church and center our emphasis upon union.

Still others believe that a new synthesis of these two concepts of unity and restoration is possible which would avoid, on the one hand, the too dogmatic claim that we alone have restored the New Testament church and, on the other hand, the indifferentism that regards the restoration concept as irrelevant to Christian unity.

VI. Baptism

Our churches have from the beginning administered the ordinance of baptism by the immersion in water of a penitent believer. Our study discloses no appreciable tendency among our churches to abandon or modify this practice. It has also been our practice, in the case of unimmersed members of other churches who sought membership with us, to receive them only on condition of their acceptance of immersion. A considerable number of our churches have, however, modified our traditional procedure at this point by receiving such applicants into membership without raising the question of baptism. This practice, commonly called "open membership," is one of the causes of tension among us. [Survey made by Chairman on behalf of Commission showed about 110 known churches.]

Some hold that, under the authority of Christ we have no right to receive any who have not been scripturally baptized, and that we are bound to apply this principle to the penitent believer and the unimmersed Christian without discrimination. It is maintained that any such discrimination is a surrender of the witness which we have been called to bear with respect to the scriptural action of baptism.

Others hold that in making the distinction between a penitent believer and one who brings credentials from a sister church of Christ, they are acting under the authority of Christ. They believe that inasmuch as Christ has received such a person into the membership of his church, they would be disloyal to Christ in not recognizing the full status of such a person as a Christian, a member of the Church of Christ, and receiving him as such without re-baptism, unless he desires to be re-baptized.

Among those who hold this view and practice it, are many who testify that, instead of surrendering or weakening our witness to immersion, it enhances it.

VII. In Faith, Unity

Our brotherhood has from the beginning rested upon a broad basis. It represented a revolt against the divisive use of human creeds as terms of admittance into the church and as authoritatively bound upon its ministers and members. In place of such creeds, there was adopted a simple, scriptural and truly catholic creed, namely, faith in Jesus Christ as the Son of God and man's Savior. A declaration of faith in the divine Lordship of Christ was the only confession required for membership in the Church or for ordination to the ministry. This faith represented not a belief about Him in terms of the historic creeds, but was a simple acceptance of the fact of His divinity and a spiritual and moral attitude toward Him. In our study of contemporary thought among our people, we have found two tendencies in the matter of faith which are a cause of tension and a peril to our unity.

Some among us seem to have abandoned the theological implications in the simple confession of Christ, and have come to regard His Lordship chiefly and essentially in ethical terms. He is the supreme moral and spiritual leader of mankind, and the confession of faith in Him is essentially a decision to follow His way of life.

Others go to the other extreme and seem to confound faith with doctrine. They insist that the Lordship of Christ must be interpreted theologically, and that their particular interpretation must be made explicit in the confession as the basis of our fellowship and unity.

Thus the traditional simple formula of faith which was to guarantee our unity as a people is challenged from two sides. From one side, by those who would abandon its implicit theological connotation; from the other, by those who would make their own particular theological connotation explicit as a basis of unity. Between these two schools of thought the main body of our people continue to use the scriptural confession without specific interpretation.

VIII. In Opinions, Liberty

The breadth of our conception of unity on the basis of the Lordship of Christ left a large place for diversity in the realm of opinion—both as to creedal opinion and practical or procedural opinion. [This means liberty in theological definitions, and also liberty in choice of procedure in practice.] In this field, the fathers hoped that a common loyalty to Christ would produce such "charity in all things" that disagreements and diversity of opinion would not impair the unity and complete fellowship of our churches. Our study of the past and the present has led us to the unhappy conclusion that we have, in practice, fallen far below their high hopes and the standard under which they summoned us to march together.

Our commission is unanimous in affirming the soundness of the two principles of unity in faith and liberty in opinion. That these principles were wrong or mistaken is, to us, unthinkable. But the divisions that have already taken place, and the dissension that exists among us today, plainly call for a re-examination of the principles upon which our movement was launched and of the spirit in which we have proclaimed and exemplified them. Such a re-examination we have been making in the deliberations of our commission.

It is apparent from this careful analysis that there were in the brotherhood three clearly defined schools of thought that may be designated as follows: (1) *The Legalistic Right Wing*: Biblical exclusivists, who while accepting the Holy Scriptures as authoritative and normative, on the basis of a literalistic interpretation of the Scriptures, refused to have fellowship with those with whom they disagreed; (2) *The Conservative Center*: Biblical inclusivists who accepted the Holy Scriptures as authoritative and normative and sought communication with all Christians; and (3) *The Liberal Left Wing*: non-Biblical inclusivists who rejected the Holy Scriptures as authoritative and normative and were prepared to accept a non-Biblical basis for an ecumenical church.

Still there were points of agreement to which all members of the Commission could subscribe. This was evident in its formal report to the 1947 International Convention:

We find that the great body of Disciples agree that:

1. The acknowledgment of Jesus Christ as Lord and Saviour is the sole affirmation of faith necessary to the fellowship of Christians.

2. The New Testament is the primary source of our knowledge concerning the will of God and the revelation of God in Christ, and is the authoritative scripture by which the will of God is conveyed to men.

3. Each local church is, under Christ, a self-governing unit; that organizations and agencies are in no sense governing bodies but may be useful instruments in carrying on Christian work and in fostering and expressing fellowship; that likewise congregations and individuals have the inherent right to initiate and carry on Christian work through directly supported enterprises without breach of the wider fellowship; and that the unity of the whole church in faith, fellowship and service is to be earnestly sought.

4. In the proclamation of the gospel of Christ as the message of salvation to the affection and intelligence of men, we have found our largest unity. The Great Commission demands that to make this "one world" we must first make it God's world, by the universal acceptance of Christ as Saviour. This acceptance of Christ can be attained only by the recovery of the apostolic passion for the proclamation of the message, regarding the method as incidental. "That the world may be saved" is our only hope of unity. The message of salvation in Christ is the only business of the Church.

5. The unity of Christians according to the program and prayer of our Lord, with Christ Himself the center of that unity, by the restoration of New Testament Christianity, is necessary to the realization of God's program for human redemption.

6. Their historical position has given them practical insight into the New Testament fellowship which they desire to share with the whole divided body of Christ.

In the light of this body of unifying principles and sentiments of faith and practice, the Commission has come to the conclusion that we ought to take courage, and address ourselves to active endeavors to magnify our unity and rally our people to ardent advocacy of these central agreements. The Commission therefore proposes:

1. That, recognizing that the unity of the Church must be maintained by constant care, all who occupy positions of trust in both congregations and general work, might well examine their work in the light of the above unifying center.

2. That we all seek opportunities of expressing our conviction that diversity

of methods in Christian activities is no barrier to the fellowship of Christian men.

3. That we all magnify our agreement in belief of the Gospel—"in faith unity": here there must be unity; and all grant freedom in opinions and methods—"in opinions liberty": here there must be liberty; and in charity and Christian love each must seek to excel the other.

4. That, since the Word of God transmitted to us in the New Testament is of primary significance to the Church, we all give ourselves to a continuous study of the New Testament Church in respect to its origin and nature, its structure and function, its mission and hope.

In loyalty to Jesus Christ, we believe, lies the hope of unity for the whole Church of Christ. To accept, let alone advocate division, would be, we believe, supreme disloyalty to our Lord. To give ourselves to advocacy of unity as encompassed above is, we believe, our mission in loyalty to our Lord (1947 *Year Book*, pp. 116, 117).

The Commission had failed to find sufficient common ground to reunite all schools of thought under the formal organization of the International Convention, as it was then constituted and controlled. It demonstrated, however, that if a broad and irenic Christian spirit could be maintained among all parties, they could sustain sufficient communication to preserve the movement.

The Commission expressed this conclusion and recommended a practical course of action in its formal report to the 1948 Convention:

The Commission would record its judgment that the most immediate problems requiring our attention in order to the preservation and development of our unity may be reduced to the following statements:

Our first major problem is to distinguish carefully the nature of our agreements and differences.

We are forced to recognize in the analyses of 1946 and 1947, that our differences deal with matters of relative emphasis, and our agreements with matters of basic importance. The differences lie in the realm of history, of theology, of application of principles to the problems of the church, of methods in labor and co-operation. The agreements are in the area of fact, of faith, and of doctrine. The differences touch only the periphery of the Christian life, but the agreements are at its center.

We hold that the divisive differences are obstacles to be overcome, while our agreements are foundations on which to build. These agreements speak of the person of Jesus Christ, confession of whom as Son of God, Lord and Savior, is the sole affirmation of faith necessary to the fellowship of Christians; of the definitive place which the New Testament holds in our personal religious lives and in the work of the Church; of the Church itself as Christ's body, making a reality on earth of the fellowship of those who are Christ's; of the unfinished business before the Church in the persons of those who have not heard or have not heeded the Gospel of Christ; and of the absolute necessity of unity among Christians as a condition to the answer of Christ's prayer that the world may believe. These matters of agreement are neither few nor trivial. They lie at the center of the faith that constitutes us a people, and a people of God.

Our second major problem is to discover, maintain and enjoy fellowship.

The discord, hatred and bitterness which evidences the alienation of this age from God, the desolation of this present world, would seem to be warning enough that God abandons to their destruction those who live in strife. We would, therefore, that our brethren seize quickly upon whatever fellowship we may have, that by cultivation we may enrich it; and that under the healing rays of the light of Christ it may be purified; so that we may exemplify the reconciled community of him whose ministry was the breaking of the walls of partition among men.

Fellowship among Christians is based on the relation they sustain to Christ. It is, therefore, personal, not organizational; religious—personal commitment to Christ—not theological; moral, not legal. The sole element of constraint is the love of Christ. Nothing must be permitted to obscure this high view of fellowship. At the same time, we may rightly appropriate all practical means of expressing this fellowship. Among such means we may note the various agencies for Christian work; direct participation by a local church in work beyond its own community; and attempts to make Christianity "one community" in fact, such as the "ecumenical movement." Each such activity may be interpreted on a subpersonal level, and so be evil; each may express an extension to personality, and so be Christian.

Our third major problem lies in educating our people to the realization, intellectually and practically, of the nature of our movement.

We cannot think of our brotherhood as a sect, but think of it rather as a demonstration of that unity to which Christ has called his whole Church. The historic distinctiveness of our people is not of our will, but has been made necessary in order that we may appropriate unto salvation the instruments of Christ's appointment for his Church. To these appointments, of belief, of ordinance, of doctrine, of polity, we lay no exclusive claim. Within these appointments we seek the unity of his Church and the salvation of men.

When we plead for the unity of the Church, it is not alone unity for unity's sake; when we plead for the Good Confession of Christ as the sole creedal requirement, it is not merely for the abolition of human creeds; but this plea for unity in faith is in order that Christ may be unobscured and that the world may believe in him, and be saved.

We are therefore persuaded that at no time has the demand been more imperative than now for a demonstration of the sufficiency and catholicity of the New Testament Church as the divine agent in human redemption.

We Therefore Sound a Call to All Disciples

That we sink into oblivion the particularisms which divide us as a people, and rally ourselves to a supreme and common effort for the realization of Christian unity, beginning each one with himself. Let each examine himself in the light of his relationship to Christ, as the center of that unity. Let each examine himself in respect to the teachings of the New Testament in his personal and corporate life. Let each one hear again the Gospel, and judge again his attitudes and sentiments, his programs and procedures, his thoughts and deeds—whether these things flow from the preaching of Christ and him crucified. Let us be no less concerned that our co-operative life shall relate itself to these same standards. Let each agency and congregation examine its stewardship, and so form and declare its policies and activities that all may rejoice in their manifest loyalty to the spirit and mandate of Christ's New Covenant.

That we evaluate our differences by treating them for what they really are, opinions which are subjects for free and open discussion, and which all are free to accept or to reject, answering only to Christ. To make these divergences from our central agreements more than this is to fall into the sin of sectarianism, and by overvaluing, actually devalue the silences of the Bible wherein we find liberty.

That we rise to a new sense of our mission to the Church and our mission to the world, noting their essential interdependence; for only if the Churches hear our Lord's prayer for unity may we expect the world to believe. Let us remember the holy purpose calling our movement into existence—the nations must wait in ignorance and destruction for Christians to unite. How can we today, standing under the impending world tragedy, do less than throw ourselves unreservedly into the one divinely commissioned business of the Church—and, using whatever means and methods may commend themselves to our Christian intelligence, seek to reach all this generation's unreached with the Gospel of our blessed Lord: We mean not alone the first proclamation of the Gospel to those who have not heard—but the continued preaching to those who have not heeded. We would reach with the Gospel those in the Church "who having ears, hear not"; we would reach the architects of our social order; we would reach all the people in all their affairs, that they may all pass under the judgment of the Gospel. Let us not be preoccupied with the dangers of disunity, but lift our eyes from the deadly concern we have for our particularistic preferences, and take to a desperate world the Gospel of its redemption! We live in this hour as men on borrowed time. Can we expend it, under God, on less than the most urgent work? Cannot we as a people point the way by our agreements to the unity of a Church resurgent, consecrated only to the Gospel of reconciliation with God through Christ Jesus, furnished in the grace of God with power to win the whole world? To do less, as we judge, is to forfeit our heritage as Disciples; nay, is to be found false stewards of the mystery of the faith.

In a time of sectarian strife, we were called into being as a people to bear witness to the unity of the Church without which its divine task could not be accomplished. Now again in a critical time of confusion we see the Church recognizing the impotency of division and seeking the power of unity. The Church will hear us now, and be restored to her might, if we but give clear voice to that plea to "unite for the conversion of the world." This is the dynamic of our mission.

We close with a fervent prayer, that God may grant us the grace of his Providence, that our concern for lost men may so burden our souls that we shall find no rest until the Church is united for the world's redemption, through the Gospel of Jesus Christ as proclaimed in the New Testament (1948 *Year Book*, pp. 120-122).

In 1949 the Commission, at its own request, was dismissed by the International Convention. The final report of the Commission suggested that it be succeeded by a Restudy Extension Committee, but this suggestion was not carried out. The Commission had hoped that study and discussion groups across the nation within local churches, ministerial associations, state ministers' meetings, conventions, conferences, and rallies might bring about a grass-roots confrontation of the issues and arouse a widespread sentiment for whatever degree of unity might be possible.

This was not to be. The *Christian-Evangelist*, the *Christian Standard*, and the *World Call*, for reasons of their own, refused to print the definitive 1946 report.

The Convention failed to underwrite or promote the study and discussion groups.

Conditions within the brotherhood apparently had deteriorated to the point where it was impossible to rally a strong concern for internal unity.

A conciliatory influence during this era was the emphasis on evangelism maintained by the National Evangelistic Association. This association had its beginning early in the present century at the Bethany (Indiana)

Assembly where it was organized by J. V. Updike, S. M. Martin, J. H. O. Smith, J. V. Coombs, and others. The Association continued for many years as a fellowship of professional evangelists. O. E. Hamilton, Charles Reign Scoville, John D. Hull, Z. T. Sweeney, Charles Medbury, and others of like faith and zeal saw in this organization a potential instrument to unite the brotherhood as an aggressive evangelistic force. During the 1921 International Convention at Winona Lake the N.E.A. conducted a "Hillside Service" each evening in addition to the scheduled convention program. So much enthusiasm was engendered that a series of evangelistic institutes were projected in various parts of the nation. In 1923 successful institutes were held in Oklahoma City, Oklahoma; Des Moines, Iowa; Louisville, Kentucky; and Pittsburgh, Pennsylvania. The N.E.A. meetings immediately preceding the International Conventions came to be anticipated events drawing hundreds of ministers and injecting a new spirit of evangelism into the whole movement.

Agitation by N.E.A. leaders prepared the way for the establishment of a Department of Evangelism in the United Christian Missionary Society, under the leadership of Jesse M. Bader, who had a distinguished evangelistic ministry with the Jackson Boulevard church in Kansas City, Missouri. Some two dozen evangelistic conferences were held each year under Bader's supervision. He appeared before state and district conventions and addressed ministerial students in the Christian colleges. A new evangelistic tract and methods literature was created and widely distributed. Schools for the training of personal workers were held in the churches.

Such was the esteem in which Bader was held by many in the brotherhood that they came to hope that he would succeed F. W. Burnham as president of the U.C.M.S. and would be able to bring all factions of the brotherhood together in its support. Opposition by liberal forces made this impossible, however, and after a series of adjustments in leadership Bader moved into interchurch work, where he became the last hope for making evangelism a major activity in the Federal Council of Churches. The Department of Evangelism in the U.C.M.S. became a mere promotional arm of the Society, and tensions mounted between it and the N.E.A.

Conservative elements in the International Convention insisted on perpetuating the preconvention sessions promoting evangelism. For many years these meetings have furnished a ground for fellowship on the part of those who still believe that the "gospel is the power of God unto salvation," and they have preserved a minimal measure of co-operation on the part of conservatives in the affairs of the convention and its associated agencies.

Parallel to and somewhat interrelated with these organized attempts at reconciliation were moves by irenic conservatives working through the *Christian Standard* as a medium of communication. Edwin R. Errett and James D. Murch were leaders in these moves.

Mr. Errett, a grandson of Isaac Errett's brother, was a graduate of

Bethany College with postgraduate studies at Yale. He was thoroughly committed to the Restoration plea, and having been through all the bruising organizational battles leading to the break-up in Memphis in 1926, he came to the editorship of the *Christian Standard* in 1930 with a scholarly understanding of the issues involved in the current controversy. He saw the fundamental objection to the liberally controlled missionary agencies, "not that they are wasteful, or present a wrong method of doing things," but that "they have abandoned the plea and forsaken the movement." With his intelligently conceived and incisive editorials he dealt with this and all the other issues of the controversy. Uncompromisingly loyal to fundamental principles of the Restoration, he devoted his energies to the encouragement and promotion of such agencies, old and new, as were committed unequivocally to the authority of the Scriptures.

At the same time Errett conferred courteously with all parties— right, left, and center—thus earning the ill will and suspicion of extremists and the respect of irenically minded Disciples everywhere. He participated eagerly and sacrificially in the work of the International Convention's Commission on Restudy and in many other conferences looking toward a better future for the brotherhood.

In 1937 he became a delegate to the World Faith and Order Conference in Edinburgh, Scotland, and when that assembly took action to join in the conversations that eventuated in the World Council of Churches, he accepted a place on the continuing committee on Faith and Order. He believed that he might be used of the Lord to bring to the attention of this world body the testimony of the Restoration movement for Christian unity on the Bible and the Bible alone as the rule of faith and practice. When it became evident that the studies on faith and order were to be smothered in the plethora of World Council ecclesiastical politics, Mr. Errett resigned.

Until his death in 1944 he continued, both through his editorship of *Christian Standard* and through personal counsel in numerous areas of brotherhood life, to give himself unstintingly toward establishing a basis for unity in obedience to the Scriptures and in liberty from human authority.

In the meantime James D. Murch, who had been with the Standard Publishing Company earlier and had left to become editor of the *Restoration Herald,* returned in 1933 to the Standard staff, bringing with him a program which he was convinced had the best possible chance of uniting the divergent forces of the brotherhood. Called "Christian Action," it had the avowed purpose of shifting emphasis from agency competition and liberal-conservative controversy to spiritual renewal, restudy of the Bible, and demonstration of Christian principles in the lives of men. Romans 12:1, 2 was the text of the crusade.

The management of the Standard Publishing Company, believing in the soundness of this spiritual approach to brotherhood problems, offered generous space for development of Christian Action in its periodicals, especially the *Christian Standard,* and promotion in other channels. Murch wrote voluminously and set up calls of spiritually committed persons in homes, churches, and communities, using specially-designed Bible studies. Christian Action conferences and rallies were held in all parts of the nation, reaching thousands. Among outstanding leaders in the crusade as it developed were C. G. Kindred, J. B. Hunley, George W. Knepper, Ernest Hunter Wray, G. Edwin Osborn, Aldis L. Webb, J. Merle Appelgate, Homer E. Sala, Basil Holt, and Charles Reign Scoville. National Christian Action gatherings were held in the late 1930's at Lake James, Indiana; Chautauqua, Ohio; and Winona Lake, Indiana.

The influence of Christian Action carried over into a series of moves—roughly contemporaneous but continuing longer—to reconcile the two associations of Christian churches and noninstrumental Churches of Christ that had separated in 1906. George A. Klingman, minister of a leading Church of Christ in Louisville, had already become professor of Old Testament in the Cincinnati Bible Seminary in 1932. Other gestures of rapprochement, spontaneous and loosely related one to another, gave evidence of the Spirit of God moving in men of both communions to heal the inconsistent breach of fellowship among folk committed to unity.

Murch was invited to Toronto, Canada, to address a rally in the old Central church. At the conclusion of an evening message an elder of a noninstrument congregation approached the speaker and remarked that such a spirit as that expressed in the present meeting might well be the means of promoting understanding and eventual unity among the people of the two bodies. Through the good offices of this elder a meeting was arranged between Murch and Claude E. Witty, minister of the large West Side-Central Church of Christ in Detroit, Michigan. They became warm friends and prayerfully considered what they might do to promote unity. They agreed that

> something should be done about the scandal of division in the ranks of the Restoration movement. . . . Tradition, creedalism, provincialism, institutionalism, Pharisaism, extremism, indifference, self-sufficiency, ignorance, proselyting, distrust, and all the imps of Satan were running riot. The leadership of the churches were not calling for unity. There was no great uprising of the rank and file demanding it. Yet we, as a people, had preached it; we ought to practice it.

By faith these two men launched an adventure for unity. They made a list of two hundred leaders in both groups and set up small face-to-face conferences with equal representation. The first was held in Cincinnati, February 23, 1937. It was so cordially received that others followed in Indianapolis, Indiana; Akron, Ohio; Los Angeles, California; Columbus, Indiana, and elsewhere. Out of these meetings developed two courses of action:

First, a five-point "Approach to Unity," which was widely publicized:

> 1. *Prayer.* Definite private and congregational prayer for unity, seeking the leadership of Christ.

2. *Survey.* Seeking to determine how much we have in common in faith and practice.

3. *Friendliness.* Establishing individual friendly relations by exchange of fraternal courtesies and through fellowship meetings.

4. *Co-operation.* Joint activity in enterprises which will not do violence to personal or group convictions.

5. *Study and Discussion.* Open-minded study and humble discussion of the things which at present divide us, in order to discover the way to complete and permanent unity.

Second, a proposal to hold a national gathering of interested brethren of both groups in which unity would be the central theme.

The first "National Unity Meeting" was held May 3, 4, 1938, in Witty's church in Detroit with capacity crowds. More than one thousand persons were in the audiences which heard major messages delivered by George Benson, H. H. Adamson, and J. N. Armstrong of the Churches of Christ, and W. R. Walker, P. H. Welshimer, and O. A. Trinkle of the Christian churches. So encouraging was the meeting that Trinkle invited the brethren to Englewood Christian Church, Indianapolis, for 1939.

Such meetings continued with encouraging interest for several years. Some fifty key men from each communion braved the criticism of many of their brethren to make valuable contributions to the venture. The chief accomplishments were (1) a growing personal acquaintance among the brethren of both groups; (2) a growing knowledge of the current status of the churches—their teaching, their programs, their problems, their aims and accomplishments; (3) a frank study and discussion of the obstacles to unity, the impelling motives toward it, and possible methods of achieving it; (4) dramatizing and publicizing the five-point approach; and (5) the creation of a spirit of prayer and surrender to God's will as supremely important requisites to any such endeavor.

A *Christian Unity Quarterly,* edited jointly by Murch and Witty, was launched as a medium of free discussion and promotion. The *Christian Standard* gave generous space to addresses delivered in the gatherings and heartily supported the effort. A tract, *Christian Unity: Churches of Christ and Christian Churches,* was distributed by hundreds of thousands of copies. The *Christian-Evangelist* was friendly. Among the more conservative periodicals of the churches of Christ, only the *Christian Leader* and the *Word and Work* were openly friendly. The *Gospel Advocate* was at first violent in its opposition, but later joined with the *Firm Foundation* in studiously ignoring the movement. The latter two were the most widely circulated and influential of these papers.

During the years of rapprochement there were many incidents which deserve a record in history. In Indianapolis a lively and enlightening exchange developed between H. Leo Boles, editor of the *Gospel Advocate,* and Edwin R. Errett, editor of the *Christian Standard,* establishing the fact that both groups were equally zealous in their acceptance of the Bible alone as their rule of faith and practice.

W. R. Walker delivered a history-making address interpreting the

275

"silences" of Campbell's dictum, "Where the Scriptures speak, we speak; where the Scriptures are silent, we are silent." Murch delivered a paper at Columbus, Ohio, on "What I Believe About Instrumental Music," giving a new approach to the problem.

The Board of Church Extension, the Pension Fund, and the National Benevolent Association offered their services without distinction or limitation, to the Churches of Christ. E. L. Jorgenson of the Churches of Christ, edited a hymnbook, *Great Songs of the Church,* which was published by the Standard Publishing Company for use in Christian churches.

Witty was invited to read a paper before the International Convention's Commission on Restudy and to speak at Butler School of Religion, Minnesota Bible College, the Michigan State Minister's Meeting of the Christian Churches, and the North American Christian Convention. Murch was invited to address a joint meeting of some sixty ministers of both groups at Louisville and to preach in Churches of Christ in Louisville, Nashville, Detroit, and other places.

An encouraging independence of friendly thought and action developed among young ministers of both communions. Lines were crossed in occasional exchanges of pulpits, and lecturers from one group were invited to speak in colleges and seminaries of the other.

Prayer meetings for unity were held at the graves of Campbell, Stone, and McGarvey, great leaders of the past whom both groups highly regard.

Some of these activities continue, with varying success and interest, in various parts of the country. One of the most significant later developments was led by Ernest Beam, a minister of the Churches of Christ in California, who in 1950 launched a new journal, *The Christian Forum,* dedicated to the promotion of unity. Until his death in the late 1950's he served as minister of congregations including members and practices of both groups. W. Carl Ketcherside, in his paper *Mission Messenger,* proposed and initiated an irenic restudy and reappraisal of the reasons for division, which continues to bear good fruit.

The decade of the 1940's, however, saw the decline of a significant number of organized efforts at reconciliation. The Christian Action Crusade ceased as a promoted campaign in 1941. Indirectly World War II was a factor in this decline with its necessary restrictions on travel and consequently on national conventions. Governmentally imposed restrictions in paper quotas forced publishing houses to take such drastic actions as putting ceilings on circulation and reducing the number of pages in their publications.

Late in 1943 the *Christian Standard* announced a "change in policy" by which, "instead of continuing chiefly as a home paper of general religious information and instruction," it would be "a rallying center for all who believe implicitly in the authority of Christ as revealed to us in the divinely inspired New Testament Scriptures." Since the announcement included the declaration that the journal would "vigorously protest every instance of the substitution of human expediency for the authority of Christ," it was interpreted by many as an abandonment of conciliation and the adoption of an extremist policy. The same announcement continued, " 'Where the Book is silent,' we shall champion the right of any Christian to uphold his own opinion in a Christian spirit," but those who were sure that the change of policy included matter and manner of doctrinal presentation as well as area of journalistic content were not convinced. When Mr. Murch was relieved of his responsibilities as editorial secretary at Standard Publishing within a year after Edwin Errett's death in 1944, they disregarded the personal issues involved and were sure that the passion for unity had departed from *Christian Standard* with these two men. Murch became editor of *United Evangelical Action,* the official organ of the growing National Association of Evangelicals.

In the same year—1944—the International Convention for the first time elected as its president an outspoken advocate of open membership. Lines of opposition and defense of the International Convention and its related agencies stiffened immediately. The Commission on Restudy made its last report and disbanded in 1948.

The series of unity meetings initiated by Murch and Witty came to an end at about the same time. Reactionary forces in the Churches of Christ rejoiced over the failure of attempts at reconciliation.

For the time being, at least, the lines of separation were drawn more closely. Each of the three parties in the Restoration movement began with renewed vigor to promote its distinctive ideas and peculiar programs of service.

In a movement which had emphasized the independence and autonomy of the local church there was a minimum of apparent friction. The religious world seemed unaware of what had taken place. Local congregations were primarily concerned with preaching the gospel, winning souls to Christ, and nurturing them in faith and life. Within two decades the total enrollment of the churches in the three companies of Christians reached the amazing total of nearly four million in America and another million in foreign lands. The story of that growth is told in the three chapters which follow.

BIBLIOGRAPHY: Chapter 17

Abbott, B. A., Willard Shelton, Raphael H. Miller, editors, *Christian-Evangelist* (1929-1945).
Boles, Leo H., and others, editors, *Gospel Advocate* (1938-1945).
Mohorter, Willard, Edwin R. Errett, and Burris Butler, editors, *Christian Standard* (1929-1945).
Murch, James DeForest, editor, *Christian Action* (1934-1945).
Murch, James DeForest, and Claude F. Witty, editors, *Christian Unity Quarterly* (1943-1945).
Peters, H. H., *Charles Reign Scoville.*
Rowe, Fred H., editor, *Christian Leader* (1938-1945).
Wallace, Foy E., editor, *Bible Banner* (1940-1945).
Reports of the Commission on Restudy of the Disciples of Christ, *Disciples of Christ Year Book* (1934-48).

Chapter 18

Leftist Status and Growth

ALMOST the entire institutional heritage of the Disciples came under the control of left-wing liberals following the Memphis International Convention. Infiltrations which were first evidenced among the Disciples by "open membership" in the Foreign Christian Missionary Society and "liberalism" in Transylvania and the College of the Bible, eventually appeared in most of the agencies of the brotherhood, and the so-called "inclusivist" strategy succeeded in capturing all key administrative and policy-making bodies. The pattern of infiltration and eventual control was similar to that in most major American denominations. This did not mean that all the agencies themselves were necessarily liberal nor that their friends and supporters were exclusively liberal. Strong evangelical elements remained the chief financial support of the agencies. Agency control, however, provided liberals with the prestige and the machinery to assure the eventual achievement of their ultimate objectives.

The extreme Left in Discipledom may be characterized as having abandoned the authority of the New Testament and its normative pattern in all matters of religion. Having undermined this foundation pillar of Thomas Campbell's platform for Christian unity, this school of thought further denies that fellowship is predicated upon a common body of doctrine. Its theology lies in the realm of expediency and opinion, consequently exalting the liberty of the human mind. Leftists favor the universal practice of "open membership" as a practical demonstration of "Christian unity." Leftists having lost the distinctive message of the Disciples have become apologists for the "historic position" of the Disciples on Biblical authority and practice, and seek to convince the religious world that they alone represent the true spirit of the communion. They cite the Stone period of history, and later aberrant historical incidents to "debunk" the century-old and well-authenticated facts about the Restoration movement. Leftists represent the Disciples as a denomination and are moving as rapidly as opposition will permit to create a full-fledged ecclesiasticism with firmly centralized authority. This institution they intend to deliver, by a series of mergers with other denominations, to the "Coming Great Church" which is the dream of modern ecumenicists.

The colleges related to the Board of Higher Education are centers of liberal strength. There are still a few evangelicals in some of them, but their major impact is in favor of liberalism and the liberal-controlled agencies of the brotherhood. An editorial in the *Christian Century* (March 25, 1959, p. 350) rejoiced over the fact that "the last stronghold among the accredited seminaries of the Disciples who opposed the co-operative policies of the denomination's major organizations" had been gathered into the liberal fold—the Christian Theological Seminary (formerly the Butler School of Religion). All the Board-related institutions were originally established and endowed by evangelically minded men thoroughly committed to the principles of the Restoration movement. Now many of them, while maintaining a nominal relationship to the "denomination," are little concerned with the aims of their founders. These universities, colleges, and seminaries maintain high academic standards, according to modern theory, and are widely recognized for the quality of their work. They add immense prestige to liberal claims and the standing of the "denomination." The list is most impressive:

Atlantic Christian College at Wilson, North Carolina, was established in 1902. After many years of struggle, it has developed into an institution enrolling more than a thousand students—the largest school of the Disciples on the Eastern seaboard.

Bethany College, the school founded by Alexander Campbell and rich with Campbellian tradition, is located in the beautiful West Virginia hills. It is well-equipped and endowed, and maintains high small-college standards.

Butler University is the outgrowth of Ovid Butler's small Northwestern Christian University, established in 1850. Today it has become the chief institution of higher learning in Indianapolis, assuming somewhat the character of a great secular municipal university. Located in former Fairview Park it has an enrollment of some seven thousand students and possesses growingly adequate equipment and endowment. Characteristic of this type of institution, the trustees, faculty, and student body are heavily weighted with non-Christian-church personnel. The fully accredited Christian Theological Seminary has an adjacent campus but now maintains a separate corporate existence. C.T.S. normally enrolls more than four hundred men and women training for the ministry.

Chapman College has had a varied educational history under several different names. It is the lineal descendant of the old Hesperian College established in 1860. Chapman serves Southern California and normally enrolls around five hundred students.

Christian College is a standard junior college for women located at Columbia, Missouri, with a student body averaging about four hundred.

Christian College of Georgia is all that remains of several adventures in higher education in this state. It is located at Athens, adjacent to the campus of the State University and serves around fifty students.

The College of the Bible, Lexington, Kentucky, is located on a comparatively new campus opposite the University of Kentucky. It has every modern facility of a standardized theological seminary and enrolls around two hundred candidates for the ministry.

Culver-Stockton College is the former Christian University founded in 1855 at Canton, Missouri. It has a commanding location on bluffs overlooking the Mississippi, offers standard liberal arts courses, and enrolls between six and seven hundred students.

Disciples Divinity House is one of the federated theological seminaries clustering about the University of Chicago. It has only a small enrollment but exercises a strong liberal influence far beyond its size among current Disciple leadership.

Drake University, like Butler, is now a municipal type institution serving the great city of Des Moines, Iowa, and is the third most heavily endowed school of the Disciples. It is recognized as one of the great universities of Iowa (four thousand students) and is noted for its educational, scientific, and athletic prowess. Its School of Religion is adequately housed and furnishes a center for liberal propaganda in the Central West.

Eureka College is the historic school of Illinois Disciples. It is an academically high-rated liberal-arts college usually enrolling around three hundred students, some forty of whom aspire to the ministry.

Hiram College has the same status in northern Ohio but because of its suburban relationship to the great city of Cleveland enrolls more than six hundred students annually.

Lynchburg College is the successor to the old Virginia Christian College but has assumed a more-or-less municipal character. It has a student body of one thousand with about one hundred ministerial aspirants.

Phillips University, located at Enid, Oklahoma (formerly Oklahoma Christian University) enrolls from twelve to fifteen hundred students in a rapidly developing metropolitan area. Its large, well-staffed and well-equipped College of the Bible and Graduate Seminary have more than three hundred enrollees.

Texas Christian University, located at Fort Worth, is the largest and richest of all the institutions of higher education related to the Christian churches. It enrolls nearly eight thousand students, whose famed football team, the "Horned Frogs" often defeat such schools as Baylor, Southern Methodist, and Notre Dame. Around two hundred of the eight thousand students matriculate annually in the Brite College of the Bible. Like Butler and Drake, T.C.U. is a municipal-type institution. It has gross assets approaching the forty-million-dollar mark and continues to grow in power and influence in the Texas area.

Transylvania College, rivalling Bethany for honors as the oldest institution of higher education among the Disciples, usually has about five hundred students enrolled, of which some seventy are undergraduate ministerial majors. Transylvania is located in Lexington, Kentucky.

William Woods College at Fulton, Missouri, is a high-grade junior college for women enrolling around 350 students each year.

Other American institutions, members of the Board of Higher Education, are of various types: College of the Churches of Christ in Canada, Toronto; College of Missions, Indianapolis, Indiana; Cotner School of Religion, Lincoln, Nebraska; Disciples Divinity House, Vanderbilt University, Nashville, Tennessee; Disciples Student Foundation of the Christian Churches of Kansas; Drury School of Religion, Springfield, Missouri; Illinois Disciples Foundation, Champaign; Indiana School of Religion, Bloomington; Iowa Department of Campus Christian Life, Des Moines; Jarvis Christian College, Hawkins, Texas; Kansas Bible Chair, Lawrence; Midway Junior College, Midway, Kentucky; Missouri School of Religion, Columbia; Northwest Christian College, Eugene, Oregon; Oklahoma Christian Foundation, Norman; Tougaloo Southern Christian College, Tougaloo, Mississippi.

A total of nearly 35,000 students is registered in the thirty-four institutions: some 2,800 are in preparation for various types of religious vocations. Educational leaders say that the number of ministerial students who graduate and actually take pulpits is inadequate to meet the needs of the churches. There are fewer volunteers from liberal churches for the ministry and the mission fields as the years pass. This problem constitutes a major concern which is accentuated by the fact that non-Board conservative schools are graduating an ever-increasing numbers of ministers.

Left-wing control of the United Christian Missionary Society gave liberal missionary leaders *carte blanche* to purge their Christian missionary heritage of all opposition. An immense complex of stations, outstations, churches, schools, hospitals, dispensaries, missionary properties and endowment funds, representing the gifts and sacrificial work of evangelicals over nearly one hundred years, passed into liberal hands. They took over some 300 missionaries, 1,700 national workers, 230 church organizations, 1,700 outstations, 560 schools and colleges, 18 hospitals, 28 dispensaries, and properties and permanent funds totaling more than four million dollars.

As hundreds of churches withdrew financial support, there was serious retrenchment. Then came two world wars. The records show tremendous losses. Five stations were closed in India. Many schools, hospitals, and dispensaries were abandoned. All the great work in China was lost, including Nantung, Nanking, Chuchow, Wuhu, and Luchowfu, with immense investments in boy's and girl's schools, academies, colleges, and hospitals. Tibet, with its Batang hospital and mission buildings, was abandoned. More than half of the work in the Philippines was taken over by the new "independent" mission, forcing the U.C.M.S. to dispose of its schools and three hospitals and to merge many of its interests with the Philippine Federation of Churches. In Japan, Drake Bible College with its distinctive program of ministerial training was closed, as was Asakusa Institute, Christy Institute, and East Tokyo Institute. All other work was merged into the Church of Christ in Japan (Kyodan). In Argentina, the Colegio Americano in Buenos Aires, was closed.

Home missionary activity in the United States ceased in Russian churches located in New York City and Chicago; Slavic missions in the

282

coke regions of Pennsylvania, Cleveland, Ohio, and Bayonne, New Jersey; Brotherhood House in Chicago; Disciples Community House in New York City; twelve churches among the French Acadians in Louisiana. Mountain schools in Livingston, Tennessee, and Martinsville, Virginia, were sold. All work on the continent of Europe, where early missionaries had been sent, was abandoned.

Despite these losses there were still enough assets with which to rebuild and develop an even greater program. It is difficult to segregate distinctly Disciples work from the interchurch missionary federations and ecumenical agencies on the various fields, but it appears that the U.C.M.S. in its world mission is now responsible for extensive operations in twelve lands:

Jamaica boasts 37 churches, 46 preaching points, and one school, a total of 5,000 members.

In Puerto Rico, 50 churches and 117 preaching points report some 6,500 members.

In Mexico 15 churches and 24 preaching points, reach less than 1,000 members. Schools are maintained in San Luis Potosi and Aguascalientes.

Argentina still has 6 churches and 11 preaching points with around 500 members.

Nearby Paraguay has the Colegio International in Asuncion which maintains high educational standards and is greatly respected by Latin Americans. At first there were no churches established in Paraguay, but today the Society reports 5 congregations, 9 preaching points, and about 200 members.

Some of the work that the independent Thomas Mission did in establishing churches among the whites in South Africa is now being supervised by the U.C.M.S. Nine churches are reported with a membership of around 500.

Africa is, however, the scene of the greatest missionary work of the Society. Here in the Republic of Congo the spirit of Royal J. Dye still lives, and there are 100,000 baptized believers in 64 churches and a thousand preaching points. Wema, Lotumbe, Moneika, Bolenge, Mondombe, and four other centers are bases for the work of 60 missionaries and nearly 2,000 native workers. It is estimated that a half million natives are being reached with the gospel. There are 441 schools with more than 8,000 students, 183 of which are studying for the ministry. Ten hospitals and dispensaries minister to the physical ills of the people. Congo Christian Institute does an increasingly effective work in higher education.

India reports ten stations, 49 missionaries, and 275 national workers. Thirty-four churches and 62 Bible schools are maintained with 4,500 members. Fifteen schools of various grades enroll 3,000 students. Five hospitals and 7 dispensaries serve the physical ills of the Indian masses. Social service centers are located at Damoh and Takhatpur.

All this work is being merged with the interdenominational India Church Council and will soon lose its distinctive testimony. Union missionary projects are carried on in Orissa and Nepal. Some 4,000 Christians are reported in Orissa where Baptists have been at work for many years.

Under the direction of Donald A. McGavran, a survey was recently made in Thailand resulting in a work being undertaken in the Sam Yek area in co-operation with the national council of the Church of Christ in Thailand.

In Japan, all the work is integrated with the Kyodan, but reports indicate the U.C.M.S. is responsible for 4 stations, 11 churches, and 18 meeting places which have a membership of 700. There is also supervision of 5 schools, enrolling 2,000 students, and of a maternity hospital. Many Disciples are confused as to the extent of their work in Japan because of U.C.M.S. reports which include all the work of the Kyodan's 1,200 churches, 7,000 ministers and workers, and 125,000 members. Eventually all the churches of the Disciples and the institutions they have built will be completely submerged in the union organization.

In the Philippines something of the same situation prevails. All of the forty-eight churches, with their 2,500 members, have been merged with the United Church of Christ. All except three of the Disciple missionaries in the Philippines are appointed to work in the United church. The Union Theological Seminary (Presbyterian, Methodist, United Brethren, Congregational, and Disciples) trains all the ministers and workers. Evangelism is of the ecumenical variety.

The U.C.M.S. publishes one of the most impressive missionary magazines in American Protestantism, *World Call*. It has a large circulation which is maintained through Christian Women's Fellowships in the local churches. The Christian Women's Fellowship is the modern organizational counterpart of the old Christian Woman's Board of Missions. It is efficiently and effectively promoted as the exclusive women's co-operative program in thousands of local churches. It constitutes the chief strength of the U.C.M.S. in the life of the brotherhood.

In the United States, the U.C.M.S. has fifteen foreign language churches. Social welfare and educational institutions include: All Peoples Church and Community Center in Los Angeles, California; Hazel Green Academy, Hazel Green Kentucky; Jarvis Christian College, Hawkins, Texas; Mexican Christian Institute, San Antonio, Texas; Mount Beulah Christian Center and Farm, Edwards, Mississippi; Tougaloo Southern Christian College, Tougaloo, Mississippi; and Yakima Indian Christian Mission, White Swan, Washington.

The United Christian Missionary Society maintains a total of 244 missionaries (compared with more than 300 in 1928), 2,200 native workers, 267 churches, and 1,430 meeting places, with a combined membership of 130,500. It has some 336 schools, 13 hospitals, and 23 dispensaries. The total value of missionary property on home and foreign fields is only slightly less than $4,000,000. The Society's net worth is $10,000,000. Its vast undertakings in other areas of church life will be treated in another portion of this chapter.

Liberal missionary leaders no longer talk about Christian missions in terms of the great commission of Jesus. Their concern is about the "ecumenical world mission" of the church. The U.C.M.S. is thoroughly committed to the new strategy which is involved in the unification of all mission work within the aegis of the World Council of Churches, minimizes evangelism, stresses the social gospel, and seeks to make a Christian impact upon varied cultures looking toward the achievement of one great world community under the fatherhood of God and the brotherhood of man.

Virgil A. Sly, as executive chairman of the new "Division of World Mission" of the U.C.M.S., is supervising this new ecumenical strategy. Basic principles are set forth in his address, "From Missions to Mission," delivered in Pittsburgh in December, 1958. "Christian mission," said the U.C.M.S. leader, "is concerned with the whole relationship of man with God and men with each other. . . . God is the Father of all mankind. Jesus Christ is the Redeemer of our world. The gospel is the instrument of God's transforming love. All mankind is heir to the dignity and spiritual equality that is their due as sons of God. Christians are one within the concern of God. . . ." Sly called upon Christians to be willing to sacrifice the essentially "Western pattern" of Christianity and accept the nonconformist church practices and procedures which may emerge in the coming ecumenical church. He urged missionary leaders to scrap their old boards and societies and delegate to new co-operative bodies the authority to project the total new ecumenical world mission. He admitted that this revolutionary idea would not be realized without a "dramatic struggle" but expressed his belief that eventually the transition "from missions to mission" would be accomplished.

In this frame of reference the U.C.M.S. will eventually disappear and the kind of missions which brought organized work among the Disciples into being will become the exclusive ministry of the Centrists and Rightists of the Restoration movement.

The International Convention of Christian Churches (Disciples of Christ) is the lineal descendant of the first General Convention held in Cincinnati in 1849. The present organization (serving churches in the United States and Canada) dates to 1917. The incorporation of the Convention was approved by the Cincinnati Assembly in October, 1949. Its present name was adopted at Des Moines, Iowa, 1956.

The Preamble of the present Constitution states the purposes of the Convention and its relationship to the local churches and member agencies:

Whereas, There is a widespread feeling among Disciples of Christ that a closer cooperation among their various missionary, educational, benevolent, and other agencies, and a more general fellowship in their common efforts for the extension of the Kingdom of God in the world would result in greater efficiency;

Therefore, We, members of Churches of the Disciples of Christ in convention assembled, reaffirming our steadfast adherence to the independence and autonomy of the local churches and disavowing any control over our congregations or missionary, educational and benevolent agencies other than that which is advisory, and inviting the fellowship of all our brethren in the accomplishment of these ends, do hereby adopt the following . . . (1948 *Year Book*, p. 39).

This statement is essentially the same as that agreed to by Left and Center parties at the Kansas City assembly in 1917, except for certain changes in phraseology which weaken the old Convention's individual voluntary character. The assembly is now a delegate meeting, representative of the participating churches. Every action that has been taken to change, amend, or interpret the Constitution since Kansas City, has encouraged centralization and denominationalization.

The structure of the Convention vests authority in the Assembly and between conventions in the Board of Trustees. There are sixteen member agencies which report to the International Convention, many of which are larger and more influential than the Convention itself and have great influence in state organizations which elect or appoint the members of the important Nominating Committee and Committee on Recommendations. In matters relating to the agencies, the Commission on Budgets and Promotional Relationships and the Council of Agencies prevent the Convention from taking actions thought to be inimical to agency policies and programs, or from admitting new agencies that might be considered competitive. So effective is this apparently democratic system that its critics often facetiously remark that "the tail is wagging the dog."

Friends of the present Convention system insist that it is thoroughly democratic in purpose, organizational structure, and operation, and that it has no motives or future intentions beyond those stated in the Preamble. They see all nonco-operative elements in the brotherhood as unduly concerned for the autonomy of the local congregation and about incipient ecclesiasticism. They feel that critics of the Convention have a spirit less than Christian and that they misrepresent it because they themselves are not in positions of leadership. Convention advocates say that if the official personnel is inclined to soft-pedal the Restoration witness, then the way to counteract this is not to set up independent agencies, but to stay in the "organized work" and bring the weight of their influence to bear through the accepted and responsible channels of the organization.

With its liberal supporters in the vast majority, the Convention and its major agencies have, since Memphis, constantly moved to the Left. In general, the left-wing group have always favored a strongly centralized organization and a frankly denominational status. Liberals have tended to say that anything the U.C.M.S. does is certain to be right and that anyone who does not support it is "out of the brotherhood." They are strongly ecumenical and they accept pronouncements of the Councils of Churches and proceed to interpret the Christian unity message of the Disciples in that frame of reference. As long as there is liberal control of the Convention and the U.C.M.S., their policies and declarations are likely to coincide with the liberal position.

Between the Convention and the United Society there has now developed a complete denominational superstructure which denominationalists of all communions recognize as somewhat synonymous with their ecclesiastical systems. The International Convention is, to all outward intents and purposes, the denomination. It is the member body of the

286

National Council of Churches and the World Council of Churches. Either the Convention or its agencies appoint representatives to all interchurch bodies. The great majority of these representatives are liberals. Because of this type of representation, the denominational world and the entire interchurch complex is led to assume that the two million Disciples (or at least the majority of them) hold the views expressed by these appointees.

The United Christian Missionary Society, since the merger of seven major agencies was authorized in Cincinnati in 1919, has become far more than a missionary society. Early in its history (1933-34) three of the uniting agencies, the Board of Church Extension, the National Benevolent Association, and the Pension Fund, withdrew because they realized the new U.C.M.S. policies would endanger their integrity and support. The United Society now supervises work of "the brotherhood" through committees and societies in state and regional organizations, and local churches. It has complete machinery in its Department of Religious Education for serving the Sunday schools and controlling curriculum. The Department maintains a liaison relationship with the Christian Board of Publication. Departments of Resources, Service, Missionary Education, and Social Welfare involve almost every conceivable operation of a "responsible" denomination. Committees and commissions deal with town and country problems, urban work, church development, ministerial services, military and veterans services, campus ministries, youth fellowships, Christian literature, evangelism, and world mission. Each of these functional arms reaches into a comparable committee in most of the well-organized state societies, and the major metropolitan and area organizations throughout the nation. The huge body of paid and voluntary personnel involved in this ecclesiastical machine exerts a determining influence in the actions of the subsidiary and related organizations of the churches.

The Code of Regulations of the U.C.M.S. in its statement of purposes and functions, provides for the unlimited scope of its activities:

> That the world may the more fully come to know Christ, the Son of God; that all men everywhere may increasingly appropriate for themselves His way of life; that a world of Christian brotherhood may be realized, and that the unity of God's people may be achieved, this Society is established.
>
> To this end the Society shall aid in the preaching of the Gospel of Christ at home and abroad; shall create and foster a program of Christian education and training to the end that men's minds may be enlightened concerning the Christian way of life; shall lend encouragement and assistance to congregations with a view to helping them become as efficient units as possible; shall interpret to the world the social implications of the teachings of Jesus; shall advance the cause of Christian womanhood; shall establish and maintain such institutions as schools, institutes, orphanages, hospitals and homes in the neglected areas of the world, and shall engage in other forms of Christian service as will help to bring in the Kingdom of God, in which His will shall be done in earth as it is in heaven.

The Board of Managers, which is the representative and authoritative body of the U.C.M.S., is chosen in state conventions. They, in turn, elect a Board of Trustees (formerly the Executive Committee) which, with the

National Cabinet, directs the affairs of the Society. The staff personnel is of a very high order in administrative ability. So capably have they acquitted themselves in interchurch affairs that its members have frequently been invited to take high posts of responsibility in state, regional, national, and world interchurch agencies. Their preparation and experience and their irenic spirit fit them to understand and appreciate denominational problems and to deal successfully with them in the larger frame of reference.

In the International Convention, the denominational pattern is more fully disclosed. The Convention is responsible for the publication of the annual *Year Book* which lists Christian churches and churches of Christ in the United States and Canada, the ministers and other full-time Christian workers, and contains the reports of its affiliated agencies. Until recent years there has been little or no complaint from even the critics of the Convention concerning the objectivity of this important document. Lately, a tendency has been noted to eliminate names of ministers and statistics of churches which do not support "the recognized agencies." Names must be cleared through state secretaries and there is a noticeable failure to consult with other agencies which might provide additional data not available through the so-called "official" channels. If this trend in *Year Book* policy is not halted, extremists of the Center may take some kind of precipitate and irresponsible action similar to that of J. W. Shepherd in 1906, which resulted in the creation of the Church of Christ which in the eyes of the government and the world, is a separate denomination or sect of Christendom.

The Christian Board of Publication was admitted to membership in the I.C.C.C. in 1952. The proposition of a "brotherhood publishing house" had been a matter of debate in the Convention since 1907. In 1909, seven weeks after the Centennial Convention in Pittsburgh, philanthropist R. A. Long purchased the property of the old Garrison-owned Christian Publishing Company in St. Louis, and in 1911, deeded it to a nonprofit organization to become the nucleus of a "brotherhood publishing house." Application was then made for recognition as a member agency of the Convention, but the controversy continued. Traditionally, all publications serving the Disciples were privately owned because of the fear that the editorial pronouncements of "official" journals would be construed as "the voice of the brotherhood" and restrict the right of free speech. With the loss of support of the major Center constituency of the Restoration movement at Memphis, Convention opposition to the Christian Board's application weakened and it has now become for all intents and purposes a part of a denominational structure. Since B. A. Abbott vacated the editorship of the *Christian-Evangelist* (now *The Christian*) it has reflected the liberal position in varying degrees of intensity and conviction. At all times it has been in substantial agreement with the liberal policies and pronouncements of the Convention and of the U.C.M.S. The Board owns a publishing plant worth some $2,000,000 and provides a complete publication service for the churches. It is implementing plans for expansion in the New Millcreek Valley Development Area of St. Louis. Under the name *Bethany Press,* Christian Board produces, on an average, twenty-three books a year. A full complement of Sunday-school periodicals and lesson quarterlies flows from its presses.

The three major agencies which withdrew from the U.C.M.S. retained affiliation with the International Convention and elicit support far beyond the Leftist orbit of the I.C.C.C.

The Board of Church Extension serves the churches through (1) loans to churches for the erection of new buildings, the remodeling of existing buildings, the purchase of sites for new buildings, and the purchase of new equipment; (2) loans to state and city societies for the purchase of parsonages for staff members; (3) interest-free loans to mission churches; (4) trust funds in which churches may deposit interest-bearing funds earmarked for new building projects; (5) financial counseling; (6) leadership in financial campaigns; and (7) architectural counseling. Its policies have permitted assistance to congregations of all types in the movement.

The Pension Fund, the lineal descendant of the Board of Ministerial Relief, serves some five thousand ministers, educators, evangelists, chaplains, missionaries, state and national agency executives, and approximately 7,900 churches desire to provide security for their ministers in old age or permanent disability. Under the Plan, member dues are 3 per cent of monthly salary; church dues are 9 per cent. Retirement pensions are paid those who become totally or permanently disabled. Widows and minor children receive pensions when members die. The highest actuarial ratings are given the Fund which now has assets of more than $25,000,000. This agency also operates on a policy that is fair and objective to all ministers of the Restoration movement.

The National Benevolent Association maintains eight homes for children: Child Saving Institute, Omaha, Nebraska; Cleveland Christian Home, Cleveland, Ohio; Colorado Christian Home, Denver, Colorado; St. Louis Christian Home, St. Louis, Missouri; Juliette Fowler Homes, Dallas, Texas; Carrie Hedrick Seay Memorial Home, Somerset, Pennsylvania; the Southern Christian Home, Atlanta, Georgia; and the Woodhaven Christian Home for Children, Columbia, Missouri. It has eleven homes for the aged: California Christian Home, San Gabriel, California; Emily E. Flinn Home, Marion, Indiana; Florida Christian Home, Jacksonville, Florida; Illinois Christian Home, Jacksonville, Illinois; Remsay Memorial Home, Des Moines, Iowa; Juliette Fowler Homes, Dallas, Texas; Northwestern Christian Home, Beaverton, Oregon; Lenior Christian Home, Columbia, Missouri; Oklahoma Christian Home, Edmond, Oklahoma; Kansas Christian Home, Newton, Kansas; and Kennedy Memorial Christian Home, Martinsville, Indiana. About two thousand persons compose the "N.B.A. Family Circle." More than thirty thousand children and aged persons have been served by the association since its founding in 1887. It has been faithful to the purpose set forth in its original charter, "To help the helpless, to give a home to the homeless, to provide care for the sick and comfort for the distressed."

Besides the agencies mentioned, the International Convention lists other "Co-operative Relationships": All-Canada Committee of the Churches of Christ; Christian Foundation; Christmount Christian Assembly; Council of Christian Unity; European Evangelistic Society; Disciples of Christ Historical Society; National Association of State Secretaries; National Christian Missionary Convention; National City Christian Church Corporation; National Evangelistic Association; Unified Promotion; Council of Agencies; State Missions Planning Council; and the state societies.

The scope of this work is too limited to permit more than passing reference to the state societies, many of which have attained a high degree of ecclesiastical efficiency. In Kansas, for example, are large permanent funds and related institutions such as the hospital and the home for the aged at Newton and the Kansas Bible Chair at the University of Kansas at Lawrence. All the state societies are gradually abandoning their former independent status under pressure from the International Convention and the United Christian Missionary Society. The device of Unified Promotion now exercises a species of control over their functions and finances. They recognize only "official agencies" in their convention programs and promotional efforts. In some states the conventions are little more than promotional instrumentalities of the International Convention and its major associated agencies. In a few states, notably Oregon and Pennsylvania, there remains a modicum of evangelical emphasis and a more-or-less free platform for the presentation of responsible non-Convention missionary, educational, and benevolent causes.

The impressive denomination-like machinery of the International Convention, the United Christian Missionary Society, and the state societies, largely under liberal control, becomes more firmly entrenched in the life of the brotherhood with the passing of the years. The liberals have culture, prestige, and administrative wisdom. They have no doctrinal or traditional inhibitions; they are *non-Biblical inclusivists*. They seek ecclesiastical status and are willing to make concessions which will promote ecumenical achievement. Their strong supporters in local churches are of similar timbre. In earlier days, the leadership of these churches had strong doctrinal commitments and held them passionately and aggressively. Today sound Biblical doctrine, the meaning of church membership, and commitment to the Restoration cause are sometimes deemed less important than social status and business success. Church members covet social and cultural relationships with the prominent churches of the community which are often affiliated with liberal-dominated councils of churches. Churchgoing has been popularized and, while it is a deeply felt and soul-searching experience for many millions of Americans, they frequently cannot hear Biblical preaching. The denomination has status and is accepted by other denominations. Disciples on the extreme Left accept this position and are glad that they have the status the International Convention can give them.

Extreme Leftists are zealous ecumenicists. They believe the movement which had its origin with the Campbells, Stone, and Scott, is primarily

290

a unity movement and that its chief function is to merge and unite. They have "written off" unity with the Center and the Right of the Restoration movement as an obstacle to their goals. In their zeal for the ecumencial church they overlook, minimize, or pervert, the historical basis of unity proposed in the early days of that movement. They have forgotten that an irreducible minimum of authority and basic belief are essential if true Christian unity is to be achieved. Since liberals acknowledge no authority outside their religious experience, the bond which would unite them with any of their religious neighbors would be a tenuous one. Unity at any price is their aim. They are schooled in the new science of ecumenics which has to do with the world community, its nature, functions, relations, and strategy. With the same cleverness which enabled them to gain control of the major educational institutions and the U.C.M.S. they are now working toward the accomplishment of "world mission." Liberals see the International Convention as the medium through which mergers with other communions can be effected and eventual union in the world ecumenical community will be realized.

The Denver International Convention in 1959 passed a resolution calling for "Brotherhood Restructure." It was the fruitage of discussions in the biennial meeting of the Council of Agencies at Culver Stockton College in July, 1958. In 1961, the Kansas City International Convention authorized a Commission on Brotherhood Structure. The commissioners were named and the program of restructure is taking shape. Propaganda and education are being disseminated through all available channels. Conferences and consultations, speakers in conventions and institutes, lectures in seminaries, articles in the church press, study courses, books, brochures, and pamphlets are preparing the minds of left-wing constituents for ultimate action. The International Convention will be the central authoritative denominational body. The state societies or associations, under the I.C.C.C., will become "associations of churches" with all essential denominational controls at the state level. The local churches are being asked to adopt new charters and constitutions which recognize the superior extracongregational authority of state and national bodies. Some state organizations have already completed their restructure. Local congregations are following the advice of state officials and are changing their legal papers, although some are loath to surrender their traditional freedom. When restructure has been completed, the new denominational leadership will be in legal position to consummate mergers with other denominations. Conversations looking to merger with the United Church of Christ are now under way.

Many Bible-believing Disciples remaining in the co-operative pattern of the International Convention and its related agencies give evidence that they are beginning to realize they must not let the Convention be the sole determining factor in fellowship with the immense body of faithful Disciples outside its aegis. They are increasingly aware of the weakness of a united brotherhood which would make tests of fellowship out of the post-office address to which the minister sends his missionary, benevolent, and educational contributions; the name of the periodical he reads; the schools where he received his college degrees; the publishing house from which he buys his Sunday-school literature; and the summer conference to which he sends his young people. They are realizing that true Christian fellowship and brotherhood co-operation come through Christ and loyalty to the teachings of the Word of God. In such a high view of co-operation n ay lie the hope of perpetuating the great principles of the Restoration movement in their purity and power, and of challenging the Christian world with its plea and program for Christian unity.

BIBLIOGRAPHY: Chapter 18

Buckner, George Walker, editor, *World Call* (1958-1959).
Cartwright, Lin D., Raphael H. Miller, and Howard Elmo Short, editors, *Christian Evangelist* (1946, 1958-1959).
Garrison, W. E., and Alfred T. DeGroot, *Disciples of Christ: A History*.
One World in Christ, 1958-1959. United Christian Missionary Society.
Official Program, 1959 Denver International Convention of Christian Churches (Disciples of Christ).
Osborn, Ronald E., editor, *Encounter* (Summer, 1959).
Reports, Panel of Scholars of the Disciples of Christ (1958-60).
Scroll, The (1958-60).
Warren, W. R., *Survey of Service*.
Whitley, Oliver Reed, *Trumpet Call of Reformation*.
Year Books (1958-61), International Convention of Christian Churches (Disciples of Christ).

Chapter 19

Centrist Status and Growth

PHENOMENAL growth has marked the activities of the great Center of the Restoration movement since the decision of its majority leadership to abandon the fight to maintain historic Restoration principles and fair balance of representation within the old traditional agencies.

In the broad sense the Center might be characterized as consisting of all those who continue to hold to the basic Biblical principles set forth in Thomas Campbell's *Declaration and Address* and Isaac Errett's *Our Position.* Let it be emphasized: *to the basic Biblical principles*—not to the historic documents themselves as such. Through one hundred years of history, Disciples had been *Biblical inclusivists,* and modern Centrists are of the same persuasion. They accept the Holy Scriptures as divinely inspired, alone and all-sufficient as the revelation of the will of God for mankind and of Christ and His gospel. They believe that the basic pattern for the church is revealed in the New Testament and that it is the duty of every faithful follower of Christ to restore and maintain that pattern. In the midst of the divided Christian world they consider themselves to be "Christians only, but not the only Christians." They are deeply concerned for the unity of all Christians and are working zealously for the attainment of the great hope of Christendom—*"Unum Corpus in Christo."* Thus the Center is inclusivist, rather than exclusivist, in spirit and purpose, but unwilling under any circumstances to abandon the Biblical revelation and New Testament standards to gain desirable ends.

Centrists in any political or social milieu partake of both the Right and the Left. The principle holds good in the fellowship of the Disciples. It is difficult to draw distinct lines between the fringe groups of the Center and border-line groups of Right and Left. No historian has the competency or omniscience to draw such lines and it is good that this is so. Whatever measure of liaison may exist is a possible basis for better understanding and eventual unity. Nevertheless, a hard core of Biblical belief and practice always distinguishes the Center, whether its fringe elements be found co-operating in the International Convention, in the

293

"independent agencies," or in no extracongregational undertakings whatsoever.

Some idea of the numerical strength of the Center may be gained from a study of the *Year Book* of the Christian churches (Disciples of Christ). Churches which fail to report gifts to International Convention agencies and, in some cases, other vital statistics, are likely to be of this persuasion. Other churches supporting Convention agencies have within their membership large conservative constituencies. In privately printed lists of churches, not including *Year Book* listings, there are probably another 200,000 members. Conservative estimates place the whole number of Centrists at considerably more than one million. The vast majority of these brethren, while strongly contending for full freedom and autonomy for the local churches, do not wish separate listing from those who do not agree with them; neither do they wish to be party to any project which would further divide the body of Christ.

Centrists are by nature co-operative. They have the conviction expressed by Alexander Campbell in the *Millennial Harbinger* in 1842 that comparatively little can be done to improve and educate a competent Christian ministry, to evangelize the world, to protect the flock from imposture and fraud, or to secure effective action in any worthwhile enterprise, without co-operation. They believe in the utmost freedom as to the method of co-operation as long as it does not by its nature defeat the purposes desired. After Memphis (1926), most of the brethren in the Center began to find their co-operative instincts best served in the variety of new educational, missionary, benevolent, and publishing agencies which were being created.

In education, a few colleges remained loyal to the Biblical faith, but they were wholly inadequate to meet the demand for the training of ministers and missionaries "true to the Book." New schools and colleges had to be created. The resources for such a courageous adventure were pitiably small, if judged by the educational standards of the new day. Dedicated educators were not certain as to what might be necessary to design and execute the new program, but they expressed faith that God would give them the answer to their problems as they arose.

These men conceived of their problem as primarily religious, and, after that, educational. There was a faith to be perpetuated—the one true, perfect plan of salvation revealed in the New Testament—the restoration of the apostolic church in doctrine, ordinances, and life. As they proceeded, they learned the deepest truth about education: that, like faith, it is an attitude of man's soul and mind. God, in His own good time, they believed, would provide the essential material resources that He had given Bethany, Hiram, and Drake in the days when they were loyal to the Restoration ideal. Beginning with a handful of loyal institutions after Memphis, higher education among the Centrists mushroomed to amazing proportions.

Centrists generally recognized and continued to support educational institutions which had their origins prior to the Great Controversy and which remained loyal to the distinctive position of the Disciples. Among them were Milligan College, Northwest Christian College, Johnson Bible College, Minnesota Bible College, and Kentucky Christian College.

Milligan College was established in eastern Tennessee by Josephus Hopwood in 1882. Hopwood and Henry J. Derthick accounted for fifty-two years of its administrative guidance, a somewhat remarkable record of educational stability. Under the presidency of Dean E. Walker, Milligan became the major liberal arts college serving evangelicals or conservatives. Three new buildings have been constructed in recent years, increasing capital assets by $2,000,000; and its enrollment has reached an all-time high. Plans are now being implemented for the creation of a strong graduate school for the Christian ministry, under the name *Emmanuel School of Religion*.

In 1893, Ashley S. Johnson founded Johnson Bible College at Kimberlin Heights, Tennessee, under the nomen *School of the Evangelists*. Originally designed to provide a self-help program for young candidates for the ministry, it has always laid great stress on the necessity of a practical knowledge and use of the Bible in an evangelistic ministry. Under R. M. Bell, it achieved its highest attainments in scholarship, buildings, equipment, and favor with the brotherhood.

Eugene Divinity School, later Eugene Bible University (still later Northwest Christian College), was opened by E. C. Sanderson in 1895. Its buildings are located near the campus of the University of Oregon in Eugene. It offers Christian instruction in a Christian atmosphere to young people who may also wish to obtain degrees at the state university. It has been granting its own degrees since 1900. Its ministerial students are advised to seek graduate degrees in standardized seminaries. Under the presidency of Ross Griffeth, N.C.C. has been firmly established and its influence broadened.

Minnesota Bible College (1913), opposite the campus of the University of Minnesota in Minneapolis, had its origin in the vision of David Eugene Olson. Olson hoped to build an "international Bible college" in which men of foreign birth would be trained to return to their native lands as preachers of indigenous churches of Christ. Two world wars served to change the institution's goals and M.B.C. became one of the strong Centrist Bible colleges. Former President Russell E. Boatman's leadership brought new strength and effectiveness, continuing under President Harry Poll.

An eastern Kentucky educator, J. W. Lusby, founded the Grayson Normal School in 1913, much in the tradition of Lower and Lehr (p. 200). In 1919 its name was changed to Christian Normal Institute, and in 1944, to Kentucky Christian College. It is a Bible college dedicated to the training of Christian workers, located on a beautiful campus at Grayson. Under the leadership of J. Lowell Lusby, it serves an ever-enlarging constituency in a five-state region.

From 1924 to the present, some thirty-five other educational institutions have been founded by evangelical groups. Some of these attempts to meet the grave needs of the hour were doomed to failure or a hand-to-mouth existence which limited their effectiveness. This situation was reminiscent of the era when the Restoration movement was beginning to solve its educational problems. It is impossible to record in the limited space available in such a comprehensive history more than the more significant of these ventures.

The Cincinnati Bible Seminary, the largest of the newer schools, is located on a beautiful twenty-five-acre campus overlooking the city. Its beginnings have already been recorded. Under the presidencies of Ralph L. Records and Woodrow W. Perry, the Seminary has taken a position of leadership in preparing youth for the ministry and the mission field. Many of the newer schools and direct-support missions have been organized by its graduates. New buildings continue to rise to care for its growing enrollment. Currently more than five hundred students are in residence. The Seminary has a Graduate School, of which Lewis Foster is dean. The annual Conference on Evangelism attracts three thousand persons from all over the nation.

In 1927, E. C. Sanderson purchased a site adjacent to the campus of what is now Kansas State University in Manhattan, and founded "Christian Workers University," now known as Manhattan Bible College. T. H. Johnson became head of the institution, guiding it during the formative years in which buildings were constructed, courses of study formulated, and faculty assembled. President Wilford F. Lown has carried on an effective moderate policy educating a leadership which will "speak the truth in love." Its graduates serve many churches in Kansas and its border states and are engaged in foreign missionary work.

On the site of the historic Civil War Battle of Atlanta rise the new buildings of Atlanta Christian College. The campus was the gift of Judge and Mrs. T. O. Hathcock. First classes were held in 1928. James C. Redmon succeeded Orval Crowder as president in 1955. Their administrations were marked by great progress and the development of a strong Centrist constituency in the South.

Pacific Bible Seminary was organized in 1928 with first classes meeting in the Alvarado church, Los Angeles. George P. Rutledge, a former editor of the *Christian Standard,* was its first president. Under the presidency of James S. Hurst, a campus was purchased opposite the Long Beach municipal golf course, and buildings erected. President Kenneth A. Stewart has stabilized the work of the Seminary and greatly expanded its influence in this burgeoning metropolitan area in the West.

Ten years later (1939), E. C. Sanderson purchased property in San Jose, California, to establish San Jose Bible College, serving the vast middle Pacific coastal area of the brotherhood. It remained for President William L. Jessup to develop the strong institution which now occupies new buildings. The College's annual Conference on Evangelism spurs the establishment of new congregations and gives an evangelistic emphasis to the work of all the churches. Alvan L. Tiffin is president.

In 1942, Ozark Bible College opened its doors in Bentonville, Arkansas. Two years later it moved to Joplin, Missouri, where it enrolls

296

some two hundred students on a new campus. It serves the growing Ozark community of churches in the four-state area of Missouri, Kansas, Arkansas, and Oklahoma, although it draws students from many other states. Under the leadership of President Don Earl Boatman and Dean Seth Wilson, great gains are being recorded. A School of Missions is being established.

Rivaling the Cincinnati Bible Seminary for numerical leadership of the new Centrist educational complex is Lincoln Christian College (formerly Lincoln Bible Institute), founded in 1944. President Earl C. Hargrove has been the moving spirit from the beginning. The institution is aiming toward the ability to grant the highest educational degrees early in the 1960's. Lincoln has become the center of area rallies and conferences resulting in new churches, new missions, and more effective evangelistic and educational work in existing churches. An entire campus of new buildings has been erected. A significant graduate program is conducted in the Lincoln Christian Seminary. Enos E. Dowling is dean.

Midwest Christian College had small beginnings in 1946 under the leadership of Vernon M. Newland. Ten years later, crowded quarters in downtown Oklahoma City were sold and the institution moved to a strategic area, the former property of a country club. New buildings are proposed under the leadership of President Lester Ford and such loyal associates as Orval M. Morgan. The annual Midwest Christian Convention, sponsored by this school, draws hundreds of constituents for inspiration and fellowship.

Roanoke Bible College was incorporated in 1948 under the laws of the state of North Carolina. It is located at Elizabeth City, and serves some one hundred churches in the Eastern seaboard area. Farther to the north is Eastern Christian College (1946), at Bel Air, Maryland, under the leadership of J. Thomas Segroves, encouraging the churches in New Jersey, Delaware, New York, and Maryland.

C. H. Phillips, founder and for eleven years principal of Alberta Bible College (serving the churches of Canada), together with E. H. Chamberlain, organized the Puget Sound College of the Bible in 1950. After beginnings in the West Seattle church, the buildings and campus of Simpson College were purchased. An enlarging educational program is serving the great Northwest, under the presidency of James Earl Ladd II.

To this list may be added Nebraska Christian College (1944); Boise Bible College (1945); Dakota Bible College (1945); Southern Christian College (1945); Intermountain Bible College (1946); Southwest Christian Seminary (1947); Midwestern School of Evangelism (1947); Central Washington School of the Bible (1948); Great Lakes Bible College (1949); Louisville Bible College (1949); Dallas Christian College (1950); Platte Valley Bible College (1952); Church of Christ School of Evangelists (1952); Grundy Bible Institute (1956); Central Christian College of the Bible (1957); St. Louis Christian College (1957); Memphis Christian College (1959); and Paducah Christian College (1962).

Two colleges in the United States are serving the Negro churches: College of the Scriptures at Louisville (1945); and Winston-Salem Bible College (1950). Colegio Biblico, at Eagle Pass, Texas (1945); and Mexican Bible Seminary, at Nogales, Arizona (1950) serve the Mexican missions.

Canada has three Bible colleges. Alberta Bible College began in 1932; Toronto Christian Seminary, in 1959; and Maritime Christian College, in 1960.

Each school in its own way is seeking to make a worthwhile contribution to Christian leadership training. More than three thousand students, most of whom are dedicated to full-time Christian service, are enrolled in these institutions.

At this stage along the road to ultimate achievement, Centrist educational leaders are becoming more objective in their thinking, evaluating their accomplishments, improving the quality of work done, revising or eliminating questionable practices, and moving toward closer co-operation in a common task. With millions of dollars already invested in buildings and equipment, Centrist schools are planning millions more of new construction to provide thoroughly adequate educational equipment and facilities. Plans are beginning to be implemented for the production of new evangelical textbooks. Involved in this move is closer co-operation of educational leaders in (1) agreement on essential curriculum; (2) qualifications of authors; (3) provision for sabbatical leaves for the preparation of manuscripts; (4) agreement on standards of production and distribution. An annual national educational conference is being projected. Standardization problems are being considered. Johnson Bible College, Manhattan Bible College, and Minnesota Bible College led the way in qualifying for membership in the Accrediting Association of Bible Colleges. Other schools have followed their example. Graduate schools, which meet high standards, are being developed.

Another development in Centrist higher educational thinking is the study of the possibilities of converting some schools into liberal arts colleges or junior colleges to serve students who are not planning to enter full-time Christian service. Many families supporting Centrist schools are insisting that something be done to provide a standardized curriculum with strong Bible courses in a distinctly Christian atmosphere. This type of institution is proving successful in Rightist education and Centrists are beginning to see its enormous possibilities.

The first concern after the Memphis convention was the care of missionary work already in existence. Hundreds of churches had withdrawn support from the United Christian Missionary Society. The undergirding of independent missions in the Philippine Islands, Mexico, Japan, and South Africa had an immediate appeal.

Leslie Wolfe's courageous stand had laid the foundation (1926) for the Philippine Christian Mission, with scores of native workers already trained and ready for service. There were 102 churches in Luzon, Mindoro, Negros, and Mindanao, with twelve thousand members. Nine of these churches were in Manila, the largest having more than one thousand members. Manila Bible Seminary enrolled more than fifty students training for Christian service. A vigorous program of tent evangelism reached thousands with the gospel. Even a world war which caused the death of Wolfe and demoralized the work for several years, was unable to wipe out the conviction and zeal of the workers. Today, there are nearly three hundred churches with 52,000 members. Annual conventions draw around four thousand persons. Manila Bible Seminary is erecting new buildings on a campus near the site of the new capitol. Strong native leadership is carrying on an aggressive program.

Also in 1926, Enrique Westrup's work in Mexico attracted considerable support. The churches which were abandoned (1919) in comity agreements by the old societies were weak, but sought to carry on. The field embraced the northern halves of Nueva Leon and Coahuila. Two primary schools—one in Monterrey and the other in Sabinas—were limping along. Westrup was printing a little tract magazine, *La Via de Paz*. The Mexican Christian Missionary Society was organized to carry on the work. Among others, Westrup's sons stepped in to help, but there was little cohesion to the program.

W. D. Cunningham and his Yotsuya Mission in Japan, begun in 1901, in 1926 had 24 organized churches, 40 trained native ministers and evangelists, and 82 Bible schools and classes. New support began to flow into the field and an expansion program began including a new Korean church. In 1936 Cunningham died; for 35 years his mission had borne fruits in Japan unequaled by any other missionary of the Christian churches. Then came World War II with its destruction of most mission property and a demoralization of all missionary work. Protestantism has never recovered its prewar grip on Japan, although there are hundreds of missionaries at work there. The Cunningham Mission all but disappeared, but other direct-support missions carried on. The Osaka Mission, founded by M. B. Madden in 1928, was another object of new support. Harold Cole set up a seminary in 1937 for the training of native workers, and the work went on in this great industrial metropolis.

India's direct-support missionary program had its beginnings in the year of the fateful Memphis convention. In 1928 the S. G. Rothermels set up a new work in Ragaul, which had been abandoned by the United Society. The Christian Mission to India still continues the work with churches in Ragaul, Madras, and Cawnpore. In the Central Provinces, the Harry Schaefers, former U.C.M.S. missionaries, opened a work at Bilaspur (1928). Under their son, the Central Provinces India Mission grew to considerable proportions. Several churches and outposts are maintained, as well as a seminary for the training of native workers, and a children's home.

Still another missionary work with beginnings prior to Memphis, was the Kalane Mission to South Africa, later known as the African Christian Mission to South Africa, and still later as the Africa Christian Missionary Society. Thomas Kalane, a native of South Africa came to the United

States for a college education and was converted by W. H. Book, whose great Tabernacle church, Columbus, Indiana, sent the young Negro back to establish New Testament churches among his people. He preached his first sermons in Kimberley in 1920. Hundreds of persons were baptized. Government requirements made it necessary to send out white supervisory aid. The African Christian Missionary Society sent O. E. Payne to assume charge of the Mission in 1923; Kalane had died the previous year. Payne was succeeded by C. B. Titus, who trained many native evangelists and helped the new churches to build chapels, before returning to America in 1932 because of failing health. Then Simon Benjamin Sibenya, a native leader of outstanding qualities, served as superintendent until his death in 1941. Great progress had been made. The church membership reached several thousand. Then in a series of unfortunate occurences the work declined. Until recently under the leadership of Max Ward Randall (arriving in 1947) and others, the South Africa Church of Christ Mission directs the work among the natives of South Africa. (Randall opened a new field in Northern Rhodesia in 1961.) Operations extend over an area of approximately 400,000 square miles with Capetown as central headquarters. There are some forty churches with many outstations and preaching points. The churches have their own chapels and are largely self-supporting.

The story of the attempts of Disciples to penetrate forbidden Tibet with the gospel reads like a missionary romance. Dr. Susie Rijnhart lost both her husband, Petrus, and their infant son, after arriving in Tibet in 1895. Then came the Ogdens, Dr. A. L. Shelton, and Dr. Z. S. Loftus. After Loftus died of deadly typhus fever and Shelton was killed by bandits, the mere mention of Tibet brought tears to missionary-minded brethren. Russell Morse had volunteered for the field under Shelton's persuasion and arrived at Batang in 1921. After Shelton's death, the U.C.M.S. closed the mission; but Morse determined to go on, alone if need be. After Memphis, non-United Society support began coming; and in 1932, the Morses reported 118 baptisms and preaching appointments in twenty-two villages. The Lisu tribes were turning to Christ in unprecedented numbers. More than one hundred native workers had been trained. Then came the Communist revolution. Morse was imprisoned. His family thought him dead. He was miraculously spared and is still doing a great work in Burma, hoping and praying that the day may come when he can carry the gospel to his dearly beloved Tibetans. The Duncans, Bares, Nichols, and Newlands also had a share in this great missionary adventure to the "roof of the world."

Confronted with the task of winning the world to Christ outside the aegis of the traditional central mission boards, Centrists began a restudy of the missionary methods of the apostolic church. This revealed that the task was primarily evangelistic and predicated on the proposition that all men outside Christ are lost and in need of a Saviour. It appeared that missionaries were set apart for their work by local churches. The technique on the field was the discovery and training of a native or national leader-

300

ship which would organize indigenous churches of Christ. The simplicity of the New Testament program had tremendous appeal to many evangelical churches and hundreds of young people volunteered for service.

Now began a surge of new missionary adventure. Only a mere sketch of this amazing development is possible in the limitations of this chapter.

The Guy Humphreyses, under the sponsorship of the African Christian Mission, opened a mission in 1948 near Stanleyville, in the Ituri Forest of the Belgian Congo. In two years, nine churches were organized and eight hundred converts recorded. A printing press and a school for native workers were set up. Howard Crowl and others carry on this growing ministry in the Republic of Congo.

The Roy Goldsberrys established the West Africa Christian Mission in Yaba, Nigeria, in 1955. The Donald Baughmans joined them in 1956 to assist in the rapidly growing work.

In the Matsai Reserve, Southern Rhodesia, a vast mission field was entered by John Pemberton (1956) and Dr. Dennis Pruett (1958). Southern Rhodesia had long been served by a mission supported by New Zealand churches of Christ. Together with Max Randall and the South Africa Church of Christ Mission, extensive plans have been carried out for a new united evangelistic, educational, and hospital program. Mashoko is the center of this development.

Japan's independent missionary work took on new life with the advent of a new generation of young leaders. Besides the work in Tokyo and Osaka, new fields were opened with preaching and teaching points in Obihiro, Sapporo, Sendai, Nagoya, Tenabe, Kutsugi, Shikoku, Kanoya, Kagoshima, Kobe, and Nishinomote on Tanegashima. Forty-nine congregations and thirteen preaching points have been reported in addition to forty-five direct-support missionaries in Japan, thirty-three native pastors, and ten lay leaders.

The work in old Mexico received a new lease on life with missionary ventures in many new fields. At Eagle Pass, across the border, Colegio Biblico was founded by Harland Cary in 1945 to train Mexicans for full-time Christian service. More than forty native churches with some two thousand members are now in operation in northern Mexico. Saltillo has a Christian school founded by Rodney Northrup, which is the center for some fifteen organized churches and many more preaching points. The Mexican Bible Institute, founded by Gerald Bowlin in Nogales (Hermasillo) serves another area of comparable strength. Under the leadership of Antonio Medina, similar centers have been set up at Chihauhua, Baja, Salinas, and Estancia to encourage a growing number of native churches. It is estimated that more than 120 organized congregations are to be found in this general fellowship with a membership of ten thousand. The spread of the gospel is contagious and missionary leaders believe the evangelization of Mexico will come largely under Mexican leadership.

From 1935-38, C. Vincent Hall established a group of new churches in the Clarendon district of Jamaica. This work was carried on and expanded by E. A. Watts, Luke Elliott, and others. Through the development of local leadership, more than six thousand Christians are now to be found in six districts of the island.

A Restoration movement which had origins in Russia (see Chapter 21) was responsible for the establishment of churches after the New Testament pattern throughout Poland, Latvia, Estonia, and border states in eastern Europe. In 1921, the Union of Churches of Christ in Poland was affiliated with the Christian Restoration Association. Prior to World War II, some forty thousand members were reported in these churches. When communism swept these lands all contact was lost, but information continues to filter through concerning thousands who still hold fast the faith. Some young men from these churches are now in independent Bible colleges training for service among their own people if and when iron curtain barriers are lifted.

A similar group of churches in Germany was responsible for the ministry of Ludwig von Gerdtell who came to America and was for a time a member of the faculty of the School of Religion at Butler University. The situation he described stirred the heart of a student, Earl Stuckenbruck, who volunteered to inaugurate a unique ministerial education project at Tubingen University, the source of early liberalism. Completing his work for a doctorate at Edinburgh University, he is now firmly established at Tubingen with the backing of the European Evangelistic Society. The James Crouches joined him in 1961. Several men trained in the new school are already evangelizing among the German people with encouraging results. Edward Fausz has a direct-support work in Frankfurt.

In Italy, where Roman Catholicism is supreme, the missionaries of the Restoration movement are doing a sacrificial work. The conservative Church of Christ evangelists are frequently in the headlines as they contend for freedom to preach the gospel. Shortly after World War II (1947), Guy Mayfield entered Bari, baptizing converts, organizing churches, and establishing a Bible seminary. The Charles Phippses, Malcom Coffeys, Charles Troyers, Evelyn Jones and Betheen Grubaugh, and others succeeded in the work at Bari and Lecce. With 96 per cent of the population Romanist, missionaries encounter real difficulties but they persevere.

In 1949, the Bertrand Smiths opened a mission in Valparaiso, Chile. After a year and a half a church was organized, and men are now being trained for the evangelization of of this South American country. The discovery of a group of independent churches holding views similar to the churches of Christ and taking the Bible alone as their rule of faith and practice has greatly encouraged them.

The first Christian church missionaries to enter Brazil (1948) were the Lloyd Sanderses. They set up headquarters in Goiania, capital of Goiaz, a city of seventy thousand. Several churches, Sunday schools, primary day schools, and the Goiania workers training school have been established. A strategic location in the new federal capital of Brasilia brings the Restoration plea to the attention of this great nation comprising two-fifths of the area of South America. The Amazon Valley Mission (1952) under the leadership of Bill Loft, Arthur Carter, and Lew Cass, is penetrating the heart of the jungle with the gospel. The Sao Paulo Christian Mission was initiated by John Nichols.

When the United States took a protectorate over the Ryukyu Islands after World War II, General MacArthur called for Christian missionaries. In Okinawa, Nago, and Miyako, Harland Woodruff (1948) and others planted New Testament churches and gave guidance to a growing native leadership.

Before Hawaii became a state, the Owen Stills opened a work (1946) in Haleiwa and Hauula. In 1954 they set up a mission in the Palolo Valley, with a day school and a number of preaching points. Several New Testament churches resulted. The Stills were later joined by other direct-support missionaries who established work in Keolu Hills, Maile, Makaha, Pearl Harbor, and Sunset Beach. The new churches now have a far greater membership than the long-established churches related to the so-called "official agencies." With a forward-looking evangelistic program, evangelicals are planning to cover the Islands with the plea.

In 1954, direct-support work began in San Juan, Puerto Rico, with the coming of the Gordon Thompsons. Several new churches have been established in the area.

In the easternmost island of the British West Indies, Barbados, a New Testament church was established by Charles C. Leacock, a native minister, in 1940. The Vernon Osbornes took charge of the work in 1953 and reorganized it into the Oistin Church of Christ, Bridgetown. Silver Sands, Spooner's Hill, and other preaching points have since been established with a ministers' training school and a Christian day school. In the Bahamas and the Cayman Islands, native Christians have established several small churches of Christ which are being shepherded from the Bridgetown base.

Expansion in the India field began when Kulpahar, an abandoned mission of the U.C.M.S., was taken over by the Tom Rashes in 1947. Now there are six churches, three schools, and three benevolent homes. The work in South India had its inception in 1936 when a native Indian converted at Ragaul organized a New Testament church. Now eighty ministers serve 111 churches with a membership of more than five thousand. The work centers in Madrappakkam. South India Christian College trains ministers and workers. A trade school and a hospital are also maintained. Other independent missionaries are at work in Thalavady, Cawnpore (Kanpur), and scattered villages.

A unique work was begun by the Schaeffers of the Central Provinces India Mission in Orissa in 1952. Five evangelistic centers, each with a training institute and about one hundred full-time workers, and preaching points in two hundred villages, with Bargarh as the operating center are maintained. A boy's hostel and a base hospital are first steps toward an institutional program.

A native Khasi tribesman, Rajani Roy Kharkhongir, began a New Testament work in the Khasi Hills of Assam about 1925. When direct-support missionaries from America discovered him, there were eleven congregations with around one thousand members. The Assam Mission

Churches of Christ was organized around this work by the Fairbrothers and Reeveses in 1953. There is a Christian day school in Mawlai, a suburb of Assam's capital, and a workers' training school. Refugees from Tibet and Nepal have considerably augmented the original work. There are now some two thousand members.

The Callaways opened the first American direct-support mission in Thailand in 1950 at Chiengkam, five hundred miles north of Bangkok. In 1952, the first Yao Christian village was founded. Nan Province has been entered and native workers maintain work in several tribes.

The first churches of Christ were planted in Korea by Koreans from the Cunningham direct-support mission in Tokyo, Japan. Twelve congregations were wiped out in World War II and the Korean War. The present work in Korea owes its origin to the John Chases, who established seven churches with some eight hundred members. The Harold Taylors later supervised a conservation program which strengthened the churches and set up schools and orphanages. There are approximately twelve hundred members, with the work centered in Seoul. A seminary has been established there.

As Alaska became an increasingly strategic possession of the United States, only a proverbial "stone's throw" from Soviet Russia, direct-support missionaries were challenged by its opportunities for planting New Testament churches. The first church was established in 1936 by Franklin Smith at Ekwak. Anchorage, Dillingham, Fairbanks, Homer, Ketchikan, Palmer, Wasilla, and other cities and towns have been added. Schools, benevolent homes, and other auxiliary work are maintained. Now that Alaska is the largest state in the Union, the importance of this adventure is multiplied. The Restoration plea now has an opportunity to grow and prosper in this rapidly-developing area.

While the discovery of new mission volunteers becomes increasingly difficult for liberal-controlled agencies, a great stream of dedicated young life is available for evangelical missions. Conviction and utter consecration impel to sacrifice and service. From Christian service camps, where decisions are made for the ministry and the mission fields, through the many new schools and colleges with constantly higher standards of training, second-generation missionaries will go out to give great stability and effectiveness to the whole program.

The question of responsibility in missionary endeavor is a matter of increasing concern among Centrist churches. A new agency, the Christian Missionary Fellowship, has been created which, its founders believe, combines the best features of the early organized work and the modern independent missions.

The C.M.F. was chartered under the laws of Kansas at Junction City on February 28, 1949, by Evelyn C. Parks, W. F. Lown, and Earl Hoyle. It came into being through the energy and foresight of O. D. Johnson, who conceived it during his service as a missionary in Jhansi, India.

The purpose of the C.M.F., as stated in its charter, is: "To evangelize the non-Christian people of the world in the order, manner, and fashion

304

of a missionary society and toward this purpose to recruit and send forth missionaries. . . ." Article I of its bylaws states the doctrinal position of the Fellowship: "The Fellowship shall accept the Christian program as presented in the New Testament Scriptures, referring all matters of doctrine to these writings for final decision."

Currently the Fellowship is operating in three fields: India, Japan, and Brazil. There are twelve affiliated missionaries: the Kent Bateses, the Chester Parkers, the Wayne Wertzes, the William Walkers, the Eugene Smiths, and the James Morgans. There are four candidates, three candidate applicants, and two volunteers. Annual receipts for all purposes were $18,000 during 1950, the first full year of operations; and in 1958 they totaled $54,000.

The structure of the Fellowship makes the contributor, both missionary and congregation or individual Christian, the foundation of responsibility. Missionaries and recruits hold voting power by virtue of their commitment of life; congregations and individual Christians hold voting power by virtue of their contribution of money. Twenty-one directors, elected by the Fellowship, in annual meeting assembled, direct the affairs of the Fellowship through appropriate committees. Missionaries are selected by the directors on the basis of their devotion to Christ and His Word, physical and emotional stability, and disposition to serve faithfully. The Fellowship is committed to the principle of indigenous Christianity.

With less than thirty-five years of experience behind them, Centrist churches loyal to the distinctive principles of the Restoration movement now have six hundred missionaries at work in eighteen lands—an achievement unprecedented in the history of Disciples of Christ.

Time would fail to tell of great Centrist expansion in America with a new church being planted almost every day. Individual congregations accept responsibility of Bible schools which develop into churches; of evangelizing fellowships, in which groups of churches participate in planting new congregations; and of aiding in the purchase of property, erection of buildings, and provision of a full-time ministry. A special type of evangelistic work in the mountains of Oklahoma, Arkansas, Colorado, Kentucky, West Virginia, Tennessee, and other states bears good fruit. Among Negroes, an evangelistic program fans out from the College of the Scriptures and Winston-Salem Bible College. Among French Acadians, there are three evangelistic centers. Among the American Indians seven such centers are maintained. And in New York, Chicago, and Toronto immigrants are served.

Christian benevolence finds its expression in a growing number of homes and schools. The Christian Women's Benevolent Association has a large home for the aged, a children's home, and a $3,000,000 hospital and nurses' training school—the only hospital now maintained by the Christian churches in America—all in the St. Louis, Missouri, area. The East Tennessee Christian Home, the Grundy (Virginia) Mountain Mission Home and School, and the Turner (Oregon) Memorial Home are among the growing number of such agencies.

305

Radio and television have been enlisted in the dissemination of the gospel and the Restoration plea. "The Christian's Hour" was established in 1943 by a group of churches in the Cincinnati area under the leadership of Ard Hoven and Harry Poll. It now has more than seventy stations carrying its radio program. The Vernon Brothers pioneered in television with their program series, "Homestead, U.S.A." The National Association of Christian Broadcasters serves about fifty Centrist radio and television broadcasters which reach an estimated three million listeners each week.

This view of Centrist growth would be incomplete without mentioning an institution, privately owned in the pure tradition of the movement's publishing concerns, which has done yeoman service in preserving and perpetuating the "faith which was once delivered"—the Standard Publishing Company, founded in 1866. Its multimillion-dollar plant, complete in the latest facilities of the graphic arts, pours out millions of copies of "true-to-the-Bible" literature every year. James N. Johnson is president, and Burris Butler is executive editor. Edwin V. Hayden is editor of *Christian Standard.* More than fifty capably staffed publications serve an ever-enlarging constituency.

When John Bolten, Sr., and his associates purchased Standard Publishing from the Errett family in 1955, the announcement was made that Standard Publishing would continue to dedicate its services to Christian churches and churches of Christ and would continue to be operated solely to advance the historic plea for the unity of Christians on the authority of the Bible as the Word of God. In response to this announcement, fifty-two leading ministers joined in issuing a call for a national meeting to "rally one another to increased zeal for and knowledge of evangelism and Christian education, particularly at the local congregational level," to elect a "Publishing Committee to represent it in determining Christian education policy and program, and in directing the management of the Foundation as to the wishes of the brethren."

In August, 1956, 1,614 persons registered for the first National Christian Education Convention in Cincinnati and elected the publishing committee. The original committee included Hugh F. Sensibaugh, of Cincinnati, chairman; Thomas W. Overton, Huntington Beach, California, secretary; Leon H. Appel, Lincoln, Illinois; Ernest H. Chamberlain, Seattle, Washington; Edwin G. Crouch, Columbus, Indiana (deceased, 1961); Mortimer A. Hawk, Valley Center, Kansas (succeeded by Harry Poll, Minneapolis, Minnesota); Olin W. Hay, Louisville, Kentucky; Ernest E. Laughlin, Springfield, Illinois; Ard Hoven, Lexington, Kentucky; Harold W. Scott, Columbus, Ohio; Alva Sizemore, Steubenville, Ohio; T. K. Smith, Columbus, Indiana; W. R. Walker, Columbus, Ohio (president emeritus of Standard Publishing); Robert O. Weaver, Lexington, Kentucky; and P. H. Welshimer, Canton, Ohio (deceased, 1957, succeeded by Joseph H. Dampier, Milligan College, Tennessee).

The 1957 meeting was at Springfield, Illinois. The publishing committee named Leonard G. Wymore to be executive secretary of the Convention.

306

In 1958, four area conventions met at Fort Wayne, Indiana; Kingsport, Tennessee; San Jose, California; and Oklahoma City, Oklahoma. By 1959, it seemed apparent that if the convention were more adequately to fulfill its purpose, smaller area meetings would be preferable to the larger national gatherings. Therefore, thirty-seven such conventions met that year. More than twelve thousand persons registered at these sessions. Since then, several area conventions have met each year. The N.C.E.C. has co-operated twice with the North American Christian Convention in joint sessions: at Columbus, Ohio, in 1960, and at Lexington, Kentucky, in 1962.

The North American Christian Convention continues to be the major forum for fellowship at the national level. Its character remains unchanged. It is in no sense an official agency and seeks to exercise no divisive influence in the brotherhood at large. Its annual meetings are planned by new continuation committees each year. The largest auditoriums in the great cities of the nation are required to accommodate the convention. In 1960 at Columbus, Ohio, in an expanded program of service, more than four thousand persons registered for the convention. Observers often remark at the youthfulness and unswerving conviction of the leadership in these gatherings—a fact which speaks volumes for the future of the Centrist conservative, evangelical testimony in the Restoration movement.

There is a growing interest in the obligations of this great host of brethren in a Christendom, now deeply concerned in the necessity for Christian unity. Plans are under consideration by which the Restoration plea may adequately be presented to challenge the modern Ecumenical movement and advance the kind of unity for which Christ prayed.

BIBLIOGRAPHY: Chapter 19

Butler, Burris, and Edwin V. Hayden, editors, *Christian Standard* (1955-1959).
Carr, James B., *The Foreign Missionary Work of the Christian Church.*
DeGroot, Alfred T., *Church of Christ Number Two.*
Gresham, Charles R., editor, *Christian Quarterly* (1957-1959).
Harrison, Lora Banks, *The Church Abroad.*
McFarland, Harrold, editor, *Horizons* (1955-1959).
Newland, Vernon M., and Ralph McLean, editors, *A Directory of the Ministry* (1955-1960).

Chapter 20

Rightist Status and Growth

SINCE 1906, when the United States Government Religious Census first listed the Church of Christ as a religious body separate from the Disciples of Christ, the "right wing" of the Restoration movement has made remarkable progress.

The 1906 figures, compiled by J. W. Shepherd, indicated that there were 2,649 congregations located in thirty-three states and territories. Of these churches, 1,979 were located in the south central states. Tennessee had 631 churches, and Texas, 627. The total membership was only 159,658, and 693 congregations were meeting in rented halls or store buildings. According to the report, members of the fellowship maintained eight colleges, employing seventy-three teachers and enrolling 1,024 students. The value of all school property was only forty thousand dollars. The *Gospel Advocate,* the *Christian Leader,* and *Firm Foundation* were the leading periodicals reflecting the beliefs and practices of the Church of Christ.

In 1960 authentic statistical sources listed 16,500 churches located in every state in the union with a membership of 2,025,000, giving the Church of Christ status with the leading religious bodies of the nation. About 80 per cent of the churches are in Texas, Arkansas, Louisiana, Tennessee, Mississippi, Alabama, and Georgia. Rightists have more congregations and more members than Centrists and Leftists combined. In greater Nashville, Tennessee, a center of Rightist strength, they have more than one hundred churches with some twenty thousand members and a co-operative program of evangelism that often packs the city's largest auditoriums. New areas are constantly being entered to plant churches following the New Testament pattern. Central Church of Christ has a large and commodious edifice in the heart of the city with adequate equipment for educational and social work, a men's dormitory, a home for working girls, a day nursery, and radio equipment for daily broadcasts of the gospel. Its membership includes many of Nashville's leading business and professional men, and not infrequently governors and other leading statesmen. The Nashville situation can be matched in many other municipalities throughout the southern states.

Rightists hold much in common with right-wing Centrists in the Restoration movement. They believe that Jesus is the Christ, the Son of God, Saviour and Lord. They accept the Bible as the inspired revelation of God's will and as the sole rule and norm of faith and practice. They preach the same gospel with faith, repentance, confession, immersion as the terms of pardon for a non-Christian. Only immersed believers are admitted to church membership. They are committed to the restoration of the New Testament church in doctrine, ordinances, and life; and they believe this will be accomplished by an appeal to the Scriptures and the abandonment of human creeds and dogmas. They accept the principle, "In faith, unity; in opinions, liberty; and in all things, charity." Both groups seek to continue steadfastly in the apostles' doctrine, in the fellowship, in the breaking of bread, and the prayers. They stress evangelism, winning men to Christ. They practice Christian stewardship in all things, including their earthly goods. They are faithful in attendance upon divine worship and the weekly observance of the Lord's Supper. Both claim to sing "with the Spirit and the understanding, making melody in their hearts to the Lord." Both claim they are seeking not to be "wise above that which is written," and they "speak where the Bible speaks" and are "silent where the Bible is silent."

In the last two areas, however, there lie differences of opinion which divide them. Rightists deny that Centrists can worship Scripturally and acceptably to God with the accompaniment of instrumental music. They also deny that Centrists properly observe the "silences" of the Scriptures. They consider these differences so serious that they refuse fellowship either with the ministers or the congregations of the Center.

A study of the churches which make up the reported census figures of the Church of Christ further reveals that there is wide divergence within its own ranks as to terms of fellowship. Beyond the basic doctrines which would seem to unite both the Centrists and Rightists there appears to be complete Church of Christ unity only on the issues of instrumental music and extracongregational agencies. It is said that there are more than twenty types of congregations within the Church of Christ, each representing disagreement over proper observance of the "silences" of Scripture. Progressive Rightist leadership deplores this situation. Earl Irvin West in his *Search for the Ancient Order* devotes an entire chapter in Volume 2 to a consideration of "extremism" but speaks optimistically of a better day. It is impossible, however, to present a realistic picture of the Church of Christ without objective reference to the facts. As the result of a careful survey it appears that major differences have to do with proper observance of the Lord's Supper, the Sunday school, the choice of elders, colleges, missionary methods, the located ministry, choirs and special music, millennial views, and the place of women in the church. Majority and minority views on some of these questions are the following:

A considerable number of churches hold only to the "divine pattern of the order of worship" (Acts 2:42) which requires that the elders go into the pulpit to read the Scripture and to pray. Then, under the supervision of the elders, the service proceeds, including (1) a few brief teaching lessons by brethren on previously assigned topics; (2) taking up the "fellowship" (offering); (3) breaking the loaf; and (4) the prayers, in which several brethren may participate.

A majority of the churches believe that the elders may break the loaf for the congregation in the Lord's Supper. Minority: The elder may break the loaf once, but each member should break off his own piece (Acts 2:42, 46; Luke 22:19; Matthew 26:26). The greater number of churches hold that individual communion cups may be used in the observance of the Lord's Supper. Minority: The Scripture says specifically that Christ took *a* cup (Matthew 26:27), so multiplicity of cups is unscriptural.

The majority of the churches now have Sunday, Lord's Day, or Bible schools directed by the eldership which is "apt to teach." Many of them have large education buildings with every modern facility for graded instruction. The minority contends that such schools are "a degenerate of denominationalism without precept, example or necessary inference in the Word of God, and therefore must rest on the silences of the Bible, as do all other inventions and devices of men." Majority: The use of quarterlies and other helps for the study of the lesson is permissible. Minority: Each pupil should use the Bible only. Helps are as evil as human creeds and dogmas.

A majority of the churches do not "elect" elders or deacons. Those who are Scripturally qualified must be "looked out" by the congregation, "chosen" by the eldership, and may be "appointed" by evangelists. Minorities insist that church leadership must be selected by the elders or by the "ruling elder": or that only the "evangelist" has the right to "appoint elders in the churches."

Voluntary Christian educational institutions such as Bible schools and colleges are viewed by the majority as having a right to exist and serve the churches provided they respect the autonomy of the local church and do not presume to exercise authority outside their field. Opposing view: Education is a Scriptural function of the local church. Bible schools and colleges are a camouflaged attempt to build an institutional hierarchy which will eventually destroy congregational autonomy. The *American Christian Review* has been the avowed enemy of Christian colleges for more than one hundred years.

Christian benevolent institutions are encouraged and supported by the majority of the churches on the ground that, although they are *un*scriptural, they are not *anti*-Scriptural. But a large minority insist that it is wrong to transfer a local church obligation to an extracongregational organization and thus build a threat to the freedom of the local church.

In the early days of the Church of Christ there were few if any "located" ministers. Now all the larger churches build parsonages and have one or more resident ministers who "do the work of an evangelist" under the direction and supervision of the eldership. Opposing view: It is unscriptural to have a paid, located ministry. The local eldership serves in this capacity. Evangelists may be sent out by local churches and their services may be requested as needed.

Choirs, soloists, quartets, and special music are considered matters of expediency in some churches, provided they do not interfere with congregational singing and worship. Some churches have well-trained a cappella choirs. Opposing view: There is neither New Testament precept or example for such "performances" which have their origin in denominationalism and are susceptible to all the evils inherent in instrumental music.

Church dinners are permissable for purposes of fellowship only. None of the congregations permit dinners or any other device for raising money. A minority opposes the use of the church building for any purpose other than teaching and worship.

Missionary methods are one of the chief items of controversy in the churches today. For many years there was little or no interest in missions, but now a large and growing number of missionaries are in the field. The majority of the churches agree that it is permissable to use a third party or agent to handle missionary funds, provided that person or agency does not appoint missionaries and otherwise take the missionary work into its own hands. Choosing, sending, supporting, and directing the missionary are obligations of the elders of the local church. Opposing view: Missionary clearing houses are "man-made," set up "to do the work of the local church," and are inherently "as dangerous as the societies of the digressives." These brethren also oppose local churches receiving offerings from other congregations to be expended in their missionary program on the ground that such procedure exalts one church above another and tends to Roman Catholic cathedralism. Many churches unable to support a missionary of their own, support none and insist that all missionary work must be done by its own members in the local community.

Most ministers and churches are postmillennial or a-millennial in their view of the second coming of Christ. While the small minority of premillennialists hold that millennial views should not be made tests of fellowship, the majority contend that premillennialism is heresy and must be rooted out of the fellowship.

Involved in the widespread habit of withdrawing fellowship from those who do not agree with particular views is the "Scriptural attitude" toward "erring brethren" and "weaklings." The majority holds that in matters of faith or explicit commands there can be no allowance of disagreement. In all other matters the "law of love" should be obeyed unless the "erring" or the "weak" should try to force his "scruples" upon others, thus creating a faction. It is necessary to "mark," "avoid," and "refuse" such. The minority gives lip service to the principle but falls short in its practice.

The "Preachers List of the Churches of Christ" is, for some, a bone of contention. There is no Scriptural or other commonly recognized authority for the publication of such a list. Men who are denied listing are often ostracized, though usually for good reasons. One of those responsible for the preparation of this useful document states the principle followed:

312

The Preachers List is a helpful medium of information which claims no official character. It lists men who are generally known as Scriptural in their belief and practice. "Unscriptural practice," if not fundamentally subversive of the faith and not practiced in such a way as to compel others to participate with it, or so to establish a faction, should be no barrier to recognition of brethren. There is, of course, no authority higher than the local congregation. In theory, when a brother is discredited or disfellowshipped by his home congregation, others should accept their judgment.

It is evident that the grave question perplexing the Restoration movement has always been and continues to be, "Where does the realm of human judgment and action begin and end?" While the Church of Christ is harassed by those who fail to understand where it *begins,* the Disciples are troubled by those who do not know where it *ends.*

Within the last generation, the Church of Christ has made a phenomenal growth. This is due to two things: (1) Its people have stood like the Rock of Gibraltar for "the faith which was once delivered unto the saints," amid the doubt and confusion superinduced by liberalism. They have challenged the spirit of compromise and worldliness and dared to be a "peculiar" people teaching and practicing what they believe is the Bible way of life. (2) They have come to realize that the silences of the Scriptures must be respected as well as the commandments of Scripture, but that obedience to its silences permits freedom of judgment and action. Old chasms of division are being replaced by ever-widening agreement and ground for fellowship.

To the educational leaders of the Church of Christ must go the praise for this encouraging development. Today there are a score of colleges and nearly the same number of high schools and elementary schools operated by members of the Church of Christ. The colleges include Abilene Christian College, Abilene, Texas; Alabama Christian College, Montgomery, Alabama; Columbia Christian College, Portland, Oregon; Florida Christian College, Tampa, Florida; Freed-Hardeman College, Henderson, Tennessee; Great Lakes Christian College, Beamsville, Ontario; Harding College, Searcy, Arkansas; Ibaraki Christian College, Ibaraki-Ken, Japan; David Lipscomb College, Nashville, Tennessee; Lubbock Christian College, Lubbock, Texas; Magic Valley Christian College, Albion, Idaho; North Central Christian College, Rochester, Michigan; Ohio Valley College, Parkersburg, West Virginia; Oklahoma Christian College, Oklahoma City; George Pepperdine College, Los Angeles, California; Southeastern Christian College, Winchester, Kentucky; Southwestern Christian College (Negro), Terrell, Texas; Western Christian College, Weyburn, Saskatchewan; and York College, York, Nebraska.

The Church of Christ institutes and schools include the following: Athens Bible Schools, Athens, Alabama; Boyd-Buchanan School, Chattanooga, Tennessee; Christian Schools, Inc., Dallas, Texas; Crowley's Ridge Academy, Paragould, Arkansas; Fort Worth Christian Schools, Fort Worth, Texas; Clifton L. Ganus School, New Orleans, Louisiana; Georgia Christian Institute, Valdosta, Georgia; Houston Christian Schools, Houston,

Texas; Madison County Bible School, Huntsville, Alabama; Mars Hill Bible School, Florence, Alabama; Memphis Christian School, Memphis, Tennessee; Nashville Christian Institute (Negro), Nashville, Tennessee; Northeastern Institute for Christian Education, Villanova, Pennsylvania; Rocky Mountain Christian School, Denver, Colorado; Wichita Christian School, Wichita, Kansas.

Only a few of these institutions can be described in the limited scope of this chapter. David Lipscomb College has an historic background of special significance to the brotherhood. It has spiritual ties to Tolbert Fanning's Franklin College (founded in 1842) and is the direct lineal descendant from the Nashville Bible School, established by David Lipscomb, William Lipscomb, and James A. Harding in 1901. In 1903 three large buildings were erected on David Lipscomb's farm on Granny White Road, Nashville, where more than twenty buildings of the modern David Lipscomb College now stand. Its history has been one of constant growth and expansion in physical and educational equipment. There is an enrollment of some two thousand in the liberal arts college, the high school, and the elementary school. D.L.C. is a senior college fully accredited by the Southern Association of Colleges and Secondary Schools. As in all Church of Christ colleges the chief feature of its program is its emphasis on the study of the Holy Scriptures and the building of Christian character. With assets of more than ten million dollars, it has a long-range development program to double its present status. The campus of D.L.C. is frequently the scene of ministerial meetings, elders conferences, evangelism clinics, study groups in Christian stewardship, youth problems, Bible-school methods, and every phase of local church activity. It has become the cultural center of the Church of Christ community which is such a dominant factor in the life of Greater Nashville.

Abilene Christian College was founded in 1906 as a Bible-centered college of liberal arts. It has an enrollment of twenty-five hundred. Its twelve-million-dollar equipment of modern, cream-colored brick buildings is a West Texas showplace, and its educational standing is fully accredited. The college was elected to the Southern Association of Colleges and Secondary Schools in 1951. The graduate school which offers Master's degrees in nine areas, was established in 1953. On its campus is held an annual Bible lecture series which features outstanding Church of Christ speakers and draws thousands of brethren. Other similar events in the fields of agriculture, and domestic arts, social science and education, journalism and English literature, music and art, make Abilene a religious, cultural, and educational center for Churches of Christ. A.C.C. has all the accoutrements of a modern institution of higher learning including top-rated football, basketball, baseball, and track teams, one of the largest college bands in Texas, a farm, etc.

Harding College has one of the most modern, well-equipped, air-conditioned small college plants in America. It has assets of more than ten million dollars, is fully accredited as a liberal arts institution and offers graduate study. It is nationally known for its contribution to the preserva-

314

tion of the American way of life and offers a wide range of studies in this field. The students' religious life is a major concern.

Freed-Hardeman College is the fruit of the educational labors of A. G. Freed and N. B. Hardeman. It has a group of excellent buildings mostly constructed during Hardeman's twenty-six-year presidency. It operates as a junior college and is a member of the Tennessee Association of Colleges and the American Association of Junior Colleges.

Oklahoma Christian College had its beginnings as Central Christian College at Bartlesville but later purchased a strategic location near the state capital, Oklahoma City. With eight modern buildings and an accredited liberal arts status it is destined to become one of the great Christian colleges of the Southwest.

In a beautiful location overlooking the Hillsborough River ten miles above the point where it empties into Tampa Bay, the Florida Christian College has five buildings and a big citrus farm. It is a fully accredited junior college in the Southern Association. It offers two years of advanced study in the Bible and religious education.

George Pepperdine College in Los Angeles rose almost overnight in 1937. It came into being because of the educational conscience of the man whose name it bears, one of America's outstanding businessmen, founder of the Western Auto Supply Company and other successful corporations. Through his munificent gifts completely modern buildings and equipment were provided on a spacious campus and a full corps of able educators were called to form its faculty. It is a fully accredited liberal arts institution with strong emphasis on Bible training and normally has an enrollment of one thousand students. Its graduate school has about seventy candidates for higher degrees.

Southeastern Christian College operates in the large, well-equipped buildings purchased from the former Kentucky Wesleyan College at Winchester, Kentucky. Magic Valley Christian College took over the three-million-dollar equipment of the state college at Albion, Idaho, in 1958.

The "rash" of new schools being set up over the nation may be typified by the Northeastern Institute for Christian Education and the Fort Worth Christian College, both founded in 1959. N.I.C.E. was sparked by a small group of Eastern churches led by Manhattan Church of Christ, New York City. Clinton Davidson, wealthy insurance executive, and Pat Boone, in the late fifties America's teen-age TV and recording idol, gave generously to purchase the twenty-four-acre estate of the late Morris Clothier, Philadelphia department store magnate, located near the great Roman Catholic Villanova University. The new school opened in the Clothier mansion with forty students and will probably grow to become the center of Church of Christ expansion in the East. In Fort Worth, under the shadow of the twenty-two-million-dollar campus complex of Texas Christian University, is Fort Worth Christian College. Its related elementary and junior-high schools enrolled 250 the first year. Evening college classes attracted forty students. In September, 1960, day classes opened in two new buildings. More than four hundred donors from the churches in the Fort Worth area made this educational venture possible. The development of Christian day schools in some Southern communities is due partially to the integration of the races in the public schools and partially to the growing conviction that the public schools have succumbed to the theory that a pluralistic society precludes religious and moral instruction in tax-supported institutions. Church of Christ leaders, while disclaiming these motives, believe strongly that Bible instruction and the maintenance of strict Christian moral principles are essential to the whole educational structure from the earliest grades to the graduate school.

The Churches of Christ may eventually develop a comprehensive educational system without peer in the Restoration movement. Such educators as Don H. Morris, of Abilene Christian College; M. Norvel Young, of Pepperdine College; Athens Clay Pullias, of David Lipscomb College; and George S. Benson, of Harding College, are widely recognized as leaders in the educational life not only of the South but of the nation.

The impact of this enlightened new leadership on the life of the brotherhood is having salutary results in many areas. It has been largely responsible for the development of a comprehensive missionary conscience in the churches. For a hundred years the Church of Christ did little or nothing in the field of foreign missions. It is true that R. W. Officer was sent in 1880 by the Gainesville, Texas, church as a missionary to the American Indians. In the same year Jules DeLaunay went to Paris, France. In 1889 Azariah Paul was sent to Armenia. These sporadic efforts received little support. It remained for W. K. Azbill and J. M. McCaleb to undertake the first major missionary effort in Japan. Azbill defected to the Disciples, largely because they were more missionary minded, but McCaleb carried on in a sacrificial work which laid the foundations for the large and substantial mission of the Church of Christ in Omika.

Today there are more than two hundred male workers, besides their wives and families, in some seventy nations, and the number is growing. There are more than sixty thousand members of the Church of Christ outside the United States.

Two missionary magazines, *World Vision* and *Christian Chronicle,* keep the churches informed concerning the work on foreign fields. Other journals furnish information about missions throughout the world.

In 1933 a mission was opened in Hong Kong. Primary emphasis for several years was on Canton Bible School, under the direction of George S. Benson. All missionaries, except Elizabeth Bernard, left China during the war. She went to Hong Kong, where she teaches. In June, 1957, Melvin Harbison and Gus Eoff went to Hong Kong and established a Christian school. Work is spreading from Hong Kong.

Shortly after the New Zealand churches established their mission in Southern Rhodesia in 1905, one of their missionaries, John Sheriff, took a strong independent stand for the principles of the Church of Christ. American brethren began to send him financial support with the result that today there are a number of separate congregations such as those at Bulawayo, Gwelo, Nhowe, Macheke, and Salisbury.

In Northern Rhodesia there is the well-known Sinde Mission seventeen miles from Livingston established in 1946. It has an orphanage located on a one-thousand-acre site. There are preaching points and small churches at Kalomo, Namwianga, Lusaka, and elsewhere.

The Philippine Islands were entered in 1948 with the famous mountain resort of Baguio as a center of operations. A church was established in Manila in 1951. Scores of churches are now reported in the Islands.

In 1957 a group of native Korean evangelists trained in Cincinnati Bible Seminary accepted the Church of Christ position and a mission was set up centering in Seoul, the capital city.

South Africa's first churches established by brethren from the British Isles used no instrumental music in worship. This tradition has been maintained. Their churches were weak and eventually found their greatest source of strength from like-minded brethren in America who sent both money and evangelists. There are now congregations in Durban, East London, Johannesburg, Welkon, Praetoria, Benoni, Port Elizabeth, and elsewhere.

Nigeria, entered in 1958, has work at Aba and Uyo with many preaching points.

There is a small church in Singapore, Malaya, supported by American brethren.

Tanganyika, East Africa, entered in 1949, is being evangelized by Church of Christ missionaries.

Nyasaland saw an evangelistic center established at Rumpi in 1957. The work has spread to Lilongwe and beyond.

In 1954 there were five small churches struggling for existence in Australia. Four of them were in the Sydney-Newcastle area and the other at Hobart, a thousand miles south. Then the College Church of Christ, Abilene, Texas, began to take an interest in these brethren and to send out money and evangelists. A small magazine, *Truth in Love,* was launched. In 1959 twenty churches were reported who have no fellowship with the Federal Conference of the Churches of Christ.

This zeal to proclaim the "only true gospel" and establish churches "after the New Testament pattern in the worship" has created a new type of missionary work in which the Church of Christ has become enthusiastic and exceedingly generous. One of the finest examples of what their enemies describe as a "proselyting ministry" is to be found in Germany. Frankfurt is the center with a large modern church and school building in the heart of the city. Here an annual European Lectureship is held, attended by representatives from fifteen nations in which more than one hundred churches have been organized since the close of World War II. In Germany there are congregations in Weisbaden, Wurzburg, Hamburg, Karlsruhe, and other cities. Denmark has churches in Copenhagen, Risskov, Klampenborg, Odense. Sweden, in Stockholm, Goteberg, Sollentuna, and Bromma. Norway, in Bergen and Oslo. Holland, in Haarlem, Bilthoven, Hilversum, Aerdenhout. France, in Paris, Loiret, Colombes, Ville d'Avray, and Lambersoit. Belgium, in Liege, Brussels, and Verviers.

Austria, in Salzburg. Switzerland, in Zurich. In Italy there are numerous assemblies, and the Church of Christ has become probably the most vigorous non-Romanist Christian testimony in the nation. There are frequent brushes with the police and suits in the courts demanding "religious freedom" under the terms of the Italian Constitution. The names of Church of Christ missionaries are often in the headlines of international news dispatches. Their well-publicized stand for the "apostolic faith" has resulted in many conversions from Roman Catholicism and good congregations in Palermo, Milan, Rome, Bologna, Frasiati, Florence, Genoa, Trieste, and many small villages. Even Sicily has a Church of Christ at Catania.

In this connection the cause in the British Isles and Canada may well be considered.

In the British Isles there are about twenty churches known as "Old Pathers," who conform generally to the Church of Christ views. In Canada there are between fifty and seventy-five congregations which do not use instrumental music in worship. Many of these churches are of early origin and are not the result of modern-day missionary endeavor; but American Churches of Christ are beginning to evangelize in Canada as well as in other Commonwealth nations, especially Australia.

Cubans converted in Florida went to the native island republic to establish a mission in 1936. The Estervez and Jiminez families have given splendid leadership to this work which centers in Pinar del Rio.

Because of a lack of communication between the churches and any central missionary information agency it is almost impossible to get a complete picture of the work being done on foreign fields. The opprobrious epithet *antimissionary* can no longer be applied to these people who are making real sacrifices to carry the gospel to "the uttermost parts of the earth."

Propaganda for Church of Christ convictions in doctrine and practice now utilizes the latest modern devices. In 1952 "The Herald of Truth," radio preaching program, went on the air under the auspices of Highland church, Abilene, Texas. Today it is heard on three hundred stations by an estimated three million listeners. An auxiliary agency produces Bible filmstrips and charts used by three thousand churches. In 1955 the Gospel Press, of Dallas, Texas, a nonprofit organization, began an advertising campaign in leading national magazines and metropolitan dailies setting forth "the New Testament position" of the Church of Christ with amazing results.

There are scores of journals produced for circulation among the churches, most of which are small and may be short-lived. A new crop seems to develop each year. However, the *Gospel Advocate,* established by Tolbert Fanning and William Lipscomb in 1855 and carried on under the outstanding leadership of David Lipscomb and E. G. Sewell for many years, remains one of the most influential periodicals. The McQuiddy family, owners of a large printing establishment in Nashville, has given liberally to maintain the magazine and to develop a high-class Bible-school and book literature as a service to the churches. Under the forward-looking editorship of B. C. Goodpasture, the churches have been guided to adopt sensible practices, Biblical in basic principles and essential to progress in the modern world. The *Advocate* has encouraged higher education, an educated ministry, missionary advance, effective education in the local church and a trained eldership and diaconate.

The *Firm Foundation,* of Austin, Texas, established in 1884 is a stalwart "defender of the faith." The Showalter family has largely sponsored its ministry. The oldest journal is the *American Christian Review,* originally founded by Benjamin Franklin in 1856. It has for several generations been edited and published by the Sommer family. It vigorously opposes all "digressive practices" including church colleges. The *Twentieth Century Christian* (1937) maintains high journalistic standards. The *Word and Work,* edited by R. H. Boll from 1915 until his death in 1956, serves the premillennial brethren. The appearance of two creditable quarterlies, *Restoration Quarterly* (1957) and *Restoration Review* (1959), marks scholarly attainment of encouraging stature. *The Minister's Monthly, Power for Today, World Vision, Christian Chronicle,* and *The Voice of Freedom* serve in specialized fields. A listing of other journals would probably be obsolete in a few years. In 1960 there were an estimated forty-five Church of Christ publications in existence.

For many years brethren in the Church of Christ have been sensitive to the claims of Christian benevolence. Homes for orphan children and for the aged and infirm have been operated by the elders of many of the stronger churches. In some cases independent boards have organized and directed such institutions, soliciting operating funds from individuals and churches. The Fanning Orphan Home and School and a Home for the Aged in Nashville, Tennessee, are the oldest such agencies in existence. The Potter Orphan Home and School in Bowling Green, Kentucky; Boles Home, Quinlan, Texas; the Christian Home and Bible School, Mount Dora, Florida; the Southern Christian Home, Morrilton, Arkansas; the Tipton Orphan Home, Tipton, Oklahoma; the Christian Children's Home, Ontario, California; the Maude Carpenter Home, Wichita, Kansas; the Home for the Aged, Houston, Texas; Home for the Aged, Romeo, Michigan; Valparaiso Orphan Home, Valparaiso, Indiana; Tennessee Orphan Home, Spring Hill, Tennessee; Lubbock Children's Home, Lubbock, Texas; Childhaven, Cullman, Alabama, are some of the larger and better equipped institutions.

It is estimated that the brotherhood gives for all educational, missionary, and benevolent purposes around fifty million dollars annually.

There is strong resistance to any co-operative enterprise that might degenerate into a sect, institution, or denomination. Church of Christ brethren believe that if all believers in Christ remain simply Christians and keep the local church free and independent, denominationalism is utterly impossible. They say pure and unadulterated Christianity is undenominational. The spirit and letter of apostolic teaching is that Christians shall be of the same mind and the same judgment and that there be no divisions among them. The purpose of all true reformers through the centuries was to set people free from ecclesiastical bondage and bring them into the liberty of the sons of God. Only their successors who were smaller souls and inclined to seek prestige and authority were responsible for sect or denominational organization. Denominationalism is built on humanly devised orders and creeds and partakes of the "beggarly elements" of Roman Catholicism. So far as ecclesiasticisms and creeds are concerned there is just as much ground for the Roman Catholic system as for Protestant systems. Members of the Church of Christ see their "erring brethren" in Left and Center as partaking of the forbidden fruit against which the Campbells and the early fathers of the Restoration movement warned. They see every believer who supports a "party" organization of any sort as lending his influence to neutralize the basic Reformation and Christian principle of freedom from ecclesiastical loyalties beyond the local congregation. They see denominationalism as a sin, because, among other things, first, it fails to give full honor to Christ as the head of the church; second, it puts human authority ahead of the divine; third, it is in conflict with the plain teachings of the Scriptures on the nature of Christian unity; fourth, it postpones the fulfillment of Christ's prayer that all His *disciples* might be one as He and Father are one, that the world may believe. Right-wing conviction is that while Rome, by its despotic formalism and blasphemous assumption of divine functions, is hindering the progress of the gospel, current denominationalism and ecumenical superchurchism are neutralizing the splendid force of the evangelical faith by its divisions, rivalries, and pretensions to ecclesiastical power and authority over the churches. There should be no religious party or extracongregational agency which does not include all Christians who are in Christ Jesus, say these brethren. There can be, therefore, only the universal church of God, or body of Christ, and there is no authority in the New Testament for any Christian to belong to anything else.

This view, carried to extremes in actual practice, keeps vast areas of the Church of Christ from any fellowship beyond their local congregations, even with others who hold the same general convictions. In the restoration frame of reference this Right-wing group may be characterized as *Biblical exclusivists,* in contrast to Centrist *Biblical inclusivists* and Left-wing *non-Biblical inclusivists.*

Some irenic spirits in the Church of Christ see hope for an era of better understanding and closer unity with many Christian churches still committed to the restoration ideal. The minister of one of their great churches has said,

> If the church of the first century had been ruled by men of the type of certain preachers and elders in the conservative churches of today, or of the type of certain leaders and preachers in the liberal churches of this age, Christianity would have perished before the end of the century in which it was born. But it was not, and the great majority of the churches of today are free from these excesses. I verily believe that there are tens of thousands of good people in both the Christian Church and the Church of Christ

who are heartbroken because of the excesses to which some churches and preachers have gone in both directions. . . . I do not expect, however, to see fellowship restored in these churches in a day. Fellowship was not broken in a day, nor will it be restored in a day. But it was broken; and in the providence of God, I believe it will be restored.

BIBLIOGRAPHY: Chapter 20

Goodpasture, B. C., editor, *Gospel Advocate* (1955-59).
Lemmons, Reuel, editor, *Firm Foundation* (1955-59).
Nichols, James W., editor, *Christian Chronicle* (1955-59).
Waggoner, W. L., editor, *World Vision* (1955-59).
West, Earl Irvin, *Search for the Ancient Order*.
Young, M. Norvel, *A History of Christian Colleges*.

Chapter 21

A World-wide Fellowship

WHILE the Restoration movement was originally a distinctly American undertaking, its principles were so broad and its aims so catholic that it appealed to men in all nations. Its spirit was consonant with that of similar religious movements in history (see Introduction, p. 9 ff.) and found sympathetic acceptance among such groups as the Scotch Baptists, the Haldanes, and the Evangelical Christians. Wherever men had tired of the ecclesiastical trappings of established churches and the intricacies of human theological systems and had turned to the Holy Scriptures to discover the patterns of apostolic faith and practice, the Restoration movement was welcomed. Its warm, irenic spirit, and its dream of a united church had an almost irresistible appeal. Churches established on the New Testament pattern began to spring up throughout the world.

North and South America

Alaska. Before Alaska was admitted to statehood in the United States, it was entered by direct-support missionaries who planted churches in Anchorage, Dillingham, Ewak, Homer, Ketchikan, Fairbanks, Kenai, Palmer, Spenard, and Wasilla. In June, 1936, the Franklin Smiths began the first church in Ewak. Small children's homes are maintained at Ketchikan and Homer, and a home for the aged, at Mountain Point.

Argentina. Buenos Aires was entered by C.W.B.M. missionaries in 1906. They established churches in Belgrano, Colegiales, and San Martin. Today there are six churches and eleven preaching points with around five hundred members. One of many reasons for slow growth is the amazing strength of the Plymouth Brethren in Argentina. With a message stressing simple New Testament doctrine and practice they have become the leading Protestant body in Argentina.

British West Indies. In the easternmost island of Barbados, at Bridgetown, a New Testament church was established by Charles C. Leacock, a native minister, in 1940. The Vernon Osbornes took charge of the work in 1953, and reorganized it into the Oistin Church of Christ. Silver Sands, Spooner's Hill, and other preaching points have since been established along with a ministers training school and a Christian day school. A native ministry is at work evangelizing and baptizing throughout the island.

In the Bahamas and the Cayman islands native Christians have established several small churches of Christ which are being shepherded from mission headquarters in Bridgetown.

Jamaica. The island of Jamaica was entered in 1858 by J. O. Beardslee, under the sponsorship of the American Christian Missionary Society, but it was not until the Christian Woman's Board of Missions came in 1876 that the work began to prosper and give promise of permanency. Today thirty-seven churches, forty-six preaching points, and one school, with about five thousand members are related to the United Christian Missionary Society.

Direct-support missionary work begun by American brethren in 1935 is to be found in six districts of the island with more than six thousand members in more than forty churches. These Jamaican Christians co-operate in the support of the Jamaica Bible Seminary, several Christian day schools, and the Jamaica Christian Boys' Home.

Brazil. In this, the fourth largest country in the world, New Testament churches are thriving since Lloyd David Sanders landed in Goiania in 1948. Today, six churches claim some three hundred members and two schools— Escola Biblica and Instituo Cristao de Goiania. In the fabulous new city of Brasilia, a well-located church flourishes. Other missionary ventures in Belem, Macapa, Iccoraci, and Sao Paulo are becoming centers for educational, benevolent, and evangelistic work. A twenty-five-year-old indigenous Brazilian movement to restore the New Testament church with thirteen well-established congregations has been discovered in the Sao Paulo area and co-operative relationships have been established.

Canada. To James Black and Joseph Ash belongs the distinction of initiating the Restoration movement in Canada. Black was a Scotch Baptist who emigrated to the West in 1820 and soon became the leader of a group of churches in Eramosa Township, later to be merged into a strong congregation in Everton, Ontario. Esquesing was founded in 1820 and Eramosa East in 1832. Ash came from Anglican and Christian church backgrounds. Both men were greatly influenced by the reading of Stone's *Christian Messenger* and Campbell's *Christian Baptist* and *Millennial Harbinger*. Ash founded the Cobourg church in 1836, and claimed that it was the oldest congregation of the Disciples in Canada. Associated with these two pioneer preachers in Ontario were James Kilgour, Dugald Sinclair, Alexander Anderson, David Oliphant, Edmund Sheppard, and Charles Lister. Black was recognized as the outstanding leader. He ranged over the whole province preaching the gospel and founding churches. He was the first agent of the British and Foreign Bible Society in Upper Canada, and is credited with founding the first co-operative work among the Disciples. For length of service, piety, vision, and understanding of the true genius of the Restoration plea, he had few equals.

324

The first annual report of Canadian Disciples in the *Millennial Harbinger* appeared in August, 1843, over the signature of James Menzies, secretary, and stated that a co-operation of various congregations had met in Esquesing "for the purpose of promoting the cause of truth and disseminating the principles of our common Christianity. . . . There are now 16 churches in various parts of the province. . . . Many of the churches are in prosperous condition, and many of the saved are constantly being added to their numbers." The nucleus of this group was the enterprising Eramosa church and its branches which soon came to number nearly one thousand members. The Wellington Co-operation and other such associations of churches grew up in Ontario and were finally all merged in a Provincial Co-operation in 1846. Reorganized in 1886, it had an unbroken history until 1922, when the All-Canada organization was conceived.

Toronto has long been the center of Christian church activity in Canada. Its first congregation was established in 1838, in Yonge Street, under the strong leadership of the Beaty family. James Beaty, Sr., was prominent in public life. He founded the daily *Leader* and also a monthly magazine, *The Christian Leader*. He was elected to Canada's first federal parliament in 1867, and served until 1873. He helped to organize the Toronto General Hospital, served as a director of one of the city's leading banks, and marched in the first Orange parade in Canadian history. He was a man of strong convictions. In later life he edited the *Christian Index* and led certain churches of Christ to separate from their brethren who preferred to worship with the aid of musical instruments. Among the casualties of Beaty controversy, was William McMaster (later to be the Honorable Senator McMaster and founder of McMaster University) who joined the Regular Baptists.

After Yonge Street, came many congregations such as Shuter Street, Louisa Street, Richmond Street, Alice Street, Pembroke Street, Bathurst Street, Cecil Street, Keele Street, Fern Avenue, Wychwood, Central, Strathmoor Boulevard, and Hillcrest. Co-operative enterprises flourished in Toronto. The *Christian Messenger,* founded by Charles T. Paul and Reuben Butchart, was published there from 1897-1922, and merged with *The Canadian Disciple* in 1923. It is the headquarters of the All-Canada Committee of the Churches of Christ and the College of Churches of Christ, which is related to the University of Toronto.

Ontario is only one of the nine provinces in Canada. The Restoration movement has had an interesting history in all the others, especially in New Brunswick, Nova Scotia, and Prince Edward Island. The first church in Nova Scotia to join with the Disciples was River John. It came out of Scotch Baptist backgrounds, founded June 18, 1815. As early as 1832, there was a strong congregation "after the New Testament pattern" at Halifax. In 1840, a meeting was held at Falmouth, with congregations reported at Rawdon, West Gore, Cornwallis, and Newport. Today there are nine churches, all of strong evangelical sympathies. In New Brunswick, the first churches were formed in Charlotte County on Deer Island. From Lord's Cove came J. A. Lord to edit the *Christian Standard* (1896-1910).

In St. John, a church was organized in 1843 on Duke Street; Coburg Street and Douglas Avenue followed. Eight congregations are now in New Brunswick, with fifteen hundred members. Prince Edward Island is the smallest province in Canada, but it has sent out the greatest number of Disciples into public and professional life. The church at Summerside, alone, produced such men as Archibald McLean, J. H. Mohorter, Neil McLeod, H. T. Morrison, E. B. Barnes, C. B. Titus, J. H. MacNeil, W. H. Harding, and A. N. Simpson. More than one hundred men have come out of P.E.I. churches to serve the brotherhood on both sides of the border. Cross Roads (Lot 48) is credited as being the first congregation, dating its history from the early 1800's. Dr. John Knox, an Anglican minister from Edinburgh, baptized at Cross Roads, became the most powerful preacher in the Island, and "moderator" of the "co-operation." In 1843 he organized the churches at Montague and East Point. Later came New Glasgow, Charlottetown, Murray Harbor. Today there are eleven co-operative congregations and a number who refuse to use instrumental music in worship. The churches in the Maritime Provinces are "slow and conservative" but they are sound in the faith and continue to build solidly for the future.

In the Canadian West, the first congregation was organized at Portage la Prairie, Manitoba, in 1881. Five churches today have less than five hundred members. In Saskatchewan, Milestone was the first church, then came Yellow Grass, Regina, Saskatoon, and Winnipeg. Alberta became the strongest province numerically in the West. The name of M. B. Ryan is associated with the planting of the earliest churches—Erskine, Lethbridge, Calgary, Edmonton, Hanna, Vulcan, Black Diamond. Alberta Bible College, founded by C. H. Phillips in 1936, is now located at Calgary, and is doing more to train Canadian ministers than any other agency in the Dominion. British Columbia is still missionary territory. The "co-operative" Central church, Vancouver, was organized in 1905. Small "nonco-operative" congregations are reported at Twelfth Avenue, Vancouver, Victoria, and Blundell. The estimated membership of all these churches in the Dominion of Canada was 6,500 in 1960.

Since 1883, when the Ontario Co-operation of Disciples of Christ was organized, there have been two distinct parties in Canada. The situation has not, however, been as tense and open as in the United States. The Canadian Rightists did not set up a divisive census listing as the Americans did in 1906, and in many areas a friendly attitude exists between congregations of varying practices. With American aid in recent years, there has been a strengthening of the old Beaty spirit in some quarters.

In 1960, the Church of Christ reported twenty-two American and forty-three Canadian preachers, and 102 congregations with 3,300 members.

Chile. Valparaiso has a congregation shepherded by Bertrand Smith, who entered Chile in 1949. With this as a center, new churches have been planted at Cerro Esperanza, Villa Alemana, and Vina del Mar. The cause is in its beginning stages in this narrow ribbon-like republic on the Pacific slope of the Andes.

Cuba. The Church of Christ has forty congregations and twenty-three hundred Christians centered in the Pinar del Rio area.

Hawaii. The first Christian church in Hawaii was organized in Honolulu in 1894, in the home of the William Hoppers. The first minister was T. D. Garvin. A chapel was erected in the downtown area in 1895. In 1920 the Kaimuki church was organized. Both have a membership of about 250 and appeal mainly to people with interests in mainland United States.

Direct-support missions made the first serious gospel appeal to the native Hawaiians. The Owen Stills began work in 1946. There are now churches at Sunset Beach, Maili, Waianas, Hauula, Palolo Valley, Makaha, Pearl City, Pearl Harbor, Keolu Hills, Wahiawa, Hilo—several with Christian day schools. A growing group of native Hawaiian ministers and workers have a vision of evangelizing all the islands.

Mexico. Christian church missionaries entered Mexico under the auspices of the C.W.B.M. in 1895, setting up a small school across the Rio Grande River from El Paso, Texas. In 1897, these workers were moved to Monterrey, where a full-fledged church and school program was inaugurated. This work expanded to Sabinas and Piedras Negras, and a group of New Testament churches grew up in this area. Unfortunately, this work was abandoned in 1919, under a controversial "comity agreement" with denominational mission boards, for a new site in central Mexico.

But the gospel seed had been sown and the Restoration plea continued to be vigorously preached and disseminated by native Mexican evangelists led by Enrique T. Westrup, editor of *La Via de Paz,* and centering in the old Central Christian Church, Monterrey. Some twenty churches are still to be found in this area, with nearly one thousand members. At Eagle Pass, the Colegio Biblico trains most of the native Mexican ministers. More than forty native churches with some two thousand members are active in northern Mexico. Saltillo has a Christian school and is a center for some fifteen organized churches and scores of preaching points. The Mexican Bible Institute in Nogales, Arizona, serves another area of comparable strength. Here all the leadership is Mexican. Similar centers at Hermosillo, Chihuahua, Baja, Salinas, and Estancia encourage large groups of native churches. It is estimated that more than 120 organized churches of Christ are in this general fellowship with a membership of ten thousand. This work is a demonstration of the fact that a trained, Bible-believing Christian leadership, made up of nationals in indigenous churches, will accomplish more in missionary results than twice the number of "foreign missionaries."

Today, fifteen churches are to be found in and around San Luis Potosi and Aguascalientes, the U.C.M.S. field, with one thousand communicants. Two day schools are conducted in this area.

Paraguay. American missionaries entered Paraguay in 1918. The work centered around the Colegio Internacional at Asuncion, which is now a union institution. In five congregations and nine preaching points there are about two hundred members.

Puerto Rico. Following the annexation of Puerto Rico by the United States, the Christian Woman's Board of Missions, in 1900, entered Bayamon, a suburb of San Juan, upon the invitation of the government to take charge of a girls orphanage. In 1901 the first church was established there. This work grew until the U.C.M.S. now serves more than fifty churches with a membership of approximately eight thousand. The territory covered included about three hundred square miles in the north-central part of the island.

Direct-support work began in San Juan in 1954 with the coming of Gordon Thompson, and has resulted in only a few churches so far.

Europe

Austria. Two small Churches of Christ, one in Salzburg, have about eighty-five members.

Belgium. In this predominantly Roman Catholic country there is a small church of Christ at Genk and a few other groups meeting in homes. This work was opened by the Deelstras and Casteleins in November, 1956. Rightist workers have set up meetings in Leige, Brussels, and Verviers.

Bulgaria. Bulgaria still has many scattered New Testament Christians who maintain a semblance of fellowship in occasional cottage meetings where they observe the Lord's Supper.

Czechoslovakia. Several churches which have their origin in the Russian Evangelical Christian movement (p. 332) are maintaining worship services.

Denmark. Church of Christ brethren have congregations in Copenhagen, Risskov, Klampenberg, and Odeuse.

Estonia. The same situation exists as in Czechoslovakia.

France. There are about eighteen small congregations of the Church of Christ in France, with about 275 members. Churches are located in Paris, Loiret, Colombes, Ville d'Avray, and Lambersoit.

Germany. A group of scattered churches in Germany strive to reproduce apostolic beliefs and practices, but political tensions between East and West Germany make interchurch fellowship impossible. Earl Stuckenbruck conducts a unique ministerial education project in Tubingen. A small church there sends out evangelists to encourage groups of believers in other communities.

American Church of Christ missionaries are meeting with remarkable success in such cities as Frankfurt. An impressive contemporary oval-shaped church building in the heart of Frankfurt is filled every Sunday, and sight-seeing guides point it out as one of the city's modern landmarks. About sixty churches of Christ in Germany do not use instrumental music in worship, and their work is prospering and expanding, with nearly two thousand members.

Great Britain. Knowledge of the origins of the Restoration movement in Great Britain is indefinite. The Glasite and Scotch Baptist antecedents of such congregations as Rose Street, Kirkcaldy, Scotland (founded in

1798) and Cam-yr-Alyn in North Wales (1799) are well known, but they came into the fold of the Campbellian movement much later.

The first intimations of the plea set forth in the *Declaration and Address* were carried to England in 1833 by Peyton C. Wyeth, of Pennsylvania. William Jones, then elder of the Scotch Baptist church in Windmill Street, Finsbury Square, London, thrilled at the story of the American "search for the ancient order," and began in 1835 to publish the *Millennial Harbinger* and *Voluntary Church Advocate*. His purpose was to introduce to British Baptists the writings of Alexander Campbell, which (for a time) he accepted as "law and gospel." After issuing sixteen monthly parts, he discontinued the publication; but James Wallis, an avid reader, founded the first church of Christ in the Restoration movement in Great Britain. Wallis, a clothier, was a member of a Scotch Baptist church in the city of Nottingham. On December 25, 1836, he and thirteen others withdrew from that church and formed a new congregation "after the New Testament pattern." By the end of 1837 there were ninety-seven members. That same year Wallis determined to perpetuate the ministry of the now defunct *Millennial Harbinger* and launched the *Christian Messenger,* which for many years under that name and later as the *British Millennial Harbinger* was the chief voice of the Restoration movement in Britain. It is interesting to note that Wallis was the grandfather of alderman and wealthy industrialist James W. Black, of Leicester, one of the foremost advocates of the plea in the 1900's and at one time president of the World Convention of Churches of Christ. In Wallis' home city of Nottingham, there are now five churches and nearly a dozen others in the surrounding district.

In 1842, the first conference of the British churches of Christ was held in Edinburgh. John Davis, of Mollington, Cheshire, presided. The next conference was called in 1847, in Chester; and Alexander Campbell, then visiting the British Isles, presided. The brethren prevailed upon him to conduct the proceedings and to make several addresses. At that time, eighty churches reported membership of around 2,500.

The conference has met annually since that time except in 1940, when war conditions made all public meetings impossible. The Conference of Churches of Christ in Great Britain is not a delegate convention, but it represents a much closer co-operation than that involved in the International Convention of their American neighbors. Official committees are concerned with the work of the churches. The training of the ministry and the work of evangelism are in the hands of the Conference. A weekly journal called the *Christian Advocate* is also Conference controlled. The British churches maintain missionaries in Thailand, India, and Nyasaland. A ministerial training school is located at Selly Oak, Birmingham. It is the lineal descendant of Overdale College, which was founded in 1920. In 1931 it was determined to join the twelve interdenominational Selly Oak colleges which co-operate in the training of ministers, missionaries, teachers, and ecumenical and social workers. Ever since this decision was made, there has been a steady decline in the membership of the churches.

Their peak strength was 16,306 in 1922; today there are only about 11,000 members. Of 155 churches, only twenty-five have a membership of more than one hundred.

Certain differences in emphasis distinguish the British churches from their brethren in America. British disciples are deeply interested in doctrinal matters and have not been too much affected by the "social gospel." In matters of worship they maintain the corporate nature of the Sunday morning worship in the pattern practiced by Alexander Campbell in the church at Bethany. For example, there are the prayers of the church in which the whole congregation participates, prayers alternating with silences, the period being closed with a short prayer offered by the presiding elder. The American idea of the pastor has been accepted by only a few congregations. Elders occupy a far more important place. If there is a full-time minister, he is known as the "evangelist" and is concerned with tasks assigned him by his superiors. Close Communion is practiced by most churches, although "guests" are sometimes recognized as worthy to partake of the emblems. Open membership is practically unknown.

In 1870 the relations of the British churches with America were marred by the decision of the Foreign Christian Missionary Society to send "missionaries" to the British Isles. This was done at the instigation of Timothy Coop, a wealthy British disciple who had progressive ideas. American methods, including open membership introduced by W. T. Moore at Southport, were most unpopular. The breach between the "American churches" in Britain and the Conference churches became serious after 1875, and was not healed until 1917, when fourteen "American churches" which practiced open Communion were received into the Conference on the ground that the local church had the right to decide its own practices.

Rightists in the British Isles had their origins in "Old Pathism," under the leadership of Walter Crosthwaite, of Scotland. Old Path leadership not only opposed the use of instrumental music in worship and refused to participate in all co-operative agencies, but it narrowed the interpretation of close Communion to exclude "co-operatives," Baptists, and Plymouth Brethren from the Lord's table and all forms of Christian fellowship. Old Path numerical strength still centers in Scotland, but there are more churches in England. In 1959 the *Christian Chronicle* reported that there were about twelve hundred brethren scattered in twenty-nine English, eighteen Scottish, and two Irish congregations.

British churches have produced a number of men of great renown. David Lloyd-George, prime minister of Great Britain during World War I and noted political leader, was a member of the church of Christ in Criccieth, North Wales, where his uncle, Richard Lloyd (who reared him) was one of the leading elders. When Lloyd-George resided in London he often attended a Welsh Baptist church where services were conducted in the Welsh language, resulting in a Baptist claim that he was of their faith. However, he maintained his membership at Criccieth until his death, and was often seen participating in the simple services of the little stone chapel along with his wife, his daughter, Lady Carey Evans, and his grandchildren.

J. B. Rotherham was a noted Bible scholar and translator of the famed *Emphasized Bible* (Rotherham Version), widely used by scholars throughout the English-speaking world. It was produced in America by the Standard Publishing Company. Robert Halliday, Joseph Smith, Lancelot Oliver, and William Robinson were widely known outside Britain's borders. Robinson served as secretary of the British Council of Churches and participated in many of the strategic meetings leading to the formation of the World Council of Churches. G. Y. Tickle and George Collin enriched the hymnody of the church.

Hungary. Under the evangelistic guidance of Frank Vass, who accepted the New Testament church position in 1921, some fifty independent churches in Hungary acted (1953-55) to join the world fellowship of churches of Christ. Most of these congregations are still in touch with their brethren across the iron curtain, and a group of well-taught evangelists itinerate among the brethren to encourage them and immerse new converts. Letters, tracts, and Scripture portions are employed to keep alive the Christian witness regardless of communist opposition.

Italy. Despite Roman Catholic opposition, the churches of Christ are thriving in Italy. Shortly after World War II (1947), Guy Mayfield entered Bari, baptizing converts, organizing churches, and establishing a Bible seminary. Small congregations exist at Latiano, Oria, Manduria, Palese, Ciampino, Lecce. Italian evangelists trained in the Seminary are now beginning to assume preaching and teaching responsibilities.

The conservative Church of Christ missionaries are conducting the most vigorous non-Romanist Christian testimony in the nation (p. 319). They have strong congregations in Palermo, Milan, Bologna, Frasiote, Florence, Genoa, Trieste, and many villages. Even Sicily has a Church of Christ at Catania.

Netherlands. Congregations which will not use instrumental music in worship are at Haarlem, Bilthoven, Hilversum, and Aerdenhout.

Norway. In 1875, a small group of churches in Norway, striving to build on "the New Testament pattern," contacted Scottish churches of Christ. R. P. Anderson was sent out from Scotland, but he was unable to effect a co-operative relationship. The F.C.M.S. helped the Norwegian churches for a period, but finally abandoned them to their peculiar practices. Some of these congregations are still in existence, but they have made little or no impact on the religious life of the nation.

Church of Christ missionaries maintain assemblies in Bergen and Oslo.

Poland. The churches of Christ in Poland, Galicia, Ukraine, and White Russia had their origin in the Evangelical or Gospel Christian movement in Russia. Evangelists distributed portions of the Holy Scriptures, preached the gospel, baptized converts, and established churches over a wide area of the Slavic speaking lands but set up no overhead organization. While some contact was maintained with the St. Petersburg center, national boundaries precluded any close co-operation.

331

Joseph Keevil, the minister of the Flatbush Christian Church in Brooklyn, New York, heard a young Pole preaching on the streets and was impressed with the fact that he expressed views of the gospel plan of salvation similar to those being preached in the Flatbush church. Upon inquiry, Keevil heard from Konstantin Jaroszewicz the story of the Polish churches and the terrible poverty in which his brethren were living. Keevil persuaded him to go to Johnson Bible College, complete his ministerial training, and return to Poland, promising him support in organizing a missionary society for the evangelization of his native land.

Returning to Poland, Jaroszewicz sought out a group of evangelists and elders who joined with him in establishing the Union of Churches of Christ in Poland. Great evangelistic meetings were held throughout the nation, with as many as one hundred converts being immersed at one time and many churches being established in small villages and towns. The Union applied for membership in the Christian Restoration Association and was for several years generously supported by American churches. It received government recognition as the chief Protestant body in Poland. In 1935, a large delegation from the Polish churches attended the World Convention of Churches of Christ in Leicester, England, where they were the center of great interest because of their colorful native costumes, their rendition of Polish hymns, and their deep devotional spirit.

Before the Republic of Poland was overrun by Soviet Russia and religious work was severely restricted, there were more than 250,000 members in churches and meetings known to the Union. There were 134 evangelists in the field; 65 organized churches, many scattered meetings, and 203 preaching points in 26 counties in 10 provinces. Since Poland has been enveloped by the iron curtain nearly all contact with their Western brethren has been cut off. Occasional intimations are that, as in Russia, many congregations are still meeting for Bible study and the observance of the Lord's Supper in barns and cellars, and praying for the day when they will again be permitted aggressively to carry on the work as before. They celebrated their fortieth anniversary in May, 1961.

Russia. The romance of the Restoration movement in Russia is one of the most thrilling bits of church history ever recorded. There had been, prior to 1870, a number of reforming Christian dissenters from the Eastern Orthodox church of Russia. Among these were the Molokans, Dukhobors, and Stundists. But about 1870, Madame Chertkova invited Lord Radstock of England to preach in St. Petersburg. Among his converts was W. A. Pashkoff, a high-ranking officer of the Czar's army. Pashkoff began an earnest study of the New Testament and became enamoured of the idea of a restoration of the apostolic church in doctrine, ordinances, and life.

General Pashkoff made his decision to set up churches of the New Testament pattern at great personal sacrifice. He was wealthy and influential in social and government circles. He was forced to renounce his army commission, and devoted his wealth and energy to the preaching of the gospel. His leadership caused him to be styled "the Alexander

Campbell of Russia"; his preaching ability earned him the title of the "Russian Moody." His followers soon became known as the "Evangelical Christians" or "Gospel Christians," and were originally unrelated to the Baptist movement under Nikita Veronin, which dated from 1869.

In 1884, Pashkoff called a meeting in St. Petersburg of all evangelical Christians in Russia for the purpose of forming a united fellowship. The police, however, broke up the meeting after a day or two, arrested the General and his associate, Count Korff, and exiled them. Pashkoff died in Rome under banishment.

Four years after this debacle, a brilliant and gigantic young man, Ivan S. Prokhanoff, arrived in St. Petersburg to undertake studies in the Government Institute of Technology, Russia's finest school of engineering. While here, he came under the dire influences of Nihilism. One night he placed a Bible and a revolver on his desk and began to wrestle with God as to whether he would commit suicide or preach the gospel. He had been converted in Vladikavkas in the Caucasus in 1886, but had strayed from his original Molokan faith. A fellow student who was an evangelical Christian persuaded him to attend one of their secret meetings, and soon Prokhanoff was a fully committed member. He went to Bristol, London, Berlin, and Paris to further fit himself for leadership. Upon his return to Russia he surreptitiously launched a hectographed periodical, *The Conversation,* which he mailed in registered letters to the scattered brethren. Traveling throughout Russia, he encouraged the churches and won thousands to Christ.

When Czar Nicholas II issued the Toleration Act of April 17, and the Manifesto of October 17, 1905, a measure of religious liberty was guaranteed the Russian people. Prokhanoff and his associates now openly issued a new periodical, *The Christian,* under a threefold standard: (1) The revelation to the Russian people of the substance of Christianity— the living Christ; (2) The evangelization of Russia with the universal slogan of "Revival, regeneration, and reformation"; (3) The unification of all the branches of living Christianity with the slogan, "In essentials, unity; in secondary things, freedom; in all things, charity." In 1910 another paper, *The Morning Star,* was launched to discuss living questions and to spur a religious awakening.

In 1909, the All-Russian Union of Evangelical Christians was formed as a fellowship of the brethren upon a purely voluntary basis. The congregations remained autonomous. The Union was a means of co-operative development in the areas of missions, education, and publications. The first conference sent out Alexander Persianoff as its first missionary. By 1928, the Union and local groups reported six hundred missionaries or evangelists working in Russia for the restoration of free New Testament Christianity. It was estimated that there were two million members of the churches in Russia and the border Slavic states.

Rumors of this almost fantastic Restoration movement which had risen in Russia under circumstances similar to those surrounding the early American movement gradually filtered through to the Disciples of

Christ. When the General Convention met in Louisville in 1912, two emissaries of the A.R.U.E.C., Alexander Persianoff and Professor Martin Schmidt, appeared to appeal for help from their American brethren. It seems that Persianoff on an evangelistic tour to Siberia had met John Johnson in an exiles' prison. Johnson had a son in America who had joined a Christian church in New York and had heard from him about the American Restoration movement. Together they prayed that contact might be established between these brethren across the world. The Louisville Convention appointed a "Russian Emergency Committee" to investigate. It was headed by Z. T. Sweeney. Other members were Joseph Keevil, George W. Kramer, C. B. Drake, and A. V. Chaney. Sweeney, accompanied by Louis R. Patmont, acting as interpreter, went to St. Petersburg. There a congregation of nine hundred greeted them. They found nine other preaching places in the city, and that there were many churches throughout the nation. The government forbade a census of their strength but admitted that there were many thousands of this faith. A Bible college had recently been established in a former high-school building where young men were being trained for the ministry. Sweeney was very much impressed and reported to the American Christian Missionary Society:

> First: The Gospel Christians are as emphatic and insistent upon New Testament Christianity as the Christians of the United States.
> Second: They have a very large measure of sympathy among the most influential and powerful people of the empire. This is due primarily to the great influence and popularity of General Pashkoff, who laid the foundations of the work. . . .
> Third: The Gospel Christians have a fine organization—better than anything we have in this country—and thus work in perfect harmony. There was not a hint of clash between rival leaders or factions.
> Fourth: All they need is a little of the "sinews of war" that could be so easily supplied out of our abundance. One hundred thousand dollars put into Russia in the next ten years would develop a half million Gospel Christians in less than a quarter of a century.
> If this is not God's opportunity to us, I don't know anything about such opportunities.

If the American brethren could have possessed the vision which might have enabled them to penetrate the curtain of the future and to foresee the black menace of world communism which was soon to arise in Russia, they might have been stirred to action by the report of the Sweeney Committee. Instead, they sent little more than $5,000 to the A.R.U.E.C. in 1913, and similar amounts in succeeding years until 1928. There was occasional exchange of visits on the part of church leaders. Prokhanoff spoke in many American churches. The A.C.M.S., the *Christian-Evangelist,* and the *Christian Standard* frequently urged the claims of the Russian brethren upon American Disciples.

When the atheistic Bolshevik Revolution broke in all its fury, religious freedom was denied to the Evangelical Christians. When they persisted in their efforts to preach the gospel and maintain their churches, it is reported that more than six hundred ministers and elders fell before Russian firing squads. Prokhanoff was banished from Russia, after spending several years in prison as an enemy of the state. He finally died in a Berlin hospital, October 8, 1935, and is buried in that city.

As the Russian situation began to stabilize, the Soviet government permitted a limited number of church organizations to resume operations. The Eastern Orthodox church was divested of its vast wealth and property and forced to limit its activities to strict government control. Protestants were grouped under a government-supervised organization known as the All-Russia Union of Evangelical Christian Baptists. Without regard to doctrinal differences, Pentecostals, Baptists, Evangelical Christians, Seventh-Day Adventists, and other sects are tolerated under this organization. All Protestants are popularly known as "Baptists." Evangelical Christians in the border states report hundreds of thousands of their brethren who still meet in homes, barns, and cellars for the observance of the Lord's Supper and the study of God's Word. These men of faith look forward to the day when the Evangelical Christians can resume their role in Russia's destiny as progenitors of the restoration of primitive Christianity.

Sweden. The Church of Christ at Munday, Texas, set in order a congregation "after the New Testament pattern" in Stockholm, in May, 1957. A splendid theater building in the heart of the city has been purchased as a center for evangelistic operations. Gotheburg was the second city entered. Then followed Sollentuna and Bromma. Other cities are marked for new church plantings.

Switzerland. There are two Churches of Christ with about thirty-five members in Switzerland. Three missionaries and two evangelists are reported.

Africa

Nigeria. Conservative Church of Christ brethren have 364 congregations, mostly in southeastern Nigeria, with a membership of twenty-five thousand, served by 415 native evangelists.

The Roy Goldsberrys established the West Africa Christian Mission at Yaba, in 1955. The work patterned after the direct-support plan grows encouragingly.

Northern Rhodesia. Conservative Church of Christ brethren have the strong Sinde Mission, seventeen miles from Livingston, established in 1946. A large orphanage and an effective evangelistic program are maintained. There are churches at Kalomo, Namwianga, Lusaka, and elsewhere—a total of fifty-five with 4,500 members.

Max Ward Randall, direct-support missionary to South Africa, moved to begin a new work in Northern Rhodesia, on the north shore of Kariba Lake, in 1961.

Nyasaland. Namiwawa, near Zomba, is the mission field of the British churches of Christ. In 1930 these brethren took over the Baptist Industrial Mission in the Gowa District. The total membership in twenty-five or thirty churches is nearly three thousand.

Church of Christ missionaries entered Rampi in 1957. The work has spread to Lilongwe and beyond. They report fifty-seven churches and sixteen hundred Christians.

Republic of Congo. In 1897 Ellsworth Faris and Dr. Harry N. Biddle entered Belgian Congo under the Foreign Christian Missionary Society. They took over from the American Baptist Missionary Union a mission territory centering in Bolenge and extending to Mondombe with a population of 1,500,000 natives. Today, twenty-four organized churches with nearly one thousand preaching points have reached a membership of about 110,000. Some three hundred schools are maintained with an enrollment of fifteen thousand. There are four hospitals and seven dispensaries. This work under the United Christian Missionary Society is the largest single mission of the Disciples of Christ.

In 1947, the Guy Humphreys, direct-support missionaries, undertook a work around Bomili in the Congo. Today, fifty churches claim some five thousand members. Beginnings have been made by Howard Crowl for a new mission centering in Stanleyville.

South Africa. In the latter part of the nineteenth century, British emigrees formed several churches in South Africa. In 1900, the churches in Britain sent R. K. Francis to minister to them. From this nucleus, the independent Thomas Mission under the American evangelists Kellems and Richards was able to establish churches at Durban, Cape Town, Johannesburg, Boksburg, Brakpan, and Benoni. The supervision of this work was taken over later by the U.C.M.S. There are now nine churches and nine preaching points with a total membership of five hundred. An equal number of white churches do not use instrumental music in worship, including a congregation in Pretoria.

The direct-support South Africa Church of Christ Mission work, begun by Thomas Kalane in 1920, centers in the great Observatory Church of Christ, Polo Road, Cape Town. A Bible institute trains students at Kimberly. The work extends over an area of approximately 400,000 square miles. Some forty Negro churches have scores of outstations and preaching points. The churches have their own chapels and are largely self-supporting. Membership is estimated at five thousand.

Southern Rhodesia. John Sheriff and F. L. Hadfield were the pioneers in establishing the cause here. The New Zealand churches sent them as missionaries in 1905. Today, forty-five churches serve five thousand members. The New Zealand churches still consider this to be their chief mission field with headquarters in Dadaya. The churches at Bulawayo and other key centers are wholly independent and there is a rising sense of national self-sufficiency. R. S. Garfield Todd, a former premier of Southern Rhodesia and a political and social leader of continental stature, also came to Africa as a missionary from New Zealand to Dadaya.

Direct-support American mission work, which centers in Mashoko and in Monjoro Springs, near the great Kariba Dam, includes some twenty churches with fifteen hundred members. Co-operating with the Southern Rhodesian churches, a new hospital and more than twenty Christian schools with more than two thousand children enrolled are maintained.

336

Direct-support plans call for rapid expansion through the whole of the territory included in the Central Africa Federation, made up of Southern and Northern Rhodesia and Nyasaland, Tanganyika, and Kenya. Through the good offices of John Sheriff, right-wing American missionaries came to Southern Rhodesia. They established churches at Bulawayo, Gwelo, Nhowe, Macheke and Salisbury. They claim sixty-two congregations and nearly three thousand members.

Asia and the Pacific

Australia. Australian Disciples date the origin of the Restoration movement in their continental dominion at 1846. It was in that year that Thomas Magarey led a group out of a Scotch Baptist church in Adelaide into a new Christian Chapel in Franklin Street. Magarey had come to Australia from Nelson, New Zealand, in 1845. At Nelson, he had learned from Thomas Jackson the teachings of the Restoration movement and he carried them with him to his new home.

In 1845, thirteen members of the Newmilns church in Scotland emigrated to South Australia and settled in the country districts. More brethren came from Mount Ayr, Beith, and other Scottish churches, so that in 1865 there were five congregations in South Australia with a membership of 253. Contacts were maintained with the homeland through copies of the *British Millennial Harbinger*.

The discovery of gold in Australia drew a great influx of immigrants from the British Isles beginning in 1850. In the state of New South Wales, gold-seeking brethren established the first church in Sydney in 1852, in the home of Albert Griffin. In 1864, a public meeting place was secured and the work grew into the Bathurst Street church. In Victoria, other gold-seeking brethren organized a New Testament church August, 1853, "in the tent of Brother Ingram" at Prahran, a suburb of Melbourne. Out of this congregation came James Service, who became a premier of Victoria. When Thomas Magarey, of Adelaide, visited Melbourne in 1860, he found twelve congregations. In 1864 a British-born American evangelist, H. S. Earl, was invited to Melbourne, and in one year, 297 persons were added to the churches. Land was secured in Lygon Street and a building seating six hundred persons was erected. The Swanston church in downtown Melbourne was established in October, 1865. In 1866 the first annual conference of the Victoria churches was held with about three hundred brethren present.

The cause was carried from Victoria to Tasmania in 1865 by the R. C. Fairlams, who set up a church in their house. Another Victorian, George Smith, moved to Hobart in 1871. After inviting another American evangelist, Oliver Carr, to Hobart, the church there grew in one year to a membership of 108.

Victoria churches were likewise responsible for introducing the Restoration plea in Queensland. In 1882, they sent a young Tasmanian schoolteacher to establish churches in Zillmere, Lancefield, and Toowoomba.

At an intercolonial conference held in Melbourne in 1889, the brethren agreed to send an evangelist to plant churches after the New Testament pattern in Western Australia. T. H. Bates began the church at Perth in 1891.

Organized work developed into the Federal Conference of Churches of Christ, a democratic co-operation which is careful to preserve congregational autonomy. Fully 90 per cent of the churches participate in its evangelistic, missionary, educational, and benevolent program. The *Australian Christian* (which succeeded the *Australian Christian Standard*) is the representative weekly journal, published by the Austral Printing and Publishing Company. This establishment also publishes graded lessons for Sunday schools, tracts, and books. A College of the Bible was founded in Melbourne in 1906, for the training of the ministry. The college buildings are now located at Glen Iris, Victoria. In 1942, another Bible College was started by the New South Wales churches, and is situated at Woolwich, a suburb of Sydney. A Preachers' Provident Fund helps aged and infirm ministers. A hospital at Claremont, homes for the aged at Oakleigh, and Pendle Hill, a boys' home, have been established. Australian churches support missions in India, the New Hebrides, New Guinea, Shanghai, and Thailand. Work among the Australian Aborigines was begun in 1945 with the purchase of twenty thousand acres near Norseman, Western Australia, and the sending of four missionaries to this area.

The vigorous churches of Christ in Australia now number approximately four hundred with a membership of approximately forty thousand, and are growing. Churches that do not co-operate in the Federal Conference number about twenty and have a membership of less than one thousand.

Guam. Church of Christ brethren own a good building at Agana and are doing commendable work.

India. The Disciples entered India at Harda in 1882. Today the U.C.M.S. India Mission is located in the urban centers at Jubbulpore and Bilaspur. It reports thirty-five churches and fifty-four preaching points with 4,500 members. Industrial schools are maintained at Damoh and Pendra Road. There are five hospitals and five dispensaries. There are sixteen schools of all grades with more than three thousand students.

British churches of Christ established a mission at Daltonganj in 1909, and later entered Mirzapur. Four churches claim some five hundred members in the United Provinces.

In 1926 the first of the many American direct-support missions was established by Dr. Zoena Rothermel at Ragaul. In 1928, the Harry Schaeffers began a work in the railway area of Bilaspur, which has grown to large proportions. Through emphasis on evangelism and church planting, there are some thirty churches of the New Testament pattern in the Central Provinces and beyond. Bilaspur, Manila, and Kulpahar are among other mission centers (p. 303). The work in South India began in 1936 through a native Indian converted at Ragaul. Real expansion began under the Arthur Morrises in 1950. Some eighty ministers now serve 111 churches, with a membership of more than five thousand. The work centers in Madrappakkam. South India Christian College trains ministers and workers. A trade school and a hospital are also maintained. Other independent missionaries are at work in Thalavady, Kanpur, and Bargarh. Membership in this combined Centrist fellowship is estimated at between ten and fifteen thousand.

A unique work was begun by the Schaeffers of the Central Provinces India Mission in Orissa, in 1952. There are five evangelistic centers, each with a training institute and about one hundred full-time workers. Preaching points in two hundred villages have Bargarh as the operating center. A boys' hostel and a base hospital are first steps in an institutional service program.

The U.C.M.S. has responsibility in a union work in Orissa where Baptists have labored for many years. There are 127 churches, 242 preaching points and a membership of 4,300. A hospital has been built in Diptipur.

A native Khasi tribesman, Rajani Roy Kharkhongir, began a New Testament work in the Khasi Hills of Assam about 1925. When direct-support missionaries from America discovered him, there were eleven congregations with around one thousand members. The Assam Mission Churches of Christ was organized around this work by the Fairbrothers and Reeses in 1953. A Christian day school in Mawlai, a suburb of Assam's capital, and a workers' training school have been established. Refugees from Tibet and Nepal have considerably augmented the original work. Some two thousand members are reported in the area.

Japan. In 1883, two missionary couples, the George T. Smiths and the Charles E. Garsts, sent out by the Foreign Christian Missionary Society, arrived in Japan to preach the simple gospel. Captain Garst was a West Pointer who had received his commission from General U. S. Grant and served eight years in the Army on frontier duty in the Indian wars. He had dreamed of becoming a missionary to the Japanese whose land, customs, and religions he had long studied. The story of his life is told in *A West Pointer in the Land of the Mikado.*

The first convert was baptized in Akita in 1884, and the work began which now, under the United Christian Missionary Society, has two schools and thirty-eight Leftist-related churches. Most of the work is done through the United Church of Christ in Japan (Kyodan).

Independent missionary work in Japan began in 1892 with the ministry of W. K. Azbill. The W. D. Cunninghams came to Tokyo in 1901 and developed the largest number of churches of Christ prior to World War II. After the war a few remained, but many of them have been absorbed by the Kyodan. In the great postwar resurgence of missionary interest, some forty-five direct-support missionaries went from America to Japan setting up new churches in Obihiro and Sapporo, Sandai, Tokyo, Nagoya, Osaka, Hirakata, Tenabe, Kutsugi, Shikoku, Kagoshima, Kanoya, and Nishinomote in Tanegashima. In these missions are thirty-three native pastors and ten lay leaders in fifty congregations and ten preaching points. Two training schools for ministers and workers are also operating. Membership reported is approximately two thousand persons. W. K. Azbill brought John McCaleb to Japan where he labored for forty-two years. McCaleb found support from the conservative Churches of Christ in America and did an especially fruitful work. In the postwar era these churches developed a keener interest in the evangelization of the world and their Japan mission expanded rapidly. Ibaraki Christian College is the center of the work which consists of seventy churches with two thousand members. There is a Christian Orphans' Home in Nakada, Ibaragiken, and the Nazarene Old Folk Home in Urizura.

Korea. The first churches of Christ were planted in Korea by Koreans from the Cunningham direct-support mission in Japan. The twelve congregations were wiped out in World War II and the Korean War. The present work in Korea owes its origin to the John Chases who established seven churches with some eight hundred members. The Harold Taylors later supervised a conservation program which strengthened the churches and set up schools and orphanages. There are approximately twelve hundred members. The work centers in Seoul.

Several churches of native origin do not use instrumental music in worship and receive support from Rightist churches in America. They report twenty-one congregations and eleven hundred Christians.

Nepal. The U.C.M.S. co-operates in the United Mission where seven "meeting places" are reported. A hospital and three schools with 140 students are maintained here.

New Hebrides. The Australian churches sent missionaries to the islands resulting in some fifty native churches with a membership of twelve or fifteen hundred. Cordial relations are maintained with the Australian brotherhood.

New Zealand. Twenty-nine years after the first Christian worship service was held on New Zealand soil, a church of Christ was organized at Nelson in November, 1843, by Thomas Jackson, an ardent Disciple from Glasgow, Scotland. He had found no one of like faith upon his arrival "down under" and proceeded to set up "a congregation according to the Apostolic order" in his own house.

When Maori persecutions and economic depression drove many members of the Nelson church to seek new homes, Thomas Magarey went to Adelaide, where he helped to organize the first church in Australia in 1845. Others went to Auckland, now one of the largest cities in the Dominion of New Zealand, and founded the work there at about the same date.

Brethren from Scotland founded the church at Dunedin in 1858. From this mother body came several suburban congregations. The same year services began in Ivercargill, the farthest south of any Christian church in the world. Wanganui, Christchurch, Wellington (the capital city), Hokitika, and Greymouth followed. Now more than fifty churches in New Zealand claim almost five thousand members.

Co-operation developed at first along sectional lines—Auckland, Middle District, and South Island. In 1901, the first Dominion Conference was held. Meetings are held every five years. Churches are admitted to the Conference by its vote in open session. Vote is by delegates chosen by the churches, but large numbers of nondelegates attend and take part in discussions. Conference committees, headed by the Conference Executive Committee, serve the churches in various functional areas. Decisions of the Conference are felt to be morally binding on the churches participating, but the body has no legislative authority. Prior to the meetings of the Conference, matters of special importance are submitted to the congregations for discussion.

Before 1927, most of the ministers of New Zealand churches were trained in the United States and Australia, but in that year a Dominion College was set up in Dunedin. A. L. Haddon was called from Sydney to be the first principal, and held that position until his death in late 1961.

A monthly magazine, the *New Zealand Christian,* was started in 1920 by resolution of the Conference. A Department of Religious Education issues the *Religious Education Quarterly* which serves the Bible schools, and *Quest,* for the youth work of the churches. In 1946, the Preachers' Provident Fund created a pension plan. A Church Extension and Property Trust Board, constituted under an act of Parliament, is trustee for funds and property of the churches. Conference churches co-operate in the National Council of Churches in New Zealand.

The Church of Christ reports five missionaries, six congregations, and eighty-five members.

Philippine Islands. In 1901 the W. H. Hannas and the Hermon P. Williamses organized a church of thirty members in Manila. This was the beginning of the Philippine Christian Mission. Previous chapters have recounted the history of the churches in the islands. Today 95 churches with twelve hundred preachings points are under the U.C.M.S. leadership with 14,500 members. All co-operate with the "United Church of Christ."

Direct-support churches (dating from 1926) number 102 in Luzon, Mindoro, Negros, and Mindanao, with twelve thousand members co-operating with the Philippine Mission Churches of Christ. Manila Bible Seminary and schools at Aparri, Davao, and Cebu, train the ministry. Independent churches of the New Testament pattern are to be found in twenty provinces and many islands. The total strength of these brethren is well over fifteen thousand.

Church of Christ missionaries entered the Philippines in 1948 with the famous mountain resort of Baguio as the center of operations. One hundred thirty-six churches are now reported in the islands, with more than five thousand members.

Ryukyu Islands. In 1945 Harland Woodruff set up the first congregation after the New Testament pattern in Nago on the island of Okinawa. Soon after, the Okinawa Bible Seminary began to train Christian workers with a goal of providing Bible teaching in every village in Okinawa within twenty years. Nakijin was the next center to be developed. By 1956 the Christians numbered more than one thousand, with twenty-six churches and some sixty-five preaching and teaching points. The work is largely indigenous with native leadership and continues to grow throughout the islands.

Thailand. British church missionaries came over the Burma border to Thailand in 1902, making contact with the Mons, and finally setting up mission headquarters at Nakon Pathom, about thirty-five miles from Bangkok. Several mission churches, with a membership of about five hundred are in this area. The distinguished services of Robert Halliday were lost in 1922, when he returned to Burma to translate the whole Bible into Mon (or Talaing) and prepare the first Mon dictionary.

The Callaways opened the first American direct-support mission in Chiengkam, five hundred miles north of Bangkok, in 1950. From this center, evangelizing missions are carried on among various tribes. In 1952, the first Yao Christian village was founded. Nan province has been entered, with native workers in several tribes maintaining small churches.

Under the direction of Donald A. McGavran, a U.C.M.S. survey of the missionary situation in Thailand resulted in a work being undertaken in the Sam Yek area in co-operation with the union "Church of Christ in Thailand." Two churches and six preaching points reach some 250 members.

World Convention

The sun never sets on the people called Disciples of Christ and their churches "after the New Testament pattern." Their testimony for Biblical faith and their dedication to the task of restoring the apostolic church "in doctrine, ordinances, and life" continue to make an ever-growing impact on the world.

World Convention. A growing vision of world fellowship including all elements in the Restoration movement eventuated in the organization of the World Convention of Churches of Christ in 1930. Jesse M. Bader led in preparing the way for this development in the co-operative life of the brotherhood. Through his visits to the churches in Great Britain in 1926, and to Australia and New Zealand in 1927, the vision began to take shape. In October, 1930, some nine thousand brethren assembled in Washington, D. C., for the first Assembly of the World Convention.

The gathering is held every five years. The second World Convention met in Leicester, England, in 1935. The third scheduled for Toronto, Canada, in 1940 was postponed because of World War II and not held until August, 1947, in Buffalo, New York. Melbourne, Australia, entertained the Assembly in 1952; Toronto, Canada, in 1955; and Edinburgh, Scotland, in 1960. The 1965 Assembly is scheduled to be held in Puerto Rico.

The World Convention "serves as an agency for the gathering and channeling of news about the churches; for the exchange of preachers, teachers and fraternal delegates; for the stimulation (not administration) of evangelism, stewardship, Christian education and missions among the churches throughout the world; and for the safeguarding and maintenance of full religious liberty everywhere." In Melbourne, the Assembly authorized a Study Program. During the time from Melbourne to Toronto six subjects were studied by twenty-five committees located in fourteen countries. These themes were discussed in group meetings at Toronto. From Toronto to Edinburgh, there were thirty-four committees working in nineteen lands on these same subjects and after open "Study Teas" at Edinburgh the results were crystallized into manuscripts to appear in book form for distribution and study in the churches.

Little effort has been made to enlist the ministers and churches of the Center and Right of the Restoration movement in this over-all voluntary gathering, but in its broad concept it offers a possible medium through which mutual recognition and fellowship might eventually be attained. At present the World Convention is looked upon by many as one of the "confessional groups" related to the World Council of Churches and meeting every five years. The others are the Methodist, the Baptist, Congregationalist, Lutheran, Presbyterian, and Reformed, and Anglican world conventions. The presidents and general secretaries of these bodies meet annually in an unofficial conference to discuss common problems, purposes, and concerns. The World Convention of Churches of Christ is not made up of national assemblies of the various nations but is a convention of brethren located in forty nations who have a common history and common goals. In this respect it differs from the others and is sufficiently "free church" in nature to appeal to all elements of the Restoration movement. Any desire to become such a comprehensive body has yet to be implemented.

While accurate figures are not available in several areas of this world-wide fellowship, a conservative estimate of the total membership would approach five million. If this vast army could present a united testimony for the gospel and the principles enunciated in the *Declaration and Address* it would have a mighty impact on the Ecumenical movement around the world.

BIBLIOGRAPHY: Chapter 21

Buckner, George Walker, editor, *World Call* (1955-59).
Butchart, Reuben, *The Disciples of Christ in Canada Since 1830.*
Butler, Burris, and Edwin V. Hayden, editors, *Christian Standard* (1955-59).
Cartwright, Lin D., and Howard E. Short, editors, *The Christian-Evangelist* (1955-59).
Goodpasture, B. C., editor, *Gospel Advocate* (1955-59).
Hudson, John Allen, *The Church in Great Britain.*
McFarland, Harrold, editor, *Horizons* (1955-59).
Maston, Aaron Burr, *Jubilee Pictorial History of Churches of Christ in Australia.*
Nichols, James W., *Christian Chronicle* (1955-59).
Prokhanoff, Ivan S., *In the Cauldron of Russia, 1869-1933.*
Stephenson, A. W., *One Hundred Years, Churches of Christ in Australia.*
Waggoner, W. L., editor, *World Vision* (1955-59).
Watters, A. C., *History of the British Churches of Christ.*

Chapter 22

Modern Disciples and Christian Unity

THE deep concern of the Disciples for Christian unity quite naturally resulted in a wide variety of serious efforts to achieve this high ideal of the Restoration movement. In preceding chapters, reference was made to a number of these adventures involving overtures to other communions and the preservation of unity within the brotherhood. This chapter proposes to deal with major endeavors since the crucial centennial year of 1909.

Almost immediately after the Pittsburgh convention, a widespread interest in Christian unity developed in all the major Protestant denominations. The Episcopalians in their General Convention in Cincinnati (1910) appointed a Commission on Christian Union. At approximately the same time, the Congregationalists set up a Committee on Comity, Federation, and Unity, in the National Council at Boston. A short time later, the Presbyterian Church in America appointed a Committee on Church Co-operation and Union. There was no collaboration in these actions. It seemed that the Spirit of God was moving. In this atmosphere and in the same year at the Topeka convention, the Disciples appointed a Commission on Christian Union.

Peter Ainslee, minister of Christian Temple, Baltimore, always an ardent crusader for unity, was president of the Topeka convention. He called a mass meeting to consider plans for more effective promotion of unity, and the following men were selected as members of the resulting Commission: Peter Ainslee, A. C. Smither, F. W. Burnham, E. M. Bowman, Hill M. Bell, W. T. Moore, M. M. Davis, J. H. Garrison, and I. J. Spencer. The number was increased to twenty-five the following year. Ainslee was a confirmed liberal, practiced open membership in his church, and had abandoned the Restoration plea for unity. His irenic spirit had led him into many compromising situations with the result that Centrists and some Leftists in the brotherhood were wary of his leadership in this new adventure. As a result, the Commission was largely Peter Ainslee. Throughout its history it has reflected his liberal views. In 1914 it was divorced from the convention and its name was changed to the Association for the Promotion of Christian Unity. Its headquarters were moved to Ainslee's church in Baltimore, and the Association was incorporated under the laws of the state of Maryland. In 1918, H. C. Armstrong, a close friend of Ainslee, was made the Commission's executive secretary. A magazine, *The Christian Union Quarterly*, expounded Ainslee's views. Ainslee continued in the presidency until 1925, when he retired under brotherhood-wide pressures. His broad views were so foreign to the spirit of the Restoration movement at that time, that he was considered disqualified to represent the Disciples and to speak for them in interchurch councils.

Nevertheless, this personally lovable Virginia gentleman won the hearts of thousands of persons, and the impact of his aggressive advocacy of Christian union had much to do with the initiatory moves leading to the modern Ecumenical movement. The interdenominational World Missionary Conference, in Edinburgh in 1910, did not include many representatives of the Disciples, despite the fact that Archibald McLean was one of the greatest missionary statesmen of the time. Indeed, Disciples of Christ were almost unknown in interchurch councils. Ainslee proceeded to change all this.

In 1911, his Commission sponsored a conference of Congregationalists, Disciples, Episcopalians, and Presbyterians in New York City to create individual friendships with denominational leaders. This personal approach was a cherished Ainslee technique. In 1928, he promoted a conference in Baltimore which drew 650 persons from twenty-five different denominations including Catholics, Universalists, and Unitarians. This was perhaps the first time in history that Romanists and Unitarians sat as equals in conversations in the interest of Christian unity. There were addresses on the Federal Council of Churches, the Stockholm conference of 1925, and the Lausanne conference of 1927, besides others on unity in worship, in education, in missions, and in social welfare, concluding with an address on "the sacrament of unity" and the celebration of the Lord's Supper. Ainslee was restive under the restrictions imposed by the official heads of participating churches in great historic world ecumenical conferences and used the Baltimore meeting to develop the short-lived Christian Unity League, composed of fully committed churchmen of distinction who were expected to infiltrate denominational structures with unity propaganda and move from the inside to weaken the walls of separation that had arisen over several centuries.

The League was largely Ainslee, and a study of its principles and methods are pertinent to developments in the field of Christian unity among the Disciples. The League Pact emphasized Ainslee's favorite text: "All Christians are equal before God." It contained three sections: (1) an affirmation of belief in a united Christendom; (2) a resolution to make practice square with the principle of the equality of all Christians before God; and (3) a pledge of brotherhood with all Christians. In its final form the Pact read:

We, Christians of various churches, believing that only in a cooperative and united Christendom can the world be Christianized, deplore a divided Christendom as being opposed to the spirit of Christ and the needs of the world. We, therefore, desire to express our sympathetic interest in and prayerful attitude toward all conferences, small and large, that are looking toward reconciliation of the divided Church of Christ.

We acknowledge the equality of all Christians before God and propose to follow this principle, as far as possible, in all our spiritual fellowships. We will strive to bring the laws and practices of our several communions into conformity with this principle, so that no Christian shall be denied membership in any of our churches, nor the privilege of participation in the observance of the Lord's Supper, and that no Christian minister shall be denied the freedom of our pulpits by reason of different forms of ordination.

We pledge, irrespective of denominational barriers, to be brethren one to another in the name of Jesus Christ, our Lord and Savior, whose we are and whom we serve.

It was not long before this document became the means of wrecking the League. Its very broadness rendered it impractical in the eyes of denominational leaders. At the 1929 conference in St. George's Protestant Episcopal Church in New York City, upon the insistence of the Bishop of New York, the Communion service was prohibited in the sanctuary because a Presbyterian minister was to act as celebrant, assisted by other non-Episcopal clerics. The service had to be transferred to the chapel of Union Theological Seminary. Other incidents of similar nature placed participating members under criticism of ecclesiastical superiors, forcing them to withdraw. Disciples, except for a few extreme liberals, were noticeable by their absence.

Ahead of his time, by the standards of modern ecumenicity, Ainslee has been dubbed one of the great "ecumenical saints." Liberal Disciples hail him as the father of Christian unity, superseding all who preceded him in the Restoration movement. His deviations from the path toward unity marked out by Thomas and Alexander Campbell are now widely accepted by Leftists in Discipledom as the new liberal "fundamentalism" in this field. After 1924, the *Christian Unity Quarterly* was financed separately from the Association. After Ainslee's death in 1934, it continued under different ownership and developed into *Christendom* (edited by Charles Clayton Morrison), the forerunner of the present *Ecumenical Review* of the World Council of Churches.

After Edinburgh (1910), Disciples were represented in all the great gatherings looking toward Christian unity at the world level. It could no longer be said that this people was not known or not given recognition in the counsels of the great. At Stockholm, Oxford, Lausanne, Edinburgh (1937), Jerusalem, and Madras, both liberals and conservatives were members of the Disciples' delegations. Their representation was as official as it could be, considering the fact that the International Convention was a purely voluntary co-operation. Disciples were given places on committees and in study groups dealing with such matters as the nature of the church and "faith and order" with a view to better understanding among the denominations.

Disciples now received high recognition in the Federal Council of Churches. When Edgar DeWitt Jones was elected to the presidency, Jesse M. Bader was given the important post of Secretary of Evangelism. Alva W. Taylor had much to do with the development of its social views. Disciples had representation on all important commissions and committees. In the International Council of Religious Education, the F.C.C.'s adjunct in the Sunday-school field, liberal Disciples furnished distinguished leadership. W. C. Bower led in the abandonment of traditional commitment to Bible-based curriculum and in the introduction of the pupil-centered principles of "progressive education." Roy G. Ross served capably as I.C.R.E. executive secretary and guided the Council into the merger with other agencies to form the National Council of Churches of Christ in the United States of America. Robert M. Hopkins became executive secretary of the World Council of Christian Education and Sunday School Association.

The Federal Council was ardently supported by International Convention officialdom but was never widely accepted by the brotherhood at large. In its Cleveland convention in 1942, Metropolitan Antony Bashir of the Syrian Antiochan Archdiocese of New York and North America conducted a worship service in which he invoked the intercessions of "our all-immaculate Theotokos and ever-Virgin Mary." Protestant distinctives were rapidly being compromised or discarded. The Council's approach to social issues were essentially humanistic. In 1935 United States Naval Intelligence branded it as "a large radical, pacifist organization." *Newsweek* magazine in 1941 called the Council "a virtual monopoly" in American Protestantism. Losses in national prestige and in popular acceptance within its own constituent denominations pressured its leaders into merger with seven other interchurch bodies to form the more effective National Council of Churches of Christ in the U.S.A. of 1950.

Despite opposition, International Convention leadership actively participated in the merger proceedings and gained almost unanimous approval of the Convention to make the Disciples of Christ a constituent denomination. Three disciples were almost immediately given positions of high authority. Roy G. Ross was made executive secretary of the N.C.C.; Mrs. James D. Wyker was named chairman of the United Church Women; and Raymond F. McLain became director of the Commission on Christian Higher Education. Scores of Disciples were given positions of importance in divisions, departments, commissions, and committees. J. Irwin Miller, of Columbus, Indiana, became the first layman president of the N.C.C. in 1961.

In 1948, the World Council of Churches was organized in Amsterdam, Holland. The International Convention likewise committed the Disciples to membership in this body. In the following chapter, further consideration will be given to the significance of this development.

Advocates of co-operation with the National and World Councils contend that they are composed of churches which accept Christ as Lord and Saviour, and believe in "one Lord, one faith, one baptism, one God

348

and Father of all," and therefore Christians of different denominations ought not to ignore or fight one another. They must try to share their unity in Christ by co-operating in witness and service. They say that the Councils are a working fellowship of churches—not a centralized ecclesiastical authority apart from the churches constituting them.

Answering the critics of the Councils, their advocates insist that they have no "superchurch" characteristics, since they cannot legislate for their member churches nor act for them unless permitted to do so. The Councils do not seek to enforce conformity or uniformity, do not negotiate mergers of churches, do not have any one theology of the nature of the church or plan for the church's unity. The Councils, they say, are merely fellowships of churches in which Christian solidarity is practiced, so that churches mutually aid each other; in which churches unite in meeting human needs; in which common witness is rendered to the lordship of Christ over the world and the church; in which the churches enter into serious discussion about their differences in creed, practical emphases, message, ministry, church government, and missionary task in the world; and in which a clear stand is taken for the unity and renewal of the church of Christ.

A majority of the larger American denominations are constituent members of the National and World Councils of Churches, but nearly twenty-five million Protestants have refused to join.

In 1943 another interchurch co-operative movement loomed on the horizon. It had its origins among irenic evangelical Protestants who were convinced that the National Council of Churches was not representative of the true Protestant spirit.

Their objections to the Council might be stated in ten propositions: (1) The Council steadfastly refused to adopt as a basis of fellowship the hard core of generally accepted Biblical Christian doctrine. (2) It admitted into its membership a host of liberals who denied these doctrines and gave them preferred status in Council leadership. (3) It had created an ecclesiastical oligarchy which might easily develop into a superchurch. (4) Non-Council churches were forced to take protective measures to insure unfettered liberty in preaching the gospel. (5) It refused to state its acceptance of the Bible as the authoritative Word of God. (6) It considered man's need and not God's grace as motivation for social action and the amelioration of the social order as of greater concern than the salvation of souls. (7) It seriously threatened a distinctly evangelistic thrust in foreign missionary work. (8) It encouraged social revolution to displace capitalism and condoned communism. (9) Its relations with the Eastern Orthodox Catholic churches and its general attitude toward Roman Catholicism threatened to weaken its Protestant testimony. (10) It deliberately omitted to include provisions for the preservation and perpetuation of all the values and liberties inherent in Protestantism.

In the preliminary conferences at St. Louis in 1942, and in the constitutional convention at Chicago in 1943, a number of Disciples were present and participated in the development of the National Association of Evangelicals, which has now grown to a constituency of some forty denominations and ten million members. Centrist ministers and churches were attracted to the N.A.E. because of its strong Biblical position and its similarity to the World Evangelical Alliance which Alexander Campbell had so generously endorsed. Among the early leaders of the Association was James D. Murch who was in 1945 appointed editor of its official organ, *United Evangelical Action.* For fourteen years he edited this journal which became in many ways in that day "the voice of evangelical Christianity in America." Murch was active in the organization and served as president of the National Religious Broadcasters, which included in its membership 150 of the major evangelical radio and television broadcasters in America; of the National Sunday School Association; of the Evangelical Press Association; and served in other evangelical enterprises. He is the author of the definitive history of the N.A.E., *Co-operation Without Compromise,* which has become the standard reference work on the Association.

The N.A.E. has never been accorded the slightest recognition by the International Convention. Its acceptance by numerous Centrist ministers and churches has been on a purely voluntary basis. In this same quarter there has been strong opposition.

James G. Van Buren in the *Christian Standard* (October 6, 1951) took a strong stand against co-operation with the N.A.E. He (1) identified the organization with "fundamentalism," (2) deplored its "creedal basis" for membership, (3) its emphasis on the Bible as "the only infallible Word of God," (4) its superchurch potentialities, and (5) indicated that membership in the N.A.E. automatically condoned denominationalism.

Murch, in his rebuttal, contended that the N.A.E. (1) was "evangelical" and not committed to narrow "fundamentalist" views; (2) was neither a church nor council of churches with a creedal test of fellowship, but required its members for purposes of organizational solidarity to sign a statement of belief; (3) held the same view of the Scriptures as that held by the Campbells; (4) was a service organization; and (5) had many members from undenominational churches and organizations.

The exchange was inconclusive and, although there have been constant additions to N.A.E. ranks from Christian churches and churches of Christ, the majority of Centrists remain unaffiliated with any interchurch body.

The Christian's Hour Broadcasting Association is a member of the N.A.E.'s National Religious Broadcasters, and several independent Bible colleges are members of the Accrediting Association of Bible Colleges. Large numbers of Centrist churches have representatives in the conventions of the National Sunday School Association.

In 1951, at Woudschoten, Holland, the N.A.E. joined with the World Evangelical Alliance (British organization), to form the World Evangelical Fellowship. It now has organizations in many lands bringing evangelicals throughout the world into a new sense of solidarity and co-operative endeavor.

In this period of ecumenical concern, Disciples made specific overtures for union to American (Northern) Baptists and Congregationalists.

350

In 1929 a joint report of two committees, Baptists and Disciples, proposed to the Northern Baptist Convention in Denver that a wide range of united activities be developed in the fields of missions, education, and evangelism. Accusations of Disciple commitment to the doctrine of "baptismal regeneration" killed the proposal. In 1946, the International Convention and the Northern Baptist Convention referred a similar plan to a standing joint committee on fraternal relations, with the added proposal of "ultimate union." Conferences were held in 1947 and 1948, and fraternization continued. The American Baptist Publication Society and the Christian Board of Publication co-operate in publishing *The Secret Place,* a guide for daily devotions, and textbooks in the field of religious education.

During the period in which so-called "official" negotiations were being carried on, the Northern Baptists were losing hundreds of churches and thousands of members to the Southern Baptists, the General Association of Regular Baptist Churches, and the Conservative Baptist Association of America. In these centrist Baptist bodies, and among brethren of like mind in the Northern Baptist Convention, there were individual pastors who were interested in rapprochement with Centrist Disciples. P. H. Welshimer and James D. Murch carried on a rather extensive correspondence with such men. The problem of "baptismal regeneration" again appeared as the chief barrier to agreement and co-operation. In correspondence with Gabriel R. Guedj, then pastor of the famed Brooklyn Temple, Murch stated the generally held Disciples' view as follows:

> Conservative Disciples believe the Bible teaches that salvation is basically by grace through faith in the atoning work of Christ. Faith, however, must be demonstrated (James 2:17; I John 5:2, 3). Christ commanded baptism (Matthew 28:18-20) and was himself baptized to fulfill all righteousness. Peter, by the Holy Spirit, commanded baptism on the Day of Pentecost (Acts 2:38). In this sense Disciples believe that baptism is essential to salvation. The Bible teaches (I John 2:3-6) that refusal to obey a command of Christ is a demonstration of a lack of saving faith. The unimmersed are therefore denied membership in local churches of Christ. Without too much concern for systematic theology Disciples accept such Scripture texts as the following as buttressing their belief in the essentiality of baptism to salvation: Romans 6:3, 4; Mark 16:15, 16; I Peter 3:21; Galatians 3:27. They would object to any such view as expressed by Dr. Strong in his *Systematic Theology:* "[Baptism] is the appointed sign but never the condition of forgiveness of sins."

A number of conservative Baptists agreed that this statement could well be a basis for friendly discussions and that such a position should not necessarily preclude eventual unity. Closer relationships between these groups wait on aggressive leadership deeply concerned for the unity of the people of God.

In 1954 the Association for the Promotion of Christian Unity voted to change its name and its character. Since that time it is known as the Council on Christian Unity and affects an official character in the International Convention enabling it to represent the Disciples in the counsels of the National and World Councils of Churches. Its purpose, as stated in its constitution, is:

To watch for every indication of Christian unity, to initiate steps for Christian union and to hasten the time of its fulfillment through intercessory prayer, friendly conferences, study of pertinent issues, publications and distribution of literature, prophetic witness to the will of Christ for his Church, and the practice of love, fellowship and mutual service among Christians. The Council shall give particular attention to the development and nurture of an ecumenical spirit among Disciples of Christ.

Membership in the C.C.U. is made up almost entirely of liberals. Its principles, policies, and programs are not at all representative of the views of majority elements in the Restoration movement.

The Restoration plea has been abandoned by the C.C.U. and the ecumenical scholars in Leftist colleges and seminaries. The St. Louis assembly of the International Convention (1958) was chosen as the launching ground for a bold new ecumenical drive. Alfred T. DeGroot, in a series of lectures in Disciple history, attacked the Restoration concept of Christian unity. He caricatured it by associating it with restoration movements in church history like Shakerism and Skoptism, and ridiculed all efforts at discovering apostolic missionary methods, church polity, or terms of salvation as a pattern for modern practice. DeGroot rejected Biblical revelation and proposed a "democratic search for truth." Ronald E. Osborn, in the closing address of the Convention, declared, "It now seems clear that restorationism has been a misguided attempt at apostolicity" and insisted that "as we Disciples face the future there is nothing we can do of greater ecumenical significance than to develop a rational churchly structure." In both addresses it was strongly intimated that the frank acceptance of denominational status was essential to effective participation in the development of the "Coming Great Church" and that Christian unity was to be achieved by the union of denominations on an institutional basis. This appeared to involve the acceptance of open membership and other non-Biblical practices to be found in the traditional ecclesiastical structures of Christendom.

The views of liberal ecumenicists among Disciples are similar to those long advocated by Charles Clayton Morrison. In his book, *The Unfinished Reformation,* he takes an entire chapter to prove that the Restoration concept of Christian unity is "an illusion." In his chapter summary he says,

That the Christian faith requires the restoration of the details of the primitive church is a belief without any foundation either in the spirit or the letter of the New Testament. Those denominations which imagine they have restored it have only created a stereotype composed of a few arbitrarily selected features of the biblical pattern and omitted other far more important features . . . The restorationist heresy has diverted the Christian mind from the path of realism into a blind alley of fantasy. The church of the New Testament was the infant church; Protestantism should be the church grown up.

But liberal Disciples do not stop at merely rejecting the Restoration plea; they go on to deny that the New Testament is in any distinctive and ultimate sense the Word of God and authoritative and normative in faith and practice. They say there can be no unity of God's people as long as the Bible is "given a place beside Christ" in the constitution of the church. To use it as such would make it a divider rather than a uniter of modern-day Christians.

Biblical doctrines which form the vertebrate strength of the Christian religion are rejected. Disciple ecumenicists say that there must be no insistence upon any form of doctrine as essential to unity. God the Creator, divine fatherhood, the incarnation and deity of Christ, the atonement, the resurrection, sin, salvation, faith, repentance, confession, baptism, divine judgment, heaven and hell, and all other Biblical doctrines without which there can be no distinctively Christian church are said to be the product of human imagination and without divine authority.

Liberal Disciple ecumenicists have rejected congregational polity. They brand the freedom of the local church as the culminating "Protestant heresy," or "the sin of Protestantism." They say that it derives chiefly "from Protestant biblicism, and from an utterly unimaginative form of biblicism."

All Disciples of this school of thought have agreed that the International Convention, its agencies and state and local societies, should be "restructured" to achieve denominational status. Oliver Read Whitley in his award-winning book, *Trumpet Call of Reformation*, labors through 252 pages to prove that the Disciples of Christ are a sociological phenomenon produced and shaped by the social, economic, and cultural conditions which existed in America from 1809 to 1959. He plots their evolution from *movement* through *sect* to *denominational* status. He holds that in this evolutionary process Disciples lost their "distinctive witness" and *raison d'etre* but became a great people. He advises that they accept their denominational status, develop into a great ecclesiastical body, and join with other denominations which are congenial and have common social and cultural mores and needs, to discover practical ways to ecumenical achievement.

In place of the historic plea of the Disciples to "restore the New Testament church in doctrine, ordinances, and life" by an appeal to the Bible as the rule of faith and practice, this new generation of Disciple ecumenicists proposes an appeal to the authority of the church. Again Charles Clayton Morrison's view is accepted. In his Lyman Beecher Lectures at Yale (1939), he proposed that the church should rely on its own revelation. The true church, he insisted, is here now, always has been, and always will be. Throughout its long tradition, the church, not the Bible, has been the perfect expression of God's will and way, and as it continues to evolve it will produce truth and practice relevant to the day and generation in which it exists. This ecumenical thesis that the church itself is God's divine revelation is as old as Greek and Roman Catholicism.

Centrist Disciples hold that this view is in essence similar to the institutional view of the Hebrew community which sent Jesus Christ to His death on the cross. Christ rejected this view in His own ministry and

353

incurred the everlasting displeasure of that institution. They say that the Morrison idea, now largely held by liberal Disciples, is of a psychological piece with the divine imperialism of all great cultures. The church as God's divine revelation, relying on its subsidiary and supporting revelations, and on its own judgment of itself and its powers, was the basic reason why mankind has had periodically to emancipate itself from ecclesiastical tyranny for the sake of cultural progress, and why the true church has been forced to initiate reformatory and restoration movements to preserve its divine purpose and the Biblical faith. Centrists and Rightists in the Restoration movement, along with a very considerable number of Leftists, see the development of this strange doctrine as a convincing revelation of hierarchical ambition to create an unified ecclesiasticism with inherent tyrannical powers. They see it as an intimation of a subtle will to the creation of a monolithic church which could be as dangerous to true Christianity as the menace of Roman Catholicism.

Around 1950 liberal Disciples moved with Congregational Christian liberals to frame an overture to all those denominations which "recognize one another's ministries and sacraments" to send delegates to a common meeting place to consider the possibility of effecting a union of their churches. This eventuated in the Conference on Christian Union in Greenwich, Connecticut, December 4-11, 1949. As a result, a definite blueprint for union was presented at a second conference in Cincinnati, Ohio, in January, 1951. After a long debate, the plan for a new "United Church of Christ" was adopted. Communions participating beside Congregationalists and Disciples included representatives of the Evangelical and Reformed church, African Methodist Episcopal Zion, Colored Methodist Episcopal, Methodist, National Council of Community Churches, and the Presbyterian Church in the United States. In its basic form, this "Greenwich Plan" became the blueprint for the merger of the Congregational Christian churches and the Evangelical and Reformed church in 1957, to form the United Church of Christ.

In 1957 the International Convention of Disciples of Christ authorized the appointment of a commission to explore the possibilities of joining the United Church of Christ. Adventures in co-operation are already bringing the two bodies together: establishment of union churches, joint administration of student work, exchanges of pulpits, and joint undertakings in higher education, missions, and theological study. While the Greenwich plan was officially "put in moth balls" in 1959, it now has practical realization in the United Church of Christ. Many observers believe that this new denomination is designed to bring together all "free churches" as a first step toward reorientation and amalgamation in the "Coming Great Church."

Under this plan, local churches may be made up of members of all denominations. Doctrinal and denominational loyalties—if any—are considered secondary to the larger ecumenical church, although subject to guidance from some central authoritative body. The program of the local church will be the program of the United church and its doctrine,

354

if any, will be the doctrine generally accepted by the ecumenical church. The pastor of the church will consider himself the local representative of the larger ecumenical church and be prepared to serve in whatever sector of the United church he may be assigned. In due time, all local churches will be subject to merger or relocation until there is, in the judgment of the proper authorities, adequate coverage of a given community, without overlapping. The territory of a local church may be reduced or enlarged. The ultimate relationship of the United church and its local congregations with the "Coming Great Church" is not clearly spelled out but there is emphasis on "One Church for One World."

This approach to unity being propagandized by the Council on Christian Unity is only one of two contrasting views held by Disciples. The view which accords with the "historic plea" of the Disciples and which is held by the great majority of Disciples is set forth by P. H. Welshimer, outstanding Centrist leader, writing in the *Christian Standard* in 1927:

> So long as the people have the same creed—which is Christ—recognize the inspiration of the Scriptures, take Christ as their authority and the Scriptures as the Revelation of that authority, adhere to the New Testament ordinances, and make Christians in the New Testament way, they will be united. . . .
> [Loyal Disciples] are a thousand times more concerned with restoring the church of the New Testament in the whole earth than they are about Christian unity, for when the church of the New Testament obtains everywhere, automatically the desired union will be present.

There is, however, a growing concern on the part of many Centrists that more aggressive and effective measures be taken to present the Restoration plea to the Christian world. Whether this can be done through media of the National and World Councils of Churches or whether through other means of communication remains in doubt.

Any confrontation of the whole Christian community with the Restoration idea by the Disciples, however, is impaired by lack of unity within their own ranks. Internal unity is, therefore, a matter of primary concern. The Council on Christian Unity has no program in this field, but a number of independent movements are developing. Wichita, Kansas, was the scene of an important Consultation on Internal Unity of Christian Churches at Friends University, June 2 and 3, 1959. Participants represented Leftist and Centrist groups, and they discussed in good spirit many of the problems that have tended to divide the brotherhood.

They decided to continue the Consultations, and meetings followed at Broadway Christian Church, Wichita, in 1960; at Camp Redlands, Stillwater, Oklahoma, in 1961, preparatory to the Third Consultation at the Wheeling Avenue Christian Church, Tulsa, in 1962. Similar sessions, not part of the formal Consultations, have been held in Owosso, Michigan, Los Angeles, California, and other cities.

Among those who have participated are Jesse M. Bader, William

Blakemore, Dyre Campbell, James B. Carr, Ting R. Champie, A. T. DeGroot, Stephen J. England, A. Dale Fiers, Robert O. Fife, Lester H. Ford, John Greenlee, Charles R. Gresham, Clifford Hauxwell, Edwin V. Hayden, W. Carl Ketcherside, Leslie L. Kingsbury, W. F. Lown, W. L. McEver, Donald McGavran, R. G. Martin, Walter H. Moore, James D. Murch, Park H. Netting, George Earle Owen, Tom O. Parish, Woodrow Phillips, Harry Poll, Wayne Reinhardt, Lester Rickman, Howard E. Short, Floyd E. Strater, Lloyd Taylor, C. K. Thomas, Fred P. Thompson, Jr., Robert Tobias, and Dean E. Walker.

Many practical problems are receiving prayerful consideration in these conferences on internal unity. There is a mood of antagonism and hostility among both "independent" and "co-operative" Disciples which needs to be superseded by the spirit of Christ. Brethren have a tendency to indulge in sweeping generalizations. "Independents" are prone to reason that since some "co-operative" churches practice open membership, therefore all such churches practice open membership. "Co-operative" brethren brand all "independents" as nonco-operative and isolationist, because they know certain "independents" who are. In this pattern of "black and white" thinking, members of each group think of themselves as faultless, and brand the others as corrupt and apostate. Beyond this mood of suspicion, the conferees in these unity meetings are facing genuine issues which tend to divide. These appear to be (1) theological liberalism, (2) the attempts to "restructure" the brotherhood along denominational lines, (3) the abandonment of the Restoration plea, (4) the making of agency support a test of fellowship.

Centrists, who have the irenic spirit of their forebears in the faith, feel as did archconservative J. W. McGarvey when he wrote in his commentary on Romans 14:3:

> In modern times controversy over meat sacrificed to idols is unknown, but the principles still apply to instrumental music, missionary societies, etc. Such matters of indifference are not to be injected into terms of salvation, or set up as tests of fellowship. As to them there is to be neither contempt on the one part nor judgment on the other.

Other Centrists and Leftists hold to the views expressed in the *Christian-Evangelist* (February 13, 1957):

> It would seem that all are included in [the brotherhood] who have accepted the Lordship of Jesus Christ and possess a brotherly spirit.
> Since it is a basic term with universal connotations, it runs beneath all types of organization among us. The support, or lack of support of agencies, methods of doing the work of the Lord, theological differences or practices cannot affect it. It is a mood and a spirit and travels only in the realm of the spirit.
> There must be room within it for all shades of honest opinion among us. It should be all-inclusive, as broad as the Kingdom of God and as wide as the gates of heaven.
> If you are a member of "the brotherhood" according to Disciple thought and practice, there is no one who can read you out of it. However, it would

seem reasonable that if one is to remain in "the brotherhood" one must show a brotherly attitude toward others in it. . . .

In 1959, the campus of Southeastern Christian College, at Winchester, Kentucky, provided the setting for a meeting between Centrist and Rightist ministers and elders looking toward better understanding and closer fellowship. W. Carl Ketcherside, editor of *Mission Messenger,* has taken the initiative in promoting several joint meetings of Rightist and Centrist brethren, which have helped to create much good will. Ketcherside sees the problem of division to be primarily "the factional spirit." He says,

[There] were innovations and it is evident that they were without scriptural warrant. But there is a difference between those things and *the division* which resulted from agitation of them. The factional spirit is sinful. The party spirit is a work of the flesh. To oppose evil from a factional standpoint is as wrong as to uphold evil from any standpoint. It is not opposition to evil but the factional spirit which is wrong. It is subversive of the divine government to create a party to oppose wrong. This is a species of doing evil with the hope that good may come.

. . . .

The restoration movement today is splintered into more than two dozen antagonistic parties. These have been created by application of the philosophy that was adopted by our fathers three-quarters of a century ago. Since the cleavage resulting from introduction of the instrument, those opposed to its use have averaged four partisan divisions for every decade of their separate existence.

This is not all. Other divisions must follow in the future. Every time a truth is discovered, every time honest investigation forces a change of mind, there will be another division. This philosophy bars the door to further scriptural research, makes real unbiased study a crime, and places a premium on mediocrity. It throws a dam across the channel of thought, freezes the acquisition of knowledge, and constitutes an unwritten creed. It makes blind conformity a blessing and enthrones orthodoxy as the ideal. If a system, like a tree, is known by its fruits, we should eliminate this one immediately (*Mission Messenger,* February, 1962, pp. 5, 6).

It is in an irenic spirit that conferences on internal unity are being held and that the divisive issues are being frankly considered. The efforts of these conferees are being reflected in pulpit exchanges, united evangelistic crusades, and co-operative activities among laymen of the churches. Ministers and congregations that have not had fellowship with one another for years are now rejoicing in new-found unity of belief and practice. Many of the barriers that have been built up through the years have been of secondary importance largely in the field of opinion and method. Adventuring on the principle, "In faith, unity; in opinions, liberty; and in all things, Christian love," real progress is being made toward a larger internal unity involving Left, Center, and Right. This sort of grassroots movement raised up by the promptings of the Holy Spirit can be more effective than carefully planned and organized strategy.

The Restoration movement which began with the realization of the principle that "the church of Christ on earth is essentially, intentionally and constitutionally one" is growingly conscious of the necessity for a re-examination of its own present situation in the light of that principle. This would involve a restudy of the spirit, the motives, and the precepts in Thomas Campbell's *Declaration and Address* and their further elaboration in the *Appendix;* the structures of ideas and practices that have been built upon the principles inherent in that document; and the relationship of the Restoration movement to the Ecumenical movement. And above all a fresh, uninhibited restudy of the Holy Scriptures to discover the emphasis which a Biblical people, 150 years after their birth, need to declare in a changing world.

BIBLIOGRAPHY: Chapter 22

Ainslee, Peter, editor, *The Christian Unity Quarterly* (1924-34).
Ainslee, Peter, *The Message of the Disciples for the Union of the Church*
Ainslee, Peter, *Towards Christian Unity.*
Ainslee, Peter, *Working With God.*
Bradshaw, Marion J., *Free Churches and Christian Unity*
England, Stephen J., *We Disciples.*
Gresham, Charles, editor, *Report of the 1959 (and 1960) Consultation on Internal Unity of the Christian Churches.*
Hutchinson, John A., *We Are Not Divided.*
Kershner, Frederick D., *How to Promote Christian Union.*
Morrison, Charles Clayton, *What Is Christianity?*
Morrison, Charles Clayton, *The Unfinished Reformation.*
Murch, James DeForest, *Co-operation Without Compromise.*
Murch, James DeForest, *The Growing Superchurch.*
Murch, James DeForest, *The Coming Great Church.*
National Council of Churches of Christ in the United States of America, *The National Council of Churches: What Is It?*
Sanford, E. B., *Origin and History of the Federal Council of Churches.*
Tobias, Robert, and Robert Heckard, editors, *Christian Unity Newsletter* (1957-59).
Tulga, Chester A., *The Case Against the National Council of Churches.*
Tulga, Chester A., *The Case Against the World Council of Churches.*
Walker, Dean E., *Adventuring for Christian Unity.*
Whitley Oliver Reed, *Trumpet Call of Reformation.*

Chapter 23

The Restoration Plea in
an Ecumenical Era: An Evaluation

THE future of the Disciples lies in an era of history in which Christendom will be chiefly concerned with Christian unity. The atmosphere is charged with ecumenicism—a concern for the development of one universal Christian church, "throughout the whole inhabited world." What might the Campbells have given to have lived in such an era!

The various churches of Christendom have in a sense been driven into a concern for Christian unity. Christians today live in a hostile world. They are beset by powerful forces of materialism, led by a rapidly expanding atheistic international communism. Less than one-third of the world's population is Christian, and Christianity is actually losing ground in its race to keep up its percentage in the rapidly increasing population figures. Christian leaders are beginning to realize that in this atomic space age, time may be running short for the human race and that Christendom can no longer afford the luxury of division. They sense the inadequacy of their traditional beliefs and practices conceived by men of another era. They yearn for some new doctrines or new techniques which will challenge the modern man. They are ready to abandon the past, to venture out of their temples and monasteries into the highways and byways and compel men. They are meeting the big social, political, and cultural questions head-on, but often with a sense of futility because they are ignorant of the divine answers to man's need. Under these crucial circumstances, the Roman church called an Ecumenical Council in 1962 and most other ecclesiastical establishments have joined in an Ecumenical movement in a quest for a united church strong enough to cope with the enemies of Christianity and to win the world to Jesus Christ.

The attitude of the Restoration movement toward the Ecumenical movement and the effectiveness with which the Restoration plea is communicated will determine our destiny. Disciples of Christ cannot ignore the evident moving of the Spirit of God to break down old denominational barriers, nor the spontaneous desire of millions of followers of Christ for a united church. While the World Council of Churches assumes the role and the nomen of the Ecumenical movement, it by no means represents all sectors of the church's life. There have been failures as well as successes in the Council's efforts, and its limitations are increasingly evident. It may or may not afford an ultimate basis for a "Coming Great Church" and the achievement of the final ideal goals of the Christian community. The Ecumenical movement is still in a formative period and susceptible to spiritual guidance and instruction. If the advocates of the Restoration plea refuse or fail to communicate the gospel, they will prove themselves unworthy of their heritage. William H. Whyte, in referring to the failure of business to communicate its "gospel" to America, quotes Dostoevsky: "If the people around you are spiteful and callous and will not hear you, fall down before them and beg their forgiveness; for in truth you are to blame for their not wanting to hear you." Disciples need to learn how to restate their message in terms of this new era, and master the techniques and discipline by which it may be communicated.

The "oldest ecumenical movement in America" needs, first of all, to familiarize itself with the modern Ecumenical movement. While the Disciples' 150 years of propaganda for Christian unity unquestionably contributed to and aided in the current adventure, the immediate motivation for it came from other sources. As it was previously indicated, there were three initiatory attempts which combined to create an interest in ecumenical advance. They represent three approaches to the problem. The first was the Edinburgh method of co-operation in evangelism and missions; the second, the Stockholm method of federation for Christian service and social action; and the third, the Lausanne method of rethinking diverse church doctrine and tradition with a view to organic church union. Edinburgh's World Missionary Movement (International Missionary Council), Stockholm's Life and Work Movement, and Lausanne's Faith and Order Movement all proved to be inadequate in themselves. The reasons for their failure cannot be delineated in this brief chapter. Suffice to say that their constituencies agreed to pool their resources and in view of the changing world situation create a new medium for ecumenical advance. In 1948 at Amsterdam the World Council of Churches came into being with "a new emphasis on the need of a rebirth or renewal of the Church . . . to serve God's purpose in this age." While enlisting great sectors of Protestantism and the Eastern Orthodox Catholic church, the World Council has thus far failed to enter the "promised land" of true Christian unity.

Spontaneous demonstrations of unity indicate that there is an increasing acceptance of the idea that "the church of Christ on earth is essentially, intentionally, and constitutionally one"; but many incidents in the World Council relations prove that there are great barriers to ultimate unity. Some progress has been made in the Division of Studies and the Ecumenical Institute, but the so-called "confessional fellowships" are being strengthened. One reason for this is the utter lack of conviction concerning any hard core of Christian doctrine and of any impelling motivation for

Christian crusade. The denominational families have strong traditional incentives to loyalty and action. They also have their internal problems of division. The ecumenical urge finds satisfaction in bringing about internal unity and renewed commitment to a common cause. The Anglican Lambeth Quadrilateral was founded in 1867; the Reformed-Presbyterian confessional group, in 1875; the International Congregational Council in 1891; the World Methodist Council in 1881; the Baptist World Alliance in 1905; the Lutheran World Federation in 1923; the World Convention of Churches of Christ in 1930; and other confessional groups which have grown in influence and power, at the same time, have served to slow down the progress of the Ecumenical movement as a whole.

The oldest of all these bodies, the Lambeth Conference, has an ecumenical testimony which it insists upon propagating as the ultimate answer to the dilemma of the World Council. Lambeth says there must be agreement on four points—the Holy Scriptures, the Apostles' and Nicene Creed, the two sacraments instituted by Christ (baptism and holy Communion) and an office recognized by all parts of the church, centered in the historic episcopate or apostolic succession. The pattern of unity recently adopted by the Church of South India, the scheme for the Church of Ceylon, the proposed constitution of the Church of North India and Pakistan, and similar proposals for Australia, New Zealand, and New Guinea, are all of the Lambeth pattern. Liberal elements in the World Council are rather enthusiastic about it. It fits into the concept of "the continuing Church of Christ" which is the sum total of the churches and whose pronouncements are considered to be of equal or superior authority to the Holy Scriptures.

The Lambeth pattern includes the acceptance of the Scriptures, but even Rome accepts the Bible as sacred, a dogma defined as the Constitution of the Catholic Faith at the Council of the Vatican in 1870. She also accepts tradition as a second source of revelation. Lambeth's concept is almost identical. It is not the doctrine of *sola scriptura* accepted by Protestantism. While holding that nothing in the church must be taught as dogma which is not grounded in Scriptures, the church alone has the right to say what the Scriptures admit or forbid. This understanding of Scripture is well stated by Geoffrey Fisher, former archbishop of Canterbury, when he says that church authority rests in the Holy Spirit who speaks to us in the Holy Scriptures, in the tradition of the church, and in the living experience of today. Lambeth's attitude toward the creeds is intimated in Anglican reticence regarding its own Thirty-nine Articles and its acceptance of the doctrinal content of the *Book of Common Prayer*. The administration of the sacraments is dependent upon the properly ordained clergy in the line of apostolic succession. The most thorny problem implicit in the Lambeth proposals is the historic episcopate which is not recognized by Rome nor by most of the Eastern Orthodox churches. Lutherans who believe in a sort of apostolic succession, insist that only the acceptance of the doctrine of the apostles qualifies the minister to administer the holy offices. All free churches look askance at the whole

Lambeth pattern as a poor imitation of Rome. Indeed, the World Council's palliation of Lambeth's infiltration of the so-called "younger churches" is causing many to be restive regarding the whole ecumenical adventure. Probably the majority of the churches composing the World Council believe that individual members of Christ's mystical body compose the true church and that this church is hidden to human eyes, *cruce tectum,* in this world and yet is of supreme reality, grounded as it is in the *sola fide*— the evangelical doctrine of the death, burial, and resurrection of our Lord. To accept any human hierarchical system in place of or as representing the revealed church of the crucified and risen Lord would to them be blasphemy. It is therefore evident that the Lambeth proposals will not completely prevail.

Liberal elements in the World Council are committed to the achievement of unity through compromise. They have experienced such radical changes in their own beliefs in the past fifty years that they are somewhat disillusioned as to the possibility of attaining unity through an acceptance of their views. They see denominational differences as sinful and believe they must be eliminated through a turn from theology to history, sociology, and ethics. Liberals see church differences as the result of social traditions, the basic cultural heritage of a people, as well as political and economic interest; not as the result of profound spiritual forces at work in the hearts of men and commitment to the commands of the gospel. This element in the leadership of the Council believes most member churches are far enough along in their historic development that they are beginning to recognize the strength of the secular world and are in the process of rethinking their beliefs in the modern social and cultural frame of reference. It is believed that the churches are ready to compromise their traditional beliefs to achieve a position of mobility, adaptivity, and universal acceptance.

Liberalism is ready for compromise in theology. The old classical liberalism is dead. The *Christian Century* was forced to admit its inadequacy in a devastating series of articles by liberalism's foremost advocate, Charles Clayton Morrison, June 7, 14, and 21, 1950. While the apparent thesis was liberalism's advance, Dr. Morrison admitted:

> First, that much of classical liberalism's thinking had been shallow, premature and, in a large measure, erroneous.
>
> Second, that early liberalism which caused such havoc in the religious world foreclosed its own case, crystallized prematurely before all the facts were in and reached conclusions which it came to hold dogmatically. While this type of liberalism is considered *passe,* it still exists as a monument to its utter failure.
>
> Third, that there is a new liberalism which rejects the conclusions of the old liberalism and that, therefore, the forces of liberalism are divided.
>
> Fourth, that the liberal tendency to give science the final word as to the nature of the universe and to shift religious interest from the cosmology of the Bible to the ethical teaching of Jesus is erroneous. It is now clear that the enduring substance and essence of Christianity is not to be found in its ethic but rather in the nature of the cosmos and the meaning of human existence.

Fifth, that liberalism was premature and unwarranted in humanizing the Bible as a whole and in regarding the idea of revelation as having no realistic foundation.

Sixth, that liberalism was wrong in conceiving of Christianity as the religion *of* Jesus in contrast with a religion *about* Jesus. Such a religion can be little more than Judaism carried to its highest ethical and universal expression.

Seventh, that liberalism has been forced by the findings of competent scholarship to abandon the view that the writings of Paul postdated the true literature of Christianity and that, therefore, his theology is an obscuration of essential Christianity as contained in the Synoptic Gospels.

Eighth, that liberalism was wrong in making its goal the "building of the Kingdom of God on earth" and in accepting the concept that all historical progress is "onward and upward forever." Furthermore, it erred in identifying the eschatology of the New Testament with "sheer obscurantism and escapism."

Ninth, that liberals now have some doubts regarding the doctrine that man is inherently good and that sin is an expression of his immaturity or ignorance or some maladjustment. They concede that some intelligent people believe in the doctrine of original sin.

Tenth, that liberalism's subservience to the dictates of human reason as it operates in science and philosophy is unfortunate and has resulted in its failure to discover the true nature of reality.

This undercurrent of self-criticism which runs throughout the three articles reached its height when, at the conclusion of the series, Morrison made bold to say,

Those who claim to have a sort of patent on liberalism have betrayed it. They have carried liberalism into a blind alley. In clinging to the earliest conclusions from modern science, biblical criticism, the psychology of religion and comparative religion, those who still wear the label of liberalism as a partisan badge are essentially dogmatists.

This new liberalism is in a state of flux, changing its doctrine as often as new discoveries of science, new dicta in philosophy, ever-changing social mores, and human experience may require. In recent years, liberal theological and philosophical fads have appeared and disappeared in rapid succession in liberal "search for truth." Human reason is still regarded as the perfect instrument which enables man to discover truth and it is also believed to be the final arbiter of truth.

In the ecumenical scene, liberalism is therefore prepared to make many concessions to those who hold other theological views in a search for a pragmatic ecumenical theology. They believe that the same metamorphosis has taken place with the old theological systems that has occurred in liberalism. They think that a large part of the theological issues dividing Protestants into Lutherans, Calvinists, and Arminians, and even a considerable part of the issues dividing Protestants from Catholics, have now become *passe.* Therefore, liberals are ready to sit down around the council table and collaborate. They optimistically hope for a synthesis of Catholic, conservative Protestant, liberal Protestant, Eastern Orthodox, neo-orthodox, and Anglican conceptions of essential Christianity. They believe that it is entirely possible to get agreement on a least common

363

denominator of the Christian faith and that old differences will form no barrier to union between them. Liberal ecumenicists think a little hard selling and shrewd bargaining between friends might produce the desired results.

All this indicates that the ecumenical situation is ripe for the introduction of certain principles of the Restoration plea into the current milieu. Everybody is confused. There is no consensus on anything. It is time to join the searching party. It is unfortunate that the distinguished representatives of the Disciples in the councils of the Ecumenical movement have abandoned the Restoration concept of Christian unity. Unless the International Convention can be persuaded to be broad enough in their choice of representatives to permit someone to present the claims of Restoration, some other means must be devised to establish communication. It is passing strange that just as there is a developing return to the Bible as a norm for Christian faith and order, the people who have insisted on that position for 150 years are without a voice in top-level ecumenical consultations.

Trends toward renewal of exploratory Biblical studies are of phenomenal proportions throughout the world. In the forefront of this development is Karl Barth and his so-called neo-orthodox theology. He is a long way from orthodoxy, but he has broken with liberalism in a number of important matters. He sees man as a creature under the sovereignty of God and accents the central fact that God is God. He then moves decisively into the Biblical frame of reference and insists that he must be theologically faithful to the message enshrined within the Holy Scriptures. While his concept of the "Word of God" is not strictly orthodox, it is certainly not strictly liberal. He sticks carefully to the words of the Bible, although he does not always identify the Word with the words. When confronted with the clear teaching of the Bible in juxtaposition to the teaching of human creeds, Barth chooses the Bible way. This is well illustrated in his recent rejection of the Reformed doctrine of infant baptism for believer's baptism and acceptance of immersion as the true form of baptism. His experience is reminiscent of that of Thomas and Alexander Campbell (page 60) and indicates a sincere desire to follow the will of Christ as revealed in the Scriptures. Barth's continuing exploratory Biblical studies are a constant challenge to liberalism and to classic creedalism.

Barth's view of the church universal coincides in many respects to the historic interpretation of the Disciples. In his small brochure, *The Church and the Churches,* he frequently refers to New Testament passages to authenticate his views. Barth insists that the church must be united "in the One, in Jesus Christ as the one Son of God, the bestower of the one Holy Spirit. Its basis does not lie . . . in any independent rights and claims of local, national, cultural or personal individuality, but . . . in God's grace and in no secondary principle distinguishable from grace." Again, Barth urges that the quest for the one church must be "concerned with the imperative content of the acknowledgement that there is one Lord, one faith, one baptism, one God above all, for all and in all. Unity in belief will not suffice: nor will any or all of the ideas or ideals which we may link with that concept. Unity in itself, even Church unity in itself is, as surely as the independent multiplicities are, merely fallen and unreconciled human nature. . . . The quest for the unity of the church must in fact be identical with the quest for Jesus Christ as the concrete Head and Lord of the Church. The blessing of unity cannot be separated from Him who blesses, for in Him it has its source and reality, through His Word and Spirit it is revealed to us, and only in faith in Him can it become a reality among us." Barth makes clear that mere union in a federation of churches is not true Christian unity. Such a union would be merely "something which the Church would have in common with human societies and undertakings in general. . . . A mere federation in itself has nothing at all to do with real Church union."

Barth expresses sympathy for all ecumenical movements but points out that their efforts will be futile if they eventuate in nothing more than "mutual tolerance, respect, and co-operation; readiness to hear and understand one another: an emotional sense of oneness in the possession of some ineffable common link, or, more than that, worshiping together in one accord." Above all, says Barth, the "decisive test of unity is joining in making a confession of our faith and unitedly proclaiming it to the world, thus fulfilling the commandment of Jesus on which the Church is based. The message and witness, given by the Church's teaching, order and life, must utter one voice, however manifold in the diversity of languages, gifts, of place and persons. A union of the churches in the sense that the task which is so seriously laid upon the Church would mean a union of all confessions into the one unanimous Confession." To arrive at this united testimony, Barth says in his closing appeal that the mere syllogistic approach based on human presuppositions is inadequate and will fall short of achieving the ultimate end. "We must listen to Christ—THE CHRIST OF THE SCRIPTURES—for the answer."

Explorations of the Study Department of the World Council of Churches—the *Ecclesia Militans* series—reveal this trend toward a Biblical approach to ultimate unity. The most important study in this series is Suzanne de Dietrich's book on *The Biblical Renewal (Le Renouveau Biblique)*, which gives information about a world-wide "back to the Bible" movement, entirely outside the aegis of the American Restoration movement. De Deitrich reveals that this development extends beyond Protestantism into the Eastern Orthodox and Roman Catholic churches. A further volume is a symposium edited by Alan Richardson and Wolfgang Schweitzer, *Biblical Authority for Today*, a Biblical study to discover a normative philosophy for the church's social and political message. In the first part of the symposium, attention is given to fundamental considerations on the authority of the Bible from the viewpoints of seven different churches. Part III deals with principles of Bible interpretation. While there is wide divergence of opinion and practice, the very fact that in our day there is a deep concern to rethink the church's view of the Holy

365

Scriptures is evidence of the relevance of the Restoration plea to the ecumenical situation.

It would appear that the day may soon come within the counsels of the Ecumenical movement when sincere advocates of Christian unity will be ready for serious discussion based on Scriptural truth. Many Christian brethren are beginning to tire of the liberal indisposition to accept any challenge to their intellectual leadership, to recognize dissent from their hegemony to be serious or intelligent. At present, however, there is a complete taboo on consideration of the Restoration plea for unity either in the tightly controlled International Convention representation in the National and World Councils, or in the Councils themselves. As long as this situation exists, purposive discourse will be postponed. Peaceable agreement within the dominating leftist school of thought is believed better than the introduction of strong differing views with the risk of precipitating debate. The passion for modulation and peace outweighs the passion for Biblical truth. The old-time liberal search for truth has been replaced by a new liberal dogmatism which has no patience with anything "controversial." Anyone who speaks up for Biblical faith is branded as a "controversial person" and is not invited to participate in "ecumenical studies." But there are evidences that this period of the ecumenical era may soon pass. There appears to be a growing desire to discover new ground for unity that offers supernatural revelation of divine truth, a positive gospel, a catholic and apostolic church, and a mission for the church which can call forth the same sacrificial allegiance that characterized the church of the New Testament. This ground the Restoration movement is prepared to propose.

Probably the greatest hurdle which Centrists and Rightists among the Disciples will have to take in this eventual confrontation with the "denominational world" is admission of the fact that their traditional presentation of "the plea" is outmoded and that they do not have all the answers to the present ecumenical situation. Many of them have become enmeshed in controversies involving outworn shibboleths which had meaning in the day they were created, but some of which are a "foreign language" now.

The principles of the *Declaration and Address* are still valid, and the truth of the Holy Scriptures is eternal; but they must be applied to an era of Christian history which is not at all like the one in which the Restoration movement was born. Pharisaical insistence that "we are right" and "they are wrong" will get no place in the counsels of men who are as eager—possibly more eager—for Christian unity as the Disciples. There must be admission of the fact that there have been misinterpretations and misapplications of Restoration and Scriptural principles, accompanied by a woeful lack of true Christian spirit.

There must be admission that the New Testament church has not yet been perfectly restored anywhere within the Restoration movement. The division into three bodies and the lack of complete unity within each of them are positive proof that the Disciples have yet much to learn about

366

what it takes to realize the answer to Christ's prayer in John 17. Moderate persons are saying now that this situation calls for penitential prayer and the demonstration of sincere repentance. A new spirit of humility must be born in those who would sit down with men in other communions and talk of the things of the kingdom. The guidance of the Holy Spirit must be sought in discovering a right approach to the modern ecumenical problem.

Thomas Campbell, in the closing phrases of his *Declaration,* describes the spirit in which he and his friends intended to approach the hidebound sectarians of his day in an adventure for Christian unity. If he could exhibit such a Christlike attitude under such deleterious circumstances, what ought Christians to do in an atmosphere charged with ecumenical hope? Said Campbell:

> May the Lord soon open the eyes of His people to see things in the true light, and excite them to come up out of their wilderness condition, out of this Babel of confusion, leaning upon their Beloved, and embracing each other in Him, holding fast the unity of the Spirit in the bonds of peace. This gracious unity and unanimity in Jesus would afford the best external evidence of their union with Him, and of their conjoint interest in the Father's love. "By this shall all men know that ye are my disciples," says He, "if ye have love one to another." And "This is my commandment, That ye love one another as I have loved you; that ye may also love one another." And again, "Holy Father, keep through thine own name those whom thou has given me, that they may be one as we are" even "all that shall believe on me; that they may all be one: as Thou Father art in Me and I in Thee, that they also may be one in Us: that the world may believe that Thou has sent Me." . . . May the Lord hasten it in his time. . . .

Campbell did not merely effervesce in a wave of spiritual emotion. In the *Appendix* of the *Declaration* he goes on to say:

> With a direct reference to the state of things, and, as we humbly think, in a perfect consistency with the foregoing . . . we declare ourselves ready to relinquish whatever we have hitherto received as matter of faith or practice, not expressly taught and enjoined, in the Word of God, so that we, and our brethren might, by this mutual concession, return together to the original constitutional unity of the Christian church, and dwell together in peace and charity. By this proposed relinquishment we are to be understood, in the first instance, of our manner of holding these things, and not simply of the things themselves; for no man can relinquish his opinions or practices until once convinced that they are wrong; and this he may not do immediately, even supposing they were so. One thing he may do: when not bound by express command, he need not impose them upon others, by any wise requiring their approbation; and when this is done, the things, to them, are as good as dead . . .

Literally millions of Christians are willing to sit down in such mutuality of spirit today, but they will not tolerate a holier-than-thou attitude from a people who have manifestly fallen far short of perfection in their plea for and practice of unity.

The Restoration plea for unity begins at a point of almost universal agreement—*the centrality of Christ.* This approach is superior to the humanistic approach in that it bypasses all the problems of diverse philosophies, creeds, traditions, and institutions, and centers the minds of men in the true source and sustenance of Christian unity—the person of the Son of God. The Disciples have long insisted that Christ is their only creed and when people present themselves for baptism and church membership they are asked only to make the same confession Peter made in Matthew 16:13-18. It was "on this rock" that Christ said He would build His church. The apostolic church was marked by a common loyalty to Jesus Christ and those doctrines which were related to obedience to Him were taken without question in every quarter. This accounts for the lack of emphasis upon many essential items in the New Testament. The concept of unity during the first century, as expressed in Ephesians 4, was one of an inner spiritual state contained within Spirit-wrought framework. Out of a sincere commitment to the lordship of Christ grew a tolerant loyalty to one another even when there was lack of uniformity in many things that some today hold to be indispensable.

It was only selfish insistence on other loyalties, secondary considerations, or human interpretations of divine truth, that led to the creation of parties and sects. The tyranny which grew out of creedal controversies broke this essential unity and put the emphasis upon doctrines instead of the person of Christ. If these "middle walls of partition" are to be removed, there must, first of all, be a return to a renewed commitment to Christ as God and Saviour. When the Jewish and Gentile Christians began to break their fellowship with one another in the apostolic era, Paul admonished them to make Christ their peace and unity and become one in Him (Ephesians 3:14-21). Through Him by the one Spirit they gained new access to the Father. Upon Him as the chief cornerstone all the building was fitly framed together, growing into a holy temple in the Lord.

If all those who are essentially one in Christ would unquestioningly and deliberately drop all concern, reference, or argument about human systems of thought and the things that divide and seek the face of Christ, think only what would please Him, do only what He commands, and acknowledge only His lordship, He would give the motivation for true unity. This involves not only an emotional and spiritual experience but also a clear understanding of the historical Jesus revealed through the mind of the earliest Christian community and recorded in the New Testament Scriptures. In the words of Karl Barth, "We must listen to Christ—the Christ of the Scriptures—for the answer" to the ecumenical problem.

The Restoration plea for unity involves a return to *Biblical authority.* God has spoken to man. The most effective revelation of His truth and His way was in Jesus Christ. The record of that revelation and of other revelations of divine truth through Spirit-chosen men are to be found only in the Holy Scriptures. There is no other tangible and objective criterion to which the human mind may appeal intelligently to apprehend God's truth and way of life and by which to judge the validity or worth of any religious belief, practice, or institution. To admit other sources is to open the gates to a flood of all manner of human subjectivisms and opinions. The acceptance of Biblical authority should not pose a difficult ecumenical problem. Every communion accepts the Scriptures as sacred because they have been written under the inspiration of the Holy Spirit, have God as their author, and are given to the church for its instruction and admonition. This doctrine is implicit in all the major creeds of Christendom. Even Rome in its Constitution on the Catholic Faith, adopted by the Council of the Vatican in 1870, admits that the Holy Scriptures are the inspired and inerrant Word of God. The trouble comes when the churches admit human opinions and traditions as of equal authority as did Rome in the Council of Trent (1545-1563). The truly catholic authority, therefore, lies in the commonly accepted Holy Scriptures.

It would appear that unity in doctrine and life for the "Coming Great Church" could come in a high decision by all Christians to abandon all human creeds and traditions and sit down together in humble and contrite study under the guidance of the Holy Spirit to determine what the Scriptures and the Scriptures alone have to say for our instruction and having reached a consensus to obey the Scriptures in all that they teach. What of those who reject the validity of the Bible? They seem to have no part nor lot in ecumenical discussions. They are subjects for prayer and loving consideration in the hope that they may be brought into submission to the revealed will of God.

The Restoration plea for unity would propose that *the church is one body in Christ,* and that its universalities may be discovered only in the New Testament Scriptures. The church is "the body of Christ." It is built on the "foundation of the apostles and the prophets, Jesus Christ himself being the chief corner stone; in whom all the building fitly framed together groweth into a holy temple in the Lord: in whom ye also are builded together for an habitation of God through the Spirit."

The book of Acts unfolds the story of the growing church and the epistles reveal the fulfillment of Christ's program for the church. Any program for the unification of the church today must take into account the characteristics of the church which Jesus built in the first Christian century. An evaluation or value judgment must be pronounced upon modern Christendom in the light of the New Covenant Scriptures and their historical message. It is in the Scriptures that the principles of catholicity requisite to a united church may alone be discovered: certainly not in the welter of opinion, methods, theologies, and experiences of man which characterize modern denominational groups, no matter how ancient they may claim to be or how powerful and important they may have become. The ecumenical problem is not to unite the "churches" or "denominations" of our time, but to restore the one church in which exist the catholic functions of which sectarian bodies have robbed it. As Thomas Campbell put it, "the church of Christ upon earth is essentially, intentionally and constitutionally one; consisting of all those in every place that profess

369

their faith in Christ and obedience to Him in all things according to the Scriptures . . ." The task is to liberate the captive church of the New Testament and restore its functions as they were in apostolic times.

As in any other organization, the constitution and form of government, qualifications for membership, the manner in which its officers and representative leaders are chosen and the extent of their authority, the method used in orderly expansion and extension, the means of inculcating sound doctrine and training future leadership, and the pattern for the substance and form of worship and public meeting must be discovered. The deeper meanings of fellowship and, above all, the overpowering sense of commitment to the mission of the church in a needy world must also be discovered. This is what the Campbells had in mind when they contended for the restoration of "the ancient order." They sought no mere form but the Biblical principles of catholicity—the universalities of the church in which lie the secret of its unity and effectiveness. Some of these catholicities may be intimated, along with experience of Disciples in their effort to restore the New Testament church.

The catholic *name* for the church is the *church of Christ*. At first the Disciples were criticized for their use of this Scriptural name for the church, but today it is the preferred name used for the council of churches, for churches seeking to manifest the ecumenical spirit of the times, and for the "Coming Great Church" which ecumenicists envision. There is no longer any argument here. Gradually the uncatholic names of denominations which give honor to men or to forms of doctrine, instead of the one Head of the church, will disappear.

The catholic *creed*—belief in Christ—emphasizes the heart of the gospel. He alone is the "good news of salvation," "the sure mercies of David." Implicit in Him are His coming, His incarnation, His teaching, His death, burial, resurrection, exaltation, His sending of the Holy Spirit, and the establishment of His church. In His acts God has "visited and redeemed his people." Man's unwithholding and complete surrender to Him so that He takes possession of body, mind, and spirit, intellect, emotions, and will, for the accomplishment of His purpose, is the complete and ultimate commitment for members of His body—the church. Obedience to His commandments are evidence of that commitment. All of the elements of the living creed are precisely delineated in the Holy Scriptures for our edification and guidance. What more could be required?

The catholic *rule of faith and practice* for the church of Christ is the New Testament. Here may be discovered the doctrine, ordinances, and life of the church. Said Thomas Campbell, human standards which would "determine the doctrine, worship, discipline and government of the church for the purpose of preserving her unity and purity and requiring approbation of them as a term of communion" must be abandoned. He saw no reason to deprive Christians of any necessary and possible assistance to understand the Scriptures or to come to a distinct and particular knowledge of every truth they contain (such as human creeds), but he held that only the Holy Scriptures should determine faith and obedience,

370

and the Christian's knowledge of the way of salvation and the mystery of the Christian life. The Scriptures are the constitution of the church. Ordinances and polity are to be found in the Word of God.

The catholic view of the *ordinances* is to be found in the New Testament. The most careful scrutiny can discover only two—baptism and the Lord's Supper. Protestant Christianity is agreed on the general definition of these ordinances: baptism being an initiatory ordinance and the Communion the rite to be observed perpetually by Christians in remembrance of Christ.

All divisions of Christendom agree on the Scriptural subjects and actions of baptism. All agree that adults coming into the church should be baptized, some Christians disagree that infants should be baptized, but there is common ground concerning believers. The action of baptism presents a similar situation. All Christians, with practically no exceptions, will accept immersion as the act of baptism. Many will not accept affusion. The catholic baptism is therefore the immersion of penitent believers.

The Lord's Supper, as the years pass, presents less and less of an ecumenical problem. Practically all Christians partake of the same emblems and practice much the same basic ritual. Some churches observe it every Sunday, some monthly, some quarterly; but if the table were to be spread every week all may be served and those who wish to abstain may do so. The Disciples from their beginnings have followed the apostolic practice and made the Communion the center of worship. This tradition has been followed by all the Catholic churches in some form or other—the Roman Catholics in the mass and the Anglicans and Episcopalians in making the emblems available every Lord's Day.

However the ordinances may be interpreted (and this is fundamentally a matter of individual conscience and judgment), the fact remains that they present common New Testament ground accepted by all Christians and therefore a substantial basis for unity.

A catholic church *polity* may be discovered in the New Testament. It is not set forth in a positive command but it is perfectly clear that the individual churches and the individual Christian possessed the largest measure of freedom. It is also clear that there is nothing of monarchical, oligarchical, or despotical government such as that assumed by the church of Rome and other similar bodies. Efforts to impose nondemocratic forms of church government have resulted in many schisms in Christendom. Even the apostles, pre-eminent as they were because of their personal acquaintance with Jesus and because of their possession of certain special powers He conferred upon them, never presumed to lord it over the churches. The churches were free churches under the leadership of Christ and the constitution of the Holy Scriptures.

Modern ecclesiastical overlords hold to the idea that the church itself is God's divine revelation through which His will is to be done. It is from these leaders that the chief opposition will come for a return to the congregational order of the early church. Such leaders seemingly are contending for the same institutional view which characterized the religious body that sent Jesus to His death. It is of a psychological piece with divine imperialisms of many false religions. The doctrine of a universal church of human origin and traditions, relying on its own subsidiary and supporting revelations of the will of God, and on its own judgment of itself and its powers, could well lead to the same evils that made the Reformation imperative. The moral ideal of the Christian religion involves freedom. Frederick D. Kershner, in *How to Promote Christian Unity,* says:

> Any form of government which destroys the idea of freedom must prove fatal to Christianity in the long run. It would not be possible to unite Christians today on any polity which does not guarantee individual liberty. The testimony of history, the voice of Scripture and the experience of present-day political institutions are at one on this point. The free and somewhat loosely organized polity of the New Testament—the simple authority of the congregational brotherhood—remains as the most satisfactory and hopeful solution for the problem of polity.

This principle of freedom allows for many divergencies of practice in churches which are in various stages of development in their search for the ancient order and the ultimate in spiritual power. Freedom under Christ and the New Testament makes for growth and progress and avoids the dangers of a monolithic superchurch with power to impose a deadening conformity. The measure of co-operative organization which may be necessary to maintain a united testimony to the world is a problem which ecumenical leaders may well consider with prayer and fasting. It is devoutly to be hoped that the heirarchy in the present councils, in an effort to co-ordinate the functions of member churches, would almost completely disappear when the New Testament pattern is achieved.

It is impossible in the limited scope of this chapter to deal with many other ecumenical problems, except to intimate possible Scriptural solutions which may result through the acceptance and implementation of Restoration principles. One further area of ecumenical concern should, however, be briefly explored, i.e., *the mission of the church.*

The Disciples have never held to a program of Christian unity for unity's sake, as laudable a goal as that might seem. They have seen the necessity of union in order to the evangelization of the world. This idea is implicit in Christ's prayer in John 17: "That they may all be one . . . that the world may believe." This was the apostolic concept of the motive for unity. The first epistle of John opens with a declaration that the apostles were honored to be used by the Lord in bringing to the attention of men the truth incarnate in the Word. On the basis of their testimony men believed and entered into a united fellowship with the Father and the Son. This unity is expressed in the fellowship of the church. In the act of their naturalization they were brought from the barren and desolate position of the sinner into the rich, holy, and joyful associations of the spiritual kingdom. As common heirs of a common salvation, brought into one brotherhood on a common level, they have been made joint partakers alike of the benefits of the Christian life. They have also become partners

372

in a great enterprise, having in view the redemption of all men out of Christ, and in this task they give themselves unreservedly to Christ and to one another. This is a fellowship *(koinonia)* which preserves the significant element of holy purpose and the Bible makes clear that it is inconceivable to think that the fellowship even exists without the purpose. Here is set forth the divine-human relationship which constitutes the church. The two divine goals implicit in Christian unity are: (1) to redeem a world of perishing sinners through the preaching of the gospel and (2) to instruct such as are saved for the dignities and benefits of eternal life. In the realization of this great mission of the church the men of all nations and all generations will be lifted from death to life, from sin to holiness, from vileness and shame to glory and honor, and the heirs of wrath will be the inheritors of eternal life in Christ.

Involved in this high sense of mission is the production of Christian character. Men who regard religion as a matter of ceremonialism in a holy institution and not a matter of character and life have never plumbed the depths of Christ's purpose in coming into the world. Christ offended the Jewish ceremonialists in His Sermon on the Mount and Christian ceremonialists scoff at puritan ideals. Horton has said, "Goodness . . . is the high note of the Church; a goodness to be maintained by teaching, by discipline, by faith and by prayer, by 'provoking one another to good works,' because the saving power of the Church depends on it." When the church loses its capacity to be a channel through which individual and social morality are developed, it has outlived its usefulness to God and to humanity. The element of love realized in actual experience in the apostolic church produced the finest spirit of brotherhood ever known to exist on this earth. The world was amazed by it and convinced that here was a way of life so superior to their own that they must of necessity learn its secret. In the literature of the apostolic age of the church, especially in the early apologies, it is this divine love of man for man which is pressed as the evidence of the divine character of the Christian church. Growing out of this good life came the principles of freedom for the individual and for the nations which have been such a blessing to the world in the Christian era of human history. The united church envisioned by the ecumenical leaders of our day must have these high motivations and this deep sense of mission in order to produce the results which its advocates anticipate.

On the facade of the great National Archives building in Washington is chiseled the legend, "Past is prologue." The history of the Restoration movement should be but the prelude to a more glorious future for the church of Jesus Christ.

With Christendom now widely concerned with its weaknesses, divisions, and inertia, and seeking to recapture the pristine purity, power, and effectiveness of the apostolic church, Thomas Campbell's *Declaration and Address* has new meaning and relevance. No proposals for Christian unity made by the ecumenical leaders of our time are more irenic and humble in spirit, more aware of the true genius of the Christian church, more sound in basic principles, more revolutionary and cathartic with respect to outworn systems and traditions, more broad in vision and constructive, or more certain to achieve the revealed purpose of Christ for His church.

Despite human weaknesses and failures, the Restoration movement which began in 1809 with some twenty earnest souls on the Allegheny frontier has grown to five million disciples of Christ around the world— the most amazing single development in modern church history. The testimony and challenge of this company of "Christians only" committed to the "restoration of the New Testament church in doctrine and life" by an appeal to "the Bible alone as a rule of faith and practice" deserves the consideration of the whole Christian world in this new day.

In this ecumenical era the church universal faces a future rich with promise. There is endless work to be done. The day of partyism is ending. Ancient inhibitions which have long obstructed progress toward a united church are rapidly being dissolved. The vast potentialities of one body in Christ, while yet all too dimly recognized, except by the imaginative and broad of vision, are beginning to be seen by the masses. Free communication is being established. Earnest prayer for divine guidance is pervading all Christians of good will. The future is unknowable in all its aspects, but the past should give us hope and courage. We cannot now precisely define the exact terms of ultimate union, but if we turn to the perfect Guide and the guide Book He has given, with pure hearts and willing minds we shall find the way.

BIBLIOGRAPHY: Chapter 23

Barth, Karl, *The Church and the Churches.*
Craig, Clarence Tucker, *The One Church in the Light of the New Testament.*
Deitrich, Suzanne de, *The Biblical Renewal.*
Dun, Angus, *Prospecting for a United Church.*
Garrison, W. E., *The Quest and Character of a United Church.*
Glover, Christopher, *The Church for the New Age.*
Horton, Walter M., *Christian Theology: An Ecumenical Approach.*
Horton, Walter M., *Toward a Reborn Church.*
Leuba, Jean-Louis, *New Testament Pattern.*
Littell, Franklin Hamlin, *The Anabaptist View of the Church.*
Minear, Paul S., editor, *The Nature of the Unity We Seek.*
Phillips, Thomas W., *The Church of Christ.*
Richardson, Alan, and Wolfgang Schweitzer, *Biblical Authority for Today.*
Robinson, William A., *What Churches of Christ Stand For?*
Robinson, William A., *The Biblical Doctrine of the Church.*
Visser t'Hooft, W. A., *The Renewal of the Church.*
Walker, Dean E., *Adventuring for Christian Unity.*

A Prayer for Unity

Gracious God, our heavenly Father, we thank Thee for the church of Jesus Christ. We thank Thee that Thou didst so love us as to send Thine only begotten Son into the world to give His life a ransom for all men who believe on His name.

We thank Thee, our God, that we have been purchased by His precious atoning blood, born again and made a part of His glorious body the church. We thank Thee for the blessed fellowship we know in Thee through Thy dear Son—one flock, one fold, and one Shepherd. We find in Jesus Christ our life, our hope, our all.

We thank Thee for thy holy Word and the Holy Spirit whereby we are grounded, upheld and guided, and preserved in holy communion with Thee.

As we look upon the outward divisions of the church in the world our hearts are pained. God, forgive our humanisms, our perversions, and our feverish ways which promote divisions, which keep us from fellowship one with another and which hinder the evangelization of the world. We long for the visible realization of the unity for which Christ prayed. We would surrender our wills completely to Thee that Thy will may be done in us to the unity of Thy people and to Thy everlasting glory.

We pray Thy divine blessing upon all those movements and agencies which seek in sincerity the true and ultimate unity of Thy people in the earth. Guide them in Thy Truth to do Thy will. Bless especially, we beseech Thee, those earnest souls who have dedicated their lives to the achievement of this holy purpose. Keep them in Thy will and way. Deliver them from presumptuous thoughts, precipitous acts, and shameful compromises.

Hinder and destroy, we beseech Thee, every device of men or of Satan which would mar the pattern of the church which Jesus built and which His chosen apostles have revealed to us in Thy holy Word.

Forbid, O God, that unity which would compromise Thy eternal truth, condone evil, dampen our zeal for lost souls, consent to barren profession, bear no spiritual fruit, take pride in outward show, seek political power, and number in its company a people who praise Thee with their lips but whose hearts are far from Thee. Fulfill the heartening promise of our Lord that the gates of hell shall not prevail against Thy church.

Help us to know the mind of Christ and His will for us in all things pertaining to His church, that in His greatness we may rise above our littleness, in His strength we shall lose our weaknesses, in His peace we may bury all discord that in His truth and righteousness we may march—the united church militant accomplishing the work Thou hast set for us in our day and time.

At last, we pray, enfold us in the one church triumphant, the family of God, to dwell with Thee forever. And unto Thee we will ascribe all honor and glory through Jesus Christ, our Lord. Amen.

Index

Bryan, William Jennings, 230
Bryant, Joseph, 59
Buchanan, James, 198
Buckner, George Walker, Jr., 263
Buffalo Creek, 41, 59, 67
Bulgaria, 328
Bullard, Chester, 127, 134
Burgess, O. A., 125, 187, 195
Burghers (see Presbyterians)
Burma, 300, 342
Burnet, David S., 79, 133, 147, 148, 153, 154, 180-182, 189, 190
Burnett, Glenn, 132
Burnett, Peter H., 132
Burnett, T. R., 217
Burnetta College, 201
Burnham, Frederick W., 249, 252, 263, 272, 345
"Burnham Interpretation," 249, 252
Burritt College, 126
Butchart, Reuben, 325
Butler, Burris, 306
Butler, J. A., 147
Butler, Ovid, 154, 199, 280
Butler, Pardee, 131, 154
Butler School of Religion (see Christian Theological Seminary)
Butler (College) University, 146, 154, 169, 201, 280

C

Caldwell Academy, 83, 84, 106
Caldwell, David, 83
Caldwell, William, 91
Calhoun, Hall L., 241, 243
California, 132, 190, 274, 280, 284, 289, 296, 313, 315, 319
Callaway, C. W., 304, 342
Calvin, John, 15
Calvinism, 32, 37, 62, 84, 114, 139, 195, 220, 363
Camden Point Female Academy (see Missouri Christian College)
Campbell, Alexander, 52, 53-81, 94, 95, 99, 110, 113, 117, 121, 124-130, 137, 148, 166, 189, 195, 276, 329, 330, 347, 350; Baptism of, 60, 364; Birth, 36; Conversion of, 54; Death, 155, 156; Debate with McCalla, 76, 77, 128, 141; Debate with Owen, 78-80; Debate with Purcell, 141; Debate with Rice, 142, 143; Debate with Walker, 69, 70, 76, 141; Education of, 36, 53-57; Family, 59, 78, 134, 136, 152, 156; His role as author, 71-76, 137, 138, 144; as citizen, 71, 80, 81, 133; as debater, 69, 70, 76-80, 141-143, 195; as editor, 70-75, 147; as educator, 38, 145, 146; as preacher, 57-59, 62, 81; as publisher, 71, 137; as theologian, 62-65, 68, 71, 73, 76, 79, 137-139, 142, 143; Migration to America, 42, 54-57; Separation from Baptists, 104, 127; from Seceders, 56, 58; Travels, 125, 126, 128-130, 133-136; Views on atonement, 63, 115; on the Bible, 62-65, 68, 71, 73, 75, 76, 114, 117, 138, 143; on baptism, 58, 60, 64, 69, 70, 76, 77, 142, 143; on Christ, 63, 64, 71, 75, 139; on the church, 9, 58, 138, 180; on church government, 58, 61, 71, 72, 116; on communion, 56, 73; on conversion, 74, 75, 117, 142; on co-operation, 61, 72, 73, 127, 139, 148, 150, 179, 259; on creeds, 58, 62, 64, 71, 142; on denominations, 58, 71, 73, 139, 140, 143; on dispensations, 62-65, 68; on ecclesiasticism, 58, 72, 116; on education, 143-146, 294; on expedients, 186; on faith, 61; on the Holy Spirit, 74, 105, 117, 139; on the law,
62; on the ministry, 71, 72, 116, 162; on missions, 64, 179, 181; on the name, 115; on open membership, 117-119; on organizations, 72, 148, 150, 179-181, 186; on restoration, 71, 72; on revivalism, 116; on Roman Catholicism, 141; on Sabbath, 61; on salvation, 74, 75, 117, 139; on sin, 63, 139; on slavery, 80, 81, 136, 137, 152, 166; on the Trinity, 114, 139; on unitarianism, 114, 115; on unity, 95, 113, 350; on war and peace, 153
Campbell, Dyre, 356
Campbell, George, 69, 238, 263
Campbell, John Poague, 91
Campbell, Laird, 55
Campbell, Robert M., 209
Campbell, Thomas, 59, 60, 65, 67, 68, 70, 78, 102, 110, 115, 128, 150, 166, 207, 215, 220, 293, 347, 358, 366, 367, 369; Ancestry, 35; Baptism, 60, 364; Birth, 35; Break with Baptists, 104; Break with Seceders, 39, 58; Conversion, 35; Death, 155; Declaration and Address, 42-51, 293, 358, 366, 367; Education, 36; Family, 36, 42, 53; Migration to America, 38, 42; Ministry in Ireland, 36-38; Ministry in America, 38-52, 128; Unity efforts, 38, 42-51; Views on baptism, 41, 52, 59, 60; on atonement, 115; on Christian character, 46, 49; on church membership, 46, 47; on communion, 39, 45, 46, 48, 51; on creeds, 45, 46, 48, 49, 62; on denominationalism, 43-45, 47, 50; on expedients, 47; on liberalism, 49; on the name, 115; on private judgment, 43, 46, 220; on restoration, 45, 47, 49, 52; on salvation, 102; on Scriptural authority, 40, 43, 45, 46, 49, 50, 367; on the Trinity, 65, 114; on unity, 40, 43-46, 48, 358, 366, 367; on war and peace, 152
Campbell, Thomas F., 194
Campbell Club, 239
Campbell-Hagerman College, 201
Campbell Institute, 237-240
"Campbellites," 77, 78, 104, 112, 132, 137, 156
Canada, 213, 281, 290, 297, 313, 318, 324-326
Canadian Disciple, 325
Cane Ridge church, 85, 88-90
Cane Ridge revival, 29, 30, 85, 86
Canton Bible School, 316
Carleton, S. P., 195
Carlton College, 201
Carpenter, Homer W., 263
Carr, Francis, 79
Carr, James B., 356
Carr, Oliver, 337
Carr-Burdette College, 201
Carroll, R. W., 170, 177
Carson, Alexander, 38, 54
Carson, "Kit," 132
Carson, Linsey, 132
Carter, Arthur, 302
Cartwright, Peter, 20
Cary, Harland, 301
Caskey, T. W., 153, 183, 195
Cass, Lew, 302
Cathars, 11
Catholicism (see Roman Catholicism)
Centennial Convention (Pittsburgh), 207-214, 238, 288, 345
Central Christian College of the Bible, 297
Centralization of authority, 10, 58, 71, 72, 88, 183-187, 254-256, 258
Central Ohio Classical and Business College, 201

Henry, John, 104
Henry, Matthew, 135
Henshall, James, 135, 147
Herald of Gospel Liberty, 33, 90, 94, 120, 147
Herald of Truth, 318
Hereford-Panhandle Christian College, 201
Hesperian College (see Chapman College)
Higdon, E. K., 248
Hill, Claude E., 249, 263
Hill, Rowland, 17, 38, 54
Hinsdale, B. A., 200
Hinson, W. B., 231
Hiram College, 124, 146, 153, 169, 197, 200, 201, 281, 294
Hoadley, Gideon, 109
Hocking, W. E., 228, 229
Hodge, William, 84
Hodges, George, 233
Hoffman, G. A., 130, 194
Holland (see Netherlands)
Holley, Horace, 77
Holt, Basil, 274
Holy Scriptures (see Bible)
Holy Spirit, 74, 93, 103, 105, 110, 116, 117, 138, 142, 172, 174, 198, 361, 369
"Holy Spirit, Discourse on the," 105
Home missions, 213, 282-284, 312
Homes for aged, 213, 250, 289, 319
Homes for children, 213, 289, 319
Hong Kong, 316, 342
Honore, H. H., 125, 177
Hook, Daniel, 128
Hopkins, Robert M., 348
Hopper, R. A., 195
Hopper, William, 327
Hopson, Winthrop H., 152, 153, 170, 217
Hopwood, Josephus, 295
Hoshour, Samuel K., 128
Houston, William C., 199
Houston, Matthew, 90
Houston Christian Schools, 313
Hoven, Ard, 306
Howard, J. R., 147
Howe, Henry, 126
Hoyle, Earl, 304
Hubbard, Ephraim P., 109
Hughes, J. A., 199
Hull, Hope, 84
Hull, John D., 272
Hume, David, 24
Humphreys, Guy, 301, 336
Hungary, 13, 331
Hunley, J. B., 274
Hurst, James S., 296
Huss, John, 13
Hussites, 12
Hutchison, John A., 232
Hygeia Female Athanaeum, 124, 201
Hymnody, 203, 204

I

Idaho, 313, 315
Iden, T. M., 202
Illinois, 125, 135, 155, 190, 204, 281, 282, 283, 289, 297
Illinois Disciples Foundation, 282
Immanence, Doctrine of, 223
Immersion, 60, 69, 70, 101, 102
Independent missions (see Direct-support missions)
India, 187, 188, 213, 248, 253, 261, 282, 283, 299, 303-305, 329, 338, 339, 361

Indiana, 124, 125, 154, 187, 204, 271, 272, 274, 275, 280, 282, 289, 319
Indiana School of Religion, 282
Indianapolis, Indiana, 124, 187, 191, 274, 275, 280
Infant baptism, 10, 41, 58, 64, 69, 77, 91, 98, 109, 176
Infidelity, 19, 20, 21, 23-27, 78
Ingersoll, Robert G., 198
Innes, George, 97
"Innovations," 157-163, 166, 167, 171, 175, 181-186, 216, 217, 311, 312, 357
Instrumental music (see Controversies)
Intelligencer, The, 165
Interchurch co-operation (see Co-operation)
Interdenominational co-operation (see Co-operation)
Intermountain Bible College, 297
Internal unity among Disciples, 263-271, 274-276, 355, 356, 357
International Convention of Christian Churches (Disciples of Christ), 239, 248, 254, 255, 257, 259, 262-272, 277, 285, 286, 293, 345, 347, 348, 352, 364, 366
International Convention of Disciples of Christ (See International Convention of Christian Churches)
International Council of Religious Education, 348
International Missionary Council, 360
International Sunday School Association, 259
Interpretation of the Scriptures, 13, 62-65, 68, 72, 73, 76
Investigator, 121, 262
Iowa, 130, 131, 190, 262, 272, 281, 282, 285, 289
Iowa Department of Campus Christian Life, 282
Ireland, 35
Irwin, Joseph I., 199
Italy, 302, 318, 331

J

Jackson, Thomas, 337, 340
Jamaica, 187, 188, 213, 283, 301, 302, 324
Jameson, Maria, 187
Japan, 188, 213, 250, 261, 282, 284, 298, 299, 301, 305, 313, 316, 339, 340
Jaroszewicz, Konstantin, 332
Jarvis Christian College, 282, 284
Jarvis Institute, 201
Jefferson, S. M., 241
Jenkins, George S., 181
Jenkins, Obadiah, 133
Jerusalem mission, 149
Jessup, William L., 296
Jesus and Jonah, 241
Johnson, Ashley S., 295
Johnson, B. W., 202
Johnson Bible College, 201, 295, 332
Johnson, James N., 306
Johnson, Jefferson, 129
Johnson, John, 334
Johnson, John T., 94, 110, 111, 113, 123, 130, 144, 147, 148, 181, 185
Johnson, O. D., 304
Johnson, Richard M., 130
Johnson, T. H., 296
Johnson, Tom L., 199
Jones, Abner, 32, 33, 90
Jones, Edgar DeWitt, 249, 263, 348
Jones, Evelyn, 302
Jones, J. Harrison, 153, 189
Jones, John T., 125

Oliver, George S., 214
Oliver, George T., 208
Oliver, Lancelot, 331
Olson, David E., 295
Ontario, 282, 298, 305, 313, 324, 325, 326
Open membership, 117-120, 157, 160-162, 238, 246-249, 253, 266, 277, 279, 330, 345, 356
Opinion, Liberty of, 43, 45, 139, 140, 157, 158, 171, 176, 186, 215, 220, 267, 279, 313
Ordinances, 76, 139, 173, 175, 198, 261, 370, 371 (see Baptism, Lord's Supper)
Ordination, 116
Oregon, 132, 133, 190, 204, 213, 282, 289, 290, 295, 306, 313
Organ controversy (see Instrumental music and Controversies)
Organic Evolution Considered, 241
Orlina, Felina S., 252
Osaka Christian Mission, 250, 299
Oskaloosa College (see Drake University)
Osborn, G. Edwin, 274
Osborn, Ronald E., 352
Osborne, Jacob, 68
Osborne, Vernon, 303, 323
Otey, James, 134
Our Position, 172-176, 293
Overdale College, 329
Overton, Thomas W., 306
Owen, George Earle, 356
Owen, Robert, 78-80
Oxford Movement, 139
Oxnam, G. Bromley, 234
Ozark Bible College, 245, 296

P

Pacific Bible Seminary (Pacifi Christian College), 245, 296
Pacifism, 153, 348
Paducah Christian College, 297
Palmer, Francis R., 129
Palmer, Joel, 131
Palmer, Potter, 125, 177
Panama, 188
Paraguay, 283, 328
Parker, Chester, 305
Parkinson, David, 126
Parks, Evelyn C., 304
Parish, Tom O., 356
Parliament of Religions, 239
Pashkoff, W. A., 332-334
Patillo, Henry, 84
Patmont, Louis R., 334
Patroon College, 201
Paul, Azariah, 316
Paul, Charles T., 325
Paulicians, 11
Payne, O. E., 253, 300
"Peace (Sweeney) Resolution," 249, 252
Pearce, W. C., 219
Pearre, Caroline Neville, 177, 187
Pemberton, John, 301
Pendergast, J N., 132
Pendleton, Edmond, 156
Pendleton, William K., 145 147, 148, 156, 176, 182, 183
Pennsylvania, 38-42, 51, 57, 58-61, 97-99, 126, 127, 190, 207-214, 283, 289, 290, 314, 315
Pension Fund, 191, 276, 287, 289
Pepperdine George, 315
Pepperdine College, 313, 315, 316
Periodicals of Disciples (see Journalism)
Perry, Ransom, 251
Perry, Woodrow W., 296

Persianoff, Alexander, 333, 334
Peter's Creek, 65
Philadelphia Confession of Faith, 62, 104, 128
Philippine Islands, 188, 213, 248, 252, 253, 261, 282, 284, 288, 298, 299, 317, 341
Phillips Bible Institute, 201, 244
Phillips, C. H., 297, 326
Phillips, Charles M., 169
Phillips, Dirk, 15
Phillips, I. N., 169
Phillips, John T., 169
Phillips, O. H., 208
Phillips, Thomas W., Sr., 169, 199, 208, 211, 212, 245
Phillips, Woodrow, 356
Phillips University, 199, 201, 281
Philputt, A. B., 255
Phipps, Charles, 302
Pietism, 10
Pinkerton, L. L., 154, 181
Pittsburgh, Pennsylvania, 39, 51, 57, 97, 98, 165, 207-214, 272
Platte Valley Bible College, 297
Plymouth Brethren, 18, 135, 323, 330
Poland, 302, 331, 332
Polity (see Congregational Polity)
Poll, Harry, 295, 306, 356
Power, Frederick D., 233, 260
Preaching among the Disciples, 145, 157, 195, 196
Presbyterians, 27, 28, 31, 69, 83-87, 97, 141, 151, 160, 195, 212, 230, 231, 345, 346, 354, 361; Anti-Burgher, 36-39, 54, 57, 58; Bible, 231; Burgher, 37; Covenanter, 35, 37, 38; Church of Scotland, 16, 17, 37, 97; Cumberland, 31, 86; New Light, 37, 84, 86, 112, 151; New Light (Seceder), 37; Old Light, 37, 112, 151; Old Light (Seceder), 37; Orthodox, 231; Reformed, 37, 160; Seceder, 35-37, 39, 106; United, 160, 212
Presbytery of Chartiers, 38, 39
Presbytery of Transylvania, 85
Price, Sterling, 153
Priesthood of believers, 52, 58, 71, 72, 89, 116
Prince Edward Island, 189, 325, 326
Princeton University, 231
Priscillian, 11
Pritchard, H. O., 249
Pritchard, Henry B., 125, 195
Proclamation and Reformer, 147
Procter, Alexander, 130, 183
Progress, 240
Prokhanoff, Ivan, 333, 335
Protestant Episcopal church, 134, 142, 151 345-347, 371
Protestantism, 19-34, 64, 141, 223-235, 239, 261 345-358, 363
Provincial Co-operation (Canada), 325
Pruett, Dennis, 301
Puerto Rico, 213, 283, 303, 328
Puget Sound College of the Bible, 297
Pullias, Athens Clay, 316
Purcell, John B., 106, 141
Puritans, 11, 16, 38
Purviance, David, 89, 91, 120
Pytt, Henri, 17

R

Radio and television, 306, 309, 318
Radstock, Lord, 332
Ralston, Samuel, 57
Randall, Max Ward, 300, 301, 335
Randolph, John, 81

Randolph College, 201
Rash, Tom, 303
Ray, Joseph, 106
Records, Ralph L., 244, 251, 296
Redmon, James C., 296
Redstone Baptist Association, 61, 62, 65, 67, 78, 114, 219
Reeves, Prior, 129
Reformation, Protestant, 14, 66
"Reformers," 94, 104, 105, 109, 110, 111, 116, 124
Regeneration, 117, 174
Reinhardt, Wayne, 356
Republican Methodists, 32, 84, 89, 90, 109, 120, 128
Restoration Herald, The, 251, 253, 273
Restoration movements in history, 9-18, 77, 352
Restoration of apostolic Christianity, 9-18, 72, 77, 123, 173, 219, 310, 359-374
Restoration principles, 72, 77, 101, 209, 210, 211, 270, 352, 357-374
Restoration Review, 319
Restoration Quarterly, 319
Restructure of the Brotherhood, 291
Revelation, Divine, 75
Reverend, The title, 71, 88, 162
Revival, Cane Ridge (see Cane Ridge Revival)
Revival, Great American (see Great American Revival)
Revival, Wesleyan, 22
Revivalism, 22, 27-31, 116, 141
Revolutionary War, 19, 83
Rice, Absolom, 129
Rice, N. L., 142, 143
Rice, Perry J., 214
Rich Hill Academy, 37, 38, 54
Rich Hill church, 38, 54, 136
Richards, Charles, 253
Richards, George, 233
Richards, J. Fraise, 200
Richardson, Alan, 365
Richardson, James D., 199
Richardson, Nathaniel, 98
Richardson, Robert, 16, 40, 98, 99, 105, 133, 145, 156, 158, 159, 215
Richardson, William, 54
Rickman, Lester, 356
Rigdon, John, 132
Rigdon, Sidney, 68, 76, 120, 121, 217
Rightist Status and Growth, 309-321, 357
Rijnhart, Petrus and Susie, 300
Riley, W. B., 231
Roanoke Bible College, 297
Roberts, C. D., 143
Roberts, W. H., 233
Robertson, James, 135
Robeson, James, 91
Robinson, J. P., 154, 169, 189, 190
Robinson, William, 331
Rockefeller, John D., 228, 231, 238, 245
Rocky Mountain Christian School, 314
Rogers, A. G., 249
Rogers, John, 86, 94, 111
Rogers, Nathaniel, 85
Rogers, Samuel, 130, 133
Roman Catholicism, 10, 11, 12, 35, 140, 141, 348, 360, 361, 363, 365, 369, 371
Roper, William, 76
Rose, J. P., 132
Rosecrans, J. H., 204
Ross, A. F., 145
Ross, Roy G., 348
Rothenburger, William F., 264

Rotherham, J. B., 331
Rothermel, S. G., 253
Rothermel, Zoena, 299, 338
Rowe, Fred L., 215, 218
Rowe, John F., 203
Rowlinson, C. C., 238
Rule, J. K., 132
Russia, 302, 332-335
Rutledge, George P., 243, 296
Ryan, M. B., 326
Ryukyu Islands, 303, 341, 342

S

Sabbath, The, 61
Sabinal College, 201
Sadler, M. E., 264
St. Louis, Missouri, 135, 191, 288, **289**
St. Louis Christian College, 297
Sala, Homer E., 274
Salvation, Plan of, 74, 75, 101-103, 106, 110, 117, 139, 172-176, 268, 310, 372
Sanders, Lloyd David, 302, 324
Sandemanianism, 18
Sand Creek Declaration, 216
Sanderson, E. C., 295, 296
Sanford, E. D., 259
San Jose Bible College, 245, **296**
Sarvis, Guy W., 246
Saskatchewan, 313
Saunders, Alvin, 198
Schaeffer, Harry, 253, 299, 303, 338, 339
Scheme of Redemption, The, 196
Schmidt, Martin, 334
School of the Evangelists (see **Johnson Bible College**)
Schools and Colleges, 146-147, 157, 199-202, 213, 214, 280-282, 294-298, 311, 313-316
Schweitzer, Wolfgang, 365
Scotch Baptists (see Baptists)
Scotland (see Great Britain)
Scott, Harold W., 306
Scott, Walter, 68, 70, 97-107, 110, 121, 134, 144, 148, 149, 166, 181, 189; Ancestry, 97; Association with Campbells, 70, 97, 99, 100, 102, 104, 105; Birth, 97; Baptism, 98, 110; Death, 155; Education, 97, 98; Evangelistic methods, 101-103, 110, 116; Family, 100; As author, 100, 105, 106; As editor, 104, 105, 124, 147, 182; As educator, 97-100, 106, 144; As evangelist, 100, 101, 102, 103, 110, 196; As preacher, 100, 101, 166; Migration to America, 97, 98; Views on atonement, 106; On baptism, 98, 101; On co-operation, 148, 149, 181; On the Holy Spirit, 105; On the name, 116; On salvation, 101-103, 106, 110; On slavery, 106, 151-155; On temperance, 106
Scoville, Charles Reign, 196, 197, 272, **274**
Search for the Ancient Order, 310
Seceders (see Presbyterians)
Second Awakening, 30
Secret Place, The, 351
Sectarianism, 21, 39, 71, 175, 270, 271, 353
Segroves, J. Thomas, 297
Selly Oak Colleges (see Overdale College)
Sensibaugh, Hugh F., 306
"Sermon on the Law," 62-65, 67-69, 220
Service, James, 337
Sewell, E. G., 318
Shakers, 90, 352
Shannon, James, 129, 144
Sharp, C. J., 244
Sharp, George, 59

389

Sharp, Thomas, 59
Shaw, Knowles, 196
Shelburne, C. F. R., 147
Shelton, A. L., 253, 300
Shelton, O. L., 264
Shelton, Willard E., 264
Shepherd, J. W., 215, 218, 288, 309
Sheppard, Edmund, 324
Sheriff, John, 316, 336
Short, Howard E., 356
Showalter, A. J., 204
Sias, Elias, 126
Sias, Gerald, 264
Sibenya, Simon Benjamin, 300
Sickafoose, K. H., 194
Simons, Menno, 15
Simpson, A. N., 326
Sin, The problem of, 63, 106, 172, 225
Sinclair, Dugald, 324
Sizemore, Alva, 306
Skaggs, James, 77
Slavery, The Disciples and, 34, 80, 81, 92, 106,
  132, 135, 136, 151, 166
Sly, Virgil A., 285
Small, James, 197
Smith, Benjamin L., 208
Smith, Bertrand, 302, 326
Smith, Charles W., 212
Smith, E. C., 227
Smith, Elias, 32, 33, 90, 147
Smith, Eugene, 305
Smith, Franklin, 304
Smith, George, 337
Smith, George Birney, 231
Smith, George T., 339
Smith, J. H. O., 257, 272
Smith, Joseph, 120
Smith, Joseph (of England), 331
Smith, Kirby, 153
Smith, "Racoon" John, 94, 104, 111, 112,
  123, 154
Smith, Sam I., 249
Smith, "Speed," 142
Smith, T. K., 264, 306
Smith, Thomas, 113
Smither, A. C., 246, 345
Smyth, John, 16
Snoddy, Elmer E., 242, 243
Snodgrass, C. E., 199
Snow, Dexter A., 128
"Social Gospel," 226, 330, 348
Socinianism, 73, 74, 78
Sommer, Daniel, 216, 217, 319
South Africa, 253, 283, 298, 300, 301, 317, 336
South Australia, 337
South Carolina, 128, 134, 135
Southeastern Christian College, 313, 315, 357
Southern Christian College, 297
Southern Christian Convention, 258
Southern Rhodesia, 301, 316, 336, 337
Southwest Christian Convention, 258
Southwest Christian Seminary, 297
Southwestern Christian College, 201, 213
Speer, Robert E., 229, 230
Spencer, Claude E., 200
Spencer, I. J., 345
Spencer, J. A., 78
Spencer, Oliver M., 79
Spotlight, The (see The Touchstone)
Springer, John, 84
Springfield, Illinois, 166
Springfield Presbytery, 87-90
Sprinkling (see Infant baptism)

390

Stambaugh, J. H., 257
Standard Oil Company, 245
Standard Publishing Company, 177, 202, 203,
  214, 244, 245, 251, 253, 272, 273, 276, 277, 306
Starnes, Shubail, 77
Starr, Henry, 79
State Mission Planning Council, 290
State organizations, Evolution of, 189, 190,
  258, 290, 291
Stevenson, William Wilson, 130, 132
Stewart, Charles, 145
Stewart, George H., 264
Stewart, Kenneth A., 296
Still, Owen, 303, 327
Stockholm Conference, 346, 347, 360
Stockton, R. H., 199
Stone, Barton W., 27-30, 90, 100, 110, 123,
  143, 144, 276; Ancestry, 83; Birth, 83; Break
  with Presbyterians, 87, 88; Conversion, 84;
  Death, 135, 155; Education, 83, 84; Family,
  86, 93, 94, 153; Ordination, 85; As editor,
  92, 147; As evangelist, 85, 86, 91; As
  preacher, 91; As theologian, 92, 93, 112;
  Views on atonement, 92, 115; On baptism,
  91, 93, 110, 117; On Bible authority, 85,
  87-89; On church government, 88, 89, 116;
  On conversion, 92, 93, 117; On deity of
  Christ, 92; On Holy Spirit, 84, 87, 93, 117;
  On the name, 89, 115; On open membership,
  93, 117-119; On pacifism, 153; On sin, 92, 93;
  On slavery, 34, 92, 153; On revivalism, 28-30,
  86, 116; On the Trinity, 65, 84, 91, 92, 114,
  115; On unity of Christians, 88, 94, 95, 111,
  112
Stone, Barton W., Jr., 153
Stoner, Bertie, 194
Stoner, J. H., 194
"Stonites," 78, 94, 112
Stowe, Calvin E., 106
Strater, Floyd E., 356
Stratton, John Roach, 231
Streator, W. S., 169
Strong, Augustus, 226, 351
Stuckenbruck, Earl, 302, 328
Stundists, 332
Sturgis, J. E., 244
Succoth Academy, 84, 106
Sulphur Fork Association, 104
Sunday School and Tract Society, 180
Sunday schools, 34, 149, 180, 202, 204, 219
Sweden, 317, 335
Sweeney, John S., 195
Sweeney, W. E., 256, 264
Sweeney, Z. T., 199, 249, 255, 272, 334
"Sweeney Resolution" (see Peace Resolution)
Switzerland, 15, 17, 318, 335
Synod of Kentucky, 87, 89
Synod of Pittsburgh, 51, 57
Synopsis of the Faith, 167, 168

T

Taborites, 13, 14
Tait, John W., 102
Talks to Bereans, 177
Tanganyika, 317
Tarbell, Ida M., 245
Tasmania, 337
Tate's Creek Association, 104
Taylor, Alva W., 240, 348
Taylor, C. C., 257
Taylor, Harold, 304, 340
Taylor, Lloyd, 356
Temperance, 34

Virginia Christian College (see Lynchburg College)
Voice of Freedom, The, 319
Voltaire, 19, 25
Voluntary Church Advocate, 329
Von Gerdtell, Ludwig, 302
Von Imbroich, Thomas, 15

W

Waldenses, 12
Waldo, Peter, 12
Wales (see Great Britain)
Walker, Dean E., 264, 295, 356
Walker, John, 38, 54
Walker, John, 69
Walker, W. R., 243, 256, 275, 306
Walker, William, 305
Wallace, Sarah, 187
Wallis, James, 329
Walnut Grove Academy (see Eureka College)
Walsh, John T., 153
Wanamaker, John, 230, 233
War, Disciples and, 152-154
Ward, William Hayes, 233
Ware, Henry, 22
Warfield, B. B., 230
Warren, Ohio, 67, 101-103, 166
Warren, P. D., 216
Warren, W. R., 208
Washington, 284, 297
Washington Association, 78
Washington, Pennsylvania, 39-41, 51, 57, 78
Washington Presbytery, 87
Waters, George, 130
Watkins, Isaac, 130
Watts, Isaac, 84, 92
Watts, E. A., 301
Weaver, Robert O., 306
Webb, Aldis L., 274
Weekly communion (see Lord's Supper)
Wellington Co-operation, 325
Wells, L. N. D., 264
Wellsburg, (West) Virginia, 67, 68
Welshimer, P. H., 249, 251, 256, 264, 275, 306, 351, 355
Wertz, Wayne, 305
Wesley, John, 22
West, Earl Irvin, 310
West Kentucky College, 201
West Virginia, 127, 190, 280, 305, 313
West, William, 68
Western Christian College, 313
Western Evangelist, 132
Western Reformer (see *Proclamation and Reformer*)
Western Reserve of Ohio, 68, 69, 102-104, 109, 110, 116, 134
Western Reserve Eclectic Institute (see Hiram College)
Westminster Confession of Faith, 37, 48, 76, 85, 98, 230
Westminster Theological Seminary, 231
Westrup, Enrique T., 250, 299, 327
Wharton, G. L., 188
White, Charles J., 176
White, Cyrus, 128
White, Henry H., 144
White, John D., 199
White, John O., 132
Whitehouse, J. J., 269
Whitley, Oliver Reed, 353
Whitman, Marcus, 132
Whyte, William H., 360

Wichita Christian School, 314
Wilcox, Alanson, 190, 205
Wilhite, H. E., 197
Wilkes, Lanceford B., 170, 195, 217
Willett, Herbert L., 214, 233, 238, 240
William Woods College, 201, 281
Williams College, 23, 27, 197
Williams, Herman P., 341
Williams, John Augustus, 111
Williams, Roger, 16
Williams, W. M., 251
Willis, Albert T., 199
Wills, M. P., 129
Wilmington College, 126, 146, 157, 200, 314
Wilson, Reuben, 126
Wilson, Robert Dick, 230
Wilson, Seth, 296
Wilson, William, 39
Wilson, Woodrow, 199
Winston-Salem Bible College, 298, 305
Wisconsin, 126, 190
Witty, Claude E., 274-276
Wolfe, Leslie, 252, 298
Women in church work, 177, 187, 188, 212, 213, 250, 257, 284
Wood, Joel M., 131
Woodruff, Harlan, 303, 341
Word and Work, 275, 319
World Call, 271, 284
World Convention of Churches of Christ, 329, 332, 342, 343, 361
World Council of Christian Education and Sunday School Association, 348
World Council of Churches, 273, 285, 287, 343, 347, 348, 351, 355, 360, 366
World Evangelical Alliance, 139, 140, 232, 259, 261, 350
World Evangelical Fellowship, 350
World Missionary Conference, 346, 360
World's Sunday School Association, 348
World Vision, 316, 319
Worley, Malcom, 90
Worship, 160, 311, 330, 348
Wray, Ernest Hunter, 274
Wright, Allen, 129, 130
Wright, John, 124
Wycliffe, John, 13, 15
Wyeth, Peyton C., 329
Wyker, Mrs. James D., 348
Wymore, Leonard G., 306
Wyoming, 194

Y

Yale Divinity School, 33, 233, 238, 239, 273
Yale University, 22, 23-27
Year Book, 288, 294
Yearly Meetings, 124, 189, 259
Yohe, W. S., 131
York College, 313
Yost, G. W. N., 169, 199
Young, Brigham, 121
Young, Charles A., 238
Young, Duke, 131
Young, M. Norvel, 316
Young Men's Christian Association, 259
Young Peoples' Standard, The (see *The Look-out*)
Youngs, Benjamin Seth, 90
Yuell, Herbert, 197

Z

Zizka, Jan, 13
Zollars, E. V., 199, 200
Zwingli, Huldreich, 15